THE SCIENCE OF FOOD

THE SCIENCE OF FOOD

MARION BENNION

Former Professor, Food Science and Nutrition
Brigham Young University

Harper & Row, Publishers
San Francisco

Cambridge
Hagerstown
New York
Philadelphia

London
Mexico City
São Paulo
Sydney

1817

To Wayne

Sponsoring Editors: John Woods and Earl Shepherd
Project Editor: Julie Segedy
Production Manager: Marian Hartsough
Cover and Interior Design: Nancy Benedict
Illustrators: Nelva Richardson and John Foster
Compositor: Bi-Comp, Inc.
Printer & Binder: R. R. Donnelley & Sons Company

The Science of Food

Library of Congress Cataloging in Publication Data
Bennion, Marion, 1925–
  The science of food.

  Includes index.
  1. Food.   I. Title.
TX354.B47   641.3   79-23464
ISBN 0-06-453532-0

CONTENTS

PART IV

PART V

PART VI

PART VII

BAKED FLOUR PRODUCTS   528

PREFACE

Food preparation and processing have been undergoing many changes in recent years, since both the food industry and the average consumer have become more sophisticated in their knowledge and approach to food. Economic and political factors have further influenced food manufacture and consumption, so not only is food complex in its chemical composition and physical structure, but it has also become complex in its economic, social, political, and emotional impact on people and populations.

This book is designed for the college student who has already had an introduction to the study of food as well as some background in chemistry. The emphasis of the book is on the chemical and physical structure of food and the effects of processing and preparation on its properties. Research studies are often cited to support the discussion, although the review of research on each topic is not meant to be exhaustive. It is expected that the student will gain a basic understanding of why foods respond as they do in preparation and processing. It is also hoped that the student will acquire an appreciation for food research and its role in expanding the frontiers of knowledge.

The subject matter is divided into seven parts. The first part is designed as an introduction and review. A discussion of food quality and evaluation serves as an introduction to the in-depth study of foods. Chapters on composition, structure, acidity, and enzymes review some basic science principles and apply them to food preparation and processing.

The second part is concerned with food preservation and it emphasizes canning and freezing. Part III is closely related to food preservation and discusses food safety and standards.

Part IV is basically concerned with carbohydrates, including a general introduction to these chemical compounds. However, other subjects are discussed as they relate to food systems in which carbohydrates play an important role. This includes a discussion of crystallization in connection with candies and frozen desserts, and a chapter on the structure of plant tissues and pigments.

Gels, emulsions, and foams in food systems are treated in Part V. The first chapter discusses basic structures for each of these food systems, since they have many characteristics in common. The following chapters treat each in more detail. The chemical and physical properties of fats are included with emulsions, while pectic substances and jellies are included in this unit as well.

Food systems that are relatively high in protein are included in Part VI. As in Part IV on carbohydrates, other properties of these food products are discussed but proteins are emphasized. The first chapter of this unit is devoted to a discussion of the general characteristics of food proteins.

The concluding part treats baked flour products. Leavening agents are generally discussed in the first chapter. The following chapters include discussions of specific flour mixtures.

The chapters may be presented to students in different order, depending upon the objectives and plan of the course. References to other related sections of the text are included throughout.

I would like to acknowledge those who have supplied illustrations for this book. Grateful acknowledgment is also included in the text. Many students and instructors with whom I have worked throughout the years have influenced the development of this book. I wish to thank them for their contributions. While it was being written, the manuscript was reviewed by several colleagues teaching this course. The comments, criticisms, and suggestions of Professors Elena Kissick and Joanne Caid, California State University, Sacramento; Louise Wakelee, Oklahoma State University; Natholyn D. Harris, Florida State University; Mary Jo Kenny, California State University, Sacramento; and Martha Stone, Kansas State University, have helped improve the text substantially. I am appreciative of the many hours spent by Florence S. Strate as she assisted in the preparation of this manuscript. I am also grateful for the support and helpful suggestions of my husband in the review of each chapter and in the final manuscript preparation.

Marion Bennion
El Paso, Texas

PART I

RELATIONSHIP OF STRUCTURE TO QUALITY IN FOOD

The chemical components in a food product and the physical orientation of these chemical substances determine the quality characteristics of that food. Part I will introduce you to some basic determinants of quality in food, beginning with a discussion of the influence of flavor on food quality and eating enjoyment. Next, the chemical composition of food will be discussed and related to its physical structure, and some effects of acidity and enzyme activity will also be treated.

CHAPTER 1

FOOD QUALITY: CHARACTERISTICS AND EVALUATION

Most of us enjoy the pleasures of the table and satisfy our physical need for food at the same time. We can survive on, thrive on, and enjoy a wide variety of foods. The types of food individuals or populations eat are influenced by many factors, including availability, technology, economics, religion, cultural habits, social conditions, nutrition, politics and taste. From infancy and early childhood on, people learn to like familiar and accustomed foods and to associate them with many feelings not necessarily related to physiological need. Individual standards for an acceptable quality of food are also established at an early age; for humans, preferred flavors of food are to a large extent learned phenomena. Preferences and standards are, however, constantly changing as the world changes and as technologies develop.

1.1

SENSORY CHARACTERISTICS OF FOOD QUALITY

Von Sydow (1971) has suggested that food quality is a complex concept involving chemistry, physics, and technology in the food; physiology, psychophysics, and social science in the human being; and the mathematical sciences in combining the two. Quality indicates the basic nature of food or its degree of excellence, and encompasses taste, aroma, texture, appearance, and nutritional content, as well as factors that determine the safety of food. The food scientist must be able to evaluate these properties in order to assure that quality has been achieved.

According to Moncrieff (1967), flavor in a broad sense is a complex sensation comprising taste, odor, roughness or smoothness, hotness or coldness, and pungency or blandness of food. Appearance, including color and form, is also an important component of food acceptance. Even sound, such as the crunchiness of crisp celery, is part of the overall flavor profile for a food. Kramer (1972) classified the sensory quality of foods according to the major senses by which it is perceived. These are 1. appearance as sensed by the eye; 2. flavor as sensed by taste buds in the mouth and olfactory cells in the nose; and 3. texture or kinesthetics as sensed by muscle endings in the mouth or on the hands. He has emphasized that the sensory quality of food does not consist of a single well-defined attribute, but is a composite of several properties perceived by the human senses individually and then integrated by the brain into a total impression of quality. Figure 1.1 illustrates how the primary sensory attributes of food quality may overlap.

APPEARANCE

The shape, size, color, gloss, and luster of a food as seen by the eye usually initiates the first phase of the perception of food quality. The appearance of a food may produce a psychological prejudgment of its quality. On the basis of past experience, one may expect a food to taste a certain way because of its color or its general appearance. For example, in a classroom experiment, a lime-flavored beverage colored red caused 50 percent of a group of judges to label it cherry, strawberry, or raspberry while only 20 percent identified the true lime flavor.

Color measurement is commonly used by the food industry to help control the quality of food, at least to the extent that color is correlated with other quality attributes. The extensive use of color additives to

Figure 1.1

Sensory attributes of food quality and how they overlap are represented schematically. The primary attributes—appearance, texture (kinesthetics), and flavor—share the periphery of the circle. At one part of the circumference—between appearance and kinesthetics—there is an overlapping zone where terms such as consistency and viscosity are placed since these attributes can be classified under both appearance and texture (kinesthetics). At the other side of the zone—where texture meets flavor—there is a similar overlapping where the term "Mouth Feel" is placed. (Reprinted from *Food Technology* Vol. 26, No. 1, p. 34, 1972. Copyright © by Institute of Food Technologists.)

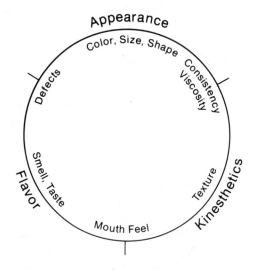

make food more attractive began in the early 1800s with the development of the food processing industry. Both synthetic and natural coloring agents have been approved for use in food by the U. S. Food and Drug Administration (FDA). With the availability of sophisticated analytical techniques, these color substances are constantly being retested for safety. Some of the synthetic coaltar derivatives have been withdrawn or delisted by FDA as a result of the retesting program. For example, FD & C Red No. 2 (amaranth) was banned by the FDA in 1976. Less than ten synthetic coloring compounds remain on the FDA list approved for use in foods.

Color is the result of reflected radiant energy which stimulates the retina of the eye. Total reflection produces whiteness while no reflection gives blackness. Reflection of energy with wave lengths between 400 and 720 millimicrons (mμ) is colored. Dominant reflection of 400–480 mμ produces blue, 480–560 mμ produces green, 560–620 mμ produces yellow, and 630–720 mμ produces red. Overlap between these wave lengths produces complementary colors.

The measurement of color is a complex process. Color belongs to the realm of sensory perception, and can thus only be directly measured in psychological terms. For example, when food color is seen by the human eye, it is interpreted in terms of the unique personality of the viewer. Additionally, physical measurements can be made, from which predictions of visual appearance are then calculated. Objective measurements allow the color of a food to be stated in numerical terms.

Approaches to the measurement of color may be classified into three areas, they are 1. visual methods; 2. spectrophotometry; and 3. tristimulus colorimetry. *Visual methods* involve color matching by an observer. Revolving discs and the projection of lights on a screen have been used to mix colors for the comparison of various foods. *Spectrophotometric methods* use an instrument to measure the light that reflects off a test sample placed against a small opening. *Tristimulus colorimetry* involves an instrument, such as a color difference meter, that has three scales for color measurement. These include an *L scale* to indicate lightness or value, an *a scale* to measure redness or greenness, and a *b scale* to measure yellowness or blueness. Because foods are often irregularly colored, irregularly shaped and vary widely in texture or consistency, many practical problems are encountered in color measurement. In spite of the difficulties in measurement, however, color remains an important quality characteristic of foods.

FLAVOR

Taste Receptors for taste, or gustatory sensations, are most numerous in the tongue, but also occur in the soft palate and throat. Taste buds, as illustrated in Figure 1.2, are found in connective tissue elevations on the tongue that are called *papillae. Circumvallate papillae,* which always contain taste buds, are the largest elevations and form an inverted *V* shape at the back of the tongue. *Fungiform papillae* are mushroom-shaped and are found primarily on the tip and sides of the tongue; most

Figure 1.2

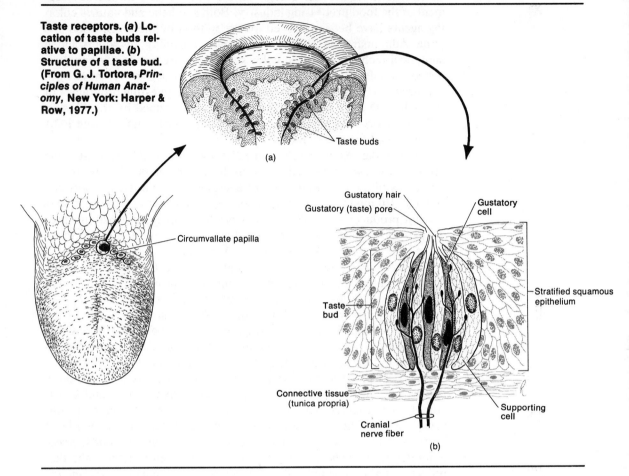

Taste receptors. (*a*) Location of taste buds relative to papillae. (*b*) Structure of a taste bud. (From G. J. Tortora, *Principles of Human Anatomy*, New York: Harper & Row, 1977.)

of them contain taste buds. *Filiform papillae* are conical or threadlike structures that cover much of the tongue surface, and contain no taste buds.

The *taste buds* are oval-shaped bodies that contain both supporting cells and gustatory cells, that are the sensing neurons for taste. A dendrite projects from each gustatory cell through an opening in the taste bud called the *taste pore*. Contact with taste-stimulating substances that are in solution is made through the taste pore and apparently involves the formation of a complex between the stimulating substance and the receptor (Price, 1969). Taste impulses are conveyed from the gustatory cells in the taste buds to the brain by cranial nerves. The *facial nerve* (VII) supplies the anterior two-thirds of the tongue; the *glossopharyngeal* (IX) supplies the posterior one-third; and the *vagus* (X) supplies the epiglottis area of the throat.

Estimates of the number of primary tastes have varied over the years. It is now generally agreed that there are four—sweet, sour, salty, and bitter. However, it is not believed that these four taste qualities can completely describe all tastes. The salty taste is characteristic of low molecular weight ionized inorganic salts, such as sodium chloride and potassium chloride. The acid taste is related to pH for inorganic acids, such as hydrochloric acid, but the relationship is not clearcut for organic acids such as citric acid (Teranishi et al., 1971). Shallenberger and Acree (1969) have suggested that the OH (glycol) groups of sugars are involved in the ability of these compounds to elicit a sweet taste. The conformation of neighboring OH groups on the sugar molecule influences the degree of sweetness. Alkaloids and glycosides are bitter, but no general relationships between chemical structure and bitterness have been established.

From studies of the electrical neural response of nerve fibers, it appears that taste cells specific for sweet, sour, bitter, and salty do not exist (Teranishi et al., 1971). A single taste cell may possess multiple receptor sites, each of which has specificity.

Various sugars differ in sweetness. The relative sweetness of sugars in solution varies with concentration. Pangborn (1963) studied the relative taste intensities of four sugars at *threshold levels* (the concentration at which a subject can detect that the solution is different from water) and at *suprathreshold levels*. Fructose was reported to be the sweetest, followed by sucrose, glucose, and lactose. Yamaguchi et al. (1970) also found fructose to be the sweetest of four sugars tested at various concentrations, but with sucrose, glucose, and xylose following in decreasing order. Relative sweetness of the sugars again differed when they were tested by Pangborn (1963) in pear nectar, suggesting that interactions in complex foods may change the results found in model systems. Pilgrim (1961) reported that when sucrose was a secondary stimulus it decreased the sourness of a primary acid solution, decreased the bitterness of a primary caffeine solution, but had no effect on the saltiness of a sodium chloride solution. Citric acid was found to enhance sweetness, bitterness, and saltiness.

A number of nonsugar substances give a sweet taste, including some amino acids and alcohols. Saccharin, a nonnutritive sweetener, has been used for many years when sugar intake must be limited. However, its safety for human consumption has recently been questioned by the FDA. Researchers are currently attempting to develop additional nonnutritive sweeteners.

It was accidently discovered that sensitivity to the bitter taste of an organic compound called *phenylthiourea* is determined by heredity. A significantly lower proportion of people who are not sensitive to this taste (*nontasters*) has been reported among Chinese and Japanese subjects than among white Europeans. An intermediate percentage of nontasters among Polish Jews was reported by Saldanha and Becak (1959). Other genetically determined differences in ability to taste may yet be discovered, and will help explain differences among individual taste preferences.

Taste thresholds may vary greatly among individuals. Korslund and Eppright (1967) reported that the median taste threshold for a group of 25 preschool children was similar to adult taste thresholds reported. Those children who had the lowest taste sensitivity tended to accept more foods and to have more enthusiasm for food than did those with the highest taste sensitivity. In a study of 45 teenagers, however, Jefferson and Erdman (1970) found a significant correlation between a low recognition threshold (concentration required for recognition of a specific taste) for the bitter taste of phenylthiourea and percentage of disliked discriminating foods. Turnip greens and beets were particularly disliked by those subjects with a low threshold, or high sensitivity, for phenylthiourea. Probably the bitter characteristics of these vegetables were more aptly detected by these people. Although the number of taste buds decreases with age, Kare (1975) reported that individuals 80–85 years of age discriminated among tastes as well as did a control group of 40–45 years of age.

Odor Receptors for the olfactory sense are found in the nasal epithelium of the nasal cavity as shown in Figure 1.3. The nasal epithelium contains both supporting cells and olfactory neurons. Dendrites, or olfactory hairs, are found at the free end of each olfactory cell or neuron, and make contact with molecules that are being smelled in the nasal cavity. The axons of the olfactory cells unite to form olfactory nerves that pass through the cribiform plate into the olfactory bulb (see Figure 1.3). From this point, nerve impulses are conveyed to the olfactory portion of the cerebral cortex by additional neurons, and once in the cortex, the impulses are interpreted as odors. During the process of swallowing, as food begins to go down the esophagus, a slight vacuum is formed in the nasal cavity. This draws odor-containing air into the nasal area, stimulating olfactory hairs. Odor thus contributes a great deal to what is commonly called taste.

The supporting cells of the nasal epithelium and tear ducts are also innervated by the trigeminal nerve (V). Stimulation of these nerve endings causes pain, cold, heat, tickling, and pressure. Substances such as pepper and onions may be irritating and cause tearing because they stimulate the receptors of the trigeminal as well as the olfactory nerves.

The nose is an extremely sensitive instrument for detecting odors. It takes only a few molecules of a substance reaching the olfactory receptors to produce an identifiable olfactory sensation. Not all molecules that are taken into the nasal cavity actually reach receptor sites. However, it has been estimated by Teranishi *et al.* (1971) that the nose can detect an odor substance when approximately 10^{-19} moles are present in the nasal cavity. This sensitivity is beyond the capability of analytical instruments in the laboratory. According to Klopping (1971), in order to be clearly odorous a substance must have both lipid and water

Figure 1.3

Receptors for olfaction. (a) Location of receptors in nasal cavity. (b) Enlarged aspect of olfactory receptors. (From Gerard J. Tortora. *Principles of Human Anatomy,* New York: Harper & Row, 1977.)

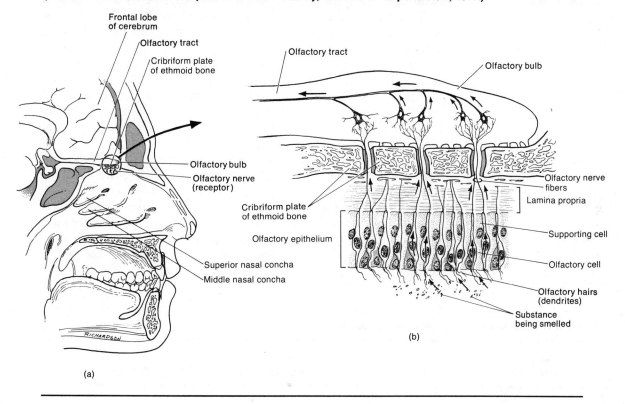

solubility, have some volatility, and be present in a certain *threshold concentration* that varies widely with the substance. There must also be direct physical contact between odor molecule and receptor site.

The problems involved in studying the nature of odor are even more complex than those concerned with taste. Olfactory cells are smaller and more numerous than taste cells, and while four basic tastes have been assumed, the nose is capable of distinguishing hundreds or thousands of different odors.

Attempts have been made to correlate the odor produced by a chemical compound with some aspect of its structure, but relationships are complex. Several olfactory theories have been suggested. From a review of the major theories, Klopping (1971) concluded that at least three main factors probably contribute to the odor quality of a molecule, namely its size and shape, its functional chemical group, and its orientation with respect to the receptor surface. In individual instances one of these factors may have the predominant influence while another factor may have little effect. The final odor quality observed appears to be the outcome of a complicated interplay of the three factors.

TEXTURE

Texture relates to the sense of touch or feel. In the ends of the muscles in the mouth there are pressure receptors and receptors for awareness of movement. Impulses are transferred to the brain by way of the trigeminal nerve (V).

Definitions of texture have changed over the years as characteristics of food have been studied. According to Kramer (1972), the term *texture* may be used for a major division of sensory quality covering all kinesthetic (or muscle) responses to foods. Thus consistency and viscosity as well as hardness, cohesiveness, brittleness, chewiness, and gumminess are characteristics of texture.

Szczesniak (1963) classified textural characteristics of food into three groups: 1. mechanical; 2. geometrical; and 3. other, referring mainly to moisture and fat content. *Mechanical characteristics* are related to the way a food reacts to stress and are measured by pressures exerted on the teeth, tongue, and roof of the mouth during eating. These characteristics are described in Table 1.1.

Geometrical characteristics are related to 1. the size and shape of the particles or 2. their shape and orientation. Examples of geometrical

Table 1.1 Mechanical Characteristics of Food Texture.

Primary characteristics	Definition	Secondary characteristics	Definition
Hardness	Force necessary to attain a given deformation		
Cohesiveness	Strength of internal bonds in a food	Brittleness	Force with which material fractures
		Chewiness	Energy required to masticate a solid food to a state ready for swallowing
		Gumminess	Energy required to disintegrate a semi-solid food to a state ready for swallowing
Viscosity	Rate of flow per unit force		
Elasticity	Rate at which a deformed food returns to its undeformed condition after deforming force is removed		
Adhesiveness	Work necessary to overcome attractive forces between the surface of other materials that it contacts		

Source: Adapted from Szczesniak, 1963.

characteristics include graininess, coarseness, grittiness, and fibrous, cellular or crystalline qualities.

1.2

FLAVOR PRECURSORS

Flavor substances may be present or developed naturally in foods through enzymatic reactions, or they may be produced by heating and other processing measures. In either case the development of flavor often involves the changing of certain molecules without particular flavor characteristics, called *flavor precursors,* into flavor molecules. The chemical reactions involved in changing precursors to flavor compounds are often complex and will require further research for full understanding.

Examples of substances occurring preformed in natural foods include the many volatile compounds, such as low molecular weight alcohols and esters, that contribute to the pleasant characteristic odors of fresh strawberries, peaches, and apples. Enzymatic production of flavor substances occurs in garlic, leek, and onion when the tissues of these vegetables are cut or bruised. Enzymes and substrates combine in the damaged cells with the rapid production of a characteristic smell. The substrates for these reactions are derived from the sulfur-containing amino acid, cysteine, and are called *alliins*. The reaction is catalyzed by the enzyme alliinase. A substance called *sinigrin* acts as a flavor precursor to form the flavorful mustard oil in fresh cabbage. The enzyme myrosinase catalyzes this reaction when cabbage is cut or bruised. Some of these enzymatic reactions are outlined in Chapter 14 (see Figures 14.1, 14.2 and 14.3).

Procedures to which many fresh vegetables are subjected, such as heating and drying, often destroy their fresh odors and tastes, yet many flavor precursors may be stable under such processing. The flavor of some vegetables can be improved after processing by adding an enzyme preparation extracted from the unprocessed material. Hewitt *et al.* (1956) reported that the flavor of dehydrated watercress was improved with the addition of an enzyme preparation from white mustard seed, which belongs to the same *Brassica* family as does watercress. Konigsbacher *et al.* (1959) found that adding flavor enzymes to dehydrated and canned vegetables strongly influenced the flavor, as reported by a panel of judges. Schwimmer (1963) reported flavor changes resulting from the addition of vegetable enzyme fractions to dehydrated cabbage, horseradish, and carrots; canned peas, beans, and tomatoes; and frozen broccoli. The flavor of the enzyme-treated processed food approached that of the fresh vegetable but was not identical to it.

Flavor precursors have been studied in a number of processed and cooked foods. Mabrouk *et al.* (1969) reported that the major portion of beef flavor precursors are low molecular weight, water-soluble compounds. The amino acids, methionine and/or cysteic acid, are apparently important contributors to cooked beef flavor and occur in the meat along with reducing sugars. Flavor precursors have also been studied in bread, roasted peanuts, cheese, and chocolate. For most effective results, the study of flavor in foods must include both natural flavor substances and flavor precursors (Rohan, 1970).

1.3

FLAVOR POTENTIATORS

A *flavor potentiator* is a compound that, when used in small quantities, has no sensory effect but increases the effect of other flavor agents in a food mixture. Glutamic acid was discovered in 1908 in edible seaweed used by the Japanese and was immediately recognized as a flavor potentiator or enhancer. Monosodium glutamate (MSG) was then commercially produced in Japan. Conflicting research findings have since been reported concerning its mode of action in flavoring food (Amerine *et al.,* 1965).

Pure MSG has a pleasant, mild flavor with a sweet and salty taste. The flavor of MSG itself is not generally detected in the amounts commonly added to foods, but might, however, enhance the flavor of other components. Some investigators have suggested that MSG changes the acuity of basic tastes, such as increasing sensitivity to sour and bitter or reducing taste thresholds for sweet and salty. Others, however, have concluded that MSG acts as a seasoning by itself and does not change taste acuity. Other amino acids, including ibotenic acid and tricholomic acid, have been reported to have flavor effects similar to those of MSG (Amerine *et al.,* 1965).

Another group of flavor enhancers includes certain 5'-nucleotides containing 6-hydroxypurine. Inosinic acid and guanylic acid are two of these nucleotides that are produced commercially for use as flavor enhancers and have been shown to enhance preference judgments for fish, poultry, and certain canned vegetables. Woskow (1969) investigated the flavor modifying properties of a 50:50 mixture of 5'-disodium inosinate and 5'-disodium guanylate. This mixture potentiated sweetness and saltiness but its strongest effects were to suppress bitterness and sourness. Because of the suppression of undesirable "off-flavors" by the 5'-nucleotides, Woskow suggested that they might more appropriately be called flavor modifiers rather than potentiators or enhancers.

There is a synergistic relationship between 5'-nucleotides and MSG in flavor activity: MSG reduces taste thresholds for the 5'-nucleotides and the nucleotides likewise reduce the threshold for MSG. If a 5'-nucleotide is present in a small amount in a food mixture, a lesser amount of MSG may be used to achieve the same flavor effect as a larger amount of MSG without nucleotides (Kuninaka, 1967).

1.4

EVALUATION OF FOOD

There are a number of reasons for evaluating quality characteristics of food. Evaluation may provide information pertinent to improving the quality of a food product produced either commercially or at home. It is essential also to assure the maintenance of high quality standards on a continuing basis. Evaluation is an important part of the process of developing new food products and of analyzing the market potential for these foods; likewise it is necessary in the study of processing and storage effects. The student of food science must be able to evaluate food products prepared in the laboratory in order to understand the effects of various food preparation and processing procedures on these foods.

When the quality of a food is evaluated by the use of human sensory organs, the food is being *subjectively* evaluated. When assessment is done with the use of instruments that do not involve the human senses, the food is said to be *objectively* evaluated. According to Amerine *et al.* (1965), objective measurements of food quality are preferable to subjective measurements only if the objective tests can provide a precise measure of a sensory quality. In the final analysis, the effects on human senses of food being eaten are of primary importance and these effects cannot be easily duplicated in the laboratory.

SUBJECTIVE EVALUATION

Human sense organs for taste, smell, sight, touch, and hearing are the instruments for subjective evaluation of food. People participating in sensory evaluation may be untrained consumers or trained laboratory taste panelists. Groups of consumers are usually used in preference testing to learn if a food product will be acceptable, the results of which are useful to food manufacturers in predicting whether or not consumers will buy a particular new product. Consumer panels are usually composed of a large number of individuals—often more than 100 people selected from a geographical area—representing the general consumer population.

A trained laboratory panel is commonly used for difference testing, scoring, or ranking. Panel members should be readily accessible to the testing laboratory and be in good health. Training increases a panel member's sensitivity and memory, permitting more precise judgments and more uniform results. The amount of training given to panel members depends on the degree of acuity required for the testing. Judges may be tested for their ability to recognize the four basic tastes— sweet, salty, sour, and bitter. The thresholds for each of the basic tastes may be determined by having the subject taste a series of solutions which gradually increase in concentration of a substance that elicits the taste. The threshold is the concentration at which the subject can first detect that the solution is different from water. Difference tests, such as the triangle test described below, using the particular foods that will be tested in the project, are useful in both screening for selection and training of panel members. The sex of the panelist, as well as smoking habits, have little influence on ability to discriminate tastes, but there is some effect of age on flavor sensitivity, particularly after age 50. In a study involving 97 individuals, Venstrom and Amoore (1968) found a 50 percent mean loss of sensitivity for odors with increasing age, in subjects representing a 22 year age range. The number of panel members may vary from four to as many as thirty, depending upon the type of testing to be done.

A special testing area should be used for sensory evaluation of food so that conditions such as lighting, temperature, atmosphere, and humidity can be carefully controlled. The testing area should be separate from the food preparation area, and judges should be separated from each other in order to allow independent judgments. Figure 1.4 shows one type of physical setup in which samples and written instructions are passed through a small opening from the preparation area to the panelist's testing booth (Larmond, 1973).

Sensory evaluation is a scientific discipline used to evoke, measure, analyze, and interpret reactions to those characteristics of foods that are perceived by the senses (Prell, 1976). Standardized sensory testing procedures have been developed, and the results analyzed statistically. The various approaches employed in sensory testing of food include use of the following tests:

Paired comparison   The judge is given two samples and asked to indicate how they differ in a particular sensory characteristic. This test is useful in the selection and training of a panel. It is also valuable in programs to control and maintain the quality of a food product. However only two samples can be compared at one time, at times necessitating a large number of comparisons.

Figure 1.4

Samples and instructions are passed through a domed hatch from the preparation area to the panelist's testing booth so that the operators do not have to serve samples in the testing room. (Reprinted from *Food Technology* Vol. 27, No. 11, p. 28, 1973. Copyright © by Institute of Food Technologists.)

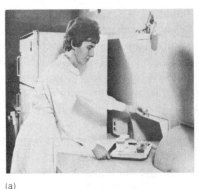
(a)

(b)

Triangle test   Three samples are presented simultaneously, two of which are identical. The judge must decide which two of the three samples are alike and which is the odd one. This test has similar advantages and disadvantages to paired comparisons, and is particularly useful when only small differences exist between samples.

Duo-trio test   One identified sample is presented first. Two coded samples are then presented, one of which is identical to the first sample. The judge must determine which of the two coded samples is like the first control sample. With this test there is a 50 percent chance of a correct answer simply by guessing. In many cases the paired comparison and triangle tests may be more useful than the duo-trio test.

Ranking   Several samples are presented simultaneously, and are ranked by the judge according to the intensity of a single sensory characteristic. This test is useful when a comparatively large number of samples are being evaluated at one time for a single quality characteristic.

Scoring   The judge rates samples according to a set of numerical standards. Standards may consider the relative importance of particular properties such as color, texture, and flavor in formulating an overall score. Scoring is called *hedonic* when the degree of liking is expressed on a scale of from five to nine points, ranging from extreme disapproval to extreme approval. Much information about the test product can be accumulated as scoring allows the collection of both qualitative and quantitative data. This type of evaluation may be difficult for an inexperienced person who does not have well-established standards by which to judge.

Flavor profile method   A specially trained panel works together in producing a written record of the aroma and flavor of a product. Aroma and flavor are examined separately and tabulated according to 1. the individually detectable components or character notes; 2. the intensity of each; 3. the order of appearance; 4. the amplitude; and 5. the aftertaste (Moriarty, 1969). This method requires a highly skilled panel that works well together. The information collected may be difficult to interpret and analyze for purposes of research.

OBJECTIVE EVALUATION

Because sensory evaluation of food is time consuming and costly, less expensive methods of analysis with laboratory instruments are desirable providing they give information that correlates well with the sensory characteristics. Objective evaluation involving instruments may be categorized into two types: imitative measurements and nonimitative measurements. Imitative measurements are done by instruments which imitate the way in which humans perceive the sensory property, such as machines that duplicate the bite of human teeth. Nonimitative measurements include any determination of chemical or physical properties of a food system that statistically correlate with sensory properties when each type of measurement is performed on a single food product. For example, the taste intensity of a particular acid solution may be predicted by determining the hydrogen ion concentration (Noble, 1975).

Texture measurement *Rheology* is a branch of physics that deals with the deformation and flow of both liquids and solids. Deformation and flow of food materials are related to their subjectively perceived textural properties. For example, the tenderness of meat is subjectively evaluated by the effort or force required for the teeth to penetrate and chew the tissue. Fresh fruit is sometimes pressed with the hand and fingers as an indication of firmness or softness.

Objective tests for measuring food texture also rely upon deformation and flow characteristics in determining how much the test sample resists applied forces greater than gravity. Instruments for texture measurement usually consist of four basic elements (Szczesniak, 1966):

1. A probe contacting the food sample. This may be a flat plunger, a rod, a spindle, a pair of shearing jaws, a tooth-shaped attachment, a cutting blade, or a set of cutting wires.
2. A driving mechanism for putting the probe in motion. The motion may be vertical, horizontal, or rotational at either a constant or a variable rate.

Table 1.2 Instruments Used for Measuring the Texture of Foods

Instrument	Description
Penetrometer	Employs a rod-like or cone-shaped probe to penetrate the test material.
Compressimeter	Uses a flat or curved plunger to test the resistance of a food sample to being compressed.
Shearing device	Uses a single- or multiple-blade-probe to shear through a sample.
Cutting device	Employs a knife-like blade or wire to cut through the test food.
Masticometer	Attempts to simulate the conditions of mastication or chewing.
Consistometer	Measures either the distance of spread when a semi-solid food sample is placed on a flat surface, or the resistance to a rotating spindle or paddle placed in a liquid food.
Viscometer	Employs capillary flow or uses a rotated spindle in the test material.
Multiple-purpose units	Perform a number of different texture tests.

Source: Adapted from Szczesniak, 1972.

3. A sensing element for detecting the resistance of the food sample to the applied force.

4. A recording system. This may be a dial showing maximum force, an oscilloscope, or a recorder tracing.

Each texture-measuring device has advantages and shortcomings that are considered when using it for the evaluation of food. Some instruments commonly used for measuring the texture of foods are described below in Table 1.2. Photographs of several instruments are also found in Figure 1.5.

In rheology, three types of deformation are generally recognized—elastic, viscous, and plastic—even though few materials show any one of these characteristics perfectly. Figure 1.6 gives a rheological model for elasticity as a spring. If a material is perfectly elastic, deformation occurs instantaneously when force is applied and completely disappears when the force is released. A rheological model for viscosity is

Figure 1.5

Instruments that measure the texture of foods. (*a*) A compressimeter with a flat plunger measures the compressibility of a slice of bread. (*b*) A Bostwick consistometer measures the distance that a semisolid substance such as tomato sauce spreads. (*c*) A Brabender Visco-amylo-graph measures the changes occurring in consistency as a starch paste is heated. (*d*) A Corn Industries viscometer with gelometer measures the consistency and gel strength of a heated and cooled starch slurry. (*e*) A Bloom gelometer with a plunger measures the force required to penetrate the surface of a gel. (Reprinted from *Food Technology* Vol. 23, No. 5, pp. 38–39, 1969. The compressimeter (*a*) photograph reprinted from Vol. 26, No. 1, Cover, 1972. Copyright © by Institute of Food Technologists.)

(a)

(b)

(c)

(d)

(e)

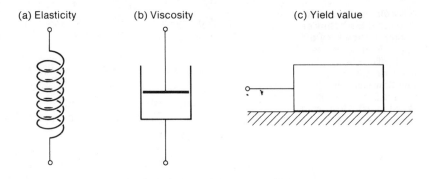

Figure 1.6

Rheological models. (a) Elasticity is represented as a spring. (b) Viscosity is represented as a dashpot. (c) Yield value is represented as a block on a flat surface. (From *Bakers Digest* Vol. 44 [Apr.], p. 41, 1970. With permission.)

(a) Elasticity

(b) Viscosity

(c) Yield value

shown in Figure 1.6 as a dashpot. A fluid in perfect viscous flow exhibits a rate of flow that is directly proportional to the applied force. Materials that show properties of both fluids and solids are called plastic substances. In these materials a force, called a *yield value,* must be first applied before flow will begin. Yield value is illustrated in Figure 1.6 as a block on a flat surface. When deformation begins the rate of deformation is proportional to the applied force.

Foods are particularly complex materials from a rheological standpoint. They are often heterogeneous and rheological properties may vary from one place to another within one food product. Most foods cannot be described by a simple rheological model since they usually possess all rheological properties to some degree. A model representing the rheological behavior of bread dough is shown in Figure 1.7 (Hlynka, 1970).

Flavor Measurement No imitative objective procedures are available to measure the taste and the aroma of food because the processes by which these senses operate are not fully understood. The closest imitative evaluation of flavor has come from research studies which measure nerve responses in experimental animals that are triggered by stimulating a taste cell.

The *gas chromatograph,* a sensitive laboratory instrument, has been widely used in the study of chemical molecules that contribute to the aroma and flavor of foods. Many different molecules may be present in the aroma from one food. For example, more than 400 components have been detected in coffee aroma and at least 120 constituents in fresh strawberry odor. A major task in aroma research is identifying these molecules and determining which ones are primarily responsible for characteristic aromas. *Gas chromatography* makes possible the separation and detection of the molecules.

The basic principles of gas chromatography are relatively simple, although modern gas chromatography equipment may be very com-

Figure 1.7

A rheological model to represent the behavior of dough shows a yield value, instantaneous elasticity, retarded elasticity, damping viscosity, and flow viscosity. (From *Bakers Digest* Vol. 44 [Apr.], p. 40, 1970. With permission.)

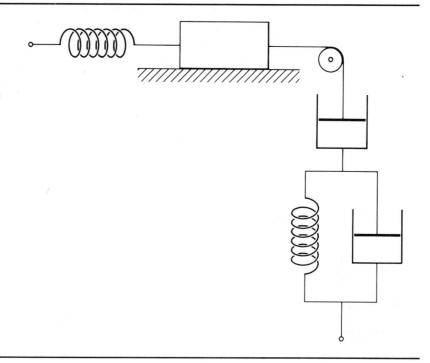

Figure 1.8

The basic parts of a gas chromatography system.

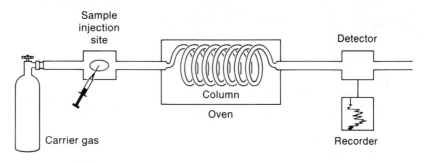

plex. A diagram representing the major parts of a gas–liquid chromatography system is given in Figure 1.8. Using a hypodermic-type syringe, a sample containing several different compounds is injected into the system which contains an inert carrier gas. The sample may be a gas or a liquid which changes to a gas at the high temperature of the heated injection chamber.

The gas carrying the sample compounds enters a long tubular column which is usually coiled like a spring. The column is packed with a finely ground inert solid support material which has been covered with a nonvolatile liquid. The column is maintained at a controlled temperature in an insulated chamber. As the sample compounds are carried through the column, they are alternatively adsorbed on the nonvolatile liquid and then reenter the gas stream in a continuous manner so that they gradually move down the column. Since some of the compounds in the sample are adsorbed on the liquid more readily and completely than are others, they move more slowly through the column. Differences in the way sample molecules partition between the stationary liquid phase and the moving gas phase separate these molecules so that they reach the end of the column at different times. Figure 1.9 illustrates the chromatographic separation of four different types of molecules as they move through a column.

A detector signals the emergence of each different compound in the sample as it activates a recording system. A peak for each separated compound is drawn on a strip chart as shown in Figure 1.10.

Figure 1.9

Chromatographic separation occurs when a sample that is a mixture of several different types of molecules is carried by an inert gas through a small packed tube or capillary. The tube is packed with a liquid that is held stationary on the surface of particles of a finely divided inert support material. Various components of the sample are adsorbed or dissolved in the liquid at different rates, and therefore are separated from each other as they move through the column. The separated components pass from the end of the column through a detector, whose output appears as a peak on a chart.

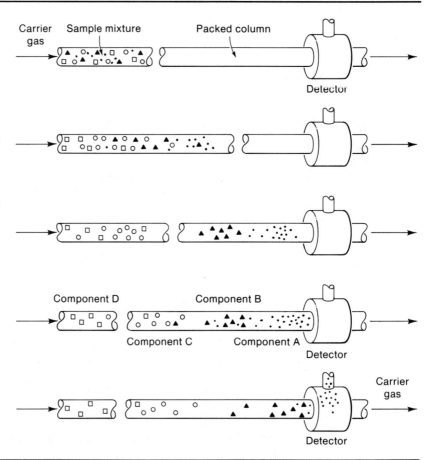

Figure 1.10

A gas liquid chromatogram. Each peak represents a different compound that was present in the original sample mixture.

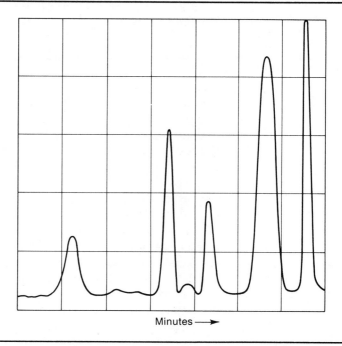

Minutes ⟶

NEED FOR FLAVOR SUBSTANCES

Changes in modern society influence the direction of change in the food industry. The production of flavorings and their use by food manufacturers has increased in recent years due to various developments throughout the world. World population growth has increased the demand for food, and so concentrated sources of protein for use as dietary components have been developed from soybeans, grains, oilseed cakes, and fish. However, for consumer acceptance these protein-rich materials must be put into an appropriately flavored form. With the high cost of producing meat, substitutes using vegetable protein concentrates or isolates are becoming popular in countries with advanced technology such as the United States. Acceptable flavoring substances may make the difference between success and failure in the marketing of these products.

During the 1950s, as part of a changing pattern of living in the United States, consumers began to use more prepared food products, the so-called "convenience foods." The food industry tried to meet and stimulate this demand with innovative products. However, it was soon apparent that research and development depended upon a better knowledge of flavor. Consumers were not willing to pay for products that did not deliver flavor to their satisfaction. The development of prepared foods, therefore, required a concurrent development of flavor substances to make these foods acceptable.

Since there are not enough available natural flavoring substances to flavor all of the foods that are being produced, synthetic flavors must also be used. Research in identifying natural food flavors will aid in developing new and improved synthetic flavor substances.

SUMMARY

Food quality is a complex concept with properties that include taste, aroma, texture, appearance, nutritional value, and safety. These properties must be evaluated by the food scientist in order to assure quality in processed and prepared food. They may be evaluated by subjective (sensory) or by objective procedures.

The sensory qualities of food may be classified according to the major senses by which they are perceived—appearance as visually observed, flavor as sensed by taste and olfaction, and texture as detected by touch. Perceptions from each of the senses are integrated by the brain into a total impression of quality. The eye sees shape, size, color, gloss, and luster as indicators of food quality. Taste buds, located in the tongue and mouth, apparently form complexes between taste stimulating substances and receptors at their surfaces and elicit four primary taste sensations—sweet, sour, salty, and bitter. A single taste cell probably possesses multiple receptor sites, each of which may have specificity for a particular primary taste. Taste thresholds vary greatly among individuals.

Many different odors can be distinguished by an individual when receptors in the epithelium of the nasal cavity are stimulated. Odor contributes greatly to what is commonly called the taste of food. At least three main factors probably contribute to the odor quality of a molecule, namely its size and shape, its functional chemical group, and its orientation with respect to the receptor surface in the nasal epithelium.

Pressure receptors and receptors for awareness of movement in the mouth are stimulated by the presence of food and send impulses to the brain for interpretation of texture. The term texture may be used for a major division of sensory quality covering all kinesthetic or muscle responses to food. Textural characteristics include 1. the mechanical properties of hardness, cohesiveness, viscosity, elasticity, and adhesiveness; 2. geometrical characteristics that are related to size, shape, and orientation of particles; and 3. other factors relating chiefly to moisture and fat content.

The development of flavor in food often involves the changing of flavor precursor molecules into flavor molecules, sometimes by enzymatic processes. The characteristic flavors of cabbage and onion develop when the cells are damaged and allow enzymes to contact appropriate substrates. Since flavor-producing enzymes are often destroyed in the processing of many vegetables, the flavor of the processed products may be improved by adding enzyme preparations after processing.

Flavor potentiators, which increase flavor without having a sensory effect of their own, include monosodium glutamate and certain 5'-nucleotides such as inosinic and guanylic acids. There is a synergistic relationship between these two types of flavor enhancers.

Subjective or sensory evaluation of food uses the human sense organs for taste, smell, sight, touch, and hearing. Groups of consumers may be used in preference testing for marketing purposes or a trained laboratory panel may perform difference testing and scoring. Standardized sensory testing procedures have been developed.

Since sensory evaluation of food is time consuming and costly, less expensive methods of analysis using laboratory instruments, have been sought. This objective evaluation of food may use imitative or nonimitative measurements of sensory properties. Many objective measurements involve the texture of food and include the determination of deformation and flow characteristics by penetrometers, compressimeters, and shearing devices. Elastic, plastic, and viscous flow are usually present to some degree in most foods.

A major task in flavor research is to identify the many different molecules that can be present in a food and to determine which ones are primarily responsible for the characteristic aroma and taste of that food. The gas chromatograph provides an effective laboratory tool for this type of study. Research in identifying natural food flavors will aid in the development of new and improved synthetic flavor substances to supplement natural flavors in the production of processed foods.

STUDY QUESTIONS

Each of the five senses affects evaluation and enjoyment of food, but the most important effects come from visual, olfactory, gustatory, and tactile stimuli.

1. Draw and label a diagram representing a single taste bud and explain how the taste bud functions in the detection of the primary tastes.
2. On a diagram of the head, locate the olfactory area in the nasal cavity and explain how this area contributes to the perception of flavor during the eating process.
3. Describe the characteristics of a food that might be perceived as a result of tactile stimuli.
4. Outline a general procedure that might be followed in humans to measure the taste threshold for any one of the four primary tastes.
5. Give an example of an inherited taste blindness.
6. Compare the following sugars for relative sweetness: glucose, fructose, sucrose, and lactose.

Flavor substances may be present naturally in foods or may be developed by heating or other processing techniques.

7. In the following list, distinguish foods in which the major flavor components are present naturally and foods that have had major flavor substances produced by processing or preparation procedures.

Foods
   rye bread
   fresh peaches
   maple syrup
   honey
   French bread
   rolled oats, boiled
   broiled sirloin steak
   potato chips
   camembert cheese
   fresh green onions
   baking chocolate
   strawberry jam

8. Discuss the reasons for adding "flavor enzyme" preparations to processed vegetables.
9. Describe the general flavor effects of the enzymes, alliinase, and myrosinase, in onion and in cabbage tissue respectively.

A flavor potentiator has no sensory effect of its own but increases the effect of other flavor agents.

10. Name three flavor potentiators that are used in seasoning food.

Characteristics of food may be evaluated by subjective (sensory) or by objective methods.

11. Below is a list of tools and instruments for evaluating food. Differentiate the tools that might be used in subjective methods of food evaluation from those that would be used in objective procedures.

Tools
   viscosimeter
   triangle test
   color difference meter
   tactile receptors
   color wheel for matching colors
   Kjeldahl protein determination
   gas chromatograph
   olfactory cell
   difference testing panel
   taste buds
   texturometer
   compressimeter
   preference testing panel
   penetrometer

12. Describe procedures generally involved in each of the following tests used in the sensory evaluation of food:
   a. paired comparison
   b. triangle test
   c. duo-trio test
   d. ranking
   e. scoring
   f. flavor profile method

13. Draw and explain rheological models for elasticity, viscous flow, and plasticity.

Gas chromatography is used in research concerned with the separation and identification of flavor components of food.

14. Outline the major parts of a gas chromatography system and explain what happens to a sample as it passes through these various parts.
15. Describe ways in which gas chromatography may be used to study the flavor of food and discuss the usefulness of the resulting information to the food industry.

REFERENCES

1. Amerine, M. A., R. M. Pangborn, and E. B. Roessler. 1965. *Principles of Sensory Evaluation of Food.* New York: Academic Press.

2. Hewitt, E. J., D. A. M. Mackay, K. Konigsbacher, and T. Hasselstrom. 1956. The role of enzymes in food flavors. *Food Technology* 10, 487.

3. Hlynka, I. 1970. Rheological properties of dough and their significance in the breadmaking process. *Bakers Digest* 44 (No. 2), 40.

4. Jefferson, S. C. and A. M. Erdman. 1970. Taste sensitivity and food aversions of teenagers. *Journal of Home Economics* 62, 605.

5. Kare, M. R. 1975. Changes in taste with age—infancy to senescence. *Food Technology* 29 (No. 8), 78.

6. Klopping, H. L. 1971. Olfactory theories and the odors of small molecules. *Journal of Agricultural and Food Chemistry* 19, 999.

7. Konigsbacher, K. S., E. J. Hewitt, and R. L. Evans. 1959. Application of flavor enzymes to processed foods. I. Panel studies. *Food Technology* 13, 128.

8. Korslund, M. K. and E. S. Eppright. 1967. Taste sensitivity and eating behavior of preschool children. *Journal of Home Economics* 59, 169.

9. Kramer, A. 1972. Texture—its definition, measurement, and relation to other attributes of food quality. *Food Technology* 26 (No. 1), 34.

10. Kuninaka, A. 1967. Flavor potentiators. In: Schultz, H. W., E. A. Day, and L. M. Libbey. *Symposium on Foods: The Chemistry and Physiology of Flavors.* Westport, Conn.: The Avi Publishing Company, Inc. pp. 515–535.

11. Larmond, E. 1973. Physical requirements for sensory testing. *Food Technology* 27 (No. 11), 28.

12. Mabrouk, A. F., J. K. Jarboe, and E. M. O'Connor. 1969. Water-soluble flavor precursors of beef. Extraction and fractionation. *Journal of Agricultural and Food Chemistry* 17, 5.

13. Moncrieff, R. W. 1967. *The Chemical Senses.* London: Leonard Hill.

14. Moriarty, J. H. 1969. The essence of flavor. *Bakers Digest* 43 (No. 4), 54.

15. Noble, A. C. 1975. Instrumental analysis of the sensory properties of food. *Food Technology* 29 (No. 12), 56.

16. Pangborn, R. M. 1963. Relative taste intensities of selected sugars and organic acids. *Journal of Food Science* 28, 726.

17. Pilgrim, F. J. 1961. Interactions of suprathreshold taste stimuli. In: Kare, M. R. and B. P. Halpern, editors. *Physiological and Behavioral Aspects of Taste*. Chicago: University of Chicago Press, pp. 66–78.

18. Prell, P. A. 1976. Preparation of reports and manuscripts which include sensory evaluation data. *Food Technology* 30 (No. 11), 40.

19. Price, S. 1969. Chemoreceptor proteins from taste buds. *Journal of Agricultural and Food Chemistry* 17, 709.

20. Rohan, T. A. 1970. Food flavor volatiles and their precursors. *Food Technology* 24, 1217.

21. Saldanha, P. H. and W. Becak. 1959. Taste thresholds for phenylthiourea among Ashkenazic Jews. *Science* 129, 150.

22. Schwimmer, S. 1963. Alteration of the flavor of processed vegetables by enzyme preparations. *Journal of Food Science* 28, 460.

23. Shallenberger, R. S. and T. E. Acree. 1969. Molecular structure and sweet taste. *Journal of Agricultural and Food Chemistry* 17, 701.

24. Szczesniak, A. S. 1972. Instrumental methods of texture measurement. *Food Technology* 26 (No. 1), 50.

25. Szczesniak, A. S. 1966. Texture measurements. *Food Technology* 20, 1292.

26. Szczesniak, A. S. 1963. Classification of textural characteristics. *Journal of Food Science* 28, 385.

27. Teranishi, R., P. Issenberg, I. Hornstein, and E. L. Wick. 1971. *Flavor Research*. New York: Marcel Dekker, Inc.

28. Venstrom, D. and J. E. Amoore. 1968. Olfactory threshold in relation to age, sex, or smoking. *Journal of Food Science* 33, 264.

29. Von Sydow, E. 1971. Flavor—a chemical or psychophysical concept? *Food Technology* 25 (No. 1), 40.

30. Woskow, M. H. 1969. Selectivity in flavor modification by 5'-ribonucleotides. *Food Technology* 23, 1364.

31. Yamaguchi, S., T. Yoshikawa, S. Ikeda, and T. Ninomiya, 1970. Studies on the taste of some sweet substances. Part I. Measurement of the relative sweetness. *Agricultural and Biological Chemistry* 34, 181.

CHAPTER 2

CHEMICAL COMPOSITION AND
PHYSICAL STRUCTURE OF FOOD

Most foods are not homogeneous. The macroscopic appearance of many foods reveals obvious differences from one portion to another. For example, a slice of fresh tomato has skin, flesh, seeds, and entrapped juices, each differing in structure. If foods are viewed microscopically, additional differences in structure are also apparent. Various types of cells and intercellular substances may be seen if fresh fruits, vegetables, or meats are examined. The electron microscope allows us to see intracellular bodies and even large molecules such as proteins.

Foods are composed of chemical molecules. Those substances, present in largest amounts and making up the gross chemical composition of food, are water, carbohydrates, fats, and proteins. (Carbohydrates are described in Chapter 10, fats in Chapter 18, and proteins in Chapter 22.) Minerals make up the noncombustible or ash portion. Many other chemical substances, including vitamins and organic acids, are present in food in small amounts. As foods undergo processing and preparation procedures, their characteristic properties, affecting their quality, are influenced by a changing chemical composition and a changing physical structure.

2.1

CHEMICAL COMPOSITION OF FOOD

A large number of analyses have been carried out, and the results published, on the chemical composition of food. In some cases, only a single chemical substance or nutrient in the food has been determined; in others, several. Published data on food composition have been compiled, evaluated, and published in comprehensive tables.

In the United States, the Department of Agriculture's Consumer and Food Economics Institute has assumed the responsibility for publishing food composition tables. This work was begun in the 1890s by W. O. Atwater, who listed the gross chemical composition of foods, according to their percentages of water, protein, fat, carbohydrate, and ash. Today a computerized bank of food composition data that includes information on up to 67 components of a food is maintained by the U. S. Department of Agriculture (USDA). Food composition data are sought by USDA from private industry, government agencies, and academic institutions. Agriculture Handbook No. 456, *Nutritive Value of American Foods,* includes nutritive values for household measures and market units of foods (Adams, 1975). Agriculture Handbook No. 8, *Composition of Foods* (Watt and Merrill, 1963) is being published by sections, in a revised and expanded looseleaf form. The first section released, No. 8–1, lists values for 144 dairy and egg products.

Food preserving techniques such as canning and freezing increase the availability of food year round. Although the effects of processing on nutritive composition have not been studied extensively, some changes apparently occur. Processing often affects texture, flavor, and appearance. Chemical and physical analyses assist the food manufacturer in evaluating both nutritional and esthetic qualities of processed foods.

A working knowledge of the gross composition of food is a valuable tool for the student of food science. Proteins, fats, and carbohydrates each have unique characteristics and can be expected to behave in reasonably predictable ways when subjected to various processing and preparation procedures. Information on the types of proteins, fats, or carbohydrates and the amounts of each in a food may be used to plan new processing techniques and to evaluate the results.

2.2

DISPERSION SYSTEMS

The way in which the chemical components of food are physically dispersed influences a number of quality characteristics. Well-emulsified mayonnaise, for example, is a satiny smooth dispersion of oil in water. When not properly prepared, this product becomes a curdled, broken emulsion, although retaining its same chemical composition. The marked differences in the appearance and texture of the two products result from a great change in the physical dispersion of their ingredients.

Chemical molecules may be present in foods in the solid state, the liquid state, or the gaseous state. In the solid state the molecules exist in a specific ordered pattern. They may vibrate in place, but they move very little. In a liquid the molecules are less ordered or organized. They move about freely and the liquid takes the shape of the container in which it is held. In a gas the molecules are completely disordered. At ordinary pressures and temperatures, they are usually widely separated in space and are constantly moving.

Energy is involved in the transformation of a substance from one state to another. The heat required to change the state of a substance without changing its temperature is called *latent heat*. When a liquid changes to a vapor, the latent heat is called *heat of vaporization* and when a liquid changes to a solid the latent heat is called *heat of fusion*. For example, changing liquid water at atmospheric pressure and 100°C (212°F) to water vapor or steam at the same pressure and temperature, requires as latent heat (heat of vaporization) approximately 540 calories per gram (g) of water transformed. This is an *endothermic* process, meaning that energy is absorbed in the transformation. An equal amount of energy is released when steam condenses to form 1 g of water. Liquid water may also be changed to solid ice in the process of freezing. This is an *exothermic* reaction which releases approximately 80 calories per gram. The same amount of energy is absorbed when 1 g of ice melts.

Foods are usually mixtures of substances in various states. The mixtures may be called *dispersion systems,* with the subdivided material or dispersed phases being scattered throughout a continuous phase called the *dispersion medium*. Dispersion systems may be classified according to the state of the matter in each phase. Using this classification method, the possible dispersion systems that are most applicable to food products are:

Dispersed phase	Dispersion medium	Example
Gas	Liquid	Whipped egg whites
Gas	Solid	Sponge cake
Liquid	Liquid	Mayonnaise
Solid	Liquid	Proteins in milk

Dispersion systems may also be classified on the basis of the size of the dispersed particles as 1. true solutions; 2. colloidal dispersions; or 3. suspensions. Some of the comparative characteristics of these dispersions are shown in Table 2.1.

In some instances the type of dispersion of substances in foods—true solution, colloidal dispersion, or suspension—may change with changing conditions. However, small molecules or ions such as sugars, salts, and vitamins are usually found in true solution; large molecules such as proteins, pectic substances, cellulose, and cooked starch are usually colloidally dispersed; clumps of molecules such as fat globules and uncooked starch granules are usually suspended and readily separate from the dispersion medium on standing.

Various treatments given to food products during processing or preparation may change the dispersion so that particles are either more finely divided and dispersed or are more aggregated. Changes in the extent of dispersion may markedly alter the properties of a food product. Therefore, it is important to know what may be expected to occur when foods are treated in various ways. Applying heat may cause either an increase or a decrease in dispersion depending upon the sys-

Table 2.1 Comparative Characteristics of Dispersions

Characteristic	True solutions	Colloidal dispersions	Suspensions
Particle size	Less than 1 millimicron (mμ) in diameter	1 mμ to 0.1 or 0.2 micrometers (μm) in diameter	Greater than 0.2 μm in diameter
Nature of particles	Ions or small molecules	Macromolecules or small groups of molecules	Large groups of molecules
Type of movement	Constant kinetic motion	Brownian movement	Gravitational movement
Type of charge on particles	Uncharged or some positive and some negative	All positive or all negative	Usually uncharged
Visibility of particles	Invisible under any microscope	Visible under electron microscope	Visible under ordinary microscope
Filterability of particles	Pass through most membranes and parchments	Pass through usual filters but not most membranes	Do not pass through filters
Stability	Very stable	Moderately stable	Unstable
Gel formation	Usually not capable of gel formation	Capable of sol-gel transformation	Not capable of gel formation

tem being heated. Heating a sugar solution, for example, increases the degree of dispersion of the sucrose molecules in water. This occurs because the kinetic energy and consequent movement of the small sugar molecules increases. Heating a gelatin gel breaks hydrogen bonds between gelatin molecules and increases the dispersion of the gelatin. On the other hand, heating egg whites causes the proteins to coagulate and bond together, resulting in a decreased degree of dispersion.

Mechanical treatments such as grinding, beating, or homogenizing may either increase or decrease the degree of dispersion. If egg whites are beaten, the degree of dispersion of the proteins is decreased as they begin to coagulate. However, grinding meat increases the degree of dispersion of the connective tissue and homogenization of milk increases the dispersion of fat globules.

The addition of acid to foods will have an effect that is related to the resulting pH. When acid is continuously added to milk in amounts that will lower the pH of the milk from approximately 6.6 to about 3.4, the casein particles will clump together in curds and separate from the whey. A decreased degree of dispersion of the casein has occurred. This process is desirable in the making of cheese but undesirable if it occurs in the preparation of tomato soup. Acid developed in bread dough during fermentation causes an increased dispersion of gluten.

The crystallization of sugar in the making of candies such as fudge and fondant is an example of changing the type of dispersion system in foods during preparation. A solution of sugar in water is concentrated by boiling and supersaturated by undisturbed cooling. Many sugar molecules from the supersaturated solution then combine in a set pattern to produce crystals that can be seen under the microscope. These crystals represent a suspension of sugar particles in a very concentrated sugar syrup. Thus, in the process of preparing the candy, the state of dispersion of some of the sugar is changed from a true solution to a suspension.

2.3

WATER AND SOLUTIONS IN FOOD

Water has unique molecular characteristics and has been called a universal solvent. It is present in foods in amounts ranging from 1 to 98 percent and plays several important roles in food preparation and processing. It is the dispersion medium for most food systems, dispersing various substances in true solution, colloidal dispersion, or suspension. It promotes ionization of electrolytes. This effect is of particular importance in such reactions as those that occur when chemical leavening agents are added to batters or doughs.

Water may be soft or hard. *Soft water* may contain some organic matter but no mineral salts. *Hard water* is of two general types, temporary or permanent. *Temporary hard water* contains bicarbonates of calcium or magnesium. These salts are precipitated as carbonates on boiling and hardness is thus eliminated. *Permanent hard water* contains calcium, magnesium, and iron sulfates that are not precipitated by boiling. They form insoluble salts with soap and decrease the cleansing effectiveness of hard water. Hard water is generally more alkaline than soft water or distilled water that is sometimes used in food research. Distilled water contains no mineral salts or organic matter. The degree of alkalinity or acidity of water may affect the quality characteristics of many foods, such as the color and texture of vegetables, and the hydrolysis of sugar in boiling solutions. (Various effects of acidity in food systems are discussed in Chapter 3.)

BOILING WATER

Water is used as a medium for applying heat in food preparation. For this purpose it may be used either in the liquid state or the gaseous state as steam. The *boiling point* of a liquid may be defined as the temperature at which the vapor pressure of the liquid is equal to the atmospheric pressure resting over its surface. At any temperature there will be some molecules that have vaporized from the surface. *Vapor pressure* is the pressure that these molecules produce. The vapor pressure increases with increasing temperature as more molecules are vaporized. At the boiling point, the vapor pressure of the liquid becomes high enough to push aside the atmospheric pressure. Bubbles of vapor form in the interior of the liquid, rise to the surface, and break the surface as they are released. Once boiling occurs, the temperature of the boiling liquid does not rise further. Any heat that is added at the boiling point is used to change the state of the water from liquid to vapor and is called latent heat. Figure 2.1 illustrates the relationships between the vapor pressure and the temperature of water.

The boiling point of a liquid depends upon atmospheric pressure and decreases as altitude increases. At sea level with an atmospheric pressure of 760 mm mercury, water boils at 100°C (212°F). For every 960 ft above sea level, the boiling point of water is decreased 1°C (1.8°F). The boiling point of water for any locality may be calculated if the altitude is known. For example, at an altitude of 5,760 ft above sea level one would divide 5760 ft by 960 ft per °C to yield 6°C, indicating that water boils at a temperature 6°C less at this altitude than at sea level. Thus the boiling point of water at 5760 ft above sea level is 94°C (201°F).

The boiling point of water is unusually high in view of the small size of the water molecule. This high boiling point results from the dipolar nature of water, as illustrated in Figure 2.2. The water molecule has two positive poles and one negative pole. This produces attraction between adjacent molecules, which tend to cluster together, bonded by hydrogen. Although the strength of a hydrogen bond is small in comparison to that of a covalent bond, additional energy is required to break these bonds and expel the water molecules from the surface of the liquid.

Figure 2.1

Comparison of vapor pressure-temperature curves for pure water and a one Molal solution.

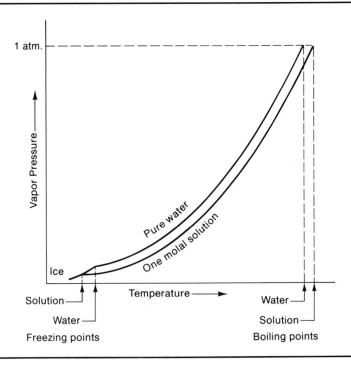

Figure 2.2

Water is a dipolar compound and water molecules bond together in clusters.

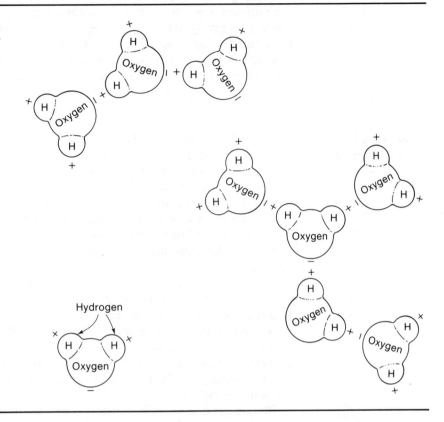

The temperature at which water will boil may be increased above its normal boiling point by use of a pressure cooker. A pressure cooker is made from a strong metal material and has a tight-fitting lid that is capable of withstanding steam pressure exerted from within. In use, a small amount of water is placed inside the cooker before it is tightly closed. As the container and its contents are heated, water molecules vaporize and produce steam which cannot escape. The trapped steam increases vapor pressure over the surface of the water. An equilibrium of pressures cannot be reached and the boiling point continues to rise as long as heating is continued. A pressure cooker is used when temperatures substantially above the usual boiling point of water are required. For example, a pressure cooker must be used in the canning of nonacid vegetables and meats where resistant bacterial spores may create potential health hazards. It may also be used to decrease the usual cooking time for various food products such as meat and vegetables.

The normal boiling point of water may be decreased by forming a partial vacuum over the surface of the water. With the creation of a vacuum, there is less pressure at the surface and less heat is required for boiling. Equilibrium between the vapor pressure of the water and the pressure above its surface is reached at a lower temperature. Boiling at a relatively low temperature is advantageous for the processing of a number of foods that require the evaporation of substantial amounts of water. Examples of such foods include evaporated milk and concentrated fruit juices. Heat-produced changes are minimized when evaporation is done under a vacuum.

SOLUTIONS AND BOILING POINTS

Water acts as a solvent to dissolve sugars and salts in many food products. When a true solution is formed, the relationship between the vapor pressure of water and its temperature is changed as illustrated in Figure 2.1. Nonvolatile solute molecules displace water molecules across the surface of the liquid and decrease the tendency for water molecules to escape as vapor. Additional heat must be applied to the system to bring about vaporization and the boiling point of the solution is therefore higher than the boiling point of the pure water solvent.

The effect of solutes on vapor pressure and boiling point is directly proportional to the number of particles that are dissolved. The *molal boiling point raising rule* describes this relationship. It states that for every *gram molecular weight* (GMW) of nonvolatile solute in 1000 g water, the boiling point is raised 0.52°C (0.94°F). With information concerning the composition of a true solution, the number of GMWs or *moles* of solute may be calculated and the theoretical boiling point of the solution estimated.

Boiling sugar solutions are basic in candymaking. The boiling point of a sugar solution is not stable. As boiling continues, water is evaporated from the solution and the concentration of the solute increases. A more concentrated solution boils at a higher temperature and the boiling temperature of the solution thus continues to rise as it is boiled. In the preparation of candies, the boiling temperature of a sugar solution is used as an indication of concentration and of doneness. (Candies are discussed in Chapter 10.)

Figure 2.1 also shows that the freezing point of a solution is lower than the freezing point of pure water. Water freezes when the vapor pressure of the liquid water is equal to that of ice; thus, an equilibrium is established. The freezing temperature of water is 0°C (32°F). Sherbets, ices, and ice creams contain sugars and salts in solution. As a result, these products freeze at a temperature that is below the freezing point of water. Just as the boiling temperature of a solution increases with continued boiling, the freezing temperature of a solution decreases with continued freezing. Ice crystallizes as freezing begins, removing pure water from the solution. The remaining solution becomes more concentrated and causes a continued lowering of the freezing point. (Frozen desserts are discussed in Chapter 11.)

2.4

COLLOIDAL SYSTEMS IN FOODS

The word *colloid* comes from the Greek language and means "glue-like." Colloids were first recognized in the 1860s by Graham who was studying the movement of various substances through fine membranes. He found that molecules like those that make up gelatin and glue did not pass through the pores or openings. At the present time, the term colloid is usually used to refer to the state or character of a dispersion system rather than as a classification of the dispersed substance itself.

STABILIZATION OF COLLOIDAL DISPERSIONS

The *colloidal state* is an intermediate one between the true solution and the suspension, as far as size of dispersed particles is concerned. Because colloidal particles are larger and have less kinetic energy than do those in true solution, they are not as stable. However, they are moderately stable and under usual conditions of food preparation and storage will stay dispersed much longer than will the particles in suspensions. There are three major factors that are responsible for the stabilization of colloidal systems in food. They are 1. Brownian movement of the dispersed particles; 2. like electric charges on the dispersed particles; and 3. water of hydration around the dispersed particles.

Colloidal particles in dispersion continue to move back and forth in all directions even though they have lost most of their kinetic energy. This type of random motion is known as *Brownian movement* and is the result of the colloidal particles being constantly and unevenly bombarded by the smaller molecules of the dispersion medium, which, in food products, is usually water. Even though Brownian movement is a slow and somewhat cumbersome type of movement, it helps to stabilize a colloidal system by decreasing the tendency for dispersed particles to settle out. Thus, the moving particles resist the downward pull of gravity.

The surfaces of colloidal particles carry electric charges. The net charge on each particle may be either positive or negative. The charge may come from the ionization of chemical groups within the colloidal molecule itself or it may result from adsorption of ions at the surface of the particle. In either case, each of the particles in the system will carry the same net charge.

Since like charges repel each other, the charge on colloidally dispersed particles stabilizes the system by keeping particles separated (Figure 2.3). When two colloidal particles approach each other, they are repulsed and prevented from clumping together to form a larger particle that is more likely to settle out.

The charges on colloidal particles are readily disturbed by the addition of small amounts of acid or base. A positively charged hydrogen ion (H^+) may neutralize negative charges on a dispersed particle while a

Figure 2.3

Like charges repel each other.

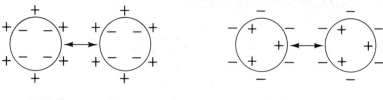

NET Charge positive   NET Charge negative

negatively charged hydroxyl ion (OH⁻) decreases the positive charge. If charges on colloidally dispersed particles are neutralized, the particles lose the repulsion that comes from the like charges and they tend to adhere to each other, forming larger particles that are unstable. The milk protein, casein, is stabilized to a great degree by net negative charges. Therefore, this protein is susceptible to precipitation by acid as the negative charges are neutralized.

A layer of water molecules may be bound to colloidally dispersed particles by hydrogen bonds. Other water molecules then bind to the first layer of water and several consecutive layers of water molecules may eventually surround a colloidal particle. This *water of hydration* or water shell moves with the colloidal particle and stabilizes the system by preventing the particles from contacting each other. The water shell acts as a buffer between dispersed particles. Colloidal particles that are attracted to the water solvent are said to be *hydrophilic*. Examples of hydrophilic colloidal food systems include gelatin and water dispersions, egg proteins in a baked custard, and starch in a cornstarch pudding. *Hydrophobic* particles are not attracted to water and are consequently not well hydrated in a water dispersion. Oil particles dispersed in the vinegar of French dressing and the casein dispersion in milk are examples of hydrophobic systems.

PROTECTIVE COLLOIDS

Colloidal substances may in certain cases act to stabilize other dispersed particles. A dispersion of oil in water, for example, is very unstable with the oil readily separating from the water. If a small amount of a hydrophilic colloid, such as the proteins of egg yolk, is added to the oil and water mixture, the egg proteins coat the dispersed oil particles and give them hydrophilic properties. The egg proteins act as protective colloids by wrapping a coating or shell around the dispersed oil particles and preventing them from clumping together. Mayonnaise is an oil in water dispersion that is stabilized by egg yolk proteins acting as protective colloids.

SURFACE PROPERTIES OF COLLOIDS

Colloid chemistry is sometimes called surface chemistry because of the relatively large amount of surface area on the finely divided particles. Therefore, *surface* and/or *interfacial tension* and effects of surface active agents play important roles in colloidal systems.

Surface tension is the tension created by unequal forces of attraction at a liquid/gas interface. The molecules of a liquid that are close to the surface do not have the same type of attractive forces surrounding them as do those molecules in the interior of the liquid. Figure 2.4 represents these forces of attraction. A molecule inside the liquid is surrounded by other similar molecules and is attracted with equal force in all directions. On the other hand, a molecule close to the surface is only partially surrounded by other similar molecules. It is less attracted to the air at the surface than it is to other liquid molecules. Unbalanced attractive forces are thus created. The unbalanced downward pull on the surface molecules is actually a force that causes the liquid to behave as though it were covered with a skin and is called surface tension. Water has a relatively high surface tension because water molecules have a great attraction for each other.

When oil and water are poured into one container, they separate into two distinct layers. The line between the two liquids is called the *interface*. The same kind of unbalanced attractive forces occur at an interface between two immiscible liquids as occurs between a liquid and a gas. A tension or force develops that is called *interfacial tension*. When interfacial tension is high, as it is between oil and water, the liquids do not mix spontaneously. They may be temporarily mixed by vigorous beating or shaking. However, if mixing is to be more permanent, a third

Figure 2.4

Unbalanced attractive forces are created at the surface of a liquid.

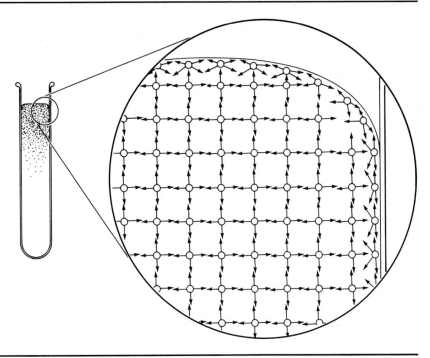

substance of a special type, called a *surface active agent,* must be added.

All surface active agents have a common molecular characteristic, that is, one part of the molecule is polar while another part is nonpolar. Another characteristic is unequal relative strengths of the polar and nonpolar groups. Some polar and nonpolar groups found on organic molecules are shown in Figure 2.5. Polar groups are hydrophilic and thus soluble in water while nonpolar groups are hydrophobic and not soluble in water. The polar part of a surface active molecule is soluble in water while the nonpolar part is not. When a surface active agent or *surfactant* is dispersed in a liquid, more of its molecules are found at the surface of the liquid than are found in the interior. The surface active molecules are oriented at the surface with their polar parts in aqueous liquid and their nonpolar parts oriented toward the air at the surface.

A number of surface active compounds are useful in food preparation as emulsifying and foaming agents. (Emulsions are discussed in Chapter 18 and foams in Chapter 19.) They are considered to be a part of colloidal chemistry because surface properties play an important role in their development and stabilization. A monoglyceride, shown in Figure 2.6, may serve as an example of a surface active agent used in food preparation. Polar parts of this molecule include the OH groups and the ester linkage. The long hydrocarbon chain is nonpolar. This compound, used as an emulsifying agent in shortened cakes, acts as a

Figure 2.5

Both polar and nonpolar groups are found on organic molecules.

Polar Groups

$$\overset{\displaystyle O}{\underset{\displaystyle \|}{}}$$
—C—OH   (carboxyl)

—OH   (alcohol)

—C—   (ketone)

—C=O (with H)   (aldehyde)

—NH₂   (amine)

—C—O—C—   (ester)

—C—O—P—O—C—   (phosphate ester)

—C=C—   (double bond)

Nonpolar Groups

—CH₃   (methyl)

—CH₂CH₂CH₂CH₂CH₂CH₂CH₂CH₂CH₂CH₂etc

(long carbon chains)

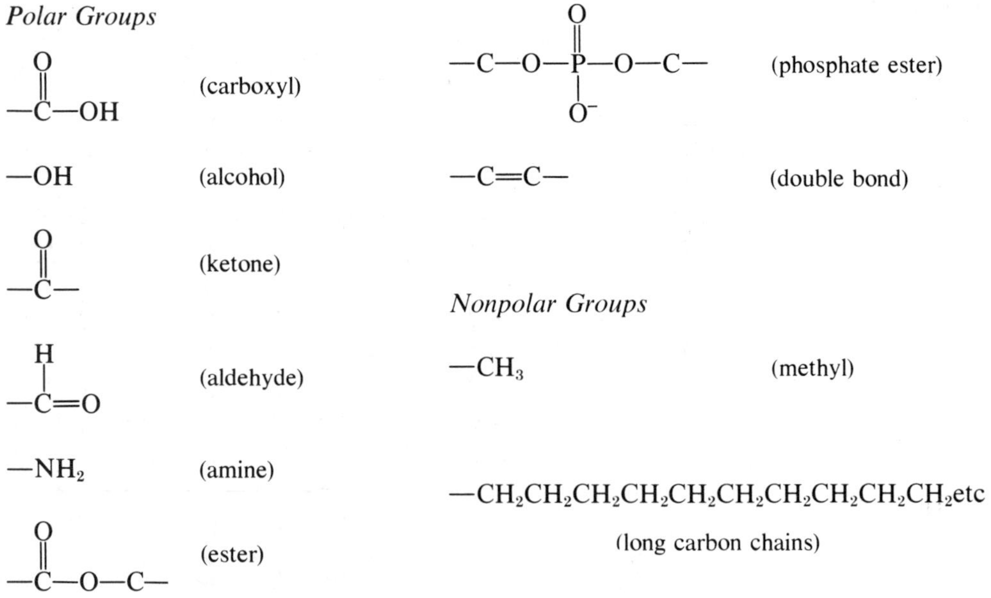

Figure 2.6

A monoglyceride molecule is a surface active agent having both polar and nonpolar groups.

Polar ester linkage

bridge between the water and fat components of cake batter, because of its orientation at the interface between fat and water, with its polar parts in the water and its nonpolar portions in the fat. Therefore, it makes possible a more than usually complete mixing of fat and water in the batter. Because of the improved mixing of fat and water, greater volume and finer texture are produced in the finished cake. Again, this illustrates the importance of physical structure as well as chemical composition in determining food quality.

SUMMARY

The characteristic properties of food, affecting its quality, are determined by both the chemical composition and the physical structure of the chemical components within the food system. Knowledge of the chemical composition of food is a valuable tool in predicting the effects of processing and preparation on the quality of the finished product. The USDA accumulates and publishes extensive information on food composition.

Foods are usually mixtures of various substances in solid, liquid, or gaseous states. These mixtures are dispersion systems containing dispersed phases and dispersion medium. Dispersion systems may be classified according to the state of matter—gas, liquid, or solid—in each phase. They may also be classified on the basis of the size of the dispersed particles as true solutions, colloidal dispersions, or suspensions. Small molecules or ions, such as sugars and salts, are usually dispersed in true solution in foods. Large molecules, such as proteins and cooked starch, are colloidally dispersed. Large fat globules and uncooked starch granules form suspensions. Various treatments given to foods during processing and preparation, such as heating, beating, homogenizing, or adding acid, may change the degree of dispersion. Dispersed particles may become more finely divided or become more aggregated.

Colloidal dispersions in foods are stabilized by Brownian movement of the dispersed particles, by like charges on the dispersed particles, and by water of hydration around the particles. Colloidal substances may also stabilize other suspended hydrophobic particles by forming a hydrophilic coating on their surfaces.

Surface phenomena play important roles in food dispersion systems. Surface active agents may be used to decrease surface or interfacial tension by allowing the mixing of two immiscible liquids such as fat and water. A surface active agent acts as a bridge between fat and water because it has both hydrophilic polar groups and hydrophobic nonpolar groups as part of its chemical structure.

Water is a unique molecule and an important constituent of foods. It serves as the dispersion medium in most food systems, promotes ionization, and provides a medium for applying heat because of its relatively high boiling point. Temperatures higher than the usual boiling point of water may be achieved by use of a pressure cooker. Lower boiling temperatures are possible with use of a vacuum. The boiling point of water is raised and the freezing point lowered by dissolving substances in true solution. These effects are of importance in boiling sugar solutions for making candies and in preparing frozen desserts such as sherbets and ice creams.

STUDY QUESTIONS

A knowledge of the chemical composition of food is useful in planning for and evaluating preparation and processing effects.

1. Compare the average gross composition of fruits, vegetables, grains, meats, and milk.

The way in which the chemical components of food are physically dispersed influences quality characteristics.

2. Describe examples of foods with the same chemical composition but differing quality characteristics due to differences in physical structure.

Dispersion systems may be classified on the basis of the state of matter in each phase or according to the size of dispersed particles.

3. What foods or food products are illustrations or examples of each of the following dispersion systems?
   a. Gas dispersed in a liquid
   b. Gas dispersed in a solid
   c. Liquid dispersed in a liquid
   d. Solid dispersed in a liquid

4. Compare each of the following characteristics for true solutions, colloidal dispersions, and suspensions.
   a. Particle size
   b. Nature of particles
   c. Type of movement
   d. Visibility of particles
   e. Filterability of particles
   f. Stability
   g. Ability to form a gel

Various types of dispersion systems may be found in food.

5. For each of the following components of food, list the usual type of dispersion (true solution, colloidal dispersion, or suspension).
   a. Sugars
   b. Uncooked starch
   c. Cooked starch
   d. Cellulose
   e. Pectic substances
   f. Proteins
   g. Fats
   h. Sodium chloride (salt)
6. Describe examples of increasing or decreasing the degree of dispersion of substances in food by use of heat, mechanical treatment, and acid.

Colloidal dispersions may be stabilized by Brownian movement, by "like" charges on the dispersed particles, and by water of hydration.

7. Explain how each of the three factors listed above may act to stabilize colloidal systems.

Tension at a gas/liquid surface or a liquid/liquid interface may be lowered by surface active agents.

8. With the use of a sketch, explain why surface or interfacial tension develops.
9. Explain how surface active agents lower surface or interfacial tension.
10. Explain why foams and emulsions are considered in a study of colloid chemistry.

The water molecule has a unique chemical structure and plays important roles in food.

11. Describe some major functions of water in food preparation and processing.
12. Show, by drawing a sketch, how water molecules associate with each other in hydrogen bonding and use this as a basis for explaining water's relatively high boiling point, heat of vaporization, and surface tension.
13. Calculate the boiling points of water at 4500 ft and at 7400 ft above sea level.
14. Give the energy involved, in calories per gram, in changing water from:
    a. Ice to liquid
    b. Liquid to ice

    c. Liquid to water vapor

    d. Water vapor to liquid

    In each case indicate if the process is endothermic or exothermic.

15. Explain how high temperatures are achieved in a pressure cooker and how low boiling temperatures may be achieved in a vacuum pan. Give examples showing advantageous use of the pressure cooker and of a vacuum in food processing and preparation.

Substances in true solution decrease the vapor pressure, increase the boiling point, and decrease the freezing point of pure water.

16. Explain why solutes affect the vapor pressure, boiling point, and freezing point of water.

17. Give examples of food products in which the effect of solute on boiling or freezing points is of particular importance.

REFERENCES

1. Adams, C. F. 1975. *Nutritive Value of American Foods*. Agriculture Handbook No. 456. Washington, D. C.: U. S. Department of Agriculture, U. S. Government Printing Office.

2. Watt, B. K. and A. L. Merrill. 1963. *Composition of Foods*. Agriculture Handbook No. 8. Washington, D. C.: U. S. Department of Agriculture, U. S. Government Printing Office.

CHAPTER 3

pH AND ACIDITY IN FOOD

The properties and quality of many different food products are affected by their *pH* or *active acidity*. After a review of some principles governing pH and acidity, several examples of the effects of acids found in foods will be described briefly. These examples will be reviewed again in the chapters dealing with food products.

3.1

REVIEW OF pH AND ACIDITY

When hydrogen ions (H$^+$) from an acid and hydroxyl ions (OH$^-$) from a base are brought together, they readily combine to form water molecules (H$_2$O). This reaction, known as *neutralization,* is typical of acids and bases. Salts, consisting of the negative ion of an acid and the positive ion of a base, are also formed in neutralization.

Strong acids such as hydrochloric acid (HCl) and strong bases such as sodium hydroxide (NaOH) are completely dissociated or ionized in dilute solution. Weak acids and weak bases are only slightly ionized in solution. Most of the acids commonly found in foods are weak organic acids. These include lactic, acetic, citric, oxalic, malic, and tartaric acids. Lactic acid is produced, in sour or cultured milks and in some pickled foods, by the action of certain bacteria. Oxalic acid forms insoluble salts with divalent ions such as calcium. This acid is present in relatively large amounts in spinach and in rhubarb. Acetic, citric, malic, and tartaric acids are widely distributed in fruit and vegetable tissues. The chemical structures for these acids are shown on the next page in Figure 3.1.

When a weak acid is neutralized by a strong base, the hydroxyl ions (OH$^-$) from the strong base combine with the small number of hydrogen ions (H$^+$) that have dissociated from the weak acid to form water. As the H$^+$ is removed by this combination, more H$^+$ will dissociate from the weak acid and this process of dissociation and neutralization will continue, as long as sufficient base is available, until all of the H$^+$ has dissociated from the weak acid.

Acidity can be measured in two ways. First, the concentration of

Figure 3.1

Chemical structures for weak organic acids commonly found in foods.

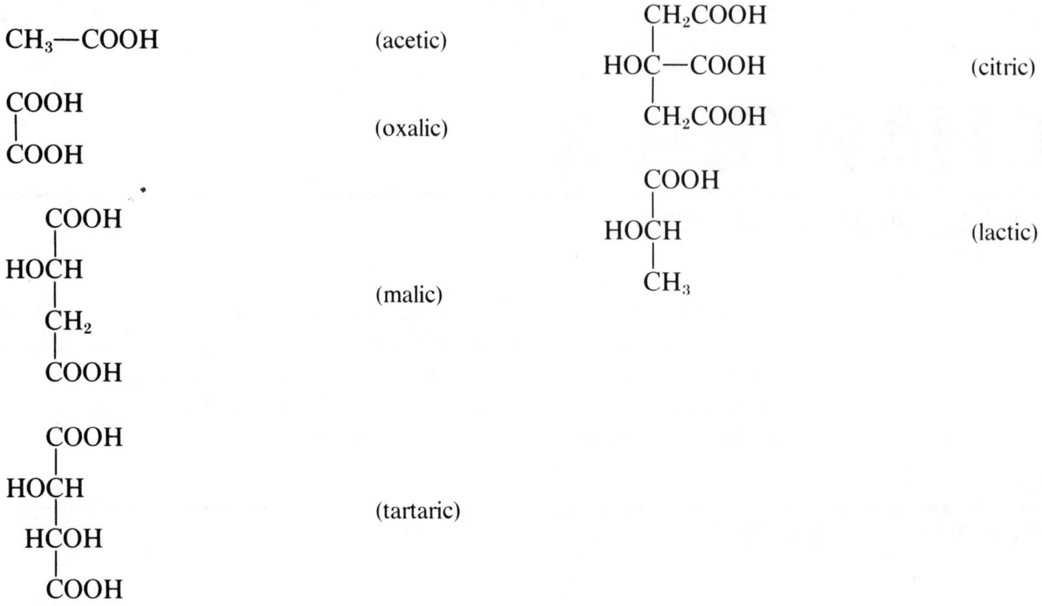

CH_3-COOH (acetic)

$$\begin{array}{l} COOH \\ | \\ COOH \end{array}$$ (oxalic)

$$\begin{array}{l} COOH \\ | \\ HOCH \\ | \\ CH_2 \\ | \\ COOH \end{array}$$ (malic)

$$\begin{array}{l} COOH \\ | \\ HOCH \\ | \\ HCOH \\ | \\ COOH \end{array}$$ (tartaric)

$$\begin{array}{l} CH_2COOH \\ | \\ HOC-COOH \\ | \\ CH_2COOH \end{array}$$ (citric)

$$\begin{array}{l} COOH \\ | \\ HOCH \\ | \\ CH_3 \end{array}$$ (lactic)

hydrogen ions that exists in solution at any one time may be measured. This is called *active* or *effective acidity* and is expressed as *pH*. Second, all of the hydrogen in the solution that can be replaced by a metal, may be measured. This is done by neutralizing the acid solution with an appropriate amount of hydroxide base and is called *titratable* or *total acidity*. All of the hydrogen in inorganic acids such as hydrochloric acid (HCl) and sulfuric acid (H_2SO_4) is readily replaceable or ionizable. However, organic acids have some hydrogen that cannot be easily replaced by a metal. In acetic acid, for example, only the hydrogen of the carboxyl group ($-COOH$) is replaceable or acidic.

By definition, a solution of an acid which contains 1 g of replaceable hydrogen per liter (l) is called a *normal* (N) *solution*. A one-half normal (0.5 N) nitric acid (HNO_3) solution has the same total acidity as a one-half normal (0.5 N) lactic acid ($HC_3O_3H_5$) solution and half as much total acidity as a one normal (1.0 N) lactic acid solution.

Water is a weak electrolyte since it is very slightly ionized according to the following equation:

$$H_2O \rightleftharpoons H^+ + OH^-$$

In pure water an equilibrium exists as:

$$\frac{[H^+][OH^-]^*}{[H_2O]} = K\dagger$$

In all dilute solutions the concentration of water can be considered constant and can be combined with K to give K_w, the dissociation constant for water. The value for K_w is 1.0×10^{-14} at 25°C (77°F), thus:

$$[H^+][OH^-] = K[H_2O] = K_w = 1.0 \times 10^{-14}$$

In pure water all of the H^+ and all of the OH^- must come from the dissociation of water molecules. There will be the same number of H^+ as OH^-. The concentration of each of these ions in water is 1.0×10^{-7} moles per l, thus:

$$[H^+][OH^-] = (1.0 \times 10^{-7})(1.0 \times 10^{-7}) = 1.0 \times 10^{-14}$$

If an acid is added to pure water, the concentration of H^+ will increase above 1.0×10^{-7} moles per l. In order to maintain equilibrium the product of $[H^+] \times [OH^-]$ must equal 1.0×10^{-14}. The concentration of OH^- must therefore decrease below 1.0×10^{-7}. Hydrogen ions and hydroxyl ions both exist in dilute aqueous solutions of acids and dilute aqueous solutions of hydroxide bases, but the H^+ concentration is greater than the OH^- concentration in acid solutions and the OH^- concentration is greater than the H^+ concentration in basic solutions. Usually the effective or active acidity of a solution is described in terms of hydrogen ion concentration even though the solution is alkaline. In dilute acid solutions H^+ is generally present as the hydronium ion (H_3O^+).

As a convenience for working with very small numbers for hydrogen ion concentration, the pH scale was devised. The mathematical definition of pH is:

$$pH = -\log_{10} [H^+] = \log_{10} \frac{1}{[H^+]}$$

In pure water $[H^+]$ is 1.0×10^{-7} moles per l. Therefore, the pH of water is equal to $-\log (1.0 = 10^{-7})$ which is 7. The $[H^+]$ of blueberry juice is approximately 1.0×10^{-3} moles per l. The pH of blueberry juice would therefore be:

$$pH = -\log(1.0 \times 10^{-3}) = 3$$

---

* Brackets [ ] indicate concentration (moles per l).
† K equals equilibrium constant.

When dealing with pH values that are whole numbers, the logarithmic relationship between pH and $[H^+]$ may be simply represented. A decrease in pH value of one integer corresponds to an increase in $[H^+]$ of ten times the original value. The value pH 2, for example, represents a $[H^+]$ of 0.01 moles per l while a value of pH 1 represents ten times that amount of 0.1 moles per l. pH values between whole numbers, such as 3.56, may be calculated using log_{10} tables.

The pH scale ranges from 1 to 14 and corresponds to concentrations of hydrogen ions ranging from 1 mole per l to 0.000,000,000,000,01 or 1.0×10^{-14} moles per l. Solutions having a greater $[H^+]$ than 1 mole per l or a greater $[OH^-]$ than 1 mole per l cannot be represented by the pH scale. Neutral solutions have a pH value of 7, acid solutions have pH values less than 7 and basic solutions have pH values greater than 7.

A normal (1.0 N) solution of an acid which is 100 percent ionized contains 1 gram* of H^+ per l of solution. All of the replaceable hydrogen is present as H^+. Its concentration of H^+ is 1 mole per l and it has a pH of 0. A normal solution of an acid that is 10 percent ionized, however, has a $[H^+]$ of 0.1 moles per l and has a pH of 1. The product of the normality of an acid and the degree of ionization (or fraction ionized) equals its $[H^+]$. For example, in a 1.0 N solution of acetic acid that is approximately 1 percent ionized, the $[H^+] = 1.0 \times 0.01 = 0.01$ moles per l $= 1.0 \times 10^{-2}$ moles per l. The pH of this solution is 2.

A *buffered solution* is one that shows little or no change in active acidity or pH when a small to moderate amount of acid or base is added to it. Pure water is not a buffered solution. If a drop of concentrated HCl is added to a l of water, the pH will decrease from about 7 to 4 or less. However, if a drop of concentrated acid is added to 1 l of buffered solution, there is no appreciable change in the pH of that solution.

A buffered solution has a latent source of alkalinity which is responsible for the removal of H^+ introduced into it. It also has a latent source of acidity which removes added OH^-. Buffer systems include 1. mixtures of weak acids and their salts, 2. mixtures of weak bases and their salts, and 3. proteins or amino acids.

An example of a buffered solution containing a weak acid and its salt is a mixture of lactic acid and sodium lactate. The latent sources of alkalinity and acidity can be explained in terms of the ions and molecules present. The lactate ion (Lac^-) is a common ion derived from either lactic acid or sodium lactate.

$$HLac \rightleftharpoons H^+ + Lac^-$$
$$NaLac \rightarrow Na^+ + Lac^-$$

---

* 1 g of H^+ is equal to 1 mole.

If a base is added to the lactate buffer solution, the H^+ that has been ionized from the weak acid, HLac, combines with the OH^- to form H_2O and thus the base disappears. Additional HLac then dissociates to H^+ and Lac^- to maintain equilibrium.

$$H^+ + OH^- \rightarrow H_2O$$
$$HLac \rightleftharpoons H^+ + Lac^-$$

If an acid is added to the solution, H^+ is removed by combination with Lac^- to form undissociated molecules of the weak acid.

$$H^+ + Lac^- \rightarrow HLac$$

In this way the buffered concentrations of H^+ and OH^- are maintained. Buffered solutions produce useful buffering over only a limited pH range as controlled by complex equilibria. After the buffering capacity of a solution is exceeded, a strong change of pH with change in concentration occurs. A mixture of acetic acid and sodium acetate, for example, buffers over the pH range of 3.7–5.6.

Proteins and amino acids function as buffers in a number of food systems. An amino acid molecule has both an acidic and a basic group. Glycine is the simplest amino acid and has the following molecular structure:

$$\begin{array}{l} CH_2-COO^- \\ | \\ NH_3{}^+ \end{array}$$

If H^+ is added to a glycine solution it will combine with the ionized carboxyl group, thus absorbing H^+.

$$\begin{array}{l} CH_2-COO^- + H^+ \\ | \\ NH_3{}^+ \end{array} \rightarrow \begin{array}{l} CH_2-COOH \\ | \\ NH_3{}^+ \end{array}$$

On the other hand, if OH^- is added to a glycine solution it may combine with the H^+ associated with the amine group, thereby removing the OH^- from solution and producing water.

$$\begin{array}{l} CH_2-COO^- + OH^- \\ | \\ NH_3{}^+ \end{array} \rightarrow \begin{array}{l} CH_2-COO^- + H_2O \\ | \\ NH_2 \end{array}$$

Proteins contain hundreds of amino acids joined together through the carboxyl and alpha-amino groups in a peptide linkage. An R represents a side chain, which is H for glycine. It varies for other amino acids and in some cases contains a -COOH or -NH_2 group.

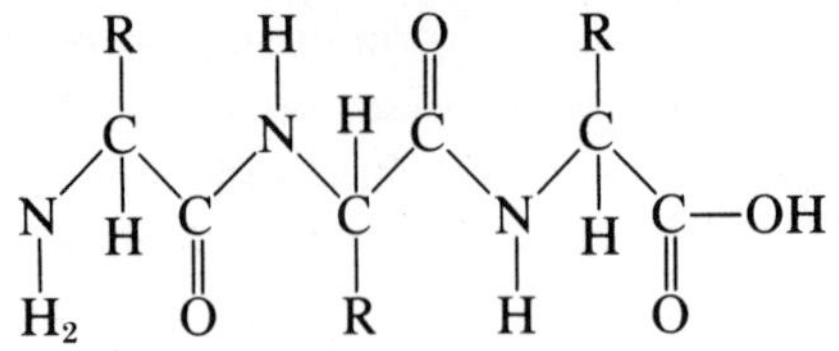

R   H   O   R

(peptide linkage structure)

peptide linkage

Proteins have free carboxyl and amino groups at the ends of the long peptide chains and also on some of the side groups of the amino acid residues in the peptide chains. In solution these carboxyl and amino groups are ionized. The degree of ionization and the net charge on the protein molecules depend on the pH of the protein dispersion. Buffering capacity results from the ability of the protein molecules to combine with either H^+ or OH^- and resist change in pH over a limited pH range.

3.2

SOME EXAMPLES OF ACIDITY IN FOODS

PREPARING FRUIT JELLIES

The pH of fruit jelly is a very important factor in the development of its gel structure. (Fruit jellies are discussed more completely in Chapter 20, but the role of acid will be emphasized in this chapter.)

The basic gel-forming substance in a fruit jelly is pectin. Pectin is a large threadlike molecule containing many units of galacturonic acid linked together. Some of the galacturonic acid residues have formed esters with methyl alcohol. Part of the free carboxyl groups (-COOH) on the pectin molecules are ionized (-COO⁻). A portion of a pectin molecule may be represented as:

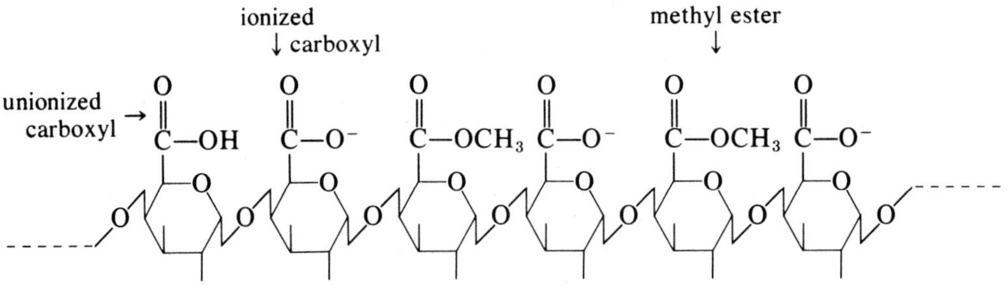

ionized
↓ carboxyl

methyl ester
↓

unionized → carboxyl

C—OH   C—O⁻   C—OCH₃   C—O⁻   C—OCH₃   C—O⁻

(pectin molecule structure)

Pectin molecules are colloidally dispersed as separated particles in fruit juice. They are stabilized in this dispersion by a net negative charge on each particle which results from ionization of the carboxyl groups. They are also stabilized by water of hydration. In order to form a gel, the effects of these stabilizing factors must be reduced to some degree so that the molecules are able to come closer together. A three dimensional crossbonded network of molecules, called a brush-heap structure, is characteristic of a gel. The pectin molecules may bond together at occasional intervals with hydrogen bonds, trapping water in the meshes between molecules, to form this structure. Figure 3.2 illustrates a possible orientation of pectin molecules in a liquid dispersion, called a *sol,* and in a rigid formation, called a *gel.*

A pH of 3.2–3.4 is required for enough destabilization of the pectin molecules to form a gel. Hydrogen ions (H^+) in the system combine with the negatively charged carboxyl groups of the pectin molecule, giving a greater number of unionized groups and a decreased total charge on the molecule.

$$-COO^- + H^+ \rightarrow -COOH$$

By decreasing the net negative charge on the particles, they are less repelled by each other and may crossbond at intervals.

In addition to the effect of active acidity on gel formation in fruit jellies, the water of hydration must be reduced. Approximately 65 percent sugar is present in the finished jelly to act as a dehydrating agent and decrease the stabilizing effect of the water held by the pectin molecules. Water is attracted to the sugar and some of the water molecules held by the pectin are therefore pulled away.

Without sufficient active acidity a gel cannot be formed with fruit juice and sugar. Some fruit juices such as currant, grape, and tart apple juices have enough acidity naturally to be successfully used. For other fruit juices, additional acid must be added. Lemon juice is usually a suitable source of acid that may be added to low acid juices.

CANNING VEGETABLES

Most vegetables are only slightly acid with a relatively high pH. Peas, corn, and lima beans have pH values as high as 6.2–6.9. A few vegetables, such as pumpkin, have a pH as low as 4.8. The relatively high pH of vegetables makes it absolutely necessary that they be processed for canning at a temperature higher than 95°–100°C (203°–212°F) in order to

Figure 3.2

Sol-gel transformation.

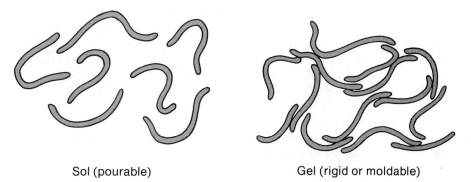

Sol (pourable)   Gel (rigid or moldable)

assure destruction of dangerous *Clostridium botulinum* spores which may be present on the vegetables. These resistant bacterial spores are not readily destroyed by heating in a boiling water bath unless the heating process is continued for several hours, in which case the food is grossly overcooked. If the *botulinum* spores are not destroyed in processing, they may vegetate as the canned food is stored and produce a deadly toxin. A pressure cooker, in which temperatures higher than 100°C (212°F) are obtained, must be used in order to safely can low-acid vegetables.

Vegetables such as beets may sometimes be pickled with the addition of vinegar which contains acetic acid. The addition of acid to a low-acid vegetable lowers the pH and makes it possible to can the product in a boiling water bath. Bacterial spores are readily destroyed when heated at the boiling temperature of water in an acid pH. It is important, however, to realize that there are buffering substances in vegetables which will absorb some added acid and sufficient amounts must be allowed to appropriately lower the pH before processing the pickled vegetables in a boiling water bath.

COOKING GREEN VEGETABLES

A loss of attractive green color usually results when green vegetables are canned or otherwise overcooked. Acid may play a role in the development of the olive-drab color.

As green vegetables are heated and part of their cells are disrupted, some organic acids are released into the surrounding tissues. When hydrogen ions from these acids come in contact with the green chlorophyll pigment, a chemical change occurs in the chlorophyll molecule. Chlorophyll is a flat disc-shaped porphyrin molecule with a magnesium atom (Mg) coordinated in the center. (The chemical structure of the chlorophyll molecule is shown in Chapter 12.) In the presence of acid, the magnesium atom is removed from the center of the chlorophyll molecule. Without the magnesium, the molecule becomes pheophytin which absorbs light differently than chlorophyll and is brownish or olive-drab in color.

To prevent the acid in a cooking vegetable from coming into contact with the chlorophyll, therefore avoiding the development of an unattractive olive-drab color, green vegetables should be cooked for a very short time in order to avoid overcooking. This procedure not only protects the attractive green color but also conserves flavor and nutritional value. Leaving the lid off the pot for the first few minutes of boiling allows some of the volatile acids to escape.

PREPARING ANGEL FOOD CAKE

An important ingredient in angel food cake is cream of tartar which is the potassium salt of tartaric acid. This ingredient, in usual amounts, produces an angel cake batter with a pH of 5.2–6.0. At this slightly acid pH, two effects on color are noted. First, a browning reaction called the *Maillard reaction,* which may occur not only on the surface but throughout the cake, is retarded. This reaction involves, as a first step, the combination of sugar and protein. Second, anthoxanthin pigments in the flour remain white at an acidic pH whereas they are yellow in a basic medium. The net effect of cream of tartar on color is to maintain whiteness.

The acid component of angel food cake has additional effects. It stabilizes the egg white foam which forms the basic structure of the cake and contributes to large volume in the finished product. It also contributes to tenderness. Therefore, if cream of tartar is not included in an angel cake recipe, the result will be a small tough cake with a yellowish color.

PREPARING DEVIL'S FOOD CAKE

Pigments in chocolate undergo color changes as the pH of the medium in which they are dispersed is changed. The characteristic chocolate flavor also decreases at high pH values. As the pH of a chocolate cake batter is adjusted, the color of the finished product changes as follows:

Color	pH
Yellowish brown	5–6
Brown	6–7
Mahogany	7–7.5
Mahogany with reddish tint	7.5–8
Reddish brown	Above 8

The typical reddish brown color of devil's food cake requires that a batter pH above 8 be produced. Baking soda is the major ingredient used to achieve this degree of alkalinity. Although the typical flavor of chocolate is actually decreased at this high pH, the luxurious reddish brown color more than compensates for many individuals who enjoy the appearance of devil's food cake.

PREPARING MILK SHERBET

The sharp, tart taste of a fruit ice, prepared by freezing a mixture of fruit juices, water, and sugar, is produced when the acidic hydrogen ion stimulates the taste buds on the tongue. If milk is substituted for the water in the recipe and a milk sherbet is thus prepared, a decrease in the intensity of the tart, sour taste may be noted. The pH of fruit sherbet is somewhat higher than that of fruit ice. Milk contains proteins which have buffering capacity and which absorb some of the hydrogen ions from the fruit juice.

Figure 3.3

Hydrogen Ion Concentration and pH of Some Common Foods

Hydrogen ion concentration and pH of some common foods. (From American Home Economics Association. 1975. *Handbook of Food Preparation,* 7th edition, p. 21. Washington, D.C. With permission.)

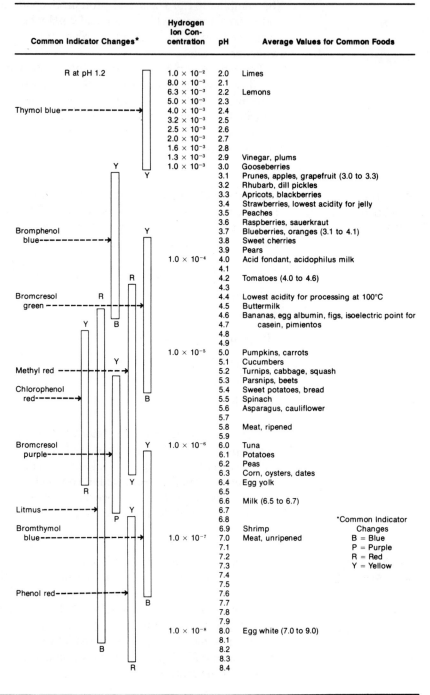

Common Indicator Changes*	Hydrogen Ion Concentration	pH	Average Values for Common Foods
R at pH 1.2	1.0 × 10⁻²	2.0	Limes
	8.0 × 10⁻³	2.1	
	6.3 × 10⁻³	2.2	Lemons
	5.0 × 10⁻³	2.3	
Thymol blue	4.0 × 10⁻³	2.4	
	3.2 × 10⁻³	2.5	
	2.5 × 10⁻³	2.6	
	2.0 × 10⁻³	2.7	
	1.6 × 10⁻³	2.8	
	1.3 × 10⁻³	2.9	Vinegar, plums
	1.0 × 10⁻³	3.0	Gooseberries
		3.1	Prunes, apples, grapefruit (3.0 to 3.3)
		3.2	Rhubarb, dill pickles
		3.3	Apricots, blackberries
		3.4	Strawberries, lowest acidity for jelly
		3.5	Peaches
		3.6	Raspberries, sauerkraut
Bromphenol blue		3.7	Blueberries, oranges (3.1 to 4.1)
		3.8	Sweet cherries
		3.9	Pears
	1.0 × 10⁻⁴	4.0	Acid fondant, acidophilus milk
		4.1	
		4.2	Tomatoes (4.0 to 4.6)
		4.3	
Bromcresol green		4.4	Lowest acidity for processing at 100°C
		4.5	Buttermilk
		4.6	Bananas, egg albumin, figs, isoelectric point for
		4.7	casein, pimientos
		4.8	
		4.9	
	1.0 × 10⁻⁵	5.0	Pumpkins, carrots
		5.1	Cucumbers
Methyl red		5.2	Turnips, cabbage, squash
		5.3	Parsnips, beets
Chlorophenol red		5.4	Sweet potatoes, bread
		5.5	Spinach
		5.6	Asparagus, cauliflower
		5.7	
		5.8	Meat, ripened
		5.9	
Bromcresol purple	1.0 × 10⁻⁶	6.0	Tuna
		6.1	Potatoes
		6.2	Peas
		6.3	Corn, oysters, dates
		6.4	Egg yolk
		6.5	
		6.6	Milk (6.5 to 6.7)
Litmus		6.7	
		6.8	
Bromthymol blue		6.9	Shrimp
	1.0 × 10⁻⁷	7.0	Meat, unripened
		7.1	
		7.2	
		7.3	
		7.4	
		7.5	
Phenol red		7.6	
		7.7	
		7.8	
		7.9	
	1.0 × 10⁻⁸	8.0	Egg white (7.0 to 9.0)
		8.1	
		8.2	
		8.3	
		8.4	

*Common Indicator Changes
B = Blue
P = Purple
R = Red
Y = Yellow

pH OF COMMON FOODS

The average pH of some common foods is given in Figure 3.3.

SUMMARY

Acidity can be measured either as total (titratable) acidity or as active (effective) acidity. The properties of many different foods are affected by their acidity, particularly active acidity or pH. Active acidity is a measure of the concentration of hydrogen ions that exist in solution at any one time. Total acidity refers to all of the hydrogen in a solution that can be replaced by a metal. It is measured by neutralizing the acid solution with an appropriate amount of hydroxide base.

All of the hydrogen in inorganic acids is replaceable and is completely dissociated in dilute solution. Organic acids have some hydrogen that is not replaceable by a metal. These acids are also weak acids and are only partially dissociated in solution. Most of the acids in foods are weak, organic acids.

The pH scale was devised as a convenient method of expressing the concentration of hydrogen ions in solution. The mathematical definition of pH is:

$$pH = -\log_{10} [H^+] = \log_{10} \frac{1}{[H^+]}$$

The pH scale ranges from 1 to 14. Neutral solutions have a pH value of 7, acidic solutions have pH values less than 7, and basic solutions have pH values greater than 7.

A buffered solution is one that shows little or no change in pH when small to moderate amounts of acid or base are added. It has the ability to absorb either H^+ or OH^- over a limited pH range. Weak acids or bases and their salts may act as buffering agents in food systems. Proteins also act as buffering agents in various foods.

Examples of the importance of acidity in foods are described. Successful jelly making requires fruit juices to have a pH of 3.2–3.4. The H^+ destabilizes the gel-forming pectin molecule by decreasing its net negative charge.

The relatively high pH of most vegetables makes it necessary that they be canned in a pressure cooker which can maintain a temperature well above the boiling point of water, because certain bacterial spores are resistant to destruction unless heating is done at a pH below 4.5.

When acid from the disrupted tissues of an overcooked green vegetable comes in contact with the vegetable's green pigment, chlorophyll, an olive-drab pigment is formed. Green vegetables should be cooked only until tender in order to retain a bright green color.

Cream of tartar in angel food cake batter produces an acidic pH which maintains a white color in the finished cake. The acidity also contributes to a large volume and a tender crumb. Devil's food cake has a pH above 8 so that a typical reddish brown color is produced. A frozen fruit sherbet made with milk is less tart than a fruit ice because the milk proteins in the sherbet have a buffering effect on the hydrogen ions of the fruit juice.

STUDY QUESTIONS

Total acidity may be measured by titration while active acidity is determined by the quantity of hydrogen ions actually present in solution.

1. Calculate the total acidity in a 0.1 N solution of acetic acid and a 0.1 N solution of hydrochloric acid. Compare the answers and explain similarities or differences found.
2. Calculate the active acidity of each of the solutions described in question 1, assuming acetic acid to be 1 percent dissociated. Compare the answers and explain similarities or differences found.
3. Define pH mathematically.
4. Write the pH scale and indicate areas of acidity, alkalinity, and neutrality.

Buffered systems resist change in hydrogen ion concentration or pH.

5. For each of the following, explain how the system acts as a buffered solution when small amounts of acid or base are added.
   a. Glycine in water solution
   b. Acetic acid plus sodium acetate in water solution
   c. A protein in water dispersion

The properties of many foods are affected by pH.

6. For each of the following processes, explain how active acidity is of importance in affecting the quality of the finished product:
   a. Preparing apple jelly
   b. Canning green peas
   c. Boiling broccoli
   d. Preparing angel food cake
   e. Preparing devil's food cake
7. List approximate pH values for each of the following foods:
   a. Lemons
   b. Tomatoes
   c. Peaches
   d. Peas
   e. Spinach
   f. Potatoes
   g. Meat, unripened
   h. Milk
   i. Egg white

CHAPTER 4

ENZYMES IN FOOD

All foods, such as meats, grains, fruits, and vegetables, were once living tissues. During the growing process and as long as the tissues are alive enzyme molecules are synthesized within the cells. The enzymes act as catalysts to facilitate chemical reactions. These complex reactions occur constantly in all living tissues even under relatively mild conditions of temperature, pressure, and acidity. The term *catalysis* was coined by Berzelius in 1836 from a Greek word meaning dissolution. A *catalyst* changes the rate of a chemical reaction without appearing in the products. Enzyme catalysts increase the rate of chemical reactions that, under the usual physiological conditions of living cells, would otherwise occur too slowly to support life.

Enzymes may remain active after cells die. Therefore, animal tissues, such as meat, fish, and poultry, and plant tissues, such as fresh fruits and vegetables, used for food, contain active enzyme systems that catalyze many different reactions. During the time between the slaughtering or the harvesting of these products and that of their preparation for consumption, one may want to either minimize or encourage the various enzymatic reactions, depending upon the particular food quality characteristics desired.

This chapter will first review the general activity and properties of enzymes. Examples of several enzymatic reactions in foods will then be discussed briefly in order to emphasize the important roles played by enzymes in food production, processing, and preparation.

4.1

CLASSIFICATION OF ENZYMES

All enzymes are proteins. The molecular weights of enzyme proteins vary widely. Many enzymes are present in living tissues as tightly organized complexes containing several enzymes and essential cofactors. *Cofactors* may be metal ions such as zinc and manganese or they may be low molecular weight nonprotein organic molecules. Several B vitamins, which are small organic molecules, function as coenzymes in cellular metabolism. The complete functional complex of an enzyme and its cofactors is called a *holoenzyme*. The protein enzyme itself, free of cofactors, is called an *apoenzyme*.

An international classification has been established defining six major classes of enzyme function with several subclasses for each class. Known enzymes within each subclass have been named so that they describe the reactions they catalyze. Common names for many enzymes, (e.g., sucrase, pepsin, and rennin), however, have been used for many years and continue to appear in the food science literature.

A summary of the international classification of enzymes follows (as found in Montgomery *et al.*, 1974):

1. *Oxidoreductases* catalyze a wide variety of oxidation–reduction reactions. Common trivial names for these enzymes include dehydrogenase, oxidase, and peroxidase.
2. *Transferases* catalyze various kinds of group transfers. Amino, carboxyl, carbonyl, methyl, glycosyl, or phosphoryl groups are commonly transferred from one molecule to another.
3. *Hydrolases* catalyze cleavage of bonds between a carbon and some other atom by the addition of water. Common trivial names for these enzymes include esterase, peptidase, amylase, phosphatase, pepsin, and trypsin.
4. *Lyases* catalyze the breakage of carbon–carbon, carbon–sulfur and certain carbon–nitrogen (excluding peptide) bonds.
5. *Isomerases* catalyze intramolecular rearrangements. Common trivial names for these enzymes include epimerase, racemase, and mutase.
6. *Ligases* catalyze the formation of bonds between carbon and oxygen, sulfur, nitrogen, and other atoms.

4.2

ENZYME PROPERTIES

Enzymes, as organic catalysts, have characteristic properties. They are effective in extremely low concentrations. The *turnover number* may be used to compare the activities of various enzymes. It is expressed as the moles of substrate (the material that is being acted upon) converted to a product per minute per mole of enzyme. This number may range from about 200 to as high as 2 million, indicating the effectiveness of very small quantities of enzymes.

Enzymes, like other catalysts, are unchanged in the reaction in which they are involved as long as the conditions for the reaction are optimal. Since enzymes are proteins, they may be denatured under some conditions such as excessive heat, cold, or acidity.

Enzymes do not change the equilibrium of a reversible chemical reaction. They speed up the approach to equilibrium. They cannot make a reaction proceed if it would not do so without the enzyme but they allow the reaction to occur rapidly under moderate conditions of temperature and pressure.

Enzymes show specificity and are very selective in the reactions they will catalyze. Some enzymes will catalyze only one very specific reaction while others may catalyze more than one. All enzymes are selective to a considerable degree.

The activity of an enzyme is influenced by the conditions around it and there are optimum conditions for the activity of each enzyme. The speed of most enzymatic reactions will increase as the temperature is increased until the temperature reaches a critical level at which denaturation of the protein enzyme occurs and activity is decreased (see Figure 4.1). There will be an optimum temperature for each enzyme at which activity is maximal and denaturation does not occur. High temperatures are used to destroy enzymes in such processes as the blanching of vegetables before freezing.

There is also a pH that is optimal for the activity of each enzyme (see Figure 4.2). The pH affects the ionization of the protein enzymes. The pH optima vary widely, although a pH value between 4 and 8 is optimal for the majority of enzymes. Some enzymes have a wide tolerance for pH while others are active only within a narrow pH range. Enzymes are denatured when they are exposed to extreme pH values.

The rate of an enzymatic reaction will increase with an increased amount of substrate up to a certain point. When there is a large amount of substrate present in proportion to the amount of enzyme, the rate of the reaction will level off and become constant.

With increasing amounts of enzyme, the rate of the enzymatic reaction increases. The increase in activity is directly proportional to the amount of the enzyme, when low enzyme concentrations are involved. At higher enzyme levels the reaction rate is no longer directly proportional to the amount of enzyme. The reaction rate increases slowly at higher enzyme concentrations.

Enzymes possess an *active catalytic site,* the nature of which has

Figure 4.1

There is an optimum temperature for maximum activity of an enzyme.

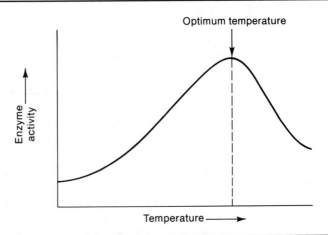

Figure 4.2

There is an optimum pH for maximum activity of an enzyme.

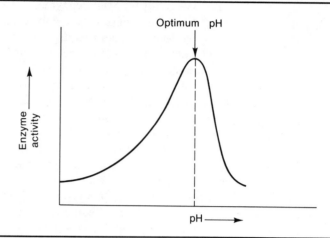

been the subject of research for many years. The concept of active site proposes that a relatively small number of the amino acids in the protein enzyme chain are active in the catalytic reaction. It has been suggested that enzymes operate by forming an intermediate compound with the substrate. Formation of the enzyme–substrate (E–S) complex involves the active catalytic site but is probably influenced by some other portion of the enzyme molecule as well. When the reaction is complete, the enzyme separates from the complex and the product is released. When a single substrate goes to a single product the reaction may be represented as:

Enzyme (E) + Substrate (S) $\rightleftharpoons$ E-S $\rightarrow$ E + Product (P)

4.3

ENZYMES IN FOOD PRODUCTS

Schwimmer (1972) has suggested that food processing and technology be considered as the art and science of the promotion, control, and/or prevention of the disruption of cells along with its metabolic consequences. The application of this technology at the right time and at the right place is extremely critical in the processing of food. The disruption of cells releases many enzymes that are present within the cells. In some cases the release of enzymes is desirable and improves food quality. For example, as dates are tree-ripened their cells become disrupted with the resulting activation of several enzymes. The released pectinases, polyphenol oxidase, invertase, and cellulase act on various substrates in the date tissue and convert a light colored, tasteless, and turgid fruit into a dark, moist, soft product of high quality. On the other hand, fresh peaches that are overripe show deleterious effects of enzyme activity resulting from a softening of the fruit and a disruption of the cells.

The control of enzyme activity must be accomplished during the processing and preparation of many food products in order to achieve and maintain quality. A few examples of the importance of enzyme activity will be given in this chapter. Others will be described throughout the text as specific foods are discussed.

FLOUR AND BREAD

Milled wheat flour contains the enzyme β-amylase, which catalyzes the hydrolysis of starch to the sugar, maltose, and to some polysaccharides of varying sizes, called dextrins. This enzyme works on the damaged starch granules in the flour that are partially hydrated during the mixing and fermentation of the dough, as yeast bread is prepared. The maltose produced by this reaction provides food for the yeast cells present in the dough.

Yeast, a single-celled microorganism used for the leavening of bread, synthesizes many different enzymes. These enzymes include maltase, which catalyzes the hydrolysis of maltose, a disaccharide, into two molecules of the simple sugar (monosaccharide), glucose. Glucose is then available to be acted upon by a group of yeast-produced enzymes in the process of fermentation whereby carbon dioxide (CO_2) and ethyl alcohol (CH_3CH_2OH) are produced. Carbon dioxide is the primary leavening agent which makes bread rise. The alcohol is volatilized during the baking.

Alpha-amylase is an enzyme that, in its first stages of activity, hydrolyzes starch primarily to dextrins with little maltose produced. Dextrins have a softening effect on the crumb of yeast bread which is desirable when dextrins are produced in controlled amounts. Alpha-amylase is not normally present in milled flour but may be added to bread dough by the commercial baker. The usual source of α-amylase is barley malt or a purified enzyme produced by microorganisms.

FRUITS AND VEGETABLES

Enzymes play important roles in the ripening of fruit. They catalyze chemical reactions that change starch to sugar and increase fruit sweetness, degrade pectic substances and contribute to the softening of fruit tissues, and synthesize pigments that produce the characteristic colors associated with ripe fruit. Dilley (1972) concluded that normal ripening of pear fruit requires the coordinated synthesis of enzymes involved in the various ripening reactions. Most of this synthesis takes place during the early stage of ripening before marked physical changes, such as softening, become apparent. Ethylene gas is produced within the fruit and it initiates the ripening process. This gas is sometimes used in the atmosphere surrounding picked fruit and tomatoes in order to encourage ripening.

Some fruits develop a brown discoloration when they have been peeled, cut, or bruised, and allowed to stand for a period of time. The brown pigment is not harmful but is unattractive and makes the food appear less appetizing. Browning results from enzyme-catalyzed reactions in the fruit tissues. The enzymes responsible are generally called polyphenoloxidases or polyphenolases. Their name suggests that they catalyze the oxidation of polyphenol compounds. A polyphenol compound has an unsaturated six-carbon ring with two or more -OH groups as illustrated below.

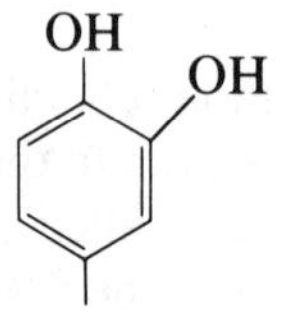

OH
OH

a polyphenol

Polyphenols readily react with oxygen, in the presence of polyphenolase, to produce oxidized compounds. Additional reactions involving the oxidized products then occur to eventually produce brownish pigments. The overall reaction may be represented as follows:

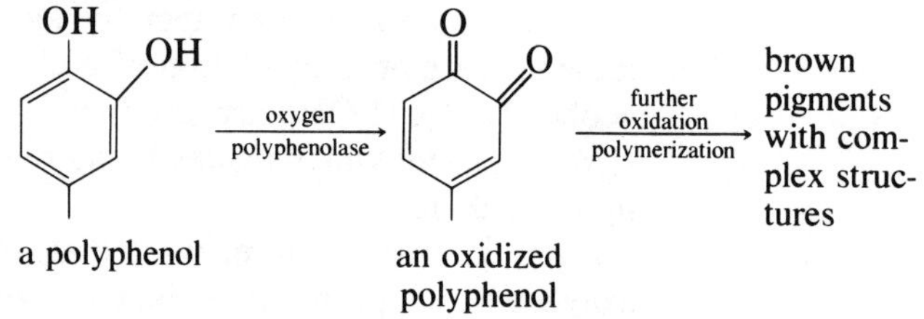

OH OH   O O
      —oxygen→   —further oxidation→   brown pigments
      polyphenolase   polymerization   with complex structures

a polyphenol   an oxidized polyphenol

Not all fruits brown readily. Some apparently do not synthesize polyphenolase enzymes. Others may not have the appropriate polyphenol substrate. Enzymatic oxidative browning is discussed in more detail in Chapter 13.

Since browning is an undesirable phenomenon in the preparation of fresh fruits, several procedures may be used to retard or prevent it. Cut surfaces of fruits, such as bananas, may be coated with lemon juice. This not only helps to protect the surface from contact with air but may inhibit enzyme activity by lowering the pH at the surface of the tissues. The fruit may be dipped into an ascorbic acid solution. Ascorbic acid is a reducing agent or antioxidant that interferes with the oxidation of polyphenols. Pineapple juice contains compounds with sulfhydryl (-SH) groups which may also act as antioxidants. Dipping cut fruits in pineapple juice is therefore an aid to preventing browning and maintaining the fresh natural fruit color. Immersing cut fruit in a dilute salt solution interferes with enzyme activity and also excludes oxygen. Exposing cut fruits to sulfur dioxide before drying helps to retain a light color in fruits such as peaches, apricots, and apples.

Heating fruits and vegetables denatures enzyme proteins and thus destroys their activity. This process is of importance in the preparation of frozen, canned, and fresh vegetables. Since enzyme activity may continue at freezing temperatures and produce undesirable changes in frozen vegetables, these plant tissues are blanched before freezing. Blanching involves heating the prepared vegetable in boiling water or steam for a specified period. Flavor and texture deterioration during frozen storage is markedly decreased by this heat treatment. Rapid heating of vegetables early in the canning process inactivates enzymes and helps to produce a high quality product. Cooking fresh vegetables in boiling water is another way of rapidly inactivating enzymes which might catalyze undesirable changes in the plant tissues if the vegetables were to be heated slowly.

4.4

USE OF ENZYMES IN FOOD PROCESSING

Enzymes have played very important roles in various segments of the food processing industry. In some cases they have made possible the development of new products and, in other cases, the improvement of traditional products.

For example, the candy industry uses an enzyme, invertase or sucrase, to prevent excessive crystallization in such products as chocolate covered cherries. Invertase is added to fondant and cherry centers that are later coated with chocolate. As the chocolates are stored, invertase begins to hydrolyze some of the sucrose in the fondant, producing the two monosaccharides, glucose and fructose. The number of sugar crystals in the fondant center is decreased by the presence of glucose and fructose so that softening or liquifaction occurs.

Glucose isomerase, an enzyme isolated from a species of bacteria, is used to convert glucose into fructose. Fructose is a sweeter, more expensive sugar than glucose. High fructose corn syrup is being produced commercially and finding many uses as a sweetener.

Pectic substances are present in fruits and vegetables. These substances are essential for gel formation in fruit jellies. However, they interfere with juice extraction and contribute to a hazy appearance in some processed fruit juices such as apple juice and grape juice. Pectinases are used commercially to break down the pectin molecules during the processing of the fruit juices, thus helping to produce clear, sparkling products.

Rennin is a protease that is widely used in the dairy industry to clot milk in the making of cheese. Rennet, a crude extract of rennin, is obtained from the fourth stomach of suckling calves. The supply on the market is supplemented by rennets with similar properties that are obtained from certain microorganisms.

Meats are tenderized by use of the enzymes papain, ficin, and bromelin. These enzymes, which are proteases, are extracted from papaya, figs, and pineapple, respectively. Papain attacks the protein in muscle fibers, primarily hydrolyzing it to smaller peptides. Ficin and bromelin more readily attack the fibrous connective tissue proteins, degrading them and thereby having a tenderizing effect on meat. The tenderizing takes place when the meat proteins are being denatured during the cooking process. There is enough time for the enzymes to catalyze the partial breakdown of the denatured proteins before the enzyme proteins themselves are denatured by the heat that is being applied.

Some foods are particularly sensitive to oxygen, their flavor deteriorating rapidly in the presence of even small quantities. An enzyme system has been successfully used to remove traces of oxygen in certain tightly packaged food products. This system includes glucose oxidase and catalase which catalyze the following reactions:

$$2 \text{ Glucose } (C_6H_{12}O_6) + 2H_2O + 2O_2 \xrightarrow{\text{Glucose oxidase}}$$
$$2 \text{ Gluconic acid } (C_6H_{12}O_7) + 2 \text{ Hydrogen peroxide } (H_2O_2)$$
$$2H_2O_2 \xrightarrow{\text{Catalase}} 2H_2O + O_2$$

It can be seen that two oxygen molecules are consumed in the reactions preceding but only one oxygen molecule is released, thus accomplishing a net removal of oxygen from the closed atmosphere in which this system is placed. It has been called an *oxygen scavenger system* because it can pick up traces of oxygen. This system is also used to remove small amounts of glucose from egg whites before drying them. Dried egg whites containing even tiny amounts of glucose are susceptible to browning during long periods of storage. This browning reaction is a specific type called the *Maillard reaction* and involves a combination of sugar and protein as the first step in a complicated series of reactions. (The Maillard reaction is discussed in Section 10.3.)

The use of immobilized enzymes may become an important processing tool for the food industry. In this process enzymes are attached, either by chemical bonding or physical binding, to insoluble substances such as glass or ceramic beads. They may also be attached to membranes or sheets of cellulose. The immobilized enzyme may be added to a reaction mixture and easily removed by filtration after the reaction is complete. Alternatively it may be packed in columns and the substrate allowed to pass through the column to react with the enzyme. If the immobilized enzymes are attached to a membrane, the necessary contact is made as the substrate passes through the membrane.

Glucose isomerase, as an immobilized enzyme, is used on a commercial scale for the production of fructose from glucose (Park and Toma, 1975). Other uses of immobilized enzymes in the food industry will become possible as various technological problems are solved (Olson and Richardson, 1974).

SUMMARY

Enzymes synthesized by plant and animal cells act as catalysts to facilitate chemical reactions that constantly occur in all living tissues. They increase the rate of chemical reactions that would normally occur too slowly to support life. Animal and plant tissues used for food contain active enzyme systems that must be properly controlled in order to maintain food quality.

All enzymes are proteins. A complex of the protein enzyme and its cofactors is called a holoenzyme while the enzyme itself is called an apoenzyme. Six major types of enzymes, as classified by their functions, are oxidoreductases, transferases, hydrolases, lyases, isomerases, and ligases.

Examination of the characteristic properties of enzymes shows that 1. they are effective in extremely low concentrations; 2. they are unchanged in the reaction if conditions are optimal; 3. they do not change the equilibrium of a reversible reaction; 4. they show specificity; and 5. their activity is influenced by temperature and pH. Enzymes possess an active catalytic site. They form an intermediate compound with the substrate in the course of a reaction.

When cells are disrupted many enzymes are released. This may have either beneficial or deleterious effects on the food. Several examples of the importance of enzyme activity in foods are discussed. Beta-amylase in milled wheat flour catalyzes the hydrolysis of starch to maltose and some dextrins. Maltose is hydrolyzed to glucose by yeast enzymes. In bread dough, the glucose is further fermented to yield the leavening gas, carbon dioxide, and alcohol. Alpha-amylase, which produces dextrins immediately and thus has a softening effect on bread crumb, may be added in commercial breadmaking.

Enzymes play important roles in the ripening of fruit. Starch is changed to sugar, the tissues soften, and the pigments are synthesized. The browning of cut surfaces of fresh fruits is a result of the oxidizing action of polyphenoloxidases in the tissues. Vegetables are blanched before they are frozen in order to destroy enzymes that cause changes in flavor and texture during their storage at freezing temperatures.

Several examples of enzymes used in food processing are discussed. Invertase is added to the fondant centers of chocolate covered cherries. This enzyme hydrolyzes some sucrose, thereby decreasing the number of sugar crystals in the fondant, and softening the chocolate center.

Glucose isomerase is used to convert glucose into the sweeter fructose. This process is carried on commercially with an immobilized enzyme system.

Pectinases are used commercially to break down pectin molecules in certain fruit juices such as apple juice in order to avoid a hazy appearance. Clear, sparkling juice is the final product.

Rennet is a crude extract of the protease rennin. It is widely used to clot milk in the making of cheese. Meats are tenderized by using the enzymes papain, ficin, and bromelin.

An enzyme system involving glucose oxidase and catalase has been used to remove traces of oxygen in tightly packaged food products. This system is also used to remove small amounts of glucose from egg whites before drying them. Browning may occur during storage if egg whites contain even small quantities of glucose.

STUDY QUESTIONS

Enzymes have certain properties when they act as catalysts.

1. From the following list of properties or characteristics identify those that could correctly be applied to enzymes.

   Properties or characteristics
   Effective in very small amounts
   Polysaccharide molecules
   Must be present in relatively large amounts for activity
   Have optimal pH for activity
   Protein molecules
   Act over a wide temperature range
   Often require other molecules as coenzymes
   Are unchanged in the reaction
   Can act either inside or outside cells
   Exhibit specificity
   Do not change the equilibrium of a reaction

Active sites on enzymes apparently bind specific molecules and guide them together to produce a chemical reaction.

2. Explain the concept of active site in enzyme action.

Enzyme activity may be influenced by a. concentration of substrate; b. concentration of enzyme; c. temperature; and d. pH.

3. Indicate how enzyme activity is affected as each of the factors listed above increases or decreases.

Enzymes are present in many food products and may have varying effects during processing, holding, or storage.

4. From the following list of food products, identify those that are likely to contain active enzymes. For those foods with enzyme activity, list some of the principal enzymes that might be expected to produce significant effects or changes in the food under proper conditions of temperature.

   Food products
   bread dough
   fresh apples
   fresh pork shoulder
   hydrogenated shortening

white granulated sugar
unaged cheddar cheese
frozen TV dinner
green bananas
frozen peas
canned beef stew
sliced ripe bananas
chocolate covered cherries

REFERENCES

1. Dilley, D. R. 1972. Postharvest fruit preservation: Protein synthesis, ripening, and senescence. *Journal of Food Science* 37, 518.

2. Montgomery, R., R. L. Dryer, T. W. Conway, and A. A. Spector. 1974. *Biochemistry*. St. Louis: The C. V. Mosby Company.

3. Olson, N. F. and T. Richardson. 1974. Immobilized enzymes in food processing and analysis. *Journal of Food Science* 39, 653.

4. Park, Y. K. and M. Toma. 1975. Isomerization of glucose to fructose by semipurified, cell bound, and immobilized glucose isomerase from Streptomyces sp. *Journal of Food Science* 40, 1112.

5. Schwimmer, S. 1972. Cell disruption and its consequences in food processing. *Journal of Food Science* 37, 530.

PART II

FOOD PRESERVATION

The primary cause of food spoilage is the action of microorganisms, but chemical changes and mechanical damage may also be contributing factors. Food is preserved when the basic causes of food spoilage are controlled. Methods for preserving food are varied and, depending upon their basic approach, may be effective for either short or long periods of storage. This Part will review some basic causes of food spoilage and discuss both the special physiological requirements of microorganisms that determine the predominant type of spoilage and the use of both high and low temperatures in food preservation.

CHAPTER 5

GENERAL PRINCIPLES AND HISTORY OF FOOD PRESERVATION

All foods are subject to decomposition with consequent deterioration in quality. Living tissues have a natural resistance to attack by microorganisms. However, when plants are harvested and animals slaughtered, their tissues' susceptibility to degradation by microorganisms becomes a problem. Deterioration in the quality of plant and animal tissues used for food is also caused by enzymatically catalyzed chemical changes.

5.1

HISTORY

Our ancestors discovered that certain types of food treatment could delay deterioration and act as a preservative for variable periods of time. This discovery ensured human survival and contributed to the expansion of the race. The development of agriculture produced a relative abundance of food at harvest time. But intermittent abundance and thus the need to save food for times of scarcity stimulated the improvement of existing methods of food preservation and fostered the development of new techniques. Satisfactory methods of preserving food have helped to make it possible for more people to include a larger variety of foods in their diets, so that the diets are more nutritionally adequate.

The role of microorganisms in food spoilage was not discovered until the time of Louis Pasteur in the 1860s. Many methods of food preservation had been discovered and were in widespread use without anyone's understanding of the underlying principles involved. Even now, much remains to be learned about the specific microorganisms that spoil food.

Preservation of foods by drying has been practiced for centuries. Such foods as harvested grains, and nuts in the shell are sufficiently dry to remain unspoiled for long periods of time under proper conditions of storage. The sun drying of fruits has long since been practiced in climates with hot sun and dry atmosphere. The smoking of meats and fish was introduced many years ago and is essentially a drying process. Mechanical driers were a later innovation while freeze drying was developed by modern technology.

CANNING

The process of canning as practiced in the present day has been developed over a period of 175 years. Goldblith (1971) has emphasized three milestones that stand out sharply in this development. They are 1. the practical work of Nicolas Appert (1752–1841) who developed a process for preserving food by bottling; 2. the contributions of Louis Pasteur during the 1860s when he elucidated the basic science underlying the process of canning; and 3. the technological developments of Underwood and Prescott toward the end of the nineteenth century as they applied basic scientific principles to the canning process, turning the art into a science.

In 1804, after successful trials of his bottled products aboard several ships, Appert, a French confectioner, founded a commercial food bottling factory. He received a prize of 12,000 francs from the French government for the development of his process. This process consisted of enclosing in bottles the foods to be preserved, corking the bottles carefully, submitting the filled bottles to the action of boiling water for various lengths of time, depending on the foods, and then removing and cooling them. Appert's book on the subject was translated into many languages and enjoyed wide distribution. He is generally recognized as the father of thermal processing (Goldblith, 1971).

In 1864, Pasteur reported that the spoilage problem troubling the wine and beer industries of France was caused by growth of a microscopic plant. His discovery of microscopic growth explained Appert's successful results with bottled food. Heat destroyed the microscopic vegetation and sealing prevented other microscopic material from entering the bottle to spoil the food. Pasteur's work formed the foundation for the science of canning.

Patents for glass and metal packaging containers for foods to be canned were received by Peter Durand of England in 1810. The canning industry expanded to the United States in the early 1800s. One of the first organizations established was the Underwood Company of Boston. The grandson of the founder of this company was William Lyman Underwood. He collaborated with Samuel Cate Prescott at Massachusetts Institute of Technology to publish a number of scientific papers of great importance in the development of canning technology. Underwood and Prescott's research showed that bacteria were the causative agents of spoilage of canned foods and that heating to temperatures above the boiling point of water was needed to achieve sterilization of that product. They showed the importance of heat penetration into the center of the can and demonstrated the need for cooling the canned foods (Goldblith, 1972a).

It was necessary to heat low-acid bottled foods in a boiling water bath for long periods of time, sometimes for several hours, in order to avoid spoilage. The development of the pressure cooker or autoclave made possible the heating of canned foods at temperatures well above the boiling point of water. Heating times could then be substantially reduced. The first patent for a pressure cooker or retort for use in canning was issued in 1874 to A. K. Shriver, a Baltimore canner (Goldblith, 1972b).

Many improvements in processing technology have occurred in the canning industry during the twentieth century. New canned products have been developed. Canning has become a well-established food preservation method that undoubtedly will continue to play an important role in the distribution of food.

COLD STORAGE AND FREEZING

In times past, some foods were stored in natural caves, holes in the ground, or cellars. These places provide a relatively uniform temperature somewhat cooler than the outside air in the summer and warmer in the winter. Ice for packing certain foods was used in the middle 1800s. Mechanical refrigeration became important in the chilling preservation of food during the late 1800s. Cold storage warehouses were then gradually established.

The preservation of food by freezing was practiced for centuries in areas where natural freezing and frozen storage were available. However, the operation of a frozen food industry on a year round basis and its growth into an industry of major importance awaited the development of mechanical refrigeration systems. About 1880, ammonia refrigeration systems were used commercially in the United States for freezing fish products and by 1890 freezing was used fairly extensively for meats. The frozen egg industry also began about this time. Between 1910 and 1926, frozen fruit production in the United States expanded to over 40 million pounds per year and by the mid-1930s a sizeable quantity of vegetables was being frozen. After World War II precooked frozen foods became important items in the industry (Goresline, 1962).

Research in the areas of product varieties best for freezing, techniques of enzyme inactivation, and maintenance of nutritional qualities, as well as packaging materials, have accompanied the development of the frozen food industry. Great growth has occurred in the production and marketing of frozen food products during the past 50 years. The frozen food industry has become a ten billion dollar a year operation. The use of home freezers has also increased, both for the storage of commercially frozen foods and for the freezing of fresh produce. (More specific treatment of canning and freezing for preservation is found in the two following chapters.)

DEFINITIONS

There is no universal definition for spoiled food. Some well-ripened meats or aged cheeses may be considered spoiled by certain individuals whereas others view them as delicacies. Many foods that have deteriorated in quality are not injurious to health, although their aesthetic appeal is decreased. On the other hand, some foods that contain hazardous toxins, such as those produced by *Clostridium botulinum* and certain staphylococcus organisms, may appear and taste normal and yet if consumed, be very dangerous to life and health. The presence of large numbers of other organisms such as salmonellae may also create health hazards without changing the taste or appearance of the food. Food which is to be consumed by humans should certainly be safe from a health standpoint as well as acceptable from an aesthetic point of view. Spoiled food therefore may be generally defined as any food that is not acceptable to an individual or group because of health hazards or aesthetic appeal.

The period of time between the manufacture and the retail purchase of a food product is termed the *shelf life* by food technologists (IFT Expert Panel, 1974). During this time, the food product is in a state of satisfactory quality in terms of nutritional value, taste, texture, and appearance. Storage studies on processed foods are part of the development program for each product. The manufacturer of a processed food attempts to provide the longest shelf life practical, consistent with costs, patterns of handling, and uses by distributors, retailers, and consumers. One of the major reasons for processing foods is to preserve them. Changes that may occur as processed foods are stored, resulting in a decrease in shelf life, include 1. loss of nutritive value; 2. spoilage by microorganisms or enzymatic action; 3. loss of aesthetic qualities such as color, flavor, aroma, and texture; and 4. loss of functional properties such as leavening activity in baking powder and thickening power in sauce mixes.

5.3

CAUSES OF FOOD SPOILAGE

Food is easily contaminated by microorganisms. They are everywhere. They are present in great abundance in the soil in which plants are grown. They are present on utensils and work counters used for food preparation. They may be carried through the air from one object to another. Most foods contain nutrients that serve well as sources of nourishment for microorganisms as well as for man. Therefore, microorganisms present in foods will grow or increase in numbers if they are given suitable environmental conditions. Microbial decomposition is the major cause of food spoilage. Spoilage may be initiated by bacteria, yeasts or molds, or a combination of these organisms, depending upon the particular conditions of temperature, acidity, availability of moisture, and presence or absence of oxygen.

A second major cause of food spoilage or deterioration is chemical change brought about by either nonenzymatic or enzymatically catalyzed reactions. Enzymes are present in both plant and animal tissues and will remain active after the harvesting of plants or the slaughtering of animals. Some of the enzymes are hydrolases and will hydrolyze proteins, carbohydrates, or fats. Oxidases may catalyze undesirable oxidation–reduction reactions, such as those occurring when the cut or torn surfaces of certain fruits and vegetables undergo browning. Unwanted changes in texture, color, odor, and flavor can result from enzymatic activity as food is held or stored after harvest.

Oxidation may also occur simply as a chemical reaction that is not catalyzed by enzymes. Oxidation of fat, producing rancid odors and flavors, causes detrimental changes in many foods containing this substance, especially when these foods are held for extended periods of time. The browning or Maillard reaction that involves an initial combination of the aldehyde group from a reducing sugar and the amino group from a protein is another type of spoilage due to a nonenzymatic chemical change. (This reaction is discussed in Section 10.3.) The Maillard reaction may occur with the long storage of such products as nonfat dry milk. Color, odor, and flavor changes occur and the biological value of the protein may be decreased because the amino acids involved in the reaction are not readily released during digestion.

A third cause of food spoilage is desiccation. This occurs as moisture evaporates from foods and it is a physical cause of deterioration in quality. Loss of water usually has a pronounced effect on texture, appearance and taste.

Additional causes of food spoilage include damage from insect infestation or from small animals such as rodents. These may be major causes of food loss, particularly in many developing countries throughout the world. Damage from mechanical bruising and tearing of tissues may also spoil foods for human consumption.

Cleanliness is extremely important in reducing the incidence of food spoilage. Sanitary procedures in the handling of food help to decrease the number of microorganisms in or on that food. Hands, counters, and utensils used in food preparation should be washed thoroughly and kept clean during the preparation period. Proper control of temperature when food is held for periods of time after its harvest or after various stages of its processing and preparation is also important in controlling spoilage. Refrigerator temperatures, preferably below 23°C or 45°F, should be used to hold perishable foods.

CHARACTERISTICS OF MOLDS, YEASTS, AND BACTERIA

Although microorganisms are the major cause of food spoilage, they also perform many useful functions in food processing and preparation. Various strains of bacteria and molds are used in the production of a wide variety of cheeses. Sauerkraut and pickles are made by use of bacterial fermentation. The yeast, *Saccharomyces cerevisiae,* is the baker's yeast of leavened bread and other baked products. Yeast fermentation is the basic process involved in the manufacture of beer, wines, and vinegar. Molds are used in the making of Oriental foods such as soy sauce, miso, and sonti. They are also employed to make citric acid, used in food manufacturing, as well as the enzyme, alpha-amylase, which may be added to breads that are baked commercially.

There are numerous genera of molds, yeasts, and bacteria that may be involved in food spoilage. The extent to which each will grow in a food depends upon the composition of the food and the presence of competing microorganisms.

MOLDS

Molds are multicellular, filamentous fungi that produce a fuzzy or cottonlike appearance when they grow on the surface of foods. The growth commonly appears white but may be colored, dark, or smoky. Molds produce a mass of branching, intertwined filaments called hyphae. The whole mass is called the mycelium (Frazier, 1967).

Molds reproduce chiefly by means of asexual spores. The spores are produced in large numbers and are small, light, and resistant to drying. They are readily spread through the air and can start new mold wherever they settle, as long as conditions are favorable for growth. There are three principal types of asexual spores. Conidia (singular conidium) are made up of chains of spores that have somewhat the appearance of little brushes. *Penicillium* molds produce conidia (see Figure 5.1). Many *Penicillium* molds produce a blue-green growth. They cause a soft rot in

Figure 5.1

Diagram of a simple *Penicillium* showing conidia. (From W. C. Frazier, *Food Microbiology,* 2nd edition, New York: McGraw-Hill, 1967, p. 16. With permission.)

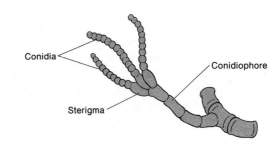

Figure 5.2

Diagram of *Rhizopus* showing sporangia. (From W. C. Frazier, *Food Microbiology,* 2nd edition, New York: McGraw-Hill, 1967, p. 12. With permission.)

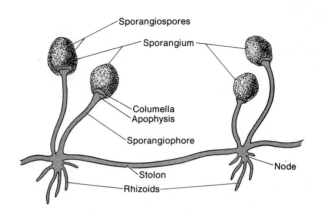

citrus fruits. *P. roqueforti* and *P. camemberti* are used to ripen Roquefort and Camembert cheeses. *Aspergillus* molds also produce conidia. These molds are widespread and many are involved in food spoilage. *A. niger* produces a black, brownish-black, or purple-brown growth.

Sporangiospores are a second type of asexual mold spore and are enclosed in a sac called a sporangium (plural sporangia) (see Figure 5.2). *Rhizopus* molds produce sporangia. *R. nigricans* is a common bread mold and is also involved in the spoilage of berries, fruits, and vegetables.

Arthrospores are a third type of asexual spore. They are formed by fragmentation of a hypha, so that the cells of the hypha become arthrospores (see Figure 5.3). *Geotrichum candidum* produces arthrospores. It is sometimes called the dairy mold and gives a white to cream-colored growth. The various morphological characteristics of molds are used in their identification and classification.

Molds generally require less available moisture than most yeasts and bacteria. Not all water in foods is available to microorganisms. Water is made unavailable by being tied up with solutes and hydrophilic colloids. Water tightly held by hydrophilic colloids is called *bound water.* Water that has crystallized as ice is not available to microorganisms. Some molds can grow on relatively dry foods.

Most molds are *mesophilic,* that is, able to grow well at ordinary temperatures. The optimal temperature for mold growth is usually about 25–30°C (77–86°F). Some molds, however, grow well at high temperatures (35–37°C or 95–98.6°F or above) while others grow fairly well at freezing temperatures or just above freezing.

Figure 5.3

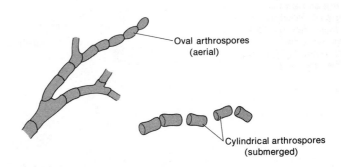

Oval arthrospores (aerial)

Cylindrical arthrospores (submerged)

Molds that grow on food are *aerobic;* that is, they require oxygen for growth. Most of them can grow over a wide range of pH (2–8.5) although the majority grow better at an acid pH. Most molds can utilize many kinds of food, ranging from simple nitrogen sources to complex proteins. Molds can thus grow on almost any food product, as long as their activity is not inhibited by the growth of other microorganisms, such as yeasts and bacteria, or by food preservation procedures.

Several molds are able to grow and elaborate toxins. These are called *mycotoxins* and cause illness when consumed by man or other animals. *Aspergillus flavus* is a common soil fungus found throughout the world and is present on such crops as peanuts, dry beans, and cereal grains. Its toxin is called aflatoxin and has been responsible for illness and death among both human and domestic animal populations in several countries (Anderson, 1977). Methods useful for the detection of mycotoxins in foods are being developed and evaluated (Ayres et al., 1970).

YEASTS

Yeasts are single-celled fungi that vary in shape and size. They may be spherical to ovoid, pear-shaped, cylindrical, or triangular. They usually reproduce asexually by budding. *True yeasts* may reproduce sexually by the production of ascospores following the conjugation of two cells (Frazier, 1967). Baker's yeast, *Saccharomyces cerevisiae,* may produce ascospores and has been selectively bred to produce desirable baking characteristics.

Unlike molds, most of the yeasts encountered in foods grow best with a generous supply of available moisture. However, some yeasts called *osmophilic yeasts* grow in the presence of greater concentrations of solutes, such as sugar or salt, than do most bacteria. This indicates that they need less available moisture.

Yeasts are mesophilic and have an optimum temperature range for growth similar to that of molds. The growth of most yeasts is favored by an acid medium, about pH 4–4.5. Yeasts grow best in the presence of oxygen (aerobic), but the fermentative types can grow slowly under *anaerobic* conditions. Anaerobic organisms do not require free oxygen and grow better in its absence.

Sugars are an excellent energy food for yeasts. They may utilize nitrogen sources that vary from simple to complex compounds. They also require accessory growth factors. Yeasts grow particularly well in fruit juices which provide large amounts of available moisture, sugars, and an acid pH.

Most of the yeasts used industrially are of the genus *Saccharomyces*. *Zygosaccharomyces* yeasts are *osmophilic* and can thus grow in relatively concentrated sugar solutions. They are involved in the spoilage of honey, syrups, and molasses. Film yeasts, such as those of the genera *Pichia* and *Candida*, grow on the surface of acid products such as sauerkraut and pickles, oxidizing the organic acids found in these products.

BACTERIA

Bacteria are one-celled microorganisms that are smaller than the fungi, molds and yeasts. They are rod-shaped (bacilli) or round (cocci). Many different families and genera of bacteria are involved in the spoilage of food (Frazier, 1967).

Bacteria generally require more available moisture than do molds or yeasts. They grow best where concentrations of sugar or salt are low. Some bacteria are *psychrophilic* (cold-loving) and grow well at refrigerator temperatures. Other are mesophilic with an optimal temperature range of 20–45°C (68–113°F). Bacteria with an optimal temperature above 45°C (113°F) are called *thermophilic* (heat-loving). Differences in the storage temperatures of foods influence the type of bacterial growth in these foods.

Each bacterium has its own optimal, minimal, and maximal pH for growth. Most bacteria, however, grow best at a pH near neutrality. Some types of bacteria are aerobic. Others are anaerobic, while still other bacteria are *facultative*, growing either with or without free oxygen. Bacteria vary greatly in nutrient requirements for growth.

Bacteria of the genera *Bacillus* and *Clostridium* form endospores which are more resistant to destruction by heat and other agents than are the vegetative forms. During the process of sporulation, the proteins within the bacterial cell are changed and special enzymes are formed. Germination of spores is favored by the usual conditions that are favorable to growth of the vegetative cells.

Bacterial genera commonly involved in food spoilage include *Pseudomonas, Acetobacter* (acetic acid-producing), *Achromobacter, Flavobacterium* (yellow to orange in color), *Proteus, Salmonella, Shigella, Micrococcus, Staphylococcus, Streptococcus, Leuconostoc, Lactobacillus, Bacillus, Clostridium* and *Microbacterium*. Bacteria in the genera *Escerichia* and *Aerobacter* are included in the coliform group. *E. coli* is considered to be indicative of sewage contamination.

The type of spoilage that occurs in a particular food depends to a large extent upon the composition of the food and conditions under which it is held. If a food is relatively moist, has a pH close to neutrality and is held at room temperature, it will likely be spoiled by bacteria. With optimal conditions for bacterial growth, this type of microorganism will usually predominate. Fresh meat, fish, and poultry are commonly spoiled by bacteria, although mold growth may occur on the surface of meats held for long periods at refrigerator temperatures. Yeast growth is favored by the presence of sugar and an acid pH. Fruit juices are readily fermented by yeasts while their acid pH discourages most bacterial growth. Molds grow readily on breads and slightly moist cereal grains, where the lack of available moisture discourages bacterial and yeast growth.

FACTORS AFFECTING HEAT RESISTANCE OF MICROORGANISMS

Figure 5.4 shows the usual temperatures required for control of bacteria in food. Several factors affect the resistance of cells and spores of microorganisms to destruction by heating. These factors must be kept in mind when heat treatment for sterilization is considered (Frazier, 1967).

Temperature–time Relationships Definite relationships exist between the temperature of heating and the time required to destroy a specified percentage of the microorganisms present. The *"D" value,* standing for decimal, designates the length of time needed at a specific lethal temperature to reduce the population of microorganisms to one-tenth; that is, to kill 90 percent of the microorganisms present (IFT Expert Panel, 1977). For example, if a given amount of food inoculated with 1000 bacterial spores is heated at 113°C (235°F) for five minutes and 900 spores have been destroyed, the "D" value for this spore at 113°C is five minutes. If the food is heated another five minutes at 113°C, 90 percent of the 100 remaining spores will be destroyed. This is a second "D" value.

Extensive laboratory testing has been done to determine the "D" value for each type of bacterial spore likely to be present in a product that is being canned. Recommended heating times for commercially canned products have been established using a wide margin of safety. To achieve acceptable sterility in a canned low-acid food, the cans or jars are heated for a period of time equivalent to 12 "D" values for the most heat-resistant spores that might be associated with that particular food (IFT Expert Panel).

The association between temperature and time of heating in relation to destruction of microorganisms was demonstrated in the work of Bigelow and Esty (1920). They reported that it would take 1200 minutes at 100°C (212°F) to kill 115,000 spores of flat sour bacteria per ml in corn juice at pH 6.1. At 115°C (239°F) it would take 70 minutes, while at 135°C (275°F) it would take only one minute to destroy all of the spores.

Figure 5.4

Temperature of food required for control of bacteria. (Courtesy of U. S. Department of Agriculture. Keeping food safe to eat. Home and Garden Bulletin No. 162.)

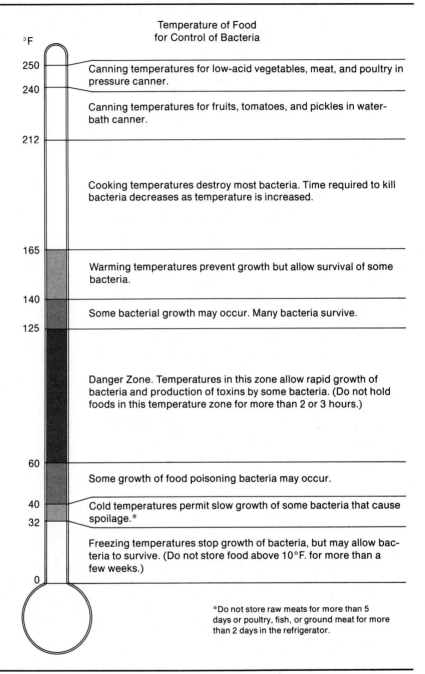

Temperature of Food
for Control of Bacteria

°F

250
240 — Canning temperatures for low-acid vegetables, meat, and poultry in pressure canner.

Canning temperatures for fruits, tomatoes, and pickles in water-bath canner.

212

Cooking temperatures destroy most bacteria. Time required to kill bacteria decreases as temperature is increased.

165

Warming temperatures prevent growth but allow survival of some bacteria.

140

Some bacterial growth may occur. Many bacteria survive.

125

Danger Zone. Temperatures in this zone allow rapid growth of bacteria and production of toxins by some bacteria. (Do not hold foods in this temperature zone for more than 2 or 3 hours.)

60

Some growth of food poisoning bacteria may occur.

40
32 — Cold temperatures permit slow growth of some bacteria that cause spoilage.*

Freezing temperatures stop growth of bacteria, but may allow bacteria to survive. (Do not store food above 10°F. for more than a few weeks.)

0

*Do not store raw meats for more than 5 days or poultry, fish, or ground meat for more than 2 days in the refrigerator.

Initial Concentration of Cells or Spores The greater number of cells or spores present in a food, the greater the heat treatment necessary to kill all of them. Bigelow and Esty (1920) showed that it took 14 minutes at 120°C (248°F) and pH 6 to destroy an initial concentration of 50,000 spores per ml of a thermophilic bacterium. When the initial concentration was 5000 spores per ml it took 10 minutes, 500 spores per ml were destroyed in 9 minutes and 50 spores per ml were destroyed in 8 minutes.

The microbial load on a food product may be partly controlled by particular attention to cleanliness throughout the food processing procedure. A relatively low level of contamination by microorganisms is desirable at the time that the product is ready for final treatment, whether the treatment is heating, freezing, or other processing.

Composition of the Substrate in which Cells or Spores Are Heated The active acidity of a food has an important effect on the heat resistance of microorganisms and their spores. In general, cells and spores are most heat resistant at or near neutrality. An increase in either acidity or alkalinity hastens killing by heat, but a change toward acid is more effective than a change toward alkalinity.

Low-acid foods have been defined as those foods having a pH of 4.6 or above. Acid foods are those having a pH of 4.5 or below. *Acid foods* include fruits and tomatoes, unless the tomatoes are low acid varieties. Because of their acidity, these foods can be safely processed at the usual temperature of boiling water. Microorganisms and their spores are less resistant to heat in the acid medium and can be destroyed in a reasonable heating period. Vegetables, meat, fish, poultry, and milk have pH values above 4.5. In order to destroy the more resistant spores during the canning of these foods, it is necessary to use a pressure cooker in which temperatures above the usual boiling point of water can be achieved and maintained. (The pH of a number of foods is given in Section 3.3.)

The nutrient substances that are present in a food may affect the resistance of microorganisms being heated in that food. The presence of sugar seems to protect some organisms but not others. Colloidal materials, especially proteins, protect microbes against destruction by heat. Fats also have a protective effect, often due to thermal insulation and a slower rate of heating. Large amounts of fatty tissue should not be included when meat is canned because of the effect this has on the rate of heating and the destruction of bacteria. Sodium chloride in low concentrations protects some bacterial spores. Moist heat is much more effective than dry heat in destroying microorganisms.

Type of Microorganism Most molds are killed by moist heat at 60°C (140°F) in 5–10 minutes. Their spores usually require, in a given time, a temperature 5–10°C higher than does mycelium. Mold spores are fairly resistant to destruction by dry heat.

Vegetative yeast cells are usually killed by heating at 50–58°C (122–136°F) for 10–15 minutes. Yeast spores are usually killed by heating at 60°C (140°F) for 10–15 minutes. The heat resistance of vegetative bacteria varies widely with the species. Some are easily killed while others which are thermophilic may require several minutes at 80–90°C (176–194°F) for destruction. The heat resistance of bacterial spores also varies greatly with the species of bacterium and the conditions during sporulation. Resistance at 100°C (212°F) may vary from less than a minute to over 20 hours (Frazier, 1967).

Clostridium botulinum is a rod-shaped, spore-forming, anaerobic bacterium. This organism may grow in a food and produce a toxin that is extremely powerful. Only a tiny amount of toxin is sufficient to cause death. Since *C. botulinum* is a soil organism, it is widely distributed in foods. Its spores are very heat resistant. If they are not destroyed during the heat processing treatment applied in the process of canning, they may vegetate and produce toxin under the relatively anaerobic conditions of a jar or can stored at moderate temperatures.

5.5

METHODS OF FOOD PRESERVATION

If food spoilage is to be prevented and food preserved, the basic causes of spoilage must be controlled. Therefore, microbial decomposition and self-decomposition from nonmicrobial causes must be prevented or delayed. Frazier (1967) has suggested that prevention or delay of microbial decomposition may be brought about by:

1. Keeping microorganisms out (*asepsis*).
2. Removing microorganisms, e.g., by filtration.
3. Hindering the growth and activity of microorganisms, e.g., by low temperatures, drying, anaerobic conditions, or chemicals.
4. Killing the microorganisms, e.g., by heat or radiations.

Prevention or delay of self-decomposition of the food is done by:

1. Destruction or inactivation of food enzymes, e.g., by blanching.
2. Prevention or delay of purely chemical reactions, e.g., prevention of oxidation by means of an antioxidant.

Some methods of food preservation involve more than one type of treatment in order to control both microbial activity and self decomposition. For example, canning employs a heat treatment sufficient to kill essentially all microorganisms and a sealing process which keeps other microorganisms out (asepsis). Vegetables are blanched before they are frozen in order to destroy enzymes and are then held at temperatures below freezing to hinder the growth and activity of microorganisms.

Methods of food preservation generally used industrially and at home may be classified in terms of the major controlling treatment.

1. Use of high temperatures to destroy both microorganisms and enzymes. Examples include pasteurization of milk and fruit juices, and canning.
2. Use of low temperatures to control the growth of microorganisms. Examples include root storage of fresh vegetables, refrigeration, and freezing.
3. Removal or tying up of moisture to control microbial growth. Examples include drying, freeze drying, adding large amounts of sugar as in jelly making.
4. Addition of chemical preservatives to inhibit microbial growth. Examples include development of acid in fermenting pickles, addition of antioxidants to lard and other fats, addition of propionates to bread as anti-molding agents.
5. Keeping microorganisms out. Examples include sealing sterilized foods and packaging foods.
6. Use of ionizing radiations to destroy microorganisms and control enzyme activity. Examples include the experimental use of pasteurizing radiation dosages for fresh strawberries and radiation of fresh potatoes to inhibit sprouting. More research data on the safety of irradiated foods are necessary before this method of preservation can gain widespread approval and use.

Effective methods of food preservation are particularly important in modern civilizations where population is concentrated in various urban centers and food is mass produced at diverse locations. Food must be transported, sometimes over long distances, and remain in marketing channels for variable periods of time. Food preservation is also important in many less developed settings in order to extend the supply of food over periods of scarcity between harvests. Although foods are processed for a number of different reasons, including palatability and convenience, the primary reason for processing food is for its preservation.

The processes used for preservation purposes may also affect the quality characteristics of a food. For example, undesirable changes in flavor, texture, and appearance occur in some foods, such as milk and eggs, with application of relatively small amounts of heat. Other foods, such as corn, can undergo a much greater heat treatment before marked changes become apparent. Frozen fruits usually retain their fresh flavors but the completely thawed product is often limp and soggy in texture. Marked changes in texture and appearance often result from drying foods.

Pasteurization involves the application of a milder heat treatment than that necessary for sterilization and effects fewer changes in the original quality characteristics. Temperatures below 100°C (212°F) are usually used in the pasteurization of such products as milk and fresh fruit juices. Pasteurization kills disease-producing microorganisms (pathogens) and most of the spoilage organisms present in a food product. However, some spoilage organisms survive and their activity must be controlled by storing the pasteurized product at a low temperature.

An inevitable consequence of food processing is some loss of nutrient content. Nesheim (1974) has reviewed these nutrient changes. The amount of loss is dependent on the susceptibility of the nutrient to the process employed, the type of process used, and the care taken to minimize the loss. Nutrient loss may occur between harvesting and processing, during processing, during holding periods after processing, and during the final preparation of the food before consumption. Heat processing enhances the digestibility of proteins generally but the Maillard or browning reaction may adversely affect protein quality when sugars are present with protein. Carbohydrates and fats are usually not adversely affected by heating.

Losses of water-soluble vitamins with heating vary widely. Vitamins may be lost in washing and blanching procedures as well as in the final heating period for canned products. Cain (1967) reviewed water-soluble vitamin changes during processing and storage of fruits and vegetables. The mean percent losses of vitamins in commercial processing of canned asparagus have been reported to be 5 percent for ascorbic acid, 6 percent for niacin, 8 percent for thiamin, and 10 percent for riboflavin. Reported losses in canned spinach were 33 percent ascorbic acid, 17 percent niacin, 15 percent thiamin, and 12 percent riboflavin. Canned citrus juices retain 92–97 percent of their ascorbic acid.

Fruits and vegetables lose their minerals as these nutrients are leached into the surrounding water or juice. This process continues to occur during storage of canned foods. In the case of canned vegetables, many nutrients are often discarded with the packing medium when the vegetables are served (Nesheim, 1974).

Freezing *per se* does not destroy vitamins in frozen vegetables, but losses may occur from the blanching process. Alternative freezing and thawing of foods and widely fluctuating temperatures during frozen storage are also destructive of vitamins.

5.6

PRESERVING FOOD AT HOME

Since commercially preserved foods are widely distributed and available in many countries of the world, home food preservation has become less important. Nevertheless, varying amounts of food are still preserved at home, depending upon individual circumstances and interests.

In deciding whether or not to preserve food at home, the consumer might consider several pertinent factors. The cost of the home-preserved product in comparison to the commercially available one may be evaluated. For example, fresh fruits and vegetables suitable for canning or freezing may not be available at a reasonable cost in some localities. Equipment necessary for processing, such as a pressure cooker for canning low-acid vegetables, should be considered in estimating costs. The amount of storage space available for keeping the finished product should be adequate. Other factors to consider include 1. the amount of time and labor involved; 2. the skill necessary or the desire to acquire the skill; 3. the quality of the finished home-preserved product in comparison to the commercial counterpart; and 4. the personal satisfaction derived from "do-it-yourself" projects.

SUMMARY

All foods are subject to deterioration in quality. Causes of food spoilage include 1. decomposition by microorganisms; 2. chemical change, either nonenzymatic or enzymatically catalyzed; 3. damage from insect infestation or from small animals; and 4. mechanical bruising and tearing. There is no universal definition for spoiled food but it is generally agreed that, from a health standpoint, food should be safe to eat. It should also be aesthetically acceptable.

Microorganisms perform many useful functions in food. For example, molds and bacteria are used to ripen cheese, yeast fermentation is used by the baking and wine industries, and various enzymes are harvested from microbial growth.

Molds reproduce chiefly by means of asexual spores. The spores are found in conidia, sporangia, or arthrospores. Yeasts are one-celled organisms that vary in shape from spherical to triangular. They usually reproduce asexually by budding but may reproduce sexually by ascospore formation. Bacteria are either rod-shaped or round. Wide variation in characteristics is found among the numerous genera.

Bacteria require more available moisture than do yeasts. Molds can grow with the least amount of moisture. Bacteria generally grow best at a pH near neutrality. Yeasts favor an acid pH of 4–4.5. Molds can grow over a wide pH range. Molds and yeasts are mostly aerobic. Some bacteria are aerobic, some anaerobic, and others are facultative. Molds and yeasts are generally mesophilic. The optimal temperature for their growth is about 25–30°C (77–86°F). Some types of bacteria are mesophilic, some are psychrophilic, and others are thermophilic. Bacteria of the genera *Bacillus* and *Clostridium* form endospores which are more resistant to destruction by heat and other agents than are the vegetative forms. Factors affecting the heat resistance of microorganisms include time–temperature relationships, the initial concentration of cells and spores, and the composition of the substrate in which the microbes are heated. The type of spoilage in a food depends both upon the composition of the food and the conditions under which it is held.

The basic causes of food spoilage must be controlled if food is to be preserved. Microbial decomposition may be prevented or delayed by 1. keeping out the microorganisms, 2. removing microorganisms, 3. hindering the growth and activity of microorganisms and 4. killing the microorganisms. Self-decomposition in food may be prevented or delayed by 1. destruction or inactivation of food enzymes and 2. prevention or delay of purely chemical reactions such as oxidation.

Methods of food preservation, which have historically developed from relatively simple to very complex processes and systems, may be classified in terms of the major controlling treatment. They are 1. use of high temperatures to destroy both microorganisms and enzymes; 2. use of low temperatures to control the growth of microorganisms; 3. removal or tying up of moisture to control microbial growth; 4. addition of chemical preservatives to inhibit microbial growth; 5. keeping out the microorganisms; and 6. use of ionizing radiations to destroy microorganisms and control enzyme activity.

Some loss of nutrients occurs with the processing of food for preservation purposes. Losses can generally be minimized by good manufacturing practices.

Commercially preserved foods are widely distributed and available. In deciding whether or not to preserve food at home, the consumer might consider costs, necessary equipment, storage space, time and labor involved, necessary skill, quality of the finished products, and personal satisfaction derived from the "do-it-yourself" project.

STUDY QUESTIONS

Present day methods of food preservation have developed over many centuries.

1. Discuss three important milestones that, according to Goldblith, stand out in the historical development of canning.
2. What major industrial developments were necessary before the frozen food industry could develop and grow? Explain.

There are several basic causes of food spoilage.

3. Describe three or four basic causes of food spoilage.

General methods of food preservation, to be effective, must be directed toward the elimination of the basic causes of spoilage.

4. List six general methods of food preservation classified according to the major controlling treatment.
5. For each of the methods listed in question 4, name the basic cause(s) of food spoilage being controlled or prevented and indicate how it is done.
6. From the following list of brief descriptions of treatments for food, identify those treatments that will increase the storage life of foods and explain why. Also classify each of these treatments according to one of the general methods of food preservation listed in question 4.

Treatments
>Heat jars of peaches in a boiling water bath for a specified time
>Blanch and freeze broccoli spears
>Harvest cherries and hold at room temperature
>Pasteurize milk
>Shell walnuts and store on the kitchen shelf
>Produce clean eggs
>Keep unshelled pecans on the kitchen shelf
>Prepare fruit salad
>Subject strawberries to a Co^{60} source
>Add sodium benzoate to margarine
>Prepare salt pickles
>Make grape jelly
>Prepare potato salad and refrigerate it
>Place sulfured apricots in the sun for several hours
>Smoke ham
>Can green beans in a pressure cooker

Molds, yeasts, and bacteria each have distinctive characteristics.

7. From the following list of characteristics, identify those that apply to molds, those that apply to yeasts, and those that apply to bacteria.

   Characteristics
   >May multiply by budding
   >May produce sporangia
   >Single-celled
   >May produce conidia
   >Some are rod-shaped
   >Some are of the genus *Rhizopus*
   >May form spores
   >Some are of the genus *Aerobacter*
   >Fungi
   >Develop mycelium
   >May produce ascospores
   >Ferment sugar readily in a slightly acid media
   >Some strains are thermophilic
   >Some are of the genus *Saccharomyces*

Certain physiological requirements of molds, yeasts, and bacteria are similar and others differ.

8. For each of the following factors, describe optimum requirements of molds, of yeasts, and of bacteria.
   a. pH
   b. Temperature
   c. Available moisture
   d. Oxygen
9. From the following list of foods, identify those that, if placed in a warm room, would most likely be spoiled first and chiefly by molds, those that would most likely be spoiled first and chiefly by yeasts, and those that would likely be spoiled by bacteria. Explain why in each case.

Foods
> enriched white bread
> soda crackers
> raw milk
> fresh lettuce in a plastic bag
> lean ground beef
> cornflakes
> pasteurized milk
> apple juice
> oranges

10. Discuss the general effect of each of the following factors on the resistance of microbes to destruction by heat.
    a. Heating time–temperature relationships
    b. Initial concentration of cells or spores
    c. Composition of the substrate in which cells or spores are heated
    d. Type of microorganism
11. List the approximate temperature required, with 5–15 minutes of heating, for destruction of most yeast and mold cells and spores.
12. Define the term thermophilic in relation to bacteria.
13. Define ''D'' value.
14. Name the organism responsible for botulism, describe the relative heat resistance of its spores, and explain why safe canning procedures must always allow for its destruction.

REFERENCES

1. Anderson, A. W. 1977. The significance of yeasts and molds in foods. *Food Technology* 31 (No. 2), 47.

2. Ayres, J. C., H. S. Lillard, and D. A. Lillard. 1970. Mycotoxins: Methods for detection in foods. *Food Technology* 24, 161.

3. Bigelow, W. D. and J. R. Esty. 1920. The thermal death point in relation to time of typical thermophilic organisms. *Journal of Infectious Diseases* 27, 602.

4. Cain, R. F. 1967. Water-soluble vitamins. Changes during processing and storage of fruit and vegetables. *Food Technology* 21, 998.

5. Frazier, W. C. 1967. Food Microbiology, 2nd edition. New York: McGraw-Hill.

6. Goldblith, S. A. 1971. The science and technology of thermal processing, Part 1. *Food Technology* 25, 1256.

7. Goldblith, S. A. 1972a. The science and technology of thermal processing, Part 2. *Food Technology* 26 (No. 1), 64.

8. Goldblith, S. A. 1972b. Controversy over the autoclave. *Food Technology* 26 (No. 12), 62.

9. Goresline, H. E. 1962. Historical development of the modern frozen food industry. In: *Low Temperature Microbiology Symposium*. Campbell Soup Company, p. 5.

10. Institute of Food Technologists' Expert Panel on Food Safety and Nutri-

tion and the Committee on Public Information. 1977. Home Canning. *Food Technology* 31 (No. 6), 43.

11. Institute of Food Technologists' Expert Panel on Food Safety and Nutrition and Committee on Public Information, 1974. Shelf life of foods. *Food Technology* 28 (No. 8).

12. Nesheim, R. O. 1974. Nutrient changes in food processing. *Federation Proceedings* 33, 2267.

CHAPTER 6

FOOD PRESERVATION BY CANNING

Microorganisms are destroyed by heating to a sufficiently high temperature. In the canning process, enough heat is applied to bring about what is called *commercial sterility*. This may not destroy every single microorganism in the food product, but the vast majority are destroyed and a safe food with a long storage life is produced (IFT Expert Panel, 1977). After sterilization, hermetic sealing guarantees that the food will not be recontaminated by microorganisms.

6.1

HEAT PENETRATION AND PROCESSING TIME

The rate of heat penetration into a food must be known in order to calculate the heat processing that will be necessary to destroy the microorganisms present. Heat penetrates from the warmer outside part of a can or jar to the cooler center portion by convection and/or conduction. In *convection* heating, heated molecules themselves move from one place to another. This can occur when liquids or gases are being heated. In *conduction,* heat is transferred from molecule to molecule through a substance. Conduction is rapid in metals but relatively slow in foods. When solid particles of food are suspended in a liquid, the particles are heated by conduction and the liquid is heated primarily by convection. Several factors determine the time required for heat to penetrate and bring the center of a container of food up to a sterilizing temperature (Frazier, 1967).

The material of which the container is made influences heat penetration. Glass has a slower rate of heat penetration than does a tin-coated iron can.

The larger the container, the longer it will take for heat to reach the center. A quart jar takes longer to heat to the appropriate temperature than does a pint jar. The shape of a container also affects heat penetration. Food in a long, slim, cylindrical can will be heated faster than the same volume of food in a shorter cylindrical can of greater diameter.

The consistency of the contents of a can and the size of the food particles in the can affect heat penetration. Heat penetrates slowly through a dense, viscous food mixture because heating is chiefly by conduction. Convection currents cannot move easily through a thickened food mixture. Cream-style corn, squash, pumpkin, and sweet potatoes may become mushy with heating. If pieces of food are small, such as green peas, and retain their identity during heat processing in a liquid media, the heating is similar to the heating of water. On the other hand, if the pieces of food are large, heating is delayed because the heat must penetrate to the center of each piece before the liquid can reach the optimal temperature.

Fat is a thermal insulator. Heat penetration is slower when large amounts of fat are present in the can or jar.

Rotation or agitation of the container during heat processing may hasten heat penetration, if the food is at all fluid, permitting heat transfer by convection. Agitation is helpful in heating foods that tend to form layers, such as spinach, tomatoes, and peach halves.

The rate of heat penetration during canning, determined for individual canned products, is used to calculate the *sterility value* or *F value*. The "F" value is the length of heat processing time at a given processing temperature necessary to obtain a 12 "D" value for destruction of heat-resistant spores. (The "D" value is discussed in Section 5.4. It is the length of time needed at a specific lethal temperature to reduce the population of microorganisms to one-tenth.) Heat processing times and conditions that are used by commercial canners for canning low-acid foods have been determined in the United States primarily by the National Canners Association. These are calculated from the results of tests on spore destruction and heat penetration in individual foods (IFT Expert Panel, 1977). In 1946, the U.S. Department of Agriculture (USDA) (Toepfer *et al.*) published the results of extensive bacteriological and heat penetration tests on home canning procedures. Recommended processing times given in USDA bulletins are based on these scientific studies.

6.2

CANNING ACID FOODS

Fruits and tomatoes have pH values less than 4.6 and may safely be canned in a *boiling water bath*. In this procedure, the cans or jars of food are immersed in boiling water and heated for a specified period of time. It is possible to use the temperature of boiling water for processing because of the lesser resistance of microbial spores in an acid medium and the inhibitory effect on microbial growth of the acid environment.

In recent years new varieties of tomatoes have been developed. Some questions have been raised as to whether or not these varieties were high enough in acidity to be canned by the boiling water method. Measurements of pH have been made within the past few years on more than 100 varieties of tomatoes grown in several locations. In most cases the pH of firm, fully colored, ripe tomatoes of each variety was below 4.6. Four varieties were found, however, which had pH values above 4.6. These varieties—Garden State, Ace, 55VF, and Cal Ace—should not be processed in a boiling water bath. A pressure canner, in which temperatures above that of boiling water can be maintained, should be used for these varieties (IFT Expert Panel, 1977). As a tomato ripens, its acidity decreases. Therefore, overripe tomatoes could reach pH values in the low-acid range and should not be processed in a boiling water bath. Savani *et al.* (1978) found that overripe Ohio 7584 tomatoes had a mean pH of 4.6 but after treatment with a water-lye solution to remove the skins the pH was 5.1. After storage of the home canned product for from 3–7 months the pH was 4.8 whether or not citric acid, cream of tartar, or ReaLemon juice had been added before processing. However, Schoenemann and Lopez (1973) reported that the addition of citric, malic, fumaric, or phosphoric acids to commercially canned tomatoes maintained a sufficiently reduced pH for canning at atmospheric pressure.

METHODS

Detailed procedures for canning fruits and vegetables at home are given in USDA Home and Garden Bulletin No. 8 (1976). The general procedure for processing fruits and tomatoes involves first the selection of fresh, firm fruits, sorted for size and ripeness. They should be washed thoroughly and may be peeled. The food, either raw or hot, may be packed into containers with recommended processing times being longer when raw packing is done. With few exceptions, some space should be left between the packed food and the lid or closure. If fruit is being processed in tin cans, it must be heated to 77°C (170°F) to drive off air before it is sealed. If fruit is being processed in glass jars having self-sealing lids, the screw band is tightened but not sealed and still allows air to escape during the boiling procedure. Sealing occurs automatically after the jar is removed from the boiling water bath.

General recommendations have been to immerse the jars or cans completely in boiling water and boil for a specified time that depends on the particular product and the size of jar or can. Harris and Davis (1976) have reported that tomato juice can be heated as rapidly with a $2\frac{1}{2}$-in. water level in the canner as with a higher water level. The time and heat energy required to preheat the water and the amount of heat liberated to the kitchen area were reduced to approximately one-fourth of the quantities used when water covered the jar tops. A close-fitting cover that holds saturated steam around and over the jars is essential when a low level of water is used. The conventional pressure canner operated with the cover closed but the vent open may be used with a low water level for canning fruits and tomatoes. Canners specially designed for steam cooking are also available.

Open kettle canning is a method in which cooked food is packed, while hot, into sterilized jars and sealed with no additional processing. Contamination by microorganisms during the filling process may easily occur. Therefore, this method is not recommended for the canning of fruits and tomatoes. It is safe only for jams and jellies containing sugar (USDA Home and Garden Bulletin No. 8; IFT Expert Panel, 1977).

6.3

CANNING LOW-ACID FOODS

Low-acid foods, such as vegetables, meat, fish, poultry, and milk, must be canned in a pressure cooker that will allow the achievement of temperatures above the usual boiling point of water. The resistance of bacterial spores to destruction by heating is increased by the relatively low level of acidity in these products. Surviving spores may also vegetate and grow more readily in the low-acid foods than in acidic fruits and tomatoes.

Proper use of a pressure canner in processing low-acid foods is essential in canning chiefly because of the danger of botulism. *Botulism* is a disease condition resulting from the consumption of the extremely potent toxin that may be produced by the anaerobic bacterium *Clostridium botulinum*. (The heat resistance of *C. botulinum* spores is discussed in Section 5.4.) Minimal heat processes for canned foods recommended by the National Canners Association are sufficient to destroy *C. botulinum* spores and allow a wide margin of safety. Most of the cases of botulism in the past 30 years have resulted from consumption of improperly processed home canned foods, although commercially canned tuna fish and some soups have also been involved.

METHODS

The preparative steps in the canning of low-acid vegetables are similar to those used for fruits and tomatoes. Good quality produce should be selected, carefully washed, and packed into jars. Packing hot is preferable to raw packing for many vegetables. It allows closer packing, drives out air and destroys enzymes that may catalyze undesirable reactions in the vegetables during slow heating. A head space is left in the top of the container. Specific directions for canning vegetables are found in the USDA Home and Garden Bulletin No. 8. Home canning of meat and poultry is treated in USDA Home and Garden Bulletin No. 106.

The pressure canner is made of materials strong enough to withstand the pressures created by confined steam. The steam is produced from 2 or 3 in. of water placed in the bottom of the canner. After placing the filled jars or cans in the canner, the cover is securely fastened so that no steam can escape except through the vent. The canner is heated until steam has escaped steadily from the vent for 10 minutes. This exhausting process drives essentially all of the air out of the canner so that the pressure created inside the canner comes completely from steam. The vent is then closed and as heating is continued the pressure gauge measures the increasing pressure inside the canner.

The temperature achieved inside the canner is proportional to the pressure. If all of the pressure comes from steam, the temperature follows the curve shown in Figure 6.1. If air is left in the canner, it will exert its partial pressure on the gauge and the temperature–pressure relationship will then deviate from that for 100 percent steam. If the canner is not completely exhausted of air, the temperature attained will be lower than expected from a reading of the pressure gauge and food may be underprocessed. Pressure canners should be tested regularly to assure accuracy.

It is important to maintain a constant pressure in a pressure canner during processing. If the pressure is allowed to fluctuate markedly, liquid will be lost from jars inside the canner. A sudden drop in pressure around the jars causes release of liquid through the unsealed lid in order to equalize pressures inside and outside the jar.

Procedures used in commercial canning to yield improved products include agitated cooking and aseptic filling. Many different types of agitating cookers are available. Agitation may be end-over-end or axial, and continuous or intermittent. Agitation increases the rate of heat transfer from container to product by renewing the surface that comes in contact with the walls of the container. Burned or cooked flavors are decreased in intensity by agitation (Desrosier, 1977).

A process for sterilizing a product prior to filling it into sterilized cans was described by Martin (1948). The product is sterilized by flash heating with immediate cooling in a heat-exchange system. Containers and covers are sterilized with superheated steam. The containers are then aseptically filled and covers applied in an atmosphere of either saturated or superheated steam. The flavor and texture, as well as the nutritive value, of the product may be improved by the shorter heating period. Chen *et al.* (1970) reported that strained peas canned by the aseptic method had higher levels of amino acids and amino nitrogen

Figure 6.1

Relationships between pressure and temperature of steam.

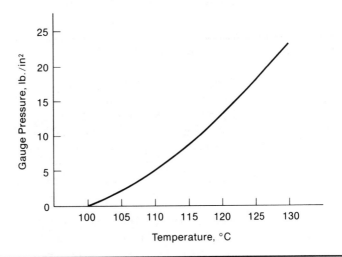

than did the same product processed in a retort. This had significance from a flavor standpoint since loss of amino acids during processing may influence the flavor acceptance of a canned product. The aseptic sample was also higher in essential amino acids, and thus nutritionally improved over the traditionally processed product. Luh *et al.* (1969) found that aseptically canned strained carrots were superior in color, aroma, and flavor to carrots canned by a retort process.

6.4

VENTING AND THE DEVELOPMENT OF A PARTIAL VACUUM

A head space, usually one-half inch, is left in filled glass jars that are to be processed. The jars are closed but not completely sealed before being placed in a boiling water bath or pressure cooker. As the heating process continues, the contents of the jar expand and fill the head space. Air trapped in the food product also expands and rises to the top of the jar where it is forced out through the unsealed top. This process is called *venting*. If insufficient head space is left in a jar, the expansion of the jar contents on heating may force a small amount of liquid through the unsealed lid. A siphoning effect then draws a large amount of liquid from the jar.

After processing has been completed, the jars are removed from the cooker. Sealing is then completed. This occurs automatically with the use of self-sealing lids in which case the sealing compound adheres to the top of the jar and hardens as it begins to cool. The sealed jar does not allow air to reenter. As the expanded contents of the jar condense with cooling, the loss of air creates a partial vacuum in the jar. The partial vacuum aids in maintaining a seal on the jar since pressure on the outside of the lid is greater than that inside. The loss of oxygen from the jar is also important in retarding oxidative changes that may occur at the surface of the product.

6.5

ADDING CALCIUM TO CANNED FOODS

The heating process required for canning some vegetables, as well as tomatoes and apples, may produce undesirable disintegrating or softening effects. The addition of calcium was shown by Kertesz as early as 1939 to have a firming effect on plant tissues.

The enzyme pectin methylesterase is present in plants. This enzyme catalyzes a reaction in which the methyl esters of galacturonic acid, the building block of pectic substances, are hydrolyzed to leave free carboxyl ($-\overset{\overset{\text{O}}{\|}}{\text{C}}\text{OH}$) groups. Calcium interacting with partially deesterified pectic substances to form insoluble calcium salts increases the firmness of plant tissues. The mechanisms for this action are not completely clarified. A heat blanching process at moderate temperatures applied during the early stages of canning fruits or vegetables will activate the pectin methylesterase enzyme.

LaBelle (1971) produced improved texture in red tart cherries by preheating them at about 60°C (140°F) for 5–20 minutes in the presence of calcium. Van Buren (1968) reported that the firmness of snap beans was directly related to the level of calcium attained in the pods by the addition of calcium chloride at various stages of processing. Calcium added before blanching was more effective than that added after blanching. Since calcium continued to have an effect on firmness after more than the amount calculated to combine with all of the polygalacturonide carboxyl groups present was added, it was postulated that other factors in addition to the formation of calcium bridges between pectin molecules were operating to produce firmness. Possible explanations for the additional firming action included promotion by calcium of coagulation between pectin molecules and binding of calcium by nonpectic substances.

6.6

SPOILAGE OF CANNED FOODS

If canned foods are underprocessed some microorganisms will survive and grow during storage of the canned products. Unless the products were grossly underprocessed the spoiled cans will contain only one microorganism type. In low-acid and medium-acid foods this will be a spore-forming organism. In acid foods it may be yeasts; molds; or acid-resistant, spore-forming, or non spore-forming bacteria (Desrosier, 1977).

Microbiological spoilage is commonly accompanied by the production of acid and gas. The ends of tin cans become bulged by the internal pressure created by the gas. The food product is usually decomposed and appears spoiled. Growth and toxin production by *C. botulinum*, however, is not always accompanied by obvious signs of spoilage. This increases the danger of one unknowingly tasting canned foods that are contaminated with toxin. It has been recommended that home canned low-acid products be boiled for 10–15 minutes before serving (IFT Expert Panel, 1977). The heat will destroy any toxin which might have formed in the food.

A type of microbial spoilage that is not accompanied by gas production and bulged ends of cans is called *flat sour spoilage*. This is characteristically caused by thermophilic bacteria which produce large amounts of acid without gas formation. Flat sour spoilage is usually the result of underprocessing or of leakage from cans, allowing contamination of the contents.

Gas production in stored canned food may result from chemical action as well as from the activity of microorganisms. Hydrogen gas can be produced by the action of high-acid foods on the iron of the can, that may be exposed from scratches or damage to the tin coating. Carbon dioxide gas in canned foods may result from decomposition of such products as molasses, malt extract, or syrups.

The stability of canned food products during long-term storage is influenced to a large degree by the temperature of storage. Storage at relatively high temperatures hastens undesirable changes in color, texture, flavor, and vitamin content. Cecil and Woodroof (1963) reported on the storage of 43 canned items for up to seven years at varying temperatures. Patterns of change in sensory quality were roughly proportional to storage temperature but were characteristic for each individual product. Storage life at 38°C (100°F) ranged from less than six months to more than three years. Storage life at 21°C (70°F) ranged from about two and one-half years to more than seven years. All products remained in fair to good condition after four years when stored at 8°C (47°F).

SUMMARY

Extensive laboratory testing has been done to determine the "D" value for each type of bacterial spore likely to be present in a product being canned. The "D" value designates the length of time needed at a specific lethal temperature to reduce the population of microorganisms to one-tenth. Recommended processing times for various canned foods can be calculated by using "D" values and test information on heat penetration during the processing of individual food products. This has been done in the United States by the National Canners Association.

Low-acid foods have been defined as those having a pH of 4.6 or above. Acid foods are those with a pH of 4.5 or below. Acid foods may be processed in a boiling water bath while low-acid foods require a pressure canner in which temperatures higher than the usual boiling point of water can be achieved.

Heat penetrates to the center of a can or jar by convection and/or conduction. Heat takes longer to penetrate to the center of a large container than a smaller one. The shape of a container also affects heat penetration. Heat penetrates slowly through a dense, viscous food mixture and more rapidly through a thin, watery product. Rotation or agitation of the container during heating hastens heat penetration.

In the home canning of acid foods, which include tomatoes and other fruits, the product may be packed into containers either raw or hot. The closed containers are then heated in a boiling water bath for a specified period of time. Relatively low levels of water may be used in the boiling process if a close-fitting cover holds saturated steam around and over the jars and cans. Heat resistance of microbes is decreased by the acid pH so that these organisms are destroyed in reasonable processing times. In addition, surviving organisms will not grow in the acid environment.

Low-acid foods, such as vegetables, meat, fish, poultry, and milk, require relatively high processing temperatures in order to destroy all sporeforming organisms, particularly *Clostridium botulinum*. Closed jars or cans are placed in a pressure canner containing 2–3 in. of water. The tightly covered canner is first heated with the vent open in order to exhaust all of the air from the cooker. The vent is then closed and the pressure increased by heating to vaporize the water as steam. The temperature inside the canner is proportional to the steam pressure produced. The canning pressure is measured by a pressure gauge.

During the processing of glass jars, the heated contents of each jar expands into the head space and pushes out air. This process is called venting. After the jars are removed from the processing equipment, sealing is completed. Then as the contents cool and contract a partial vacuum is formed in each jar. This aids in holding the seal and in decreasing oxidative changes at the surface of the food.

The addition of calcium to some canned fruits and vegetables contributes to a firm texture. The calcium apparently forms an insoluble salt with pectic substances.

Canned foods will spoil by the action of microorganisms if they are under-processed. Microbial spoilage is commonly associated with gas and decomposition. However, spoilage by *C. botulinum* may occur without apparent signs. Since this organism produces a potent toxin, it is recommended that home canned low-acid foods be boiled for 10–15 minutes before serving in order to destroy any toxin that may have formed. Chemical spoilage of canned foods may result from the action of acid foods on iron and tin from the can. Canned foods maintain quality characteristics for a longer period of time when stored at temperatures below 21°C (70°F) than when stored at higher temperatures.

STUDY QUESTIONS

Heat penetrates canned foods at varying rates.

1. Define convection and conduction in relation to the heating of canned foods.
2. Describe several factors that affect the penetration of heat into the center of canned foods.
3. Define "F" value and discuss its use in calculating processing times for canned foods.

Acid foods may be processed in a boiling water bath.

4. Explain why the above statement is true.
5. Describe the major steps involved in the home canning of tomatoes and other fruits. Explain why each step in the procedure is important to the final product.
6. Describe how a partial vacuum is formed in bottled fruit and explain its usefulness.

7. Explain why open kettle canning is not recommended for use, except in the preparation of jellies and jams containing high concentrations of sugar.

Low acid foods must be processed in a pressure canner.

8. Explain why the above statement is true.
9. Define low-acid foods; acid foods.
10. Describe the major steps involved in the home canning of vegetables. Explain why each step in the procedure is important to the final product.
11. Explain why exhausting a pressure canner is an essential step in the process of canning low-acid foods and describe the possible consequences of not doing it.
12. Choose a satisfactory canning method for each food in the following list and explain why the method chosen would be most satisfactory.

Foods
  green peas
  beef chuck
  peaches
  raspberries
  stewing hen
  green lima beans
  apricots
  tomatoes
  pickled beets
  spinach

A young homemaker canned green beans in glass jars using a pressure canner and processed the beans for the time recommended in a USDA bulletin on home canning. However, many of her jars spoiled, as evidenced by gas formation and an "off-odor," after short storage. In addition, she noticed at the completion of the canning process that the jars had lost much of the liquid originally in them. She would like to know what she might have done wrong so that she can avoid these problems in the future.

13. What questions would you ask of her in order to understand what she had done? Give some explanations for her results.

REFERENCES

1. Cecil, S. R. and J. G. Woodroof. 1963. The stability of canned foods in long-term storage. *Food Technology* 17, 639.

2. Chen, K. C., B. S. Luh, and M. E. Seehafer. 1970. Chemical changes in strained peas canned by the aseptic and retort processes. *Food Technology* 24, 821.

3. Desrosier, N. W. 1977. *The Technology of Food Preservation*, 4th edition. Westport, Conn.: Avi Publishing Company.

4. Frazier, W. C. 1967. *Food Microbiology*, 2nd edition. New York: McGraw-Hill.

5. Harris, H. and L. M. Davis. 1976. Use of low water level in boiling water bath canning. Circular 226, Alabama Agricultural Experiment Station, Auburn.

6. Institute of Food Technologists' Expert Panel on Food Safety and Nutrition and the Committee on Public Information. 1977. Home canning. *Food Technology* 31 (No. 6), 43.

7. Kertesz, Z. I. 1939. The effect of calcium in plant tissues. *Canner* 88, 26.

8. LaBelle, R. L. 1971. Heat and calcium treatments for firming red tart cherries in a hot-fill process. *Journal of Food Science* 36, 323.

9. Luh, B. S., J. Antonakos, and H. N. Daoud. 1969. Chemical and quality changes in strained carrots canned by the aseptic and retort processes. *Food Technology* 23, 377.

10. Martin, W. M. 1948. Flash process, aseptic fill are used in new canning unit. *Food Industries* 20, 832.

11. Savani, J., N. D. Harris, and W. A. Gould. 1978. Survival of *Clostridium sporogenes* PA 3679 in home-canned tomatoes. *Journal of Food Science* 43, 222.

12. Schoenemann, D. R. and A. Lopez. 1973. Heat processing effects on physical and chemical characteristics of acidified canned tomatoes. *Journal of Food Science* 38, 195.

13. Toepfer, E. W., H. Reynolds, G. Gilpin, and K. Taube. 1946. Home canning processes for low acid foods. USDA Technical Bulletin No. 930.

14. U. S. Department of Agriculture. 1976. Home canning of fruits and vegetables. Home and Garden Bulletin No. 8.

15. U. S. Department of Agriculture. 1975. Home canning of meat and poultry. Home and Garden Bulletin No. 106.

16. Van Buren, J. P. 1968. Adding calcium to snap beans at different stages in processing: Calcium uptake and texture of the canned product. *Food Technology* 22, 780.

CHAPTER 7

FOOD PRESERVATION BY FREEZING

The length of time that foods can be kept edible is generally determined by the storage temperature. As temperatures are decreased, metabolic changes, both in living plant tissues and in microorganisms, are retarded.

7.1

LOW TEMPERATURES AND FOOD PRESERVATION

The usual temperatures for cold storage rooms in which foods are held without freezing depend upon the food products being stored. Consideration is given to retarding microbial activity without causing injury to the tissues of the fresh food products. Dairy foods and fresh meats are commonly held at 0°–2.2°C (32°–36°F). The ideal storage temperature for eggs is −1.7°C (29°F). Fresh fruits and vegetables are actively metabolizing and produce some heat during cold storage. This must be considered in planning for maintenance of cold storage temperatures. Some fruits and vegetables are susceptible to cold injury when stored at only moderately low temperatures. Lemons, bananas, winter squash, sweet potatoes, and mature green tomatoes are best held at 10°–14.4°C (50°–58°F). Others such as cucumbers, eggplants, grapefruit, limes, cantaloupes, papayas, sweet peppers, and mature green pineapples should not be held at temperatures below 7.2°C (45°F) if cold injury is to be avoided.

Chilling at or below the freezing point of water, at about −2°C (28°F), is gradually assuming greater commercial importance for the storage of some food products. Foods do not freeze at this temperature but are in the nearly frozen zone. The usable shelf life of poultry meat was extended 12 days when the meat was stored at −2°C (28°F) as compared with poultry stored at 0°C (32°F). Red meat and poultry will continue slowly in their aging process, which increases their tenderness, during storage in the nearly frozen zone, sometimes called *latent-zone chilling*. This temperature also offers possibilities for lengthening the storage life of many prepared foods without freezing them (Smith, 1976).

Preservation of foods by freezing is based on the retardation of microbial growth to the point where no decomposition occurs in the food. The growth of most microorganisms is stopped at temperatures of from 0° to −4°C (from 32° to 24.8°F), although molds and yeasts may grow slowly in frozen foods at −8.9°C (16°F) (Frazier, 1967). It is generally recommended that all frozen foods be held at −18°C (0°F) or lower, however. Changes in flavor, texture, and nutritive value are retarded at this low storage temperature. Bacteria die most rapidly in the range of from −1° to −5°C (from 30.2° to 23°F). Some microorganisms die during the frozen storage of foods. Insect larvae also die. However, freezing is not a sterilizing process and microorganisms in the food may multiply during the thawing process as temperatures become favorable for their growth. The process of freezing also provides an opportunity for microbial growth throughout the time required to reduce the temperature of the food to its freezing point. The freezing rate is, therefore, a critical factor to be controlled for microbiological safety.

The microbial load on frozen foods should be kept as low as possible during preparation for freezing in order to minimize changes that may occur if the frozen foods are temporarily subjected to temperatures above freezing. Hands, counters, and equipment used in the preparation of the food for processing should be clean. The mishandling of commercially prepared frozen foods in market channels and after they are brought into the home or institutional kitchen, may create health hazards in terms of microbial spoilage.

7.2

CHANGES OCCURRING DURING FREEZING AND FROZEN STORAGE

FORMATION AND GROWTH OF ICE CRYSTALS

Water is the basic dispersion medium in most foods that are frozen. When pure water is subjected to temperatures below 0°C (32°F), it gradually changes to its solid form, ice, in a manner illustrated in Figure 7.1. As sensible heat is removed from the water, the temperature falls. Not uncommonly, supercooling will occur before freezing begins. As soon as ice starts to crystallize, the temperature returns to 0°C (32°F), the true freezing point of water, and remains at that temperature until all of the water has been changed to ice. Further removal of heat causes the ice to decrease in temperature below the freezing point of water.

When food is frozen at a moderately slow rate, the change in temperature with time may be similar to that depicted in Figure 7.2. As sensible heat is removed from the product, the temperature falls. Since the food contains various substances in true solution, its freezing point is depressed below that of pure water. Most foods will begin to freeze between −0.8° and −2.8°C (from 30.5° to 26.9°F). Supercooling usually occurs before ice crystallization begins. As ice crystals form, the temperature will rise to the true freezing point of the food involved.

A temperature plateau does not occur in the freezing of a food as it does with pure water. As freezing begins and pure ice forms, the sol-

Figure 7.1

Freezing curve for pure water.

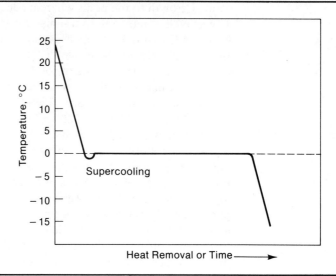

Figure 7.2

Freezing curve for a typical food frozen at a moderately slow rate.

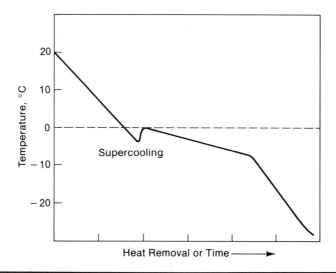

utes in the food are left in a gradually decreasing amount of unfrozen water. The more concentrated solution that is left after the ice crystallizes has a lower freezing point than the original food. This process of ice crystallization continues and results in a gradually dropping freezing temperature. Solutes become increasingly more saturated and may approach supersaturation as freezing becomes more extensive. Ice crystals grow and become larger in size. Some unfrozen water will remain in most frozen foods while they are stored at −18°C (0°F).

Ice crystals grow from tiny nuclei as additional water molecules become attached to them. The crystals vary in size. They tend to be small and numerous in rapidly frozen foods and are large and fewer in number when the food is frozen slowly. Fast removal of heat energy in the rapid freezing process probably causes many nuclei to form with each one growing to only a limited extent (Brown, 1976).

Slow freezing of plant and animal tissues generally causes ice crystals to form in extracellular spaces. With slow freezing there is maximum dislocation of water in the tissues, large ice crystals, and a shrunken appearance of cells in the frozen state. Rapid freezing results in the formation of many intracellular ice crystals, minimum dislocation of water, a frozen appearance which is similar to the original unfrozen appearance, and food quality that is often superior to that resulting from slow freezing. As ice forms slowly in extracellular regions during slow freezing, the solute concentration gradually increases. This more concentrated solution outside the cell may draw water from the less concentrated solution present intracellularly, depositing water molecules from inside the cell on the already formed extracellular ice crystals. When freezing is rapid, there is more opportunity for supercooling of cell contents and formation of nuclei intracellularly on which ice crystals may grow (Fennema *et al.*, 1973).

MECHANICAL DAMAGE

Pure water at 0°C (32°F) expands approximately nine percent when changed into ice at the same temperature. Most foods also expand upon freezing, although to a lesser extent than pure water. Damage may occur in some frozen plant and animal tissues as a result of the increase in volume. Damage to the texture is more likely in plant tissue because of its rigid structure and poorly aligned cells than it is in muscle tissue with its pliable consistency and parallel arrangement of cells. Damage to tissues may come from large ice crystals (Fennema *et al.*, 1973).

Sterling (1968) reported that slow freezing of apple tissue caused ice crystals to separate the cells, crush them and rupture cell walls. This mechanical damage occurred during freezing rather than during thawing. The firmness of frozen apple tissue was much lower than that of raw tissue.

RECRYSTAL-LIZATION

Ice crystals are not always stable after they are initially formed. During the frozen storage of foods they may undergo a number of changes in size, shape, and orientation that are collectively called *recrystallization*. Ice crystal enlargement has been observed in fish muscle exposed to temperatures fluctuating between −14° and −7°C (between 6.8° and 19.4°F). Initially small ice crystals in rapidly frozen fruits were found to be the same size as the larger ones in slowly frozen fruits after several months of frozen storage (Fennema *et al.*, 1973).

FREEZER BURN

Freezer burn is the term applied to describe a dehydrated surface on a frozen food that may range from just detectable mat-white patches to areas of continuous greyish-white blemish. It is caused by the sublimation of ice from the surface of the frozen product. Freezer burn readily occurs when stored frozen foods are not adequately packaged with moisture-proof materials.

There is a difference between the vapor pressure of ice in a frozen food and the partial pressure of water vapor in the air that is around the food in a freezer. This difference in vapor pressures encourages sublimation of ice from the frozen food in order to reach vapor pressure equilibrium with the surrounding air. When the packaging material is permeable to water vapor, these pressures are not easily equalized. Loss of water results in a desiccated area on the surface of the frozen food.

Increased velocity of air in commercial freezers contributes to the development of freezer burn. A relatively rapid freezing rate was also shown to result in greater freezer burn on liver tissue and muscle tissue than did a slow freezing rate. A histological study showed that the freezer burn region in rapidly frozen muscle consisted of cavities which were previously occupied by ice crystals and which were enlarged by shrinkage of the muscle fibers during dehydration. Just below the freezer burn region there was a compacted layer consisting of a dense mass of fibers formed by displacement of tissue into some of the spaces originally occupied by ice crystals. In slowly frozen muscle a compacted layer of fibers was formed on the surface of the muscle, thereby acting as a barrier to water transfer and delaying the development of freezer burn (Fennema, 1973; Kaess and Weidemann, 1967).

OXIDATION

During freezing and frozen storage, a number of fruits or vegetables may undergo oxidative changes resulting in browning. The reactions usually involve the oxidation of polyphenolic substances in the plant tissue and are catalyzed by polyphenolase enzymes. These reactions can usually be prevented in fruits by the addition of ascorbic acid or sulfur dioxide. The addition of sucrose also helps to protect against browning, probably to a large extent by the exclusion of oxygen. Fruits are not blanched, as are vegetables, to destroy enzymes that may catalyze undesirable reactions during storage. The desirable fresh characteristics of fruits would be changed by the heat treatment involved in the blanching process.

Autoxidation of fats during frozen storage may produce rancid "off-flavors." Polyunsaturated and monounsaturated fatty acids are susceptible to oxidation in the presence of oxygen. (The process involved in the oxidation of fats to produce hydroperoxides is discussed in Section 18.5.)

The rate and extent of lipid oxidation in frozen muscle tissues depends on 1. the degree of fatty acid unsaturation; 2. the prefreezing holding period; 3. the duration and temperature of frozen storage; 4. the oxygen content of the environment; and 5. the presence of prooxidants and antioxidants (Fennema, 1973). Extended chilling periods before freezing tend to increase lipid oxidation during frozen storage. Storage at $-18°C$ ($0°F$) or below decreases oxidative changes in comparison to higher storage temperatures. The presence of naturally occurring tocopherols (vitamin E) aids in retarding oxidation. Hematin compounds and iron in muscle tissue (hemoglobin, myoglobin, and cytochrome C) may act as prooxidants. Proper packaging with oxygen-impermeable materials is recommended for frozen muscle tissues.

CHANGES IN COLLOIDAL SUBSTANCES

A number of colloidally dispersed substances present in food may undergo changes with freezing and frozen storage. Following the heating and gelatinization of starch, retrogradation or gel formation occurs. (Retrogradation of starch is discussed in Section 16.4.) Retrogradation is usually accompanied by shrinkage and loss of moisture in a process called *syneresis,* particularly in products which contain relatively large amounts of water such as thickened puddings and sauces. Freezing a starch gel increases syneresis. Alternate freezing and thawing greatly reduces its moisture-reabsorbing capacity (Reeve and Brown, 1966). Starches containing a comparatively small quantity of the linear starch fraction, amylose, are more stable to frozen storage than are high amylose starches.

Changes in cellulose may occur as a result of freezing and thawing. Cellulose in the cell walls of vegetables may become more crystalline and toughened by freezing (Reeve and Brown, 1966).

Emulsions, such as those present in mayonnaises and salad dressings, tend to break when frozen and thawed. This apparently results from changes in the colloidal substances acting as emulsifying agents as well as from changes in the volume of the oil and water phases upon crystallization. The lipoproteins of egg yolk, which emulsify the oil in mayonnaise, are dehydrated during freezing and precipitate as a gummy mass on thawing. Their effectiveness as emulsifiers is thus decreased.

7.3

FREEZING METHODS

Commercial freezing processes differ markedly from home freezing processes. Several systems may be used commercially. In home freezers, however, foods to be frozen are simply placed, after proper packaging, against freezing plates or coils. Usually no more than two or three pounds of food to each cubic foot of freezer capacity should be frozen at one time. Overloading slows down the rate of freezing.

Commercial freezing methods may remove heat by convection or conduction (Rasmussen and Olson, 1972). *Air-blast tunnel freezing* speeds freezing by using very fast air movement and air temperatures of $-37°$–$-40°C$ ($-35°$–$-40°F$). Heat removal is by convection. Packaged or unpackaged items are commonly put on trays which are stacked on dollies or trucks. The trucks are placed in the tunnel. In an alternate method, conveyors are used which move the food on an endless belt or chain through the freezing zone of rapidly moving air at $-37°C$ ($-35°F$) or carbon dioxide gas at or near $-73.3°C$ ($-100°F$). Individually proportioned foods, such as meat patties, chicken parts, and bakery goods, are frozen in such units. Bulk unpackaged green peas, cut corn, beans, and strawberries may be frozen in minutes at a faster rate than occurs when they are packaged.

In *plate freezing,* heat transfer is by conduction. In this system, metal plates which are cooled by a refrigerant come in direct contact with packaged foods. A series of plates may be enclosed in an insulated cabinet and are loaded by hand. Plate freezing systems are also automated.

The most rapid method of freezing food is by direct immersion in a liquid refrigerant or spraying the liquid on the food. Brines and alcohols may be used as refrigerants. For extremely low temperature freezing, called *cryogenic freezing,* the media include liquid nitrogen, liquid air, liquid carbon dioxide, and solid carbon dioxide. These systems operate at $-73.3°C$ ($-100°F$) or below. Liquid nitrogen has had the widest commercial development. Instant freezing of small unpackaged products is possible with this method.

The freezing rate is slow when foods are frozen in still air in a suitable freezing room or compartment. *Still air freezing* is, however, the least expensive method. The freezing time is dependent upon the freezing temperature, the type and size of food product, and the arrangement of the packages. Individual strawberries on trays at a room temperature of $-31.7°C$ ($-25°F$) will freeze in five hours or less. A 55-gallon barrel of strawberries will take several days to freeze in a room at $-18°C$ ($0°F$) (Desrosier, 1977).

Proper packaging is essential in any freezing and frozen storage system in order to minimize loss of water from the frozen foods. The package also protects the food from oxidation and contamination from the atmosphere within the freezing cabinet. Packaging materials should be moisture-vapor-proof. Metal, glass, plastic, and laminated paper materials have been successfully used commercially for frozen foods.

For home freezing, containers should be easy to seal. They should also be durable and must not become so brittle at low temperatures that cracking occurs. Many bags, waxed cartons and sheets of cellophane, heavy aluminum foil, pliofilm, polyethylene, or laminated papers, made especially for the packaging of frozen foods at home, are not moisture-vapor-proof but are sufficiently moisture-vapor-resistant to retain satisfactory quality in many foods during freezer storage. Rigid containers made of aluminum, glass, plastic, tin, or heavily waxed cardboard are especially suitable for liquid packs (USDA, Home and Garden Bulletin No. 10).

FREEZING FRUITS AND VEGETABLES

Fruits and vegetables of high quality and suitable maturity should be selected for freezing. Some varieties produce better quality frozen products than do other varieties of the same fruit or vegetable. State Agricultural Extension Services often maintain lists of locally grown varieties that are most suitable for freezing. (Detailed procedures for the home freezing of fruits and vegetables are given in the USDA Home and Garden Bulletin No. 10.)

For the best quality in the finished product, vegetables should be frozen as quickly as possible after harvesting. Neumann *et al.* (1967) reported that "off-flavor" developed in peas that were commercially vined and held in metal bins for 2, 3, and 6 hours of storage at 26.7°, 17.2°, and 10.0°C (80°, 63°, and 50°F), respectively. The flavor differences between peas stored before processing and peas commercially processed as controls were detected by an untrained panel of 50 people.

Some fruits and vegetables do not freeze satisfactorily using presently available technology. These include green onions, lettuce and other salad greens, radishes, and tomatoes. Hoeft *et al.* (1973) compared the quality of 6 mm thick tomato slices frozen rapidly with liquid nitrogen, with slices frozen slowly. Four tomato breeding lines and calcium pretreatments were studied. All treatments resulted in poorer texture than the unfrozen controls, although slices frozen in liquid nitrogen were firmer and more acceptable than those frozen at −34°C (−29.2°F). Research may later provide acceptable methods for freezing these types of products.

CONTROL OF CHEMICAL CHANGES DURING FREEZING AND FROZEN STORAGE

Although microbial growth ceases during the frozen storage of food at temperatures of −7°C (19.4°F) or below, chemical changes may occur. These changes include 1. reactions associated with the development of "off-odors" and "off-flavors"; 2. enzymatic browning; 3. pigment degradation; and 4. autoxidation of ascorbic acid (Fennema *et al.*, 1973). Many of the changes can be satisfactorily controlled by prefreezing blanching of vegetables, addition of sugar syrup to fruits, and storing at −18°C (0°F) or below.

Development of "Off-Odors" "Off-odors" in unblanched or underblanched frozen vegetables have been attributed to the accumulation of volatile carbonyl compounds ($-\overset{\overset{\textstyle O}{\|}}{C}-$) during frozen storage. Two types of enzymatic reactions may contribute to the formation of these compounds. The anaerobic metabolic pathway whereby pyruvate is converted, by the action of several enzymes, through acetaldehyde to ethanol may be responsible for the presence of both acetaldehyde and ethanol in the frozen vegetable. In addition, the enzyme, lipoxidase, catalyzes the oxidation of polyunsaturated fatty acids. A variety of aldehydes and ketones may result from this reaction.

Chow and Watts (1969) reported that rancid odors in frozen green beans were related to malonaldehyde values, used as an index of unsaturated fatty acid oxidation. These workers concluded that both lipid oxidation and anaerobic fermentation contributed to flavor deterioration in frozen green beans. Unblanched frozen beans were unacceptable to a group of judges. Blanched samples were progressively less acceptable as the heat treatment exceeded the minimum necessary for inactivation of the enzyme systems responsible for "off-odor" development. Therefore, it appears to be important to blanch vegetables before freezing, by the use of either boiling water or steam. The time of blanching should be kept to a minimum to ensure enzyme destruction yet avoid any additional detrimental effects on palatability.

Rates of deterioration of frozen vegetables have been shown to increase as storage temperatures increase. Boggs $et\ al.$ (1960) reported that deterioration rates for commercially frozen peas approximately doubled for each 2.8°C (5°F) increase in temperature between $-18°C$ (0°F) and $-3.9°C$ (25°F). Similar deterioration rates were reported for frozen spinach (Dietrich $et\ al.$, 1960) and for cauliflower (Dietrich $et\ al.$, 1962).

Enzymatic Browning When some fruits and vegetables are frozen, stored, and thawed, undesirable brown pigments are formed. Products particularly susceptible to this type of browning include apples, peaches, pears, cherries, potatoes, and cauliflower. Browning is usually the result of the oxidation of phenolic compounds by polyphenoloxidases in the presence of oxygen. Disruption of cells by ice crystals can initiate the reaction by facilitating contact between the enzyme and its substrate. Surface browning is usually greater than internal browning, however, because of the higher level of oxygen at the surface. (Enzymatic oxidative browning of fruits and vegetables is discussed in Section 13.4.)

Browning can be minimized or prevented by excluding oxygen with proper packaging and by the addition of browning inhibitors such as ascorbic acid. Covering fruit with a sugar syrup also keeps out oxygen and retards browning. Blanching to destroy the enzymes is effective in retarding browning. This process is acceptable in vegetables that will be cooked or in apple slices that will be used for pies. However, in most fruits blanching produces cooked flavors and decreases the desirable fresh fruit odors and flavors.

Ponting and Jackson (1974) compared several prefreezing treatments for Golden Delicious apple slices. They reported that after freezing and thawing the highest quality slices resulted from soaking the slices in a solution containing from 20 to 30 percent sugar, from 0.2 to 0.4 percent calcium (to maintain firmness), and from 0.2 to 1.0 percent ascorbic acid or 0.02 percent sulfur dioxide. Ascorbic acid is an effective reducing agent to control the oxidative browning reaction.

Pigment Degradation During the frozen storage of unblanched green vegetables, the bright green color of chlorophyll slowly changes to the olive green color of pheophytin. Blanching inhibits this conversion. However, some conversion of chlorophyll to pheophytin occurs during the blanching process. The amount of conversion depends on the blanching temperature and duration. The rate of pigment change varies with individual green vegetables.

Alkaline additives to retard the formation of pheophytins from chlorophyll may sometimes be used in commercial freezing processes. Undesirable texture changes can occur with the use of many of the alkaline compounds, however. Eheart and Odland (1973) showed that ammonium bicarbonate effectively improved the color of frozen green vegetables as judged either instrumentally or by a taste panel. Texture was adversely affected by higher concentrations of the compound but low concentrations were used successfully. The optimal amount varied with the individual vegetables from 0.1 to 0.2 percent.

The color of most fruits is not significantly affected by freezing. The anthocyanin pigments in some varieties of strawberries, however, may not be present in the appropriate amounts to make them suitable for freezing. Wrolstad et al. (1970) reported that the anthocyanin content should be in the approximate range of 450–700 μg per g for strawberries to have acceptable color quality when frozen. They also calculated that berries should have a pH of 3.51 or lower to have an acceptable color after freezing, since pH influenced color stability.

Oxidation of Ascorbic Acid Ascorbate oxidase is present naturally in many plant tissues and will catalyze the oxidation of ascorbic acid if it is not inactivated. Blanching will inactivate this enzyme. The pattern of retention of ascorbic acid in frozen vegetables has been shown to vary from one vegetable to another. Some loss of ascorbic acid occurs after blanching, even though this process inactivates ascorbate oxidase. An additional loss has been reported after freezing the blanched vegetable. Gordon and Noble (1959) reported that a six month storage period at −18°C (0°F) resulted in small losses of ascorbic acid not accounted for in the blanching and freezing of vegetables. The majority of frozen vegetables studied were neither more nor less susceptible to cooking losses after freezing than were fresh vegetables. Fennema (1977) has reviewed the losses of vitamins in frozen vegetables. With the exception of small loss values of ascorbic acid for asparagus and large loss values for spinach, losses average about 50 percent. Losses are largely attributable to blanching (especially water blanching) and prolonged frozen storage (from 6 to 12 months).

RATE OF FREEZING	All research reports do not agree concerning the effect of the freezing rate on the textural characteristics and consequent quality of frozen fruits and vegetables (Fennema *et al.*, 1973). Rapidly freezing vegetables, such as green beans, in liquid nitrogen causes cracking if the vegetables are held in the freezant too long after being completely frozen. When precautions are exercised to avoid cracking, the rapidly frozen vegetables have been found to have a firmer texture than similar vegetables frozen slowly. No differences were found in frozen lima beans and corn when rapidly or slowly frozen, however. Slow freezing of fruits, with a resulting large proportion of intercellular ice crystals, can damage the cell walls and produce a soft texture in the thawed product. Slowly frozen strawberries have been reported to have a large amount of drip on thawing as compared to rapidly frozen berries. Ponting and Jackson (1972) found that very rapid freezing improved the crispness of apple slices.

7.5

FREEZING MEAT, FISH, AND POULTRY

Freezing is an excellent method for preserving meat, fish, and poultry. (Detailed procedures for freezing meat and fish in the home are given in USDA Home and Garden Bulletin No. 93. Procedures for the home freezing of poultry are given in USDA Agriculture Information Bulletin No. 371.) Only high quality products should be frozen since freezing does not improve quality. Meat should be chilled after slaughter and held long enough to allow the disappearance of rigor mortis before it is frozen. Beef and lamb are usually held from 5 to 7 days while pork and veal may be held only 1 or 2 days.

When postrigor muscle is frozen rapidly, ice crystals form *intracellularly* within the muscle fibers. With a slow rate of freezing the crystals are formed between the cells (*extracellularly*). Some changes in the microstructure of muscle occur during the period of ice crystal formation and frozen storage. Awad *et al.* (1968) studied the chemical deterioration of frozen beef muscle when stored at $-4°C$ (24.8°F). They found a decrease in the total extractable protein content ranging from 91 to 51 percent, accompanied by a decrease in the water-binding capacity of the muscle. This was primarily caused by the insolubilization of proteins. An increase in free fatty acids also occurred. The extent of oxidation of lipids in frozen muscle is dependent on the degree of unsaturation of the fat, prefreezing holding treatment, the duration and temperature of frozen storage, and the oxygen present in the environment (Fennema *et al.*, 1973). The heme pigment found in hemoglobin may act as a prooxidant for fat oxidation during the frozen storage of meats. Frozen cooked meats and frozen ground meats are more susceptible to the development of oxidized flavors during freezer storage because heme or iron are more available to catalyze oxidation in disrupted tissues.

From studies on poultry meat, Kahn and van den Berg (1967) suggested that rapid freezing preserves the integrity of muscle proteins to a greater extent than does slow freezing. Freezing pork loin chops rapidly in liquid nitrogen produced superior appearance as compared to chops frozen by homefreezing methods (Bannister *et al.*, 1971). However, the quality of the home-frozen product after it was cooked was comparable to that of the liquid nitrogen-frozen product. Rates of freezing and thawing, as studied for lamb chops by Lind *et al.* (1971), did not significantly affect flavor, juiciness, water-holding capacity, total moisture, overall acceptability, and tenderness, as indicated by shear values. Tenderness scores resulting from evaluation by a panel of judges were lower for meat frozen slowly than for the meat frozen extremely rapidly. Weight losses during cooking were also lower for the slower process than for rapid freezing, although the differences were not always significant. Reported results on the effect of the rate of freezing on tenderness have not always been in agreement. Effects would appear to be slight. The tenderness of postrigor muscles is sometimes increased by the freezing process itself, but this effect is usually detectable only if frozen storage is limited to a few days (Fennema *et al.*, 1973).

7.6

FREEZING EGGS

When fluid egg yolk is frozen, stored at a temperature of $-6°C$ (21.2°F) or lower, and then thawed it develops a high degree of viscosity or gumminess which has been called gelation. Experimental studies support the suggestion that gelation is due to aggregation of low density lipoproteins in the yolk. They form complexes with each other, in which form they exhibit excellent water-binding capacities. Apparently ice formation with a resulting increase in the concentration of salts in the unfrozen liquid is responsible for disruption of tiny egg yolk granules containing low density lipoproteins. These lipoproteins plus those already present in the egg yolk plasma are involved in the aggregation process. At a temperature of $-6°C$ or below, sufficient ice crystals are apparently formed to produce a critical level of salt concentration (Chang *et al.*, 1977).

Gelation may be prevented by the addition of certain substances to the fluid yolk before it is frozen. As little as 1 percent sucrose added to whole egg has been shown to inhibit gelation, probably by binding free water. Fructose, arabinose, galactose, glucose, and glycerol also restrict gelation, as does sodium chloride. The choice of adding salt or sugar to egg yolks frozen at home depends upon the final use planned for the product. The addition of a proteolytic enzyme, such as papain, is effective in inhibiting gelation of yolk during freezing. This effect is probably a result of the hydrolysis by the enzyme of the low density lipoproteins. Homogenization of yolk or subjection to shearing treatments prior to freezing can lessen the gelation (Fennema *et al.*, 1973).

Egg whites may be frozen with no effect on viscosity or functional properties, although pasteurization before freezing may affect whipping properties to some degree. (The pasteurization of egg products is discussed in Section 23.4.) Although whole eggs are often frozen without addition of substances to control gelation, they will probably retain functional properties better if a small amount of sugar or salt is added before freezing.

7.7

FREEZING PREPARED FOODS

A wide variety of frozen prepared foods is marketed. Many such foods may also be frozen at home. (USDA Home and Garden Bulletin No. 40 discusses the preparation of combination main dishes for storage in the home freezer.) A number of problems have been encountered in the freezing of prepared foods and modern technology has answered many of them.

Starch thickened gravies and sauces often curdle and undergo syneresis when they are frozen and then thawed. Retrogradation of starch during frozen storage is a major factor in the instability, although other ingredients such as milk and flour probably exert some effect (Osman and Cummisford, 1959). Starch products with potential for freeze–thaw stability were tested in frozen gravies by Baldwin et al. (1972). These were cross-bonded waxy milo starch, modified waxy maize starch, and unmodified waxy rice flour. The modified waxy starches performed more satisfactorily, in terms of their contributions to desirable texture, consistency, "mouth-feel", and flavor, than did the waxy rice flour. A wide variety of modified starches is available commercially and a starch can be selected according to the particular thickened product to be manufactured. Modified starches are not generally available to the consumer for use in the home.

Salad dressing emulsions may break during freezing with the separation of oil and water phases. Oil separation can be minimized by the use of an oil that does not solidify in a crystalline form at the storage temperature to be used (Hanson, 1964).

Fried chicken is a widely distributed frozen prepared food. However, the failure of batter coatings to adhere to the chicken during frozen storage affects the quality of the reheated product. Cooking chicken parts in order to shrink them before the application of the batter was found to effectively reduce the peeling tendency of coatings on frozen fried chicken. Thinner coatings also reduced the peeling tendency. Mixtures of thickening agents may be chosen to achieve good adhesive qualities, desirable thickness, crispness, color, and attractive appearance (Hanson and Fletcher, 1963).

Frozen precooked meat products, such as beef patties, retain high quality for longer periods of time in frozen storage if they are covered with gravy than they do if they are frozen without gravy. The gravy helps to prevent desiccation of the meat. Frozen entree items enriched and extended with vegetable protein will maintain high quality during storage at −20°C (−4°F) for from three to six months (Kramer *et al.*, 1976).

SUMMARY

Preservation of foods by freezing is based on the retardation of microbial growth to the point where no decomposition occurs in the food. The growth of most microorganisms is stopped at temperatures from below about 0° to −4°C (from 32° to 24.8°F). However, frozen foods should be stored at −18°C (0°F) or lower to minimize changes in flavor, texture, and nutritive value. Freezing does not kill all bacteria and microorganisms in the food may multiply during the thawing process.

A number of changes occur in foods during freezing and frozen storage. Ice crystals form and grow in size. They tend to be small and numerous in rapidly frozen foods and are large and fewer in number when the food is frozen slowly. Slow freezing generally causes ice crystals to form in extracellular spaces. The crystals are mostly intracellular when feeezing is done rapidly. Mechanical damage that affects the texture of the thawed product is likely in frozen plant tissues. Ice crystals may change in size, shape, and orientation in a recrystallization process during frozen storage.

When dehydration occurs in an area on the surface of a frozen food, it is called freezer burn. It is caused by inadequate packaging which encourages sublimation of ice from the surface of the food. This is a result of differences between the vapor pressure of ice in the food and the partial pressure of water vapor in the surrounding air. Oxidation of polyphenolic substances in plant tissues by the action of polyphenolases may occur during frozen storage. This results in undesirable browning. Blanching vegetables will destroy the enzyme which causes browning. Browning in fruits can be prevented by the application of ascorbic acid or sulfur dioxide. The addition of a sugar syrup also protects fruits against browning. Oxidation of fats during frozen storage may produce rancid "off-flavors". Changes in colloidal substances, such as retrogradation of starch and toughening of cellulose, may occur during frozen storage.

Several different methods may be used commercially to freeze foods. Heat is removed by convection using air-blast tunnel and conveyor tunnel freezing. Heat is transferred by conduction in plate freezing. The most rapid method of freezing food is by direct immersion in a liquid refrigerant or by spraying the refrigerant liquid on the food. For extremely low temperature freezing, called cryogenic freezing, the media include liquid nitrogen, liquid air, liquid carbon dioxide, and solid carbon dioxide. Instant freezing of small unpackaged products is possible. Proper packaging of frozen food is essential in order to minimize the loss of water and to protect against contamination and oxidation during freezer storage.

Fruits and vegetables of high quality and suitable maturity should be selected for freezing. For the best quality, vegetables should be frozen as quickly as possible after harvesting. "Off-flavors" may develop in some vegetables held for only a few hours before freezing. Some vegetables such as tomatoes and cucumbers do not freeze satisfactorily under any circumstances.

Accumulation of carbonyl compounds in unblanched frozen vegetables apparently contributes to the development of "off-flavors." Blanching before freezing, either by use of boiling water or steam, destroys enzymes that are responsible for the development of "off-flavors." It also controls undesirable changes in texture and color. The conversion of the bright green chlorophyll to the olive green pheophytin is inhibited by the blanching process.

Ascorbic acid is oxidized during frozen storage. Blanching vegetables inhibits this oxidation by inactivating ascorbate oxidase. Some loss of ascorbic acid occurs during the blanching process, however. Additional ascorbic acid is lost with long periods of frozen storage.

Rapid freezing of some vegetables and fruits would appear to improve their texture in comparison to similar slowly frozen products. However, all research reports do not agree concerning the effect of the freezing rate on the textural characteristics and consequent quality of frozen fruits and vegetables.

Freezing is an excellent method for preserving meat, fish, and poultry. Some changes in the microstructure of muscle tissue occur during the period of ice crystal formation and frozen storage. The freezing rate does not appear to have a significant effect on the quality of frozen meats after they are cooked, although some differences have been reported. The amount of drip after thawing muscle tissue can be reduced by increasing the rate of freezing. Inconsistent results of tests carried out to determine the effect of freezing on the tenderness of meat have been reported.

Frozen egg yolk stored at a temperature of $-6°C$ ($21.2°F$) or lower undergoes gelation upon thawing. This effect is apparently due to aggregation of low density lipoproteins in the yolk. Ice crystal formation concentrates salts in the unfrozen liquid and is responsible for disruption of egg yolk granules containing low density lipoproteins. Substances such as sugar or salt added to the yolk before freezing will prevent gelation on thawing. The addition of proteolytic enzymes also restricts gelation.

A wide variety of prepared foods may be satisfactorily frozen. Modified waxy starches show freeze–thaw stability and are used in some frozen gravies and sauces. Oil separation in frozen salad dressings can be minimized by use of an oil that does not solidify in a crystalline form at the storage temperature used. Frozen precooked meat products retain high quality for longer periods of time in frozen storage if they are covered with gravy than they do if they are frozen without gravy.

STUDY QUESTIONS

As temperatures are lowered, metabolic changes are retarded in both plant tissues and in microorganisms.

1. Discuss the usual temperatures achieved, the types of food products usually stored, and explain the relative effectiveness for food preservation by:
   a. Chilling or refrigeration
   b. Freezing
2. Explain why the recommended temperature for frozen storage of food is $-18°C$ (0°F) or below.

A number of changes occur during the freezing and frozen storage of food.

3. Describe and explain changes that occur in frozen foods in each of the following areas:
   a. Crystallization
   b. Mechanical damage
   c. Desiccation
   d. Oxidation
   e. Colloidal change

Food may be frozen by one of several methods.

4. Describe the usual method for freezing food at home.
5. Describe several commercial methods for freezing food, indicate the general process by which heat is removed from the food, and discuss the advantages and the disadvantages of each method.
6. Suggest and explain important criteria to apply in choosing packaging materials for use in home freezing.

Chemical changes may occur in frozen foods during freezer storage.

7. Explain the purpose of blanching vegetables before freezing and describe changes in texture, flavor, color, and ascorbic acid content that may occur in unblanched vegetables that are held in frozen storage.
8. Describe two methods for blanching vegetables that may be used at home.
9. Describe and explain the usual cause of browning in frozen fruits such as peaches and apples.
10. Describe several treatments that will prevent or retard the browning of fruits during freezer storage and explain why each treatment is effective.
11. Give several examples of vegetables that do not usually freeze well.
12. Discuss possible effects on frozen fruits, vegetables, and meats of a rapid vs. a slow rate of freezing.
13. Explain why ground meats and cooked meats are more susceptible to fat oxidation during freezer storage than are whole, raw cuts of meat.
14. Describe and explain undesirable changes in consistency that usually occur in thawed egg yolks that have been frozen and stored at a temperature of $-6°C$ (21.2°F) or below.

15. Describe procedures that may be used to prevent unwanted changes in the consistency of egg yolks that have been frozen.
16. Describe and explain problems commonly encountered in the freezing of starch thickened products and salad dressings and suggest possible solutions to these problems.

REFERENCES

1. Awad, A., W. D. Powrie, and O. Fennema. 1968. Chemical deterioration of frozen bovine muscle at − 4°C. *Journal of Food Science* 33, 227.

2. Baldwin, R. E., D. Moody, M. Cloninger, and B. Korschgen. 1972. Stability of gravies to freezing. *American Dietetic Association Journal* 60, 218.

3. Bannister, M. A., D. L. Harrison, A. D. Dayton, D. H. Kropf, and H. J. Tuma. 1971. Effects of a cryogenic and three home freezing methods on selected characteristics of pork loin chops. *Journal of Food Science* 36, 951.

4. Boggs, M. M., W. C. Dietrich, M. Nutting, R. L. Olson, F. E. Lindquist, G. S. Bohart, H. J. Neumann, and H. J. Morris. 1960. Time–temperature tolerance of frozen foods. XXI. Frozen peas. *Food Technology* 14, 181.

5. Brown, M. S. 1976. Effects of freezing on fruit and vegetable structure. *Food Technology* 30 (No. 5), 106.

6. Chang, C. H., W. D. Powrie, and O. Fennema. 1977. Studies on the gelation of egg yolk and plasma upon freezing and thawing. *Journal of Food Science* 42, 1658.

7. Chow, L. and B. M. Watts. 1969. Origin of off odors in frozen green beans. *Food Technology* 23, 973.

8. Desrosier, N. W. 1977. *The Technology of Food Preservation*, 4th edition. Westport, Conn.: Avi Publishing Company.

9. Dietrich, W. C., M. M. Boggs, M. Nutting, and N. E. Weinstein. 1960. Time–temperature tolerance of frozen foods. XXIII. Quality changes in frozen spinach. *Food Technology* 14, 522.

10. Dietrich, W. C., M. Nutting, M. M. Boggs, and N. E. Weinstein. 1962. Time–temperature tolerance of frozen foods. XXIV. Quality changes in cauliflower. *Food Technology* 16 (No. 10), 123.

11. Eheart, M. S. and D. Odland. 1973. Quality of frozen green vegetables blanched in four concentrations of ammonium bicarbonate. *Journal of Food Science* 38, 954.

12. Fennema, O. 1977. Loss of vitamins in fresh and frozen foods. *Food Technology* 31 (No. 12), 32.

13. Fennema, O. R., W. D. Powrie, and E. H. Marth. 1973. *Low-temperature Preservation of Foods and Living Matter*. New York: Marcel Dekker.

14. Frazier, W. C. 1967. *Food Microbiology*, 2nd edition. New York: McGraw-Hill.

15. Gordon, J. and I. Noble. 1959. Effects of blanching, freezing, freezing-storage, and cooking on ascorbic acid retention in vegetables. *Journal of Home Economics* 51, 867.

16. Goresline, H. E. 1962. Historical development of the modern frozen food industry. In: *Low Temperature Microbiology Symposium*. Campbell Soup Company, p. 5.

17. Hanson, H. L. 1964. Recent research on prepared frozen foods. *American Dietetic Association Journal* 45, 523.

18. Hanson, H. L. and L. R. Fletcher. 1963. Adhesion of coatings on frozen fried chicken. *Food Technology* 17 (No. 6), 115.

19. Hoeft, R., R. P. Bates, and E. M. Ahmed. 1973. Cryogenic freezing of tomato slices. *Journal of Food Science* 38, 362.

20. Kaess, G. and J. F. Weidemann. 1967. Freezer-burn as a limiting factor in the storage of animal tissue. V. Experiments with beef muscle. *Food Technology* 21, 461.

21. Khan, A. W. and L. van den Berg. 1967. Biochemical and quality changes occurring during freezing of poultry meat. *Journal of Food Science* 32, 148.

22. Kramer, A., R. L. King, and D. C. Westhoff. 1976. Effects of frozen storage on prepared foods containing protein concentrates. *Food Technology* 30 (No. 1), 56.

23. Lind, M. L., D. L. Harrison, and D. H. Kropf. 1971. Freezing and thawing rates of lamb chops: Effects on palatability and related characteristics. *Journal of Food Science* 36, 629.

24. Neumann, H. J., W. C. Dietrich, and D. G. Guadagni. 1967–1968. Delay in freezing harvested peas results in detectable off-flavor. *Quick Frozen Foods* Dec. 1967, p. 101 and Jan. 1968, p. 64.

25. Osman, E. M. and P. D. Cummisford. 1959. Some factors affecting the stability of frozen white sauces. *Food Research* 24, 595.

26. Ponting, J. D. and R. Jackson. 1972. Pre-freezing processing of Golden Delicious apple slices. *Journal of Food Science* 37, 812.

27. Rasmussen, C. L. and R. L. Olson. 1972. Freezing methods as related to cost and quality. *Food Technology* 26 (No. 12), 32.

28. Reeve, R. M. and M. S. Brown. 1966. Some structural and histochemical changes related to frozen fruits and vegetables. *Cryobiology* 3, 214.

29. Smith, D. P. 1976. Chilling. *Food Technology* 30 (No. 12), 28.

30. Sterling, C. 1968. Effect of low temperature on structure and firmness of apple tissue. *Food Technology* 33, 577.

31. U. S. Department of Agriculture. 1976. Freezing Combination Main Dishes. Home and Garden Bulletin No. 40.

32. U. S. Department of Agriculture. 1977. Freezing Meat and Fish in the Home. Home and Garden Bulletin No. 93.

33. U. S. Department of Agriculture. 1971. Home Freezing of Fruits and Vegetables. Home and Garden Bulletin No. 10.

34. U. S. Department of Agriculture. 1975. Home Freezing of Poultry and Poultry Main Dishes. Agriculture Information Bulletin No. 371.

35. Wrolstad, R. E., T. P. Putnam, and G. W. Varseveld. 1970. Color quality of frozen strawberries: Effect of anthocyanin, pH, total acidity, and ascorbic acid variability. *Journal of Food Science* 35, 448.

PART III
FOOD STANDARDS AND SAFETY

Governmental agencies are becoming more and more involved in the regulation of the food supply by setting standards for quality and establishing regulations for safety. The standards, including grade standards, serve as aids in the marketing of food and provide valuable information to consumers about the foods they purchase. The problem of food safety is a very old one and still has many unsolved facets. The most prevalent hazard is foodborne disease of microbial origin. Other possible food hazards include environmental contaminants, pesticide residues, food additives, and natural toxicants. This Part concentrates on food additives and foodborne disease of microbial origin. Other hazards, as well as some food standards for quality, are treated briefly. (Grade standards are discussed in various chapters of the book in connection with specific food products, such as meats.)

CHAPTER 8

CHEMICAL ADDITIVES IN FOOD

Consumers in the United States have come to expect convenience, high quality, and stability in the food products that are marketed through retail channels. They also want the food supply to be safe. Chemical preservatives of various kinds are used to increase the shelf life of many food products. Telephone surveys of approximately 200 households in the Seattle-Everett, Washington area in 1974 and 1976 indicated that there was concern among almost half of the participants about the safety of preservatives in food (Martinsen and McCullough, 1977).

The responsibility for assuring the safety of food supplies in the United States falls to several governmental units at both the federal and local levels. Controlling the chemicals added to food is but one aspect of food safety assurance, although it is an extremely important one. Chemical substances are added to food for several purposes in addition to that of preservation. (Certain additives are discussed in other chapters in connection with specific uses.)

8.1

HISTORICAL BACKGROUND

Although the time when scientific attention was first focused on food safety is not clearly documented, the writings of Fredrick Accum in England during the early part of the nineteenth century apparently produced a public awareness of the problem (Day, 1976). One of Accum's best known books was entitled: *A Treatise on Adulterations of Food, and Culinary Poisons, Exhibiting the Fraudulent Sophistications of Bread, Beer, Wine, Spirituous Liquors, Tea, Coffee, Cream, Confectionery, Vinegar, Mustard, Pepper, Cheese, Olive Oil, Pickles, and Other Articles Employed in Domestic Economy, and Methods of Detecting Them.* A number of years passed, however, before effective legislation was approved in England and other European nations. In 1875, a law was passed regulating the sale of food and drugs. The law remained the basis for British legislation of this type for many years.

Concern about food adulteration and unsafe practices in the United States increased during the latter part of the nineteenth century and the early part of the twentieth century. In 1883 Harvey W. Wiley became head of the Chemical Division (later the Bureau of Chemistry) of the Department of Agriculture. He was very interested in food quality and had his laboratory begin a systematic study of adulterated foods (Figure 8.1). He exerted strong influence to have effective federal legislation passed. The original Food and Drug Act finally became law on June 30, 1906. The stated purpose of this law was "for preventing the manufacture, sale or transportation of adulterated or poisonous or deleterious foods, drugs, medicines and liquors, and for regulating traffic therein."

In 1938, federal legislation in the area of food safety was strengthened by the passage of the Food, Drug and Cosmetic Act. This law has been expanded and amended several times since its original passage, and is administered by the Food and Drug Administration (FDA) of the Department of Health, Education and Welfare. It is the principal law designed to protect the consumer from harmful food ingredients in foods entering interstate commerce. However, some areas of food safety are within the province of other governmental units. The Department of Agriculture is responsible for meat and other products of animal origin; the Department of Commerce is responsible for marine food products; and the Environmental Protection Agency is responsible for the control of pesticides and environmental pollutants. Individual states have separate regulations that govern intrastate commerce (Siu *et al.*, 1977).

There have been several important amendments to the 1938 law. A 1954 pesticide amendment empowers the FDA to set allowable toler-

Figure 8.1

Dr. Harvey W. Wiley climaxed 20 years of scientific investigation of food adulteration with his "Poison Squad" experiment in 1903. He fed measured amounts of chemical preservatives to 12 young volunteers. The project caused a nationwide sensation and dramatized need for a federal pure food law. (Courtesy of Food and Drug Administration, U. S. Department of Health, Education and Welfare.)

ances or safe amounts of pesticide residues that may remain on fresh fruits, vegetables, and other raw agricultural products. The 1958 food additives amendment requires that any additive that is to be used in food must be carefully tested and shown to be safe before it can be added to food. Petitioners for food additives are required to present evidence of the usefulness and the harmlessness of the ingredient that they propose to add to food. Exceptions to coverage by this amendment were substances in common use at the time that were generally recognized as safe. The food additives amendment, through the Delaney clause, forbids the use, in any amount whatsoever, of a substance that is found to induce cancer in man or animals. The color additives amendment of 1960 places all color substances in a separate category from food additives, requiring prior testing for safety, and forbids any cancer-inducing substances to be used.

8.2

DEFINITIONS AND GRAS SUBSTANCES

The law, according to the 1958 food additives amendment, defines a food additive as:

Any substance the intended use of which results or may reasonably be expected to result, directly or indirectly, in its becoming a component or otherwise affecting the characteristics of any food (including any substance intended for use in producing, manufacturing, packing, processing, preparing, treating, packaging, transporting, or holding food; and including any source of radiation intended for any such use), if such substance is not generally recognized, among experts qualified by scientific training and experience to evaluate its safety, as having been adequately shown through scientific procedures (or, in the case of a substance used in food prior to January 1, 1958, through either scientific procedures or experience based on common use in food) to be safe under the conditions of its intended use.

By this statement the legislation specifically exempts from the legal definition of food additives a long list of substances in common use. These substances became known as GRAS, an acronym for "generally recognized as safe." Examples of GRAS substances include acetic acid, alum, ascorbic acid, baking soda, benzoic acid, caffeine, calcium citrate, carbon dioxide, corn starch, sugar, salt, monoglycerides, lactic acid, and lecithin. The food additives amendment took away any authority from the FDA to require scientific evidence supporting the safety of GRAS substances for use in food. Instead, FDA is required to demonstrate that they are unsafe before they can be removed from use.

In 1969, the President of the United States instructed the FDA to update the GRAS safety assessments in terms of currently available scientific data and judgment of scientists. Additional research involving new techniques of analysis and testing sometimes bring into question the safety of substances that have been used in food for many years. Therefore, the FDA contracted for a federation of scientific societies to provide a Select Committee on GRAS Substances. This committee evaluated GRAS food ingredients on a case-by-case basis and submitted reports to the FDA (Siu *et al.*, 1977). The committee pointed out the many problems inherent in passing scientific judgments on the safety of food ingredients, as decisions are often not clearcut.

The legal definition of food additives is not very useful in dealing with practical problems from the consumer point of view. Therefore, the Committee on Food Protection of the National Research Council (NRC) suggested another definition for general use. According to this definition, a food additive is:

A substance or a mixture of substances, other than a basic foodstuff, that is present in a food as a result of any aspect of production, processing, storage, or packaging. (The term does not include chance contaminants.)

An additive may be classified as *intentional* if it is purposely introduced into a food product to perform a specific function. An additive is called *incidental* if it happens to get into a food from some phase of production, handling, or packaging. In both cases new additives must receive prior approval from the FDA before they can be used.

8.3

JUSTIFIABLE USES FOR FOOD ADDITIVES

Additives may play a variety of roles in food but they must have a useful purpose. They cannot be added indiscriminantly by the food manufacturer. The NRC Committee on Food Protection (1973) has suggested several legitimate purposes for food additives:

1. *Improve or maintain nutritional value.* Vitamins and minerals used in enrichment and fortification of foods are included under this purpose. Examples are the addition of thiamin, niacin, riboflavin, and iron to white flour and bread; vitamin D added to milk; iodine incorporated in iodized salt; and vitamin A added to margarine. Antioxidants may maintain nutritional quality by preventing oxidation of certain nutrients, particularly essential fatty acids and fat soluble vitamins.
2. *Enhance quality and consumer acceptability.* Coloring agents, stabilizers, emulsifiers, thickeners, clarifiers, bleaching agents, and flavoring substances aid in producing manufactured foods that have attractive appearance, appropriate texture, and desirable flavor.
3. *Reduce wastage and improve keeping quality.* Waste is associated

with food spoilage from both microbial and chemical causes. Antimicrobial agents such as sodium propionate in bread and sorbic acid in cheese are examples of preservatives restricting mold growth. Antioxidants greatly reduce waste resulting from the oxidation of fat in such foods as baked goods, dry breakfast cereals, lard, and shortening. The shelf life of many products may be extended by the judicious use of additives. This makes possible a wide distribution of foods through the usual marketing channels.

4. *Facilitate preparation of food.* A number of additives act as essential aids in food processing and preparation. Acids, alkalis, and buffers make possible the maintenance of an appropriate pH in a wide variety of foods. Emulsifiers allow the uniform dispersion of fat and water in such products as mayonnaise, salad dressings, sauces, and margarine. Sodium lauryl sulfate is an effective foaming agent in angel food cake mix. Stabilizers and thickeners aid in the production of smooth textured ice creams, icings, cheese spreads, and chocolate flavored drinks.

8.4

CLASSES OF INTENTIONAL ADDITIVES

PRESERVATIVES AND ANTIOXIDANTS

Microbial growth is prevented or inhibited by certain substances added in very small amounts to food. Different compounds are used, depending upon the food product and the particular spoilage organisms concerned. Antioxidants retard the chemical changes involved in oxidation of fatty foods. Certain acidic substances—that is, citric acid, ascorbic acid, and phosphoric acid—enhance the effectiveness of antioxidants and are frequently used in combination with them. The oxidation of polyphenols in frozen fruits is prevented by ascorbic acid.

Examples:

Calcium or sodium propionate Sodium diacetate	Mold and rope inhibitors in bread
Sodium benzoate	Preservative in margarine, bottled soft drinks, and Maraschino cherries
Sorbic acid	Fungistat in cheese wrap and cakes
Ascorbic acid	Antioxidant in frozen fruit and canned mushrooms
Butylated hydroxyanisole (BHA) Butylated hydroxytoluene (BHT) Propyl gallate	Antioxidants in fats and dry prepared cereals
Sulfur dioxide	Preservative in dried fruits

EMULSIFYING, FOAMING, STABILIZING, AND THICKENING AGENTS

Emulsifiers and foaming agents are surface active compounds and aid in the mixing of usually immiscible substances. Emulsifiers facilitate the dispersion of fat in a water-based system. Foaming agents stabilize the dispersion of a gas in a liquid media. Volume and texture of many baked products are improved by emulsifiers. A variety of substances stabilize food systems and give body or improve texture.

Examples:

Mono- and diglycerides Lecithin	Emulsifiers in margarine, shortening, salad dressings, bakery products
Sodium alginate	Stabilizer in ice cream
Carrageenan (Irish moss)	Stabilizer in evaporated milk
Gum tragacanth Gum karaya	Stabilizers in confections and salad dressings
Modified starch	Thickener in frozen foods

BLEACHING AND MATURING AGENTS

White flour freshly milled from wheat has a pale yellowish tint. Upon storage the flour undergoes an aging process and slowly becomes white. Improved baking properties accompany the change in color. Certain oxidizing agents added to the flour accelerate this aging process, thus reducing storage costs and the dangers of insect and rodent infestation during long storage periods. Oxidizing agents added to the bread dough have similar effects.

Examples:

Potassium bromate Potassium iodate	Bread dough improvers
Chlorine dioxide Chlorine Acetone peroxides Azodicarbonamide	Bleaching and maturing agents for white flour

ACIDS, ALKALIES, AND BUFFERS

The degree of acidity is an important factor in the processing and preparation of many foods. The pH of foods may affect their color, texture, and flavor. Adjustment and stabilization of acidity is necessary in the manufacture of a number of food products.

Examples:

Acetic acid	Acidulant in sirups, sherbets, ices, beverages, bakery products, and confections
Calcium hydroxide	Used to stabilize the potassium iodide of iodized salt
Calcium oxide (lime)	Neutralizer in ice cream mixes

| Sodium bicarbonate | Leavening agent in baking powders |
| Citric acid | Used to adjust the pH of fruit juices, jams, jellies, and carbonated beverages |

FLAVORING SUBSTANCES

A large number of compounds, both natural and synthetic, are used in the flavoring of manufactured foods. They are added in small amounts ranging from a few to 300 parts per million.

Examples:

Aconitic acid Benzaldehyde Benzyl acetate Cinnamic acid	Synthetic flavors used in beverages, ice cream, candy, and baked goods
Annatto extract	Used in spice flavors, beverages, baked goods, margarine, and breakfast cereals
Wintergreen oil	Used in fruit and spice flavors, beverages, ice cream, candy, baked goods, and chewing gum

FOOD COLORS

Both natural and synthetic colors are used extensively in processed foods. They play a major role in increasing the attractiveness and acceptability of these foods. However, food colors should not be used to conceal inferior quality.

Examples:

Synthetic colors with FD&C Numbers such as FD&C Yellow No. 5 (Tartrazine)	Used in prepared breakfast cereals and bottled soft drinks
Carotene	Vegetable dye used in butter, margarine, and buttermilk
Turmeric	Vegetable dye used in meat products

OTHER ADDITIVES

Sequestering or Chelating Agents These additives tie up in an inactive form unwanted minerals, such as iron and copper, that may be present in trace amounts. Some minerals act as catalysts for undesirable oxidation in fat-containing foods or are responsible for cloudy precipitates in clear beverages. An example of a chelating agent is ethylenediaminetetracetic acid (EDTA) which may be used in some soft drinks.

Humectants Humectants aid in the retention of moisture and prevent the drying out of certain types of confections and of shredded coconut. Examples of humectants include glycerine, sorbitol, and propylene glycol.

Curing or Color Fixing Agents The pink color of cured meats is developed and fixed by the addition of small amounts of sodium nitrite. The nitrite also inhibits the activity of *Clostridium botulinum* organisms which may be present in the meat. Carcinogenic substances called nitrosamines may be produced when nitrite combines with secondary amines under appropriate conditions. For this reason the level of nitrite in cured meats is carefully regulated.

Artificial Sweeteners Sugar substitutes are used in foods for persons who must restrict their intake of ordinary sweets. Saccharin and xylitol are used for this purpose. However, the safety of saccharin has been questioned by the FDA.

8.5

EVALUATION OF SAFETY

The rationale usually given for government regulation of consumer products is that, in a complex society, individual consumers can no longer protect their own interests and the government must therefore do it for them. This rationale is now almost universally accepted. It implies that there is something against which the public needs protection and that without governmental intervention some consumer products would be marketed without adequate assurance of safety and effectiveness. From a historical point of view, this appears to be true in some instances. In other instances, however, the danger has been largely speculative (Hutt, 1977). Although the merits of government intervention remain controversial, considerable legislation regulating the safety of the food supply and chemical additives in particular, has been enacted and is being enforced. Recommendations on safety testing have been made by the FDA for the prior approval of food additives. These recommendations are reviewed and revised periodically.

Results of well designed tests of the physiologic, pharmacologic, and biochemical effects of a proposed food additive form the basis for the evaluation of the safety of the additive. Testing procedures always involve feeding the substance to test animals at large dose levels and an intensive and extensive search for any ill effects. Although tests on experimental animals cannot provide proof of the safety of a substance for humans, they can be useful and are essential. Basic minimum requirements in the design of studies with test animals include observations on growth, food intake, clinical manifestations, hematology, blood chemistry, urinalysis, gross pathology, and histopathology (Friedman and Spiher, 1971). Unless there are persuasive reasons to the contrary, an additive will be limited in use to a level not more than 1 percent of the highest level at which there was no adverse effect in test animals. Safety depends on the dose. For almost every substance, there is a level of intake at which it is safe and another level at which it is harmful (Wodicka, 1977).

With changing techniques for evaluation, additional tests for safety may be required. Acute and subacute toxicity tests have traditionally been performed. Tests to determine whether or not the additive is mutagenic can be done in the laboratory using cell cultures. A series of metabolism tests can help to determine what the body does with the test substance. If it is absorbed from the intestinal tract, tests should be designed to determine where it goes and how it is handled in the body. Effects on several animal species should be studied. Lifetime feeding tests can include feeding the additive to the female animal prior to conception of the offspring to be used in the tests. Test animals should undergo at least two cycles of reproduction while teratogenic and mutagenic data are collected (Wodicka, 1977; Friedman and Spiher, 1971).

The testing of a food additive is a very expensive and time consuming process. This expense is borne by the food manufacturer who must petition the FDA with documented evidence that the additive is needed and is safe. Scientists from the FDA then evaluate the submitted evidence and make a decision for approval or rejection.

Various avenues have been used to gather information on the patterns of consumption of food additives in the United States. A so-called Market Basket Analysis has been completed at periodic intervals. In this analysis, foods representing the 7-day intake of an 18-year-old male are purchased through usual retail outlets and appropriate meals are prepared. The foods are then composited and analyzed for various additives. Consumer exposure to food additives has been determined through calculation of annual per capita disappearance from marketing channels. A knowledge of the annual U. S. production and import of the food additive in question is necessary, as well as an assumed U. S. population. Dietary survey data may also be used to generate information on consumer exposure to food additives. This type of information on consumption of food additives is necessary in the evaluation of the safety of food additives for the U. S. population (Filer, 1976).

It is of interest to note that many natural foods normally contain toxic substances. Examples include solanine alkaloids in the potato. These substances are present close to the skin of a potato, particularly when greening has occurred through exposure of the potato to sunlight. Unripe grapefruit contains naringen, a glycoside that is irritating to the gastrointestinal tract. Hydroxyphenylisatin derivatives in prunes have potent laxative properties. Nitrates may reach relatively high levels in vegetables grown in soils that are high in nitrate. Serotonin is present in banana, pineapple, tomato, pumpkin, squash, and cucumber. A variety of common foods contain goitrogens (substances having antithyroid activity). These include rutabaga, turnip, cabbage, kale, Brussels sprouts, broccoli, cauliflower, and chard. Small amounts of estrogenic activity have been detected in many common foods, including wheat, oats, barley, rice, soybeans, potatoes, apples, plums, and cherries. Amygdalin in the bitter almond liberates hydrocyanic acid when taken into the stomach. Lemon and sesame oils have been shown experimentally to possess cocarcinogenic properties (Coon, 1969).

Foods containing natural toxicants have found wide use throughout the years because they do not contain enough of the toxic substances to be harmful when consumed in reasonable quantities or because cooking has eliminated the toxic components. However, if the criteria applied to the evaluation of food additives were applied to some of the natural chemical components of foods, many of them would not pass the test for acceptance. This illustrates the extent of efforts that are being made to maintain a safe food supply in the United States. Continued testing and evaluation of both food additives and natural food toxicants will be useful in planning for the total food supply.

SUMMARY

Consumers expect convenience, high quality, stability, and safety in the food supply. The use of food additives contributes to the food industry's ability to meet consumer demands.

Concern about food adulteration and unsafe practices in the United States eventually led to the passage of the first Food and Drug Act in 1906. Legislation in this area was strengthened in 1938 by enactment of the Food, Drug and Cosmetic Act. Several amendments, including the 1958 food additives amendment, have further expanded this legislation which is administered by the FDA.

The legal definition of food additives is complex and exempts a long list of substances in common use that are "generally recognized as safe" (GRAS). As a more useful definition for the consumer, a food additive is a substance or a mixture of substances, other than a basic foodstuff, that is present in a food as a result of any aspect of production, processing, storage, or packaging. An additive is classified as intentional if it is purposely introduced into a food product to perform a specific function. It is called incidental if it happens to get into a food from some phase of production, handling, or packaging. In both cases new additives must receive prior approval from the FDA before they can be used.

Justifiable uses for food additives include 1. improvement or maintenance of nutritional value; 2. enhancement of quality and consumer acceptability; 3. reduction of waste and improvement of keeping quality; and 4. facilitation of food preparation. Intentional additives are often grouped according to their major functions in food. Such groups include preservatives and antioxidants; emulsifying, foaming, stabilizing, and thickening agents; bleaching and maturing agents; acids, alkalies and buffers; flavoring substances; food colors; sequestering agents; humectants; curing agents; and artificial sweeteners.

Recommendations on safety testing have been made by the FDA for the approval of food additives before they can be used. Results of well designed tests of the physiologic, pharmacologic, and biochemical effects of a proposed food additive form the basis for the evaluation of its safety. Acute and subacute toxicity tests on experimental animals have traditionally been performed, although the limitations of animal testing are recognized. Additional tests may include mutagenicity, metabolic fate in the body, and lifetime feeding studies. The testing of an additive is time consuming and expensive. The cost is borne by the food manufacturer who must petition the FDA with documented evidence that the additive is needed and is safe.

STUDY QUESTIONS

Several pieces of federal legislation have been passed to regulate food additives.

1. Give a chronological description of major federal legislation involving food additives from the beginning of the twentieth century until the present time. Indicate the major purpose of each and the agency responsible for enforcement.
2. Define food additives in terms that are useful to the consumer. Explain the implications of the legal definition of food additives in terms of substances in common use as additives before 1958.
3. Explain the meaning of GRAS and describe the present status of this group of substances.
4. Define the terms intentional additive and incidental additive.

Food additives must be useful as well as safe.

5. List four general purposes for using food additives and give examples of additives that serve each purpose listed.
6. Give examples of additives that are preservatives and antioxidants; emulsifying, foaming, stabilizing, and thickening agents; bleaching and maturing agents; acids, alkalies, and buffers; flavoring substances; food colors; sequestering agents; humectants; curing agents; and artificial sweeteners.
7. Discuss some of the major problems involved in the evaluation of food additives. Describe the usual methods for collecting data on their safety and the process involved in gaining approval for new additives.
8. Give examples of natural toxicants in foods and discuss implications of these substances in general in terms of the safety of the national food supply.

REFERENCES

1. Committee on Food Protection, Food and Nutrition Board. 1965. *Chemicals Used in Food Processing.* Publication 1274. Washington, D.C.: National Academy of Sciences—National Research Council.

2. Committee on Food Protection, Food and Nutrition Board. 1973. *The Use of Chemicals in Food Production, Processing, Storage and Distribution.* Washington, D. C.: National Academy of Sciences—National Research Council.

3. Coon, J. M. 1969. Naturally occurring toxicants in foods. *Food Technology* 23, 1041.

4. Day, H. G. 1976. Food safety—then and now. *American Dietetic Association Journal* 69, 229.

5. Filer, L. J., Jr. 1976. Patterns of consumption of food additives. *Food Technology* 30 (No. 7), 62.

6. Friedman, L. and A. T. Spiher, Jr. 1971. Proving the safety of food additives. *FDA Papers* (Nov.), p. 13.

7. Hutt, P. B. 1977. Balanced government regulation of consumer products. *Food Technology* 31 (No. 1), 58.

8. Martinsen, C. S. and J. McCullough. 1977. Are consumers concerned about chemical preservatives in food? *Food Technology* 31 (No. 9), 56.

9. Siu, R. G. H., J. F. Borzelleca, C. J. Carr, H. G. Day, S. J. Fomon, G. W. Irving, Jr., B. N. La Du, Jr., J. R. McCoy, S. A. Miller, G. L. Plaa, M. B. Shimkin, and J. L. Wood. 1977. Evaluation of health aspects of GRAS food ingredients: Lessons learned and questions unanswered. *Federation Proceedings* 36, 2527.

10. Wodicka, V. O. 1977. Food ingredient safety criteria. *Food Technology* 31 (No. 1), 84.

CHAPTER 9

FOOD STANDARDS AND SAFETY

Regulation of the safety of foods and protection of the consumer is a vital issue for government, industry, and consumer groups alike. In many cases, governmental regulation of the American food supply has become very controversial. In spite of the controversy many standards have been set and are being enforced at both the federal and the local levels. Several governmental agencies are involved. Concern for both chemical and microbiological safety of food is expressed through the many regulations and programs that are in effect. (Chemical additives to food are discussed in Chapter 8.)

9.1

FEDERAL AGENCIES THAT REGULATE FOOD

The number of federal governmental agencies involved in the regulation of food and food processing has expanded in recent years. Organizational changes within each of the various governmental agencies sometimes make it difficult for both the food scientist and the consumer to stay abreast of current regulations (Semling, 1978). The U. S. Food and Drug Administration (FDA) operates under the federal Food, Drug and Cosmetic Act. It is responsible for regulating all foods except red meats, poultry, and eggs. It also administers the Fair Packaging and Labeling Act and the Public Health Service Act which concerns sanitation in milk processing, shellfish, restaurant operations, and interstate travel facilities.

The U. S. Department of Agriculture (USDA) is involved with food through a variety of activities. The Food Safety and Quality Service (FSQS) within USDA is responsible for the federal inspection of meat and poultry products for wholesomeness and truthful labeling under the federal Meat Inspection Act and the Poultry Products Inspection Act. Additionally, the FSQS is responsible for the inspection of imported meat and poultry and also for guarding against illegal chemical residues in agricultural products. The Agricultural Marketing Services (AMS) is responsible for livestock grade standards.

Within the Commerce Department, the National Marine Fisheries Service (NMFS) provides a voluntary grading and inspection program for seafood. The service complements the Food and Drug Administration which has regulatory jurisdiction over seafood products.

The Federal Trade Commission (FTC) is charged with promoting free and fair competition and protecting the public against unfair and deceptive business practices, both within and without the food industry. The Occupational Safety and Health Administration (OSHA) is concerned with health hazards of the work environment, which includes food processing plants. The Environmental Protection Agency (EPA) attacks problems of air and water pollution, solid waste management, toxic substances, pesticides, and radiation. It sets environmental standards that affect food processing plants.

9.2

FOOD STANDARDS

Under the federal Food, Drug and Cosmetic Act, the FDA is authorized to formulate definitions and standards for food when this will promote honesty and fair dealing in the interest of consumers. These include standards of identity, standards of quality, and standards of fill of container.

A *standard of identity* describes the food and lists required and optional ingredients. A food must meet these standards or it cannot be labeled as that particular food. For example, if a sample of ice cream does not meet the standard of identity for ice cream, it must be labeled *imitation* ice cream. The standards of identity are constantly being revised as new food additives are approved and new technological developments occur.

Standards of identity have been adopted for many foods, including chocolate and cocoa products, wheat and corn flour and related products, macaroni and noodle products, bakery products, milk and cream, cheeses and cheese products, dressings for food, canned fruits and fruit juices, fruit butters, jellies, preserves and related products, shellfish, canned tuna fish, eggs and egg products, oleomargarine and margarine, canned vegetables and vegetable products, and peanut butter. A listing of ingredients on the product label is not required for foods that meet a standard of identity.

Standards of quality specify minimum quality characteristics such as tenderness, color, and freedom from defects. These standards have been set for some canned fruits and vegetables. If a product does not meet these standards, it must be labeled "Below Standard in Quality," followed by a statement indicating the way in which it fails to meet the standard.

Standards of fill of container tell the packer how much the container must contain to avoid deception. These standards, based on weight rather than volume, are important for products that settle after filling.

Nutrition labeling is a program developed by the FDA and the food industry to provide consumers with nutrition information on individual foods. It is voluntary except for special dietary foods, but is appearing on many products. Nutrient information is listed on the label on the basis of one serving of food. The number of kilocalories and the amount of protein, carbohydrates, and fat are listed first. Below this is given the percentage of the U. S. RDAs of protein and seven vitamins and minerals in a serving of the product. U. S. RDAs are selected from tables of Recommended Dietary Allowances published by the Food and Nutrition Board of the National Academy of Sciences—National Research Council. (U. S. RDAs are listed in Table 9.1.)

Grade standards for meat, poultry, eggs, fruits, vegetables, butter, and cheddar cheese are formulated by USDA. These standards are used extensively in the marketing of food. Grading is voluntary and the grading service is paid for by the processor. Grade standards for fishery products are set by the National Marine Fisheries Service.

USDA grades are designed to meet the needs of consumers as well as the producers of food products. Hutchinson (1970) therefore surveyed 3000 sample households to ascertain consumers' knowledge and use of government grades. The results of the survey indicated that most

Table 9.1   U. S. Recommended Daily Allowance (U. S. RDA) (for use in nutrition labeling of foods).

	Adults and children over 4 years	Children under 4 years	Infants under 13 months	Pregnant or lactating women
Protein	65 g*	28 g*	25 g*	65 g*
Vitamin A	5,000 IU	2,500 IU	2,500 IU	8,000 IU
Vitamin C	60 mg	40 mg	40 mg	60 mg
Thiamin	1.5 mg	0.7 mg	0.7 mg	1.7 mg
Riboflavin	1.7 mg	0.8 mg	0.8 mg	2.0 mg
Niacin	20 mg	9.0 mg	9.0 mg	20 mg
Calcium	1.0 g	0.8 g	0.8 g	1.3 g
Iron	18 mg	10 mg	10 mg	18 mg
Vitamin D	400 IU	400 IU	400 IU	400 IU
Vitamin E	30 IU	10 IU	10 IU	30 IU
Vitamin B_6	2.0 mg	0.7 mg	0.7 mg	2.5 mg
Folacin	0.4 mg	0.2 mg	0.2 mg	0.8 mg
Vitamin B_{12}	6 mcg	3 mcg	3 mcg	8 mcg
Phosphorus	1.0 g	0.8 g	0.8 g	1.3 g
Iodine	150 mcg	70 mcg	70 mcg	150 mcg
Magnesium	400 mg	200 mg	200 mg	450 mg
Zinc	15 mg	8 mg	8 mg	15 mg
Copper	2 mg	1 mg	1 mg	2 mg
Biotin	0.3 mg	0.15 mg	0.15 mg	0.3 mg
Pantothenic acid	10 mg	5 mg	5 mg	10 mg

* If protein efficiency ratio of protein is equal to or better than that of casein, U. S. RDA is 45 g for adults and pregnant or lactating women, 20 g for children under 4 years of age and 18 g for infants.

U. S. consumers know little about federal grades for the foods they purchase but that those who are aware of grades find them helpful in making their buying decisions.

9.3

MICROBIOLOGICAL SAFETY

Foodborne hazards of microbial origin are real problems in the United States, as well as elsewhere in the world. In the U. S. they may account for as many as 2 million cases of illness annually. The severity of the outbreaks ranges from death due to botulism or infection in very susceptible or weak individuals to the relatively mild discomfort of what is often called the "24-hour flu" (Roberts, 1978).

A diversity of microorganisms is responsible for foodborne disease. Some act through toxic metabolites formed when the organisms grow in the food prior to consumption. These include the toxin-forming *Clostridium botulinum* and food poisoning strains of *Staphylococcus aureus.* Killing or removing these organisms after they have grown does not eliminate the danger if active toxin remains in the food. Other types of foodborne disease are true infections. Ingestion of only a few active cells may be sufficient to initiate gastrointestinal symptoms when the organism is one of the *Salmonella* species. Still another type of food poisoning occurs only when the causal organisms are ingested in very large numbers, perhaps tens of millions per gram. *Clostridium perfringens* produces this type of illness when the ingested organisms sporulate in the digestive tract, releasing a toxic substance into the gut (Foster, 1978).

Parasites such as *Trichinella spiralis* may be carried in foods such as undercooked pork or bear meat, resulting in trichinosis. Viral agents such as hepatitis A may also be transmitted by food. Toxins may be produced by molds, such as *Aspergillis,* growing on food. However, bacterial agents account for the great majority of cases of food poisoning attributed to microorganisms. Table 9.2 summarizes major characteristics of the various types of food poisoning. Information about foodborne disease outbreaks is collected and published by the Center for Disease Control in Atlanta, Georgia.

BOTULISM

Although less than 50 cases of botulism are reported in the United States annually, it is the most feared of food poisonings. A death rate from this disease of approximately 60 percent a few years ago has dropped to about 20 percent. This is probably due to early diagnosis and improved supportive treatment. Botulism is a paralytic disease resulting from the action of a neurotoxic protein elaborated by *Clostridium botulinum.* This organism is a spore-forming bacillus that grows only in the absence of free oxygen. Seven distinct types are recognized on the basis of the serologic specificity of their toxins. They are designated A through G, with types A, B, and E responsible for most human disease. Botulism is rare because four conditions must be met simulta-

Table 9.2 Food Intoxication and Infection.

Disease	Cause	Incubation Time	Symptoms	Duration	Mortality	Foods Commonly Involved
Botulism	Neurotoxin produced by *C. botulinum*	12–36 hours	Early nausea, vomiting, and diarrhea. Double vision, difficulty in swallowing, inability to talk, and finally respiratory paralysis	1–10 days	20%	Low-acid canned foods, such as vegetables, meat, fish, and soups, improperly processed
Staphylococcal food poisoning	Enterotoxin produced by certain strains of *Staphylococcus aureus*	1–6 hours	Nausea, vomiting, abdominal pain, and diarrhea	1–2 days	Essentially zero	Roast fowl, baked ham, salads containing meat, poultry, and potatoes, cream-filled baked goods, fermented sausages, and cheese
Salmonellosis	Infection with comparatively small numbers of organisms of the *Salmonella* species	12–18 hours	Nausea, diarrhea, abdominal pain, and fever	Usually 2–3 days	1%	Poultry, eggs, and pork not properly cooked; unpasteurized milk
C. perfringens poisoning	Ingestion of large quantities of *C. perfringens* that release a toxin in the gut	8–18 hours	Nausea, abdominal pain, and diarrhea	1 day	Zero	Meat or poultry products held warm for several hours

Source: From Foster, 1978; Frazier, 1967.

neously before a hazard can exist. Viable cells or spores of *C. botulinum* must be present in the food. The composition of the food must be suitable for growth and toxin development. This includes a pH above 5, water activity above 0.93, the absence of free oxygen, and the absence of nitrite. The food must be stored long enough at a suitable temperature for growth and toxin production. Finally, the food must be eaten without being cooked. Heating for a few minutes at boiling temperature destroys the toxin (Foster, 1978). Electron photomicrographs of *C. botulinum* cells and spores are shown in Figure 9.1.

Reports of botulism outbreaks have appeared in the scientific literature (Eadie *et al.,* 1964; Foster *et al.,* 1965; Merson *et al.,* 1974). Thirty outbreaks of foodborne botulism involving 91 cases were reported to the Center for Disease Control between 1970 and 1973. Vegetables were the most commonly implicated foods, and peppers were incriminated in seven of the 13 outbreaks due to vegetables. Fish were implicated in six outbreaks. Three of the 30 outbreaks were due to commercially canned foods and involved vichyssoise soup, a pepper product, and a meatball and spaghetti sauce mixture. Faulty home canning practices account for most cases of botulinum food poisoning in the United States.

Prevention of botulism requires the use of proper processing methods which will accomplish the destruction of the bacteria and of their very heat-resistant spores (IFT, 1972). (Procedures for the canning of low acid foods are discussed in Chapter 6.)

Figure 9.1

Scanning electron photomicrographs of (*top left*) a cell of *C. botulinum,* Type A, prior to sporulation and (*top right*) another type A cell during actual sporulation. At *bottom* are spores of Type B (*left*) and Type E (*right*). (Kautter and Lynt, 1972.) (Courtesy of Food and Drug Administration, U. S. Department of Health, Education and Welfare.)

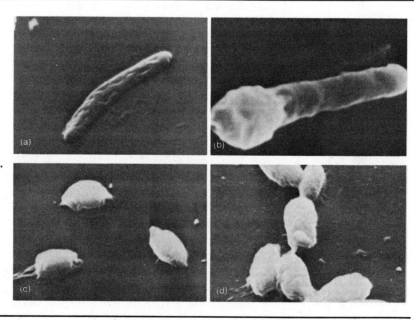

STAPHYLOCOCCAL FOOD POISONING

Staphylococcus aureus is a common contaminant of the human skin, nose, and throat. Certain strains of this organism produce a potent toxin that causes severe gastrointestinal symptoms. The toxic substance is a protein that is quite resistant to heating even at a boiling temperature. Ordinary cooking procedures will not inactivate staphylococcal enterotoxin once it has formed, thus the avoidance of illness requires prevention of the growth of the microorganisms by storage of the susceptible foods at refrigerator temperatures.

Staphylococcal poisoning is the most common of the foodborne diseases in the United States. Its mortality rate is essentially zero but it could be fatal in severely malnourished infants or in infirm adults. Its symptoms are gastrointestinal and appear soon (1–6 hours) after consuming the spoiled food. Three conditions are necessary for an outbreak of staphylococcal food poisoning. Food poisoning staphylococci must be present in the food. These usually come from food handlers but may originate from other animal sources. Composition of the food must permit growth and toxin formation. The food must be held sufficiently long at a temperature satisfactory for growth of staphylococci. The foods most commonly involved include roast fowl, baked ham, meat, poultry and potato salads, and cream-filled baked goods (Foster, 1978). Control of staphylococcal food poisoning requires constant vigilance in the handling of food by the food processor, the manager in commercial food service, and the consumer in the kitchen (de Figueiredo, 1971).

SALMONELLOSIS

Salmonella gastroenteritis is the most important foodborne disease in the United States in terms of severity and incidence. An estimated 2 million Americans suffer from this disease each year with at least half the cases attributable to contaminated food. The economic impact of an outbreak of foodborne salmonellosis affecting approximately 125 individuals was estimated at $28,733, mostly in lost salaries and productivity (Levy and McIntire, 1974). Gastrointestinal symptoms usually appear within 12–18 hours after ingesting the organisms. Most cases recover within 2 or 3 days but some develop complications that persist for weeks or months. Salmonellosis is an intestinal infection caused by various bacteria of the genus *Salmonella*. These organisms may be carried in the intestine after symptoms of the disease have subsided. Since a small number of viable cells can apparently cause illness, any detectable salmonellae are potentially hazardous (Foster, 1978).

The main health hazard to man for the development of salmonellosis comes from the constant introduction of contaminated animal products into the food supply. Chickens, turkeys, and swine often carry salmonellae. Eggs are also a common source of these organisms. Frozen or dried eggs are always pasteurized before processing to destroy any salmonellae that may be present. Salmonellosis has also resulted from the consumption of contaminated nonfat dry milk (Collins *et al.*, 1968). Processing conditions must be adequate to destroy any salmonellae that may be present. Outbreaks of salmonellosis due to commercially baked meringue pies have been reported (Ager *et al.*, 1967). A food-borne institutional outbreak at a Massachussetts hospital was traced to frozen, unpasteurized egg yolks used in the preparation of ice cream (Morse and Rubenstein, 1967).

Salmonellosis can be prevented by proper cooking and careful food handling practices which maintain scrupulous cleanliness. An alternative approach and one that has received little attention is to eliminate all infections from herds and flocks (Foster, 1978). Poultry must be adequately cooked in order to destroy any organisms that may be present. Time and temperature relationships are important in achieving proper degrees of doneness. Mabee and Mountney (1970) reported that *Salmonella senftenberg* 775W was not recovered from inoculated chicken legs, breasts, or wings that were deep-fat fried at atmospheric or 15 lb pressure for 11 minutes. Wings reached the highest internal temperature, legs the lowest, and breasts an intermediate level in the poultry tested.

CLOSTRIDIUM PERFRINGENS POISONING

Spores of *C. perfringens* are widespread in nature and are common in the intestinal tract of man and other animals. Certain strains of this organism produce an enterotoxin that causes mild gastrointestinal illness (Foster, 1978). During 1970, *C. perfringens* was responsible for 22.4 percent of foodborne outbreaks and 37.8 percent of cases of food poisoning reported to the Center for Disease Control. The specific food involved, when known, was usually a meat or poultry product. Other foods affected included dairy products, fruits, vegetables, and Chinese food (Loewenstein, 1972). *C. perfringens* food poisoning is usually associated with foods that are held at warm temperatures for several hours.

SUMMARY

Several governmental agencies are involved in regulating food safety and protecting the consumer. The Food and Drug Administration (FDA), under the Food, Drug and Cosmetic Act, regulates all foods except red meats, poultry, and eggs. It also administers the Fair Packaging and Labeling Act and the Public Health Service Act which concerns sanitation. The U. S. Department of Agriculture (USDA) is responsible for inspection of meat and poultry products and sets grade standards for agricultural products. The National Marine Fisheries Service in the Department of Commerce provides inspection and grading service for seafood.

The FDA monitors chemical additives in food. It also establishes standards of identity, standards of quality, and standards of fill of container. Nutrition labeling is under the jurisdiction of FDA. A standard of identity describes the food and lists required and optional ingredients. These standards have been set for many foods. Standards of quality specify minimum quality characteristics and have been set for some canned fruits and vegetables. Standards of fill of container tell the packer how much the container must contain to avoid deception. Nutrition labeling provides consumers with nutrition information on individual foods. Nutrients are given in percentages of the U. S. RDAs in one serving of the product.

Foodborne hazards of microbial origin are real problems in the United States. A diversity of microorganisms is responsible for foodborne disease. *Clostridium botulinum,* an anaerobic spore former, elaborates a neurotoxin which produces botulism. This disease affects a mortality rate of about 20 percent. Before botulism is produced, viable cells of *C. botulinum* must be present in the food. The composition of the food must be suitable for growth and toxin development. The food must be stored long enough at a suitable temperature for toxin production and the food must be eaten without cooking. These conditions rarely occur simultaneously. Improperly canned foods, particularly low-acid home-canned products, are responsible for much of the botulism that develops in the United States.

Certain strains of *Staphylococcus aureus* produce a potent toxin that causes severe gastrointestinal symptoms. The toxin is heat resistant and avoidance of illness requires prevention of the growth of the microorganism so that toxin will not be formed. Storage at refrigerator temperatures inhibits growth. For an outbreak of staphylococcal food poisoning the organism must be present in the food. It usually comes from the skin, nose, or throat of food handlers. The composition of the food must be suitable to the organism's growth and the food must be held long enough at a temperature satisfactory for its growth. Poultry, meat, meat salads, and cream-filled baked goods are often incriminated in this type of poisoning.

Salmonellosis results from the ingestion of microorganisms of the *Salmonella* species. Only a small number of viable cells is necessary to cause illness. This is the most important foodborne disease in terms of severity and incidence. The main sources of contamination are chickens, turkeys, and swine. Salmonellosis can be prevented by the proper cooking of these foods and by careful food handling practices.

Certain strains of *Clostridium perfringens,* when consumed in very large quantities, sporulate in the intestinal tract and produce an enterotoxin that causes mild gastrointestinal illness. This type of poisoning is usually associated with meat or poultry that is held at warm temperatures for several hours.

STUDY QUESTION

Many federal agencies are involved in setting standards for food and regulating its safety.

1. Describe the basic functions of each of the following agencies in the regulation of food standards and safety:

a. U. S. Food and Drug Administration (FDA)
b. U. S. Department of Agriculture (USDA)
c. National Marine Fisheries Service (NMFS)
d. Federal Trade Commission (FTC)
e. Environmental Protection Agency (EPA)
2. What is meant by each of the following in terms of FDA standards?
a. Standard of identity
b. Standard of quality
c. Standard of fill of container
3. How might nutritional labeling of foods benefit the consumer?

A diversity of microorganisms is responsible for foodborne disease.

4. For each of the following organisms, describe the type of disease that may occur as a result of their growth in food, the foods commonly concerned, and the procedures for preventing the development of the disease:
a. *Clostridium botulinum*
b. *Staphylococcus aureus*
c. *Salmonella* spp.
d. *Clostridium perfringens*

REFERENCES

1. Ager, E. A., K. E. Nelson, M. M. Galton, J. R. Boring III, and J. R. Jernigan. 1967. Two outbreaks of egg-borne salmonellosis and implications for their prevention. *Journal of the American Medical Association* 199, 122.

2. Collins, R. N., M. D. Treger, J. B. Goldsby, J. R. Boring III, D. B. Coohon, and R. N. Barr. 1968. Interstate outbreak of *Salmonella newbrunswick* infection traced to powdered milk. *Journal of the American Medical Association* 203, 838.

3. Eadie, G. A., J. G. Molner, R. J. Solomon, and R. D. Aach. 1964. Type E botulism. *Journal of the American Medical Association* 187, 496.

4. de Figueiredo, M. P. 1971. Staphylococci control and the food processor. *American Dietetic Association Journal* 58, 109.

5. Foster, E. M. 1978. Foodborne hazards of microbial origin. *Federation Proceedings* 37, 2577.

6. Foster, E. M., J. S. Deffner, T. L. Bott, and E. McCoy. 1965. *Clostridium botulinum* food poisoning. *Journal of Milk and Food Technology* 28 (No. 3), 86.

7. Frazier, W. C. 1967. *Food Microbiology,* 2nd edition. New York: McGraw-Hill.

8. Hutchinson, T. Q. 1970. Consumers' knowledge and use of government grades for selected food items. U. S. Department of Agriculture, Marketing Research Report No. 876.

9. Institute of Food Technologists' Expert Panel on Food Safety and Nutrition and the Committee on Public Information. 1972. Botulism. Chicago: Institute of Food Technologists.

10. Kautter, D. A. and R. K. Lynt, Jr. 1971. Botulism. *FDA Papers* 5 (No. 9), 16.

11. Levy, B. S. and W. McIntire. 1974. The economic impact of a food-borne salmonellosis outbreak. *Journal of the American Medical Association* 230, 1281.

12. Loewenstein, M. S. 1972. Epidemiology of *Clostridium perfringens* food poisoning. *New England Journal of Medicine* 286, 1026.

13. Mabee, M. S. and G. J. Mountney. 1970. Time-temperature patterns during deep fat frying of chicken parts and their relation to the survival of *Salmonella*. *Food Technology* 24, 808.

14. Merson, M. H., J. M. Hughes, V. R. Dowell, A. Taylor, W. H. Barker and E. J. Gangarosa. 1974. Current trends in botulism in the United States. *Journal of the American Medical Association* 229, 1305.

15. Morse, L. J. and A. D. Rubenstein. 1967. A food-borne institutional outbreak of enteritis due to *Salmonella blockley*. *Journal of the American Medical Association* 202, 939.

16. Roberts, H. R. 1978. Principal hazards in food safety and their assessment. *Federation Proceedings* 37, 2575.

17. Semling, H. V., Jr. 1978. 1978 guide to government agencies. *Food Processing* 39 (No. 7), 24.

PART IV

CARBOHYDRATES IN FOOD SYSTEMS

Carbohydrate substances, from simple sugars to complex polysaccharides, are widely distributed in nature. Comparatively large proportions of carbohydrates are found in certain plant tissues. Sugars and starches are extracted from plants for use in concentrated forms. They play a variety of roles as ingredients in various food products. In the plant, carbohydrates may act as structural components, as storage compounds, and as readily available sources of energy for the plant cells. Although in addition to carbohydrates many other substances are present in plant tissues and are discussed in this Part, emphasis is placed on the carbohydrates.

The Part begins with a chapter on sugars and candies and is followed by a chapter on frozen desserts. Candies and frozen desserts both contain comparatively large amounts of sugar. They also have in common the phenomenon of crystallization—that of sugar in the case of candies, and that of water in the case of frozen desserts. A general discussion of the structure of plant tissues is given in a separate chapter. Plant pigments, although noncarbohydrate substances, are also included. Three chapters then discuss quality and preparation of fruits and vegetables and the structure and milling of cereal grains. Characteristics and uses of starch, the plant storage carbohydrate, are included in the final chapter of this Part.

CHAPTER 10

SUGARS AND CANDIES

Sugars are carbohydrates. They are ingredients of many food products and are naturally present in fruits and other plant tissues. As components of diverse food products, sugars play several different roles. They function primarily as sweetening agents in a variety of foods which include beverages, puddings, custards, sauces, pies, stewed fruits, ice creams, and gelatin desserts. Sugars are added as sweeteners to many prepared cereals. Several types of sugars are available for use by the food processor. These sugars include glucose, sucrose, corn syrup and high fructose corn syrup, which is being used in increasing quantities.

Sugar acts as a tenderizing agent in baked products such as cakes, cookies, and quick breads. In the mixing of wheat flour batters and doughs a tough protein complex called gluten is formed. The structural contribution of gluten is reduced by the addition of sugar. Sugar increases the fluidity of batters. (A more complete explanation of the role of sugar in baked products is given in Part VII.) Sugars participate in nonenzymatic browning reactions that are desirable in baked products but undesirable in other foods such as nonfat dry milk and dried eggs.

Sugar is an essential ingredient in fruit jellies. In this case it acts as a dehydrating agent for the gel-forming pectin molecules. (The preparation of fruit jellies is discussed in Chapter 20.)

Sugar is the principal ingredient of candies and forms the basic structure of these products. It may be in a crystalline or noncrystalline form. Appropriate control of crystallization is the major aim of the candymaker. It should be pointed out that purified sugars are essentially 100 percent carbohydrate. They are fascinating ingredients as they play many functional roles in food products. However, from a nutritional standpoint, sugars should be consumed in relatively small quantities as they provide no other nutrients than carbohydrates. This recommendation is made so that individuals will avoid consuming a disproportionate number of calories without a corresponding proportion of vitamins, minerals, and proteins (Sipple and McNutt, 1974).

CARBOHYDRATES

Carbohydrates, or saccharides, are polyhydroxy aldehydes ($-\overset{\displaystyle O}{\overset{\|}{C}}H$) or

ketones ($-\overset{\displaystyle O}{\overset{\|}{C}}-$) and their derivatives. They have the empirical formula $(CH_2O)_n$. Carbohydrates are commonly classified as monosaccharides, oligosaccharides, and polysaccharides. Monosaccharides are simple sugars and consist of a single polyhydroxy aldehyde or ketone. The simplest monosaccharides are the three-carbon trioses, glyceraldehyde and dihydroxyacetone. If the carbon chains of the trioses are extended by adding atoms, tetroses (four-carbon compounds), pentoses (five-carbon compounds), hexoses (six-carbon compounds), and heptoses (seven-carbon compounds) are formed. Pentoses are important in foods because of their presence as building blocks in some of the plant polysaccharides (complex carbohydrates), including the hemicelluloses and other vegetable gums. Pentoses that may be present in these types of compounds include xylose, arabinose, and ribose.

The most abundant hexose in foods is D-glucose. It has an aldehyde group on the first carbon. D-fructose, which is sometimes called levulose, is a hexose with a ketone group on the second carbon. It is widely distributed in fruits and vegetables. Honey is a rich source of fructose. Galactose is another hexose that is important in the study of food science because it is one of the two monosaccharides that make up milk sugar or lactose. Galactose and its derivative, galacturonic acid, are also building blocks for some polysaccharides distributed in plant tissues, including pectic substances, gum arabic, and carrageenan (a vegetable gum extracted from seaweed). Galactose is produced in yogurt by the action of fermenting bacteria on lactose and small quantities may be present in aged cheese. The chemical structures for D-fructose and D-galactose are given in Figure 10.1, along with that of D-glucose.

Disaccharides are formed by combining two monosaccharides. The most common disaccharides in foods are sucrose, lactose, and maltose. Sucrose is not a reducing sugar because the two monosaccharides, glucose and fructose, are joined through their aldehyde and ketone carbons, respectively. These groups are, therefore, not free to participate in oxidation–reduction reactions. Sucrose is found abundantly in the plant world, with sugar cane and sugar beets being some of the most concentrated sources. Lactose occurs only in milk or products made from milk. It is produced by joining D-glucose and beta D-galactose. Maltose is formed as an intermediate compound when starch is hydrolyzed. It contains two D-glucose units. The chemical structures for sucrose, lactose, and maltose are found in Figure 10.2.

Figure 10.1

CH$_2$OH

α-D-Glucose

CH$_2$OH

α-D-Galactose

α-D-Fructose

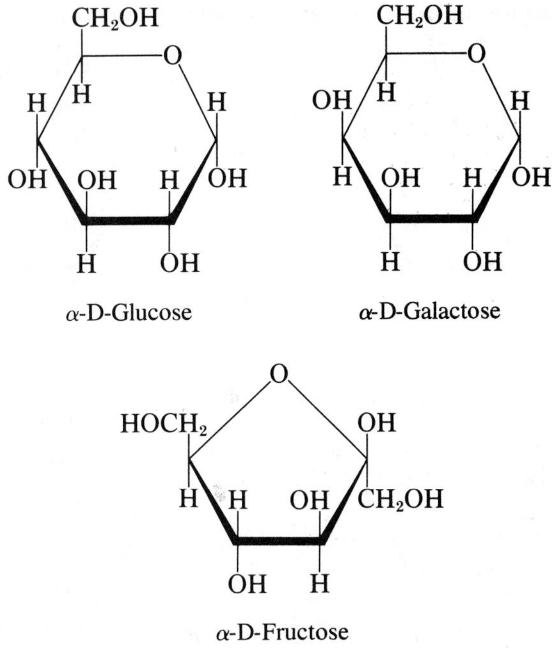

The term oligosaccharide is used to designate any sugars which contain from two to ten monosaccharide units. Disaccharides are thus included in this general classification. Examples of other oligosaccharides are raffinose, a trisaccharide which contains fructose, glucose, and galactose, and panose, a trisaccharide containing three glucose molecules in a straight chain.

Hexoses with aldehyde groups (aldohexoses) react with alcohols (−OH), under appropriate conditions, to form glycosides. For example, glucose may form a glucoside with methanol.

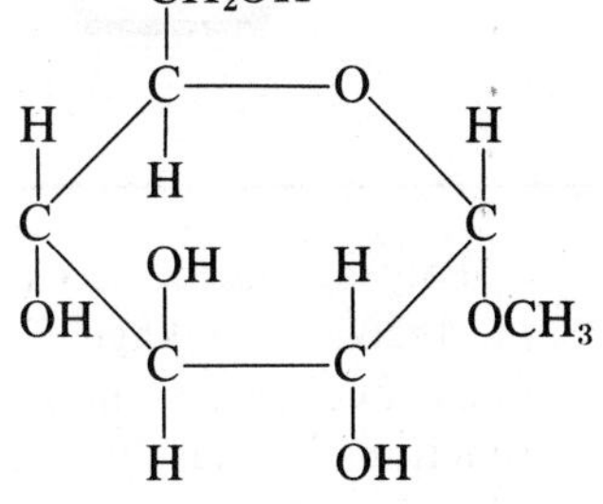

CH$_2$OH

OCH$_3$

Anthocyanin pigments are examples of glycosides in plant tissues. Anthocyanidin pigments combine with monosaccharides through hydroxyl groups.

Figure 10.2

Chemical structures for disaccharides commonly occurring in foods.

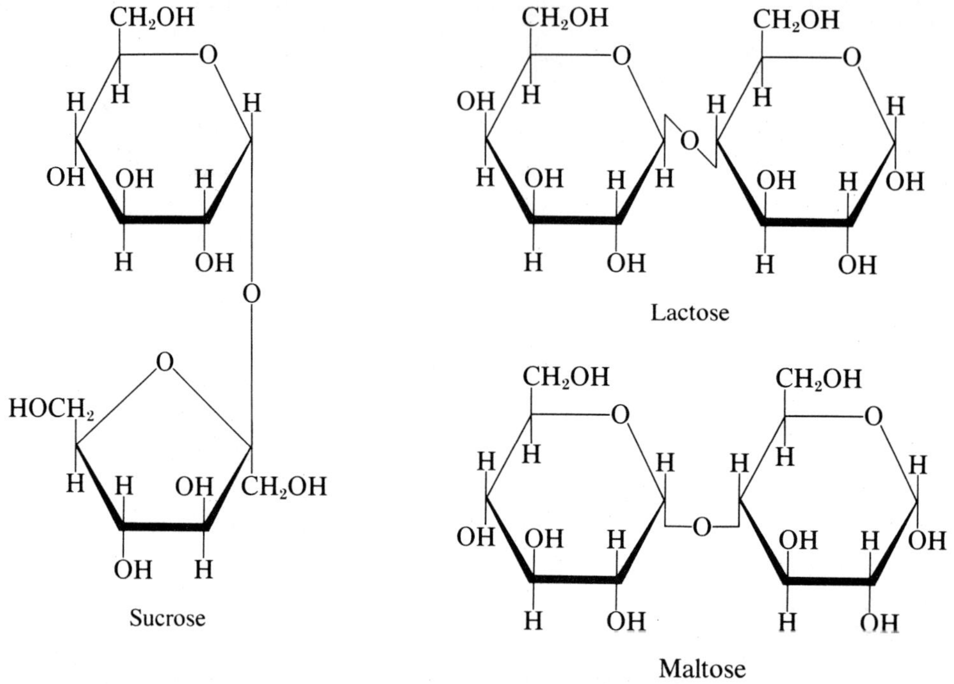

Sucrose

Lactose

Maltose

Figure 10.3

In cellulose, glucose units are combined through β-(1→4)-linkages into long chains.

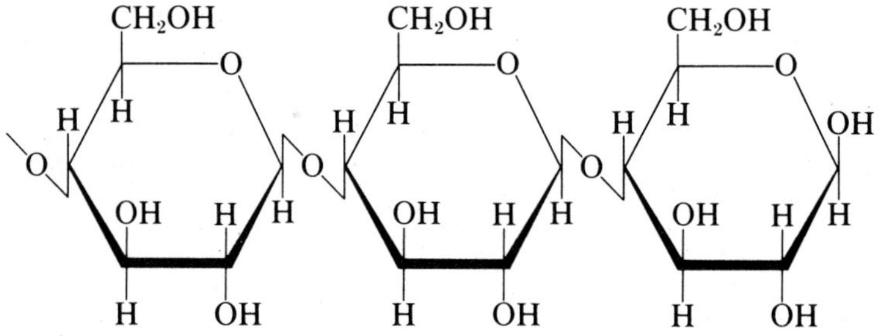

Polysaccharides contain many monosaccharide units joined together in glycosidic linkage. On complete hydrolysis, polysaccharides yield monosaccharides and/or their derivatives. Polysaccharides may be functionally classified as storage or structural compounds. Starch, composed of hundreds to thousands of α-D-glucose units, is the most widely distributed plant storage polysaccharide. Glycogen is a storage polysaccharide of animal origin. (The properties of starch are discussed in Chapter 16.) The most important structural polysaccharide is cel-

Table 10.1 Vegetable Gums and Their Major Monosaccharide Components

Gum	Major monosaccharides
Agar	D-galactose, 3,6-anhydro-L-galactose.
Algin	D-mannuronic acid, L-glucuronic acid.
Carrageenan	D-galactose, 3,6-anhydro-D-galactose.
Locust bean gum	D-galactose, D-mannose.
Guar gum	D-mannose, L-arabinose, L-rhamnose.
Gum tragacanth	L-arabinose, D-xylose, L-fucose, D-galactose.
Gum arabic	D-galactose, L-arabinose, L-rhamnose, D-glucuronic acid.
Gum karaya	D-galacturonic acid, L-rhamnose, D-galactose.

Source: From Matz, 1962.

lulose, which is composed of from 300 to 3000 D-glucose units in β-(1→4)-linkages, as illustrated in Figure 10.3. It makes up more than 50 percent of the total organic carbon in the biosphere. Cellulose is present in plant cell walls in the form of fibrils that are built up from bundles of cellulose molecules oriented together in a parallel fashion. The fibrils are cross-linked by hydrogen bonds.

Other structural polysaccharides found with cellulose in cell walls include hemicelluloses and pectic substances. Hemicelluloses are polymers of D-xylose in β-(1→4)-linkage with side chains of arabinose and other sugars. They are water insoluble but alkali soluble. (Pectic substances are polymers of galacturonic acid, a derivative of galactose, and are discussed in Chapter 20.)

A number of polysaccharide vegetable gums are used in the food industry. Some of these gums, such as carrageenan and algin, are extracted from seaweed products. Most of the vegetable gums are heteropolysaccharides, having two or more recurring monosaccharide units. Examples of vegetable gums are given in Table 10.1.

10.2

PRODUCTION OF SUGARS AND SYRUPS

SUCROSE

Sucrose is commonly known as table sugar, cane sugar, or beet sugar. World production of sucrose in 1972 was about 74 million metric tons. More than 10 million tons is marketed as food in the United States annually, approximately 70 percent of which is used by the baking, confectionery, ice cream, beverage, and other food industries. Annual consumption of 102.5 lb per person of cane and beet sucrose in the United States, as indicated by measuring the disappearance of sugar from marketing channels, changed little from 1925 to 1970 (Life Sciences Research Office, 1976).

Sucrose, or table sugar, is produced commercially from sugar cane or sugar beets. It is of high purity and readily available at relatively low cost.

Extraction of Sucrose from Plants Columbus brought sugar cane to the new world. The Spaniards then developed cane production on a commercial scale in the West Indies. Juice is extracted from the cane by crushing it between a series of rollers. After straining, the juice is clarified by the use of lime in order to remove nonsucrose substances. Water is then evaporated from the juice under vacuum and crystallization occurs when the solution becomes supersaturated. The crystals are separated in a centrifuge. Molasses syrup is spun off from the sugar crystals in a revolving drum leaving the unwashed sugar crystals in the drum. The crystals are called raw sugar at this point and sugar is generally shipped in this form for world trade. Sugar companies in the United States refine the raw sugar further by repeating the clarification process, passing the sugar liquor through charcoal filters to remove color substances and other impurities, crystallizing the sucrose, separating the sugar crystals in a centrifuge, and removing the remaining moisture by heat (Borgstrom, 1968).

The sugar beet came to the United States from Europe. The first beet sugar in this country was produced in Northampton, Massachusetts in about 1836. The processing of beet sugar bears many similarities to but also differs from, the processing of cane sugar. The beets are washed and cut into thin strips which are soaked in hot water in a continuous diffusion process. The raw juice resulting from this treatment contains many nonsugar substances which are precipitated by a clarification procedure, using lime and carbon dioxide. They are later removed by filtration. The juice is concentrated in an evaporator and boiled in vacuum pans. The thick liquid is seeded with a small amount of pulverized sugar and crystallization takes place. When the crystals are of an appropriate size they are separated from the syrup in the centrifuge. These crystals constitute refined sugar (Borgstrom, 1968).

Granulated sucrose (table sugar) is available in a wide range of particle sizes. These include standard granulated, fine, extra fine, and fruit granulated sugars which have been separated by screening. Pulverized or powdered sugars are produced by reducing the particle size of refined sugar and usually contain anti-caking agents such as starch or silica gel. Powdered sugars vary in fineness and are used chiefly in icings and fillings for bakery products. Finer grain sugars will dissolve more rapidly than coarser grain sugars and are used where this property is desirable. Liquid sugars are prepared by dissolving granular refined sucrose in water to achieve a solids level of about 67 percent. Liquid sugar is particularly useful in automated industry systems which involve weighing and dispensing of ingredients.

Brown sugar is composed of clumps of sucrose crystals coated with a molasses film. Brown sugars contain about 3.5 percent invert sugar which may participate in the nonenzymatic browning or Maillard reaction when brown sugar is used in baked products. A small amount of organic acid is also present in brown sugar.

LACTOSE

Lactose, or milk sugar, is a disaccharide containing glucose and beta galactose linked between the aldehyde group of galactose and the number four carbon atom of glucose as shown in Figure 10.2. It is a reducing sugar because the aldehyde group of the glucose moiety is not tied up in linkage.

Lactose is produced commercially by crystallization from whey solutions. Dried whey contains about 73 percent lactose. To manufacture lactose as alpha lactose monohydrate, whey is treated with lime, heated, and filtered to remove the precipitated proteins and calcium phosphate. It is then concentrated to about 30 percent solids and refiltered to remove any protein and salts that have separated out during the concentration process. The whey is further concentrated and the lactose crystallized. The crystals are separated in a centrifuge. They may be dissolved again in water and treated with activated carbon to decolorize the solution before recrystallizing. The finished product contains 99.8 percent alpha lactose monohydrate and 0.1 percent moisture (Guy, 1971). Anhydrous beta lactose is also produced but less widely used than the monohydrate form. Lactose may be used as a partial replacement for sucrose in a number of bakery products.

GLUCOSE

Glucose, which is sometimes called dextrose, is a monosaccharide with the chemical structure shown in Figure 10.1. It is found naturally in a wide range of foods and is the building block of starch and cellulose. In starch it is linked in the alpha form and in cellulose in the beta form.

Glucose is produced commercially by the complete hydrolysis of starch. Both acid and enzyme hydrolysis have been used. The liquor from the hydrolysis process is purified. It is then seeded with glucose crystals and crystallized under carefully controlled conditions. A centrifuge is used to separate the crystals. Glucose is available in particle sizes ranging from granular to a pulverized powder. The monohydrate form contains about 8 percent water and the anhydrous form less than 1 percent water. Glucose is also available in a liquid form with approximately 68 percent solids. This product must be kept at elevated temperatures in order to prevent crystallization.

Glucose is used in yeast doughs as a fermentation substrate for yeast. It is also used to control crystallization of sucrose in candies, for its moderate degree of sweetness and for its water-holding or hygroscopic properties. It is an ingredient in many bakery products, soft drinks, jams and jellies, puddings, and confectionery.

CORN SYRUP

Corn syrup is manufactured by the hydrolysis of corn starch. Acid treatment, sometimes combined with enzymes, is used. Starch is composed of large numbers of α-D-glucose molecules linked together.

(Starch is discussed in Chapter 16.) In the making of corn syrup, the starch molecules are broken down into sub-units of varying size. Among the products present are glucose, maltose, maltotriose and panose (trisaccharides), oligosaccharides with higher numbers of glucose units, and dextrins. The degree of hydrolysis of corn starch is controlled to produce the type of syrup desired, differing in the proportions of glucose, maltose, and higher saccharides. When enzyme hydrolysis is used in combination with acid hydrolysis, a high proportion of maltose results. Corn syrup is available in dry form as well as liquid form. To produce the dry corn syrup solids, refined corn syrup is usually dried in spray or vacuum drum driers to a moisture content less than 3.5 percent.

The term *dextrose equivalent* (D.E.) is used as a measure of the degree to which the starch chain has been hydrolyzed in the making of corn syrup. Dextrose equivalency indicates the total reducing sugar content on a dry basis. Low conversion syrups have D.E. values between 28 and 37, regular conversion syrups between 38 and 47, intermediate conversion syrups between 48 and 57 and high conversion syrups 58 D.E. and over (Keal, 1973). As D.E. values increase, sweetness, fermentability, hygroscopicity, and the capacity to participate in the Maillard or browning reaction increase. Viscosity decreases with increasing hydrolysis and D.E. value. Carbohydrate composition of some of the major commercially available corn syrups is given in Table 10.2.

HIGH FRUCTOSE SYRUPS

Dextrose, or glucose, is only 70–75 percent as sweet as sucrose while fructose or levulose is sweeter than sucrose. Ways to increase the sweetness of corn syrups have been sought for many years. In the 1960s the enzyme glucose isomerase became available from the *Streptomyces* microorganisms, making possible the production of high fruc-

Table 10.2 Carbohydrate Composition of Commercial Corn Syrups

	% Saccharides (on basis of total carbohydrate)					
	Mono-	Di-	Tri-	Tetra-	Penta-	Hexa- and higher
Low conversion (D.E. 27, acid conversion)	9	9	8	7	7	60
Regular conversion (D.E. 42, acid conversion)	20	14	12	9	8	37
High conversion (D.E. 65, acid and enzyme conversion)	39	31	7	5	4	14

Source: From Corn Refiners Association, Inc., 1976.

tose syrup from high dextrose corn syrup. This enzyme may be immobilized on an inert support so that the production of high fructose syrup is a continuous process. The glucose-containing corn syrup is passed through a reactor containing the immobilized enzyme and approximately half of the glucose is converted to fructose by action of the enzyme. The resulting product contains about 71 percent total solids with approximately 42 percent fructose, 50 percent glucose, and minimal amounts of higher saccharides (Mermelstein, 1975).

High fructose corn syrup (HFCS) is being used in the manufacture of soft drinks. Its use is advantageous because of its intense sweetening power, thus allowing lesser quantities to be used than when sweetening is accomplished with corn syrup or sucrose. This decreases the cost to the manufacturer and also may decrease the total sugar intake of the consumers of soft drinks. HFCS can serve the same function as invert sugar in the making of candies, that is, to control crystal size. It may be substituted for all or a portion of other sweeteners in the preparation of pickles, relishes, maraschino cherries, and similar preserved foods. A nutritive medium for yeast growth may be provided by HFCS in the making of yeast breads. It may also be used as a partial replacement for sucrose in soft, moist types of cookies (Fruin and Scallet, 1975). Other uses will undoubtedly be developed in the future.

Sorbitol is a sugar alcohol similar to glucose in structure except that it has an alcohol group instead of an aldehyde group on the first carbon atom. It is used as a stabilizer and sweetener in frozen desserts, cookies, and candies that are prepared for special dietary uses.

10.3

NONENZYMATIC BROWNING

Sugar may participate in several ways in the nonenzymatic browning of food products. Caramelization of dry table sugar when it is heated to very high temperatures produces brown-colored products as described in Section 10.4. Probably the most important nonenzymatic browning reaction involving sugar in foods was first described by Maillard in 1912. The initial step in this reaction is the combination of a reducing sugar and an amino compound. The general reaction is called the *Maillard reaction,* and it is responsible for both desirable and undesirable effects in food products. The browning of bread during baking is due primarily to the Maillard reaction. The browning of other baked products also involves this reaction. Flavor substances as well as color are produced. The brown color which develops in caramels during cooking is due chiefly to the Maillard reaction as the reducing sugars in the corn syrup combine with amino groups on the milk proteins. Undesirable effects of the Maillard reaction occur in dehydrated products such as dry milk and eggs when they are stored for long periods of time.

A series of chemical steps is involved in the Maillard reaction. The first step is the formation of a glycosylamine. For example, glucose may react with an amino group on a protein (indicated by R) as follows:

$$\text{D-glucose} + \text{NH}_2-\text{R} \leftrightarrow \text{D-glucosylamine} + \text{H}_2\text{O}$$

D-glucose   an amine   D-glucosylamine   water

The glycosylamine is rearranged chemically and then undergoes a complex series of changes. Eventually brown pigments are produced by polymerization of compounds formed during the series of reactions.

Reducing sugars that may participate in the Maillard reaction include glucose, fructose, galactose, lactose, and maltose. Sucrose is not a reducing sugar.

The Maillard reaction is affected by the pH of the food involved. An increase in pH (increased alkalinity) causes the browning to occur more rapidly than at lower pH values. The rate of browning is also increased as the water content of the system is decreased to about 18 percent with peak activity at approximately 13 percent (Schultz *et al.,* 1969). Increasing the temperature increases the rate of browning. However, browning may occur with long periods of storage even at relatively low temperatures.

10.4

PROPERTIES OF SUGARS

RELATIVE SWEETNESS OF SUGARS

Sugars are characteristically sweet. Sweetness is a property that is detected by taste. Therefore, the measurement of sweetness for sugars is a subjective measurement that is susceptible to the usual problems of organoleptic evaluation (see Sections 1.1 and 1.4). Taste thresholds differ from one individual to another. Some people are more sensitive than others in detecting sweetness from dilute solutions. Relative sweetness of sugars has often been compared using dilute solutions of pure sugars. The relative sweetness may change if the concentration of the sugar solutions is changed. In addition, if substances other than sugar are present in the solution being tested, the relative sweetness may change. In most testing, sucrose has been used as a standard for comparison with other sugars.

From a number of reports in the scientific literature, some of which are discussed in Section 1.1, it has been determined that fructose is the sweetest of the common sugars. This is followed by sucrose and glucose, respectively. Lactose is the least sweet of the sugars that have been tested.

Table 10.3 Effect of Temperature on the Solubility of Sucrose.

Temperature (°C)	Amount of sucrose soluble in 100 g water (g)
0	179.2
20	203.9
40	238.1
50	260.4
100	487.2
115	669.0

Source: From Browne, 1912.

SOLUBILITY

The solubility of a sugar affects its use in food preparation and processing. If it is very soluble, there is less tendency for the sugar to crystallize out of concentrated solutions, such as those found in jellies and syrups. Solubility increases as the temperature of a solution is raised. The slope of a curve representing increasing solubility with increasing temperature will not be the same for each of the sugars, however. This means that their solubilities must be compared at a specific temperature. At room temperature, fructose is the most soluble of the common sugars, followed by sucrose, glucose, maltose, and lactose respectively. The solubility of sucrose at various temperatures is given in Table 10.3. (The effect on solubilities of mixing two or more sugars is discussed in Section 10.5.)

EFFECT ON BOILING POINT OF WATER

Sugars form true solutions in water. They therefore raise the boiling point of water according to the molal boiling point raising rule discussed in Section 3.4. For every gram molecular weight (GMW) of sugar dissolved in 1000 g of water the boiling point is raised 0.52°C (0.94°F).

Since the boiling point of a sugar solution is directly related to the number of molecules (particles) present, it is an indicator of the concentration of sugar at any point in the boiling process. This is part of the procedure followed in candymaking. Concentration of sugar affects the consistency of finished candy. For a particular formulation of ingredients, there will be a concentration that gives the most desirable consistency in the finished candy. Therefore, the final boiling temperature of a candy mixture is commonly used as an indicator for doneness.

The theoretical boiling point of a sugar solution may be calculated according to the following formula:

$$\text{Boiling Point at sea level (°C)} = 100 + \frac{1000\,(0.52)}{W}\left[\frac{S_1}{M_1} + \frac{S_2}{M_2} + \cdots \frac{S_n}{M_n}\right]$$

S_1 to S_n = grams of each sugar or other solute in true solution
M_1 to M_n = gram molecular weight for each of the sugars or other solutes
W = grams of water in the solution

When dry sucrose is heated it will melt at 160°C (320°F) and form a colorless liquid. If heating continues beyond this point, the color of the material changes from yellow to brown and eventually to black. Sweetness is decreased and eventually lost completely as heating continues. Many complex chemical changes occur during this process which is called *caramelization*. Although these changes are not completely understood, they may first involve the decomposition of sucrose to produce a molecule of glucose and one of fructosan. Fructosan is produced from fructose by the loss of a molecule of water. Removal of a molecule of water from the glucose molecule to produce glucosan may also result during the heating process. These dehydrated monosaccharide molecules tend to combine and polymerize into large molecules. Caramel is probably composed of the dehydrated monosaccharides and their polymers. Sugar acids are also produced in the thermal decomposition process as evidenced by the sudden release of carbon dioxide when soda is added to peanut brittle at the end of the cooking period.

The caramel substances produced when dry sucrose is heated to high temperatures contribute characteristic flavor and color to brittles and similar hard candies. They apparently aid in preventing the crystallization of sugar in these candies.

10.5

CRYSTALLIZATION

When the molecules or atoms of which a substance is composed are arranged in a fixed, orderly pattern the material is called *crystalline*. Each crystal has a definite geometric form that is characteristic of the substance. The crystal pattern repeats itself throughout the entire structure. Crystals are bounded by plane surfaces called *faces*. The faces always intersect at angles peculiar to the substance. Sucrose usually forms crystals having 18 faces (see Figure 10.4). Sodium

Figure 10.4

Sucrose crystals. (Reprinted with permission from Miller, M. D. and G. E. Spaulding, Jr. Free-flowing brown sugars ease handling problems. *Food Engineering,* 1965 [May].)

chloride generally crystallizes as a cube. Water forms six-sided ice crystals.

Although the pattern, and thus the shape, of a crystal is generally characteristic for a given substance, it is possible in some cases to produce different crystal forms of the same substance. This is called *polymorphism* (capable of existing in many forms).

The ease of crystallization of a substance is related to its solubility. The greater the solubility of a solute, the lower will be its tendency to form crystals. Increasing the temperature of a solution increases the solubility of some substances but has little effect on others. The solubility of sucrose is increased with rising temperature and its tendency to crystallize is thus decreased at relatively high temperatures. At 40°C (104°F) 238 g of sucrose are soluble in 100 g of water. At 100°C (212°F) 487 g of sucrose are soluble and at 115°C (239°F) 669 g of sucrose are soluble in 100 g of water.

Assuming that the temperature is constant, a concentrated solution will crystallize more easily and rapidly than a less concentrated one. However, the concentration must be greater than the solubility at that temperature in order for crystallization to occur. An *unsaturated* solution is one to which more solute can be added, a small amount at a time, to produce a series of solutions with successively increasing concentration. The process of adding solute cannot go on indefinitely. Eventually a stage will be reached, distinctive for each substance, at which added solute remains undissolved. In this case a *saturated* solution has been produced, representing the limit of solubility.

It is possible to prepare a solution that has a higher concentration of solute than does a saturated one. This type of solution is called *supersaturated* and is unstable in that the solute will separate or crystallize out very easily. A supersaturated solution of some solutes may be prepared by heating a solution containing excess solute until additional solute dissolves. Cooling this solution very carefully so that crystallization does not occur produces a solution having a concentration of solute higher than that corresponding to a saturated solution. A supersaturated solution is very unstable and crystallization occurs readily. Molecules that are in excess of saturation tend to combine and form nuclei upon which other molecules are deposited to produce crystals. These processes take place in the preparation of crystalline candies such as fondant and fudge. In these products, crystallization proceeds from a supersaturated sucrose solution.

The rate of crystallization and the size of crystals formed from a solution are influenced by temperature. For example, the sucrose in a fondant mixture will crystallize more rapidly if it is beaten when hot (100°C or 212°F) than if it is cooled to 40°C (104°F) before beating. In either case the stirring initiates crystallization by disturbing an unstable solution. However, crystallization occurs more rapidly at the higher temperature because of the more rapid movement of the molecules at that temperature. Sugar crystals will be larger in the fondant crystallized at the higher temperature. The degree of supersaturation is less than at the lower temperature and therefore fewer nuclei are available on which crystals may form. In addition, the great kinetic energy of the sugar molecules at the higher temperature allows them to move quickly onto an already formed crystal, making it larger.

Stirring or agitating a crystallizing solution generally aids in the formation of many small crystals. Mechanical stirring increases surface area and encourages the formation of many small nuclei for crystallization, probably by increasing the rate of heat removal so that the temperature decreases to a point favorable for nucleation. If beating stops or if crystallization occurs in an unstirred solution, fewer nuclei are available for crystal formation. The few crystals present grow into larger ones since the excess molecules of solute coming out of solution are undisturbed and free to migrate to sites on the already formed crystals.

When several substances are present together in solution, the solubility of each of the components may be altered by the presence of the other components. This is the case with a mixture of sugars. For example, the solubility of total sugar is increased above the solubility for any of the separate components when sucrose is present in solution with glucose, fructose, or an equimolecular mixture of glucose and fructose (invert sugar). Figure 10.5 illustrates this effect for a mixture of sucrose and invert sugar in water. The effect of the addition of invert sugar in decreasing the rate of crystallization of sucrose is shown in Figure 10.6. Added invert sugar interferes with the crystallization of sucrose and aids in keeping the crystals small.

Lactose solubility throughout a temperature range was reported by

Figure 10.5

The effect on solubility of mixing sucrose and invert sugar. (After Bates, 1942.)

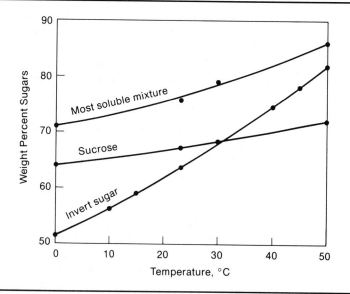

Figure 10.6

Effect of invert sugar on the rate of sucrose crystallization. (After Van Hook, 1946.)

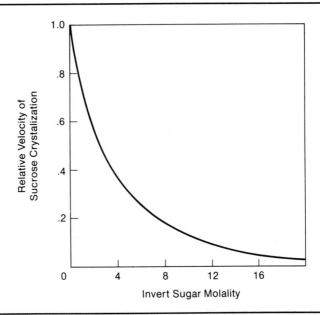

Nickerson and Moore (1972) to be decreased to 40–80 percent of normal by the presence of 40–70 percent sucrose. At a given temperature, lactose solubility decreased as sucrose concentration increased. In contrast, the solubility of sucrose was decreased only slightly by the presence of lactose. Mixtures of lactose and sucrose are present in ice creams.

Substances that form colloidal dispersions or suspensions may change the rate and ease of crystallization of a substance present in true solution. For example, the nonsugar components of a crystalline candy, including milk proteins, butterfat, margarine, and chocolate, may interfere with the crystallization of sucrose by making it more difficult for the sucrose molecules to combine or cluster. Similar ingredients in ice creams and sherbets interfere with the formation of large ice crystals.

10.6

PREPARATION OF CANDIES

CLASSIFICATION

A wide variety of candies are made, both commercially and at home. Several classifications of candies have been proposed. As a simple classification they may be placed into two groups—crystalline and noncrystalline or amorphous. Crystallization is carefully controlled in the preparation of crystalline candies so that the crystals produced are usually very small and not detectable in the mouth. Crystalline candies are characterized by their soft consistency and smooth, creamy texture. They contain approximately 8–13 percent moisture in the final

Table 10-4 Crystalline and Noncrystalline or Amorphous Candies

Type of candy	Final cooking temperature at sea level		Behavior when a small sample is placed in cold water
	(°C)	(°F)	
Crystalline	112–116	234–240	Forms a soft ball which does not retain its shape

Creams
   Fondant
   Butter
Fudge
Pinoche			

Noncrystalline Caramels	118–121	244–250	Forms a firm ball which holds its shape
Marshmallows	121–130	250–266	Forms a hard ball
Butterscotch Taffy	132–143	270–290	Forms hard threads
Brittles Toffee	149–154	300–310	Forms brittle threads

product. Table 10.4 lists a number of crystalline and noncrystalline candies and the final cooking temperature range for each at sea level.

Crystallization is generally prevented in amorphous candies by one or both of two methods. First, in noncrystalline candies such as caramels, a large number of substances are present that interfere with the crystallization of sucrose. These substances include butterfat and milk proteins. Large amounts of glucose are also present in the corn syrup that is used in the preparation of caramels. Glucose affects the solubility of sucrose and interferes with its crystallization.

A second factor that is influential in the prevention of crystallization in amorphous candies is the high degree of concentration of the sugar mixtures. Many of these candies are cooked to very high final temperatures, thus concentrating the mixtures so that they contain only 1–2 percent moisture. Noncrystalline candies such as brittles that are cooked to 149–154°C (300–310°F) will cool very rapidly when they are poured onto a cold, hard surface such as a marble slab. They solidify immediately into a rigid mass and sugar molecules are therefore unable to move into ordered crystals.

CRYSTALLINE CANDIES

A variety of ingredients are used in the preparation of crystalline candies. Sugar (sucrose) is, of course, the major ingredient in each case. A simple fondant may be prepared with sugar and water only. However, small amounts of either cream of tartar (which produces invert sugar) or glucose (in the form of corn syrup) are usually included in fondant recipes that are made at home to aid in the control of sucrose crystal formation. Commercially glucose or invert sugar are commonly used. Creams that are used as the centers for chocolates usually contain a source of fat, such as butter or cream, to give increased richness and ensure small sugar crystal formation. Chocolate fudge usually contains milk, butter, and corn syrup, as well as cocoa or baking chocolate. Chocolate fudge is sometimes made with a comparatively large amount of marshmallow creme added. The marshmallow is a noncrystalline mixture containing egg whites and other stabilizers. It acts as an interfering agent for the crystallization of sucrose and aids in the production of a smooth texture achieved without the usual necessary precautions taken in the cooling and beating of the candy. Pinoche is made with brown sugar and milk.

Major steps in the preparation of all crystalline candies include:

1. Dissolving the sugar completely.
2. Concentrating the solution to the appropriate degree.
3. Supersaturating to the appropriate degree.
4. Crystallizing to give the desired size of sugar crystals.

Dissolving In the preparation of candies, the sugar must be completely dissolved so that no crystals will remain to seed the cooked candy solution and start premature crystallization. Therefore, a relatively large amount of liquid is used in proportion to the amount of sugar in the mixture. Stirring and heating aid in dissolving the sugar. All sugar crystals should be removed from the sides of the pan above the surface of the boiling liquid. This may be done by washing the sides with a small brush dipped in water or by using any butter or margarine in the recipe to rub off the crystals as the fat melts. The fat may be held in the bowl of a wooden spoon. The sugar solution is unsaturated at this point.

Concentrating There are two methods or tests for measuring the degree of doneness in candies. One method, the *cold water test,* measures the consistency of the cooled candy mixture. This may be done by placing a small sample ($\frac{1}{2}$–1 tsp) of the boiling mixture in cold water. Table 10.4 describes the results of these cold water tests as they correspond to various final cooking temperatures. Evaluation of cold water test results is very subjective and subject to error, particularly for the inexperienced individual.

The second method of indicating doneness involves *temperature measurement.* As water is vaporized during the boiling of a candy mixture, the solution gradually becomes more concentrated. The sugar is not volatile and remains in the pan. As concentration thus increases, the boiling point of the solution increases. As the temperature is raised, the solubility of the sugar increases and more can be held in solution.

The boiling point is an indicator of sugar concentration, which is generally related to the consistency of the finished candy. Crystalline candies such as fondant and fudge cooked to a final temperature of 112–116°C (234–240°F) at sea level are generally soft but moldable. Adjustments in the final cooking temperature are made for altitude and for fluctuations in barometric pressure. This is done by adding the desired elevation of temperature above the boiling point of water at sea level to the boiling temperature of water at a particular altitude and barometric pressure. As an approximation, the final cooking temperature will decrease 1°C (1.8°F) for each 960 ft above sea level.

The types of sugars and other substances present in true solution in a candy mixture influence its boiling point and thus the boiling temperature is usually not a true measure of sucrose concentration. The precise optimal final cooking temperature must be determined for each formulation. Glucose and/or invert sugar are often present in crystalline candy mixtures. They raise the boiling point and also affect the consistency of the finished product since they interfere with sucrose crystallization. Proteins and fats do not affect the boiling point of a mixture to any appreciable degree because they are comparatively large particles. However, they do affect the consistency by interfering with crystallization.

Glucose is commonly added in the form of corn syrup to candies made at home. Invert sugar is usually produced from some of the sucrose in fondant during the boiling process by action of the acid salt, cream of tartar, although other sources of acid could be used. The H^+ acts as a catalyst for the hydrolysis of sucrose, yielding invert sugar that is a mixture of equal molecular amounts of glucose and fructose.

$$C_{12}H_{22}O_{11} + H_2O \xrightarrow{\text{H}^+} C_6H_{12}O_6 + C_6H_{12}O_6$$

$$\underset{\text{sucrose}}{} \qquad \underset{\text{glucose}}{} \quad \underset{\text{fructose}}{}$$

$$\underset{\text{invert sugar}}{}$$

The amount of invert sugar produced during the boiling of a candy mixture is variable. More invert sugar will be produced as the amount of added cream of tartar is increased. With approximately $\frac{1}{16}$ tsp (0.2 g) of cream of tartar added to 1 cup (200 g) of sucrose, about 6.5 percent invert sugar was found by Woodruff and Van Gilder (1931) to be present in the finished fondant, while the addition of twice this amount of cream of tartar produced 11.1 percent invert sugar. Approximately 6–15 percent invert sugar appears to be the limit for convenient molding of fondant. Woodruff and Van Gilder (1931) also reported that with 16.3 percent invert sugar a very soft fondant was produced after 50 minutes of beating. Fondant syrups containing 43.4 percent or more invert sugar would not deposit any sucrose crystals even after extended beating and standing times.

The rate of heating will influence the amount of invert sugar formed. A long, slow heating period produces more invert sugar than does a short, rapid period in achieving the same final boiling temperature. When no acid is used in a fondant, only traces of invert sugar are produced.

Supersaturating A crystalline candy mixture is cooled after the appropriate final cooking temperature has been achieved. If it is poured out of the cooking pan onto a hard, cold surface such as a marble slab it will cool rapidly with minimum danger of premature crystal formation. As it cools, undisturbed, it becomes increasingly more supersaturated. A highly supersaturated solution is in a precarious state since it is holding more solute in solution than is ordinarily soluble at that temperature. It will crystallize readily if it is seeded with anything that can act as a nucleus on which crystals may form. Introduction of sugar crystals from a spoon, thermometer, or pan may start crystallization. Even dust particles or rough surfaces may initiate the process, as will agitating the cooling syrup.

Cooling to approximately 40°C (104°F) allows the development of a highly supersaturated solution and yet one that is not too viscous to be easily beaten. A highly supersaturated solution has many nuclei, consisting of a few sugar molecules aggregated together, on which crystals may form.

Crystallizing The final step in the preparation of a crystalline candy is to bring about the formation of many small crystals from the supersaturated sugar solution. The presence of many nuclei in a highly supersaturated solution favors this process since many crystals will form simultaneously. Rapid beating of the mixture also encourages the formation of many nuclei and the production of small crystals because of the moving surfaces and increased surface area created. The candy will suddenly begin to lose its glossy appearance, becoming somewhat opaque and lighter in color, as crystallization occurs. It will also soften slightly as the heat of crystallization is given off. Beating should be continued until the candy is cool and crystallization is essentially complete, as indicated by the change in appearance resulting from the way light is reflected from the crystalline structure. During this stage in the preparation of a crystalline candy a supersaturated solution has become a saturated one.

The sucrose crystals in crystalline candies such as fondant and fudge are suspended in a heavy sugar syrup or a saturated sucrose solution. This saturated solution is in equilibrium with sucrose in solid crystalline form. Figure 10.7 shows a photomicrograph of sugar crystals in fondant.

If fondant is held for 12–24 hours, it becomes somewhat more moist and kneads more easily than when it was first made. This change is called *ripening*. Small crystals in the fondant may dissolve, letting the larger crystals move about more easily.

NONCRYSTALLINE CANDIES

The classification of noncrystalline candies includes hard candies, such as toffee, peanut brittle and lollipops, and chewy candies, such as caramels. In either case, crystallization of sugar does not occur.

In the preparation of hard candies, the major steps are similar in some ways and different in other ways from the steps followed in

Figure 10.7

Sugar crystals in fondant prepared in various ways. (*a*) Crystals from fondant made with sugar, water and cream of tartar; boiled to 115°C and cooled to 40°C before beating. (*b*) Crystals from fondant made with sugar and water with 7 percent glucose added; boiled to 115°C and cooled to 40°C before beating. (*c*) Crystals from fondant made with sugar and water only; boiled to 115°C and cooled to 40°C before beating. (*d*) Crystals from fondant made with sugar and water only; boiled to 115°C and beaten immediately. (Reprinted with permission from Woodruff, S. and H. Van Gilder. 1931. Photomicrographic studies of sucrose crystals. *Journal of Physical Chemistry* Vol. 35, p. 1355. Copyright © by the American Chemical Society.)

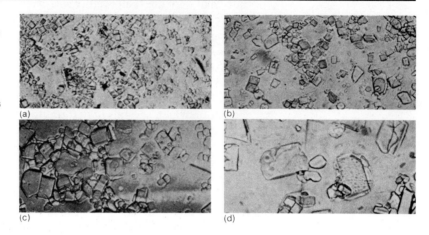

preparing crystalline candies. The first step, that of completely dissolving the sugar, is the same for both types. The second step, concentrating the sugar to an appropriate degree, is also the same. However, the appropriate degree of concentration differs considerably. While most crystalline candies are heated to 112–116°C (234–240°F), brittles and toffees are heated to 149–154°C (300–310°F). The degree of concentration is such that the finished hard candies contain only 1–2 percent moisture. Rapid solidification of the candies on cooling produces a rigid mass that prevents an orderly crystalline pattern from developing within the candy.

The last two major steps in the preparation of candies are different for noncrystalline and crystalline candies. While in crystalline products, securing a high degree of supersaturation and carefully controlling the formation of crystals are essential for success, in noncrystalline candies steps are taken to avoid crystallization completely. A comparatively large quantity of substances that interfere with crystal formation is present in noncrystalline candies such as caramels. Caramels are made with sugar, corn syrup, butter and cream, or evaporated milk.

The ingredients form a thick syrup which is heated only to 118–121°C (244–250°F), at which temperature the syrup forms a firm ball when placed in cold water. Thus the finished caramel may contain from 8 to 22 percent moisture. Glucose from the corn syrup, fat from the butter and cream, and proteins from the milk all interfere with sucrose crystal formation. The brown color and caramel flavor of caramels come primarily from the Maillard or browning reaction.

In brittles and toffee, the high boiling temperature allows some caramelization of sucrose to occur, giving a characteristic brown color and caramel-like flavor. Caramel substances may interfere with sugar crystallization. Some invert sugar may also be produced during cooking. The presence of fat interferes with crystallization of sucrose.

SUMMARY

Sugars are carbohydrates and may be classified as mono- and oligosaccharides. Polysaccharides are composed of many monosaccharide units linked together. Table sugar or sucrose plays diverse roles in various food products. It is a sweetening agent in many foods, a tenderizing agent in baked products, a dehydrating agent in jellies, and the principal ingredient of candies. Sucrose is commercially produced from sugar cane or sugar beets. The juice is extracted from cane by crushing and from beets by soaking. After the juice is clarified to remove nonsucrose impurities, it is concentrated by evaporation under vacuum. The sucrose crystallizes from a supersaturated solution and is separated in a centrifuge. Granulated sucrose is available in a wide range of particle sizes and in powdered form.

Lactose is produced by crystallization from whey dispersions. It may be used as a partial replacement for sucrose in some bakery products.

Glucose is produced by the complete hydrolysis of starch. Acid and/or enzyme catalysts are used in this process. Glucose is crystallized from the hydrolysis liquor. Glucose is useful as a fermentation substrate for yeast, to control crystallization of sucrose in candies, to provide a moderate degree of sweetness, and for its hygroscopic properties.

Incomplete hydrolysis of corn starch yields corn syrup containing a mixture of products which include glucose, maltose, maltotriose, panose, larger oligosaccharides, and dextrins. The degree of hydrolysis of the starch is controlled to produce the type of syrup desired. The term dextrose equivalent (D.E.) is used as a measure of the degree to which the starch chain has been hydrolyzed in the making of corn syrup.

High fructose corn syrup is produced from high glucose corn syrup by the action of the enzyme glucose isomerase. This syrup is very sweet and may be used as a replacement or partial replacement for other sugars in many food products.

The most abundant hexose monosaccharides in foods are D-glucose and D-fructose. D-galactose is one of the monosaccharides making up the disaccharide lactose, the other being glucose. Sucrose is a disaccharide that is found abundantly in the plant world. It contains one molecule of glucose and one of fructose. Maltose is a disaccharide containing two glucose molecules and is formed during the hydrolysis of starch.

Fructose is the sweetest of the common sugars. It is followed by sucrose, glucose, maltose, and lactose. The solubility of sucrose is increased when it is present in solution with either invert sugar or glucose. Sugars raise the boiling point of water. The boiling temperature of a candy solution therefore gives an indication of the concentration of sugar. The final boiling temperature of a candy mixture is commonly used as a test for doneness since sucrose concentration is related to the consistency of the finished candy.

Dry sucrose melts at 160°C (320°F). If heating is continued, caramelization occurs. This involves complex chemical changes that include hydrolysis of sucrose and degradation of the products. Changes in color and flavor accompany the chemical changes.

Candies may be classified as crystalline, including fondant and fudge, and noncrystalline, including caramels, taffy, brittles, and toffee. In the preparation of crystalline candies the major steps are 1. dissolving the sugar completely; 2. concentrating the solution to the appropriate degree; 3. supersaturating to the appropriate degree; and 4. crystallizing to give the desired size of sugar crystals. All of the sugar must be dissolved in order to avoid seeding the cooked mixture with crystals and starting premature crystallization. Crystalline candies are usually cooked to a final boiling temperature of 112–116°C (234–240°F) at sea level. Glucose or invert sugar is commonly used in crystalline candies to interfere with crystallization of sucrose. Invert sugar may be produced during boiling by the action of H+ (from cream of tartar) on sucrose.

A highly supersaturated solution is produced by cooling the candy mixture to about 40°C (104°F). This solution will have many nuclei on which crystals may form as the mixture is beaten. Crystallization is controlled by beating the highly supersaturated solution. The resulting crystals are numerous and small in size.

Crystallization is prevented in noncrystalline candies by 1. adding a comparatively large quantity of substances that will interfere with the crystallization of sucrose, such as invert sugar, glucose, protein, and fat, and/or 2. concentrating the mixture to a high degree. The highly concentrated candy mixture rapidly solidifies into a rigid mass upon cooling and sugar molecules are unable to move into ordered crystals.

Sugars and syrups are produced in considerable quantity in the United States.

1. Name the two most common sources of commercially produced sucrose.
2. Describe the general procedures used for the production of lactose, glucose, corn syrup, and high fructose syrup.
3. Define monosaccharide, disaccharide, and polysaccharide. Give examples of each.
4. Which of the following sugars are pentoses and which are hexoses?

    Sugars
      arabinose
      fructose or levulose
      galactose
      glucose or dextrose
      ribose
      xylose

5. List important food sources of glucose, fructose, galactose, sucrose, lactose, and maltose.

Sugars differ from one another in sweetness and in solubility.

6. Rank fructose, glucose, lactose, and sucrose in order of increasing sweetness.
7. Rank fructose, glucose, lactose, maltose, and sucrose in order of decreasing solubility.

Sucrose melts and then decomposes in a caramelization process when heated to high temperatures.

8. Describe changes in physical appearance and chemical structure as dry sucrose is heated to 160°C (320°F) and above.
9. Describe and explain possible effects of caramelized sugar on the crystallization of sucrose in certain types of hard candies.

Sugars in solution raise the boiling point of water.

10. Calculate the theoretical boiling point of the following mixture:
       400 g (2 cups) sucrose
       25 g ($\frac{1}{4}$ cup) glucose
       474 g (2 cups) water
    GMW sucrose, 342; glucose, 180)
11. Define invert sugar.
12. Write a reaction for the production of invert sugar during the preparation of fondant, including the catalyst for the reaction.
13. Explain how invert sugar aids in controlling the size of sucrose crystals in crystalline candies.

Candies may be classified into two groups on the basis of crystallization.

14. List examples of each of two types of candies classified on the basis of crystallization.
15. Describe and explain the effect of each of the following on the ease and rate of crystallization of sucrose from a solution:

a. Concentration and degree of supersaturation.
b. Temperature.
c. Stirring or agitation.
d. Presence of invert sugar or glucose.
e. Presence of fat and proteins.

16. Describe each of the major steps involved in the preparation of a crystalline candy such as fondant or fudge and explain what is happening at each step.
17. Describe and explain the major purpose(s) or role(s) in candymaking of cream of tartar, corn syrup, butter or margarine, milk, and chocolate.

The internal structure of a crystalline candy consists of a complex system of dispersed particles in a water-based dispersion medium.

18. Using fondant made with sugar, water, and cream of tartar, describe and explain the probable types of dispersion systems present in the finished product.

The preparation of noncrystalline candies differs somewhat from that of crystalline candies.

19. Describe the major steps involved in the preparation of hard noncrystalline candies, such as brittles and toffee, and of chewy noncrystalline candies such as caramels.
20. Explain the development of brown color and caramel flavor in caramels.
21. Explain how crystallization is prevented in both the hard and the chewy types of noncrystalline candies.

Doneness may be assessed in candies by use of a thermometer measuring final cooking temperature or by the cold water test measuring consistency.

22. Describe advantages for each of the tests mentioned above and explain what is being measured in each case.
23. Indicate standard temperature ranges at sea level for soft ball, firm ball, hard ball, soft crack, and hard crack cold water tests.
24. Calculate the most appropriate final cooking temperature for a fondant mixture at an altitude of 4800 ft above sea level.

Theoretical information may be applied to solve the practical problems of making candies at home.

25. Explain the problems and make recommendations for the following situation:

    Ms. B, who lives in the mountains at 4500 ft above sea level, decided to make fudge. She measured the ingredients carefully, mixed them together, and boiled the mixture to 114°C (236°F). She let the mixture stand in the pan in which it was cooked for about 10 minutes after cooking was completed. Then she stirred the mixture vigorously. The finished candy was coarse-textured or grainy and very hard. She threw it away before the other family members came home.

REFERENCES

1. Bates, F. J. and Associates. 1942. Polarimetry, saccharimetry and the sugars. Washington, D. C.: U. S. National Bureau of Standards Circ. No. 440.

2. Borgstrom, G. 1968. *Principles of Food Science,* Vol. 1. New York: Macmillan Company.

3. Browne, C. A. 1912. *A Handbook of Sugar Analysis*. New York: John Wiley and Sons.

4. Corn Refiners Association, Inc. 1976. Nutritive sweeteners from corn. Washington, D. C.: Corn Refiners Association, Inc.

5. Fruin, J. C. and B. L. Scallet. 1975. Isomerized corn syrups in food products. *Food Technology* 29 (No. 11), 40.

6. Guy, E. J. 1971. Lactose. *Bakers Digest* 45 (Apr.), 34.

7. Keal, E. J. 1973. Sweeteners for baked foods. *Bakers Digest* 47 (Oct.), 80.

8. Life Sciences Research Office. 1976. Evaluation of the health aspects of sucrose as a food ingredient. Prepared for the Food and Drug Administration. Bethesda, Maryland: Federation of American Societies for Experimental Biology.

9. Mermelstein, N. H. 1975. Immobilized enzymes produce high-fructose corn syrup. *Food Technology* 29 (No. 6), 20.

10. Nickerson, T. A. and E. E. Moore. 1972. Solubility interrelations of lactose and sucrose. *Journal of Food Science* 37, 60.

11. Schultz, H. W., R. F. Cain, and R. W. Wrolstad, editors. 1969. *Carbohydrates and Their Roles*. Westport, Conn.: Avi Publishing Co.

12. Sipple, H. L. and K. W. McNutt, editors. 1974. *Sugars in Nutrition*. New York: Academic Press.

13. Van Hook, A. 1946. Kinetics of sucrose crystallization. Sucrose-nonsucrose solutions. *Industrial and Engineering Chemistry* 38, 50.

14. Woodruff, S. and H. Van Gilder. 1931. Photomicrographic studies of sucrose crystals. *Journal of Physical Chemistry* 35, 1355.

CHAPTER 11

FROZEN DESSERTS

Most of the ice cream consumed in the United States is manufactured commercially. However, some is still made at home, particularly on special occasions. Homemade ice creams differ from those made commercially because stabilizing ingredients and freezing equipment are different. Principles of ice crystallization are the same in both products.

11.1

FREEZING POINTS OF SOLUTIONS

A pure liquid freezes at a specific temperature. The *freezing point* is that temperature at which a liquid and its solid form remain in equilibrium indefintely. *Equilibrium* exists at the temperature at which the vapor pressure of the liquid equals that of its solid form. Figure 2.1 shows the temperature at which the vapor pressure of water is equal to the vapor pressure of ice. This temperature, 0°C (32°F), is the freezing point of pure water.

When a solute is added to water, the freezing point of the solution is lowered below that of pure water. The molal freezing point lowering rule states this relationship as follows:

For every gram molecular weight (GMW) of solute in 1000 g of water the freezing point is lowered 1.86°C (3.35°F).

The vapor pressure of water is decreased by the presence of solute particles. The decrease is apparent at all temperatures, as illustrated for a one molal solution in Figure 2.1. Therefore, when the temperature of an aqueous solution is lowered to 0°C (32°F) the vapor pressure of the solution is not equal to the vapor pressure of the ice. Equilibrium does not occur until the temperature is lowered to −1.86°C (28.7°F). This temperature, then, represents the freezing point of a one molal solution. If the solute ionizes in solution and thus separates into two or more particles, the effect on the freezing point is increased in proportion to the number of particles produced. With formation of two ions, such as $NaCl \rightarrow Na^+ + Cl^-$, the effect on the freezing point is doubled. If three ions are formed, the effect is tripled.

11.2

FREEZING MIXTURES OF ICE AND SALT

When water and ice are mixed, a temperature of 0°C (32°F) is achieved as equilibrium is established. A mixture of water and ice cannot be used to freeze food products, including frozen desserts, because the freezing points of these products are all below 0°C (32°F). When salt (usually sodium chloride) and crushed ice are mixed, however, a temperature lower than 0°C (32°F) is produced.

At any temperature above the freezing point of water, water will be present on the surface of ice as it begins to melt. When salt is mixed with the ice, some of it dissolves in this water, forming a concentrated salt solution or brine. The solution and the ice are not in equilibrium with each other because the vapor pressure of the solution differs from that of ice. In an attempt to reach equilibrium, more ice melts. The melting of ice is an endothermic process, absorbing 80 calories per gram of ice as latent heat. This heat is absorbed from the surroundings, including the brine itself. Since cold is merely the absence of heat, cooling occurs in this mixture as ice melts.

As more ice melts, in an ice and salt mixture, more salt dissolves. The concentrated salt solution again upsets the equilibrium in terms of vapor pressures and stimulates the additional melting of ice. This process continues as long as there is ice to melt and salt to dissolve. The temperature of the ice and salt mixture will decrease until it reaches the freezing point of a saturated salt solution, at which point no more salt can dissolve. The freezing point for a saturated sodium chloride solution is approximately −21°C (−6°F).

Salt and ice mixtures may be used for the freezing of ice cream and other frozen desserts. The brine becomes very cold, considerably below the freezing point of ice cream, as ice continues to melt and absorb heat. Heat is absorbed by the brine from the ice cream mix which is placed in a metal container and surrounded by the ice and salt mixture. Metal is an excellent conductor and allows the passage of heat from the ice cream mix to the brine.

An effective proportion of salt to ice for freezing ice cream is approximately one part to eight parts, by volume. A somewhat higher proportion of salt to ice may be used for freezing fruit ices because they have a larger concentration of sugar and, therefore, a lower freezing temperature than do ice creams. After freezing has been accomplished, the frozen dessert is repacked with a higher proportion of salt to ice, approximately one part to four parts, for hardening.

An ice cream freezer usually consists of an inner metal container which holds the mix that is to be frozen. A dasher is placed in this container and scrapes the sides of the container as the freezer is turned, stirring the mix during the freezing process. A space between the inner and an outer container holds the ice and salt mixture. The freezer may be turned by an electric motor. Freezers which may be placed in a freezing compartment for operation are also available. The freezer container should not be filled more than two-thirds full in order to allow for expansion of the mix during freezing. The freezer should be turned slowly at first. This prevents churning or de-emulsification of fat particles in the mixture while it is being cooled to the point where ice crystallization begins. The freezer should then be turned rapidly while crystallization is occurring. This aids in keeping crystals small by scraping them off the sides of the container as they form and preventing their growth. It also incorporates air into the mixture.

11.2

COMPOSITION AND PROPERTIES OF FROZEN DESSERTS

For regulatory purposes, ice creams and similar products, sometimes called frozen dairy foods, are classified on the basis of composition. Table 11.1 gives such a classification. The federal standard for minimum weight per gallon of ice cream is 4.5 lb.

Quality in frozen desserts is concerned with texture, body, and flavor. Texture is determined by "mouth feel". Usually a smooth, fine texture is preferred with no detectable feel of ice crystals. Therefore, ice crystals must be small and numerous. Frozen desserts should be firm enough to hold their shapes. The hardness or softness is determined by the amount of water frozen or the proportion of ice crystals to unfrozen syrup. Body refers to melting characteristics. As an ice cream melts it may range from watery to very viscous. A moderate degree of viscosity as it melts is usually desirable. Body is influenced by the characteristics of the unfrozen syrup.

Ingredients are important in determining quality. Each ingredient contributes in a particular way to the characteristics of the final product.

FAT

The federal Standard of Identity published by the U. S. Food and Drug Administration specifies that ice cream must contain at least 10 percent butterfat. Most state standards also require a 10 percent minimum. The butterfat content of commercial ice cream is usually 10–12 percent. Fat gives richness and promotes desirable textural qualities that are apparent through "mouth feel". It contributes flavor and is a good carrier and synergist for added flavor compounds (Arbuckle, 1972).

Butterfat globules distributed in an ice cream mix are protected and kept separated by a protein film on their surfaces. The average size of the fat particles in their natural state is about $5\mu m$ in diameter. This is reduced to about $1-2$ μm by homogenization of the mix. During the whipping and freezing of ice cream the protective protein layer rup-

Table 11-1. Classification of Frozen Dairy Foods

Type	Distinguishing characteristics	Suggested regulatory limitations
Frozen custard	High in egg yolk solids, cooked to a custard before freezing. Medium to high in milk fat and milk solids not fat. With or without fruit, nuts, bakery products, candy, etc.	Not more than 0.5% edible stabilizer. Not less than 1.4% egg solids for plain and 1.12% for bulky flavors. Not less than 10% milk fat. Not less than 20% total milk solids.
Plain ice cream	Medium to high in milk fat and milk solids not fat. With or without egg products. Without visible particles of flavoring material. With the total volume of color and flavor less than 5% of the volume of the un-frozen ice cream.	Not more than 0.5% edible stabilizer. Not less than 10% milk fat. Not less than 20% total milk solids.
Composite ice cream or bulky flavors	Medium to high in milk fat and milk solids not fat. With or without egg products. With the total volume of color and flavor material more than 5% of the volume of the unfrozen ice cream or with visible particles of flavorings such as cocoa, fruit, nuts, etc.	Not more than 0.5% edible stabilizer. Not less than 8% milk fat. Not less than 16% total milk solids.
Ice milk	Low in milk fat. With or without egg products, chocolate, fruit, nuts, etc.	Not more than 0.5% edible stabilizer. Not less than 2% nor more than 7% milk fat. Not less than 11% total milk solids.
Sherbet	Low in milk solids not fat. Tart flavor.	Not less than 0.35% acidity. Not less than 2% nor more than 5% total milk solids.
Ice	No milk solids. Tart flavor.	
Imitation ice cream	Proper labeling required. Mellorine-types have butter-fat replaced by another fat. Parevine-types contain no dairy ingredients.	

Source: Adapted from Arbuckle, 1972.

tures and allows clustering or de-emulsification of fat globules to a limited extent. Extensive de-emulsification is hindered by the simultaneous formation of ice crystals, which average 20–40 μm in diameter. Whipping apparently distributes the solidified fat particles throughout the liquid syrup phase between air cells and among ice crystals (Shama and Sherman, 1966).

The federal Standard of Identity for ice milk requires a minimum of 2 percent butterfat and a maximum of 7 percent. As a consequence of lower fat content, ice milk is less rich and smooth than ice cream. The Standard of Identity for milk sherbet does not specify fat content. Very little is present in sherbet and none in ices.

MILK SOLIDS NOT FAT

Milk solids not fat (MSNF) contain approximately 36.7 percent protein, 55.5 percent lactose and 7.8 percent minerals. The proteins contribute to good body and smoothness in ice cream. Govin and Leeder (1971) found that MSNF, at the level normally used in ice cream, had sufficient emulsifying capacity to emulsify the fat present in a standard ice cream mix. The lactose adds to the sweet taste of ice cream and the minerals contribute a salty flavor. Since lactose is relatively insoluble, it may crystallize and cause a sandy texture if MSNF are used in ice cream in excessive amounts (Arbuckle, 1972).

SWEETENERS

A proper balance of sugar should be added to ice cream in order to produce acceptable sweetness and enhance the flavor of other ingredients while not masking desirable flavors with excessive sweetness. Sugar increases the viscosity of the mix and improves body and texture in the frozen product. Since it forms a true solution, it lowers the freezing point of the mix. The amount added is usually 14–16 percent. For many years sucrose was the only sweetening agent used. However, in recent years other sweeteners have been employed as a partial replacement for sucrose. Corn syrups and corn syrup solids are used commercially for ice cream in the interest of economy, good body, and smooth texture. A flavor defect has been noted when some corn sweeteners are added to ice cream. Eskamani and Leeder (1972) fractionated the various saccharide components of corn syrup and used each of them in the preparation of ice cream. They concluded that a group of oligosaccharides was responsible for the so-called syrup flavor. Others had previously suggested that the high molecular weight saccharides in corn syrup were the responsible agents for the flavor defect.

Simpfendorfer and Martin (1964) prepared ice milks containing 5 percent corn syrup solids of different dextrose equivalents (D.E.) combined with 12 percent sucrose. These products had satisfactory body, texture, and sweetness and were similar in quality to ice milk made with sucrose alone. It was only in a few instances that quality differences between samples were great enough to be detected by two consumer groups.

Several researchers have reported on consumer preferences for ice creams containing varying amounts of sugar. Pangborn *et al.* (1957) presented, to over 6000 consumers, samples of vanilla ice cream containing 11, 13, 15, 17, or 19 percent sugar. The ice creams with the three higher levels of sugar were equally well liked but were preferred to a significant degree over the samples with the 11 and 13 percent levels. Pangborn and Nickerson (1959) found that 650 consumers, as well as a trained laboratory panel, preferred strawberry ice cream containing 19.2 percent sugar over samples with 15.9, 17.6, and 20.8 percent sugar. Chocolate ice creams containing 13, 15, 17, and 19 percent sugar were presented to 718 consumers by Finnegan and Sheuring (1962a). The 17 percent and 19 percent sugar-containing ice creams were preferred over the 18 percent and 15 percent samples.

Sherbets and ices contain tart fruits or fruit juices. They require more sugar for sweetening than do ice creams.

EGG YOLK SOLIDS Egg yolk solids give a characteristic delicate flavor to ice cream and aid in obtaining a desirable blending of other flavors. They increase the viscosity of the mix and improve the body and texture of the frozen ice cream. They also improve whipping ability (Arbuckle, 1972).

STABILIZERS Most ice creams that are made commercially employ stabilizers. The use of stabilizers 1. improves smoothness; 2. aids in preventing ice crystal formation during storage; 3. gives desired resistance to melting; and 4. improves handling properties (Arbuckle, 1972). A maximum of 0.5 percent stabilizer is allowed in the federal standards for ice cream. Usually from 0.2 to 0.3 percent is used. Finnegan and Sheuring (1962b) prepared chocolate ice cream samples with varying content of an emulsifier-stabilizer mixture (0.14, 0.24, 0.34, and 0.44 percent). A group of 1073 consumers evaluated the products. They preferred the ice cream with 0.24 percent emulsifier-stabilizer over the other three samples. The preferred sample was described as creamier, smoother, and with a more delectable chocolate flavor than the other samples.

Stabilizers used extensively in frozen dairy foods include (Arbuckle, 1972):

Sodium and propylene glycol alginates
Carboxymethylcellulose
Guar gum
Locust bean gum
Carrageenan (Irish moss extract)
Gelatin
Pectin

Pectin is used in combination with vegetable gums as a stabilizer in sherbets and ices. Commercial stabilizer products are usually blends of the various stabilizing substances. These stabilizers, with the possible exception of gelatin, are not often used in preparing home ice creams.

EMULSIFIERS

Mono- or diglycerides are commonly used as emulsifying ingredients in the manufacture of ice cream for improved whipping quality, body, and texture. The total emulsifier content should not exceed 0.2 percent. Two polyoxyethylene-type emulsifiers may be used in amounts up to 0.1 percent.

For many years, it was assumed that emulsifiers reduced the interfacial tension between the fat phase and the aqueous phase in ice cream. This supposedly permitted a finer dispersion of the fat in the mix, produced a fine air cell structure, and improved whipping ability. Based on later work, it would appear that the role of an emulsifier, in the complex system that is ice cream, is not this simple. Lin and Leeder (1974) have suggested that different emulsifiers act differently in ice cream. They proposed that emulsifiers with strong lipophilic (fat-loving) groups become firmly associated with fat globules. They may then aid in maintaining stability of the fat emulsion during agitation and freezing. An emulsifier with a stronger hydrophilic (water-loving) group, on the other hand, may be more loosely held by the fat globule and is more easily swept off during agitation in the freezer. This would allow more de-emulsification to occur among the fat globules. Govin and Leeder (1971) suggested that the chief role of the emulsifier may lie in producing a controlled de-emulsification of the fat globules for the development of desired structure, stiffness, and melt resistance.

11.4

STRUCTURE OF ICE CREAM

Frozen ice cream, according to Sherman (1965), is an aerated emulsion, or foam (see Figure 11.1). It contains a dispersion or suspension of air in a liquid (unfrozen syrup containing sugar in true solution), with the liquid being dispersed in sheets called *lamellae*. Air may constitute about 50 percent of the total volume. Ice crystals are suspended in the lamellae. Fat globules are dispersed among the ice crystals. A colloidally dispersed protein film is adsorbed around the fat globules. Protein also envelops the air cells as the foam is formed.

Most structural changes in ice cream occur during the freezing process. The development of satisfactory texture in the frozen product is influenced by the presence of fat globules of small size and by a controlled level for the coalescing of fat globules (Sherman, 1965). The physical actions in the freezer are apparently some of the main factors affecting the de-emulsification of the fat (Lin and Leeder, 1974).

11.5

PREPARATION OF ICE CREAM

The commercial preparation of a high quality ice cream requires first the selection of high quality ingredients and the blending of these ingredients in the proper proportions into a mix. The mix is then processed

Figure 11.1

The internal structure of ice cream. (a) Ice crystals—average size, from 45 to 55 microns. (b) Air cells—average size, from 110 to 185 microns. (c) Unfrozen material—average distance between ice crystals or ice crystals and air cells, from 6 to 8 microns. Average distance between air cells—from 100 to 150 microns. (Reprinted with permission from Arbuckle, W. S. 1972. *Ice Cream,* 2nd edition, p. 246. Westport, CT. Copyright © Avi Publishing Company.)

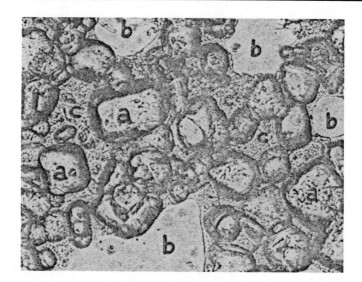

through several basic steps. These include pasteurization, homogenization, cooling, aging, flavoring, freezing, packaging, and hardening storage. The procedure used for making ice cream may range from a small batch operation to a large automatic continuous operation with the metering of ingredients into the batch (Arbuckle, 1972).

Pasteurization of the ice cream mix is required to destroy any pathogenic microorganisms that might be present. It also aids in blending the ingredients. It may be done by the batch method at 68°C (115°F) for not less than 30 minutes, by the high temperature-short time method at 79°C (175°F) for not less than 25 seconds, or at an ultra high temperature.

The homogenization process involves forcing the mix through a small orifice under suitable conditions of temperature and pressure. The size of the fat globules in the mix is reduced to a very small diameter, preferably less than 2 μm. The separation of fat from the mix is prevented by homogenization. Homogenization also contributes to the production of a smooth-textured ice cream and improves the ice cream's whipping properties. The surface area of fat globules is greatly increased as the size of the particles is reduced. MSNF participate in the process of coating the newly formed fat surfaces. There is not enough of the protein-phospholipid material that was present on the original fat globules to put a protective coat on all of the newly formed ones.

The homogenized mix is cooled immediately to about 4.4°C (40°F). This aids in controlling the viscosity. It also retards the growth of bacteria.

After homogenization and cooling, the mix is held at 2.2–4.4°C (36–40°F) for a few hours in a process called aging. During this time the fat is solidified and the viscosity is increased. If gelatin has been used as a stabilizer, it swells and absorbs water during this period. Smooth texture in the frozen ice cream, resistance to melting and ease of whipping are benefits of aging the ice cream mix. After aging, the mix is ready for freezing. Color and flavoring materials are usually added at the freezer.

The freezing process brings about the crystallization of water to ice and, at the same time, agitation during freezing incorporates air into the mixture. Air bubbles are stabilized by proteins from milk or cream that are denatured at the air–liquid interface. A foam is thus formed during the freezing process.

Small ice crystals are essential for a smooth texture in frozen ice cream. When commercial freezing equipment is used, with its powerful mixing action, fast freezing contributes to the development of many small crystals. The ice crystals are essentially pure water in a solid form. Freezing removes water which is acting as a solvent from the solution. The sugar and other solutes in the mix become more concentrated as the freezing process continues to remove water. The freezing point of the ice cream mix decreases as the solution becomes more concentrated. The temperature of the freezing ice cream is thus gradually lowered. This process continues until the concentration of solute is so great that freezing will not occur. All of the water in an ice cream does not freeze. From 33 to 67 percent of the water may be frozen in the first phase of freezing. Additional ice crystallizes as the frozen ice cream is packaged and placed in a hardening room. It achieves a temperature of −18°C (0°F) or lower at this stage.

During the freezing process, as ice crystals are forming in the lamellae between air cells, solidified fat particles are deposited among the ice crystals. Some of them are de-emulsified as the agitation of the freezing process removes their protective protein and emulsifier coating. Both the ice crystals and the fat globules give structure to the ice cream. Milk proteins, sugars, salts, and stabilizers are dispersed in the liquid phase of the ice cream.

Commercial ice cream must withstand the usual handling procedures of marketing. These include storage at variable freezing temperatures and short periods of exposure to heat. Frazeur and Harrington (1968a) reported that ice creams frozen at −9.3°C (15°F) in a low temperature ice cream freezer resisted the effects of storage, changing storage temperatures, and heat shocking better than did similar ice creams frozen in a conventional freezer at −6.1°C (21°F). Temperature of freezing was more important than length of storage time, temperature of storage, and severity of heat shocking in contributing to satisfactory body and texture in the ice cream (Frazeur and Harrington, 1968b).

Overrun is defined as the volume of ice cream obtained in excess of the volume of the mix (Arbuckle, 1972). It is usually expressed as *percent overrun* and is composed mainly of air incorporated during the freezing process. Too much air produces a fluffy ice cream while too little gives a heavy, soggy product. Ice creams with a higher total solids content may be of better quality with higher overrun than are ice creams with lower solids. A satisfactory amount of overrun in many packaged ice creams is 70–80 percent. Bulk ice creams often have 90–100 percent overrun. Sherbets commonly have 30–40 percent overrun.

Homemade ice creams that are stirred during freezing are usually made in a freezer which uses an ice and salt mixture to achieve low temperatures. Overrun is generally less in homemade ice creams than in commercial products. It may be 35–50 percent.

Ingredients used in homemade ice creams usually include sweetened milk and cream with flavoring. Additional MSNF or stabilizing substances such as egg and gelatin may be used to increase the body of the product and contribute to smoothness. The ice crystals appear to be smaller when such products are used. Stirring helps to keep the ice crystals small and air incorporated.

If ice creams are frozen without stirring, ice crystals tend to be larger than if they are stirred. Rapid freezing and using a relatively large proportion of substances that interfere with ice crystal formation are measures that help to produce a smooth ice cream. These substances include cream, MSNF, gelatin, pectin, egg, and chocolate. The mixture may be removed from the freezing compartment at intervals and stirred during freezing in order to incorporate some air. Whipping cream, with a fat content of approximately 35 percent, is effective in interfering with ice crystal formation. A mousse is made of sweetened and flavored whipped cream and is frozen without stirring.

SUMMARY

Most of the ice cream consumed in the United States is manufactured commercially although some is still made at home. Ingredients and freezing equipment differ from home to factory but the principles of ice crystallization are used in both types of production.

The freezing point of a pure liquid is that temperature at which the liquid and its solid form remain in equilibrium indefinitely. They are in equilibrium when their vapor pressures are the same. The freezing point of water is lowered by the addition of a solute. The effect is greater for substances which ionize because more than one particle is produced from one molecule.

A mixture of coarse salt (usually sodium chloride) and crushed ice is used to freeze ice cream and other frozen desserts at home. When salt is mixed with the ice, some of it dissolves in the small amount of liquid present on the ice, forming a brine. The salt solution and the ice are not in equilibrium. In an attempt to reach equilibrium, more ice melts, absorbing heat in an endothermic process. More salt then dissolves and the process is repeated. Cold is merely the absence of heat and the rapid melting of ice removes heat from its surroundings, including the brine itself. The temperature of the ice and salt mixture decreases until it reaches the freezing point of a saturated sodium chloride solution, approximately $-21°C$ ($-6°F$).

About one part of salt to eight parts of ice, by volume, can be effectively used to freeze ice cream. The dessert may be hardened with a mixture of from one part of salt to four parts of ice.

Frozen desserts may be classified as frozen custard, plain ice cream, composite ice cream or bulky flavors, ice milk, sherbet, ice, and imitation ice cream. Small ice crystals in each of these products contribute to a smooth texture. The hardness or softness is determined by the amount of water that is frozen. Body is influenced by the characteristics of the unfrozen syrup.

The federal Standard of Identity specifies that ice cream must contain at least 10 percent butterfat, 20 percent total milk solids, and weigh at least 4.5 lb per gallon. Most state standards also require these minima. Fat gives richness and promotes desirable textural qualities. It contributes flavor. Butterfat globules in ice cream mix are kept separated by a protein film on their surfaces. During agitation and freezing some de-emulsification of the fat globules occurs.

Milk solids not fat (MSNF) contributes to good body and smoothness in ice cream. It emulsifies the fat present in an ice cream mix after it is homogenized. Lactose is insoluble and may crystallize in the ice cream if MSNF is used in excessive amounts.

Sugar sweetens ice cream. It also increases the viscosity of the mix and improves body and texture in the frozen product. Corn syrups and corn syrup solids may be used as a partial replacement for sucrose. Several studies have reported that consumers prefer ice creams with higher sugar content than is commonly employed in the manufacture of commercial ice cream (14–16 percent).

Egg yolk solids increase the viscosity of the ice cream mix and improve body and texture in the frozen product. Stabilizers, such as alginates, carboxymethylcellulose, carrageenan, and gelatin, improve smoothness, aid in preventing ice crystal formation during storage, give desired resistance to melting, and improve handling properties. The role of emulsifiers in ice cream is complex. They may produce controlled de-emulsification of the fat globules during freezing and thus contribute to the development of desired structure, stiffness, and melt resistance.

Ice cream is an aerated emulsion, or foam. Air is dispersed in a concentrated sugar syrup. Ice crystals are suspended between air cells. Fat globules are dispersed among the ice crystals and are surrounded by colloidal protein films.

Processes included in the production of commercial ice cream are pasteurization, homogenization, cooling, aging, flavoring, freezing, packaging, and hardening. Pasteurization destroys pathogenic microorganisms and aids in the blending of ingredients. Homogenization decreases the size of the fat globules and prevents fat separation. It improves whipping ability. During aging the fat is solidified and the viscosity is increased.

Freezing brings about the crystallization of water to ice and also incorporates air with agitation. Small ice crystals are produced with fast freezing and whipping. The freezing point of an ice cream mix decreases as freezing proceeds. From 33 to 67 percent of the water may be frozen in the first phase of freezing. Additional ice crystallizes with the hardening of the ice cream at low temperatures. Low temperature freezing apparently improves ice cream's resistance to improper handling procedures.

Overrun is the volume of ice cream obtained in excess of the volume of the mix. It is usually 70–80 percent in packaged ice creams and 35–50 percent in homemade ice creams stirred while freezing.

Homemade ice creams may be stirred or left unstirred during freezing. If they are frozen without stirring, rapid freezing and the addition of substances that will interfere with ice crystal formation contribute to smooth texture. Interfering substances may include cream, MSNF, gelatin, pectin, egg, and chocolate.

STUDY QUESTIONS

A pure liquid freezes at a specific temperature.

1. Define the freezing point of a liquid.

Energy transformations occur when water is frozen and thawed.

2. List the calories per gram released or absorbed as water is frozen or thawed.

Ice and salt mixtures may be used to produce low temperatures.

3. Explain why a solute lowers the freezing point of pure water.
4. Explain, in terms of the absorption of heat by melting ice and the lowered freezing point of a salt solution, why low temperatures result from ice and salt mixtures.

Frozen desserts may be classified, for regulatory purposes, on the basis of composition.

5. List and describe each of seven categories of frozen desserts in terms of composition.
6. From the following information concerning the composition of a frozen dessert, classify it into one of the categories listed in question 5.

Information on composition
Butterfat 12 percent
Egg solids 1.5 percent
Sugar 15 percent

Each ingredient contributes in a particular way to the characteristics of a frozen dessert.

7. Describe and explain the role(s) of each of the following ingredients in ice cream or ice milk:
   a. Butterfat
   b. Milk solids not fat
   c. Sucrose and corn syrup
   d. Stabilizers
   e. Emulsifiers

The internal structure of ice cream is a complex system of dispersed ingredients.

8. Describe the usual internal structure of a good quality ice cream. Account for air, water, fat, proteins, sugars, salts, and ice crystals.
9. Explain how the physical dispersion of air, fat, and ice crystals may affect the texture and the body of frozen ice cream.

The preparation of commercial ice cream involves several processes.

10. Describe the general process and explain the main purpose(s) for each of the following in the preparation of ice cream:
    a. Pasteurization
    b. Homogenization
    c. Aging
    d. Freezing
    e. Hardening

Different processes operate to control ice crystal size in stirred and unstirred frozen desserts.

11. Describe and explain procedures that will help to control the size of ice crystals in the preparation of still-frozen ice cream at home.

Freezing points of ice creams differ from those of sherbets and ices.

12. Rank the following three frozen desserts in decreasing order of temperature at which freezing will begin. Explain any differences in freezing points among the desserts.

Mixture 1	Mixture 2	Mixture 3
2 cups sugar	2 cups milk	2 cups sugar
2 cups orange juice	$\frac{1}{2}$ cup sugar	3 cups pineapple juice
$\frac{3}{4}$ cup lemon juice	1 cup whipping cream	$\frac{1}{3}$ cup lemon juice
1 cup water	1 tsp vanilla	2 cups water

(Note: Consider fruit juices to contain 12 percent glucose and 88 percent water; milk, 3.5 percent protein, 4 percent fat, 5 percent carbohydrate, 87 percent water; and cream, 35 percent fat, 3 percent protein, 3 percent lactose, 58 percent water.)

REFERENCES

1. Arbuckle, W. S. 1972. *Ice Cream,* 2nd edition. Westport, Connecticut: Avi Publishing Company.

2. Eskamani, A. and J. G. Leeder. 1972. Contribution of specific saccharide fractions of corn syrup to the syrup flavor of ice cream mix. *Journal of Food Science* 37, 328.

3. Finnegan, E. J. and J. J. Sheuring. 1962a. Consumer preferences for sugar levels in ice cream and frozen desserts. I. Sugar levels in chocolate ice cream. *Food Technology* 16 (No. 2), 72.

4. Finnegan, E. J. and J. J. Sheuring. 1962b. Consumer preference for sugar levels in ice cream and frozen desserts. II. Emulsifier-stabilizer levels in chocolate ice cream. *Food Technology* 16 (No. 3), 113.

5. Frazeur, D. R. and R. B. Harrington. 1968a. Low temperature and conventionally frozen ice cream. 1. The effect of storage conditions and heat shocks on body and texture. *Food Technology* 22, 910.

6. Frazeur, D. R. and R. B. Harrington. 1968b. Low temperature and conventionally frozen ice cream. 2. Interrelationships associated with selected factors affecting body and texture. *Food Technology* 22, 912.

7. Govin, R. and J. G. Leeder. 1971. Action of emulsifiers in ice cream utilizing the HLB concept. *Journal of Food Science* 36, 718.

8. Lin, P. and J. G. Leeder. 1974. Mechanism of emulsifier action in an ice cream system. *Journal of Food Science* 39, 108.

9. Pangborn, R. M. and T. A. Nickerson. 1959. The influence of sugar in ice cream. II. Consumer preferences for strawberry ice cream. *Food Technology* 13, 107.

10. Pangborn, R. M., M. Simone and T. A. Nickerson. 1957. The influence of sugar in ice cream. I. Consumer preferences for vanilla ice cream. *Food Technology* 11, 679.

11. Shama, F. and P. Sherman. 1966. The texture of ice cream. 2. Rheological properties of frozen ice cream. *Journal of Food Science* 31, 699.

12. Sherman, P. 1965. The texture of ice cream. *Journal of Food Science* 30, 201.

13. Simpfendorfer, S. and W. H. Martin. 1964. Effect of corn syrup solids on the quality and properties of ice milk. *Food Technology* 18, 357.

CHAPTER 12

STRUCTURE OF PLANT TISSUES AND PLANT PIGMENTS

The cells of all plants have numerous characteristics in common. However, through the process of differentiation many distinctive types of cells and tissues are produced, resulting in various structures and textures in the parts of plants that are used for food. Fruits, vegetables and cereal grains are the principal plants consumed by humans.

Several groups of plant pigments have been studied as they occur in fruits, vegetables, and cereal grains. Each group has common characteristics regardless of where it is found in the plant kingdom.

12.1

CHEMICAL COMPOSITION OF PLANT TISSUES

Plants contain both inorganic and organic compounds. Plant tissues have been subjected to intensive study using modern methods of chemical analysis.

WATER

Water is present in plant tissues in amounts ranging from approximately 10 percent in dry seeds to 95 percent in green leaves. Living plant tissues generally contain 80–90 percent water. Water serves as a medium for transportation of various chemical substances from one part of the plant to another. It is also the medium in which chemical reactions occur. It is an important structural component of plant tissues. Water makes up more than 90 percent of the protoplasm of plant cells. Vacuoles within the cells are filled with water in which is dissolved a variety of chemical molecules. Cell walls and spaces between cells are saturated with water. The pressure exerted by water-filled vacuoles on the cytoplasm, pressing it against the partially elastic cell walls, produces crispness in plant tissues. This is called *turgor pressure*. Loss of moisture from harvested fruits and vegetables to the air causes loss of turgidity and the tissues become limp.

MINERALS, ACIDS, AND BASES

Plants obtain mineral elements from the soil and combine them as ions of salts. Nitrate (NO_3^-), ammonium (NH_4^+), sulfate (SO_4^{--}), phosphate (PO_4^{---}), potassium (K^+), and calcium (Ca^{++}) and magnesium (Mg^{++}) are examples of ions commonly found in plant tissues.

The ions necessary for the formation of most of the common inorganic acids and bases are present in plants. However, strong acids and bases are not found in appreciable concentrations in plant tissues because the ions are not present in large quantities. In addition, the plant tissues are highly buffered by the presence of many organic acids and other weak acids and their salts (see Chapter 3).

Organic acids commonly found in plant tissues include citric, malic, succinic, fumaric, and acetic acids. They are present in relatively large amounts in fruits.

CARBOHYDRATES

Carbohydrates make up the bulk of the dry weight of plants. They are the basic molecules produced by the plants during the process of photosynthesis. A variety of carbohydrate molecules are synthesized. Complex carbohydrates such as cellulose are structural components of cell walls. Starch is the basic storage carbohydrate. Sugars provide energy for plant respiration and growth processes. Simple carbohydrates are the raw materials for the synthesis of other organic compounds by the plant cells.

Glucose is one of the most abundant sugars found in plants. It is the basic monosaccharide unit from which both starch and cellulose are synthesized. Fructose, also called fruit sugar, is another monosaccharide present in plants in relatively large amounts. The 5-carbon sugars (pentoses) are present in plants in lesser amounts than are the hexoses, glucose and fructose. Pentoses are rather quickly used in metabolic reactions after they are formed. A number of the complex carbohydrates found in plant cell walls contain the pentoses xylose and arabinose as basic units. The disaccharide sucrose is also widely distributed in plant tissues.

Starch and cellulose are the two most abundant polysaccharides found in plants. Starch is stored as tiny starch granules in the seeds, roots, and stems of plants. In cell walls, cellulose molecules are combined as microfibrils which contain many well-ordered crystalline areas. These crystalline areas may include portions of many individual cellulose molecules as they are aligned with each other in a parallel manner. Some areas of the microfibrils have cellulose molecules that are in a disordered array. Thus cellulose exists in fibrils with a mixture of crystalline and noncrystalline or amorphous areas. Pectic substances and hemicelluloses, as well as the non-carbohydrate substance lignin, are found in plant cell walls. Indigestible dietary fiber includes cellulose, hemicelluloses, and pectic substances.

Inulin is a polysaccharide composed of fructose subunits. It is the storage carbohydrate of certain plants such as the Jerusalem artichoke and the dandelion.

**PROTEINS
AND LIPIDS**

Each specie of plant and animal synthesizes many kinds of proteins that are different from those of all other species. Therefore, there are millions of distinct kinds of proteins in existence. Many of the proteins found in plant tissues are enzymes which catalyze the numerous metabolic reactions that occur. Some plant enzymes are extracted and used in food processing and preparation. Examples are papain which is extracted from papaya and bromelin which is extracted from pineapple. These enzymes are proteases and are used as meat tenderizers.

Fruits contain very small amounts of protein and do not make a significant contribution to the dietary protein needs of humans. Vegetables vary greatly in protein content, depending on the part of the plant that is used for food. Dry seeds, such as dried beans and peas, contain the largest proportion of protein and make significant contributions to the protein intake of many people of the world. In general, dry beans and peas are limited by their content of the essential amino acid methionine, making them nutritionally incomplete protein sources. Soybeans contain higher quality protein than do other legumes.

About 5 percent of the dry weight of plant roots, stems, and leaves is fat. Fats are deposited as storage compounds in plant seeds and serve as a source of energy during the early stages of plant growth. Fats, mainly triglycerides, are extracted from soybeans, peanuts, corn, and other fruits and seeds. These purified fats are important items of food for many populations. Phospholipids are present as essential components in plant cells. Plant waxes are constituents of cutin, which covers the epidermis of leaves, stems, and fruits, and of suberin, an insoluble material in the walls of certain cells.

VITAMINS

Plant tissues are important sources of vitamins for humans. Dark green, leafy vegetables are good sources of provitamin A (synthesized from carotenoids), ascorbic acid, iron, and riboflavin. Calcium is supplied by many green leaves although it is unavailable in members of the goosefoot family, including spinach. Yellow vegetables and fruits are also good sources of provitamin A. Many vegetables contain small amounts of thiamin. Seeds are relatively good sources of this vitamin. Certain fruits and vegetables, including citrus, strawberries, cantaloupe, tomatoes, green peppers, cabbage, and broccoli, are excellent sources of ascorbic acid.

12.2

THE PLANT CELL

The cell is the basic structural unit of plant tissues. The light microscope reveals many parts of the cell and emphasizes differences among various types of cells. Use of the electron microscope, with its greater resolving power, allows observation of many details in the fine structure of the cell. This microscope is capable of resolving objects with a diameter of 0.001 μm.

Higher plant cells vary greatly in size, shape, internal organization, and wall characteristics. However, they have many fundamental similarities. They each consist of a tiny amount of living substance, called protoplasm, encased in a nonliving wall composed of cellulose, hemicelluloses, and other polymers. Because of specialized functions of cells in various parts of the plant, the contents of each type of cell are organized uniquely and the cellulose walls may be modified by the presence of other substances. Thus it is not possible to identify one cell that is typical of all cells. A *composite cell* has been described, however, embracing many cellular features (Greulach and Adams, 1967). Figure 12.1 diagrams the major parts of a plant cell. Figure 12.2 shows a three dimensional diagram of a green plant cell.

PROTOPLAST

The protoplast of plant cells is a term used to designate the functional unit of the cell that is bounded by the cell wall. It may be said to contain three parts—the plasma membrane, the cytoplasm, and the organelles.

The *plasma membrane* is a delicate, two-layered structure that appears to be an integral part of the cellular membrane system. It forms the outer boundary for the protoplasm and separates the cell wall from the cytoplasm. The *cytoplasm* is the living matter inside the plasma membrane and outside the nucleus. *Organelles* are highly organized and specialized portions of the cytoplasm that perform various func-

Figure 12.1

Diagram showing the major parts of a composite plant cell.

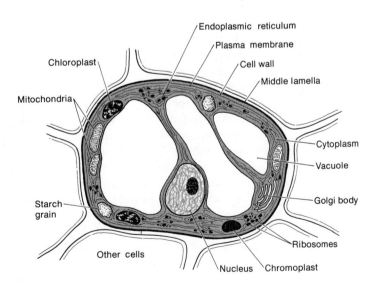

Figure 12.2

Semidiagram of green plant cell. Shown in sectional view below. (From Greulach, V. A. and J. E. Adams. *Plants: An Introduction to Modern Botany,* 2nd edition. Copyright © 1967 John Wiley & Sons, Inc. Reprinted by permission of John Wiley & Sons, Inc.)

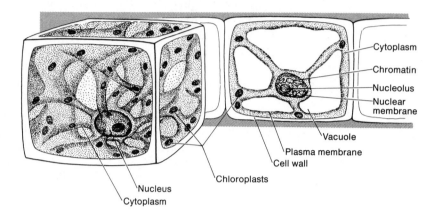

tions in cell maintenance and growth. They include the nucleus, various plastids, mitochondria, ribosomes, golgi bodies, and endoplasmic reticulum.

The *plastids* are distinctive for plant cells. They include chloroplasts, chromoplasts, and leucoplasts. *Chloroplasts* in higher plants are elaborately organized, disc-shaped bodies. About 20 percent of the volume of leaf cells, which are actively photosynthesizing, is occupied by chloroplasts. The chief component of chloroplasts is chlorophyll, primarily the blue-green chlorophyll *a* and the yellow-green chlorophyll *b*. Associated with the green chlorophyll pigment in the chloroplast are the yellow, orange, or red carotenoid pigments—carotenes and xanthophylls. Since chlorophyll accounts for approximately two-thirds of the pigments in the chloroplasts, the dominant color is green.

Chromoplasts are red, orange, or yellow in color due to their content of carotenes, xanthophylls, and related compounds. These may be plastids from which chlorophyll disappears or they may originate directly without chlorophyll. During the ripening of fruit, chlorophyll is destroyed and carotenoid pigments develop.

Leucoplasts are colorless bodies. They have various irregular shapes. Starch is accumulated in leucoplasts as it is stored in roots and tubers. Some leucoplasts participate in the accumulation of oil in the seeds of the plant.

VACUOLES

Vacuoles are a distinctive feature of plant cells. A vacuole is a cell inclusion that is surrounded by a single-layered membrane. Vacuoles begin in young cells as droplets of a watery solution and enlarge upon the maturation of the cells. As they enlarge they displace the cytoplasm. The solution in the vacuoles is called *cell sap* or *vacuolar sap*. Dissolved substances include salts, sugars, organic acids, soluble proteins, and some water-soluble pigments such as anthocyanins.

CELL WALL

The *cell wall,* also distinctive for plant cells, is produced by the protoplast and deposited on its surface over the plasma membrane. Cell walls function to protect and support. They determine the shape and the texture of plant cells and tissues. The initial wall is called the *primary wall.* It is relatively thin and capable of extension as the cell increases in size. The cells of many fruits, roots, fleshy stems, and leaves have only a primary cell wall. Other mature plant cells have a *secondary wall* that is considerably thicker than the primary wall. The cellulose fibrils are more compact in the secondary wall. In addition to cellulose, hemicelluloses, and pectic substances that are present in the primary cell wall, the secondary cell wall may contain lignin (Tortora *et al.,* 1970). *Lignin* is a noncarbohydrate material with a chemical structure derived from benzene. It contributes woody characteristics to a plant. Cooking does not soften lignin. Mature vegetables such as carrots and broccoli (stalks) may contain lignified tissues.

The *middle lamella* is a thin layer of intercellular material that is formed between adjacent cells during division. It is composed of pectic substances, calcium, cellulose, and other polymers. It is viscous and jellylike and serves as an intercellular cementing material.

12.3

STRUCTURE OF PLANT TISSUES

Working groups of cells constitute the tissues of a plant. Permanent tissues that are stable and are no longer actively dividing may be either simple or complex. *Simple tissues* are composed of cells that are structurally and functionally similar. *Complex tissues* contain various types of tissues which differ in structure and function but are involved in interrelated activities (Tortora *et al.,* 1970).

Several types of cells may comprise simple tissues (Tortora *et al.,* 1970). *Epidermal cells* form the surface layer of leaves, flowers, young stems, and young roots. The epidermis is usually only one cell layer in thickness. The cells are generally flat, with large vacuoles and a small amount of cytoplasm. Their outer walls are covered by cutin to protect against water loss and injury.

Parenchyma cells are found in roots, stems, and leaves. They have thin primary (inner) cell walls and no secondary (outer) wall. They are almost spherical in shape. Parenchyma cells carry on most of the basic metabolic functions of the plant. Some of them contain chloroplasts and are active in photosynthesis. Others, found in roots and stems, are colorless and function in food and water storage.

Collenchyma cells have unevenly thickened primary walls. Their function is primarily for mechanical support and strength, particularly in young stems and leaves.

Sclerenchyma cells are characterized by thickened cell walls. They have secondary cell walls which may be impregnated with lignin. The protoplast dies as lignin collects. There are two general types of sclerenchyma cells—*sclereids* and *fibers. Sclereids,* or *stone cells,* are irregular in shape but usually not elongated. *Fibers* are many times longer than they are wide and have tapering ends. Because sclerenchyma cells are tough and strong, their primary function is support.

The *vascular tissue* of plants is complex, consisting of more than one type of tissue. The two principal types of vascular tissue are *xylem* and *phloem.* They both include tubular elements that function in the transport of substances throughout the plant. The *xylem* generally conducts water and dissolved substances from the roots to the leaves. The *phloem* functions primarily in the transport, through sieve cells, of dissolved organic substances from the leaves to the roots.

12.4

PLANT PIGMENTS

Pigments give color and add interest to many plants used for food, particularly fruits and vegetables. The pigments have been divided into three classes on the basis of chemical structure and properties. These classes include 1. chlorophylls; 2. carotenoids; and 3. flavonoids. The *flavonoids* constitute a heterogeneous group which includes anthocyanins, flavones, flavonols, flavanols, leucoanthocyanins, and other phenolic compounds. The chlorophylls and carotenoids are fat-soluble while the flavonoids are water-soluble. Fat-soluble pigments are generally found in the plastids of plant cells and water-soluble pigments are present in the cell sap.

Pigments may undergo various changes during the processing and preparation of fruits and vegetables. Because color is such an important characteristic for these foods, a considerable amount of research has been devoted to isolating various pigments from plant tissues and studying their properties. For example, carotenoids have recently been characterized in Montmorency cherries (Schaller and von Elbe, 1971), in the avocado pear (Gross *et al.,* 1972), and in tangerines (Philip, 1973). Anthocyanins have been studied in strawberry, rhubarb, radish, onion (Fuleki, 1969), sour cherries (Shrikhande and Francis, 1973), seedless grapes (Philip, 1974), and pomegranate (Du *et al.,* 1975).

CHLOROPHYLLS *Chlorophylls* are the green pigments that play a vital role in the process of photosynthesis whereby light energy is used to convert carbon dioxide and water to complex organic compounds. The chemical structures of chlorophyll molecules have been well established. Their precise function in relation to structure, however, requires further clarification. Chlorophyll apparently functions as a photocatalyst in photosynthesis. It is present in the chloroplast of the cell in organized structures called "grana." *Grana* are stacks of membranous sacs called *lamellae* (Rabinowitch and Govindjee, 1965). A chloroplast is shown in Figure 12.3.

The chemical structure for chlorophyll *a* is presented in Figure 12.4. Four 5-membered pyrrole groups are joined together to form the basic porphyrin ring with a magnesium atom coordinated in the center. The system of conjugated double bonds in the ring is responsible for the green color. Phytol alcohol forms an ester with one of the side chains on the porphyrin ring. This long-chain compound confers fat solubility on chlorophyll. Chlorophyll *b* differs slightly in structure from chlorophyll *a*, with a $-CHO$ group instead of a $-CH_3$ group on one of the pyrrole rings (see Figure 12.4). Chlorophyll *a* and *b* occur together in land plants in a ratio of approximately $1:2.5$. Chlorophyll *a* is a blue-green while chlorophyll *b* is a more dull yellow-green color.

During the preparation and processing of fruits and vegetables, changes may occur in the chlorophyll molecule. These changes are summarized in Figure 12.5. In the presence of heat and acid, magnesium is displaced from the center of the porphyrin ring and replaced by hydrogen. The resulting compound is called *pheophytin*. Pheophytin *a*, which comes from chlorophyll *a*, is a green-gray color while pheophytin *b* is an olive-green. If zinc or copper ions are present in the

Figure 12.3

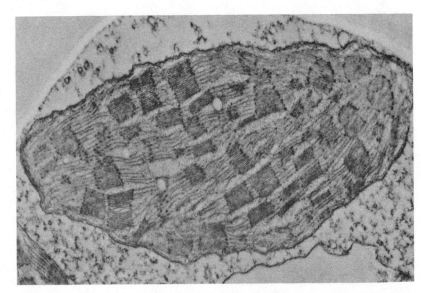

Photosynthesis takes place within the chloroplast. Chlorophyll is contained in grana, seen here in the cross section of a maize cell chloroplast enlarged 19,000 diameters. Electron micrograph made by A. E. Vatter. (Reprinted from Rabinowitch, E. I. and Govindjee. 1965. The role of chlorophyll in photosynthesis. *Scientific American* Vol. 213, No. 1, p. 74. All rights reserved.)

Figure 12.4

Chemical structure for chlorophyll.

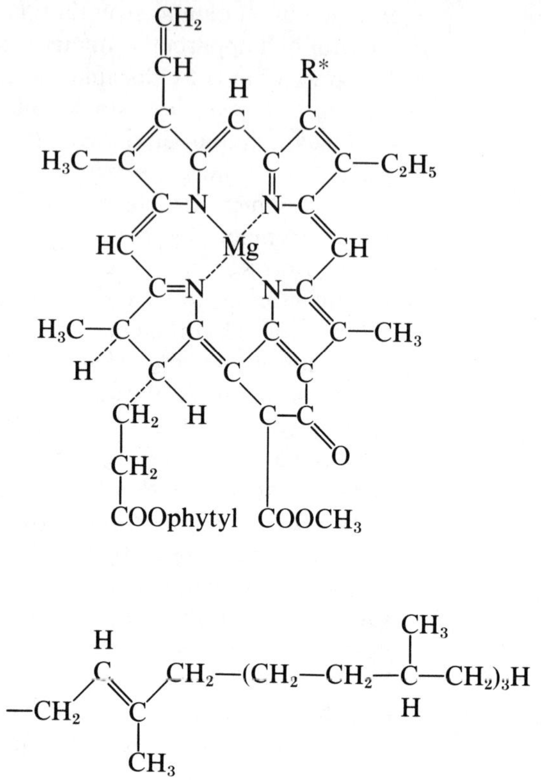

* R = —CH₂ in chlorophyll *a*
R = —CHO in chlorophyll *b*

phytyl group

heated mixture, they may replace the magnesium giving a stable bright green complex.

A second reaction occurring with chlorophyll during the processing of fruits and vegetables involves the hydrolysis of the phytol group. This may be catalyzed by the enzyme chlorophyllase. The resulting compound, which lacks the phytol group, is called *chlorophyllide* and is soluble in water. Chlorophyllide is bright green in color.

If both the removal of magnesium and the hydrolysis of the phytol ester occur during the processing of green plants, the changed chlorophyll molecule is known as a *pheophorbide*. When chlorophyll-containing vegetables are heated with enough sodium bicarbonate (baking soda) to more than neutralize the acids in the cooking water, both the phytol and the methyl esters on the porphyrin ring are hydrolyzed and a sodium salt is formed with the de-esterified chlorophyll. This compound is called *chlorophyllin* and is an intense green color. Since hemicelluloses are soluble in alkali, cooking vegetables with soda tends to produce a very soft or mushy texture in a comparatively short cooking period. The alkalinity produced by the addition of soda also increases the destruction of certain vitamins, particularly ascorbic acid and thiamin.

Degradation of chlorophyll involving breaking of the porphyrin ring may occur during the storage and processing of green plant foods. Destruction of chlorophyll during the storage of plant tissues is thought to be an enzymatic process but little is known concerning the mecha-

Figure 12.5

Summary of changes that may occur in the chlorophyll molecule during food preparation.

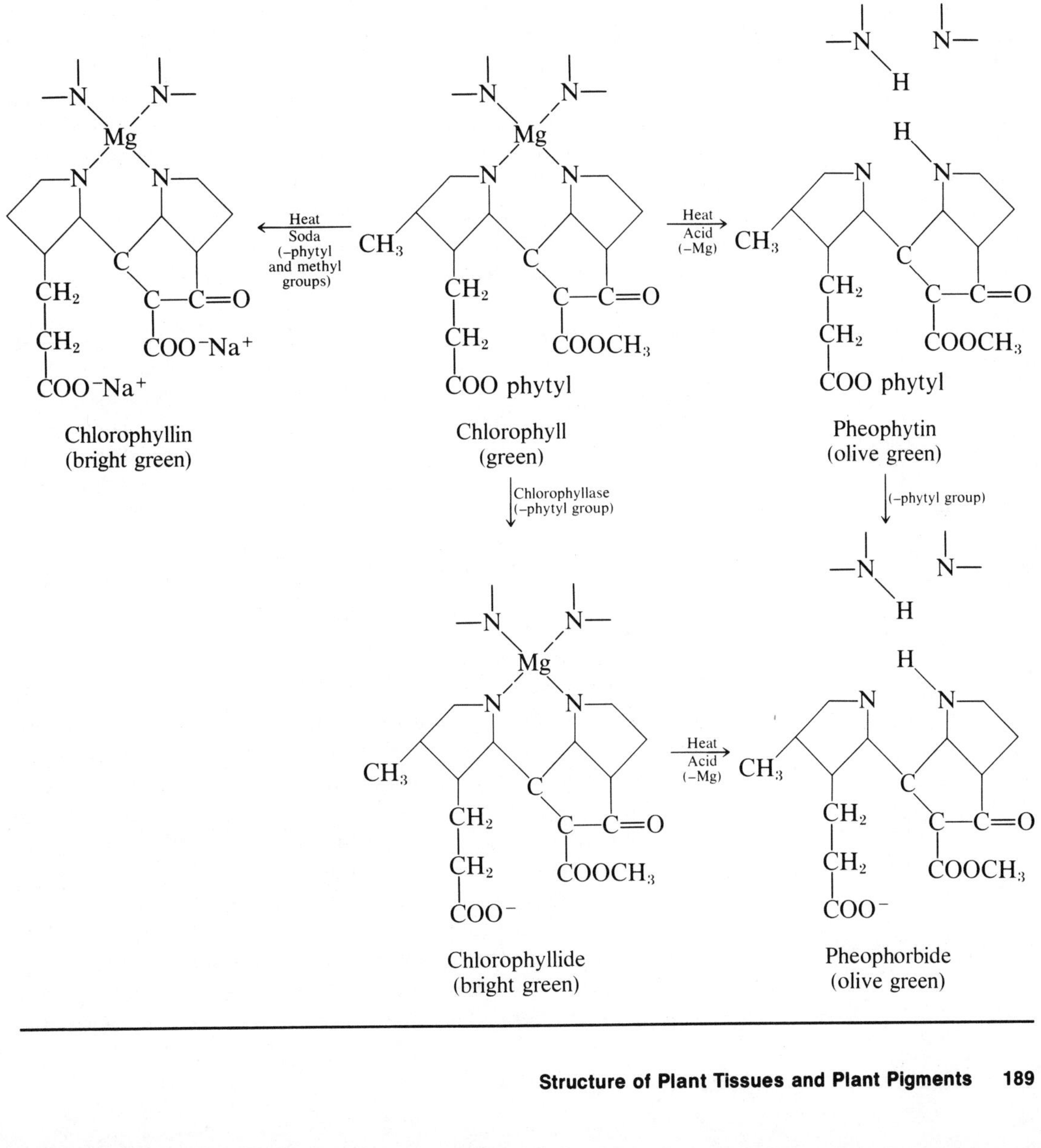

Chlorophyllin
(bright green)

Chlorophyll
(green)

Pheophytin
(olive green)

Chlorophyllide
(bright green)

Pheophorbide
(olive green)

nisms involved (Hulme, 1971). Chlorophyll degradation in some frozen vegetables has been related to lipid oxidation (Hulme, 1971). Chlorophyll loss occurs during the boiling of green vegetables. Sweeney and Martin (1958) reported that the loss of chlorophyll *a* and *b* from broccoli increased as the boiling period increased from 5 to 20 minutes. Less than one-third of the chlorophyll remained after cooking the broccoli for 20 minutes. Chlorophyll *a* was degraded more rapidly than was chlorophyll *b*.

CAROTENOIDS

Carotenoids are fat-soluble pigments of a yellow to orange-red color. Some of these pigments are present in the plastids with chlorophyll, some are found without chlorophyll in chromoplasts, and some are present as small crystals in the cytoplasm of cells. After chlorophyll is destroyed in green leaves, carotenoids remain and give orange-red colors to autumn leaves.

Chemically, there are two types of carotenoids: 1. carotenes that contain carbon and hydrogen only and 2. xanthophylls that contain oxygen in addition to carbon and hydrogen. The structures are known for well over two hundred naturally occurring carotenoids. Synthetic compounds are also produced. Carotenoids are used to color a wide variety of manufactured foods (Bauernfeind, 1975). Ting and Hendrickson (1969) suggested adding to orange juice a concentrate of carotenoids extracted from orange peel.

The structure for β-carotene is shown in Figure 12.6. The system of conjugated double bonds, commonly occurring in the all-*trans* form as shown in Figure 12.6, is responsible for the color. In lycopene, a red-orange pigment found in tomatoes, the 6-membered ionone rings at the ends of the molecule are open rather than closed as they are in β-carotene (see Figure 12.6). Carotenoids that have at least half of their structures equivalent to the vitamin A molecule may be transformed into vitamin A within body cells and are called *provitamins* or *precursors* for this vitamin. The structure for vitamin A is shown in Figure 12.6.

The *trans* form of double bonds in the carotenoid pigments may be changed to a *cis* configuration. This isomerization of the molecule occurs when carotenoid-containing vegetables are heated in the presence of acid. The change in shape of the molecule that accompanies isomerization produces a change in the intensity of the color. For example, β-carotene becomes a more pale yellow-orange color when some bonds are changed to the *cis* form. Isomerization from the *cis* to the *trans* form may also occur during heating. When this occurs in fruits and vegetables that originally contained the *cis* compound, the yellow color is intensified. Oxidation of the double bonds in carotenoid pigments causes a lightening of the color. This occurs during bleaching of white wheat flour. Kanner *et al.* (1977) reported that carotene-bleaching activity in red pepper tissue was due to a peroxidase-like protein. Processing of fruits and vegetables in the presence of oxygen causes the

Figure 12.6

Chemical structures for some carotenoids and vitamin A.

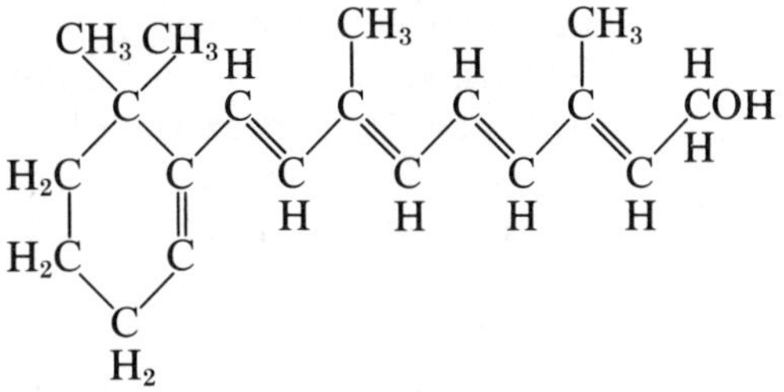

Vitamin A

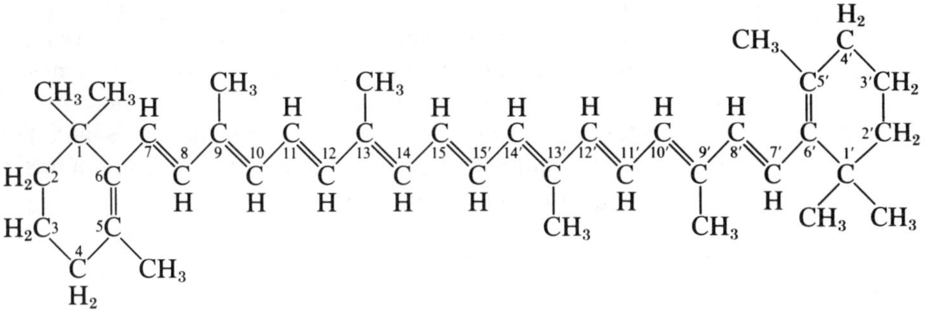

B–carotene
(all-trans)

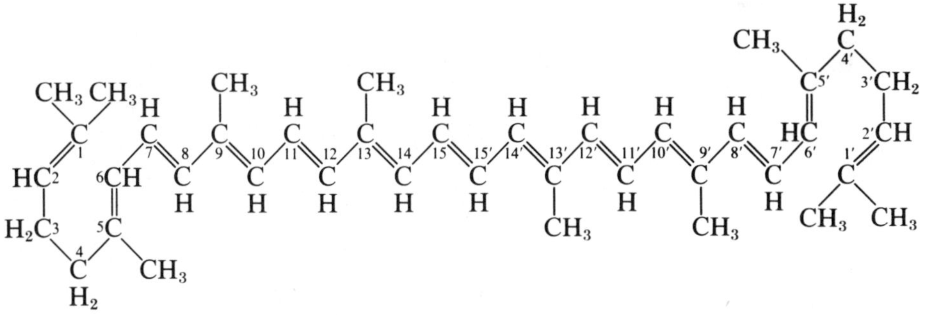

Lycopene

oxidation of carotenoids, although the stability of these pigments in plant tissues varies widely (Hulme, 1971).

The color changes occurring upon the heating of mature carrots, sweet potatoes, yellow crookneck squash, and table red tomatoes were studied by Purcell *et al.* (1969). A color shift from orange to yellow in carrots and sweet potatoes and from red to orange-red in tomatoes was attributed to the physical degradation of chromoplasts and the solution of the carotenoids in other cellular lipids. The color changes could not be completely explained by a change in total carotenoid content nor by isomerization to *cis* forms. Color changes did not occur with the heating of Yellow Crookneck squash. It was suggested that this was because carotenoids are not located in discrete chromoplasts in this vegetable but are dissolved in cellular lipids in the fresh tissue.

FLAVONOIDS

Flavonoid pigments are widely distributed in fruits and vegetables as water-soluble substances present in the cell sap. They are phenolic compounds. Most of them have the basic ring structure shown in Figure 12.7. Anthocyanins are responsible for the attractive red colors of many fruits, vegetables, and flowers. The basic chemical structure for anthocyanins is the flavylium ion presented in Figure 12.7. Other groups of colorless or slightly colored (ivory or cream-colored) flavonoids include the flavones, the flavonols, the flavanones, and the proanthocyanins (leucoanthocyanins) (Paul and Palmer, 1972). Differences in the center ring structure for flavones, flavonols, and flavanones are given in Figure 12.7. These three types of compounds may be grouped together and called *anthoxanthins*.

Figure 12.7

Flavonoid structures.

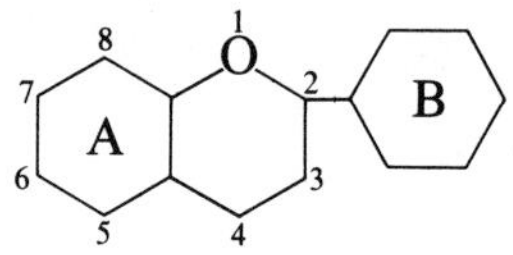

Basic Flavonoid Structure

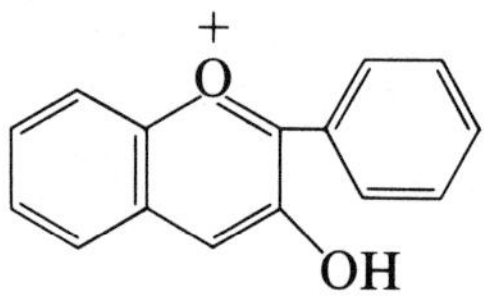

Basic Anthocyanin Structure
(flavylium ion)

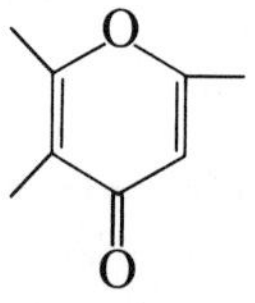

Flavone 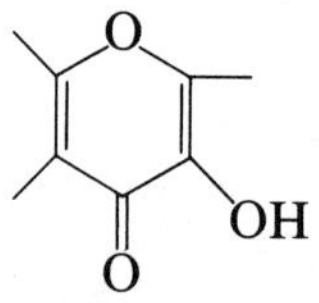 Flavonol 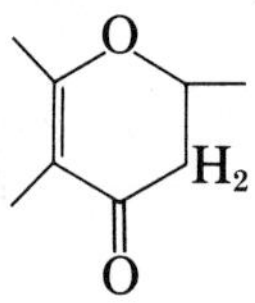 Flavanone

Figure 12.8

Chemical structure for
delphinidin.

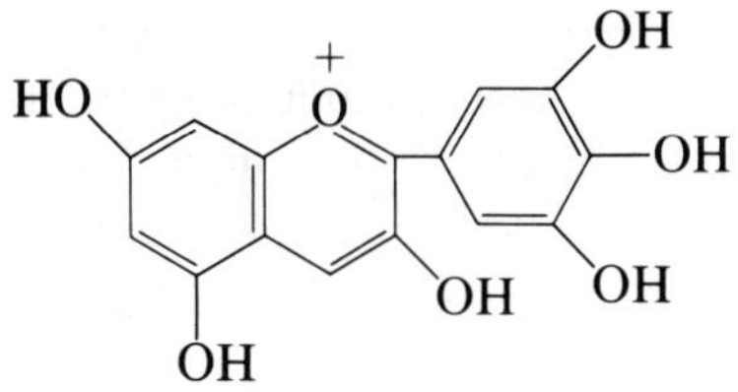

Delphinidin

Figure 12.9

Anthocyanins change
with changing pH.

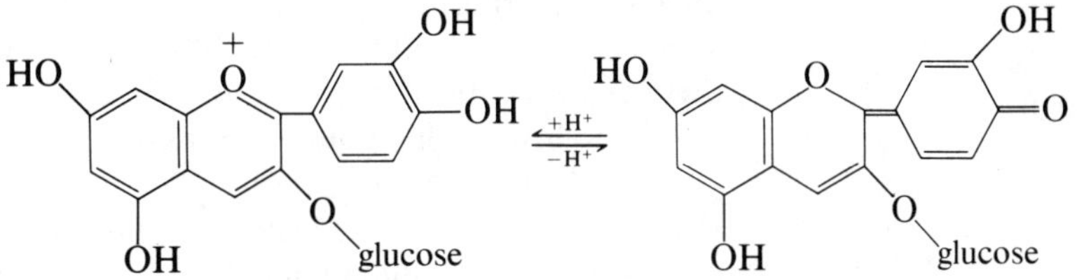

Flavylium Ion
(red)

Quinone-type
Anhydro Base
(violet)

Anthocyanins *Anthocyanins* are glycosides with sugars commonly attached through hydroxyl (−OH) groups. Hydroxyl groups are often found on the basic ring structure at carbons 3, 5, and 7 and also on carbons of the B-ring (see Figure 12.7). The pigment molecule without the sugar(s) attached is called an aglycone. Aglycones are designated as anthocyanidins. Three commonly occurring anthocyanidins are pelargonidin, cyanidin, and delphinidin. They each have hydroxyl groups at carbons 3, 5, and 7 but differ in the hydroxyl substitution of the B ring. The structure for delphinidin is shown in Figure 12.8. In general, the addition of hydroxyl groups changes the color of anthocyanin pigments from red to blue. Sugars are commonly attached by glycosidic linkage at carbons 3 and 5. The glycosidic linkage at carbon 3 stabilizes the natural pigment. The addition of a sugar shifts the color of the pigment towards red, but a pigment with two sugars attached is more blue than is a pigment with only one sugar. Glucose is the sugar most commonly found linked with the anthocyanidins (Paul and Palmer, 1972).

Many anthocyanins change color with a change in pH and are unstable at pH values above 4. In acid medium, these compounds are ionized as flavylium or oxonium ions and are reddish in color. As the pH increases, a quinone-type anhydro base is formed which is violet in color (see Figure 12.9). This compound is hydrated to form a colorless carbinol (pseudobase). Decomposition of the colorless compound may occur on long standing (Jurd, 1972). Changes in color with changing pH vary from one fruit or vegetable to another, depending upon the number and position of hydroxyl groups.

Anthocyanin anhydro bases may form colored compounds with metals if they have two or more adjacent unsubstituted hydroxyl groups. These complexes are sometimes very stable. Anthocyanins react with iron, aluminum, or tin to form greenish, blue, or slate-colored chelates. Because of this, foods that contain anthocyanins, such as cherries and raspberries, are processed in enamel-lined rather than plain tin cans (Paul and Palmer, 1972).

The stability of anthocyanins during processing is dependent upon the pH of the media. At a low pH more of the pigment is in the stable flavylium ion form and less is in the pseudobase form, that is relatively unstable. During heat processing of anthocyanin-containing fruits and vegetables, the equilibrium is shifted toward the pseudobase, which is then depleted through oxidation mechanisms (Hulme, 1971). Little (1977) followed the course of anthocyanin degradation and brown polymer formation during storage of strawberry preserves and canned strawberries. Her data suggested that on processing and during storage, some anthocyanin pigment becomes incorporated into a polymeric moiety. Encapsulation into the polymer is apparently protective to the pigment and leads to increased color stability.

Beet root contains two groups of nitrogen-containing pigments that are related to the flavonoids. The *betacyanins* are violet-red compounds that were originally thought to be anthocyanins. *Betanin* is the major violet-red beet pigment (Paul and Palmer, 1972). Von Elbe *et al.* (1974) reported that the color of betanin is stable at appropriate pH values (pH 4–6) in model systems and may find application as a food colorant. Beet root also contains yellow pigments called *betaxanthins* that are related to the yellowish flavonoid pigments.

Other Flavonoids Flavonoids other than anthocyanins do not contribute importantly to the usual colors of plants since they are cream-colored or colorless. However, these compounds are often present with anthocyanins and may act as copigments with them to influence color by the formation of polymers (Singleton, 1972). Flavones and flavonols chelate with metal ions such as aluminum, iron, or copper to produce colored compounds. A complex with aluminum by some flavones produces a bright yellow color. Iron and copper interaction causes blue-black and red-brown discoloration. Colorless leucoanthocyanins may be changed to the corresponding anthocyanins when they are heated in the presence of acid and oxygen. Luh *et al.* (1960) suggested that this type of reaction is responsible for the pink coloration of overprocessed canned pears. Chandler and Clegg (1970a,b,c) reported that pink discoloration in canned pears is due to the development of an insoluble tin-anthocyanin complex. This complex is derived from the reaction of stannous ions from the can with leucocyanins in the pear fruit in the

Table 12–1.   Changes in the Color of Plant Pigments Under Varying Conditions

Pigments	Color	Effect of acid	Effect of alkali	Effect of metals	Effect of prolonged heating
Chlorophylls	a, blue-green	a, green-gray	Bright green	Zn or Cu complex	Olive-drab
	b, yellow-green	b, olive-green Production of pheophytin or pheophorbide (irreversible)	Production of chlorophyllin (Na salt) (irreversible)	Bright green	
Carotenoids	Orange-red	Pale yellow-orange Isomerization of *trans* to *cis*	Little effect	Little effect	Orange to yellow change
Anthocyanins	Blue-red	Red Flavylium ion formed (reversible)	Violet May form colorless pseudobase (irreversible on long standing)	Fe, Al, Sn complex Greenish, blue, or slate-colored	Equilibrium shifted toward pseudobase
Flavones and Flavonols (anthoxanthins)	Colorless or Cream-colored	Cream-colored	Yellowish	Al complex Bright yellow Fe and Cu complex Blue-black and red-brown	Some colorless leucocyanins changed to pink anthocyanins

presence of acid and heat. Colorless flavonoids, as phenol compounds, may participate in browning reactions of both enzymatic and nonenzymatic types.

Alkali intensifies the color of the ivory or cream-colored flavones and flavonols. They appear yellow in an alkaline medium and light or colorless in an acid environment. Table 12.1 summarizes the effects of acid, base and certain salts on the color of plant pigments.

SUMMARY

Both inorganic and organic compounds are present in plant tissues. Living plants generally contain from 80 to 90 percent water that performs various functions. Water is an important structural component as well as a medium for transporting chemical substances throughout the plant. A variety of minerals are combined in plant tissues as ions of salts. Carbohydrates make up the bulk of the dry weight of plants. Cellulose and hemicelluloses are structural carbohydrates while starch is a storage compound. Several sugars are also present. Simple carbohydrates are the raw materials used by plant cells in the synthesis of other organic compounds. Protein is found in plants in amounts varying from about 1 percent in green leaves to 22 percent in dry beans. About 5 percent of the dry weight of roots, stems, and leaves is fat. Plant tissues are also important sources of vitamins.

The cell is the basic structural unit of plant tissues. Although higher plant cells vary greatly in size, shape, internal organization, and wall characteristics, they are fundamentally alike. A composite cell has been described which embraces many cellular features. The protoplast is the functional unit which is surrounded by the cell wall. It is made up of the plasma membrane, cytoplasm, and organelles. The organelles are highly organized and specialized portions of the cytoplasm that perform various functions in cell maintenance and growth. The plastids are organelles which perform distinctive functions for plant cells. They include chloroplasts, chromoplasts, and leucoplasts.

Vacuoles and cell walls are also distinctive features of plant cells. Vacuoles begin in young cells as droplets of a watery solution and enlarge upon the maturation of the cells. The solution is called cell sap. Dissolved substances include salts, sugars, organic acids, soluble proteins, and some water-soluble pigments. The cell wall is produced by the protoplast and deposited on its surface. The primary cell wall is thin while the secondary wall is relatively thick and contains more compact cellulose fibrils. The middle lamella is a thin layer of intercellular material that is formed between adjacent cells during division.

Plant tissues may be either simple or complex. Basically one type of cell is found in simple tissues. Epidermal cells form the surface layer of leaves, flowers, young stems, and young roots. Parenchyma cells are found in roots, stems, and leaves. They have thin primary cell walls, no secondary wall, and carry on most of the basic metabolic functions for the plant. Collenchyma cells have unevenly thickened primary walls and function primarily in mechanical support, particularly in young stems and leaves. Sclerenchyma cells are characterized by thickened cell walls. They include two types—sclereids or stone cells and fibers.

The vascular system of plants is complex tissue, consisting of more than one type of cell. The two principal types of vascular tissue are xylem and phloem. They both include tubular elements that function in the transport of substances throughout the plant.

Pigments give color and interest to plants used for food. Three classes of pigments are chlorophylls, carotenoids, and flavonoids. Chlorophylls are the green pigments that play a vital role in photosynthesis as photocatalysts. Their basic chemical structure is a porphyrin ring with a magnesium atom coordinated in the center. The system of conjugated double bonds in the ring is responsible for the green color. A phytol alcohol side chain confers fat solubility on the chlorophyll molecule. In the presence of heat and acid, magnesium is displaced from the center of the porphyrin ring and replaced by hydrogen. The resulting compound is called pheophytin. If the phytol ester is hydrolyzed, a bright green compound called chlorophyllide is produced. This hydrolysis may be catalyzed by the enzyme chlorophyllase. If both the removal of magnesium and the hydrolysis of the phytol ester occur, the resulting molecule is known as a pheophorbide. Chlorophyllin, an intense green compound, results when both the phytol and the methyl esters on the porphyrin ring are hydrolyzed and a sodium salt is formed.

Carotenoids are fat-soluble pigments of a yellow to orange-red color. Chemically, there are two types: carotenes that contain carbon and hydrogen only and xanthophylls that contain oxygen in addition to carbon and hydrogen. A system of conjugated double bonds, commonly occurring in the all-*trans* form, is responsible for the color. Isomerization to a partial *cis* configuration, upon heating in the presence of acid, decreases the intensity of the color. Oxidation of the molecule bleaches the yellow color.

Flavonoid pigments are water-soluble substances present in the cell sap. They constitute a heterogeneous group which includes anthocyanins, flavones, flavonols, flavanols, leucoanthocyanins, and other phenolic compounds. Anthocyanins have a basic flavylium ion structure and are responsible for many attractive red colors. The other groups of flavonoids are colorless or slightly colored (ivory or cream-colored) and differ in the degree of oxidation of the basic phenolic ring structure. They may act as copigments with anthocyanins to influence color by the formation of polymers. They also chelate with metal ions to produce colored compounds. They may participate in browning reactions of both enzymatic and nonenzymatic types.

Anthocyanins are glycosides with sugars attached to the basic ring structure through hydroxyl groups. In general, the addition of sugars shifts the color of the pigment toward red. Additional hydroxyl groups change the color from red to blue. Anthocyanins are sensitive to pH and change from red in an acid medium to violet in a more basic environment. Hydration of the quinone-type base produces a colorless carbinol (pseudobase) that may decompose on long standing. The stability of anthocyanins during processing is dependent upon the pH of the media.

STUDY QUESTIONS

Plants contain both inorganic and organic substances.

1. Describe the chemical components present in plant tissue.

The cell is the basic structural unit of plant tissues.

2. Describe the distinctive characteristics of plant cells.
3. Distinguish among chloroplasts, chromoplasts, and leucoplasts.
4. Explain the relationships between the texture of vegetables and the characteristics of the secondary cell wall.
5. Draw a diagram of a composite plant cell and label the major parts.

Plant tissues are composed of working groups of cells.

6. For each of the following types of plant tissues, describe the general characteristics and function.
   a. Epidermal
   b. Parenchyma
   c. Collenchyma
   d. Sclerenchyma
   e. Xylem
   f. Phloem

Pigments give color and add interest to many plants used for food.

7. For chlorophylls, describe:
   a. The basic molecular structure
   b. The solubility
   c. The location in the cell
   d. The effect of heat and acid on chemical structure and color
   e. The effect on chemical structure and color of heating with baking soda
   f. The differences in chemical structure between chlorophyll and pheophytin; chlorophyllin; chlorophyllide; pheophorbide
8. For carotenoids, describe:
   a. The particular part of the molecular structure most responsible for the color
   b. The solubility
   c. The location in the cell
   d. The effect on color of isomerization from the *trans* to *cis* form and *vice versa*
   e. The relationship to vitamin A
   f. The effect of oxidation and of heating in acid medium on color and chemical structure
9. For anthocyanins, describe:
   a. The structure of the basic chemical unit and common positions for glycosidic linkages
   b. The effect of increasing or decreasing the number of hydroxyl groups on redness or blueness
   c. The solubility and location in the cell
   d. The effect of pH on chemical structure and color
   e. The effect on color of interaction with aluminum, iron, or copper
10. Distinguish chemically among flavone, flavonol, and flavanone.
11. Discuss the contributions that may be made by flavonoids other than anthocyanins to color in fruits and vegetables.

REFERENCES

1. Bauernfeind, J. C. 1975. Carotenoids as food colors. *Food Technology* 29 (No. 5), 48.

2. Chandler, B. V. and K. M. Clegg. 1970a. Pink discoloration in canned pears. I. Role of tin in pigment formation. *Journal of the Science of Food and Agriculture* 21, 315.

3. Chandler, B. V. and K. M. Clegg. 1970b. Pink discoloration in canned pears.

II. Measurement of potential and developed colour in pear samples. *Journal of the Science of Food and Agriculture* 21, 319.

4. Chandler, B. V. and K. M. Clegg. 1970c. Pink discoloration in canned pears. III. Inhibition by chemical additives. *Journal of the Science of Food and Agriculture* 21, 323.

5. Du, C. T., P. L. Wang, and F. J. Francis. 1975. Anthocyanins of pomegranate, Punica granatum. *Journal of Food Science* 40, 417.

6. Fuleki, T. 1969. The anthocyanins of strawberry, rhubarb, radish and onion. *Journal of Food Science* 34, 365.

7. Greulach, V. A. and J. E. Adams. 1967. *Plants. An Introduction to Modern Botany.* New York: Wiley.

8. Gross, J., M. Gabai, and A. Lifshitz. 1972. The carotenoids of the avocado pear *Persea americana,* Nabal Variety. *Journal of Food Science* 37, 589.

9. Hulme, A. C., editor. 1971. *The Biochemistry of Fruits and their Products.* Vol. 2. New York: Academic Press.

10. Jurd, L. 1972. Some advances in the chemistry of anthocyanin-type plant pigments. In *The Chemistry of Plant Pigments,* C. O. Chichester, editor. New York: Academic Press.

11. Kanner, J., H. Mendel, and P. Budowski. 1977. Carotene oxidizing factors in red pepper fruits (*Capsicum annuum* L.): Peroxidase activity. *Journal of Food Science* 42, 1549.

12. Little, A. C. 1977. Colorimetry of anthocyanin pigmented products: Changes in pigment composition with time. *Journal of Food Science* 42, 1570.

13. Luh, B. S., S. J. Leonard, and D. S. Patel. 1960. Pink discoloration of canned Bartlett pears. *Food Technology* 14, 53.

14. Matz, S. A. 1962. *Food Texture.* Westport, Conn.: Avi Publishing Co.

15. Paul, P. C. and H. H. Palmer. 1972. *Food Theory and Applications.* New York: Wiley.

16. Philip, T. 1973. The nature of carotenoid esterification in tangerines. *Journal of Food Science* 38, 1032.

17. Philip, T. 1974. Anthocyanins of beauty seedless grapes. *Journal of Food Science* 39, 449.

18. Purcell, A. E., W. M. Walter, Jr., and W. T. Thompkins. 1969. Relationship of vegetable color to physical state of the carotenes. *Journal of Agricultural and Food Chemistry* 17, 41.

19. Rabinowitch, E. I. and Govindjee. 1965. The role of chlorophyll in photosynthesis. *Scientific American* 213 (No. 1), 74.

20. Schaller, D. R. and J. H. von Elbe. 1971. The carotenoids in Montmorency cherries. *Journal of Food Science* 36, 712.

21. Shrikhande, A. J. and F. J. Francis. 1973. Anthocyanin pigments of sour cherries. *Journal of Food Science* 38, 649.

22. Singleton, V. L. 1972. Common plant phenols other than anthocyanins, contributions to coloration and discoloration. *Advances in Food Research* Supplement 3, p. 143.

23. Sweeney, J. P. and M. Martin. 1958. Determination of chlorophyll and pheophytin in broccoli heated by various procedures. *Food Research* 23, 635.

24. Ting, S. V. and R. Hendrickson. 1969. Natural color enhancers—orange peel carotenoids for orange juice products. *Food Technology* 23, 947.

25. Tortora, G. J., D. R. Cicero, and H. I. Parish. 1970. *Plant Form and Function*. Toronto: Macmillan.

26. von Elbe, J. H., I. Maing, and C. H. Amundson. 1974. Color stability of betanin. *Journal of Food Science* 39, 334.

CHAPTER 13

FRUITS

The botanist describes a *fruit* as a structure composed of one or more ripened ovaries together with accessory flower parts that may be associated with the ovaries (Tortora *et al.*, 1970). This definition includes grains, nuts, and legumes as well as fleshy fruits. (This chapter discusses only the fleshy fruits and limits the discussion of these fruits to those that are sweet tasting and are commonly used as fruits in meal preparation.)

13.1

CLASSIFICATION OF FRUITS

The fruits of different species are of many sizes, shapes, structures, and textures. They are classified in terms of their differences. Flowers from which fruits develop also differ greatly in size, shape, and arrangement. However, they have a basic structure in common. The parts of a typical flower are shown in Figure 13.1. Most plants require pollination for the development of fruit. *Pollen* is produced by the *stamens*. The *pistil* occupies the central position in the flower and contains the *ovary* as the basal part with the *style* and *stigma* above it. The ovary contains one or more *ovules* (future seeds).

The main structure of many fruits is the *pericarp* which develops from the wall of the immature ovary. Figure 13.2 shows a diagram representing the pericarp of a peach. The pericarp consists of three parts. The *exocarp* is the outer layer of cells. The *mesocarp* is the middle layer of tissue which varies in thickness and is often composed of parenchyma and vascular tissue. The endocarp is the inner part and is the most variable in structure, texture, and thickness. The *endocarp* is the stony pit which encloses the seed in such fruits as the cherry and peach (Tortora *et al.*, 1970).

Fruits may be classified into three main groups: 1. simple, 2. aggregate, and 3. multiple. *Simple fruits* are derived from the ovary of one pistil. Examples are given in Table 13.1. *Aggregate fruits* are formed by

Figure 13.1

The parts of a typical flower. (Reprinted with permission of Macmillan Publishing Co., Inc., from Tortora, G. J., D. R. Cicero, and H. I. Parish. *Plant Form and Function.* **Copyright © 1970.)**

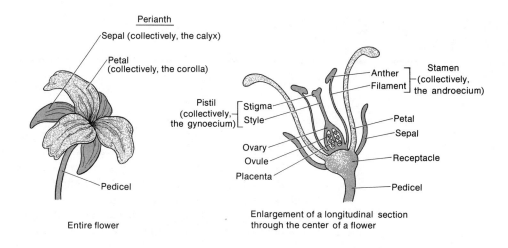

Entire flower

Enlargement of a longitudinal section through the center of a flower

a single flower containing several separate pistils on an enlarged receptacle. In some aggregate fruits, such as the raspberry and blackberry, each ovary develops into a small drupe (see Table 13.1 for a definition of drupe). In other aggregate fruits, such as the strawberry, the receptacle develops into the fleshy part of the fruit and a seed from each ovary is attached to a section of the fruit. *Multiple fruits* are formed from many flowers and remain together as a single mass. Examples are pineapple and fig (Tortora *et al.*, 1970).

Figure 13.2

Diagrammatic representation of the pericarp showing its three subdivisions as they appear in a peach. (Reprinted with permission of Macmillan Publishing Co., Inc. from Tortora, G. J., D. R. Cicero, and H. I. Parish. *Plant Form and Function.* **Copyright © 1970.)**

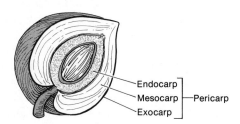

Endocarp
Mesocarp — Pericarp
Exocarp

Table 13.1 Classification of Simple Fleshy Fruits

Simple Fleshy Fruits (at least a part of the pericarp is soft and fleshy).

1. Fruits derived from the pericarp only.
    a. Berry
       The entire pericarp is fleshy. Examples are grape, date, avocado, citrus fruits, and tomato.
    b. Drupe
       The pericarp is divided into the exocarp (skin), mesocarp (fleshy pulp) and endocarp (stone or pit). Examples are peach, plum, cherry, olive, and apricot.
2. Fruits derived from the pericarp plus parts of the flower
    a. False berry
       Similar to the berry with parts of the flower included in the fruit. Examples are banana, cantaloupe, and cranberry.
    b. Pome
       Fleshy parts are all derived from the flower and enclose the portions produced by the pericarp. Examples are apple and pear.

Source: From Tortora *et al.*, 1970.

13.2

COMPOSITION AND NUTRITIVE VALUE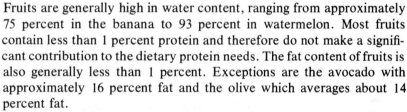

Fruits are generally high in water content, ranging from approximately 75 percent in the banana to 93 percent in watermelon. Most fruits contain less than 1 percent protein and therefore do not make a significant contribution to the dietary protein needs. The fat content of fruits is also generally less than 1 percent. Exceptions are the avocado with approximately 16 percent fat and the olive which averages about 14 percent fat.

The solids of fruits are primarily carbohydrates. Starch in an immature fruit gradually changes to sugar during the ripening process. The relatively high sugar content of ripened fruits is responsible for their sweet taste. The total carbohydrate content varies from approximately 6 percent in watermelon and avocado and 8 percent in strawberries to 15 percent in pears and 22 percent in bananas. Most fruits contain between 10 and 15 percent total carbohydrate.

The carbohydrate in fruits is made up principally of sugars, including glucose, fructose, and sucrose. Other carbohydrates present in smaller amounts in fruits include cellulose, hemicelluloses, and pectic substances. These polysaccharides constitute the indigestible fiber in fruits.

Organic acids are dissolved in the cell sap of fruit tissue. These acids are responsible for the tart flavor of many fruits. The pH of most fruits and fruit juices is less than 4.5. The average pH of several fruits is given in Figure 3.3. Limes and lemons, with a pH of 2–2.2, have the lowest pH of common fruits. Bananas have a high pH in comparison to other fruits. It is approximately 4.6.

Figure 13.3

Contribution of fruits and vegetables to selected nutrients in the U. S. food supply, 1971. (Courtesy of U. S. Department of Agriculture.)

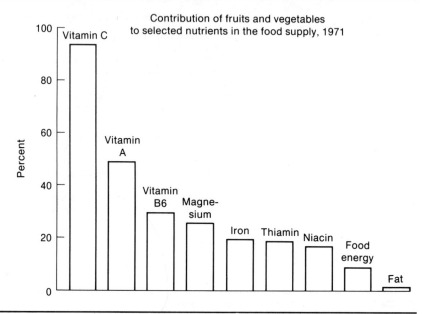

Contribution of fruits and vegetables to selected nutrients in the food supply, 1971

Fruits and vegetables as a food group may make important dietary contributions of vitamins and minerals as well as fiber. Figure 13.3 shows the contribution of fruits and vegetables to selected nutrients in the United States' food supply for 1971. Over 90 percent of the ascorbic acid (vitamin C) in the food supply for that year was supplied by fruits and vegetables. Other vitamins and minerals were supplied in lesser amounts. From marketing surveys the total consumption of fruits and vegetables in the United States, both fresh and processed, has been reported to have increased from 498 lb per capita in 1925, to 539 lb in 1947. Consumption declined slightly in the 1950s and early 1960s, but then increased again to 532 lb per capita in 1971. Within these totals, the consumption of fresh fruits and vegetables declined while that of the processed products sharply increased—from 84 lb per capita in 1925, to 293 lb in 1971 (White and Selvey, 1974). These weights of processed fruits and vegetables are expressed in terms of fresh fruit and vegetable equivalents. Figure 13.4 graphically demonstrates the changes in consumption of processed fruits.

The shift to more processed fruits and vegetables caused a decline in the contribution that this food group made to certain nutrients in the food supply. Losses of some nutrients occur in connection with processing and storage of fruits and vegetables. The contribution of ascorbic acid by fruits did not change, however, because there is a high level of retention of this vitamin in processed citrus products. Also, some fruit drinks have been fortified with ascorbic acid in recent years.

Figure 13.4

Fruit consumption per capita in the United States. (Courtesy of U. S. Department of Agriculture.)

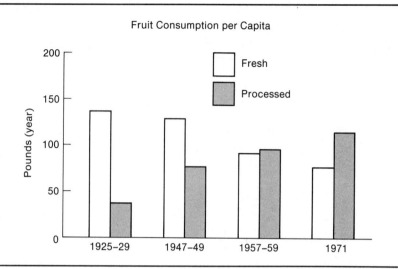

Fruit Consumption per Capita

13.3

CHANGES IN RIPENING AND SENESCENCE

Biochemical changes occurring during the latter phase of fruit maturation and ripening have been extensively studied for several plant species. Study has often been stimulated by problems encountered during harvesting, storage, and marketing. However, the internal factors that control and regulate these changes have not been well defined. Plant hormones that are produced by the plants themselves apparently regulate the ripening and *senescence* (aging) processes. Chemical compounds that can function much as do the natural plant hormones have been synthesized. This allows some external control of the ripening process. For example, preharvest sprays of gibberellic acid keep lemons and navel oranges on the tree beyond the time for normal maturity. This treatment retards chlorophyll degradation, increases peel firmness, and delays the accumulation of carotenoid pigments. Postharvest treatment of tomatoes with gibberellic acid retards ripening. The metabolic inhibitor, cycloheximide, prevents ripening in pears. Flesh softening, chlorophyll degradation, and ethylene synthesis are inhibited (Salunkhe, 1974).

In some cases it may be desirable to increase the rate of ripening. For example, it is important to quality that apples used for making sauce be processed at an appropriate stage of ripeness. Increasing the rate of ripening for processing apples may allow greater flexibility in scheduling the processing while still maintaining good quality in the product. Massey *et al.* (1977) reported that the application, by dip or spray, of ethephon to early-harvested apples shortly after harvest, accelerated the normal ripening processes when the fruit was held at 21°C (70°F). Sauce made from these artificially ripened apples was much improved over sauce made from unripened fruit, provided that the fruit was harvested and the treatment performed approximately three weeks prior to the conventional harvest date. Ethephon (2-chloroethylphosphonic acid) is absorbed by plant tissues where it spontaneously rearranges its molecular structure to form ethylene gas. Ethylene is a ripening hormone. Paynter and Jen (1976) reported that ethephon treatment of detached mature green tomatoes advanced the color development and softening of tissues.

Ripening of fruits includes obvious changes in color, texture, sweetness, astringency, and flavor. However, before visible changes become apparent, changes in respiration occur in many fruits. Respiration, as indicated by the measurement of carbon dioxide production in the tissue, begins to rise. This marked rise in respiration is called the *climacteric* and it stimulates the production of ethylene gas. Ethylene apparently initiates ripening, although other factors may participate with ethylene in this process (Reid *et al.,* 1973). It has been suggested that the mechanism for initiation of ripening by ethylene involves a modification of the pattern of ribonucleic acid (RNA) synthesis (Hulme, 1971). Synthesis of enzymes that are involved in the various biochemical reactions associated with the ripening of fruit takes place, for the most part, during the early phase of ripening before physical changes are apparent. A net increase in protein nitrogen thus accompanies ripening (Dilley, 1972).

Organic acids decrease in ripening fruit. In the apple, for example, malic acid utilization by the metabolizing tissues increases, beginning during the period of the climacteric (Hulme, 1971). The types of acid present may also change during ripening. For example, unripened Concord grapes contain malic acid in greater quantities than they do tartaric acid. However, as the grapes ripen, malic acid is apparently metabolized more rapidly than is tartaric acid so that tartaric becomes the dominant acid present in the fully ripened fruit (Cash *et al.,* 1977). Changes in organic acids and in the resulting pH may influence the flavor of the fruit and color of the pigments such as anthocyanins.

Changes in color occur during ripening. Breakdown of chlorophyll begins at the onset of the climacteric and continues throughout the ripening period. Carotenoids generally increase. Katayama *et al.* (1971) reported that β-carotene was the predominant pigment of apricot tissue and accumulated rapidly during ripening. In peach tissue, β-carotene, β-cryptoxanthin, and violaxanthin were synthesized in almost equal amounts during ripening. Anthocyanin pigments may increase in some fruits during ripening.

Starch is present in immature fruits. As previously mentioned, starch gradually disappears as the fruits ripen and as the content of sugars increases.

The texture of fruit softens during ripening. The softening appears to be a complicated process and the mechanisms which produce it vary from one fruit to another. Pectic substances and their combinations with calcium appear to play an important role. The activity of polygalacturonase, the enzyme that hydrolyzes complex pectic substances, increases during the ripening of freestone peaches (Pressey *et al.*, 1971). The softening of these peaches is accompanied by conversion of pectinic acid or pectin from large insoluble to smaller soluble forms. However, in cling peaches, which tend to remain firm, the pectic substances vary little with fruit maturity (Shewfelt, 1965). In apples, the softening appears to be due to an enzymatic breakdown of the parent pectic substance, protopectin. Chains of protopectin may be crosslinked in various ways with metals, such as calcium, and with hydrogen bonding, giving firmness to the immature fruit. Pears soften more than do apples during ripening. The softening in pears is apparently connected with activity of the enzyme, polygalacturonase. The protopectin content, as well as the viscosity of pectic substances, decreases in sweet cherries during ripening (Hulme, 1971).

Flavor changes occur during ripening. The fruit becomes less tart. A decrease in organic acids and an increase in sugar change the balance between sugar and acid. A decrease in polyphenol compounds in some fruits, such as sweet cherries, may be related to a decrease in astringency. Astringency has been described as a "puckery," tightening, or constricting feeling in the mouth. A large number of volatile compounds contribute to the aroma and taste of fruits. One hundred volatile organic substances were reported to be present in orange essence that was stripped from fresh orange juice (Schultz *et al.*, 1968). As many as 120 compounds are allegedly involved in apple aroma from various varieties. The banana contains at least 200 individual volatile components. Many of these are produced during the ripening period and are influenced by the conditions under which ripening occurs. Apricots and peaches harvested green and ripened in air containing ethylene lack the aroma and flavor of tree-ripened fruit. Although optimal eating quality may be obtained in dessert varieties of apples ripened on the tree, the usual commercial practice is to pick the fruit before the onset of ripening. It is more easily handled at this stage and ripening can be delayed for marketing purposes (Hulme, 1971).

CONTROLLED ATMOSPHERE STORAGE

Knowledge of the biochemical changes occurring during the maturation of various fruits has aided in developing optimal storage conditions for the harvested product. The use of controlled atmospheres in cold storage facilities has increased the life and improved the marketing quality of several fruits, particularly apples. Controlled atmosphere storage emphasizes the living nature of fruit tissues. The object of this type of storage is to control the respiration of fruit cells through manipulation of the oxygen and/or carbon dioxide content in the atmosphere in which the fruit is stored. As the proportions of oxygen and carbon dioxide are changed, the equilibrium of biochemical reactions in the metabolizing cells is changed. The oxygen content of atmospheric air is approximately 21 percent. Lowering and controlling this concentration to the range of about 2.5–5 percent markedly decreases the rate of respiration in fruit tissues. Biochemical processes involved in maturation are delayed and the life of the fruit is extended (Salunkhe, 1974). Carbon dioxide in amounts higher than those usually found in air may also decrease the respiratory rate. Levels of 2.5–10 percent or higher have been tried in the storage of various fruits. The inert gas, nitrogen, usually forms the basis of the controlled atmosphere, with desired proportions of oxygen and carbon dioxide added. Fruits other than tropical fruits are generally stored at 0°–4°C (32°–39°F). Tropical fruits, such as mango, banana, and pineapple, may suffer chill injury when stored at temperatures less than 10°–13°C (50°–55°F).

The use of an atmosphere of 2.5–3 percent oxygen with no carbon dioxide appears to be ideal for many varieties of apples. Controlled atmospheres have been used successfully for the short-term storage of soft fruits such as berries. Strawberries have been held successfully at 0.4° or 10°C (33° or 50°F) with 15 percent carbon dioxide. Ripening was delayed with no impairment of texture in Eldorado plums by holding them for several weeks at 0°–1°C (32°–34°F) in an atmosphere containing 7 percent oxygen and 7 percent carbon dioxide (Hulme, 1971). Davis *et al.* (1973) reported that there was a shift to anaerobic respiration in the controlled atmosphere storage of citrus fruits. The concentration of oxygenated flavor compounds may be lowered in this case.

13.4

PREPARATION AND PROCESSING

Because of the generally desirable flavor and texture of fresh fruits, they are often served raw. Preparation for serving fresh fruit is minimal, involving primarily thorough washing and, in some cases, paring. Treatment to control the browning of cut surfaces is required for certain fruits. Fruits are often processed for ease of marketing and preservation and to add variety to meal preparation. (Canning and freezing as methods of preservation are discussed in Chapters 6 and 7, respectively.)

ENZYMATIC OXIDATIVE BROWNING

When cell organization is disrupted in the tissues of fruits and vegetables by cutting or other mechanical injury, rapid browning of exposed surfaces may result. The chemical reactions responsible for this type of browning involve several steps, some of which are catalyzed by enzymes. The colors produced vary from one fruit or vegetable to another. Apples, apricots, cherries, peaches, and pears turn brown but never black. Bananas and potatoes first turn pink and then brown (Paul and Palmer, 1972). Because of their high acidity, citrus fruits do not undergo enzymatic browning.

Colorless polyphenolic compounds present in plant tissues are oxidized through the action of an enzyme or enzyme complex to which several trivial names have been applied. These include polyphenolase, phenolase, polyphenol oxidase, tyrosinase, and catecholase. An o-quinone-type compound results. This compound is rearranged, undergoes nonenzymatic oxidation, and is finally polymerized to produce colored melanin compounds, which vary from gray to black. An example of the oxidation constituting the first step in the browning process is given in Figure 13.5 with 3,4-dihydroxy phenylethylamine (Dopamine) which is found in banana.

Both the activity of polyphenol oxidase and the concentration of phenolic compounds in relation to browning have been studied in a number of fruits and vegetables. Benjamin and Montgomery (1973) purified and characterized polyphenol oxidase from Royal Ann cherries. They reported that the polyphenol oxidase system in this product is composed of three enzymes. Weaver and Charley (1974) found that the activity of polyphenol oxidase in bananas as they ripened was not significantly correlated with browning. A decrease in the concentration of dopamine as the bananas ripened correlated best with an increase in browning when measured over a 30 minute period. The characteristics of polyphenol oxidase in cling peaches were studied by Luh and Phithakpol (1972). They suggested that enzymatic browning may occur in peaches during the canning process before the enzymes have been inactivated by heating. Guadagni *et al.* (1949) suggested that enzyme activity was most important in determining the initial extent of browning in peaches but that the amount of oxidizable substrate influenced the total browning.

Ranadive and Haard (1971) found that the browning tendency of pears correlated well with the total phenolic content and, in particular, with the amount of chlorogenic acid and catechins. Durkee and Poapst (1965) isolated a number of phenolic substances from the core tissue of McIntosh apples. These were oxidized in the presence of crude apple

Figure 13.5

The first step in enzymatic oxidative browning involves the production of an o-quinone which leads to the formation of melanin-type pigments.

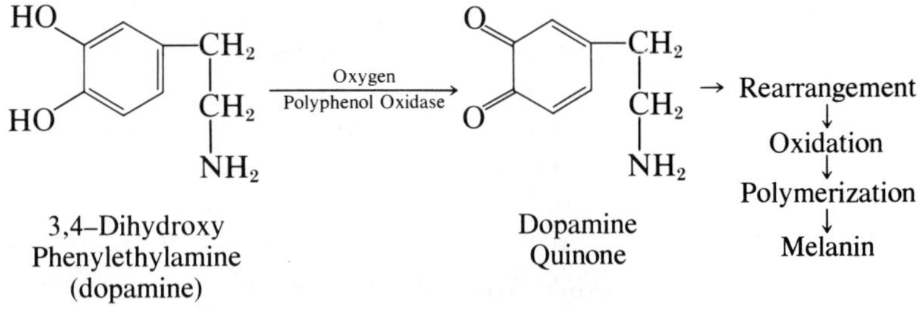

3,4–Dihydroxy
Phenylethylamine
(dopamine)

Dopamine
Quinone

Rearrangement
↓
Oxidation
↓
Polymerization
↓
Melanin

phenolase and may be considered as possible substrates in enzymatic apple core-browning reactions.

Several methods may be used to control oxidative enzymatic browning during the preparation and processing of fruits and vegetables. The enzyme may be inactivated by heating but the texture and flavor of the fruit are markedly changed. Lowering the temperature retards enzymatic activity to some degree but browning still occurs with holding at refrigerator temperatures. Lowering the pH by dipping fruit in an acid juice retards browning. Enzymatic activity is inhibited when the pH is decreased below the optimum for polyphenol oxidases. The pH optimum for pear polyphenol oxidase was reported by Tate *et al.* (1964) to be 6.2. Ascorbic acid inhibits browning by acting as an antioxidant. It apparently reduces the quinones that are formed in the first stage of the browning process and thus interferes with the chain of reactions that leads to the development of brown pigments. Dilute sodium chloride solutions may inhibit browning temporarily. The chloride ion is apparently responsible for this inhibition. The solution also excludes oxygen from the fruit surface. Covering fruit with a sugar sirup aids in excluding oxygen from the tissues and helps to control browning. Sulfur dioxide also inhibits enzymatic oxidative browning. Embs and Markakis (1965) studied this effect in model systems. They concluded that sulfite prevented browning by combining with the enzymatically produced o-quinones and stopped their condensation to melanin pigments. For many years, sulfuring has been used to assure a light color in dried fruits such as apricots, apples, and peaches. The product may be exposed to sulfur dioxide gas or it may be dipped in a dilute solution of sulfite or bisulfite. Dipping fruit in pineapple juice effectively controls browning. Sulfhydryl (—SH) compounds present in pineapple juice may act as antioxidants.

COOKING FRUITS

Fresh fruit may be cooked in water or sugar syrup. The cooked fruit may be made into sauce, such as applesauce. The texture of stewed fruit is affected by the medium in which it is cooked. When heat is applied to plant tissues, the cell membranes are disrupted and lose their selective permeability. Both water and solute can then pass through the membranes by the process of diffusion. If pieces of fruit are heated in water, sugars diffuse out of the cells and water moves into the fruit tissue in an attempt to equalize the concentration differences in the system. Pressure is higher in fruit tissue than in pure water because of the higher solute concentration in the tissue. Movement of water into fruit tissues tends to expand them and contributes to their breaking up. This may be desirable in fruits that are to be made into sauce. Dried fruits, that require rehydrating, are appropriately cooked in water.

When fruit is heated in a sugar syrup that is more concentrated than the cell sap, sugar diffuses from the solution into the tissues and water comes from the fruit into the surrounding solution. The different pressures from differing concentrations in the sugar solution and fruit tissue are responsible for the diffusion. The loss of water from the tissues causes some shrinkage and the presence of comparatively large amounts of sugar in the tissues contributes to firmness. The pieces of fruit cooked in a sugar solution tend to retain their original shapes to a greater degree than they do when cooked in water alone. Cooking soft berries in a sugar syrup aids in the retention of their original shape and form.

Calcium ions are used commercially to reduce the tissue breakdown in fruits such as apples that are subjected to thermal processing. The calcium ions react with structural polysaccharides in the tissues, particularly pectic substances, to form insoluble salts which lend strength to the tissues. In order to be effective, calcium must penetrate the tissues. Only the surface area of the slices is affected when they are dipped or soaked in a calcium salt solution. Use of a vacuum-pressure technique while the slices are submerged in a calcium solution allows satisfactory even impregnation of the tissues (Collins and Wiley, 1967).

FRUIT JUICES

During the 1930s a flash pasteurization process was developed for canned fruit juices. The process was relatively simple and produced a good quality juice with true fruit flavor and aroma. This initiated a marked rise in the production of canned fruit and tomato juices which continued during the 1930s and the 1940s. Frozen concentrated citrus juices became available after 1945 and have replaced much of the canned citrus juice. Almost two-thirds of the oranges produced in the United States are processed and, of those, approximately 99 percent are used for making some form of juice product or marmalade (Tressler and Joslyn, 1971).

When juice is extracted from citrus fruit, the cellular integrity of the juice cell is destroyed and enzymes are released. Many of the enzymes are not active at the acid pH of the juice. However, pectinesterase is active in juice and may have undesirable effects on the quality of the product unless its activity is controlled during processing. Pectinesterase catalyzes the hydrolysis of the methyl ester from pectic substances (Tressler and Joslyn, 1971).

Fresh orange juice contains finely divided particles in suspension. This gives it a cloudy appearance. The particles are composed almost exclusively of pectin, protein, and lipid. When this unstable *colloidal cloud* collapses, an unattractive product results consisting of a flocculant sediment in a clear serum. Pectinesterase removes the methyl ester from soluble pectin, converting it to a low-methoxyl pectin which reacts readily with divalent ions, such as calcium, to form insoluble pectates. The insoluble pectates apparently remove the *cloud particles* as they precipitate. Pasteurization of citrus juices destroys pectinesterase and stabilizes the product against cloud loss (Baker and Bruemmer, 1972). (Pectic substances are discussed in Chapter 20.)

Soluble pectin in the particles is not necessary for *cloud stability* and it is the source of the destabilizing low-methoxyl pectin. Based on these factors, Baker and Bruemmer proposed an alternative method to heat pasteurization for stabilizing citrus juice. This method involves the controlled degradation of pectin. They reported that commercial pectinases added to the juice would depolymerize pectin, producing small molecules. Insoluble pectates do not form with these hydrolyzed pectin molecules and the cloud remains stable.

Pectinases may be used to clarify juices such as apple juice and berry juice. The enzymes hydrolyze pectin and thereby reduce the viscosity of the juice so that it can be more easily filtered. The hydrolysis of pectin also contributes to the breaking up and settling out of particles from the clear portion of these juices (Tressler and Joslyn, 1971).

SUMMARY

A broad definition describing fruit as a structure composed of one or more ripened ovaries together with accessory flower parts includes grains, nuts, and legumes as well as fleshy fruits. Fleshy fruits are classified into three groups: simple, aggregate, and multiple. Simple fruits are derived from the ovary of one pistil. They include berries, drupes (stone fruits), and pomes (apple and pear). Aggregate fruits are formed by a single flower containing several separate pistils. They include the raspberry and the strawberry. Multiple fruits, such as pineapple, are formed from many flowers and remain together as a single mass.

Fruits contain 75–93 percent water. The solids are primarily carbohydrate, that is mostly sugar with small amounts of indigestible fiber. Organic acids are dissolved in the cell sap. Fruits and vegetables make substantial dietary contributions of vitamins and minerals. There has been a trend in recent years toward the consumption of more processed and fewer fresh fruits and vegetables.

Many biochemical changes occur during the ripening of fruits. Plant hormones apparently regulate the ripening and senescence processes. Some external control of the ripening process is possible through use of chemical compounds that function much as do the natural plant hormones. Ripening involves a net increase in protein synthesis as enzymes are produced to catalyze the biochemical reactions that occur. A marked rise in respiration, called the climacteric, precedes obvious signs of ripening. Organic acids decrease, chlorophyll is degraded, carotenoid and anthocyanin pigments are synthesized, starch decreases, and sugars increase, and the texture softens as changes occur in pectic substances and flavor substances develop during the ripening process.

The use of controlled atmospheres in cold storage facilities has increased the life and improved the marketing quality of several fruits, particularly apples. The respiration rate of fruit cells is decreased and ripening delayed through the manipulation of the oxygen and/or carbon dioxide content in the atmosphere in which the fruit is stored. The oxygen content of the atmosphere may be controlled at levels between 2.5 and 5 percent. Carbon dioxide may range from 0 to 15 percent or higher. Inert nitrogen gas usually makes up the remainder of the atmosphere.

Because of the desirable flavor and texture of fresh fruits, they are often served raw. Cut or bruised surfaces of many fruits are susceptible to enzymatic oxidative browning. In this browning process, colorless polyphenolic compounds present in plant tissues are oxidized through the action of enzymes that have been called polyphenolases, phenolases, polyphenol oxidases, tyrosinase, and catecholase. An o-quinone-type compound results. This compound is rearranged, undergoes nonenzymatic oxidation, and is finally polymerized to produce melanin compounds that are gray to black in color. Browning has in some cases been correlated with the activity of polyphenol oxidase in fruit tissues and in other cases with the total phenolic content.

Oxidative enzymatic browning of fruit may be controlled by lowered pH with an acid juice dip, by added ascorbic acid as an antioxidant, by immersion in a dilute sodium chloride solution where oxygen is excluded and the chloride ion has an enzyme-inhibiting effect, by treatment with sulfur dioxide, or by immersion in a sugar syrup. Pineapple juice contains sulfhydryl compounds that act as antioxidants in retarding browning when cut fruit is dipped in this juice.

The texture of stewed fruit is affected by the medium in which it is cooked. When heat is applied to plant tissues, the cell membranes are disrupted and lose their selective permeability. If the fruit is heated in water alone, sugars diffuse out of the cells of the fruit and water moves into the fruit in order to equalize the differing solute concentrations in the system. When fruit is heated in a sugar syrup that is more concentrated than the cell sap, the opposite type of movement occurs. In this case, loss of water from the tissues causes some shrinkage and the presence of large amounts of sugar in the tissues contributes to firmness. Calcium ions reduce the tissue breakdown in fruits that are processed. They react with pectic substances to form insoluble salts that strengthen the tissues.

The consumption of fruit juices has increased during the past 30 years. Almost two-thirds of the oranges produced in the United States are processed into juice. A cloudy appearance in citrus juices, resulting from a stabilized suspension of tiny particles, is desirable. Pectinesterase, which is released from cells as juice is made, removes the methyl ester from soluble pectin, and converts it to a low-methoxyl pectin. The low-methoxyl pectin reacts readily with divalent ions, such as calcium, forming insoluble pectates that remove the cloud as they precipitate. Pasteurization of citrus juices destroys pectinesterase and stabilizes the cloud. An alternative method of cloud stabilization involves depolymerizing the pectin to very small molecules that do not form insoluble salts by adding commercial pectinase. Pectinase may also be used to clarify juices such as apple and berry by breaking up the particles and decreasing the viscosity of the juice so that filtering is facilitated.

STUDY QUESTIONS

Fruits may be classified on the basis of their differences in development.

1. Describe the characteristics and give several examples of simple fruits, aggregate fruits, and multiple fruits.
2. List the approximate percentage of water, carbohydrate, and protein present in fruits.

Chemical and physical changes occur during the ripening of fruit.

3. As fruits ripen, describe the type and direction of change that occurs in respiration, acidity, color, texture, flavor, and astringency.
4. Describe and explain procedures that may be followed in commercial practice in order to speed up or delay the ripening process.
5. Explain the basic principles underlying controlled atmosphere storage for fruits and vegetables. Give examples of its use.

Fresh fruits and vegetables may be subject to enzymatic oxidative browning.

6. List the essential components and conditions that must be present if browning is to occur in fresh fruits and vegetables.
7. Diagram and explain the probable series of reactions involved in the production of melanin-type pigments on the cut or bruised surfaces of fresh fruits and vegetables.
8. Give examples of fresh fruits that are particularly susceptible to browning.
9. Describe and explain several treatments or procedures that might be followed to retard browning during food preparation and processing.

Fruits may be cooked in water or a sugar syrup.

10. Describe and explain differences in appearance and texture between samples of a fruit cooked either in water or a sugar syrup.
11. Give examples in which cooking fruit in water is desirable and examples in which cooking fruit in syrup is preferable.
12. Explain why calcium ions may be added to apples that are to be canned for use in making pies.

Some fruit juices are processed to be clear while others are processed to have a stable cloud.

13. For each of the following, describe and explain a role in fruit juice production and processing:
    a. Pectinesterase
    b. Pasteurization
    c. Insoluble calcium pectates
    d. Low-methoxyl pectins
    e. Commercial pectinase

REFERENCES

1. Baker, R. A. and J. H. Bruemmer. 1972. Pectinase stabilization of orange juice cloud. *Journal of Agricultural and Food Chemistry* 20, 1169.

2. Benjamin, N. D. and M. W. Montgomery. 1973. Polyphenol oxidase of Royal Ann cherries: Purification and characterization. *Journal of Food Science* 38, 799.

3. Cash, J. N., W. A. Sistrunk, and C. A. Stutte. 1977. Changes in nonvolatile acids of Concord grapes during maturation. *Journal of Food Science* 42, 543.

4. Collins, J. L. and R. C. Wiley. 1967. Penetration and distribution of calcium ions in thermal-processed apple slices. *Journal of Food Science* 32, 185.

5. Davis, P. L., B. Roe, and J. H. Bruemmer. 1973. Biochemical changes in citrus fruits during controlled-atmosphere storage. *Journal of Food Science* 38, 225.

6. Dilley, D. R. 1972. Postharvest fruit preservation: Protein synthesis, ripening and senescence. *Journal of Food Science* 37, 518.

7. Durkee, A. B. and P. A. Poapst. 1965. Phenolic constituents in core tissues and ripe seed of McIntosh apples. *Journal of Agricultural and Food Chemistry* 13, 137.

8. Embs, R. J. and P. Markakis. 1965. The mechanism of sulfite inhibition of browning caused by polyphenol oxidase. *Journal of Food Science* 30, 753.

9. Guadagni, D. G., D. G. Sorber, and J. S. Wilbur. 1949. Enzymatic oxidation of phenolic compounds in frozen peaches. *Food Technology* 3, 359.

10. Hulme, A. C., editor. 1971. *The Biochemistry of Fruits and their Products.* Vol. 2. New York: Academic Press.

11. Katayama, T., T. O. M. Nakayama, T. H. Lee, and C. O. Chichester. 1971. Carotenoid transformations in ripening apricots and peaches. *Journal of Food Science* 36, 804.

12. Luh, B. S. and B. Phithakpol. 1972. Characteristics of polyphenoloxidase related to browning in cling peaches. *Journal of Food Science* 37, 264.

13. Massey, L. M., Jr., B. R. Chase, and T. E. Acree. 1977. Ripening of processing apples with postharvest ethephon. *Journal of Food Science* 42, 629.

14. Paul, P. C. and H. H. Palmer, editors. 1972. *Food Theory and Applications.* New York: Wiley.

15. Paynter, V. A. and J. J. Jen. 1976. Comparative effects of light and ethephon on the ripening of detached tomatoes. *Journal of Food Science* 41, 1366.

16. Pressey, R., D. M. Hinton, and J. K. Avants. 1971. Development of polygalacturonase activity and solubilization of pectin in peaches during ripening. *Journal of Food Science* 36, 1070.

17. Ranadive, A. S. and N. F. Haard. 1971. Changes in polyphenolics on ripening of selected pear varieties. *Journal of the Science of Food and Agriculture* 22, 86.

18. Reid, M. S., M. J. C. Rhodes, and A. C. Hulme. 1973. Changes in ethylene and CO_2 during the ripening of apples. *Journal of the Science of Food and Agriculture* 24, 971.

19. Salunkhe, D. K., editor. 1974. *Storage, Processing, and Nutritional Quality of Fruits and Vegetables*. Cleveland, Ohio: CRC Press.

20. Schultz, T. H., D. R. Black, J. L. Bomben, T. R. Mon, and R. Teranishi. 1968. Volatiles from oranges. 6. Constituents of the essence identified by mass spectra. *Journal of Food Science* 32, 698.

21. Shewfelt, A. L. 1965. Changes and variations in the pectic constitution of ripening peaches as related to product firmness. *Journal of Food Science* 30, 573.

22. Tate, J. N., B. S. Luh, and G. K. York. 1964. Polyphenoloxidase in Bartlett pears. *Journal of Food Science* 29, 829.

23. Tortora, G. J., D. R. Cicero, and H. I. Parish. 1970. *Plant Form and Function*. Toronto: Macmillan.

24. Tressler, D. K. and M. A. Joslyn. 1971. *Fruit and Vegetable Juice Processing Technology*, 2nd edition. Westport, Conn.: Avi Publishing Company.

25. Weaver, C. and H. Charley. 1974. Enzymatic browning of ripening bananas. *Journal of Food Science* 39, 1200.

26. White, P. L. and N. Selvey, editors. 1974. *Nutritional Qualities of Fresh Fruits and Vegetables*. Mount Kisco, New York: Futura Publishing Company.

CHAPTER 14

VEGETABLES

Vegetables are a variable group in terms of composition because different parts of the plant are used for food. They are sometimes classified as leaves, stems, bulbs, roots, tubers, flowers, fruits, and seeds on the basis of the part of the plant consumed. Examples of vegetables in each of these classifications are given in Table 14.1. The per capita consumption of vegetables, not including potatoes, in the United States increased from around 150 lb per year in the 1920s to over 210 lb per year in 1971. Within this total, fresh vegetable consumption declined while processed vegetable intake increased (White and Selvey, 1974).

Vegetable preparation for eating is usually a relatively simple process. However, it is very important that this preparation be done in such a manner that vitamin and mineral content is preserved and that flavors and textures remain enticing. Vegetables make an important nutritional contribution to the diet.

Table 14.1.   Parts of Plants Used as Vegetables

Leaves	Stems	Bulbs	Roots	Tubers	Flowers	Fruits	Seeds
Beet greens	Asparagus	Garlic	Beet	Artichoke	Artichoke	Cucumber	Beans, dry
Brussels sprouts	Celery	Leek	Carrot	(Jerusalem)	(Globe)	Eggplant	Corn
Cabbage	Kohlrabi	Onion	Parsnip	Potato	Broccoli	Okra	Lentils
Chard		Shallot	Radish	(Irish)	Cauliflower	Pepper	Peas
Chinese cabbage			Rutabaga			Pumpkin	Soybeans
Collards			Sweet			Snap beans	
Dandelion			potato			Squash	
Endive			Turnip			Tomato	
Kale							
Lettuce							
Mustard greens							
Parsley							
Spinach							
Turnip greens							
Watercress							

COMPOSITION OF VEGETABLES

The gross composition of a vegetable is greatly dependent upon the part of the plant from which it comes. Each part has a specific function to perform in the living plant and its composition is closely related to this function. Leaves are the actively metabolizing parts of the plant. They contain the chlorophyll that participates in the process of photosynthesis whereby carbon dioxide from the air and water from the soil are used to synthesize carbohydrates. Simple organic molecules move from the leaves to other parts of the plant and are the building blocks for the synthesis of more complex substances. Leaves contain comparatively large amounts of water (91–96 percent). The solids content of leaves is composed mostly of carbohydrate with small amounts of protein. Stems are similar in composition to leaves. The approximate gross composition of various parts of plants is presented in Table 14.2. Green leaves are excellent sources of carotenoid pigments that have vitamin A value. They are also good sources of ascorbic acid, riboflavin, iron, and other vitamins and minerals. (Some trends in the consumption of fruits and vegetables in the United States are discussed in Section 13.2.)

Roots and seeds are common storage depots where plants lay down carbohydrates and protein. As root and seed vegetables mature and are harvested, sugar changes to starch and the products become less sweet. For example, a loss in sugar from 1 to 27 percent was reported for commercially handled sweet corn where transit and holding times of the loads ranged from $3\frac{1}{2}$ to 20 hours and the average temperature of the loads ranged from 10° to 32°C (from 50° to 90°F). The greater loss of sugar occurred with longer holding times and higher temperatures (White and Selvey, 1974). Roots and seeds are generally high in car-

Table 14.2. Gross Composition of Vegetables from Various Parts of the Plant

	Water (%)	Carbohydrate (%)	Protein (%)	Ash (%)
Leaves and stems, raw	91–96	2–6	1–3	0.5–2.0
Roots and tubers, raw	72–89	10–25	1–2	0.5–1.5
Legumes, dry	9–11	60–64	20–24	2.5–4.0
Legumes, cooked	64–69	21–26	8–9	1.2–1.5
Soybeans, dry, mature	10	34	34	4.7
Soybeans, cooked	71	11	11	1.5
Fruit-vegetables	85–95	4–12	1–2	0.5–0.8

Source: From Watt and Merrill, 1963.

bohydrate, chiefly starch. Legumes, particularly soybeans, are also high in protein.

The sprouting of soybean and mung bean seeds was developed centuries ago by the Chinese. Sprouts from many different seeds have recently become popular as vegetables in the United States with the growth of the so-called natural food movement. Fordham *et al.* (1975) reported on the nutrient composition of seeds and sprouts. All data were presented on a wet weight basis. The protein content of bean and pea sprouts (removed from the seed coat) was relatively low (2.7–5.0 percent), primarily due to the large increase in water content upon sprouting. The dry seeds contained from 2.2 to 9.0 mg/100 g of total ascorbic acid. The total ascorbic acid content of the pea seed sprouts ranged from 18.8 to 50.0 mg/100 g while that of the bean sprouts ranged from 12.6 to 42.2 mg/100 g. These authors concluded that sprouting selected varieties of seeds may provide a significant source of ascorbic acid, thiamin, riboflavin, and some minerals. Sprouts have a relatively high nutrient/energy ratio. They could be of value as fresh vegetables grown indoors in any season.

Vegetables generally contain more cellulose and hemicelluloses than do fruits. Some of the mature tissues may contain lignin. *Lignin* is a complex macromolecule made up predominantly of phenylpropane

units (⬡—C—C—C). Lignified cells give to vegetables a woody

texture that is not softened by cooking. It is particularly likely to accumulate in the vascular tissue of vegetables. For example, the inner core or xylem of root vegetables such as carrots and parsnips may be lignified in mature plants. The lower part of the stalks of broccoli and asparagus and the stems and midribs of older leaves of kale and spinach may also be lignified (Charley, 1970).

Organic acids are present in vegetables. However, the concentration of acid is lower in vegetables than it is in fruits. Tomatoes have the highest acidity (lowest pH) of the common vegetables, the pH ranging from 4.0 to 4.6. The pH of several vegetables is given in Figure 3.3.

14.2

QUALITY CHARACTERISTICS

Because of their rich and variable color, texture, flavor, and nutritive value, vegetables are important in meal planning. A close correlation usually exists between the retention of vitamins in fresh fruits and vegetables and the retention of their color, texture, and flavor. Similar conditions affect quality and vitamin retention. The pigments, chlorophyll, carotenoids, and anthocyanins are responsible for the bright colors of fresh vegetables. (These pigments are discussed in Section 12.5.)

The texture of fresh vegetables is an important quality characteristic. Turgidity contributes to crispness in plant tissues. It is produced by the pressure of water-filled vacuoles in the cells on the cytoplasm. The cytoplasm, in turn, exerts pressure on the cell walls, keeping them firm. Loss of moisture from the tissues must be prevented in harvested vegetables in order to maintain crispness. This is particularly critical for leaves and stems, which wilt easily. Home storage of these vegetables in a refrigerated vegetable crisper or a closed plastic bag will aid in preventing moisture loss. Some vegetables, such as cucumbers and tomatoes, may be coated with a water soluble wax to reduce moisture loss during marketing.

In general, as vegetables become more mature they become less tender and more fibrous. Secondary cell walls thicken and are sometimes lignified. Young, succulent, tender, crisp, and nonfibrous tissues are desirable in fresh vegetables of high quality.

FLAVOR

Many different chemical compounds undoubtedly contribute to the taste and aroma of vegetables. Vegetables are generally lower in sugar and acid content than are fruits and, therefore, taste may be less important in the total flavor profile for vegetables than for fruits. Volatile flavor compounds that contribute to the characteristic aroma of some vegetables have been studied. A variety of aldehydes, ketones, and alcohols have been reported to occur in tomatoes and processed tomato products. Kazeniac and Hall (1970) reported that many factors were important for the development of certain tomato volatile substances. These included the fruit maturity and physical condition, the crushing of the fruit, the holding time of the juice or pulp after crushing, heat, and oxygen. The fatty acid, linolenic acid, appeared to be the precursor of cis-3-hexenal, a compound that develops during tissue maceration. This compound intensifies the fresh tomato flavor notes. A thiazole compound is responsible for the characteristic flavor of certain tomato varieties.

Heatherbell et al. (1971) identified 23 volatile compounds in aqueous extracts of raw carrots. Differences in volatile substances among several varieties of carrots were quantitative rather than qualitative. Variation in the concentration of individual substances chemically known as terpenes appeared to be consistent with descriptions of the flavor characteristics of different varieties (Heatherbell and Wrolstad, 1971).

The activity of a number of enzymes in plant tissues is important in determining the volatile substances formed. The roles of lipoxygenases and alcohol oxidoreductases in the development of green bean flavor were studied by de Lumen et al. (1978). A number of different volatile compounds were formed in beans from radioactive linoleic and linolenic acids, at least partially under the influence of lipoxygenase. Green beans showed the highest lipoxygenase activity of several fruits and vegetables that were compared.

Onions and garlic offer a classic illustration of enzymatic development of flavor substances and have been extensively studied. These vegetables belong to the genus *Allium,* as do also chives and leeks. Typical garlic odor is derived from an odorless precursor called *alliin.* Chemically, this compound is (+)-S-allyl-L-cysteine sulfoxide. By action of the enzyme, alliinase, that contacts its substrate when garlic tissues are crushed or cut, alliin is changed to allicin (diallyl thiosulfinate) plus pyruvic acid and ammonia. Allicin is unstable and gives rise to diallyl disulfide and allyl thiosulfonate. The diallyl disulfide is responsible for the characteristic garlic odor (Paul and Palmer, 1972). This series of reactions is shown in Figure 14.1.

A similar type of reaction in onion is responsible for the production of a *lachrymatory* (tear-producing) factor in cut or bruised tissues. In this reaction (shown in Figure 14.2), (+)-S-(prop-l-enyl)-L-cysteine sulfoxide is converted to propenylsulphenic acid, which is the lachrymatory constituent, plus pyruvic acid and ammonia. The irritating compound is unstable and rapidly decomposes (Paul and Palmer, 1972).

Sulfur compounds contribute to flavor in vegetables of the genus *Brassica.* This group includes cabbage, cauliflower, broccoli, Brussels sprouts, kale, mustard, rutabagas, and turnips. Cabbage contains an isothiocyanate glucoside called *sinigrin.* When cabbage tissues are cut or bruised, this compound comes in contact with the enzyme myrosinase which catalyzes the hydrolysis of glucose from the sinigrin

Figure 14.1

Typical garlic odor is produced from a precursor molecule by an enzymatic process.

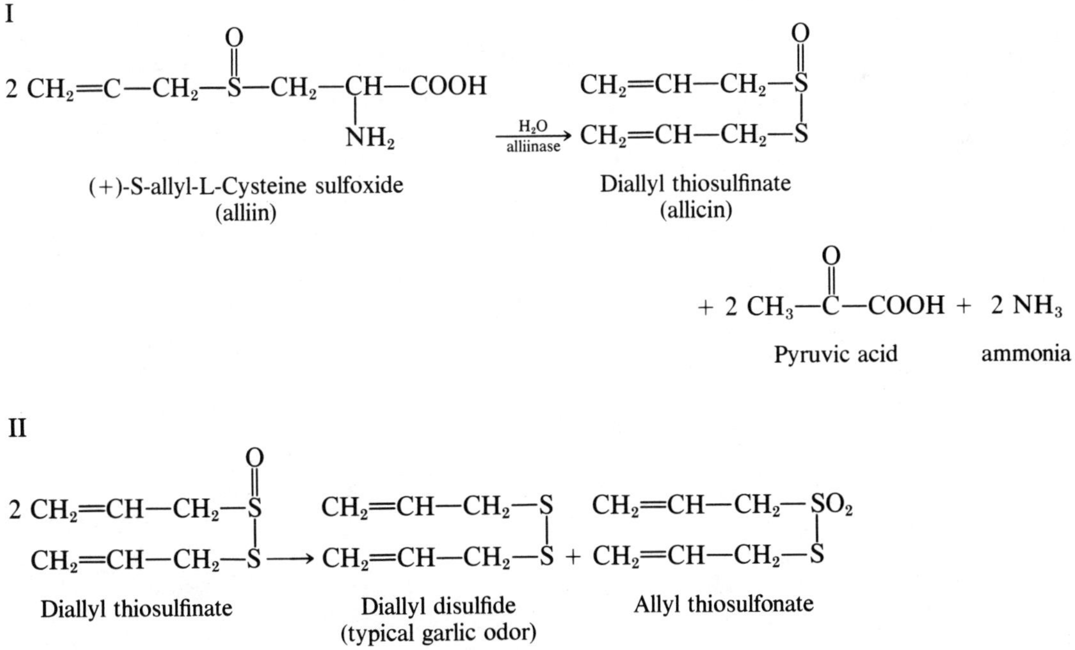

I

$$2\ CH_2{=}C{-}CH_2{-}\underset{\displaystyle \parallel}{S}{-}CH_2{-}\underset{\underset{\displaystyle NH_2}{|}}{CH}{-}COOH \xrightarrow[\text{alliinase}]{H_2O}$$

(+)-S-allyl-L-Cysteine sulfoxide
(alliin)

$$CH_2{=}CH{-}CH_2{-}\overset{\displaystyle O}{\underset{\displaystyle \parallel}{S}}$$
$$CH_2{=}CH{-}CH_2{-}S$$

Diallyl thiosulfinate
(allicin)

$$+\ 2\ CH_3{-}\overset{\displaystyle O}{\underset{\displaystyle \parallel}{C}}{-}COOH\ +\ 2\ NH_3$$

Pyruvic acid   ammonia

II

$$2\ \begin{matrix} CH_2{=}CH{-}CH_2{-}\overset{\displaystyle O}{\underset{\displaystyle \parallel}{S}} \\ CH_2{=}CH{-}CH_2{-}S \end{matrix} \longrightarrow \begin{matrix} CH_2{=}CH{-}CH_2{-}S \\ CH_2{=}CH{-}CH_2{-}S \end{matrix}\ +\ \begin{matrix} CH_2{=}CH{-}CH_2{-}SO_2 \\ CH_2{=}CH{-}CH_2{-}S \end{matrix}$$

Diallyl thiosulfinate   Diallyl disulfide   Allyl thiosulfonate
(typical garlic odor)

Figure 14.2

A lachrymatory substance in onion results from an enzymatic reaction.

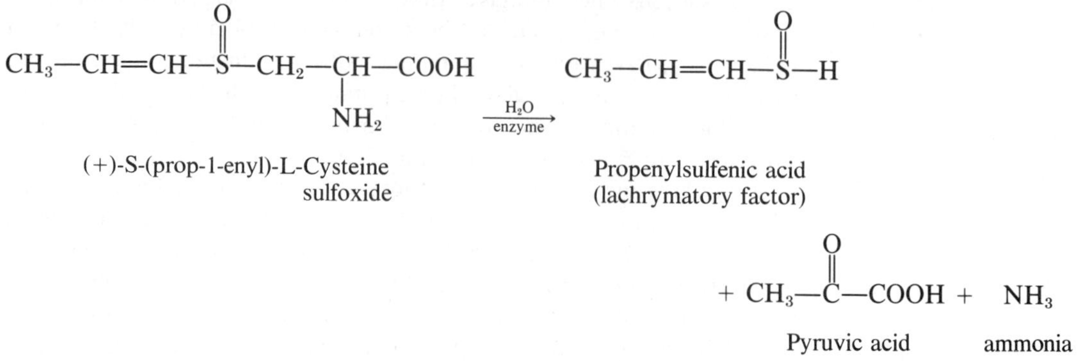

$$CH_3-CH=CH-\overset{\overset{\displaystyle O}{\|}}{S}-CH_2-\underset{\underset{\displaystyle NH_2}{|}}{CH}-COOH \quad\quad CH_3-CH=CH-\overset{\overset{\displaystyle O}{\|}}{S}-H$$

$$\xrightarrow[\text{enzyme}]{H_2O}$$

(+)-S-(prop-1-enyl)-L-Cysteine sulfoxide

Propenylsulfenic acid (lachrymatory factor)

$$+ \ CH_3-\overset{\overset{\displaystyle O}{\|}}{C}-COOH \ + \ NH_3$$

Pyruvic acid   ammonia

molecule. A rearrangement of the molecule in connection with the enzymatic reaction results in the loss of sulfate. This reaction is shown in Figure 14.3. Allyl isothiocyanate (mustard oil), which is produced from sinigrin, is the major mustard oil contributing to the flavor of raw cabbage. Another sulfur-containing compound in cabbage and other members of this family, (+)-S-methyl-L-cysteine sulfoxide, is of importance in flavor development. Dimethyl sulfide, which is responsible for a characteristic flavor note in cooked cabbage, comes from this compound (Paul and Palmer, 1972).

CHANGES DURING STORAGE AND HANDLING OF FRESH VEGETABLES

Vegetables may be stored after harvesting, either before processing or before preparation as fresh cooked products. Respiration continues in vegetable tissues after harvest and rapidly respiring vegetables have a very short storage life. Wax emulsions applied to the surfaces of vege-

Figure 14.3

Characteristic raw cabbage flavor is produced by an enzymatic reaction.

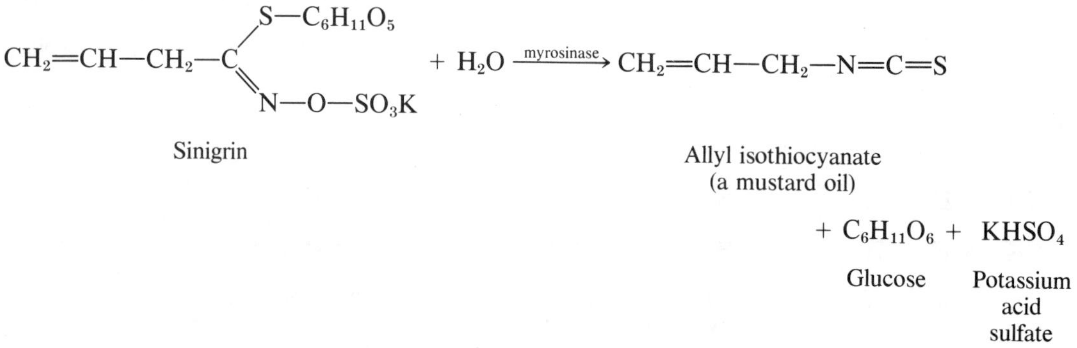

$$CH_2=CH-CH_2-C\overset{\displaystyle S-C_6H_{11}O_5}{\underset{\displaystyle N-O-SO_3K}{<}} \quad + \ H_2O \ \xrightarrow{\text{myrosinase}} \ CH_2=CH-CH_2-N=C=S$$

Sinigrin

Allyl isothiocyanate (a mustard oil)

$$+ \ C_6H_{11}O_6 \ + \ KHSO_4$$

Glucose   Potassium acid sulfate

tables provide a thin coating which retards the respiration process. Singh *et al.* (1973) reported that an emulsified vegetable oil applied to the surface of green snap beans significantly decreased the respiration rate of the beans during the first ten days of storage at 4.4°C (40°F).

The respiration rate of vegetable tissue is decreased by storage at low temperatures. Lebermann *et al.* (1968) found that the average respiration rate of broccoli heads stored in air for 11 days at 0.6°C (34°F) was 37 percent of that stored at 7.2°C (45°F). Controlled atmosphere storage (discussed in Section 13.3) of vegetables has been investigated. Singh *et al.* (1972) reported that lettuce heads could be stored for as long as 75 days at 1.7°C (35°F) in an atmosphere of 2.5 percent carbon dioxide and 2.5 percent oxygen. Increased pH and decreased total acidity was reported for asparagus stored in 5 percent carbon dioxide at 1.7°C (35°F) and 95 percent relative humidity. Degradation of chlorophylls was found to decrease with increasing pH. All vegetables do not respond alike to controlled atmosphere storage. Reduction of the respiration rate for fresh spinach was produced by storing the product in atmospheres containing as much as 9.5 percent carbon dioxide at 0.6°C (34°F) and 7.2°C (45°F). However, this did not result in improved flavor, color, or texture of the spinach. The organoleptic evaluation showed that samples stored in air were generally as good as the best products stored in modified atmospheres (McGill *et al.*, 1966).

The ascorbic acid content of fresh vegetables generally decreases with storage. The loss of this vitamin increases with higher storage temperatures and with longer storage periods. Mechanical injury to plant tissues during harvesting and handling may also contribute to ascorbic acid loss. (Enzymatic oxidative browning of plant tissues is discussed in Section 13.4.)

Although loss of ascorbic acid is commonly associated with the storage of fresh vegetables, increases in this vitamin during short-term storage have been reported. Eheart and Odland (1972) found that fresh broccoli stored in air for one week at 2°C (36°F) did not lose reduced ascorbic acid whereas green beans lost as much as 88 percent in six days. Eheart (1970) found that frozen uncooked and cooked broccoli stored for two or four days at 3.3°C (38°F) prior to blanching was significantly higher in reduced and total ascorbic acid than that blanched and frozen immediately after harvest. Payne (1967) measured ascorbic acid in frozen corn and found that this vitamin was significantly increased immediately after freezing and that it increased after certain periods of storage in the frozen state. Adequate explanations for ascorbic acid increases are not available.

Quality characteristics and optimal storage conditions vary among fresh vegetables. A consumer's guide to buying these products is given in USDA Home and Garden Bulletin No. 143, How to Buy Fresh Vegetables.

GRADING OF VEGETABLES AND FRUITS

U. S. grades have been established to identify the degrees of quality in many food products. They are based on uniform standards set by the federal government and their use is supervised by qualified government graders. Grading services are provided by the Agricultural Marketing Service of the U. S. Department of Agriculture (USDA). Grading of foods is voluntary and is paid for by the packer or processor who requests it. Grades offer the purchaser a reliable guide to quality.

USDA grades are widely used at the wholesale level. Less grade labeling is found on consumer products. This is particularly true for fresh fruits and vegetables. Hutchinson (1970) reported on a survey to determine consumers' knowledge and use of government grades for selected food items. The survey revealed that most U. S. consumers know little about federal grades for the foods they buy, but those who are aware of grades find them helpful in their buying decisions.

Standards have been set for both fresh and processed fruits and vegetables. These standards usually define such factors as color, shape, size, maturity, and number and degree of defects. For some products, flavor and tenderness are also rated. Most fresh fruits and vegetables are sold at the wholesale level on the basis of U. S. grades. The typical range of grades for fresh fruits and vegetables includes U. S. Fancy, U. S. No. 1, and U. S. No. 2. *U. S. No. 1* means good quality and is the chief grade for most fruits and vegetables. *U. S. Fancy* means premium quality and only a few fruits and vegetables are packed in this grade. The difference between the grades is mainly in appearance and waste. Nutritional value is similar among the grades (USDA Home and Garden Bulletin No. 196).

Most canned, frozen, and dried fruits and vegetables are packed according to grade although the U. S. grade is not commonly carried on the label. The three grades used are U. S. Grade A, U. S. Grade B, and U. S. Grade C. Most of the products sold are at least Grade B quality, which is quite good. *Grade A* is excellent quality and is commonly used where appearance and texture are important. *Grade B* fruits and vegetables are not as uniform in size and color as are Grade A products, nor quite as tender or free from blemishes. *Grade C* products are of fairly good quality and are as nutritious as the higher grades. Continuous inspection during the processing of fruits and vegetables is available from the USDA grading service. The grade shield for processed fruits and vegetables is shown in Figure 14.4 (USDA Home and Garden Bulletin No. 196).

Generic or unbranded foods are now appearing at some markets. Most of these items are comparable to the standard minimum specifications for USDA Grade C with some (about 20 percent) comparable to USDA Grade B. Private brand label products are about 20 percent USDA Grade B quality and the remainder USDA Grade A.

Figure 14.4

14.4

COOKING VEGETABLES

Although vegetables are sometimes served raw as relishes or in salads, they are more often cooked. Cooking brings about a number of changes. The texture becomes less firm as heating softens fibrous tissue, hydrolyzes some pectic substances, and brings about separation of cells. Proteins become denatured and flavor changes are produced. Microorganisms are also destroyed by cooking. Vegetables, such as potatoes, that contain appreciable quantities of starch are improved in palatability and digestibility as the starch is at least partially gelatinized. Plant acids are released and may come in contact with the chlorophyll of green vegetables, encouraging the production of the olive-drab pheophytin.

Vegetables may be cooked by a variety of methods. Boiling is probably the most common method used. Other methods include steaming, baking, panning, cooking by microwaves, and frying. Vegetables should be washed thoroughly as a first step in preparation. Inedible parts are discarded. The usual percentage of refuse from selected vegetables as purchased is given in Table 14.3. The amount of waste is affected by the method of removing refuse. The careless paring of vegetables wastes nutritious tissue. Cooking potatoes in their skins conserves nutrients. After cooking, the peel may be easily removed as a thin layer.

BOILING

Variables that may markedly affect the palatability and nutritive value of boiled vegetables are the surface area exposed, the amount of water used, and the length of the cooking period. With a sturdy saucepan and a tight-fitting lid, vegetables may be cooked with no additional water besides that adhering to the tissues after washing. With this so-called *waterless* cooking, heat must be adjusted and kept low in order to avoid

Table 14.3. Refuse from Vegetables

Vegetable	Source of refuse	Refuse (%)
Asparagus	Butt ends	44
Beans, snap	End, strings, trimmings	12
Broccoli	Tough stalks, trimmings	22
Cabbage	Outer leaves, core	21
Carrots, without tops	Scrapings	18
Cauliflower, untrimmed	Jacket leaves, inner leaves, stalk, base, core	61
Celery	Leaves, root ends, trimmings	25
Corn, sweet, with husk Without husk	Husk, silk, cob, trimmings Cob	64 45
Cucumber, pared	Parings, ends, bruised spots	27

Lettuce, crisphead varieties
    Good quality
    Fair quality
	
	Core
	Coarse leaves, core
		
		5
		26

Onions	Skins, ends	9
Potato	Parings, trimmings	19
Squash, winter	Cavity contents, rind, stem ends, trimmings	29
Tomato, peeled	Skins, hard cores, stem ends, trimmings	12

Source: From Watt and Merrill, 1963.

scorching the vegetable. Alternatively, varying amounts of water, from approximately one inch in the bottom of the pan to water that covers the vegetable, are used in cooking. With comparatively large amounts of cooking water and surface area of vegetable exposed, leaching of both flavor substances and nutrients occurs. The cooking liquid from vegetables is usually not served with the product. If it is discarded, valuable vitamins and minerals are lost.

Ascorbic acid is the nutrient in vegetables that is most easily lost in cooking. It is lost by the process of oxidation. Ascorbic acid may also be leached into the cooking liquid. Charles and Van Duyne (1954) cooked asparagus, broccoli, Brussels sprouts, cabbage, cauliflower, peas, and snap beans in waterless cookware. They also cooked these vegetables in a tightly covered pan with water equal to half the weight of the vegetables. All of the pans used in this study were made of aluminum. The vegetables cooked in the waterless cookware retained from 72 to 91 percent of the ascorbic acid present in the raw vegetable. The vegetables cooked in the tightly covered pan with a small amount of water retained from 73 to 88 percent ascorbic acid. These differences were not statistically significant. They rated the vegetables cooked in the small amount of water as generally superior in appearance, color, and flavor to those prepared in the waterless cooker but both products were considered satisfactory.

Gordon and Noble (1964) reported that several vegetables cooked in sufficient boiling water to cover them were greener than those cooked by a waterless method. Broccoli and cauliflower were milder in flavor when cooked in water. Cabbage and turnips, on the other hand, were milder when cooked without water. The retention of ascorbic acid was greater in the waterless cooker than in the boiling water method when cabbage, cauliflower, rutabagas, and turnips were cooked. The reverse was true for broccoli and Brussels sprouts.

Gilpin et al. (1959) and Sweeney et al. (1959) found that cooking in large amounts of water caused excessive leaching of ascorbic acid from the tissues of broccoli. Some color and flavor loss also occurred with large amounts of water. Color and flavor deteriorated when broccoli was cooked beyond a tender stage. Generally the flavor was best developed when the texture was nearest optimum.

Noble (1967) cooked green beans, broccoli, Brussels sprouts, cabbage, cauliflower, onions, rutabagas, and turnips in boiling water until they were tender. These vegetables were also cooked for 5, 10, and 50 minutes beyond the tender stage. The retention of ascorbic acid, in comparison to the raw state, ranged from 33 to 56 percent, with a mean of 44 percent. Overcooking for 5 minutes reduced the mean retention to 41 percent. At 10 minutes overcooking, 39 percent was retained and at 50 minutes, 35 percent. These differences were statistically significant, although not great. The largest proportion of the ascorbic acid lost during cooking was dissolved in the cooking liquid. The hues of the green vegetables progressed from a green-yellow toward yellow as the cooking period increased. All showed considerable change by the end of the shortest overcooking period.

Stereoisomers of carotene in selected vegetables were determined by Sweeney and Marsh (1971). These stereoisomers differ in provitamin A biologic activity. During cooking of fresh and frozen vegetables, some of the all-*trans* carotenes were converted to *cis*-isomers with lower vitamin A value. It was estimated that the vitamin A value of the average green vegetable would be decreased by about 15–20 percent by cooking. For yellow vegetables the decrease might be as large as 30–35 percent. The biologic values decreased more with longer cooking times.

The flavor volatiles of cabbage cooked for different lengths of time were studied by MacLeod and MacLeod (1970c) using gas chromatography. Certain volatile substances increased with increased cooking periods. The relative percentages of the volatile saturated aldehydes increased as did the sulfides, including dimethyl sulfide. Allyl isothiocyanate increased to a maximum of 15 percent at 20 minutes cooking time and then decreased. Sinigrin is the precursor for this compound. The authors concluded that presumably normally desirable volatile substances can be present in possibly detrimentally excessive amounts, making the major difference between properly cooked and slightly overcooked cabbage. Flavor volatiles were also reported for cooked Brussels sprouts, cauliflower, and runner beans (MacLeod and MacLeod, 1970a). Many differences in flavor volatiles were found between fresh cooked cabbage and the dehydrated product. The changes generally indicated the less desirable flavor of the preserved product. In particular, allyl cyanide was much increased in the dehydrated samples, whereas the important allyl isothiocyanate was virtually lost in dehydration (MacLeod and MacLeod, 1970b). The identification and measurement of flavor volatiles by gas chromatography offers an important tool for the study of flavor in vegetables. The aim of such studies is to improve the flavor of cooked and processed products.

The heating of sweet corn results in the development of dimethyl sulfide from precursor molecules. Dimethyl sulfide was reported by Flora and Wiley (1974) to be the most abundant volatile aroma substance in cooked sweet corn. Williams and Nelson (1973) found that blanching produced extreme losses of the dimethyl sulfide precursor and therefore the dimethyl sulfide potential of sweet corn. Various sweet corn hybrids were found to vary in their dimethyl sulfide potential.

Although reported findings concerning the relationships among cooking methods, nutrient retention and quality characteristics of cooked vegetables differ, general recommendations can be made for boiling vegetables. Fresh and frozen vegetables should be placed in a minimum amount of boiling water. A tight-fitting lid on the pan will retard loss of water during the cooking period. As soon as boiling resumes, the heat should be lowered to maintain slow boiling and the vegetables should be cooked until they are crisp tender. Overcooking should be avoided in the interest of both nutrient retention and quality characteristics. If the cooking period is short, green color will be retained. If green vegetables require longer than 7–8 minutes of cooking time, the changing of some chlorophyll to pheophytin results in a lessening of the bright green color. In this case, cooking in water to cover with the lid off to allow the escape of volatile acids is sometimes recommended. Retention of chlorophyll is favored in the absence of the acids. Compact, strong flavored vegetables such as cabbage should be shredded or cut so that they can be cooked quickly in order to avoid the unpleasant flavor that may come from changes in sulfur compounds when long cooking periods are employed. With a short cooking period and a small amount of water, the lid should be left on the pan during cooking. Because frozen vegetables have been blanched before freezing, cooking times are shorter than for fresh raw vegetables.

STEAMING AND PRESSURE COOKING

In steaming, heat is transferred to the vegetable by steam. The vegetable is placed in a perforated container above rapidly boiling water. The cooking time is usually longer than for boiling vegetables since heat penetration is slower. However, less leaching of nutrients and flavor substances occurs in steaming than in boiling vegetables. Munsell *et al.* (1949) reported the retention of 67 percent ascorbic acid, 88 percent thiamin, and 100 percent riboflavin in steamed cabbage as compared with the retention of 30 percent ascorbic acid, 43 percent thiamin, and 50 percent riboflavin in boiled cabbage. McIntosh *et al.* (1940) found that Brussels sprouts retained 77 percent ascorbic acid by boiling, 91 percent by steaming, and 97 percent by pressure cooking. Similar figures for cauliflower were 81 percent by boiling, 77 percent by steaming, and 92 percent by pressure cooking.

Cooking in a pressure saucepan is cooking with steam but the steam is under pressure so that the temperature is elevated. Ten pounds pressure is commonly used for cooking vegetables. This is equal to a temperature of 116°C (240°F) at sea level. Because of the increased temperature, vegetables cook in a relatively short time but the danger of overcooking is increased.

MICROWAVE COOKING

Microwave ranges are being more and more widely used in both home and institutional kitchens. Several research reports have been concerned with the cooking of vegetables in the microwave oven. Chapman *et al.* (1960) reported that the times for cooking fresh broccoli stems to optimum tenderness electronically were about six minutes compared to 13 minutes by boiling them in a small amount of water. The flavor of the broccoli cooked to the optimum texture of its stems electronically and by boiling was about the same. Color retention was slightly better in the microwave oven and ascorbic acid retention was higher. Campbell *et al.* (1958) also found the retention of ascorbic acid in fresh and frozen broccoli to be generally higher in microwave cooking than with conventional cooking methods. Eheart and Gott (1964) reported that frozen spinach retained significantly more ascorbic acid when cooked by microwave methods than it did when boiled in a small amount of water. However, for peas, broccoli, and potatoes, the differences were not significant between microwave and conventional methods when the amount of cooking water was constant. Carotene in peas was completely retained by both microwave and conventional methods. No large differences in eating quality were apparent.

Bowman *et al.* (1971) cooked 13 fresh and nine frozen vegetables by three different methods. The vegetables were cooked in a microwave oven, cooked in a pressure saucepan, or boiled in a saucepan, all at an altitude of 5000 feet. Each method was satisfactory but no single method was consistently best. Mean judging panel scores were highest for the color 1. of frozen Brussels sprouts and lima beans cooked in the microwave range; 2. of zucchini, frozen broccoli, and onion in the saucepan; and 3. of frozen peas in the pressure saucepan. Mean flavor appraisals were superior 1. for red McClure potatoes, frozen Brussels sprouts, and Burbank potatoes cooked by microwaves; 2. for frozen spinach, onions, zucchini, and frozen broccoli by the saucepan; and 3. for frozen lima beans cooked using the pressure saucepan procedure. Mean tenderness scores were best for cabbage, cauliflower, turnips, frozen Brussels sprouts, and onions after saucepan cookery. The texture scores for cauliflower, turnips, frozen Brussels sprouts, onions, frozen peas, and marble head squash were also superior. The tenderness of Burbank potatoes, frozen broccoli and lima beans, and the texture of Burbank potatoes and frozen broccoli were rated highest after pressure saucepan cooking. Microwave cooking appears to offer an additional satisfactory method for cooking vegetables.

PANNING

Panning uses leafy or succulent vegetables that are shredded or cut into thin strips. A heavy pan with a tight-fitting lid is essential. A small amount of fat in the pan keeps the vegetables from sticking to the pan in the first stages of cooking as they are stirred. The vegetables are then covered and are cooked primarily by steam that comes from water clinging to the vegetables or that which seeps from the tissues. The vegetables must be in small pieces so that they will cook quickly. A panning method, sometimes called stir-frying, for cooking fresh vegetables is widely used by the Chinese.

Eheart and Gott (1965) compared an adapted Chinese stir-fry method for cooking broccoli and green beans with microwave and conventional cooking methods. The stir-fry method gave the least conversion of chlorophyll to pheophytin. Stir-fried broccoli rated highest in all panel scores, whereas stir-fried green beans rated highest only for color. For broccoli, none of the cooking methods studied retained more ascorbic acid than stir-frying. Slightly more ascorbic acid was retained in the green beans boiled in a small amount of water than in those cooked by the other methods.

The use of a variety of cooking methods for vegetables may increase their acceptance and consumption. Walker et al. (1973) studied factors which influence acceptance or rejection of vegetables and fruits among school children. Although no quantitative data were reported, some trends were suggested. Children who had experienced a wide range of vegetables and fruits seemed both to accept and to like a great variety of these products. Acceptability appears to influence household consumption of fruits and vegetables, since most mothers are inclined to limit fruits and vegetables served to only those acceptable to their families.

14.5

POTATOES

The tuber is a thickened underground stem and botanically resembles the aerial stem of the plant. Each eye is a rudimentary scale leaf or leaf scar with its axillary buds. The Irish potato is the tuber most widely

Table 14.4 Proximate Composition of the Potato, Raw

Water	79.8%
Protein	2.1%
Fat	0.1%
Carbohydrate	
total	17.1%
crude fiber	0.5%
Ash	0.9%

(Source: From Watt and Merrill, 1963.)

used in the United States and in many other parts of the world. The average proximate composition for the potato is given in Table 14.4.

The average consumption of fresh Irish potatoes and sweet potatoes in the United States in 1971 was about 62 lb per person per year. A similar quantity was processed, giving a total consumption figure of 124 lb per capita per year (White and Selvey, 1974). Frozen and dehydrated potato products account for the largest share of the processed potato market.

POTATO TEXTURE

One of the most important single factors determining the suitability of potatoes for use, either prepared directly or in processed products, is textural quality. The texture of potatoes is influenced by starch granule size and composition, by cellular characteristics, and by pectic substances. Cell structure and starch characteristics are interrelated and it has been difficult to separately measure the various attributes of potato texture.

Mealiness is a desirable characteristic for many potato products, particularly for baked, fried, and mashed potatoes. The other extreme of mealiness has been considered to be waxiness. The cells tend to separate in mealy potatoes and to adhere in waxy ones. High solids potatoes are mealy when cooked and starch makes up the major portion of the solids. High starch content is thus associated with mealiness. High specific gravity is also associated with mealiness. Mealy potatoes tend to have larger tissue cells and larger average starch granule size while waxy potatoes are characterized by smaller cells and starch granules. Mealiness has been evaluated by "mouth feel" and by appearance or feel on manipulation with a fork. Zaehringer and Le Tourneau (1962) reported that the most sensitive method of evaluating potato texture was mild mashing, using a labeled sample as a reference. Le Tourneau *et al.* (1962) proposed an objective method for evaluating texture. This method involved rapid cooking in water with mechanical agitation of the potatoes that were cut into $\frac{3}{16}$-in squares. The amount of sloughing of the potato tissue was calculated. The objective method correlated well with subjective taste-panel appraisals of texture. Woodman and Warren (1972) separated the assessment of "mouth feel" from the breakdown of cellular tissue by using certain objective measurements. A Kramer Shear Press gave an indication of mealiness. The amount of breakdown was measured by sedimentation of sloughed tissue. From their data, these authors concluded that mouth feel is a rheological property controlled primarily by solids content while breakdown is due to a failure of intercellular adhesion.

Pectic substances are present in the middle lamella of plant tissues and play a role in the intercellular cementing process. They have, therefore, been implicated in the textural characteristic associated with cell separation. Pectic fractions of potatoes increase from the beginning of tuber growth to harvest time. During storage, free soluble pectins increase and the other fractions decrease. Soft-cooking potatoes contain more water-soluble pectin and less insoluble pectin, as well as less hemicellulose, than do hard-cooking tubers. More sloughing occurs in the soft-cooking potatoes. The addition of calcium, with the formation of pectic salts, may aid in controlling undesirable sloughing in such products as canned potatoes (Reeve, 1967).

Surface crispness and rigidity are important characteristics of French fried potatoes, many of which are produced commercially. These characteristics depend on the quality of the raw potato and are variable throughout the year as the source of potato supply changes. Nonaka et al. (1972) described a surface texturizing process for par-fried potatoes (potatoes subjected to a preliminary frying period) that controls crispness and contributes to uniformity in the finished product. This process involves 1. an initial surface freeze, 2. a leaching or blanching process to remove sugar from the surface, 3. par-frying, and 4. a second freeze. A strong outer shell is formed on the potatoes by this process. The texturizing process has also been reported to improve the quality of frozen French fried potatoes that are baked in the oven as the final preparation step (Nonaka and Weaver, 1973). Nonaka et al. (1978) used a three step drying, steaming, and re-drying process to make crisp French fried potatoes from mashed potatoes. Fabricated French fries are competing with fries made directly from raw potatoes because the quality of the finished product can be more easily and consistently controlled.

Sticky or gummy texture in dehydrated mashed potatoes results from excessive amounts of gelled starch extruded from ruptured cells. The percentage of cells ruptured thus provides an index for textural quality (Reeve and Notter, 1959).

SUGAR CONTENT

The sugar content of potatoes may vary from only a trace to as much as 10 percent of the dry weight. Sugar concentration is determined by the variety and by the temperature at which the potatoes are held. At storage temperatures below about 10°C (50°F) the percent of total and reducing sugars increases. The rate and extent of the increase is greater as the temperature decreases toward the freezing point. The sugar content increases at the expense of starch content, which decreases. When potatoes are stored in nitrogen at low temperatures, there is a complete suppression of sugar accumulation. However, some starch decomposition still occurs. Samotus and Schwimmer (1963) suggested that the decrease in starch content of nitrogen-stored tubers may be accounted for largely by an increase in volatile substances. When potatoes are held for 2–3 weeks at room temperature, after having been stored at low temperatures, the sugar content gradually decreases.

Potatoes with a high sugar content taste sweet and have less of a desirable texture when they are cooked. The poor texture may be related to the decreased starch content associated with increased sugar accumulation. The color development in potato chips and French fried potatoes is dependent on sugar content. The Maillard reaction, involving as a first step the combination of sugars and amino acids, appears to be chiefly responsible for the formation of brown pigments during frying. Dehydrated potatoes made from raw potatoes that are high in sugar also tend to darken on storage as the Maillard reaction occurs. The browning of processed potato products is generally controlled by proper storage temperatures for the raw potatoes and by careful testing for sugar content. Certain varieties of potatoes form less sugar than do others. Sugar accumulation in the tubers during storage at 4°C (39°F) can be prevented by temporary anoxia. A storage period of about 20 days without oxygen with subsequent exposure to normal atmosphere at 4°C for three months was reported by Amir *et al.* (1978) to be successful in controlling both sugar accumulation and injury to the tubers.

COLOR CHANGES

The phenolic compounds in potatoes are associated with color changes in the raw peeled or bruised product. (Enzymatic, oxidative browning of vegetables and fruits is discussed in Section 13.4.) The most common commercial method for inhibiting the enzymatic darkening of peeled potatoes is by the use of sodium bisulfite ($NaHSO_3$) or a combination of bisulfite and citric acid. Muneta and Wang (1977) reported that the inactivation of polyphenol oxidase by bisulfite was a function of time and was pH dependent. Rapid inactivation of the enzyme occurred at pH 4 while inactivation occurred much more slowly at pH 5, 6, and 7. At a pH of 4, the pH alone was an effective enzyme inhibitor. A pH of 5 or lower was found to also inhibit the nonenzymatic reactions that lead to the formation of brown pigments after the initial enzymatic reaction involving polyphenol oxidase (Muneta, 1977).

A bluish-grey discoloration occurs in certain varieties of potatoes after they have been cooked. It is usually more prominent at the stem end of the tuber. The darkening is probably due to a complex of ortho-dihydroxy phenols, such as chlorogenic acid, and iron. Enzymes in the raw potato maintain reducing conditions so that iron remains in the ferrous state. The cells also remain intact so that complexing does not occur. After the disruption of the cells by cooking and the destruction of enzymes, iron comes in direct contact with the phenolic substrate and forms a complex. On standing in air, the ferrous iron is oxidized to the ferric form, that produces a colored substance as it is present in combination with the phenolic compound (Hughes *et al.*, 1962).

The concentration of citric acid in potato tissues affects the intensity of the color development. With a greater concentration of citric acid, the color decreases, possibly because the citrate ties up the iron in the potato tissues and prevents it from participating in the blackening reaction (Hughes and Swain, 1962a,b). A decrease in pH also aids in preventing darkening. About $\frac{1}{2}$ tsp. of cream of tartar for each pint of cooking water, added in the middle of the cooking period, may be used with potatoes that are susceptible to after-cooking darkening.

Whenever potatoes are exposed to light during post-harvest handling and storage, chlorophyll develops immediately beneath the skin and produces a green appearance. Greening in potatoes is objectionable because of the appearance and because it is also accompanied by the formation of solanine, an alkaloid that has a bitter taste and leaves a burning sensation in the throat. Solanine is a toxic substance and its presence in increased amounts may constitute a health hazard. It is present in even higher concentration in sprouts than in the tuber itself. Dark colored polyethylene bags are commonly used for the retail marketing of potatoes in order to minimize greening. Forsyth and Eaves (1968) reported that exposing potatoes to an atmosphere containing at least 15 percent carbon dioxide prevents greening without affecting palatability. This may be accomplished by hermetically sealing potatoes inside a 4-mil polyethylene bag and by keeping them in the dark for 48 hours or more. Sufficient carbon dioxide will develop from the metabolism of the tissues. Subsequent exposure of the bag of potatoes to light will then not cause the undesirable greening.

14.6

LEGUMES

Legumes include dried beans, peas, and lentils that belong to the Leguminosae family. The following species, with common names, are grown commercially in the United States:

Phaseolus vulgaris	common beans
Vigna unguiculata (*sinensis*)	blackeye bean (pea), cow peas
Cicer arietinum	garbanzos, chick peas
Pisum sativum	dry peas
Phaseolus lunatus	lima beans
Lens escultenta	lentils

Within the specie of common beans, there are at least twelve commercial classes produced in the United States each year. They include:

Navy (pea bean)	Pink
Great northern	Small Red
Small white	Cranberry
White marrow	Yellow eye
Pinto	Flat small white
Red kidney, light and dark	Black turtle

Legumes contain the highest protein content of all commercial seed crops. Protein is present in the dry beans of the *Phaseolus vulgaris* group at a level of 20–25 percent. Legumes are generally deficient in the essential amino acid, methionine, that decreases the biological value of the protein below that of most animal proteins. However, combining legumes with other methionine-rich proteins, such as meats and cheese, enhances their protein value. A combination of legumes and cereal grains generally complement each other in terms of essential amino acids, cereals providing the methionine lacking in legumes and legumes providing the lysine lacking in cereals. Soybeans are higher in protein than are other legumes. They also have a better balance of essential amino acids, giving them a relatively high biological value for protein.

COOKING LEGUMES Legumes are susceptible to hardening during storage. In this condition, called *hard-shell,* they do not imbibe water readily as they are rehydrated during soaking and cooking. Hard-shell seeds are difficult to sprout. The development of hard-shell during storage appears to be related to the initial moisture content of the legume, the length of storage, and the temperature of storage. Morris and Wood (1956) reported that beans with an initial moisture content above 13 percent deteriorated significantly in flavor and texture after six months of storage at 25°C (77°F) and in 12 months they became unpalatable. Beans with below 10 percent moisture content maintained their quality for two years at 25°C. Muneta (1964) found wide differences in cooking times (59 *vs.* 231 minutes) after extended storage within a single variety of bean grown in Michigan or in Idaho. He reported a correlation coefficient of +0.80 between initial moisture content and cooking time. Dawson *et al.* (1952) found that pea beans stored for one year at 24°C (75°F) required a longer cooking time than those stored at 4.4°C (40°F). Burr *et al.* (1968) confirmed the previous reports that beans of high moisture content stored for long periods of time at high temperatures sometimes require excessive cooking or heat processing. From such studies it has been determined that the use of a low storage temperature (about 4°C) and/or storing legumes with a low moisture content (around 8–10 percent) at relatively low humidity will minimize the development of hard-shell.

Molina et al. (1976) reported that subjecting whole black beans to heat treatment in a retort for up to ten minutes at 121°C (249.8°F) or up to 30 minutes under steam at 98°C (208°F) decreased the development of the hard-to-cook phenomenon after nine months of storage without affecting the physical appearance of the seeds. Unfortunately, the changes produced by the heat treatment in retarding hardening were not completely explained by the data collected. Because beans are a staple diet item in many countries, a simple means of improving storage quality would be of great economic value.

Hard- and soft-cooking dried peas differ in phytic acid content. It has been suggested that, as peas cook, the phytate complexes with calcium and magnesium ions that would otherwise form insoluble salts with pectic substances in the cell wall and the middle lamella and contribute to hardening. The insoluble phytate salts apparently do not affect cell adhesion (Paul and Palmer, 1972). Kon (1968) measured the pectic substances of stored dry beans. He found no significant difference in the total pectic substances extracted from the high and low moisture beans that varied in their cooking time.

Elbert and Witt (1968) studied the gelatinization of starch in small white beans of varying initial moisture content both before and after cooking in water. In fresh, moist beans (57–63 percent moisture), birefringence of the starch granules, as observed under the microscope, almost disappeared after a one hour cooking period. This indicated that the starch had gelatinized. The starch of dry beans (9 percent moisture), however, failed to gelatinize fully even after soaking for two hours at 70°C (158°F) and cooking for 60–80 minutes. These results suggest that the organization and/or composition of starch granules in *P. vulgaris* seeds may change with maturation and drying.

Dawson et al. showed in 1952 that a rapid method of soaking and cooking dry beans produced satisfactory products. The beans may be added to boiling water, boiled for two minutes, removed from the heat, and allowed to soak for one hour in the hot water before they are cooked in their soaking liquid. Alternatively, dry beans may be soaked overnight in cold water before cooking. Even with overnight soaking, it is still advantageous to start with a two minute boiling period because this leads to fewer hard skins. Boiling briefly also prevents the beans from souring if they are left in a warm room. Although soaking overnight in salt water is sometimes recommended, USDA has suggested that salt should only be added to the beans after soaking since salt toughens the surface of the beans during the soaking and thus increases the cooking time (USDA, 1970).

Dawson et al. (1952) reported that the addition of a small amount of baking soda (0.5 g in 623 ml water) added to dry beans during the soaking or cooking period, reduced cooking time by approximately one-third, and had only a slight effect on flavor. The greater loss of thiamin produced by the increased alkalinity is probably balanced by the decreased loss resulting from a shorter cooking period.

Legumes have been processed into pre-cooked powders for use in convenience foods. Cooked powders prepared so that the cellular integrity of the beans is preserved retain their flavor and can be substituted for beans in any food recipe (Kon *et al.,* 1974).

Soybeans are finding wide useage as a raw material for the food industry. (They are discussed in Chapter 27.)

SUMMARY

Vegetables vary in composition, depending upon the part of the plant being used. Leaf vegetables come from actively metabolizing parts and contain comparatively large amounts of water (91–96 percent). The solids content of leaves is mostly carbohydrate with small amounts of protein. Stems are similar in composition to leaves. Roots and seeds are storage depots and are generally high in starch. Legumes are also high in protein. Vegetables generally contain more cellulose and hemicelluloses than do fruits. Some of the mature tissues contain lignin, a noncarbohydrate structural material.

The texture of vegetables is an important quality characteristic. Loss of moisture must be prevented in harvested vegetables to preserve their crispness. As vegetables become more mature, they generally decrease in tenderness and increase in fiber.

Many different chemical compounds contribute to the taste and aroma of vegetables. These include aldehydes, ketones, and alcohols. In vegetables such as garlic, onions, and cabbage, typical flavor substances are produced from precursor molecules by the action of enzymes. These reactions take place when the tissues are cut or bruised as the enzymes come in contact with appropriate substrates. Typical garlic odor is derived from a precursor called alliin by the action of the enzyme, alliinase. In cabbage, the enzyme myrosinase is instrumental in producing a flavorful mustard oil from the precursor sinigrin.

Respiration continues in vegetable tissues after harvest and rapidly respiring vegetables have a short storage life. The respiration rate is decreased by storage at low temperatures. Controlling the composition of the atmosphere in which vegetables are stored may lengthen the effective storage life for some vegetables but not for others. Losses of ascorbic acid and other vitamins generally occur during storage.

Grade standards have been set for both fresh and processed vegetables and fruits. They define such factors as color, shape, size, maturity, and number and degree of defects. For some products, flavor and tenderness are also rated. Grades for fresh fruits and vegetables are more commonly used at the wholesale than at the retail level. They include U. S. Fancy, U. S. No. 1, and U. S. No. 2. Processed fruits and vegetables may be graded as U. S. Grade A, U. S. Grade B, and U. S.

Grade C. Continuous inspection during the processing of fruits and vegetables is available from the USDA grading service.

A number of changes occur during the cooking of vegetables. These include the softening of fibrous tissue, hydrolysis of pectic substances with the separation of cells, denaturation of proteins, destruction of microorganisms, change in flavor, and gelatinization of starch.

Vegetables are often cooked by boiling. When whole vegetables are cut into small pieces and large amounts of cooking water are used, both flavor substances and nutrients are leached from the vegetables. Over-cooking also produces losses in nutrients and flavor. A number of research studies have documented these losses. Some desirable flavors are produced by cooking. For example, dimethyl sulfide is an important flavor molecule produced during the heating of sweet corn. Less leaching of nutrients and flavor substances occurs in the steaming than in the boiling of vegetables. Vegetables cooked by microwaves are generally satisfactory in terms of flavor and nutritive value. In comparisons of a variety of vegetables cooked by several different methods, it appears that no single method is consistently best for all vegetables. Because frozen vegetables have been blanched, a shorter cooking time is used than for raw fresh vegetables. Most frozen vegetables are not thawed before cooking.

The potato is a vegetable with relatively high starch content. The texture of this vegetable, which is an important quality characteristic in determining its use, is influenced by the starch granule size and composition, by cellular characteristics, and by pectic substances. Starch makes up the major portion of the solids of potatoes and high solids potatoes tend to be mealy in texture. Mealy potatoes have larger than average starch granules and larger cells. Texture of potatoes may be evaluated by "mouth feel," mild mashing, and measurement of sloughing. Pectic substances have been implicated in the textural characteristic associated with cell separation. Soft-cooking potatoes contain more water soluble pectin and less insoluble pectin than do hard-cooking potatoes.

The sugar content of potatoes increases at storage temperatures below about 10°C (50°F). This increase is at the expense of starch, that decreases. Potatoes with a high sugar content taste sweet and have a less desirable texture when cooked. The color development in fried potato products is dependent on sugar content, and thus the sugar in tubers processed in this manner must be carefully controlled.

Pared potatoes are susceptible to oxidative, enzymatic browning. Bisulfite and citric acid are commonly used to control browning. An after-cooking darkening in certain varieties of potatoes involves the development of a complex between phenolic compounds and ferric iron.

Legumes contain the highest protein content of all commercial seed crops, being present at a level of 20–25 percent in the dry product. They form a staple in the diets of many people throughout the world but are not usually a major food item for families in the United States. Legumes are susceptible to hardening during storage with consequent difficulty in rehydration and cooking. A moisture content above 13 percent, a relatively high storage temperature, and long storage periods encourage the development of hard-shell. A heat treatment prior to storage has been suggested as a means of decreasing the development of the hard-to-cook phenomenon. Phytic acid and pectic substances have been implicated in the hardening of dried peas. The phytate may complex with calcium and magnesium ions, preventing the formation of insoluble salts with pectic substances and thus retarding the hardening process.

STUDY QUESTIONS

The composition of a vegetable is dependent upon the part of the plant from which it comes.

1. List approximate percentages of water, carbohydrate, and protein for leaf- and stem-vegetables, roots and tubers, dry and cooked legumes, and fruit-vegetables. Relate the composition of each group of vegetables to its general function in the living plant.

Color, texture, and flavor are important qualities of vegetables.

2. What is lignin? How is it related to the texture of vegetables?
3. What is turgor pressure or turgidity and how does it contribute to the texture of vegetables?
4. Give several examples of vegetables in which typical flavor substances are developed through enzymatic action.
5. List several types of chemical compounds that have been identified in the aroma of various vegetables.
6. Explain how each of the following chemical compounds is involved in the development of the typical flavors and odors of cabbage or garlic.
   a. (+)-S-allyl-L-cysteine sulfoxide (alliin)
   b. Diallyl disulfide
   c. Diallyl thiosulfinate (allicin)
   d. Allyl isothiocyanate (mustard oil)
   e. Sinigrin
   f. (+)-S-methyl-L-cysteine sulfoxide
   g. Dimethyl sulfide
7. What is the significance of myrosinase and of alliinase in vegetable flavor development?
8. Discuss how the quality characteristics of vegetables may be affected by storage and handling conditions.

U. S. grades have been established for fresh and processed fruits and vegetables.

9. Discuss advantages to the consumer for the use of grades in the marketing of fruits and vegetables.
10. List typical grades for fresh and for processed vegetables and fruits.

Vegetables may be cooked by a variety of methods.

11. From the following list of changes or effects, identify those that apply to boiled vegetables as compared to the raw product.

   Hardening of cellulose
   Separation of cells
   Hydrolysis of protopectin
   Loss of ascorbic acid
   Production of lignin
   Denaturation of protein
   Leaching of flavoring substances
   Production of pheophytin in green vegetables
   Gelatinization of starch
   Production of carotenes in yellow vegetables
   Destruction of microorganisms
   Softening of texture

12. Cite several research studies in an explanation of the effects of the amount of water used and the length of the cooking period on the palatability and nutritive value of boiled vegetables.
13. Describe two general processes by which vitamins may be lost in the cooking of vegetables and suggest ways of minimizing these losses.
14. A salesman of waterless cookware insists that the only way to prepare nutritious vegetables is by using his product. Discuss his premise in light of extant research data dealing with various methods of cooking vegetables.

Characteristics of processed potatoes are affected by the composition and the variety of the raw potato.

15. Distinguish between mealiness and waxiness in potatoes.
16. Describe several factors that are likely to influence mealiness and suggest methods for evaluating this characteristic.
17. French fried potatoes, cooked for a reasonable length of time, are very dark in color and have an undesirable texture. Give possible explanations for this and suggestions for how the problem may be remedied in the future.
18. Describe a probable reaction to explain the blackening of cooked potatoes and recommend a method for minimizing the blackening in susceptible potatoes.

Legumes are susceptible to hardening during storage.

19. Describe the effect of initial moisture content, length of storage, and temperature of storage on the development of hard-shell in dry legumes.
20. Give a possible explanation for hard-cooking properties of dried peas as related to phytic acid, pectic substances, and inorganic salts.

REFERENCES

1. Amir, J., V. Kahn and M. Unterman. 1978. Temporary anoxia as a means of preventing sugar accumulation in potato tubers during storage at 4°C. *Journal of Food Science* 43, 706.

2. Bowman, F., E. Page, E. E. Remmenga, and D. Trump. 1971. Microwave *vs*. conventional cooking of vegetables at high altitude. *American Dietetic Association Journal* 58, 427.

3. Burr, H. K., S. Kon, and H. J. Morris. 1968. Cooking rates of dry beans as influenced by moisture content and temperature and time of storage. *Food Technology* 22, 88.

4. Campbell, C. L., T. Y. Lin, and B. E. Proctor. 1958. Microwave *vs*. conventional cooking. I. Reduced and total ascorbic acid in vegetables. *American Dietetic Association Journal* 34, 365.

5. Chapman, V. J., J. O. Putz, G. L. Gilpin, J. P. Sweeney, and J. N. Eisen. 1960. Electronic cooking of fresh and frozen broccoli. *Journal of Home Economics* 52, 161.

6. Charles, V. R. and F. O. Van Duyne. 1954. Palatability and retention of ascorbic acid of vegetables cooked in a tightly covered saucepan and in a "waterless" cooker. *Journal of Home Economics* 46, 659.

7. Charley, H. 1970. *Food Science*. New York: Ronald.

8. Dawson, E. H., J. C. Lamb, E. W. Toepfer, and H. W. Warren. 1952. Development of rapid methods of soaking and cooking dry beans. U. S. Department of Agriculture Technical Bulletin No. 1051.

9. Eheart, M. S. 1970. Effect of storage and other variables on composition of frozen broccoli. *Food Technology* 24, 1009.

10. Eheart, M. S. and C. Gott. 1965. Chlorophyll, ascorbic acid and pH changes in green vegetables cooked by stir-fry, microwave and conventional methods and a comparison of chlorophyll methods. *Food Technology* 19, 867.

11. Eheart, M. S. and C. Gott. 1964. Conventional and microwave cooking of vegetables. *American Dietetic Association Journal* 44, 116.

12. Eheart, M. S. and D. Odland. 1972. Storage of fresh broccoli and green beans. *American Dietetic Association Journal* 60, 402.

13. Elbert, E. M. and R. L. Witt. 1968. Gelatinization of starch in the common dry bean, Phaseolus vulgaris. *Journal of Home Economics* 60, 186.

14. Flora, L. F. and R. C. Wiley. 1974. Sweet corn aroma, chemical components and relative importance in the overall flavor response. *Journal of Food Science* 39, 770.

15. Fordham, J. R., C. E. Wells, and L. H. Chen. 1975. Sprouting of seeds and nutrient composition of seeds and sprouts. *Journal of Food Science* 40, 552.

16. Forsyth, F. R. and C. A. Eaves. 1968. Greening of potatoes: CA cure. *Food Technology* 22, 48.

17. Gilpin, G. L., J. P. Sweeney, V. J. Chapman, and J. N. Eisen. 1959. Effect of cooking methods on broccoli. II. Palatability. *American Dietetic Association Journal* 35, 359.

18. Gordon, J. and I. Noble. 1964. "Waterless" *vs*. boiling water cooking of vegetables. *American Dietetic Association Journal* 44, 378.

19. Harris, R. S. and E. Karmas. 1975. *Nutritional Evaluation of Food Processing*, 2nd edition. Westport, Conn.: Avi Publishing Co.

20. Heatherbell, D. A. and R. E. Wrolstad. 1971. Carrot volatiles. 2. Influence of variety, maturity and storage. *Journal of Food Science* 36, 225.

21. Heatherbell, D. A., R. E. Wrolstad, and L. M. Libbey. 1971. Carrot volatiles. 1. Characterization and effects of canning and freeze drying. *Journal of Food Science* 36, 219.

22. Hughes, J. C., J. E. Ayers, and T. Swain. 1962. After-cooking blackening in potatoes. I. Introduction and analytical methods. *Journal of the Science of Food and Agriculture* 13, 224.

23. Hughes, J. C. and T. Swain. 1962a. After-cooking blackening in potatoes. II. Core experiments. *Journal of the Science of Food and Agriculture* 13, 229.

24. Hughes, J. C. and T. Swain. 1962b. After-cooking blackening in potatoes. III. Examination of the interaction of factors by *in vitro* experiments. *Journal of the Science of Food and Agriculture* 13, 358.

25. Hutchinson, T. Q. 1970. Consumers' knowledge and use of government grades for selected food items. U. S. Department of Agriculture, Marketing Research Report No. 876.

26. Kazeniac, S. J. and R. M. Hall. 1970. Flavor chemistry of tomato volatiles. *Journal of Food Science* 35, 519.

27. Kon, S. 1968. Pectic substances of dry beans and their possible correlation with cooking time. *Journal of Food Science* 33, 437.

28. Kon, S., J. R. Wagner, and A. N. Booth. 1974. Legume powders: Preparation and some nutritional and physicochemical properties. *Journal of Food Science* 39, 897.

29. Lebermann, K. W., A. I. Nelson, and M. P. Steinberg. 1968. Post-harvest changes of broccoli stored in modified atmospheres. 1. Respiration of shoots and color of flower heads. *Food Technology* 22, 487.

30. de Lumen, B. O., E. J. Stone, S. J. Kazeniac, and R. H. Forsythe. 1978. Formation of volatile flavor compounds in green beans from linoleic and linolenic acids. *Journal of Food Science* 43, 698.

31. MacLeod, A. J. and G. MacLeod. 1970a. Flavor volatiles of some cooked vegetables. *Journal of Food Science* 35, 734.

32. MacLeod, A. J. and G. MacLeod. 1970b. The flavor volatiles of dehydrated cabbage. *Journal of Food Science* 35, 739.

33. MacLeod, A. J. and G. MacLeod. 1970c. Effects of variations in cooking methods on the flavor volatiles of cabbage. *Journal of Food Science* 35, 744.

34. McGill, J. N., A. I. Nelson, and M. P. Steinberg. 1966. Effects of modified storage atmospheres on ascorbic acid and other quality characteristics of spinach. *Journal of Food Science* 31, 510.

35. McIntosh, J. A., D. K. Tressler, and F. Fenton. 1940. The effect of different cooking methods on the vitamin C content of quick-frozen vegetables. *Journal of Home Economics* 32, 692.

36. Molina, M. R., M. A. Baten, R. A. Gomez-Brenes, K. W. King, and R. Bressani. 1976. Heat treatment: A process to control the development of the hard-to-cook phenomenon in black beans (*Phaseolus vulgaris*). *Journal of Food Science* 41, 661.

37. Morris, H. J. and E. R. Wood. 1956. Influence of moisture content on keeping quality of dry beans. *Food Technology* 10, 225.

38. Muneta, P. 1977. Enzymatic blackening in potatoes: Influence of pH on dopachrome oxidation. *American Potato Journal* 54, 387.

39. Muneta, P. 1964. The cooking time of dry beans after extended storage. *Food Technology* 18, 1240.

40. Muneta, P. and H. Wang. 1977. Influence of pH and bisulfite on the enzymatic blackening reaction in potatoes. *American Potato Journal* 54, 73.

41. Munsell, H. E., F. Streightoff, B. Bendor, M. L. Orr, S. R. Ezekiel, M. H. Leonard, M. E. Richardson, and F. G. Koch. 1949. Effect of largescale methods of preparation on the vitamin content of food. III. Cabbage. *American Dietetic Association Journal* 25, 420.

42. Noble, I. 1967. Ascorbic acid and color of vegetables. *American Dietetic Association Journal* 50, 304.

43. Nonaka, M., R. N. Sayre, and K. C. Ng. 1978. Surface texturization of extruded and preformed potato products by a three-step, dry-steam-dry process. *Journal of Food Science* 43, 904.

44. Nonaka, M. and M. L. Weaver. 1973. Texturizing process improves quality of baked French fried potatoes. *Food Technology* 27 (No. 3), 50.

45. Nonaka, M., M. L. Weaver, and E. Hautala. 1972. Texturizing process controls crispness and rigidity of French fried potatoes. *Food Technology* 26 (No. 4), 61.

46. Paul, P. C. and H. H. Palmer. 1972. *Food Theory and Applications*. New York: Wiley.

47. Payne, I. R. 1967. Ascorbic acid retention in frozen corn. *American Dietetic Association Journal* 51, 344.

48. Reeve, R. M. 1967. A review of cellular structure, starch, and texture qualities of processed potatoes. *Economic Botany* 21, 294.

49. Reeve, R. M. and G. K. Notter. 1959. An improved microscopic method for counting ruptured cells in dehydrated potato products. *Food Technology* 13, 574.

50. Samotus, B. and S. Schwimmer. 1963. Changes in carbohydrate and phosphorus content of potato tubers during storage in nitrogen. *Journal of Food Science* 28, 163.

51. Singh, R. P., F. H. Buelow, and D. B. Lund. 1973. Storage behavior of artificially waxed green snap beans. *Journal of Food Science* 38, 542.

52. Singh, B., C. C. Yang, D. K. Salunkhe, and A. R. Rahman. 1972. Controlled atmosphere storage of lettuce. 1. Effects on quality and the respiration rate of lettuce heads. *Journal of Food Science* 37, 48.

53. Sweeney, J. P., G. L. Gilpin, M. G. Staley, and M. E. Martin. 1959. Effect of cooking methods on broccoli. 1. Ascorbic acid and carotene. *American Dietetic Association Journal* 35, 354.

54. Sweeney, J. P. and A. C. Marsh. 1971. Effect of processing on provitamin A in vegetables. *American Dietetic Association Journal* 59, 238.

55. Le Tourneau, D., M. V. Zaehringer, and A. L. Potter. 1962. Textural quality of potatoes. II. An objective method for evaluating texture. *Food Technology* 16, 135.

56. U. S. Department of Agriculture. 1967. How to buy fresh vegetables. Home and Garden Bulletin No. 143.

57. U. S. Department of Agriculture. 1970. How to buy dry beans, peas, and lentils: Home and Garden Bulletin No. 177.

58. U. S. Department of Agriculture. 1977. How to use USDA grades in buying foods. Home and Garden Bulletin No. 196.

59. Walker, M. A., M. M. Hill, and F. D. Millman. 1973. Fruit and vegetable acceptance by students. *American Dietetic Association Journal* 62, 268.

60. Wang, S. S., N. F. Haard, and G. R. DiMarco. 1971. Chlorophyll degradation during controlled-atmosphere storage of asparagus. *Journal of Food Science* 36, 657.

61. Watt, B. K. and A. L. Merrill. Revised 1963. Composition of foods. U. S. Department of Agriculture. Agriculture Handbook No. 8.

62. White, P. L. and N. Selvey. 1974. *Nutritional Qualities of Fresh Fruits and Vegetables*. Mount Kisco, New York: Futura Publishing Company.

63. Williams, M. P. and P. E. Nelson. 1973. Effect of hybrids and processing on the dimethyl sulfide potential of sweet corn. *Journal of Food Science* 38, 1136.

64. Woodman, J. S. and D. S. Warren. 1972. Texture of canned potatoes: Use of new objective methods to separate the attributes of mouthfeel and breakdown. *Journal of the Science of Food and Agriculture* 23, 1067.

65. Zaehringer, M. V. and D. Le Tourneau. 1962. Textural quality of potatoes. I. Comparison of three organoleptic methods. *Food Technology* 16, 131.

CHAPTER 15

CEREAL GRAINS AND MILLING

Cereals have been staple crops throughout the world for thousands of years. They are the fruits of cultivated grasses and belong to the monocotyledonous family Gramineae. The principal cereal crops are wheat, maize or corn, rice, barley, oats, rye, sorghum, and millet.

15.1

STRUCTURE OF GRAINS

The anatomical structure is basically similar for all grains. It consists of a fruit coat or pericarp and a seed. The seed is comprised of a seed coat, germ, and endosperm. Each of the main parts of the kernel is further subdivided into various layers, tissues, or regions, as shown in Figure 15.1 for the wheat grain. Oats, barley, and rice have an additional husk outside the fruit coat (Kent, 1975).

The various grains differ in size and shape. Usual dimensions for several of the grains are given in Table 15.1.

Wheat grains are ovoid in shape and rounded at both ends. The presence of a longitudinal crease in the kernel complicates the milling processes that are used to separate the endosperm from the surrounding layers. Rye resembles wheat in structure but is slightly longer and not as wide. Rice is flattened laterally and has a small point at one end. The oat grain is cylindrical in shape, blunted at the germ end, and pointed at the beard end. Barley is spindle-shaped, thicker in the center, and tapering toward each end. Corn is much larger than any of the other cereals.

The endosperm of cereal grains is composed of an aleurone layer and a starchy endosperm. In wheat, the endosperm makes up nearly 90 percent of the total weight of the kernel. The aleurone in this grain is a single layer of thick walled cubical cells surrounding the starchy endosperm. The aleurone cell contains tiny aleurone grains that consist mostly of phytic acid with some protein (Kent, 1975). The major concentration of niacin, pyridoxine, pantothenic acid, and riboflavin is in the aleurone tissue. The major share of the kernel's thiamin is found in

Figure 15.1

Diagrammatic longitudinal section of wheat grain through crease and germ. (From Kent, N. L. *Technology of Cereals,* 2nd edition. Oxford: Pergamon Press Ltd., 1975. With permission.)

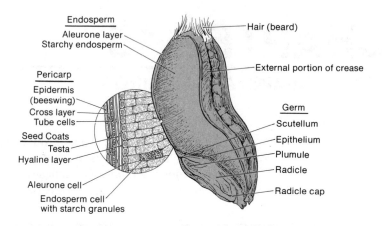

the germ, with the next largest portion in the aleurone. The vitamin content of wheat flours thus decreases as the percent of the endosperm extracted decreases (Inglett, 1974).

TYPES OF WHEAT

Each variety of wheat is commonly classified according to the texture of the ripened kernel endosperm, the color, and the growing season. The texture may be hard and vitreous or soft and floury. The color, produced by various combinations of carotenoid and other pigments, may be red or white. In relatively mild climates, some varieties of wheat may be planted in the fall and harvested in June or July. These

Table 15.1   Dimensions for Selected Cereal Grains

	Length (mm)	Width (mm)
Wheat	5–8	2.5–4.5
Rye	4.5–10	1.5–3.5
Rice	5–10	1.5–5
Oats	6–13	1–4.5
Barley	8–14	1–4.5
Corn	8–17	5–15

varieties are called *winter wheat*. In northern areas of the United States where severe winters are usual, wheat is commonly planted in the spring and harvested in the fall. This is called *spring wheat*. Various types of wheat thus include hard red winter, hard red spring, soft red winter, and white wheats, that are generally soft. Durum wheat is a hard amber wheat used for making macaroni products. The areas of the United States where the various kinds of wheat are grown are shown in Figure 15.2.

During the process of milling, the endosperm of hard wheats breaks between the cells and produces a granular flour. The soft wheat endosperm tends to pulverize with few cells remaining intact. The flour from soft wheats is softer to the touch. The baking qualities differ with the type of wheat. (Baking properties are discussed in Chapter 28.)

Hard wheats tend to be higher in protein content than *soft wheats*. However, this variation does not appear to be responsible for the characteristic differences between hard and soft wheats. A soft wheat

Figure 15.2

The map indicates the general areas in which the various kinds of wheat are grown. (Courtesy of Wheat Flour Institute and Kansas Wheat Commission.)

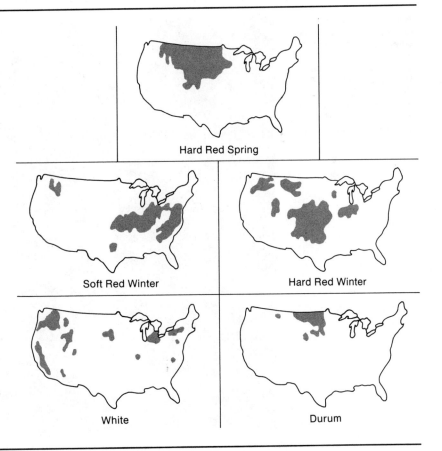

Hard Red Spring

Soft Red Winter

Hard Red Winter

White

Durum

variety grown under conditions which produce higher than normal protein content still exhibits characteristics of a soft wheat. Neither do inherent differences in the protein or starch components of hard and soft wheat explain the differences in hardness.

Hoseney and Seib (1973) used scanning electron microscopy to view the structure of wheat and its fractions using both hard and soft varieties. These studies strongly suggest that the hardness of wheat is determined by the strength of the protein–starch bond, with a stronger bond being associated with harder wheat. Figure 15.3 shows hard winter wheat endosperm. The large starch granules are flat and round in one view but rather thin when seen from the other direction. The protein appears to adhere tightly to the starch with relatively little of the starch surface exposed. The starch and protein are tightly packed and there appears to be little or no air space in the endosperm. Fractured starch granules are seen, indicating that starch–protein adherence is strong enough to break the starch granule rather than to separate at

Figure 15.3

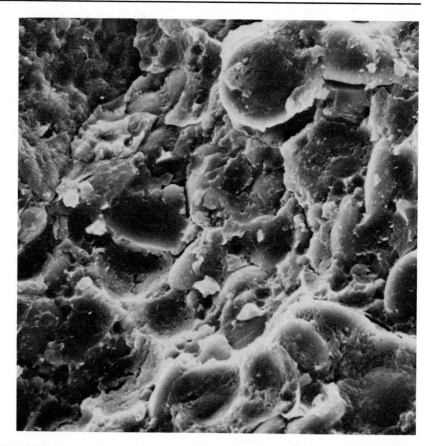

A scanning electron micrograph of hard winter wheat endosperm magnified 800×. (Reprinted with permission from Hoseney, R. C. and P. A. Seib. 1973. Structural differences in hard and soft wheat. *Bakers Digest* 47 [Dec.], 26.)

Figure 15.4

A scanning electron micrograph of soft winter wheat endosperm magnified 800×. (Reprinted with permission from Hoseney, R. C. and P. A. Seib. 1973. Structural differences in hard and soft wheat. *Bakers Digest* 47 [Dec.], 26.)

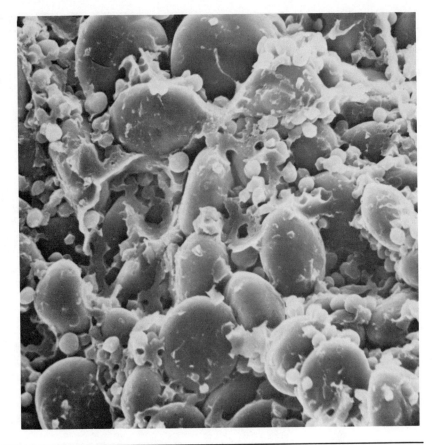

the interface when the kernel is broken. Figure 15.4 shows soft winter wheat endosperm. In this photomicrograph the protein matrix does not appear to be continuous and the surface of the starch granules is more exposed. This endosperm has a much looser structure, with many intergranular air spaces. The air spaces diffract light and give the kernel an opaque or nonvitreous appearance. No broken starch granules are seen, indicating that the bond between the protein and the starch granules breaks before the starch granule does. Figures 15.5 and 15.6 show scanning electron photomicrographs of soft winter wheat flour and hard winter wheat flour, respectively. In the soft wheat flour, the starch–protein matrix has lost most of its structure, leaving a mixture of free starch granules, free protein, and small aggregates of protein and starch. The integrity of the starch–protein matrix is maintained in the hard wheat flour, even though the particle size is greatly reduced. Many of the starch granules are damaged.

Figure 15.5

A scanning electron micrograph of soft winter wheat flour magnified 800×. (Reprinted with permission from Hoseney, R. C. and P. A. Seib. 1973. Structural differences in hard and soft wheat. *Bakers Digest* 47 [Dec.], 26.)

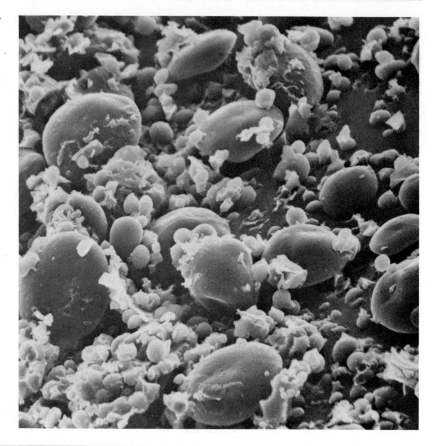

15.2

CHEMICAL COMPOSITION OF CEREAL GRAINS

The grain of common cereals consists of carbohydrates, nitrogenous compounds (mainly protein), lipids, mineral salts, vitamins, enzymes, and small amounts of other substances. (The proximate composition of several dry cereal grains is given in Table 15.2.)

CARBOHYDRATE

Carbohydrate is quantitatively the most important component of grains. It constitutes about 83 percent of the total dry matter of wheat, barley, rye, corn, and rice and about 79 percent of oats (Kent, 1975). Starch is the predominant carbohydrate and is discussed in detail in Chapter 16. Other carbohydrates include cellulose, hemicelluloses, pentosans, dextrins, and sugars. Cellulose and hemicelluloses are part of the complex of substances that make up what is called fiber. They are found in the cell walls of plants along with variable amounts of

Figure 15.6

A scanning electron micrograph of hard winter wheat flour magnified 800×. (Reprinted with permission from Hoseney, R. C. and P. A. Seib. 1973. Structural differences in hard and soft wheat. *Bakers Digest* 47[Dec.], 26.)

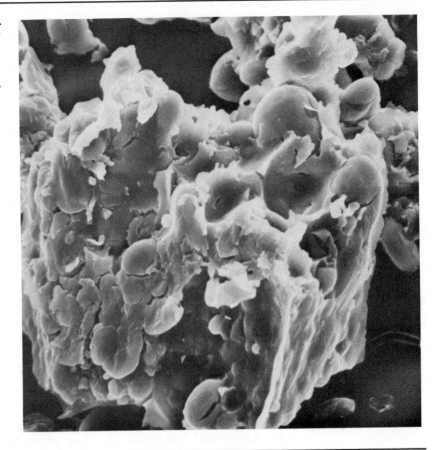

lignin, a noncarbohydrate substance. Pentosans are classified as hemicelluloses.

The importance of dietary fiber in human nutrition and gastrointestinal disease has recently been emphasized. Cereal brans contain appreciable amounts of fiber and have been used as a source of this substance, as has purified cellulose, in the commercial production of high fiber breads. The use of additional wheat gluten is necessary in high-fiber breads produced commercially because of the increased strain on the natural gluten resulting from additional fibrous materials (Pomeranz, 1977).

Several methods have been used for the determination of crude fiber in cereal grains. Depending upon the method, variable amounts of cellulose are measured, along with a certain amount of lignin, hemicelluloses, and pentosans. An enzymatic method does not destroy the hemicelluloses, pentosans, and lignin in the sample and gives higher results for fiber than does a long-used method involving acid and al-

Table 15.2 Proximate Composition of Dry Cereal Grains and Flours, 100 g, Edible Portion

	Water (%)	Kcal.	Protein (g)	Fat (g)	Carbohydrate total (g)	Carbohydrate fiber (g)	Ash (g)
Wheat, whole-grain							
Hard red spring	13.0	330	14.0	2.2	69.1	2.3	1.7
Hard red winter	12.5	330	12.3	1.8	71.7	2.3	1.7
Soft red winter	14.0	326	10.2	2.0	72.1	2.3	1.7
White	11.5	335	9.4	2.0	75.4	1.9	1.7
Durum	13.0	332	12.7	2.5	70.1	1.8	1.7
Wheat flours							
Whole (from hard wheats)	12.0	333	13.3	2.0	71.0	2.3	1.7
Patent:							
All-purpose flour	12.0	364	10.5	1.0	76.1	0.3	0.43
Bread flour	12.0	365	11.8	1.1	74.7	0.3	0.44
Cake or pastry flour	12.0	364	7.5	0.8	79.4	0.2	0.31
Rye, whole-grain	11.0	334	12.1	1.7	73.4	2.0	1.8
Rice							
Brown	12.0	360	7.5	1.9	77.4	0.9	1.2
White (fully milled)	12.0	363	6.7	0.4	80.4	0.3	0.5
Oats, rolled	8.3	390	14.2	7.4	68.2	1.2	1.9
Barley, whole-grain*			11.8	1.8	78.1	5.3	3.1
Pearled, light	11.1	349	8.2	1.0	78.8	0.5	0.9
Corn, field, whole-grain	13.8	348	8.9	3.9	72.2	2.0	1.2

Source: From Watt and Merrill, 1963.
* Watson, 1953.

kaline treatment. Generally, crude fiber as determined in the laboratory is not synonomous with dietary fiber, the indigestible residue from consumed food. Varying figures for crude fiber content of cereals have been reported in the literature. For U. S. wheat samples, the crude fiber content varies from 1.98 to 3.02 percent (Inglett, 1974).

The sugar content of wheat is about 2.5 percent. Sugars in wheat include glucose, fructose, sucrose, maltose, and several oligosaccharides that yield glucose on hydrolysis. Dextrins, polysaccharides that are smaller than starch, are also present (Kent, 1975).

Hemicelluloses and Pentosans   Hemicellulose is the name proposed by Schulze in 1891 to designate those polysaccharides that are extractable from plants by aqueous alkali, are stable end products, and are not part of a dynamic system. Their function appears to be structural. The hemicelluloses are polysaccharides, containing many simple sugars linked together, and are commonly classified according to the type of sugar residues present. Most of them are heteroglycans, containing two to four different types of sugar residues, and usually have a branched structure (D'Appolonia and Kim, 1976). The hemicelluloses of wheat are essentially composed of the five-carbon sugars, arabinose and xylose. They differ by the presence of other minor constituents that include glucose, galactose, polyuronic acids, and proteins (Inglett, 1974).

Pentosans are hemicelluloses. The pentosans of white wheat flour apparently come from the cell walls of the endosperm and have been studied because of their roles in bread dough development. Wheat flour pentosans have two unique properties that distinguish them from the common hemicelluloses of the plant cell wall. First, about 20–25 percent of the total pentosans in a white wheat flour are soluble in water and form a highly viscous solution. Second, aqueous flour extracts or solutions of purified flour pentosans form solid gels upon the addition of minute amounts of oxidizing agents. These properties are apparently due to special structural features not found in other pentosans or related gums (Neukom *et al.*, 1967).

Both water-soluble and water-insoluble wheat pentosans have been studied. Early investigators used the term hemicellulose to refer to the water-insoluble nonstarchy polysaccharides and the term pentosan to refer to the water-soluble polysaccharides. However, others have simply utilized the term water-soluble pentosan for that material extracted by water and the term water-insoluble pentosan for the pentosans that are water-insoluble (D'Applonia, 1971).

The basic structure of the water-soluble pentosans is a long straight chain of anhydro-D-xylose residues linked beta-1,4, to which are attached single anhydro-L-arabinose residues at the two or three positions of the D-xylose units. The structure of the water-insoluble pentosans appears to be similar to that of the water-soluble substances, but may be less linear and larger in molecular size. Some pentosans are linked to a peptide or protein. These glycoproteins have been shown to participate in a gelation reaction (D'Appolonia and Kim, 1976).

Pentosans in wheat flour play an important role in the water absorption properties of dough and affect dough rheology (flow characteristics). Wheat flour contains about 2–3 percent water-soluble and water-insoluble pentosans, with water-soluble pentosans making up only about 0.5–0.8 percent of the total weight of wheat flour. Jelaca and Hlynka (1971) reported that the water-soluble pentosans from Canadian hard red spring wheat flour absorbed 9.2 times their weight of water and the water-insoluble pentosans absorbed 8.0 times their weight (dry basis).

LIPIDS

The lipid content of wheat, rye, barley, and rice is generally 1–2 percent. Corn and oats contain 4–7 percent lipid. The lipids are unevenly distributed throughout the kernel. In wheat, the germ contains 6–10 percent lipid, the bran 3–5 percent, and the endosperm 0.8–1.5 percent (Kent, 1975). The lipids of cereals are chiefly triglycerides (esters of glycerol with three fatty acids). Phospholipids are present in lesser amounts. Fat-soluble tocopherols, with vitamin E activity, are also found in cereals, primarily in the germ. Price and Parsons (1975) reported the fatty acid composition of total lipid to be similar for samples of barley, corn, rye, wheat, sorghum, and triticale. Lipids are comparatively minor components of flour but have some important functions in breadmaking.

The lipids in milled cereal products are susceptible to oxidative deterioration through the action of the enzyme lipoxidase. They may also be oxidized nonenzymatically in the presence of oxygen. Rancid odors and flavors are produced. Tocopherols are natural antioxidants that help to control unwanted oxidative reactions. Additional antioxidants may be added to processed breakfast cereals. The separation of the germ, that contains most of the fat, from the endosperm in the milling of wheat flour improves the keeping quality of the flour.

The pigments in wheat include the fat-soluble carotenes and xanthophylls that impart a yellow color. Flavones and degradation products of chlorophyll are also present. In the United States and some other countries, wheat flour is bleached to achieve the whiteness desired.

PROTEINS

Cereal grains vary in protein content from 7 to 14 percent. The protein is unevenly distributed throughout the kernel. The wheat embryo contains 26 percent protein and the aleurone contains 24 percent. The outer endosperm averages 16 percent protein and the inner endosperm averages approximately 8 percent (Inglett, 1974). The study of wheat proteins is as old as protein chemistry itself. By 1838, when Mulder proposed the name "protein," wheat gluten was recognized as a simply prepared, relatively pure protein because of the demonstration by Beccari in 1728 that gluten could be produced by washing the starch and water-soluble components from dough as it was kneaded under running water (Inglett, 1974). Gluten is the substance that is primarily responsible for the excellent breadmaking properties of wheat flour. (Gluten and other wheat proteins are discussed in detail in Chapter 28.)

Grain kernels contain many different protein enzymes that are responsible for their propagation. These enzymes are distributed throughout the kernel of the grain. The process of milling disrupts the kernel and enzymes are redistributed into the various milled fractions. Some of the enzymes that are of particular importance in the milling and baking industry are α-amylase, β-amylase, proteases, lipid esterases, phytase, lipoxygenase, peroxidase, and ascorbic acid oxidase (Inglett, 1974).

TRITICALE

Triticale is a hybrid cereal derived from crossing wheat and rye (Hulse and Spurgeon, 1974). Reports of a wheat–rye crossbreed date back to about 1875. However, because the cross was sterile, little notice was taken of the grain until 1937. It was then discovered that treatment of the seedling with the drug colchicine rendered it partly fertile. Much genetic improvement has since occurred and work is continuing in order to eliminate defects in the triticale strains.

The major advantages of the use of triticale for human as well as animal food are comparatively high crop yields and high protein content. Some varieties also have higher lysine values than does wheat. The protein content of triticale has been reported to range from 11.8 to 16.8 percent. In triticale strains that characteristically have somewhat shrivelled kernels, the percent of the grain extracted as flour is lower than that for wheat. Thus the protein content of these milled triticale flours may not be higher than that of wheat flour (Lorenz, 1974).

Haber *et al.* (1976) evaluated the baking quality of commercial hard red winter wheat, rye, and triticale flours. Triticale doughs had lower water absorption and poorer baking quality than those made from wheat flour. Modified mixing and/or fermentation techniques are required for triticale doughs. Certain dough conditioners may also improve the bread baking quality of flour from this grain. Continuing research may allow this new cereal grain to reach its full potential in commercial baking use.

15.3

PROCESSING READY-TO-EAT CEREALS

A wide variety of ready-to-eat breakfast cereals, as well as cereals to be cooked, is available in the U. S. marketplace. Most of the ready-to-eat cereals are fortified to a comparatively high degree with vitamins and minerals (Hayden, 1973), a single serving often containing levels of 25 percent or higher of the U. S. RDA for these nutrients. Many of them are highly advertised and carry extensive nutritional information on their labels. Anderson *et al.* (1976) studied the effects of processing and storage on micronutrients in breakfast cereals. They found indigenous folic acid, biotin, and pantothenic acid to be relatively stable during processing. Minerals were not lost in processing. Vitamins for nutritional fortification are generally added to cereals at processing stages beyond which they are not subject to destruction. No substantial losses of added vitamins were found during the normal shelf lives of several breakfast cereals, except possibly vitamins A and C. About 15 percent of vitamin A may be lost when flaked or puffed cereals are stored for three months at 40°C (104°F), but no appreciable losses were noted when stored at 22°C (72°F) for six months. Vitamin C showed a slight loss at 40°C in some cereal tests but not in others. The stability possibly results from the low moisture content of these products.

A number of different processes are used in the preparation of ready-to-eat cereals. These include flaking, puffing, shredding, and production of granules. Most of the common grains are used in the preparation of breakfast cereals, often in combination. The basic cereal sometimes contains sweetening agents such as sugars and syrups.

In the production of flaked cereals, the whole grain is cleaned, conditioned to a suitable moisture content, and lightly rolled between smooth rolls to fracture the outer layers. This product is then cooked, often at elevated pressure, and the flavoring substances, such as malt, sugar, and salt, are added. They penetrate the rolled grain. The cooked cereal is dried, conditioned, flaked on heavy flaking rolls, toasted, cooled, and packaged (Kent, 1975).

For puffed cereals, the whole grain is cleaned, conditioned, and the pericarp removed by a wet scouring process. Alternatively, a stiff dough may be made from blended cereal flours and added sugar and salt. The dough is cooked, dried to a level of 14–16 percent moisture and pelleted by extrusion through a die. The prepared grain or pelleted dough is put into a pressure chamber. The chamber is sealed and heated both externally and by the injection of steam so that the internal pressure rapidly builds to about 200 lb/sq in. The pressure is then suddenly released. The expansion of water vapor on release of the pressure puffs up the grains or pellets to several times their original size. At the moment before expansion, the cereal product requires cohesion to prevent shattering and elasticity to permit expansion. The balance between these two characteristics may be varied by adding starch with its cohesive properties. The puffed product is dried to 3 percent moisture by toasting, cooled, and packaged (Kent, 1975).

A white, starchy wheat is used for shredding. The whole grain is cleaned and then cooked with water in such a way that the cooked grain is soft and rubbery. The moisture content is about 43 percent and the starch fully gelatinized. The cooked grain is cooled, conditioned, and fed to shredders. The shredders consist of a pair of metal rolls, one smooth and the other with circular grooves between which the cereal emerges as long parallel shreds. A thick mat of shreds is built up by superimposing several layers on one another. The mat is cut into the desired size, baked, dried to 1 percent moisture, cooled, and packaged (Kent, 1975).

In the preparation of granular breakfast cereals, a yeasted dough is made from a blend of fine flours with added salt. The dough is fermented and made into large loaves that are baked. The baked loaves are broken up, dried, and ground to a standard fineness (Kent, 1975).

15.4

MILLING OF WHEAT

Wheat and other grains have been milled since prehistoric times to separate the outer bran and germ from the endosperm. Primitive methods of milling utilized hollow stones or mortars in which the grain was pounded. Power from air and water sources was later used to turn heavy millstones. Roller milling became widely used about 1833 when refinements were made in this process. The introduction of the middlings purifier in 1865 further advanced the milling evolution. Through this invention, coarse middlings (floury particles) are purified by passing them over a vibrating screen with an upward current of air that lifts off most of the light bran particles. The best grades of flour are made by regrinding the purified middlings. Many improvements and refinements of milling machinery over the years have contributed to the development of the modern wheat mill (Inglett, 1974).

The purposes of milling are twofold, to separate as much of the endosperm as possible from the bran and germ and to reduce the endosperm to fine particles. To do this, the roller mills use a particular form of grinding that is a combination of shearing, scraping, and crushing. The grain is gradually reduced to flour in a succession of steps. At each step the severity of grinding is adjusted so that only a portion of endosperm fragmentation and bran cleaning occurs. The basic processes in roller milling are 1. grinding or breaking—fragmenting the grain or its parts with some dissociation of the anatomical parts of the grain from one another; 2. sieving or bolting—classifying mixtures of particles of differing particle size into fractions of narrower particle size range; and 3. purifying—separating mixtures of bran and endosperm particles by means of air currents (Kent, 1975).

Flour extraction rate refers to the proportion of flour by weight, derived by milling, from a known quantity of wheat. The usual commercial extraction rate from wheat is in the range of 68–77 percent. It may rise above this when wheat is scarce or when regulations based on special nutritional considerations apply. After World War II, for example, the extraction rate rose to 80 percent in the United States and to 90 percent in Britain. If the extraction is 75 percent, a white flour is implied. If it exceeds 80 percent, the flour will contain a significant proportion of nonendosperm particles. The color changes relatively rapidly with an increased extraction rate above 75 percent. Whole wheat flour is specified to approach 100 percent extraction (Pomeranz, 1971).

The physical dough, baking, and nutritional qualities of flours with extended extraction rates were studied and compared with straight grade flours of 69.6–77.2 percent extraction by Watson *et al.* (1977). The experimental flours were produced from hard red spring wheats with extended extraction rates of about 80 percent. Since mixograms and baking qualities were similar for the straight grade and extended extraction flours for each wheat variety studied, these workers concluded that the current flour extraction rates can be increased by at least 5 percent. The increase would not substantially affect the quality of the bread but would increase its nutritional value with respect to its mineral, thiamin, and lysine content.

The modern milling process is a complex one with many streams of flour being produced and mixed together to create various grades of white flour. After the wheat has been cleaned and conditioned, it is sent through the first set of spirally fluted, chilled rolls called *break rolls*. The two break rolls are driven at different speeds and the grain is sheared with a scissor action. The products of the first break are sifted through a series of sieves. The coarsest portion goes to the second break rolls, intermediate coarse particles go to the middlings purifier and the finest particles go to smooth reduction rolls where they are reduced in size.

Each break also produces some flour that goes through the sifter with the finest mesh. Usually the coarse grain particles go through four or five break processes. Each set of break rollers has finer corrugations and each is followed by a sifting and purifying process.

The wheat particles are gradually reduced to granular material called *middlings*. The basic concept of the action of a middlings purifier is shown in Figure 15.7. The middlings pass over a vibrating screen. Air currents lift off most of the light bran particles. Purified middlings of various sizes sift to the bottom. *Tailings* include flattened and coarse particles that do not go through the sifter. *Purified middlings* of small size go through reduction rolls. These rolls are smooth with no flutings and are driven at almost equal speeds. Endosperm particles are generally reduced in size by the reduction rolls. Bran and germ particles are flattened. Eight to sixteen sets of reduction rolls may be involved in the milling process. Photographs of grinding, sifting, and purifying machinery used in modern mills are shown in Figure 15.8.

Important developments in flour milling in recent years have made it possible to obtain, from a single wheat flour sample, flours that differ markedly in protein content and can be used for different purposes. Particles in the flour that result from milling are of varying sizes and

Figure 15.7

Basic concept of the middlings purifier.

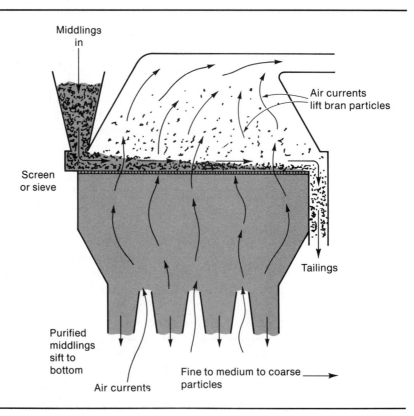

Figure 15.8

Rolling, sifting and purifying processes are repeated many times in the milling of white flour. (Courtesy of Wheat Flour Institute and Kansas Wheat Commission.)

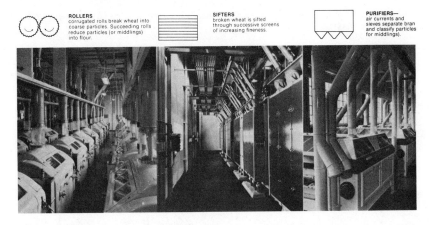

ROLLERS
corrugated rolls break wheat into coarse particles. Succeeding rolls reduce particles (or middlings) into flour.

SIFTERS
broken wheat is sifted through successive screens of increasing fineness.

PURIFIERS—
air currents and sieves separate bran and classify particles for middlings).

composition. Free starch granules are present with a wide range of sizes. Some of the smaller flour particles are pieces of free protein. Other particles include small clusters containing fragments of protein matrix in which are embedded small starch granules. Larger pieces of endosperm cells are also present with a composition similar to that of the original flour (Pomeranz, 1971).

Air classification is one scheme for separating the various flour particles into more uniform groups. Milled flour is first further reduced in particle size by use of a high-speed grinder. The reground flour is then introduced into a column of air whirling in a cyclone separator. The larger, heavier particles tend to move toward the wall and then fall to the bottom of the air classifier while the smaller particles, called *fines*, are pulled to the center, lifted up by the circulating air, and separated out. Figure 15.9 shows how flour may be separated by air classification into three fractions. A low protein mixture resulting from the fractionation may contain 20–30 percent of the initial flour. This starchy product from high protein flours is sometimes suitable for making cakes and pastries. However, Bean *et al.* (1969) found that the low protein fraction of some varieties of hard red winter wheats were unsatisfactory for cookies and layer cakes even at reasonable protein levels. A fine fraction resulting from air classification may contain from 15 to 22 percent protein and represent from 5 to 15 percent of the original flour. This product may be blended with other flours when a high protein flour is desirable.

GRADES OF FLOUR

Many streams of white flour are produced from the various sifting processes that occur in milling wheat. Grades of flour are determined by combining certain millstreams. Figure 15.10 diagrams the various grades of flour that result from the milling process. The blending of all of the flour streams results in *straight grade* flour. *Long, medium,* and

Figure 15.9

Flour may be separated into fractions of varying composition. (Courtesy of Wheat Flour Institute and Kansas Wheat Commission.)

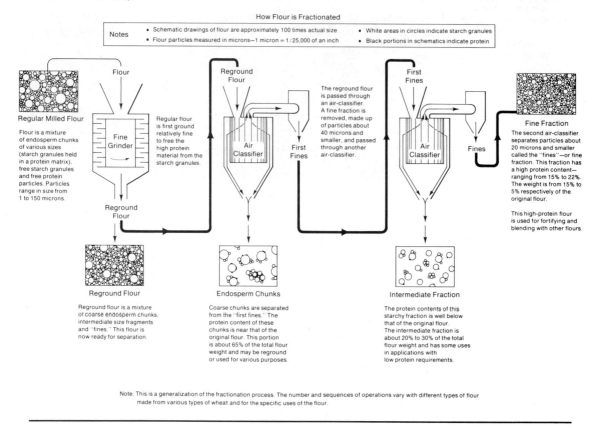

How Flour is Fractionated

Notes
- Schematic drawings of flour are approximately 100 times actual size
- Flour particles measured in microns—1 micron = 1/25,000 of an inch
- White areas in circles indicate starch granules
- Black portions in schematics indicate protein

Regular Milled Flour

Flour is a mixture of endosperm chunks of various sizes (starch granules held in a protein matrix), free starch granules and free protein particles. Particles range in size from 1 to 150 microns.

Regular flour is first ground relatively fine to free the high protein material from the starch granules.

The reground flour is passed through an air-classifier. A fine fraction is removed, made up of particles about 40 microns and smaller, and passed through another air-classifier.

Fine Fraction

The second air-classifier separates particles about 20 microns and smaller called the "fines"—or fine fraction. This fraction has a high protein content—ranging from 15% to 22%. The weight is from 15% to 5% respectively of the original flour.

This high-protein flour is used for fortifying and blending with other flours.

Reground Flour

Reground flour is a mixture of coarse endosperm chunks, intermediate size fragments and "fines." This flour is now ready for separation.

Endosperm Chunks

Coarse chunks are separated from the "first fines." The protein content of these chunks is near that of the original flour. This portion is about 65% of the total flour weight and may be reground or used for various purposes.

Intermediate Fraction

The protein contents of this starchy fraction is well below that of the original flour. The intermediate fraction is about 20% to 30% of the total flour weight and has some uses in applications with low protein requirements.

Note: This is a generalization of the fractionation process. The number and sequences of operations vary with different types of flour made from various types of wheat and for the specific uses of the flour.

short patent flours contain from 95 to 40 percent of the millstreams. *Clear grade* flours are those not included in the patent grade flours. Shorts consist of fine particles of bran and germ with some flour. The various grades of flour find uses in many different products. The longer patent flours generally go into breadmaking while the short patents are usually used for cake and cookie flours. *Second clear grade* flour is used for the extraction of wheat gluten and starch (Inglett, 1974). Clear flours may also be used in the various flour products such as pancake mixes.

TYPES OF FLOUR

The terms flour, white flour, wheat flour, and plain flour are synonymous, according to regulations and standards of the U. S. Food and Drug Administration. The standard of identity for flour specifies a certain fineness of granulation and a low ash content. Presence of bran particles increases the ash.

Figure 15.10

Various grades of flour are produced from 100 pounds of wheat. (Courtesy of Wheat Flour Institute and Kansas Wheat Commission.)

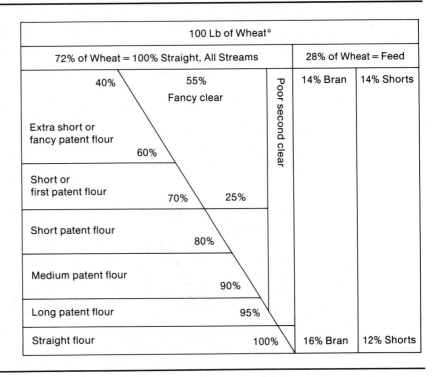

Various types of flour are available to meet specific uses. These include bread flour, all-purpose or family flour, pastry flour, and cake flour. In general, hard wheat flours are most effectively used for bread flours. Pastry and cake flours are produced from soft wheats or low-protein fractions of some hard wheat varieties. The wheat used for milling all-purpose flours may differ, depending upon the part of the United States in which the mill is located. However, wheats are often blended at the beginning of the milling process to produce a flour with characteristics intermediate between hard and soft wheat flours.

Phosphated soft wheat flours contain monocalcium phosphate. The phosphate counteracts the effect of excessive soda when these flours are used for making sour milk biscuits. It also strengthens the gluten of soft wheat flours. Self-rising flours contain salt and baking powder.

ADDITIVES TO FLOUR

Flour contains yellowish pigments, chiefly the carotenoid xanthophylls. Bleaching of these pigments occurs naturally when the flour is exposed to air. This process is accelerated by the use of various chemical substances. Only one chemical with the single function of bleaching is allowed for use in flour by the Food and Drug Administration in the United States. This is benzoyl peroxide that reacts with the carotenoid pigments of flour. Bleaching of the pigments with benzoyl peroxide has no effect on the baking properties of the flour.

The baking performance of flour improves with age. This maturing process apparently involves oxidation of proteins in the flour. Yoneyama et al. (1970a) reported that the most significant change observed in freshly milled wheat flours stored for 90 days at 30°C (86°F) was a decrease in the sulfhydryl (−SH) content of a water-soluble extraction of the flour. The change in sulfhydryl content appeared to be directly responsible for changes in rheological properties of the dough with decreased extensibility and increased resistance to extension. This may result from cross-linkage of the protein chains by disulfide bonds (−S−S−). There was no change in soluble −SH content and rheological properties for flour samples stored below 0°C (32°F) (Yoneyama et al., 1970b).

Various compounds have been approved by the U. S. Food and Drug Administration for use as chemical maturing agents in flour, by the use of which similar changes to those occurring during natural aging are engendered. The maturing agents also have some bleaching effect. Flours milled from different types of wheat have different requirements of maturing compounds and the rate of treatment must be controlled. Undesirable baking characteristics result from overtreatment with maturing agents. Substances allowed include chlorine dioxide gas, acetone peroxides, and azodicarbonamide, which does not react until the flour is made into a dough. Gaseous chlorine, or a mixture of chlorine with nitrosyl chloride, is widely used in the treatment of soft wheat flours and low-protein air-classified hard wheat flours used for cakes, certain types of nonspread cookies, and certain pastries (Pomeranz, 1971). Kulp (1972) reported that the reaction of chlorine with soft wheat flour produced changes on the surface of starch granules. It also increased the dispersability of proteins by gradually disrupting inter- and intra-molecular noncovalent bonds and breaking certain peptide linkages. He concluded that the improving effect of chlorine on cake flour is the result of changes produced in certain flour components, with concomitant alteration of their interaction properties. Treatment of cake flour with chlorine results in higher volume, superior grain, and more tender texture in cakes prepared from this flour as compared to untreated flour.

15.5

MILLING OF RYE, RICE, OATS, AND CORN

Rye is milled by a process similar to that used for the production of wheat flour. However, in rye milling, the endosperm is reduced to flour fineness more readily than is wheat endosperm but the flour is difficult to sift. The endosperm is also separated from the bran with more difficulty in rye than wheat milling. Therefore, a large amount of rye flour is made on the break rollers and fewer middlings are produced. Rye flour averaging 83.5 percent extraction is produced in the United States (Kent, 1975).

Rice is commonly cleaned, hulled, and milled—a process whereby the bran and germ are partially or wholly removed by an abrasive scouring or pearling process. The polishing of rice, after milling, is done in a brush machine that removes the aleurone layer and any adhering particles. Polishing makes the surface shiney and also minimizes the tendency for the milled grain to develop oxidative rancidity. Rice is traditionally parboiled in India and Pakistan by steeping the rough rice in hot water, steaming it, and then drying it to a suitable moisture content for milling. The original purpose was to loosen the hulls. However, there is also nutritional improvement since the process causes vitamins and minerals in the hulls and bran coat to move into the endosperm. There is, therefore, less loss of these nutrients in milling. The modern process of parboiling is called *conversion*. Some converted rice is sold in the United States. Nonconverted white rice is generally fortified with thiamin, niacin, and iron (Kent, 1975).

The adherent husk of the oat grain is tough and fibrous and is removed in a special shelling process. Only the kernel (*groat*) is used for human food. The bran of the oat kernel is relatively thin and pale in color. It is not separated from the endosperm in the manufacture of oatmeal and rolled oats. Lipase is inactivated, often by steam, before or during the milling of oat products to avoid undesirable flavor changes. Shelled groats are brushed or scoured to detach the fine hairs on their surface. For the production of oatmeal, they are then cut transversely, each kernel yielding four or five pieces. Finer cuts of oatmeal are made by grinding. Rolled oats are produced by steaming the whole or cut groats and then rolling and drying them. The amount of cooking required in the preparation of rolled oats depends to a large extent on the processes of cutting, steaming, and flaking. Quick cooking rolled oats are made from smaller particles of groat than are regular oats (Kent, 1975).

Corn grits (endosperm), cornmeal, and flour are produced by a dry milling process. The grain is cleaned, conditioned to a specific moisture content, degerminated, and dehulled by abrasive action. Milling is done on roller mills involving a number of stages. Some parts of the process are similar to the milling of wheat into flour (Kent, 1975). Corn starch is produced by a wet milling process.

SUMMARY

Cereal grains are the fruits of cultivated grasses. The principal cereal crops are wheat, maize or corn, rice, barley, oats, rye, sorghum, and millet. All grains have a similar anatomical structure. It consists of a fruit coat or pericarp and a seed. The seed is comprised of a seed coat, germ, and endosperm. The endosperm is composed of an aleurone layer and a starchy endosperm.

Each variety of wheat is commonly classified according to the texture of the ripened kernel endosperm, the color, and the growing season. The texture may be hard and vitreous or soft and floury. The color may be red or white. Wheat may be planted in the fall and harvested in June or July and is called winter wheat. Alternatively, wheat may be planted in the spring and harvested in the fall and is called spring wheat. Various types of wheat thus include hard red winter, hard red spring, soft red winter, and white wheats, that are generally soft. It has been suggested that the hardness of wheat is determined by the strength of the protein–starch bond in the endosperm, with a stronger bond being associated with harder wheat. Hard wheats are generally used for making bread flours while soft wheats provide pastry and cake flours. All-purpose flours are often milled from a blend of wheats to give characteristics intermediate between hard and soft wheat flours.

Grains contain carbohydrates, nitrogenous compounds (mainly protein), lipids, mineral salts, vitamins, enzymes, and small amounts of other substances. Carbohydrate is quantitatively the most important component, constituting about 83 percent of the total dry matter of wheat. Starch is the predominant carbohydrate. Cellulose, hemicelluloses, pentosans, dextrins, and sugars are also present. Cellulose and hemicelluloses are part of the fiber complex.

Pentosans are hemicelluloses. However, they have unique properties which distinguish them from the common hemicelluloses of the plant cell wall. About 20–25 percent of the total pentosans in wheat flour are soluble in water. These soluble extracts form solid gels upon the addition of minute amounts of oxidizing agents. Water-insoluble pentosans are also present in wheat flour. The basic structure of wheat flour pentosans is a long straight chain of anhydro-D-xylose residues to which are attached single anhydro-L-arabinose residues. Pentosans play an important role in the water absorption properties of wheat flour doughs and affect dough rheology.

The lipid content of most cereals is from 1 to 2 percent. Corn and oats contain from 4 to 7 percent lipid. Cereal grains vary in protein content from 7 to 14 percent.

Triticale is a hybrid cereal derived from crossing wheat and rye. This grain has a high crop yield and high protein content. Modified mixing and/or fermentation techniques are required for triticale doughs.

A variety of ready-to-eat breakfast cereals is available in the United States. Most of these cereals are fortified to a comparatively high degree with vitamins and minerals. No substantial losses of added vitamins apparently occur during normal shelf storage. Processes for the production of breakfast cereals include flaking, puffing, shredding, and granule formation.

Wheat and other grains have been milled since prehistoric times but roller milling is a nineteenth century development. With modern developments milling has become a complex process with many millstreams being produced and mixed together to create various grades of white flour. The purposes of milling are twofold, to separate as much of the endosperm as possible from the bran and germ and to reduce the endosperm to fine particles. In roller milling the grain is gradually reduced to flour in a succession of steps. The basic processes are 1. grinding or breaking—fragmenting the grain or its parts with some dissociation of the anatomical parts of the grain from one another, 2. sieving or bolting—classifying mixtures of particles of differing particle size into fractions of narrower particle size range; and 3. purifying—separating mixtures of bran and endosperm particles by means of air currents. In usual practice, from 68 to 77 percent of the wheat grain is extracted as white flour.

In the process of milling, the grain is first sent through a set of break rolls. These rolls are driven at different speeds and the grain is sheared with a scissor action. The products of the first break are sifted through a series of sieves. The coarsest portion goes to the second break rolls, intermediate coarse particles go to the middlings purifier, and the finest particles go to smooth reduction rolls where they are reduced in size. Each break also produces some flour directly. The coarse grain particles go through four or five break processes. Each set of break rollers is followed by a sifting and purifying process. Particles in the flour that result from milling are of varying sizes and composition.

Air classification is a scheme for separating various flour particles of differing size into more uniform groups. Air currents are used to lift the fine particles, that are high in protein, and separate them from the larger starchy particles. Low-protein and high-protein fractions have several uses in the baking industry.

Grades of flour are determined by combining various millstreams. When all flour streams are used, straight grade flour results. Long, medium, and short patent grade flours contain from 95 to 40 percent of the millstreams. Clear grade flours are those not included in the patent flours.

Several types of white flour are commonly produced. Bread flour is made by milling hard wheats. Pastry and cake flours come from soft wheats. All-purpose flour may be prepared from a blend of hard and soft wheats.

White flour is commonly bleached to produce a white product. Benzoyl peroxide has been approved in the United States for this purpose. Additional compounds may be used as maturing or oxidizing agents to improve the baking properties of flour. Allowed substances include chlorine dioxide gas, acetone peroxides, and azodicarbonamide. Gaseous chlorine is widely used in the maturing of soft wheat flours used for cakes.

Rye and corn flours are milled by processes that resemble the production of wheat flour in some respects. Rice is milled by an abrasive scouring. The bran of oats is not generally removed in the milling of this grain.

STUDY QUESTIONS

Grain kernels are made up of several distinct parts, the composition of which varies widely.

1. Draw and label the major parts of a kernel of wheat. Also describe what happens to each of the major parts of the grain during the process of roller milling to produce white flour.
2. Compare the chemical composition of the major parts of a wheat kernel.
3. Explain the relationship between hemicelluloses and pentosans and discuss possible reasons for the study of wheat flour pentosans.

Wheat may be classified as hard or soft.

4. Compare the growing season, chemical composition, physical characteristics, and baking properties of flour made from hard and soft wheat varieties.
5. Explain possible effects of the protein–starch bond in determining hardness or softness in wheat.
6. For each of the following flours, indicate whether predominantly soft wheat, hard wheat, or a mixture of both is commonly used in milling:
   a. cake flour
   b. pastry flour
   c. bread flour
   d. all-purpose flour
7. Indicate in the following list of baked products those items that could probably best be made from each of the types of flour listed in question 6.

   Baked Products
   oatmeal cookies
   blueberry muffins
   white bread
   plain pie crust
   yellow layer cake
   brownies
   plain muffins
   popovers
   quick nutbread

A wide variety of ready-to-eat breakfast cereals is produced.

8. Briefly describe the general processes involved in the production of flaked, puffed, shredded, and granular breakfast cereals.

The various parts of the wheat kernel are separated from each other by the process of milling.

9. Describe the purposes of milling wheat into flour.

10. Describe the major procedures usually involved in the process of roller milling for wheat flour production.
11. Explain the purpose and principle involved in the fractionation of white wheat flour by air classification.
12. Define flour extraction rate. What is the usual commercial extraction rate for wheat? Discuss advantages and/or disadvantages of increasing or decreasing the extraction rate.
13. Explain general differences among straight, patent, and clear grades of white wheat flour and list approximate percentages of total white flour usually included in each grade category. What are common uses for each grade of flour?
14. Distinguish between bleaching and maturing of flour and explain what is probably happening to the flour components in each case.
15. List chemical agents that are allowed by the U. S. Food and Drug Administration for use in flour bleaching and maturing.

REFERENCES

1. Anderson, R. H., D. L. Maxwell, A. E. Mulley, and C. W. Fritsch. 1976. Effects of processing and storage on micronutrients in breakfast cereals. *Food Technology* 30 (No. 5), 110.

2. Bean, M. M., E. Erman, and D. K. Mecham. 1969. Baking characteristics of low-protein fractions from air-classified Kansas hard red winter wheats. *Cereal Chemistry* 46, 35.

3. D'Appolonia, B. L. 1971. Role of pentosans in bread and dough. A review. *Bakers Digest* 45 (Dec.), 20.

4. D'Appolonia, B. L. and S. K. Kim. 1976. Recent developments on wheat flour pentosans. *Bakers Digest* 50 (June), 45.

5. Haber, T., A. A. Seyam, and O. J. Banasik. 1976. Hard red winter wheat, rye and triticale. *Bakers Digest* 50 (June), 24.

6. Hayden, E. B. 1973. New mileposts in nutrition. *Cereal Science Today* 18 (No. 5), 120.

7. Hoseney, R. C. and P. A. Seib. 1973. Structural differences in hard and soft wheat. *Bakers Digest* 47 (Dec.), 26.

8. Hulse, J. H. and D. Spurgeon. 1974. Triticale. *Scientific American* 231 (No. 2), 72.

9. Inglett, G. E., editor. 1974. *Wheat: Production and Utilization.* Westport, Conn.: Avi Publishing Co.

10. Jelaca, S. L. and I. Hlynka. 1971. Water-binding capacity of wheat flour crude pentosans and their relation to mixing characteristics of dough. *Cereal Chemistry* 48, 211.

11. Kent, N. L. 1975. *Technology of Cereals,* 2nd edition. New York: Pergamon.

12. Kulp, K. 1972. Some effects of chlorine treatment of soft wheat flour. *Bakers Digest* 46 (June), 26.

13. Lorenz, K. 1974. Triticale. *Bakers Digest* 48 (June), 24.

14. Neukom, H., L. Providoli, H. Gremli, and P. A. Hui. 1967. Recent investigations on wheat flour pentosans. *Cereal Chemistry* 44, 238.

15. Pomeranz, Y. 1977. Fiber in breadmaking. *Bakers Digest* 51 (Oct.), 94.

16. Pomeranz, Y. 1971. *Wheat Chemistry and Technology*. St. Paul, Minn.: American Assoc. of Cereal Chemists, Inc.

17. Price, P. B. and J. G. Parsons. 1975. Lipids of seven cereal grains. *Journal of the American Oil Chemists Society* 52, 490.

18. Watson, C. A., W. C. Shuey, R. D. Crawford, and M. R. Gumbmann. 1977. Physical dough, baking, and nutritional qualities of straight-grade and extended-extraction flours. *Cereal Chemistry* 54, 657.

19. Watson, S. J. 1953. The quality of cereals and their industrial uses. The uses of barley other than malting. *Chemistry and Industry* (Jan. 31), p. 95.

20. Watt, B. K. and A. L. Merrill. 1963. *Composition of Foods*. Agriculture Handbook No. 8.

21. Yoneyama, T., I. Suzuki, and M. Murohashi. 1970a. Natural maturing of wheat flour. I. Changes in some chemical components and in farinograph and extensigraph properties. *Cereal Chemistry* 47, 19.

22. Yoneyama, T., I. Suzuki, and M. Murohashi. 1970b. Natural maturing of wheat flour. II. Effect of temperature on changes in soluble SH content, and some rheological properties of doughs obtained from the flour. *Cereal Chemistry* 47, 27.

CHAPTER 16

STARCH

Starch is stored in the cells of plant roots and seeds as water-insoluble particles called granules. The starch granules are laid down in small bodies called plastids, that are dispersed in the cytoplasm of the cell, and the starch is stored in this form for long periods of time.

Starch is a polysaccharide, a polymer of α-D-glucose. It is readily assimilated by the body and is an important source of energy in the human diet. Starch has many industrial uses. Approximately one-half of the starch produced is used to make syrups and sugars. Starch, including many chemically modified starches, is used in the manufacture of a wide variety of processed foods such as sauces, casserole mixes, puddings, and pie fillings. Starch plays an important structural role as a component of flour in baked products.

16.1

STARCH MOLECULES AND GRANULES

Starch granules are well organized accumulations of numerous starch molecules. The molecules are of two major types. One component, amylose, is essentially a linear chain of α-D-glucose molecules linked between carbon atoms 1 and 4. The other component, amylopectin, has a highly branched structure.

AMYLOSE

In *amylose,* α-D-glucose molecules in the pyranose (6-membered ring) form are linked together through the aldehyde group of the number 1 carbon atom and the hydroxyl group of the number 4 carbon. This is an acetal linkage of one monosaccharide unit to another and is shown in Figure 16.1. Amylose molecules are not all the same size. They contain many thousands of glucose units, the actual molecular size depending on the source of the starch and its stage of maturity. In general, amylose molecules from roots and tubers have longer chains and thus higher molecular weights than amylose molecules from cereal grains. Although most of the amylose molecules are linear, there is a limited

Figure 16.1

The linear fraction of starch, amylose, is composed of α-D-glucose units linked through carbon atoms 1 and 4.

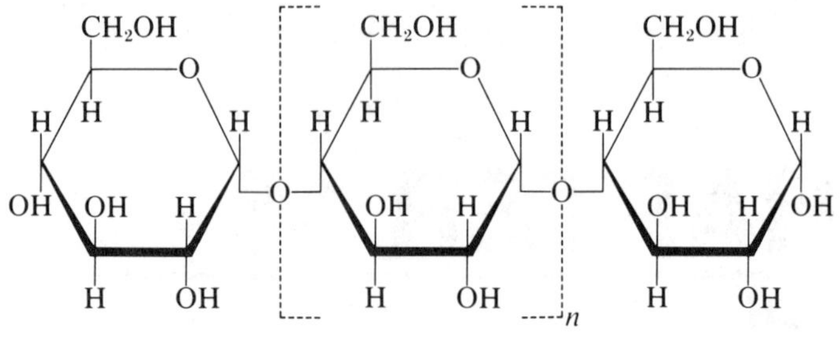

amount of branching in some molecules of the amylose fraction of starch. The branches are apparently several hundreds or even thousands of glucose residues in length.

Amylose in solution apparently assumes the form of a long flexible coiled spring, a loose helix that can be bent into wormlike configurations. When this molecule complexes with iodine or similar materials that occupy the center of the helix the helix becomes more rigid and rod like (Paul and Palmer, 1972).

AMYLOPECTIN

Amylopectin contains relatively short chains of α-D-glucose units linked through carbons 1 and 4. These chains are joined in a branching structure through carbon atoms 1 and 6. Figure 16.2 shows a point of branching where one chain is joined to another. A randomly branched or treelike structure for amylopectin was proposed as early as 1940. The unit chains are variable in length. In general, amylopectin shows two major overlapping distributions of chain length in which the most numerous chains occur at degrees of polymerization (number of glucose units) of 19 and 60 (Pomeranz, 1976). Figure 16.3 gives a proposed structure for amylopectin from potato. The major branches of the proposed molecule, called *B chains,* are longer than the subsidiary branches, called *A chains.* There is only one free reducing or aldehyde group in the amylopectin molecule. The other aldehyde groups are tied up in linkages. Amylopectin molecules are larger than amylose molecules but they are more bushy and compact in shape. Molecular weight estimations for amylopectin molecules have ranged from as low as 65 million to about 500 million (Pomeranz, 1976). These large values make amylopectin one of the largest of the natural polymers.

Various methods have been used to study the structure of amylose and amylopectin. Early chemical studies involved complete methylation of the free hydroxyl groups on starch, followed by hydrolysis of the starch to glucose, and measurement of the various types of methylated glucose molecules. The hydroxyl groups that were tied up in

Figure 16.2

In the branched fraction
of starch, amylopectin,
the point of branching
occurs through carbon
atoms 1 and 6.

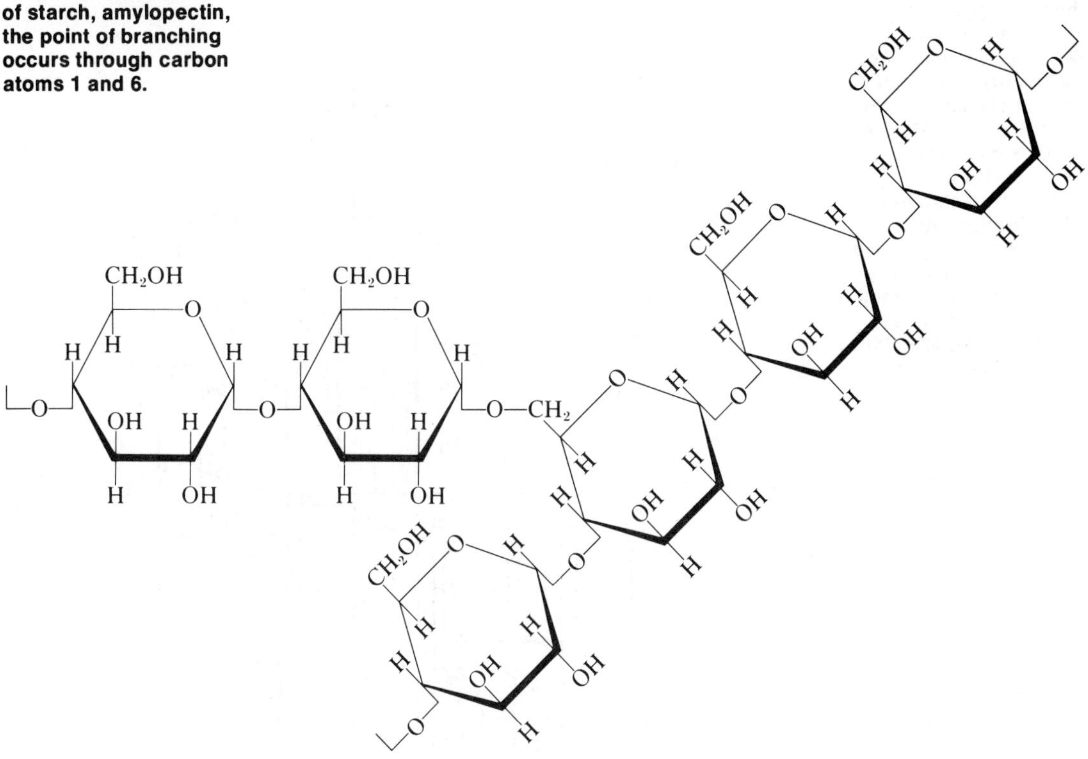

linkage were not methylated. Thus information was gained on how the glucose molecules were linked together and the length of the chains.

Various enzymatic exploration studies have contributed to the present knowledge of starch structure. Information is collected on chain length and types of linkage by studying the pattern of starch hydrolysis using α-amylase, β-amylase, and debranching enzymes. (The action of the amylases is discussed in Section 16.2.) Behavior of the starch fractions in water, viscosity measurements, and iodine reactivity have also contributed knowledge concerning the structure of starch molecules.

STARCH GRANULES　　The physical structure of starch as it is laid down in granules, as well as the chemical structure of the starch components, affects its properties when used in food products. *Starch granules* may be viewed under an ordinary light microscope. A starch sample from a single plant source exhibits granules of characteristic shape and range of sizes that make specific identification possible. Photomicrographs of several common

Figure 16.3

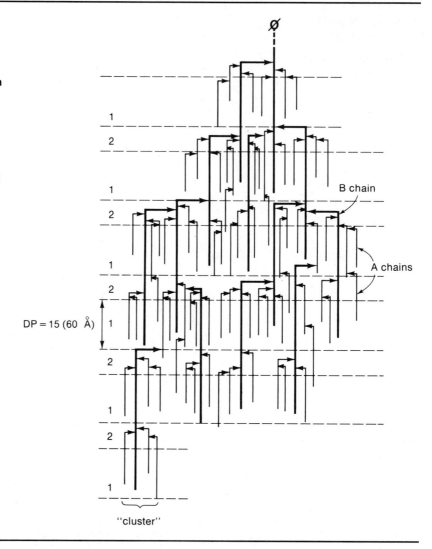

Proposed structure for potato amylopectin. 1 = compact area; 2 = less compact area rich in branching points; ϕ = reducing unit. (From Robin, J. P., C. Mercier, R. Charbonniere, and A. Guilbot. 1974. Lintnerized starches. Gel filtration and enzymatic studies of insoluble residue from prolonged acid treatment of potato starch. *Cereal Chemistry* 51, 389. With permission.)

B chain

A chains

$DP = 15 \ (60 \ \overset{\circ}{A})$

"cluster"

starches are shown in Figure 16.4. When raw starch granules are viewed under polarized light, they show birefringence (see Figure 16.5). This is observed as luminous Maltese crosses through the granules. Birefringence suggests sphero-crystalline structure. Scanning electron micrographs of starch granules give a three-dimensional image showing typical angles and rounded surfaces (see Figure 16.6)

Amylose and amylopectin, in proportions that are characteristic for a particular plant variety, are laid down as a semi-crystalline material when the granule is formed. The crystalline pattern of starch granules, as determined by use of X-ray diffraction techniques, differs for cereal

Figure 16.4

Starch granules magnified 500×. (*a*) Corn starch (*b*) Waxy corn starch (*c*) Wheat starch (*d*) Potato starch (*e*) Tapioca starch (*f*) Rice starch (Courtesy of Northern Regional Research Center, U. S. Department of Agriculture.)

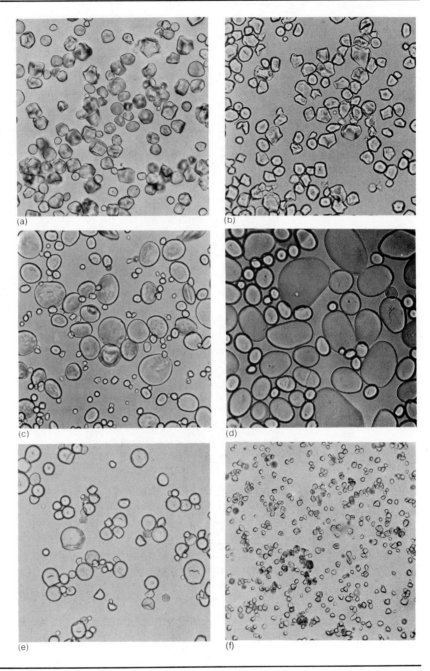

(a)

(b)

(c)

(d)

(e)

(f)

Figure 16.5

Starch granules viewed under polarized light, magnified 500×. (a) Corn starch (b) Wheat starch (c) Potato starch (Courtesy of Northern Regional Research Center, U. S. Department of Agriculture.)

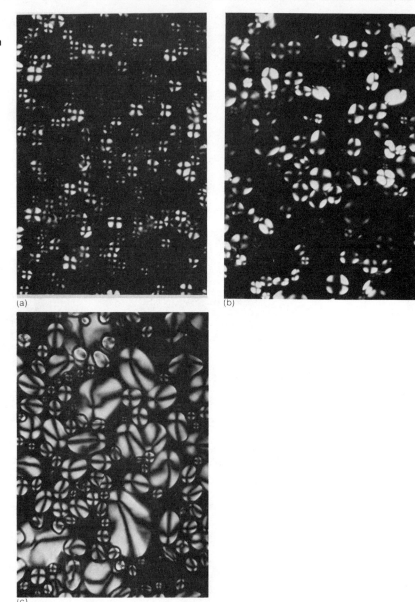

(a)

(b)

(c)

starches, root starches, and legume starches. Much research has been reported concerning the way in which the amylose and amylopectin molecules are arranged within the granule (Banks and Greenwood, 1975). A clear picture of the arrangement, however, has not yet emerged. A schematic representation of intermingling amylose and

Figure 16.6

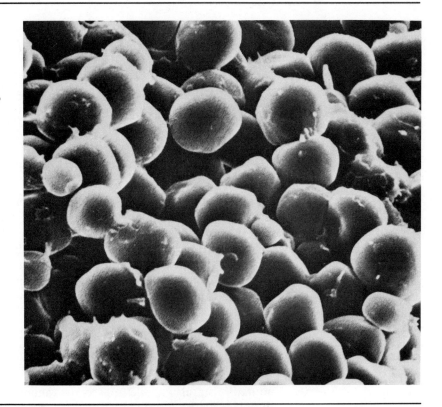

amylopectin molecules, with crystalline areas, was suggested by Meyer and Bernfeld in 1940 and is shown in Figure 16.7.

Both amylose and amylopectin are present in most plant starches. The proportion of amylose varies between 17 and 32 percent of the total starch. Of the common starches, tapioca has one of the lowest levels of amylose, it being about 17 percent. Potato starch has from 20 to 23 percent amylose, wheat starch from 25 to 26 percent, and corn starch from 24 to 28 percent (Wurzburg and Szymanski, 1970; Greenwood, 1964). The remainder of the starch in the granules is amylopectin. The proportions of the two starch fractions present in a plant depend upon the activity of various starch-synthesizing enzymes that is determined by the genes of the plant. The cooking characteristics of a starch are affected by the proportion of amylose and amylopectin. Waxy varieties of several plants, including corn, rice, and sorghum, produce only amylopectin. The starches from these plants are nongelling because of the lack of amylose and are stable to freezing and thawing. They thus find wide use in frozen food products. High amylose starches have also been developed through genetic manipulation. A high amylose corn, called amylomaize, has an amylose content of approximately 70 per-

Figure 16.7

Proposed structure of molecules in a layer of starch granule according to Meyer and Bernfeld. Chains are associated in the dark, thickened areas.

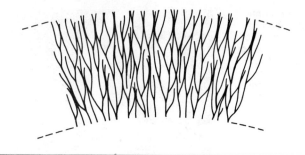

cent and is marketed commercially. High-amylose starches exhibit a unique ability to form films and to bind other materials and are finding many uses in the food industry. For example, high amylose starches have been used 1. to set a quick gel in gum drops; 2. in the blanching water for potatoes that are to be par-fried with a resultant decrease in fat absorption during frying; 3. as texturizers in tomato paste and apple sauce; and 4. as binders in the production of meat analogs (Hullinger *et al.,* 1973).

16.2

STARCH-DEGRADING ENZYMES

The native starch granule apparently cannot be degraded by starch-splitting enzymes. Starch granules that are damaged in milling or other processing procedures, however, can be attacked by enzymes. The action of starch-degrading enzymes is important in the baking industry, in the production of corn syrup and in other industrial areas.

A variety of enzymes have been isolated that have the ability to hydrolyze amylose and amylopectin molecules. Some of these enzymes start at the nonreducing end of a straight-chain amylose molecule or a branch of an amylopectin molecule and break off maltose or glucose. They are called *exo-enzymes* because of this pattern of action. Beta-amylase, phosphorylase, and glucoamylase are starch-splitting exo-enzymes. Beta-amylase removes two glucose units at one time to yield maltose (See Figure 16.8). Phosphorylase hydrolyzes one glucose unit at a time and produces glucose-l-phosphate. These two enzymes do not have the ability to hydrolyze a point of branching on the amylopectin molecule. Therefore their activity stops when the outer branches of an amylopectin molecule have been hydrolyzed, leaving a high molecular weight dextrin. Glucoamylase hydrolyzes one glucose unit at a time, yielding glucose, and also has the ability to hydrolyze the 1,6-linkage at a point of branching. It can, therefore, convert amylopectin completely to glucose (Banks and Greenwood, 1975).

Figure 16.8

Points of attack by β-amylase in the hydrolysis of amylose are indicated by arrows (↓).

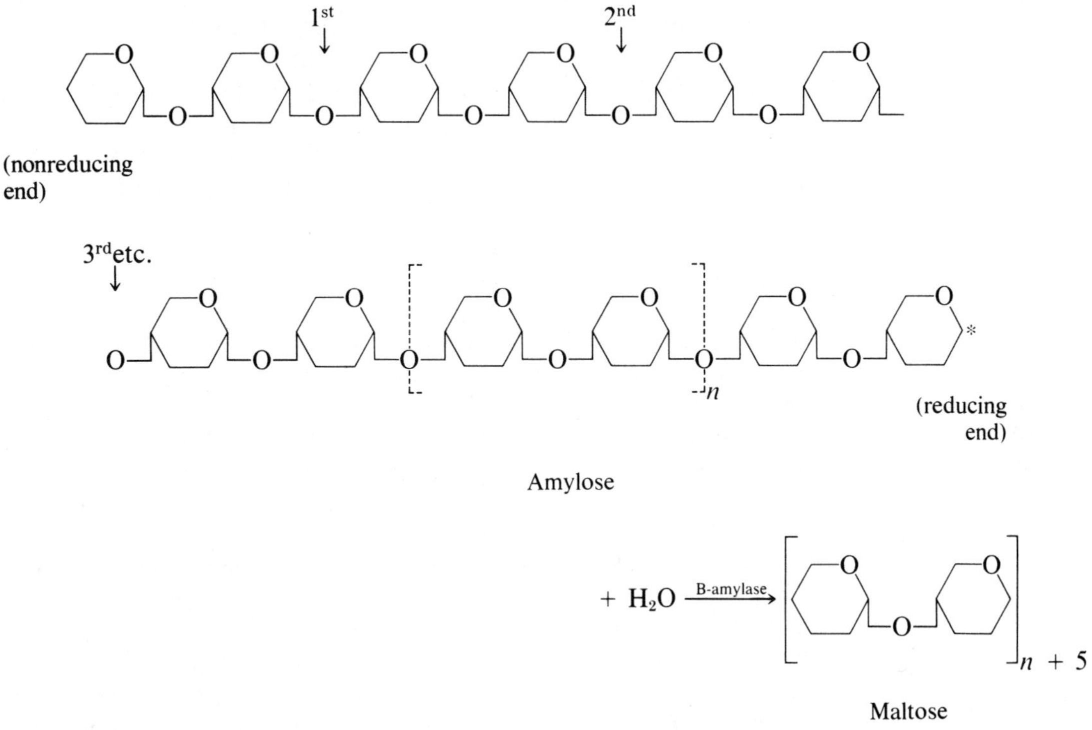

Amylose

Maltose

Alpha-amylase is an endo-enzyme. It may attack the amylopectin molecule on either side of a point of branching. The action of alpha-amylase on starch produces a rapid increase in dextrins, as it breaks the starch molecules into large pieces, while producing comparatively small amounts of sugars. Ultimately, however, alpha-amylase yields glucose and maltose from the dextrins.

Several debranching enzymes have been isolated and studied. These enzymes hydrolyze the bond between the sixth carbon atom of one glucose molecule and the first carbon of another that exists at a point of branching. Debranching enzymes include R-enzyme, that was isolated from broad beans and malted barley; pullulanase, that is elaborated by the bacterium, *Aerobacter aerogenes;* and isoamylases, that have been isolated from yeast and bacteria.

Beta-amylase activity is present in wheat flour. Alpha-amylase may be added in commercial breadmaking. (The effect of alpha-amylase in bread dough is discussed in Section 32.1.)

MANUFACTURE OF FOOD STARCHES

Commercial markets for starch grew at a steady rate for more than 25 years. Annual consumption of starch in the United States expanded from about 650 million lb in 1937 to nearly 2.5 billion lb by 1964. During the late 1960s and early 1970s many new starch derivatives with new functional properties were developed and the use of starch by the food industry expanded further. These new starches are playing important roles as low-cost stabilizers and thickeners for many new fabricated or engineered foods (Casey, 1978).

Starch processing is a very old industry, dating back about 3000 years. Historically, starch has been obtained from many cereal grains and root vegetables such as potatoes. A commercial process to extract starch from cereals was developed in the early 1840s and the corn refining industry was founded at this time. Corn has since become the best available source of starch, although other commercial starch sources include wheat, grain sorghum or milo, tapioca (cassava or manioc), potato, and arrowroot. Waxy varieties of corn and sorghum are also commercially processed for the recovery of starch.

A *wet milling process* is commonly used for the recovery of starch from cereals. This process begins with soaking or steeping the grain to soften the kernel and facilitate separation of the starch granules from the protein. The soft kernels are then torn apart and the germ separated from the other components. The coarse particles of the remaining material are ground to release the starch. The milled slurry, containing ground starch, gluten, and hulls, is screened and the coarse fibers removed. The remaining starch and gluten slurry contains from 5 to 8 percent protein. The gluten is separated from the starch by use of high-speed centrifuges since the starch is heavier than the protein. The starch is then dried (Inglett, 1970). Starch may also be recovered by a wet process from dry-milled flour fractions. However, percentage recoveries from the dry-milled flours are less than recoveries from whole grain by wet-milling procedures (Peeples and Marshall, 1970).

MODIFIED STARCHES

Natural starches are chemically and/or physically modified to meet the particular needs of a manufactured food product. Starches can be tailored to any convenience food. Numerous chemically-modified starches are being produced and have broadened the scope of usefulness of starch. Some of the more common types are described below:

Pregelatinized Starches Starches that have been precooked and then dried are dispersible in cold water, producing a thickened product without reheating. (Gelatinization of starch is discussed in Section 16.4.) There is some rupturing of the swollen starch granules as they are cooked and then dried. Therefore, a greater weight of pregelatinized starch is required to produce a given viscosity and the texture is somewhat different than that of regularly cooked starch pastes. Pregelatinized starches have wide usage in instant puddings and other starch-thickened prepared mixes. They may be useful wherever starch pastes are desired without cooking. Addition of from 3 to 3.5 percent pregelatinized starch to cake batter has been reported to give improved cake moisture content and quality scores (Boettger, 1963).

Acid-modified Starches Raw starches may be heated in very dilute acid below their gelatinization temperatures. Limited hydrolysis occurs. When these starches are then heated in the gelatinization process, they have decreased viscosity yet they form a strong gel when the mixture is cooled. This property of limited viscosity on heating and strong gel formation on cooling is desirable in making various confections and fillings for bakery products. The starches are called *thin-boiling* (Pomeranz, 1971).

Cross-linked Starches Bonding between neighboring starch molecules is produced by treating the intact starch granules with reagents such as phosphorus oxychloride, metaphosphates, epichlorohydrin, citric acid, or adipic acid. The properties of cross-linked starches vary, depending upon the degree of cross-linking. When only a small amount of cross-linking is produced in waxy corn starch, about one cross-link per 9000 glucose units, the swelling of the granules on cooking is little affected. However, after swelling, the granules resist rupture so that a thicker, less stringy starch paste results. With greater degrees of cross-linking, the swelling of starch granules is decreased. Cross-linking makes granules less fragile and more resistant to rupture during cooking. By adjusting the degree of cross-linking, starches can be tailored to perform under a wide variety of pH, temperature, or shear conditions (Wurzburg and Szymanski, 1970).

Derivatized or Stabilized Starches While cross-linking makes a hot starch paste more resistant to rupture, further treatment is required to control gelling and *syneresis* (*weeping*) of the cold, stored paste. Treating the starch granule with hydroxypropyl, phosphate, or acetyl groups allows starch derivatives to be formed. In the case of hydroxypropyl addition, a starch ether (Starch—O—C—) is produced. Phosphate

$$\overset{\text{O}}{\overset{\|}{}}$$

and acetyl groups are added as starch esters (Starch—O—C—) (Mitchell, 1972; Katzbeck, 1972).

Waxy starches, which contain only the branched or amylopectin fraction of starch, benefit greatly for many food uses by treatment for cross-bonding and stabilization. These modified waxy starches maintain viscosity during cooking and cooling, resist retrogradation and syneresis when stored at cold temperatures and produce clear pastes with nonstringy texture. (Retrogradation of starch is discussed in Section 16.4.)

16.4

HEATING OF STARCH GRANULES

When starch is to be used as a thickening and/or gelling agent, it is heated in the presence of water. The structure and integrity of the starch granule is of primary importance to the function of starch as a thickener. A series of changes occurs in the organization of starch molecules in the granule during heating and subsequent cooling.

When starch is heated in the absence of moisture, some hydrolysis of the starch molecules occurs in a process called *dextrinization*. The hydrolysis of starch molecules to dextrins decreases the thickening power of the starch granules.

GELATINIZATION

The term *gelatinization* is used to describe a swelling and disorganization process that occurs in starch granules when they are heated in the presence of water. Although this term is widely used, Elbert (1965) pointed out that specific definition of the term has been inconsistent. Gelatinization has been referred to as swelling of granules, increase in viscosity and translucency, increasing solubility, and loss of birefringence when granules are viewed under the microscope. The so-called *gelatinization temperature,* that is characteristic for each type of starch, is really a range of temperatures because large granules begin to swell before small ones. This range may be as great as 50°C for potato starch when measured from the time swelling commences until granules attain maximum size.

As starch is heated to the gelatinization temperature, the heat energy begins to dissociate the more weakly bonded regions within the starch granule, water moves into the granule and it begins to swell. The swelling continues as the temperature is raised. Some of the shorter linear molecules actually diffuse out of the swollen granule into the surrounding liquid. However, the longer linear chains wander through the granule among the bushy amylopectin molecules and act to keep the granule together and prevent complete solubilization. As the granules take up water and swell, they occupy more space and friction is created between granules. The starch paste becomes thicker, the consistency reflecting the resistance to stirring of the mass of swollen particles. The greater the granule swelling, the higher will be the viscosity. However, swollen granules are fragile and are deformed and fragmented by stirring with the consequent thinning of the mixture (Schultz *et al.,* 1969). Figure 16.9 shows several stages in the gelatinization of corn starch and potato starch. Scanning electron photomicrographs of gelatinized starch granules indicate that the gelatinized granules collapse after maximum swelling. They appear deformed, in relation to their original

Figure 16.9

Photomicrographs of starch granules during gelatinization. *(a)* **Corn starch ungelatinized** *(b)* **Corn starch pasted at 72°C** *(c)* **Corn starch pasted at 90°C** *(d)* **Potato starch ungelatinized** *(e)* **Potato starch pasted at 65°C** *(f)* **Potato starch pasted at 75°C (Reprinted with permission from Schoch, T. J. 1965. Starch in bakery products.** *Bakers Digest* **38 [Apr.], 48.)**

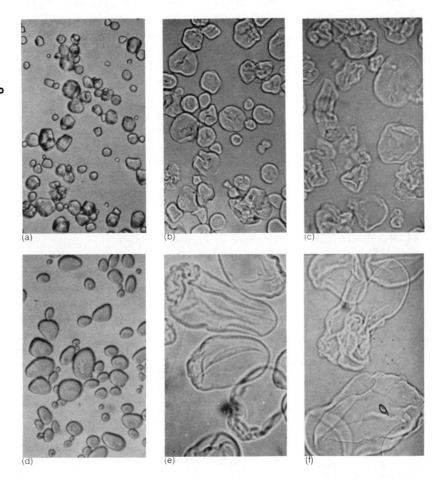

structure, and are often folded (Hoseney *et al.,* 1978). In general, starches from root vegetables and waxy varieties of cereals begin to swell at lower temperatures than do other cereal starches. The root starch pastes are also more clear than are the cereal starch pastes.

The changes in consistency as a starch slurry is heated have often been measured by using a Brabender amylograph (Anker and Geddes, 1944). This instrument is a recording viscometer. It charts the viscosity as a starch slurry is heated at a constant rate to 95°C (203°F), stirred at that temperature for an hour, cooled to 50°C (122°F), and held an hour. Starches from different plant sources behave differently as they are heated in the amylograph. Figure 16.10 shows some typical curves for pasted starches. The viscosity is given in Brabender units. Several other instruments that are similar to the amylograph are also used in starch research and quality control.

From Figure 16.10 it is apparent that corn starch gives a relatively low peak viscosity. This is because the granules are only moderately swollen. This peak is followed by some breakdown during cooking as a result of granule fragmentation under shear stresses. On cooling, gelation occurs and the viscosity increases substantially. Potato starch granules swell markedly and a high viscosity is recorded early in the heating period. Potato starch paste does not gel to as great an extent as does corn starch paste on cooling. Waxy sorghum starch, as well as tapioca, swell considerably in the early stages of heating and a high peak viscosity is noted. However, the fragile overswollen granules rupture and the paste thins during stirring. Waxy sorghum shows very little thickening or gelation on cooling since it contains essentially no amylose. Cross-bonding decreases the degree of swelling for waxy sorghum starch granules and stabilizes the paste viscosity (Schultz *et al.*, 1969).

RETROGRADATION   Amylose molecules, being highly polar linear polymers, show strong tendencies to associate and link together through hydrogen bonding. Figure 16.11 suggests possible mechanisms of bonding for amylose molecules as a hot solution is cooled to room temperature. If the solution is relatively concentrated, it will rapidly congeal to a rigid irreversible gel with cross-bonding at random intervals. A more dilute solution of amylose will slowly form an insoluble precipitate as the molecules align themselves in parallel fashion (Inglett, 1970). This process of gel formation or precipitation is called *retrogradation*.

Figure 16.10

Brabender viscosities of various starches. Concentration given in grams dry starch per 500 ml. (From Schoch, T. J. Starches in foods. In: *Carbohydrates and Their Roles*, H. W. Schultz, R. F. Cain, and R. W. Wrolstad, editors. Westport, CT: Avi Publishing Company, 1969. With permission.)

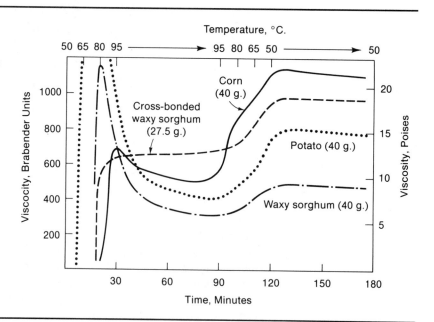

Figure 16.11

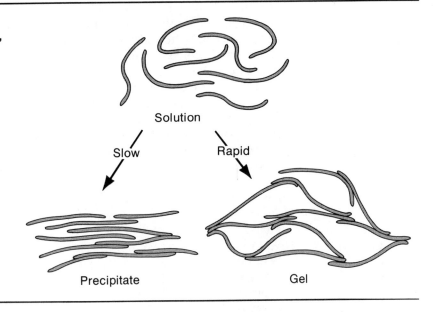

**Mechanisms of retro-
gradation. (From Schoch,
T. J. Starches in foods.
In:** *Carbohydrates and
Their Roles,* **H. W.
Schultz, R. F. Cain, and
R. W. Wrolstad, editors.
Westport, CT: Avi Pub-
lishing Company, 1969.
With permission.)**

Most starches contain both amylose and amylopectin molecules in the granule structure. The bushy, nonlinear amylopectin molecule shows much less tendency to retrograde than does amylose. Gel formation in commonly used cooked starch mixtures is due primarily to the presence of amylose. During the process of gelatinization, some amylose molecules diffuse out of the granule into the surrounding liquid. As the paste cools, the kinetic energy decreases and the amylose molecules are no longer kept apart. They form hydrogen bonds at periodic intervals with other amylose molecules and with branches of the amylopectin molecules, producing a network that traps water in its meshes. A gel results, its rigidity depending upon the concentration of starch and the particular source of starch. Starches vary in amylose content and in average length of amylose chains. Waxy starches, that contain no amylose, do not gel. The starch gel is also influenced by the presence of other ingredients in the starch mixture.

**FACTORS
AFFECTING
GELATINIZED
STARCH PASTES**

Type of Starch   It has long been recognized that starches from different botanical sources differ in properties. Additional differences are produced as starch is chemically modified for use in various food products. Purified starches, such as wheat starch, have more thickening power than flour, such as wheat flour, because the concentration of starch differs in these two types of products. Under relatively slow heating conditions for sauces and gravies, the amylase in wheat flour may be responsible for decreased thickness. As gelatinization begins, the starch granules become susceptible to attack by amylase in the flour that may hydrolyze some starch molecules before it is destroyed by continued heating (Trimbo and Miller, 1971).

Osman and Mootse (1958) compared the properties of several starch samples when heated with water. They used concentrations of the test starches that would produce nearly the same maximum viscosity. More than three times as much wheat starch as potato starch was needed to produce the same maximum viscosity. The concentrations of tapioca and waxy sorghum starches needed were about the same. However, tapioca reached its maximum viscosity at a temperature 20°C lower than waxy sorghum. The waxy starches did not produce gels. Neither did the potato and tapioca starches, although some gel formation with these starches has been reported by other workers. The concentration (percent dry substance) in water required for similar maximum viscosities was:

Potato	1.96
Waxy corn	2.98
Waxy rice	3.13
Waxy sorghum	3.42
Tapioca	3.54
Arrowroot	4.37
Sorghum	4.66
Corn	4.90
Rice	5.49
Wheat	6.44

Addition of Sugar Many starch-thickened puddings and sauces are sweetened with sugar. Sugars have been reported to decrease the swelling of the starch granules during gelatinization, apparently by competing with the starch for the water present, thus decreasing the viscosity of the cooked paste. The effects on swelling power are small at sugar concentrations of 5 and 20 percent of the weight of the water but viscosity development is delayed (Savage and Osman, 1978). The gelatinization temperature range may be increased by sugars if they are present in relatively high concentrations (about 50 percent). Different sugars have varying effects on gelatinization, disaccharides impeding the process to a greater degree than monosaccharides (Paul and Palmer, 1972; Bean and Osman, 1959; Hester *et al.*, 1956). Savage and Osman (1978) studied photomicrographs of gelatinized starch pastes containing 50 percent of the weight of water as sugar. They reported that disaccharide sugars had a more pronounced inhibiting effect on the swelling of granules than did monosaccharides. No birefringent granules were found in starch pastes made without sugar and heated to 75°, 85°, or 95°C (103°, 121°, or 139°F), indicating that complete gelatinization had occurred. However, in gelatinized pastes containing 50 percent of any of the test sugars, birefringent granules were still present when pastes were heated to 85°C. Those pastes containing sucrose or lactose had some unswollen and birefringent granules even at 95°C, although this was not true for pastes containing glucose, fructose, and galactose.

Starch-thickened puddings generally contain from 10 to 20 percent sugar (calculated as percent of the water) and about 7 percent starch. Some starch-thickened sauces or puddings may contain much larger amounts of sugar and require additional starch to give desirable thickness because of the effect of the sugar on granule swelling. The starch–water slurry may be gelatinized with only part of the total amount of sugar desired and the remainder of the sugar added after gelatinization is complete.

Addition of Acid Starch-thickened food products often contain acid ingredients such as fruit juices or vinegar. During cooking at a pH below 4 fragmentation of starch granules and some hydrolysis of starch molecules occurs, resulting in a thinning of the starch pastes. Modified starches that are somewhat acid-resistant are available to food manufacturers. Cross-linked waxy starches are often used in fruit pie fillings because of their greater acid resistance, clarity, and nongelling characteristics. Interactions between sugar and acid in a starch paste occur. Acid tends to fragment starch granules whereas sucrose tends to protect starch granules from fragmentation (Campbell and Briant, 1957).

Lemon pie filling is thickened with starch and contains both sugar and acid (in lemon juice). In order to avoid fragmentation of starch granules by acid during cooking, the acid juice may be added after the starch has been gelatinized. Adding lemon juice at the end of the cooking period also gives a more fresh lemon flavor because fewer flavoring substances are volatilized by the heat of cooking.

SUMMARY

Starch is stored in the cells of plant roots and seeds as water-insoluble granules. Starch granules are well organized accumulations of numerous starch molecules that are of two distinct types. One type or fraction of starch is amylose that consists of long chains of α-D-glucose linked $1 \rightarrow 4$. Amylopectin, the second starch fraction, is a highly branched molecule. It consists of relatively short chains of α-D-glucose units linked $1 \rightarrow 4$. These chains are joined in a branching structure through carbon atoms 1 and 6. Starch granules also contain some amylose-like molecules with limited branching of long chains.

Starch granules may be seen under an ordinary light microscope. Granule shape and range of size is characteristic for a particular plant source. Granules show birefringence when they are viewed under polarized light, suggesting a sphero-crystalline arrangement of the molecules.

Both amylose and amylopectin are present in most starches. The proportion of amylose varies between 17 and 32 percent of the total starch. Tapioca has about 17 percent amylose while corn has from 24 to 28 percent. Waxy varieties of corn, rice, and sorghum produce only amylopectin. Cooking characteristics of starches are affected by the amount of amylose they contain. Amylose is responsible for gelation in cooled, cooked pastes.

Certain enzymes may break down starch that is present in damaged granules. Beta-amylase, phosphorylase, and glucoamylase start at the nonreducing end of a chain and break off maltose, glucose-1-phosphate, and glucose, respectively. Alpha-amylase first attacks the starch molecules at random points, producing dextrins. Ultimately this enzyme produces glucose and maltose from the dextrins. Several debranching enzymes have been isolated.

Starch processing is a very old industry, dating back 3000 years. In recent years, however, many new chemically-modified starches have been produced. A wet milling process is commonly used for the recovery of native starch from cereals. The natural starches may then be modified for specific uses. Pregelatinized starches are precooked and then dried. They are dispersible in cold water and produce a thickened mixture without recooking. They are used in such products as instant puddings.

Raw starches may be heated in very dilute acid below their gelatinization temperature. Limited hydrolysis of the molecules causes the starches to form thin pastes during gelatinization yet subsequent gel formation is unaffected. Various confections and fillings for baked products benefit from these characteristics.

Cross-linked starches are produced by treating the intact starch granule with various reagents that participate in bonding neighboring molecules together. Cross-bonding may decrease granule swelling and decrease breakdown when the granules are heated in water. Starches may be further stabilized to control gelling and syneresis on its standing by forming esters or ethers with some of the free hydroxyl groups on the starch. Waxy starches benefit by cross-bonding and stabilization. These modified starches maintain viscosity during cooking and cooling, resist gelling and syneresis when stored, and produce clear pastes with nonstringy texture.

The term gelatinization describes a swelling and disorganization process that occurs in starch granules when they are heated in the presence of water. Water gradually moves into the granules and they swell. Friction is created between swollen granules and thickening occurs. A generally accepted precise definition of gelatinization is not available. Swelling of granules, increase in viscosity and translucency, increasing solubility, and loss of birefringence have all been used as indicators of gelatinization. An amylograph is commonly used to chart the viscosity as a starch slurry is heated and cooled. Characteristic patterns are seen for various starches.

Amylose molecules show strong tendencies to link together through hydrogen bonds. As a relatively concentrated solution containing amylose is cooled, cross-bonding occurs at random intervals and a gel structure is formed. This process of gelation is called retrogradation. Since amylose is primarily responsible for gel formation, waxy starches containing only amylopectin do not form gels.

Various factors affect the characteristics of gelatinized starch pastes. Each type of starch exhibits a characteristic gelatinization pattern. The presence of sugar decreases the swelling of starch granules and thus decreases viscosity. At a pH below 4, fragmentation of starch granules and some hydrolysis of starch molecules occurs with the thinning of cooked starch pastes.

STUDY QUESTIONS

Two types of starch molecules include a linear and a branched fraction.

1. Write the chemical structure for the basic monosaccharide unit of starch.
2. Write representative structural formulas for each of the two major fractions of starch, amylose and amylopectin. Describe in words and diagrams the general shape and size of representative molecules of each fraction.
3. Arrange the following starches in the order of increasing amylose content.

   Starches
   corn
   tapioca
   waxy corn
   wheat
   potato
   amylomaize
   waxy sorghum

Natural starches may be chemically or physically modified for specific uses.

4. For each of the following starches, describe chemical or physical modifications and explain the effect of the modification on functional properties in food preparation.

   Starches
   pregelatinized starch
   thin-boiling starch
   cross-bonded starch
   derivatized starch

5. Mr. Rogers plans to open a pie shop. He will sell cream pies, fruit pies, and frozen fruit pies. He needs some advice on the general types of thickening agents to use. Please advise him and explain why you make your suggestions.

Starch molecules may be hydrolyzed by various enzymes, by acid, and by heat.

6. Compare the action of alpha- and beta-amylase on starch hydrolysis, indicating the end-products of hydrolysis in each case.

7. Explain a possible relationship between starch hydrolysis and thin brown gravy.
8. Name some products of starch hydrolysis commonly used in food preparation.

Gelatinization of starch involves the swelling of starch granules when they are heated in water, with resultant thickening.

9. Using words and diagrams, describe the overall process of gelatinization, including the effect of heat and water on granule structure and the change in appearance of the paste. Give a possible explanation for the increased viscosity during gelatinization. Suggest indicators that might be used to measure gelatinization.

Retrogradation of starch pastes (gel formation) involves the realignment of molecules of the gelatinized starch, particularly amylose, into more parallel positions with cross-bonding between them.

10. Using words and diagrams, describe the overall process of retrogradation in starch pastes.
11. For each of the following starch pastes, describe clarity and tendency to gel when cold. Relate these characteristics to the chemical composition of the starch.

Starch pastes from
corn
tapioca
potato
waxy corn
cross-bonded waxy corn

12. Give a probable explanation of how the chemical composition of starch influences its tendency to gel a cooked paste when it is cooled.
13. Explain the effects of varying concentrations of starch, addition of sugar, and addition of acid on the consistency of white sauces, puddings, and gravies.

REFERENCES

1. Anker, C. A. and W. F. Geddes. 1944. Gelatinization studies upon wheat and other starches with the amylograph. *Cereal Chemistry* 21, 335.

2. Banks, W. and C. T. Greenwood. 1975. *Starch and Its Components*. New York: Wiley.

3. Bean, M. L. and E. M. Osman. 1959. Behavior of starch during food preparation. II. Effects of different sugars on the viscosity and gel strength of starch pastes. *Food Research* 24, 665.

4. Boettger, R. M. 1963. The effect of pregelatinized starches on cake quality. *Cereal Science Today* 8, 106.

5. Campbell, A. M. and A. M. Briant. 1957. Wheat starch pastes and gels containing citric acid and sucrose. *Food Research* 22, 358.

6. Casey, J. P. 1978. The future for corn wet milling. *Food Technology* 32 (No. 1), 72.

7. Elbert, E. M. 1965. Starch: Changes during heating in the presence of moisture. *Journal of Home Economics* 57, 197.

8. Greenwood, C. T. 1964. Structure, properties, and amylolytic degradation of starch. *Food Technology* 18, 138.

9. Hester, E. E., A. M. Briant, and C. J. Personius. 1956. The effect of sucrose on the properties of some starches and flours. *Cereal Chemistry* 33, 91.

10. Hoseney, R. C., D. R. Lineback, and P. A. Seib. 1978. Role of starch in baked foods. *Bakers Digest* 52 (No. 4), 11.

11. Hullinger, C. H., E. Van Patten, and J. A. Freck. 1973. Food applications of high amylose starches. *Food Technology* 27 (No. 3), 22.

12. Inglett, G. E., Editor. 1970. *Corn: Culture, Processing, Products.* Westport, Conn.: Avi Publishing Company.

13. Katzbeck, W. 1972. Phosphate cross-bonded waxy corn starches solve many food application problems. *Food Technology* 26 (No. 3), 32.

14. Meyer, K. H. and P. Bernfeld. 1940. Recherches sur l'amidon. VII. Sur la structure fine du grain d'amidon et sur les phénomènes du gonflement. *Helvetica Chimica Acta* 23, 890.

15. Mitchell, W. A. 1972. Analyzing the metaphosphate stabilization reaction of starch by acid titration. *Food Technology* 26 (No. 3), 34.

16. Osman, E. M. and G. Mootse. 1958. Behavior of starch during food preparation. I. Some properties of starch-water systems. *Food Research* 23, 554.

17. Paul, P. C. and H. H. Palmer, editors. 1972. *Food Theory and Applications.* New York: Wiley.

18. Peeples, M. L. and J. T. Marshall, Jr. 1970. Process for obtaining starch from selected grain sorghum fractions. *Journal of Food Science* 35, 377.

19. Pomeranz, Y., editor. 1976. *Advances in Cereal Science and Technology.* St. Paul, Minn.: American Assoc. of Cereal Chemists.

20. Pomeranz, Y., editor. 1971. *Wheat Chemistry and Technology.* St. Paul, Minn.: American Assoc. of Cereal Chemists.

21. Savage, H. L. and E. M. Osman. 1978. Effects of certain sugars and sugar alcohols on the swelling of cornstarch granules. *Cereal Chemistry* 55, 447.

22. Schultz, H. W., R. F. Cain, and R. W. Wrolstad, editors. 1969. *Carbohydrates and Their Roles.* Westport, Conn.: Avi Publishing Company.

23. Trimbo, H. B. and B. S. Miller. 1971. Factors affecting the quality of sauces (gravies). *Journal of Home Economics* 63, 48.

24. Wurzburg, O. B. and C. D. Szymanski. 1970. Modified starches for the food industry. *Journal of Agricultural and Food Chemistry* 18, 997.

PART V

GELS, EMULSIONS, AND FOAMS IN FOOD SYSTEMS

Gels, emulsions, and foams are all colloidal systems that play important roles in a variety of food products. Basic structures for each of these systems are described in the introductory chapter of this Part to emphasize their similarities. Separate chapters are devoted to a more detailed discussion of emulsions and foams in food systems and, since one phase of food emulsions is always fat, a discussion of fats is included in the chapter on emulsions. Gels produced by pectin and by gelatin are also treated in separate chapters. (Starch gels were discussed in the chapter on starch found in Part IV.)

CHAPTER 17

BASIC STRUCTURES IN EMULSIONS, FOAMS, AND GELS

Most foods are complex dispersion systems. (The physical structure of dispersions is generally described in Section 2.2 and colloidal systems in food are discussed in Section 2.4.) Two special types of dispersion systems that are commonly included in a study of colloid chemistry are emulsions and foams. These systems play important roles in a number of food products. They are similar in that they both involve a surface active agent in their formation and stabilization. A number of colloidally dispersed substances can undergo transformation from a liquid sol to a gelled structure. Several of these systems are represented in various food products. A detailed discussion of emulsions in food products is found in Chapter 18 and foams in Chapter 19. Pectin gels and gelatin are treated in Chapters 20 and 21, respectively. Starch gels are discussed in Section 16.4.)

17.1

SURFACTANTS AND STABILIZERS IN FOOD

A surface active agent or surfactant is a substance that, when present in a system at low concentration, adsorbs onto the surfaces or interfaces of the system and alters to a marked degree their surface or interfacial free energies (Rosen, 1972). The term *interface* indicates a boundary between any two immiscible liquids while the term *surface* denotes a liquid–gas boundary.

The interfacial free energy is the minimum amount of work required to create or to expand that interface per unit area. *Interfacial free energy* is what is measured when surface or interfacial tension is determined. (Surface and interfacial tensions are discussed in Section 2.4.) When a surface or interface is expanded, the minimum work required to create the additional surface is the product of the surface or interfacial tension (σ) times the increase in area (A) of the surface ($W_{min} = \sigma \times A$). When a surface active agent adsorbs at some or all of the interfaces in a system, it decreases the surface tension and thus reduces the amount of work required to expand the surface. In the processes of emulsification and foaming the surface or interfacial area is greatly expanded. The presence of a surface active substance facilitates these processes by reducing the work needed in the surface expansion (Rosen, 1972).

A surface active agent characteristically has a molecular structure that is both polar and nonpolar (see Section 2.4). The chemical groups on the molecule that have a strong attraction for the solvent are called *lyophilic* and those having little attraction for the solvent are termed *lyophobic.* When the solvent is water, the terms used are *hydrophilic* and *hydrophobic,* respectively. Polar groups are hydrophilic and nonpolar groups are hydrophobic. Because of its lyophilic and lyophobic nature, a surfactant distorts the structure of the solvent or liquid phase in which it is dispersed. The surfactant is pushed toward the surface (between the liquid and air) or the interface (between two liquids) and is oriented with its lyophilic groups in the solvent and its lyophobic portions away from the solvent. A new intermediate layer is formed between the two phases and the tension between them decreased. The two immiscible phases are thus linked by chemical adsorption (Chwala and Anger, 1971; Rosen, 1972). The shape and size of the polar and nonpolar portions of a surfactant affect its activity as a surface active agent.

A number of substances are used in food products primarily for their surface active properties. These include lecithin, mono- and diglycerides, diacetyl tartaric acid esters of mono- and diglycerides, polyoxyethylene (20) sorbitan monostearate, stearyl-2-lactylic acid, and sodium lauryl sulfate. Egg yolk contains lipoproteins that are excellent emulsifying agents. The proteins in egg white are responsible for foam formation when this product is beaten.

The term stabilizer is used in a general sense to refer to a group of chemical substances that have the ability to significantly and usefully change a variety of important physical parameters in food systems. Effects of stabilizers include stabilization of emulsions and foams. They also include modification of water-binding capacity; reduction of evaporation rate; alteration of freezing rate; modification of ice crystal formation; regulation of rheological properties; and suspension of insoluble particles. Stabilizers are commonly hydrocolloid substances—colloidally dispersed polymers that interact with water and modify surface properties of materials (Blanshard, 1970). Examples of hydrocolloid substances include gelatin, starch, carboxymethylcellulose, pectin, agar, carrageenan, and other vegetable gums.

Hydrocolloids operate primarily as auxiliary agents in emulsification and foaming by increasing viscosity. However, some effects on reducing interfacial tension and forming strong interfacial films have also been shown.

A number of hydrocolloids, including gelatin, starch, and some vegetable gums, participate in gelation reactions. These substances apparently affect the structure of the water in the dispersion system and reduce its mobility. The evaporation rate of water may also be decreased. Hydrocolloid gels decrease diffusion rates and are widely used to control crystal size and recrystallization in such products as frozen desserts (Blanshard, 1970).

17.2

STRUCTURE OF EMULSIONS

An *emulsion* has often been defined as a dispersed system consisting of a liquid in a liquid. The two liquids are immiscible and separated or discontinuous particles of one liquid are dispersed in a continuous phase of the other. Becher (1965) has included the stability of the system and the size of the dispersed particles in his definition of an emulsion, which is:

An emulsion is a heterogeneous system, consisting of at least one immiscible liquid intimately dispersed in another in the form of droplets, whose diameters, in general, exceed 0.1 μm. Such systems possess a minimal stability, which may be accentuated by such additives as surface active agents, finely divided solids, etc.

The two phases of an emulsion should be clearly distinguished when discussing this system. The phase that is present as finely divided droplets is called the *disperse, internal,* or *discontinuous* phase. The phase that forms the matrix in which these droplets are suspended is called the *external* or *continuous* phase.

Although the definition of an emulsion usually speaks of two liquids dispersed in one another, the food technologist broadens this definition to include combinations of liquids and solids (Lissant, 1974). Emulsions in foods have historically been considered as dispersions of oil and water. The oil may be solid fat, as it is in many baked products, butter, margarine, and sausages.

Typical emulsion systems are divided into two types. An *oil-in-water* (O/W) emulsion consists of a dispersion of oil as the discontinuous phase and water as the continuous phase. A *water-in-oil* (W/O) emulsion consists of a dispersion with oil as the continuous phase and water as the discontinuous phase. Emulsions in food products are most commonly those of the oil-in-water type. Mayonnaise and salad dressing are typical examples. Butter and margarine are examples of water-in-oil emulsions.

The dispersed particles in dilute emulsions are essentially spherical. However, dispersed droplets in more concentrated emulsions are susceptible to deformation by mutual pressure. The droplets are not uniform in size. By measurements on a high power microphotograph, it has been shown that particles even in a typical emulsion with a relatively high degree of homogeneity vary considerably in particle diameter (Becher, 1955). The majority of particles in this case are approximately 2 μm in diameter, but an appreciable number of the particles are

Figure 17.1

Distribution of spherical droplets in an emulsion.

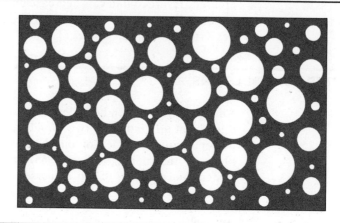

very small while others have diameters as large as 6 μm. An emulsion of nonuniform spherical droplets might look something like the representation in Figure 17.1. Figure 17.2 shows photomicrographs of meat emulsions prepared from poultry meat, ice, poultry fat, and spices. The dispersed fat particles, seen as white droplets in the photograph, are generally spherical and vary in size. The emulsion made with prerigor muscle contains a much finer dispersion of fat than does that made with postrigor muscle.

Figure 17.2

Meat emulsions. (*a*) Photomicrograph of emulsion made from prerigor muscle (400× magnification). (*b*) Photomicrograph of emulsion made from postrigor muscle (400× magnification). (Reprinted with permission from Froning, G. W. and S. Neelakantan. 1971. Emulsifying characteristics of prerigor and postrigor poultry muscle. *Poultry Science* 50, 839.)

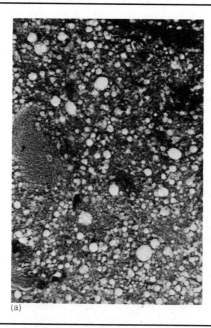

(a)

(b)

Figure 17.3

Orientation of emulsifier molecules in an oil in water emulsion.

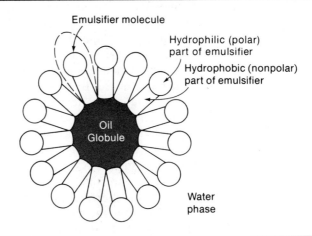

Emulsifier molecule

Hydrophilic (polar) part of emulsifier

Hydrophobic (nonpolar) part of emulsifier

Oil Globule

Water phase

Surface active agents that are added to an emulsion to aid in its formation and increase its stability by interfacial action are known as *emulsifiers* or *emulsifying agents*. The emulsifier lowers the interfacial tension between the two immiscible phases of an emulsion, allowing one phase to more readily surround droplets of the other phase. This substantially increases the ease with which an emulsion may form. The emulsifier is also important in the formation of a stable emulsion that does not readily separate into the two original phases on standing. The emulsifying agent is apparently concentrated at the interface between the suspended droplets and the continuous phase. It may form a tightly packed film around the suspended droplets. The nature of a surface active emulsifier is such that it has both polar and nonpolar parts. The polar parts of the molecule are oriented toward the aqueous phase of the system while the nonpolar parts are more soluble in the oil phase. The probable orientation of an emulsifier film around dispersed oil droplets is illustrated in Figure 17.3. Film formation at the interface between oil droplets and water has been reported to occur for a wide variety of substances. Acton and Saffle (1972), using a photomicrograph technique, reported interfacial film development with salt soluble protein of cow meat and beef hearts, sodium caseinate, and gum acacia. No films were observed using soy sodium proteinate or propylene glycol alginate.

17.3

STRUCTURE OF FOAMS

Foams are agglomerations of gas bubbles that are separated from each other by thin liquid films. They are gas in liquid dispersions. Foams, like emulsions, are formed and stabilized by surface active agents. In the case of foams, these substances are called *foaming agents*.

Pure liquids will not produce foams. Some impurity, in at least minute amounts, must be present for foam production. As a liquid is shaken or a stream of gas is passed through it, a foam forms. The surface area of the liquid is greatly enlarged in a foam, in comparison to the original surface. A surface active agent in the liquid orients itself at any available liquid–gas surface because of its partial incompatability with the liquid phase. Its lyophilic groups are in the liquid phase and its lyophobic groups are oriented toward the gas phase. A foaming agent is thus concentrated in the foam that forms on the surface of a bulk liquid.

The individual bubbles pressed against each other in a foam are separated by very thin films that are approximately parallel to the plane of the bubble surface. Certain regions of the films around the gas bubbles, however, are thickened and have a more concave shape. The molecules of an effective foaming agent are packed closely together at the gas–liquid surface to give mechanical strength to the liquid film. The lyophobic or hydrophobic portions of the foaming agent molecules should be of sufficient length to allow close packing. At the same time, there should be sufficient interaction of the hydrophilic groups of the foaming agent with the water in the system to include some bound water molecules in the surface film. This increases the stability of the foam (Rosen, 1972).

After a foam is formed, certain factors operate to decrease its stability. Because of the more concave shapes of the thicker regions of liquid around the gas bubbles, a capillary pressure is produced between these areas and the thinner portions of the film. This tends to drain the liquid from the thin films into the thicker portions. In addition, since the curvature of the thickened ribs often varies, capillary transfer of liquid may take place from some thicker parts (with smaller curvature) to others. Hydrostatic pressure also operates in a foam to cause the liquid to drain toward the bottom of the foam. As a result of these two factors, foams gradually lose some of the liquid contained in them, a process called *syneresis* or *weeping,* and the films become thinner. The breakdown or collapse of a foam is due to the eventual rupture of the films surrounding the gas bubbles (Sheludko, 1966).

17.4

STRUCTURE OF GELS

A *sol* is a dispersion of colloidal particles in a liquid dispersion medium. Depending upon the density of the dispersed particles in a sol, they may *sediment* or *cream* (*settle to the bottom* or *rise to the top*) and coagulate when the dispersion becomes unstable. The dispersion is generally stabilized, as discussed in Section 2.4, by 1. Brownian movement of the dispersed particles; 2. like electric charges on the dispersed particles that repel each other; and 3. water of hydration around the dispersed particles. A sol is similar to dilute emulsions and foams in the problem of maintaining stability by keeping the dispersed particles separated.

However, the problems of stabilizing concentrated emulsions and foams differ in that the particles are more tightly packed and are in continuous contact.

Many sols, particularly those containing long, thin macromolecules, have the ability to undergo sol → gel transformation under appropriate conditions of temperature, pH, etc. While a sol consists of dispersed particles in a continuous dispersion medium and is a pourable mixture, a gel has a variable degree of rigidity. It can be molded and will take the shape of the container. Intermolecular contact occurs between molecules in the sol to create a network system that is responsible for the rigid character of the gel.

A *gel* is defined as a two-phase system with a high degree of interface between a continuous (or at least intermeshed) system of solid material that holds a finely dispersed liquid phase (Paul and Palmer, 1972). In food products, the liquid phase is water and the gel-forming molecules have a considerable attraction for water. The intermolecular contacts are usually limited to a small number and are stabilized by secondary forces, such as hydrogen bonds, rather than by covalent bonds. Because the balance between solvent-solute and solute-solute is particularly delicate in a gel system when secondary forces stabilize the structure, the type of gel formed is dependent on the temperature and the solvent environment. The structure of the network may differ, depending on the way the gel is formed (Ward and Courts, 1977). Figure 17.4 illustrates a sol → gel transformation and the interlocking network of a gel structure. Gel structure has been likened to a three-dimensional brush-heap.

Gels generally exhibit some elasticity. The flexibility of the long, thin molecules making up the network and the relatively few links between molecules contribute to this characteristic. The strength of the intermolecular bonds influences the response of the gel to temperature change and mechanical agitation (Paul and Palmer, 1972).

Figure 17.4

Schematic representation of chain orientation in gel formation. (a) Random distribution of long, thin molecules in sol. (b) Development of crystalline or organized areas (indicated by dotted enclosures) in gel formation. (From Paul, P. C. and H. H. Palmer. *Food Theory and Application.* Copyright © 1972 John Wiley & Sons. Reprinted by permission of John Wiley & Sons, Inc.)

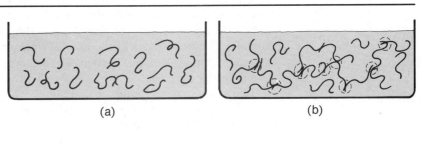

(a)　　　　　(b)

SUMMARY

Emulsions, foams, and gels are all colloidal systems that are important structural components of various food products. Surface active agents are involved in the formation of emulsions and foams. Some of the hydrocolloid stabilizers used in various food products act as auxiliary agents in emulsification and foaming. A number of these stabilizers also participate in gelation reactions.

A surface active agent or surfactant, when present in a system at low concentration, adsorbs onto the surfaces or interfaces of the system and alters to a marked degree their surface or interfacial free energies. The interfacial free energy is the minimum amount of work required to create or to expand that interface per unit area. It is what is measured when surface or interfacial tension is determined. The presence of a surfactant facilitates the great expansion of surface area that occurs in the processes of emulsification and foaming.

A surface active agent has a molecular structure that is both polar and nonpolar. By virtue of these characteristics, it forms a new intermediate layer between two immiscible phases and decreases the tension at their interface.

The term stabilizer is used to refer to a group of chemical substances that have the ability to significantly and usefully change a variety of important physical parameters in food systems. Stabilizers are commonly hydrocolloids. They interact with water and modify surface properties of substances in foods.

An emulsion is a heterogeneous system, consisting of at least one immiscible liquid intimately dispersed in another in the form of droplets. The size of the dispersed particles generally exceeds 0.1 μm in diameter. Surface active agents, known as emulsifiers, aid in the formation and increase the stability of an emulsion. The interfacial tension between the two immiscible liquids is lowered, allowing one phase to more readily surround droplets of the other phase. The emulsifier is concentrated at the interface between the suspended droplets and the continuous phase. It forms a tightly packed film around the suspended droplets. The polar parts of the emulsifying agent are oriented toward the aqueous phase of the system while the nonpolar parts are more soluble in the oil phase.

Foams are gas in liquid dispersions. They, like emulsions, are formed and stabilized by surface active agents. The surface area of a liquid is greatly enlarged when a foam is formed and thin liquid films form around gas bubbles. The surface active agent, called a *foaming agent,* orients itself at any available liquid–gas surface because of its partial incompatability with the liquid phase. Its lyophilic groups are in the liquid phase and its lyophobic groups are oriented toward the gas phase.

Certain regions of the films around the gas bubbles in a foam are thickened and have a concave shape. Because of this, a capillary pressure is produced between these areas and the thinner portions of the film. This tends to drain the liquid from the thin films into the thicker portions. Hydrostatic pressure also operates in a foam to cause the liquid to drain toward the bottom of the foam. As a result, foams gradually lose some of the liquid contained in them, a process called syneresis. Eventual rupture of the films is responsible for breakdown of a foam.

Many sols, particularly those containing long, thin macromolecules, have the ability to undergo sol → gel transformation under appropriate conditions of temperature, pH, etc. While a sol is pourable, a gel has a variable degree of rigidity. Intermolecular contact occurs between molecules in the sol to create a network system that is responsible for the rigid character of the gel.

A gel is defined as a two-phase system with a relatively high degree of interface between a continuous system of solid material that holds a finely dispersed liquid phase. The actual intermolecular contacts are usually limited to a small number and are stabilized by secondary forces rather than by covalent bonds. The structure of the network may differ, depending on the way in which the gel is formed. Gel structure has been likened to a three-dimensional brush-heap.

STUDY QUESTIONS

Surfactants play important functional roles in many food products.

1. Explain the significance of the following equation in emulsification and foaming:

$$W_{min} = \sigma \times A$$

W_{min} is minimum amount of work required; σ is surface tension; and A is area.

2. Describe the role of a surface active agent in the general processes of emulsification and foaming, keeping in mind the equation discussed in question 1.
3. What are the distinguishing chemical characteristics of a surfactant?
4. Give several examples of surfactants used in food products.

Hydrocolloid stabilizers usefully change a variety of physical parameters in food systems.

5. Describe several general effects of stabilizers in food systems.
6. Give examples of hydrocolloid stabilizers commonly used in food products.

Emulsions, foams, and gels are all colloidal systems that play important roles in food preparation and processing.

7. Define an emulsion and describe its structure.
8. Define a foam and describe its structure.

9. Describe the factors that operate to decrease the stability of a foam on standing.
10. Define a sol; a gel.
11. Describe the structure of a gel.

REFERENCES

1. Acton, J. C. and R. L. Saffle. 1972. Film observations at an oil-water interface. *Journal of Food Science* 37, 795.

2. Becher, P. 1965. *Emulsions: Theory and Practice,* 2nd edition. New York: Reinhold.

3. Becher, P. 1955. *Principles of Emulsion Technology.* New York: Reinhold.

4. Blanshard, J. M. V. 1970. Stabilizers—their structure and properties. *Journal of the Science of Food and Agriculture* 21, 393.

5. Chwala, A. and V. Anger. 1971. Surfactants. *Endeavour* 30 (No. 110), 97.

6. Lissant, K. J., editor. 1974. *Emulsions and Emulsion Technology.* Part I. New York: Marcel Dekker, Inc.

7. Paul, P. C. and H. H. Palmer. 1972. *Food Theory and Applications.* New York: Wiley.

8. Rosen, M. J. 1972. The relationship of structure to properties in surfactants. *Journal of the American Oil Chemists Society* 49, 293.

9. Sheludko, A. 1966. *Colloid Chemistry.* New York: Elsevier.

10. Ward, A. G. and A. Courts, editors. 1977. *The Science and Technology of Gelatin.* New York: Academic Press.

CHAPTER 18

FATS AND EMULSIONS IN FOOD

Fats are present in most foods in variable amounts and are important ingredients in baked products. They are a concentrated source of energy and generally increase the palatability of food. Neutral fats (triglycerides or triacylglycerols) are the principal fatty substances in foods, although phosphoglycerides, fatty acids, and sterols are also present in some tissues used for food. Triglycerides are subject to hydrolysis and oxidation whereby characteristic "off-flavors" are produced.

Fat or oil constitutes one phase of an emulsion. Any food product that contains both fat and water as ingredients and does not have an apparent separation of the two, will have the fat and water emulsified at least to a partial degree. Many factors influence the type of emulsion produced. The structure of emulsions is described in Section 17.2.

18.1

CHEMISTRY OF FATTY SUBSTANCES

The term lipid is used to describe water-insoluble organic substances found in animal and plant tissues that are extractable by nonpolar solvents such as chloroform, ether, and benzene. Lipids include the following groups of substances:

Fatty acids

Neutral fats (triglycerides or acylglycerols)

Phosphoglycerides

Steroids

Fat-soluble vitamins

The older term *triglyceride* will be used in this chapter to refer to *triacylglycerols*. Triglycerides are quantitatively the most important lipid component of foods. Some phosphoglycerides function in foods as emulsifiers.

Table 18.1　Some Naturally Occurring Fatty Acids

Common Name	Systematic Name	Number of:		Structure	Melting Point (°C)
		Carbon Atoms	Double Bonds		
Butyric	–	4	0	$CH_3(CH_2)_2COOH$	– 7.9
Lauric	Dodecanoic	12	0	$CH_3(CH_2)_{10}COOH$	44.2
Myristic	Tetradecanoic	14	0	$CH_3(CH_2)_{12}COOH$	53.9
Palmitic	Hexadecanoic	16	0	$CH_3(CH_2)_{14}COOH$	63.1
Stearic	Octadecanoic	18	0	$CH_3(CH_2)_{16}COOH$	69.6
Oleic	Octadecenoic	18	1	$CH_3(CH_2)_7CH=CH(CH_2)_7COOH$	13.4
Linoleic	Octadecadienoic	18	2	$CH_3(CH_2)_4CH=CHCH_2CH=CH(CH_2)_7COOH$	– 5.0
Linolenic	Octadecatrienoic	18	3	$CH_3CH_2CH=CHCH_2CH=CHCH_2CH=CH(CH_2)_7COOH$	–11.0

Fatty acids occur free in tissues in only small amounts. However, they are building blocks for a variety of lipids, including triglycerides and phosphoglycerides. A fatty acid consists of a chain containing carbon and hydrogen atoms with a terminal carboxyl group ($-\overset{\overset{\text{O}}{\|}}{\text{C}}-\text{OH}$). The hydrocarbon chains are of varying length. They may be saturated with hydrogen or they may be unsaturated. *Unsaturated* fatty acids may contain one double bond (*monounsaturated*) or more than one. Common terminology for fatty acids with two or more double bonds is *polyunsaturated*. A representative fatty acid structure may be written as:

$$CH_3(CH_2)_n-\overset{\overset{\text{O}}{\|}}{\text{C}}-OH$$

Naturally occurring fatty acids in higher plants and animals generally have an even number of carbon atoms. The chains are often from 14 to 22 carbons in length with molecules of 16 or 18 carbons being the most abundant. Some fats, such as butterfat and coconut oil, contain a relatively large proportion of short-chain fatty acids. Some naturally occurring fatty acids are listed in Table 18.1. Fatty acid content of selected food fats is given in Table 18.2.

Table 18.2 Fatty Acid Content of Selected Food Fats (Grams per 100 g ether extract or crude fat)

Source of Fat	Saturated Fatty Acids			Unsaturated Fatty Acids			
	Total	Palmitic	Stearic	Total	Oleic	Linoleic	Linolenic
Beef	48	28	19	47	44	2	trace
Pork, back	38	26	12	58	46	6	
Chicken	32	24	7	64	38	20	2
Eggs, chicken	32	25	7	61	44	7	1
Butterfat	55	25	12	39	33	3	1
Lard	38	31	7	57	46	10	1
Shortening, vegetable (varies with source of fat)	23	14	6	72	65	7	trace
Cacao butter	56	23	33	39	37	2	
Corn oil	10	8	2	84	28	53	1
Cottonseed oil	25	22	2	71	21	50	
Safflower oil	8	3	4	87	15	72	
Soybean oil	15	9	6	80	20	52	7

Source: From Goddard and Goodall, 1959.

Figure 18.1

**Triglycerides are formed
by esterifying glycerol
with three fatty acids.**

Ester linkage

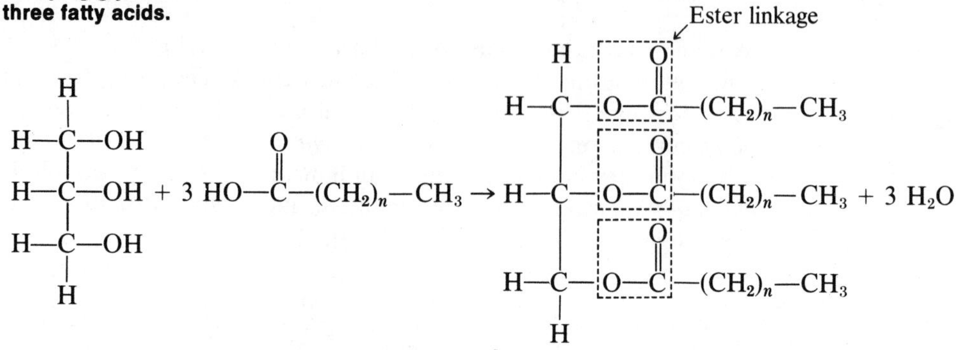

Glycerol   Fatty Acids   Triglyceride   Water

TRIGLYCERIDES

Glycerides are fatty acid esters of glycerol. (An *ester* combines an alcohol with an organic acid). Triglycerides are formed by esterifying glycerol with three fatty acids, as shown in Figure 18.1. Some mono- and diglycerides, glycerol esterified with one and two fatty acids, respectively, are used in food products as emulsifying agents. General structures for mono- and diglycerides are given in Figure 18.2.

Figure 18.2

**Chemical structures for
mono- and diglycerides.**

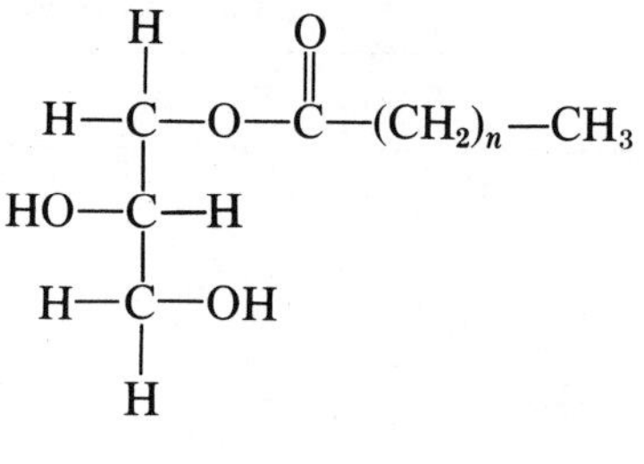

1–Monoglyceride

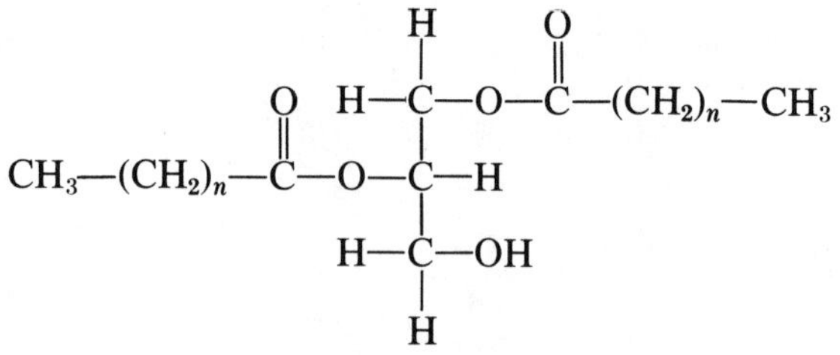

1,2–Diglyceride

Triglycerides are of different types, depending upon the fatty acids esterified to the glycerol. Those containing only one kind of fatty acid in all three positions are called *simple triglycerides*. Those containing two or more different fatty acids are called *mixed triglycerides*.

18.2

MELTING POINTS AND CRYSTALLIZATION

MELTING POINTS　　The melting point of a fat gives an indication of the strength of forces that bond adjacent triglyceride molecules together. The types of fatty acids in the triglycerides determine their melting points. In general, the melting point increases as the length of the carbon chain increases. Therefore, fats that contain a relatively high proportion of long-chain fatty acids, such as beef or mutton fat, have a higher melting point than do fats with a greater proportion of short-chain fatty acids, such as butterfat. The long carbon chains allow greater attraction or bonding between triglyceride molecules than do short chains, as illustrated in Figure 18.3. Considerable heat energy is required to move the long chains apart as they change to a completely liquid phase in melting.

The melting point also decreases with increasing degree of unsaturation or number of double bonds. For example, stearic acid, a completely saturated fatty acid, has a melting point of 69.6°C. Oleic acid, with one double bond, melts at 13.4°C. Linoleic acid, with two double bonds, has a melting point of −5°C. This effect is again related to the ability of the triglycerides to pack closely together. The presence of a double bond in a fatty acid changes the shape of the molecule as illustrated in Figure 18.3. The particular molecular shape produced by a double bond is dependent upon the configuration of the bond—*cis* or *trans*. An unsaturated fatty acid with a *trans* configuration

$$-C \diagdown \quad \diagup H$$
$$\quad C=C$$
$$H \diagup \quad \diagdown C-$$

has a higher melting point than does a similar fatty acid with a *cis* configuration

$$H \diagdown \quad \diagup H$$
$$\quad C=C$$
$$-C \diagup \quad \diagdown C-$$

because the *trans* molecules fit together well and greater forces of attraction are produced (see Figure 18.3). For example, elaidic acid, an 18 carbon fatty acid similar to oleic acid but with a *trans* double bond, melts at 43.7°C. Oleic acid, that has a *cis* double bond, melts at a lower temperature (13.4°C).

Figure 18.3

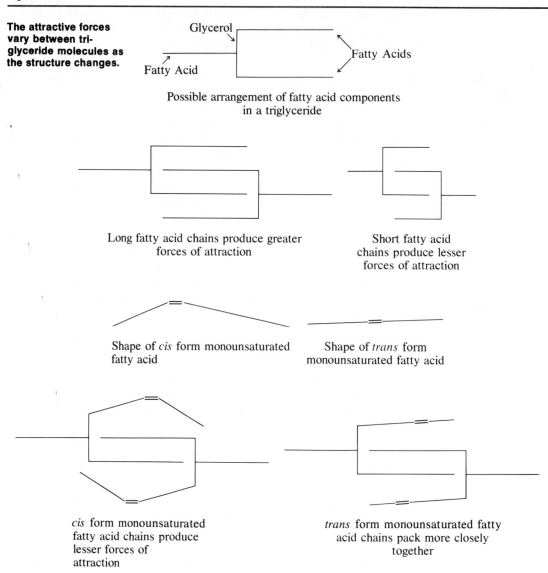

The attractive forces vary between tri-glyceride molecules as the structure changes.

Possible arrangement of fatty acid components in a triglyceride

Long fatty acid chains produce greater forces of attraction

Short fatty acid chains produce lesser forces of attraction

Shape of *cis* form monounsaturated fatty acid

Shape of *trans* form monounsaturated fatty acid

cis form monounsaturated fatty acid chains produce lesser forces of attraction

trans form monounsaturated fatty acid chains pack more closely together

Differences in melting points among food fats may be explained in terms of the factors discussed above. In general, vegetable oils contain a relatively high proportion of unsaturated fatty acids and have a lower melting point than do meat fats which contain more saturated fatty acids. Butterfat, which has a comparatively high proportion of short-chain fatty acids, melts at a lower temperature than does pork fat. Pork fat contains very few short-chain fatty acids. The process of hydrogenation of oils to produce shortenings causes an increase in the melting point. This is due primarily to the increase in degree of saturation of the fatty acid components. However, the production of some *trans* fatty acids in place of the *cis* form also contributes to an elevated melting point.

Most naturally occurring fats melt over a relatively wide temperature range. This is because most fats contain many different kinds of triglycerides, each with its own melting behavior. One notable exception to the general tendency toward wide melting point ranges is the range of cocoa butter. It melts over a relatively narrow temperature range that is just below body temperature. This is because about two-thirds of the triglyceride molecules in cocoa fat are similar types of molecules. Many of them have one molecule of palmitic acid, one of oleic acid, and one of stearic acid esterified to one glycerol molecule. The narrow temperature range for melting is responsible for the characteristic pleasant "mouth-feel" of good quality chocolate.

CRYSTALLIZATION

Most fats that are solid at room temperature can be molded into different shapes. They demonstrate the rheological property of plasticity that is discussed in Section 1.4. When a substance shows plasticity, a minimum force must be applied before it begins to move. After this force, called a *yield value,* is once applied, the substance moves in direct proportion to the additional force applied to it.

A plastic fat, such as hydrogenated shortening or lard, is a two-phase system. It has a solid phase made up of crystals of triglyceride molecules and a liquid phase that is composed of noncrystalline or individually separated triglyceride molecules. The solid crystals give rigidity to the fat. The liquid phase allows movement to occur. The individual molecules in the liquid phase move around the crystals as the fat is creamed. The solid phase must be sufficiently finely divided to hold the mass together without the liquid separating out. The ratio of solid to liquid fat depends on the temperature.

The formation of crystals in plastic fats is the result of attractive forces between the triglyceride molecules. Fats are polymorphic, meaning that they can exist in more than one crystalline form. Each crystal form has a characteristic melting point, size, and shape. The crystal forms vary, depending upon the shape and symmetry of the triglyceride molecules and the ease of close packing. Three, four, or more forms have been suggested and are called α, β', intermediate, and β (Hoerr, 1960). When melted fats are cooled rapidly, they tend to crystallize in the form of very small, delicate needles that are relatively low melting. Some fats remain in this form indefinitely, whereas others transform to a larger, higher-melting crystal. Additional transformations to still larger crystals may also take place upon standing as molecules pack more closely together. Molecules that are all alike can readily align themselves with each other and pack together, forming large

Figure 18.4

A replica of lard that was treated with 35 percent aqueous detergent to remove the liquid phase and then slowly cooled. Crystals (C) composed of layers of crystallites (K) can be clearly seen. (Reduced approximately 45 percent.) (Reprinted with permission from Jewell, G. G. and M. L. Meara. 1970. A new and rapid method for the electron microscopic examination of fats. *Journal of the American Oil Chemists Society* 47, 535.)

crystals. If molecules are not all the same shape and configuration, they cannot pack together as closely and transformation to the higher melting polymorphic forms is impeded (Hoerr, 1967).

Ordinary lard consists of a relatively limited assortment of triglyceride molecules in which the palmitic acid components are almost all located on the central carbon atom of glycerol. Since these similar molecules pack well, lard has three or four crystal forms and generally produces large crystals (Hoerr, 1967). Figure 18.4 shows crystals of

Figure 18.5

A replica of vegetable oil shortening which was treated with 15 percent aqueous detergent to remove the liquid phase and then slowly cooled. A highly crystalline surface is evident. (Reduced approximately 45 percent.) (Reprinted with permission from Jewell, G. G. and M. L. Meara. 1970. A new and rapid method for the electron microscopic examination of fats. *Journal of the American Oil Chemists Society* 47, 535.)

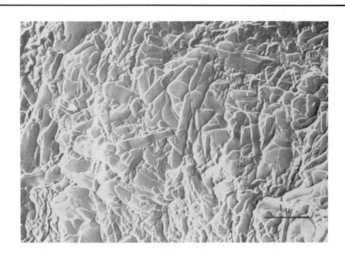

lard as seen with electron microscopic examination of a commercial sample (Jewell and Meara, 1970). The size of the lard crystals may be compared with those of a partially hydrogenated vegetable oil shortening shown in Figure 18.5. The small shortening crystals are a result of the diversity of triglyceride types contained in this product. Close packing and consequently large crystal size are less likely to occur in this case.

Processing procedures may be selected that will yield products with the most desirable crystallization characteristics for a particular use. A fat with small crystals, such as many hydrogenated shortenings, performs best in a shortened cake where creaming is part of the preparation procedure. Lard, with its larger crystals, may be more useful in the preparation of a flaky pie crust.

18.3

MODIFICATION OF NATURAL FATS

HYDROGENATION
Plastic fats are produced by the process of hydrogenation from vegetable oils that are liquid at room temperature. Liquid vegetable oil is exposed to hydrogen gas in the presence of a catalyst, such as nickel, palladium, copper, or mixtures of various metals. Hydrogen atoms add to the double bonds of unsaturated fatty acid components. The conditions of hydrogenation, including temperature, pressure, type and concentration of catalyst, and intensity of agitation of the mixture, affect the hydrogenation process. Thus selective hydrogenation may occur. For example, at high temperatures, high concentration of catalyst, low pressure of hydrogen, and low intensity of agitation, the partial hydrogenation of linoleic acid to produce oleic acid is favored as a first step. Oleic acid is later saturated to produce stearic acid (Eckey, 1954). The use of copper as a catalyst has also been shown to selectively hydrogenate linolenic acid in soybean oil (Mounts *et al.*, 1978). Some *trans* double bonds are produced during hydrogenation of oils. Hydrogenation is commonly done as a batch process in commercial operations. However, use of a continuous hydrogenation process with stationary catalysts over which the oil flows has been reported (Mukherjee *et al.*, 1975).

An alternative method of preparing hydrogenated shortenings involves blending a small amount of highly hydrogenated fat with unhydrogenated vegetable oil. This process preserves a larger quantity of polyunsaturated fatty acids, particularly linoleic acid, in the finished shortening.

After hydrogenation, liquid shortenings are charged with inert nitrogen gas, cooled rapidly to about 18°C (65°F) and agitated to bring about crystallization. A sudden pressure drop disperses the nitrogen gas and containers are then filled with the shortening. Tempering at a carefully controlled temperature for 24–48 hours ensures the proper crystal size and shape (Sanders, 1959).

INTERESTERIFI-CATION

A process called *interesterification* or *rearrangement* is used to change the arrangement of fatty acids on triglyceride molecules to produce a more random distribution. Although the fatty acid composition of the processed fat is unchanged, the rearrangement of fatty acids on the glycerol molecules produces changes in consistency. For example, lard normally has a somewhat ordered, nonrandom distribution of fatty acids among the triglyceride molecules. The similarity of a relatively large number of the triglyceride molecules in lard is responsible for the tendency of this fat to form large crystals and to change into several crystalline forms. By heating lard to about 110°C (230°F) in the presence of a catalyst, such as sodium methoxide, the fatty acids become more randomly distributed on the glycerol molecules, resulting in a larger number of dissimilar molecules. These molecules do not fit together as well and form relatively small crystals. Interesterified lard thus becomes more like hydrogenated shortenings.

If interesterification is carried out at a temperature just below the melting point of the fat, triglycerides containing three saturated fatty acids (*trisaturates*) begin to precipitate as they form and are thus removed from the reaction mixture. They continue to precipitate as the liquid phase continues to seek equilibrium in the production of these particular types of triglyceride molecules. This process, called *directed interesterification,* produces a relatively large proportion of trisaturated triglycerides that have an additional stiffening effect on the fat (Sanders, 1959).

WINTERIZING

Winterizing is used to remove high-melting triglycerides from liquid salad oils. The oil is simply cooled to about 7.2°C (45°F) and the crystallized materials removed by filtration. Winterized oils are useful in the preparation of salad dressings. The oil in the dressings will not crystallize and disrupt the emulsion when it is stored at refrigerator temperatures (Sanders, 1959).

18.4

SMOKE POINT AND FRYING

Fats are used as a medium for the transfer of heat when foods are fried. A desirable property of fats used for frying is a high smoke point. The smoke point of a fat is the temperature to which the fat may be heated, under controlled conditions, before the appearance of steady puffs of smoke from the surface of the fat. In overheated fats glycerol, produced by the hydrolysis of some triglycerides, is decomposed to produce acrolein. This pungent substance is irritating to mucous membranes.

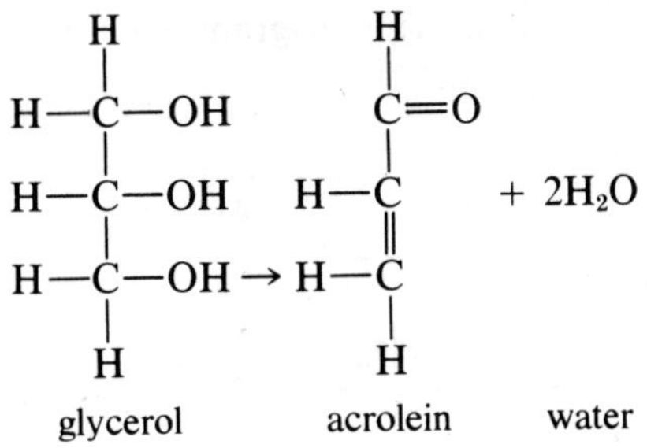

Smoke points for some types of fats are given in Table 18.3. The presence of mono- and diglycerides in fats lowers the smoke point since these emulsifiers smoke at a relatively low temperature.

Fats to be used for frying should be chosen on the basis of their resistance to smoking at the temperatures used. The production of free fatty acids by hydrolysis of some triglycerides during the frying process causes a decrease in smoke point. The presence in the fat of small particles that come from the food being fried also lowers the smoke point.

18.5 DETERIORATION OF FAT

The term *rancidity* is used to describe specific types of disagreeable odors and flavors in fatty substances. Hydrolytic rancidity results from hydrolysis of triglycerides to produce glycerol and free fatty acids with undesirable odors and flavors. *Oxidative rancidity* is produced by the process of autoxidation whereby unsaturated fatty acid components spontaneously take up oxygen.

HYDROLYTIC RANCIDITY

The enzyme lipase catalyzes the hydrolysis of triglycerides. The general reaction yields glycerol and three free fatty acids as shown in the

Table 18.3 Smoke Points of Selected Fats

Type of Fat	Smoke Point (°C)	Smoke Point (°F)
Steam rendered lard	189	372
Cottonseed oil	229	444
Peanut oil	230	446
Combination shortening I*	191	376
Combination shortening II*	177	319

Source: From Bennion and Hanning, 1956.
* Contains interesterified lard plus vegetable fat and mono- and diglycerides.

following diagram, where R represents the hydrocarbon chain of a fatty acid.

$$
\begin{array}{l}
\text{H}_2\text{C}-\text{O}-\overset{\displaystyle\text{O}}{\overset{\|}{\text{C}}}-\text{R}_1 \\[2pt]
\;\;| \qquad\qquad \overset{\displaystyle\text{O}}{\;\;} \\
\text{HC}-\text{O}-\overset{\displaystyle\text{O}}{\overset{\|}{\text{C}}}-\text{R}_2 \;+\; 2\,\text{H}_2\text{O} \xrightarrow[\text{Lipase}]{} \\[2pt]
\;\;| \qquad\qquad \overset{\displaystyle\text{O}}{\;\;} \\
\text{H}_2\text{C}-\text{O}-\overset{\displaystyle\text{O}}{\overset{\|}{\text{C}}}-\text{R}_3
\end{array}
\qquad
\begin{array}{l}
\text{H}_2\text{C}-\text{OH} \\
\;\;| \\
\text{HC}-\text{OH} \;+\; 3\,\text{R}_{(1-3)}\overset{\displaystyle\text{O}}{\overset{\|}{\text{C}}}-\text{OH} \\
\;\;| \\
\text{H}_2\text{C}-\text{OH}
\end{array}
$$

| A triglyceride | Glycerol | Fatty acids |

The odors or flavors associated with hydrolytic rancidity vary with the particular free fatty acids that are released. Short-chain fatty acids, such as butyric, caproic, and capric acids, have disagreeable odors and are volatile at room temperature. These components are present in the triglycerides of butterfat and make this product susceptible to undesirable flavor changes resulting from hydrolysis. Long-chain fatty acids, that make up the major portion of the fatty acids in vegetable oils and meat fats, are not volatile at room temperature and do not usually contribute substantially to "off-flavor" unless oxidation also occurs. Lipase is destroyed by heating. Hydrolytic randicity is, therefore, most commonly encountered in products that are not heated during processing (Paul and Palmer, 1972).

OXIDATIVE RANCIDITY

The extent of oxidation of a fat may be followed by measuring the uptake of oxygen by the fatty material. When a sample of fat is held at a constant temperature, the curve for volume of oxygen absorbed plotted against time shows that initially the rate of oxygen absorption is small and continues to be so during a period of time that is called the *induction period*. At the end of the induction period, the rate of oxygen uptake increases rapidly until it reaches a much higher level that then remains more or less constant until a large volume of oxygen has been absorbed (Eckey, 1954). This curve indicates that once the level of oxidation rises above a low minimum, it proceeds very rapidly. Food technologists are concerned, therefore, with lengthening the induction period for a fat-containing food so that its storage life is increased. The use of antioxidants is often effective for this purpose.

The unsaturated fatty acid components of triglycerides are primarily responsible for the development of oxidative rancidity (Dugan, 1961). Various mechanisms for this oxidative process have been proposed over the years. The hydroperoxide mechanism appears to offer the best explanation. Hydroperoxides (—OOH) may form through a free-radical chain reaction. According to this theory of oxidation, a free radical (R ·) is produced initially when a H atom, with its electron, is removed from the carbon atom adjacent to one involved in double bonding. Heat, light, and metals such as iron and copper are probably some of the factors involved in initiating this first production of a free radical.

$$-CH_2-CH=CH- \xrightarrow{-H} -CH\cdot-CH=CH-$$

    Fatty acid   Free radical
    component

Oxygen from the environment is then added to the free radical.

$$-CH\cdot-CH=CH- \xrightarrow{+O_2} -CH(OO\cdot)-CH=CH-$$

    Free radical

This resulting oxygen-containing molecule is still very reactive, however, acting much like a free radical itself, and reacts immediately with another unsaturated fatty acid in the mixture. It removes a H atom from this fatty acid in order to form a somewhat more stable hydroperoxide. The removal of a H atom from the second fatty acid component leaves a second free radical and propagates the chain reaction whereby this process keeps repeating itself until oxidation of all of the fatty acid components has occurred.

$$-CH(OO\cdot)-CH=CH- + -CH_2-CH=CH-$$

                             2nd fatty acid
                               component

$$\rightarrow -CH(OOH)-CH=CH- + -CH\cdot-CH=CH-$$

              Hydroperoxide   2nd free radical

Hydroperoxides themselves do not produce "off-odors" in oxidizing fats. However, they are comparatively unstable compounds and decompose into a variety of small volatile aldehydes, ketones, and acids that are responsible for the characteristic rancid odor of oxidized fatty substances.

A second mechanism for oxidation of polyunsaturated fatty acids with unconjugated double bonds in the positions found in linoleic acid involves the enzyme lipoxidase. This reaction produces hydroperoxides but is not a chain reaction as is autoxidation.

The quality of a fat and the extent of oxidative deterioration have been evaluated with the use of both chemical tests and flavor scores. A simple and rapid colorimetric method for measuring hydroperoxides in vegetable oil as an assessment of rancidity was reported by Eskin and Frenkel (1976). The thiobarbituric acid (TBA) test measures an aldehyde, malonaldehyde, that is produced in oxidizing fat. Peroxide values are measured and expressed as millimoles of peroxide per kilogram of fat (Gray, 1978). Pohle *et al.* (1964) reported that the flavor score could not be estimated for any given fat from either the peroxide value or the TBA value. However, Warner *et al.* (1978) correlated flavor scores with concentration of the aldehydes, pentanal and hexanal, in vegetable oil. These aldehydes were measured by direct gas chromatography of the oil samples.

Soybean oil is particularly susceptible to a special type of oxidative deterioration called *flavor reversion*. Linolenic acid appears to be the most important precursor of this "off-flavor" (Evans *et al.*, 1965). Various methods are used industrially to control flavor reversion. They include selective hydrogenation, controlled deodorization procedures, and inactivation of metallic impurities (Paul and Palmer, 1972).

Certain factors act as prooxidants in encouraging the autoxidation of fats. Traces of heavy metals, such as copper and iron, reduce the length of the induction period before oxidation begins (Schultz, 1962). Demetalization of soybean oil was reported by Vioque *et al.* (1965) to increase its oxidative stability. Iron-containing heme pigments have been reported to be catalysts for oxidative deterioration of the fat in cooked meats, that tends to become rancid with even short storage periods (Younathan and Watts, 1959; Love and Pearson, 1971). However, Love and Pearson (1974) found that iron in the reduced ferrous state, that could be extracted from cooked meat, was an effective prooxidant while metmyoglobin (heme pigment) had no effect on oxidation at concentrations of 1–10 mg per g of cooked meat. Thus it may be the ferrous iron in cooked meat that catalyzes oxidation of fat rather than the heme pigment. Table salt (sodium chloride) accelerates the oxidation of meat fats although the mechanism for this effect is not completely known. The chloride ion may be the active agent in this case. Light and ionizing radiations also accelerate fat oxidation.

ANTIOXIDANTS

An antioxidant, when present in a mixture in even small quantities, inhibits the autoxidation of fat and prolongs the shelf life of a food product. Most antioxidants that function in food systems are phenolic compounds. The chemical structures for three phenolic substances approved by the U. S. Food and Drug Administration for use in food are given in Figure 18.6. They include butylated hydroxyanisole (BHA), butylated hydroxytoluene (BHT), and gallic acid or propyl gallate. Each of these compounds has a readily available source of hydrogen from OH groups, usually in the ortho or para position, that can stop the chain reaction involved in autoxidation. The following illustration, using hydroquinone, demonstrates how an antioxidant may supply hydrogen. However, hydroquinone is not an approved antioxidant for food use.

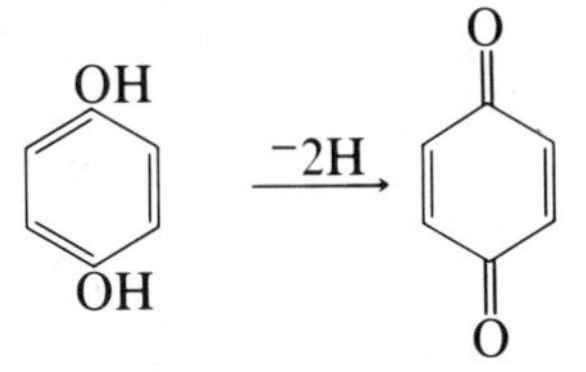

Hydroquinone   Quinone

The chain reaction of fat autoxidation is initiated and propagated by the formation of free radicals, as previously described. An antioxidant of the phenolic type supplies hydrogen to react with the free radical initially formed and breaks the chain reaction before the end products responsible for rancid "off-odors" have been produced. The compound formed in the phenolic antioxidant structure after the release of hydrogen is stable, odorless, and harmless (Sherwin, 1972).

Initiation of chain reaction	$ROO\cdot$ + Fatty acid free radical	AH_2 Phenolic antioxidant molecule, hydro-quinone-type	→	$ROOH$ + Hydro-peroxide	$AH\cdot$ Stable free radical of phenolic antioxidant	Chain reaction stopped
Another initiation of chain reaction	$ROO\cdot$ + Another fatty acid free radical	$AH\cdot$ Stable free radical of phenolic antioxidant	→	$ROOH$ + Hydro-peroxide	A Phenolic antioxidant quinone-type	Chain reaction stopped

Figure 18.6

Antioxidants used in food products.

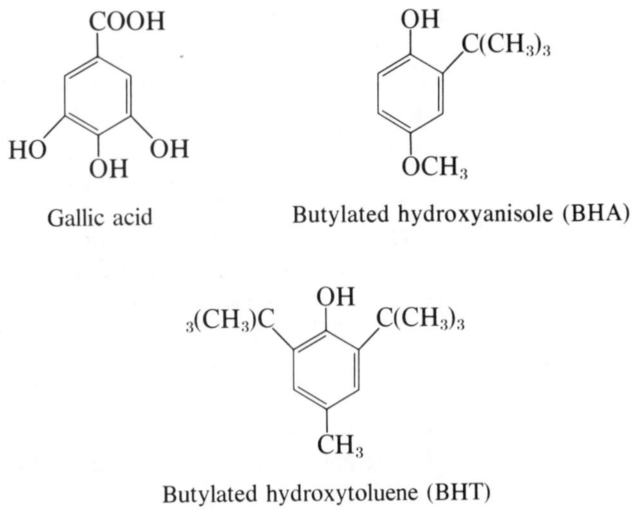

Gallic acid   Butylated hydroxyanisole (BHA)

Butylated hydroxytoluene (BHT)

Antioxidants increase the length of the induction period before the oxidation of fat becomes a rapid reaction. Whenever a free radical is initiated, antioxidants stop the chain reaction that otherwise would be propagated. However, when the antioxidant has released all of its available hydrogen, it is no longer effective and autoxidation may then proceed uninhibited. It is important that antioxidants that are to be combined with foods be added as early as possible in the processing procedures. Oxidized fats cannot be restored to their original quality by addition of antioxidants after oxidation has once occurred.

Some compounds can act as synergists to antioxidants. A *synergist* increases the effectiveness of the primary antioxidant although it is not an effective antioxidant when used alone. Di- or tricarboxylic organic acids, such as citric acid, are effective synergists in antioxidant mixtures because they *chelate* or *bind* metals such as iron and copper which can act as prooxidants. Ascorbic acid esters with long-chain fatty acids, that make these compounds soluble in fats and oils, have been investigated as antioxidants (Pongracz, 1973). Combinations of ascorbic acid esters with several antioxidants and synergists, including tocopherols (vitamin E), propyl gallate, and lecithin, have demonstrated good antioxidative properties. Lecithin acts as a synergist in these mixtures.

The trend in recent years toward the use of more highly unsaturated fats in the diet has led to changes in the susceptibility of many processed foods to oxidative deterioration (Sherwin, 1972). Antioxidants are important in controlling the quality of products such as lard and shortenings containing animal fats, margarines, prepared breakfast cereals, cake and frosting mixes, pudding and sauce mixes, whipped toppings, and many other convenience foods.

18.6

CHARACTERISTICS OF EMULSIONS

Fat is one component of food emulsions. An *emulsion* is formed when one liquid is dispersed in another liquid with which it is ordinarily immiscible. Food emulsions have been defined to include both liquid and solid fats. (The basic structure of emulsions is discussed in Section 17.2.)

The major characteristics of emulsions are generally controllable, over reasonable ranges, as the emulsions are formed. They often depend on the composition of the system and the mode of preparation.

APPEARANCE

The appearance of an emulsion varies widely and depends on the ingredients used, their color and difference in refractive index, and particle size of the dispersed phase. The color of the continuous phase is usually the controlling color for the product. Very small dispersed particles contribute to clarity (Lissant, 1974, p. 254). A milky white emulsion has particles greater than 1 μm in diameter.

VISCOSITY

Emulsions can be thin or thick fluids, pastes, or gels. Their viscosity is similar to that of the external phase as long as this phase represents more than half of the volume of the emulsion. The viscosity of the *external* or *continuous phase* may be increased by adding thickening or gelling agents that are compatible with the emulsifier. Carboxymethylcellulose and various vegetable gums may be added for this purpose.

When the *internal* or *dispersed phase* of the emulsion is greater in volume than that of the external phase, the apparent viscosity increases. This is due to the crowding of particles in the emulsion. Under these conditions, particle size and electrical charge assume greater importance in determining emulsion viscosity. Reducing the particle size increases viscosity. The charge on dispersed particles may result from the dissociation of ionic emulsifying agents or possibly from frictional electricity. Theoretically, the maximum volume that can be occupied by dispersed spherical particles of a uniform size is 74 percent of the total volume. Emulsions may be prepared that have more than 90 percent internal phase, however. In these cases, the dispersed particles must be of variable sizes and there is considerable crowding and distortion of the particles (Griffin, 1965).

PARTICLE SIZE

Particle size generally decreases with more vigorous agitation of an emulsion. The amount and type of emulsifying agent used also affects the particle size. Most commercial food emulsions have a particle diameter of 0.5–2.5 μm. Fine, relatively uniform particle size is usually an indication of stability (Lissant, 1974).

STABILITY

Emulsions are inherently unstable. This is because the system has a large interfacial surface area and an interfacial surface energy that is proportional to this area. A reduction of the total surface energy will bring the system into a more stable state. If dispersed droplets coalesce, surface energy is decreased (Bennett *et al.,* 1968). Various factors in emulsion preparation influence the stability of the finished product.

Emulsion instability is evidenced by *creaming* (or *sedimentation*) and by *phase separation*. Since the dispersed particles are freely suspended in a liquid, they obey the laws of sedimentation. If the dispersed phase has a lower specific gravity than the continuous phase, the dispersed particles will move upward. They will move downward if their specific gravity is greater than that of the dispersion medium. In an oil-in-water emulsion such as mayonnaise, the lower density of the oil particles causes them to move upward if creaming occurs. In general, the greater the difference of the specific gravity between the two phases, the more rapid and complete the separation will be. The dispersed droplets of an emulsion can carry an electric charge. Since all particles will carry the same charge, and like charges repel each other, this may be helpful in keeping dispersed particles separated. A high viscosity in the continuous phase and small particle size will also retard creaming of the dispersed particles (Griffin, 1965).

Phase separation involves breaking of the emulsion. When the interfacial film ruptures at the point where two particles of the discontinuous phase can rub together, coalescence occurs. Eventually all of the dispersed particles coalesce and the two phases of the emulsion separate. The nature of the emulsifier, and particularly its balance of hydrophilic and lipophilic groups, is of great importance in providing stability against coalescence. Fine particle size, properly induced particle charges, and high viscosity of the emulsion and its component phases are additional factors that contribute to a stable dispersion of the phases (Griffin, 1965).

Many emulsions may be unstable to freeze–thaw cycling. Apparently the instability is due to the destruction of the interfacial film by ice crystals that are formed during freezing. Choice of emulsifier and use of an adequate amount of emulsifier can markedly increase the resistance to this form of destruction (Griffin, 1965).

Emulsions are often unstable to elevated temperature. This instability may be due to changes in the solubility of the emulsifier in one or the other of the phases at increased temperatures, thus altering its distribution and affecting the interfacial film. A decrease in viscosity with increased temperature may also contribute to emulsion instability (Griffin, 1965).

18.7

EMULSIFYING AGENTS

Emulsifiers are a subdivision of the general class of surface active agents. Their role in emulsification is to increase the ease of formation and promote stability of the emulsion. When chosen so that they are compatible, emulsifiers may be used in combination.

Emulsifying agents are classified as anionic, cationic, nonionic, and amphoteric. *Anionic* and *cationic* emulsifiers cannot be used together since they tend to react with each other. *Nonionic* emulsifiers are completely covalent and show no tendency to ionize. *Amphoteric* emulsifiers may act as either anionic or cationic substances, depending upon the pH of the environment. Hundreds of different emulsifiers are available commercially for various uses. They are present in many convenience foods produced for use in the home. Classes of major synthetic food emulsifiers include (Lissant, 1974):

Fatty acid soaps	Ionic
Simple fatty acid ester	Nonionic
Modified fatty acid ester	Nonionic

Fatty acid ether ester	Nonionic
(polyoxyethylene or polyglycerol	
fatty acid ester)	
Fatty alcohol ether	Nonionic
(polyoxyethylene fatty alcohols)	

Petrowski (1975) published a list of food grade emulsifiers and their trade names. Baur (1973) reviewed analytical methodology for emulsifiers used in fatty foods.

Egg, particularly egg yolk with its high content of lipoproteins, is commonly used as an emulsifying agent in home food preparation. Hydrocolloids that function as secondary emulsion stabilizers include starch, flour proteins, and gelatin. Commercially, a variety of vegetable gums and isolated proteins are also used as hydrocolloids. The chemical structure of a monoglyceride is shown in Figure 18.2 and a lecithin is given in Figure 18.7. These are emulsifying agents commonly used in foods.

HYDROPHILE–LIPOPHILE BALANCE

The hydrophile–lipophile balance (HLB) is an expression of the relative simultaneous attraction of an emulsifier for water and for oil. It would appear to be determined by the chemical composition (the proportion of polar and nonpolar groups) and the extent of ionization of the emulsifier. The HLB number generally ranges from 1 to 20. The higher the HLB number, the greater the proportion of hydrophilic groups. HLB values can be calculated from either theoretical composition or analytical data (Griffin, 1965). Mickle *et al.* (1971) reported that a gas–liquid chromatography method appeared to accurately measure the HLB numbers of seven emulsifiers that were used in model systems.

The HLB is an important property to consider when choosing emulsifiers for specific purposes. Titus *et al.* (1968) found that as the fat content of a model system increased, the optimum HLB decreased until an HLB of 5 was optimal in the systems containing 90 percent fat.

Figure 18.7

A lecithin.

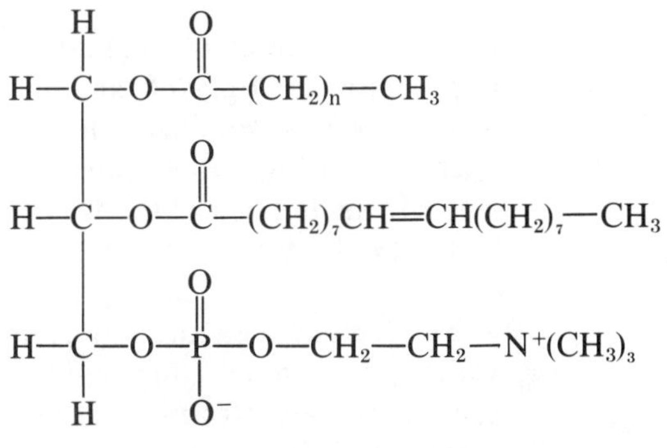

$$H-\overset{\displaystyle H}{\underset{\displaystyle |}{C}}-O-\overset{\displaystyle O}{\overset{\displaystyle \|}{C}}-(CH_2)_n-CH_3$$

$$H-\overset{\displaystyle |}{C}-O-\overset{\displaystyle O}{\overset{\displaystyle \|}{C}}-(CH_2)_7CH=CH(CH_2)_7-CH_3$$

$$H-\overset{\displaystyle |}{\underset{\displaystyle |}{C}}-O-\overset{\displaystyle O}{\underset{\displaystyle |}{\overset{\displaystyle \|}{P}}}-O-CH_2-CH_2-N^+(CH_3)_3$$
$$H \qquad\quad O^-$$

Increasing the level of emulsifier increased the stability of the model system up to a point, after which continued increases caused little additional increase in stability. The optimal amount of emulsifier varied with the fat content of the system and the HLB. Titus *et al.* found that emulsifier efficiency for use in butter cakes could be predicted from their action in model systems of similar composition.

18.8

EMULSIFICATION

A single scientific theory of emulsification has not been agreed upon. Specialized systems of emulsions have been more commonly studied. The formation of an emulsion requires work to expand the interfacial area between oil and water. Mechanical agitation of the system is employed. The surface active emulsifying agent is adsorbed at the newly formed interfaces. It is oriented with the polar groups toward the water phase and the nonpolar hydrocarbon chains toward the oil, forming a monomolecular layer around the dispersed droplets. The HLB of the emulsifier affects the type of emulsion formed—oil-in-water or water-in-oil. The geometrical shape of the emulsifier also apparently affects the type of emulsion (Becher, 1965).

Lowering interfacial tension increases the ease of emulsion formation but contributes in a less than major way to the stability of the formed emulsion. The formation of a rigid interfacial film is a more important factor operating in stabilization. A mixture of emulsifiers is often more effective than a single agent in forming a tightly packed, strong film around the dispersed particles. Emulsifiers that ionize contribute a charge to the film. This may aid in stabilizing the emulsion by keeping the dispersed particles separated (Lissant, 1974). Finely divided solids, such as spices, can also stabilize emulsions by being adsorbed at the surface of the dispersed particles.

18.9

FOOD EMULSIONS

Many foods are emulsion systems. Some foods are emulsified as they occur naturally. Egg yolk and milk are examples of this. The fat globule membrane that stabilizes the emulsion of fat in milk is discussed in Section 24.1. As whole milk is homogenized, the emulsion of fat in water is made finer as the fat particles are reduced to such small size that they do not rise to the surface on standing. Emulsions are produced during the processing and preparation of a wide variety of foods. These include peanut butter, margarine, whipped toppings, coffee whiteners, candies and confectionery coatings, icings, puddings, sauces, gravies, frozen desserts, beverages, and flavoring oils. Emulsions are produced in sausages and frankfurters. Emulsifiers play important roles in a variety of baked products. Mayonnaise and salad dressings are classical examples of food emulsions.

An emulsifier that is to be used in food must meet certain requirements. It should:

1. Contain both polar and nonpolar parts.
2. Decrease the surface tension of one liquid more than the other.
3. Be adsorbed on the surface of the droplets that constitute the dispersed phase.
4. Be chemically stable, that is, not easily altered.
5. Be pleasing in flavor and odor or have no flavor at all.
6. Be light in color or colorless.
7. Be edible (nontoxic).

SALAD DRESSINGS AND MAYONNAISE

A wide variety of salad dressings is marketed or prepared in the home. Salad dressing contains oil, egg yolk, acid substances, and a cooked starch ingredient. The egg yolk contains emulsifying substances and the starch acts as a hydrocolloid stabilizer. Additional emulsifiers may be added in commercial salad dressing production. It must contain not less than 30 percent by weight of vegetable oil.

Salad dressings tend to separate on freezing and thawing. Hanson and Fletcher (1961) discussed factors that influence this oil and water separation. They found that separation is minimized when the oil used does not crystallize readily at temperatures below 0°C (32°F). Waxy rice flour is superior to other cereal thickening agents commonly used in salad dressings because of its slower rate of retrogradation on freezing. Increasing the amount of egg yolk increases stability. Increasing salt from 0.5 percent to 1.7 percent increases emulsion stability. Jordan (1962) also reported that the addition of 0.5 g or more of salt to 15 g egg yolk produced emulsions of increased stability over those made without salt. The increased viscosity of the egg yolk with the addition of salt was suggested as a factor in its stabilizing effect.

French dressing, as usually prepared at home, is a temporary emulsion of oil in water. The two phases separate as the dressing stands. Commercial dressings of this type may include emulsifying agents that will produce a permanent emulsion. French dressings must have at least 35 percent by weight of edible vegetable oil.

Mayonnaise contains not less than 65 percent by weight of edible vegetable oil and is a semi-solid emulsified product. It also contains egg yolk and acid ingredients.

In the preparation of mayonnaise, it is important that an emulsion be formed in the early stages of mixing. Oil is then gradually added to this emulsion. The emulsion is coarse at first with large dispersed oil droplets. As additional oil is added to the emulsion and mixing is continued, the oil droplets are decreased in size, and the mixture becomes more viscous (Paul and Palmer). Figure 18.8 shows mayonnaise in four stages of preparation.

Figure 18.8

Mayonnaise. Magnifica-
tion approximately
200×. (*a*) A coarse
emulsion is formed after
the addition of 1 table-
spoon of oil. The vinegar
and seasonings were
added to the egg yolk
before the oil was
added. (*b*) After adding $\frac{1}{4}$
cup of oil. (*c*) After ad-
ding $\frac{3}{8}$ cup of oil. (*d*) After
the addition of $\frac{1}{2}$ cup of
oil. (From Paul, P. C. and
H. H. Palmer. *Food
Theory and Application.*
Copyright © 1972, John
Wiley & Sons. Reprinted
by permission of John
Wiley & Sons, Inc.)

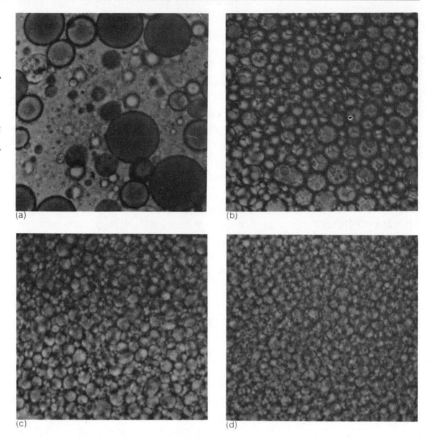

A broken mayonnaise emulsion may be reformed by adding the mixture gradually to a new egg yolk or a tablespoon of water or vinegar.
Thorough beating after each addition is important in producing a
reemulsified product.

MEAT EMULSIONS   Emulsions make up the basic structure of a variety of sausages and
frankfurters. These emulsions have the additional stress of being heat
processed during production and in many cases are heated again by
consumers before they are eaten. Loss of fat should be minimal during
these procedures.

The dispersed phase in meat emulsions is fat; the continuous phase
is water, that also contains various water-soluble components; and the
emulsifying agent is the soluble meat proteins, especially those which
are salt-soluble. Some of the dispersed fat particles are very large and a
thousand-fold difference in particle size exists in many meat emulsions.
This may tend to decrease emulsion stability (Saffle, 1968).

Some melting of meat fat occurs during comminution of the meat as the sausages are made. Swift *et al.* (1968) reported that high-melting pork and beef fats yielded stable emulsions and low-melting oily fats yielded unstable emulsions, irrespective of the temperatures attained during emulsification.

The ability of meat proteins to emulsify fat appears to depend, at least in part, on the shape of the molecule and its net charge (Carpenter and Saffle, 1965). Swift and Sulzbacher (1963) reported that the effectiveness of emulsification in a meat emulsion is influenced by pH and sodium chloride concentration. Increasing either pH or salt or increasing both of these factors simultaneously improved emulsification, possibly by increasing the extraction of proteins from the meat.

Borchert *et al.* (1967) observed meat emulsions with the aid of an electron microscope. Fat globules as small as 0.1 μm in diameter had distinct protein membranes. After thermal processing the globule membranes were highly disrupted and the protein of the continuous phase was coagulated into dense, irregular zones. Figure 18.9 shows electron micrographs of uncooked and cooked meat emulsions.

EMULSIFIERS IN BAKED PRODUCTS

One of the largest uses of emulsifiers is in the various shortenings that are offered to the baker, cake mix manufacturer, and consumer. The baking industry may use specialty shortenings that contain emulsifiers tailored to meet specific product needs. All-purpose shortenings for consumer use generally contain from 1.5 to 4 percent (w/w) mono- and diglycerides. Cake mix shortenings often contain from 8 to 12 percent mono- and diglycerides. Other emulsifiers in this shortening may in-

Figure 18.9

(a) An electron micrograph of an uncooked meat emulsion. G indicates fat globule surrounded by dense membrane. Arrows designate muscle cell organelles. (33,091×) *(b)* An electron micrograph of a thermally processed meat emulsion. G indicates fat globules. Arrows show pores or openings in membranes. (33,091×) (Reprinted with permission from Borchert, L. L., M. L. Greaser, J. C. Bard, R. G. Cassens, and E. J. Briskey. 1967. Electron microscopy of a meat emulsion. *Journal of Food Science* 32, 419.)

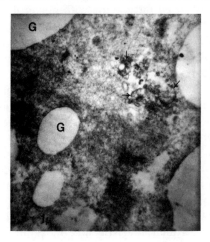
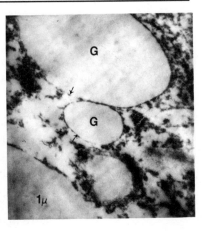

clude polysorbate 60, sorbitan monostearate, propylene glycol monoesters, and glycerol lacto esters. A different combination of emulsifiers is commonly used in bread and rolls (Nash and Brickman, 1972).

Emulsifiers in bread and rolls perform two basic functions. They act as softeners and antistaling agents. They also perform as dough conditioners to improve the dough tolerance to bakery operations. Mono- and diglycerides affect the softness of bread. The mechanism of their action has not been completely explained. Commonly used dough conditioners include calcium or stearyl lactylate, ethoxylated monoglycerides, and polysorbate 60. These substances complex with starch (Nash and Brickman, 1972).

Emulsifiers affect the distribution of fat in cake batters, producing a finer emulsion. Since the shortening holds air, a more even distribution of air in the batter also occurs. Hunt and Green (1955) reported that the volume of cakes was somewhat improved with the addition of an emulsifying agent to butter used as a cake ingredient. The batter was also more smooth and less curdled with an added emulsifier.

SUMMARY

The term lipid is used to describe water-insoluble organic substances that occur in animal and plant tissues and that are extractable by nonpolar solvents. Lipids include fatty acids, triglycerides, and phosphoglycerides. Fatty acids are building blocks for triglycerides and phosphoglycerides. Many different fatty acids occur naturally. They vary in length of carbon chain and degree of unsaturation. Fatty acids containing two or more double bonds are called polyunsaturated. Triglycerides are esters of three fatty acids with glycerol.

The melting points of triglycerides are determined by their constituent fatty acids. The melting point generally increases with increasing chain length and decreases with increasing degree of unsaturation. These effects are related to the ability of the triglycerides to pack closely together. Triglycerides containing unsaturated fatty acids with a *trans* configuration have higher melting points than similar acids with a *cis* form. Most naturally occurring fats melt over a relatively wide temperature range because of the diversity of types of triglyceride molecules in these products.

Plastic fats contain both a solid phase made up of triglyceride crystals and a liquid phase of the noncrystallized molecules. The ratio of solid to liquid fat depends on the temperature. Solid fats can exist in more than one crystalline form and are called polymorphic. Each crystal form has a characteristic melting point, size, and shape. Various forms are called α, β', intermediate, and β. Molecules that are alike can readily align themselves with each other and form relatively large crystals. Triglyceride molecules in lard exhibit these characteristics. Hydrogenated shortenings contain a greater diversity of triglyceride molecules and tend to form small crystals.

Hydrogenation of vegetable oils produces solid shortenings. The oil is exposed to hydrogen gas in the presence of a catalyst and hydrogen adds to the double bonds. The conditions of hydrogenation affect the mode of this reaction. A number of isomers are produced.

Interesterification is used to change the arrangement of fatty acids on triglyceride molecules in order to produce a more random distribution. Lard may be interesterified so that it will form small crystals and cream easily. Directed interesterification produces a relatively large proportion of trisaturated fatty acids and has a stiffening effect on the fat.

Winterizing involves cooling a vegetable oil until some molecules crystallize and then removing the solid material by filtration. These oils are useful in the preparation of salad dressings. Fats used for frying require a high smoke point.

The term rancidity describes specific types of disagreeable odors and flavors that develop in fatty substances as a result of hydrolysis or oxidation. The enzyme lipase catalyzes the hydrolysis of triglycerides. If volatile short-chain fatty acids such as butyric acid are released, characteristic unpleasant odors result.

The unsaturated fatty acid components of triglycerides are responsible for the development of oxidative rancidity. A theory involving hydroperoxides explains this process. Initially, a free radical is produced when a H atom is removed from the carbon atom adjacent to one involved in double bonding. Oxygen is then added to the free radical. The oxygen derivative still acts like a free radical, however, and removes a H atom from another unsaturated fatty acid in the mixture to form a hydroperoxide. The removal of a H atom from the second fatty acid component leaves a second free radical and propagates a chain reaction. The hydroperoxides are comparatively unstable and decompose into a variety of small volatile aldehydes, ketones, and acids that are responsible for the characteristic rancid odor of oxidized fat. Heavy metals, such as copper and iron, act as prooxidants. Sodium chloride, light, and ionizing radiations also encourage oxidation.

Antioxidants inhibit the autoxidation of fat. Most food antioxidants are phenolic compounds that supply hydrogen to stop the chain reaction. Antioxidants increase the length of the induction period before the oxidation of fat becomes rapid. Certain compounds such as citric acid act as synergists to primary antioxidants.

The characteristics of an emulsion are affected by the composition of the system and the mode of preparation. The appearance depends on the ingredients used, their color and difference in refractive index, and the particle size of the dispersed phase. Very small dispersed particles contribute to clarity.

The viscosity of emulsions may vary. It is similar to that of the external phase if this phase represents more than half of the volume of the emulsion. The apparent viscosity increases when the dispersed phase is greater in volume than that of the external phase. This is due to the crowding of particles in the emulsion. Reducing the particle size also increases the viscosity of the emulsion. Most commercial food emulsions have a particle diameter of 0.5–2.5 μm. Fine, relatively uniform particle size is usually an indication of stability.

Emulsion instability is shown by creaming and by phase separation. A high viscosity in the continuous phase, a charge on the dispersed particles, and small particle size retard creaming. Phase separation involves breaking of the emulsion with coalescence of the dispersed particles. The proper choice of emulsifier, fine particle size, properly induced particle charges, and high viscosity of the emulsion and its component phases contribute to a stable dispersion of the phases. Emulsions may be unstable to freezing and thawing and to elevated temperatures.

Emulsifiers are classified as anionic, cationic, nonionic, and amphoteric. Many synthetic food emulsifiers are available for commercial use. Egg yolk is a commonly used emulsifying agent in home food preparation. Hydrocolloids that function as secondary emulsion stabilizers include starch, flour proteins, and gelatin.

The hydrophile–lipophile balance (HLB) is an expression of the relative simultaneous attraction of an emulsifier for water and for oil. The higher the HLB number, the greater the proportion of hydrophilic groups. The HLB should be considered when choosing an emulsifier for a particular product.

The formation of an emulsion requires work to expand the interfacial area between oil and water. Mechanical agitation is employed. The emulsifier is adsorbed at the newly formed interfaces. It is oriented with the polar groups toward the water phase and the nonpolar groups toward the oil, forming a monomolecular layer around the dispersed droplets. Lowering the interfacial tension increases the ease of emulsion formation but the formation of a rigid interfacial film is more important in emulsion stabilization. A mixture of emulsifiers is often effective in forming a tightly packed film. Many foods are emulsion systems.

Egg yolk contains emulsifying substances that function in salad dressings and mayonnaise. A cooked starch ingredient in salad dressing acts as a hydrocolloid stabilizer. Salad dressings tend to separate on freezing and thawing unless special precautions are taken. Mayonnaise contains at least 65 percent oil. An emulsion is formed in the early stages of mayonnaise preparation. Oil is then gradually added and the particle size decreases in the later stages of mixing.

Soluble meat proteins act as emulsifiers in a variety of sausages and frankfurters. The ability of these proteins to emulsify fat appears to depend, in part, on the shape of the molecule and on its net charge. With an electron microscope, membranes can be seen around the dispersed fat globules. These membranes are highly disrupted after thermal processing.

Emulsifiers perform various functions in a variety of baked products. In bread and rolls they act as softeners and antistaling agents. They also perform as dough conditioners. Emulsifiers produce a fine fat dispersion in cakes. The batter is smooth and the volume of the cakes somewhat higher than in cakes made without emulsifier.

STUDY QUESTIONS

Saturated and unsaturated fatty acids differ in the amount of hydrogen present.

1. Write structural formulas for each of the following fatty acids and identify the saturated and the unsaturated compounds in the group.

   Fatty acids
   butyric
   palmitic
   stearic
   oleic
   linoleic
   linolenic

2. Identify food products that are comparatively rich sources of polyunsaturated fatty acids; of saturated fatty acids; of short-chain fatty acids; and of long-chain fatty acids.

Triglycerides are esters of glycerol and fatty acids.

3. Write structural formulas for triglycerides that might typically be found in foods.
4. Write structural formulas for diglycerides and for monoglycerides and discuss their usefulness in food processing.

The chemical structures of triglycerides affect their melting points and crystallization properties.

5. For each of the following structural characteristics, explain (with the use of both diagrams and words) the effect on melting point and/or crystallization properties:
   a. Length of fatty acid carbon chains.
   b. Presence of double bonds.
   c. Presence of *cis* or *trans* configurations.
   d. Large proportion of similar triglyceride molecules.
   e. Random distribution of fatty acids on glycerol.
6. Explain differences in melting points among the following fats:

   corn oil
   lard
   butter
   hydrogenated vegetable shortening

7. Describe the melting characteristics of cocoa butter and discuss the significance of this behavior to the eating quality of chocolate.
8. Why do hydrogenated shortenings and lard tend to form different crystal structures? Explain.

9. List and explain three factors that influence the formation of small crystals and the development of good creaming properties in plastic fats such as hydrogenated shortenings.

Natural fats may be modified by several industrial processes.

10. What is meant by selective hydrogenation?
11. Describe two methods for preparing hydrogenated shortenings and suggest advantages for each.
12. How might isomerization during hydrogenation affect the consistency of the finished shortening? Explain.
13. Give an example of a useful purpose served by interesterification of triglycerides.

Fats are subject to the development of rancidity.

14. Present a scheme that describes the hydroperoxide theory for the development of oxidative rancidity in fats. What is meant by induction period?
15. List types of compounds that are responsible for the rancid odor of oxidized fats and explain their origin.
16. List several prooxidants and suggest ways of avoiding them in the processing or storage of fatty foods.
17. Present a scheme that describes the action of phenolic antioxidants in inhibiting the development of oxidative rancidity.
18. List antioxidants commonly used in food products.
19. Write a chemical reaction representing the development of hydrolytic rancidity in fat. Explain why this type of spoilage is a greater problem with butter than with vegetable oils or hydrogenated shortenings.

The major characteristics of emulsions are generally controllable as the emulsions are formed.

20. Describe the following characteristics of emulsions and explain possible influences on them:
    a. Appearance
    b. Viscosity
    c. Particle size
    d. Stability

The formation of an emulsion is a complex process requiring work.

21. Using lecithin as an example of an emulsifier, describe and explain the process of emulsion formation and stabilization that is likely to occur when mayonnaise is prepared.
22. List several classes of synthetic food emulsifiers.
23. Describe how monoglycerides probably function as emulsifying agents.
24. What is an HLB value and what purpose may it serve in food processing?

Many food products contain fat and water in an emulsified system.

25. From the following list of food products identify those that are examples of emulsion systems. Also indicate whether the emulsion is usually oil-in-water or water-in-oil, temporary or relatively permanent, and coarse or relatively fine.

Food Products
whole milk	applesauce
homogenized milk	cream of mushroom soup
carrots	cream puffs
spaghetti sauce	French dressing
butterscotch pudding	white cake
canned peaches	mayonnaise

26. Describe requirements that an emulsifier should meet if it is to be used in foods.
27. Describe the emulsion system in sausages and explain what probably happens to this system during the cooking of these products.
28. Discuss the use of emulsifiers in baked products.

REFERENCES

1. Baur, F. J. 1973. Analytical methodology for emulsifiers used in fatty foods: a review. *Journal of the American Oil Chemists Society* 50 (No. 3), 85.

2. Becher, P. 1965. *Emulsions: Theory and Practice,* 2nd edition. New York: Reinhold.

3. Bennett, H., J. L. Bishop, Jr., and M. F. Wulfinghoff. 1968. *Practical Emulsions.* Vol. I. New York: Chemical Publishing Company.

4. Bennion, M. and F. Hanning. 1956. Effect of different fats and oils and their modification on changes during frying. *Food Technology* 10, 229.

5. Borchert, L. L., M. L. Greaser, J. C. Bard, R. G. Cassens, and E. J. Briskey. 1967. Electron microscopy of a meat emulsion. *Journal of Food Science* 32, 419.

6. Carpenter, J. A. and R. L. Saffle. 1965. Some physical and chemical factors affecting the emulsifying capacity of meat protein extracts. *Food Technology* 19 (No. 10), 111.

7. Dugan, L. R., Jr. 1961. Development and inhibition of oxidative rancidity in foods. *Food Technology* 15 (No. 4), 10.

8. Eckey, E. W. 1954. *Vegetable Fats and Oils.* New York: Reinhold.

9. Eskin, N. A. M. and C. Frenkel. 1976. A simple and rapid method for assessing rancidity of oils based on the formation of hydroperoxides. *Journal of the American Oil Chemists Society* 53, 746.

10. Evans, C. D., H. A. Moser, D. G. McConnell, J. C. Cowan, J. L. Cartter, and F. I. Collins. 1965. Flavor evaluation of natural soybean oils of high and low linolenate content. *Journal of the American Oil Chemists Society* 42, 736.

11. Goddard, V. R. and L. Goodall. March 1959. Fatty acids in food fats. U. S. Department of Agriculture Home Economics Research Report No. 7.

12. Gray, J. I. 1978. Measurement of lipid oxidation: A review. *Journal of the American Oil Chemists Society* 55, 539.

13. Griffin, W. C. 1965. Emulsions. In: *Encyclopedia of Chemical Technology.* Vol. 8, 2nd edition, pp. 117–154. New York: Wiley.

14. Hanson, H. L. and L. R. Fletcher. 1961. Salad dressings stable to frozen storage. *Food Technology* 15, 256.

15. Hoerr, C. W. 1967. Changing the physical properties of fats and oils for specific uses. *Bakers Digest* 41 (Dec.), 42.

16. Hoerr, C. W. 1960. Morphology of fats, oils, and shortenings. *Journal of the American Oil Chemists Society* 37, 539.

17. Hunt, F. E. and M. E. Green. 1955. Physical properties of cake as affected by method of butter manufacture and addition of an emulsifying agent. *Food Technology* 9, 241.

18. Jewell, G. G. and M. L. Meara. 1970. A new and rapid method for the electron microscopic examination of fats. *Journal of the American Oil Chemists Society* 47, 535.

19. Jordan, R. 1962. Salt as a factor in the stability of emulsions. *Journal of Home Economics* 54, 394.

20. Lissant, K. J., editor. 1974. *Emulsions and Emulsion Technology.* Part I. New York: Marcel Dekker.

21. Love, J. D. and A. M. Pearson. 1974. Metmyoglobin and nonheme iron as prooxidants in cooked meat. *Journal of Agricultural and Food Chemistry* 22, 1032.

22. Love, J. D. and A. M. Pearson. 1971. Lipid oxidation in meat and meat products—A review. *Journal of the American Oil Chemists Society* 48, 547.

23. Mickle, J. B., W. Smith, J. M. Tietz, T. C. Titus, and M. Johnston. 1971. Influence of emulsifier type and solubility on the stability of milk fat-water emulsions. *Journal of Food Science* 36, 423.

24. Mounts, T. L., S. Koritala, J. P. Friedrich, and H. J. Dutton. 1978. Selective hydrogenation of soybean oil: IX. Effect of pressure in copper catalysis. *Journal of the American Oil Chemists Society* 55, 402.

25. Mukherjee, K. D., I. Kiewitt, and M. Kiewitt. 1975. Stationary catalysts for the continuous hydrogenation of fats. *Journal of the American Oil Chemists Society* 52, 282.

26. Nash, N. H. and L. M. Brickman. 1972. Food emulsifiers—Science and art. *Journal of the American Oil Chemists Society* 49, 457.

27. Paul, P. C. and H. H. Palmer. 1972. *Food Theory and Applications.* New York: Wiley.

28. Petrowski, G. E. 1975. Food-grade emulsifiers. *Food Technology* 29 (No. 7), 52.

29. Pohle, W. D., R. L. Gregory, and B. Van Giessen. 1964. Relationship of peroxide value and thiobarbituric acid value to development of undesirable flavor characteristics in fats. *Journal of the American Oil Chemists Society* 41, 649.

30. Pongracz, G. 1973. Antioxidant mixtures for use in food. *International Journal of Vitamin Nutrition and Research* 43, 517.

31. Saffle, R. L. 1968. Meat emulsions. *Advances in Food Research* 16, 105.

32. Sanders, J. H. 1959. Processing of food fats—A review. *Food Technology* 13, 41.

33. Schultz, H. W., E. A. Day, and R. O. Sinnhuber, editors. 1962. *Lipids and Their Oxidation.* Westport, Conn.: Avi Publishing Company.

34. Sherwin, E. R. 1972. Antioxidants for food fats and oils. *Journal of the American Oil Chemists Society* 49, 468.

35. Swift, C. E. and W. L. Sulzbacher. 1963. Comminuted meat emulsions: Factors affecting meat proteins as emulsion stabilizers. *Food Technology* 17, 106.

36. Swift, C. E., W. E. Townsend, and L. P. Witnauer. 1968. Comminuted meat emulsions: Relation of the melting characteristics of fat to emulsion stability. *Food Technology* 22, 775.

37. Titus, T. C., N. N. Wiancko, H. F. Barbour, and J. B. Mickle. 1968. Emulsifier efficiency in model systems of milk fat or soybean oil and water. *Food Technology* 22, 1449.

38. Vioque, A., R. Gutierrez, M. A. Albi, and N. Nosti. 1965. Trace elements in edible fats. IX. Influence of demetalization on the oxidative and flavor stabilities of soybean oil. *Journal of the American Oil Chemists Society* 42, 344.

39. Warner, K., C. D. Evans, G. R. List, H. P. Dupuy, J. I. Wadsworth, and G. E. Goheen. 1978. Flavor score correlation with pentanal and hexanal contents of vegetable oil. *Journal of the American Oil Chemists Society* 55, 252.

40. Younathan, M. T. and B. M. Watts. 1959. Relationship of meat pigments to lipid oxidation. *Food Research* 24, 728.

CHAPTER 19

FOAMS IN FOOD

In the process of preparation, many food products are mixed or beaten and bubbles of gas are dispersed in them. Foams contain an appreciable quantity of dispersed gas particles. When a limited amount of gas is dispersed and the volume of the liquid is much greater than the volume of the gas, the product is not usually designated as a foam.

Foams are similar to emulsions except that the dispersed foam droplets are gaseous. Gas is always the discontinuous phase in a foam. (The structure of foams is discussed in Section 17.3.) A surface active foaming agent is essential for the formation of a stable foam. The foaming agent lowers the surface tension of the liquid phase and allows expansion of its surface area. The surfactant forms a closely packed film around the dispersed gas bubbles. This surface layer must have a certain amount of strength or rigidity for foam stability. The layers of the film that are adjacent to the gas phase have been shown to exhibit a viscosity that is greater than that of the dispersion medium.

Cumper (1953) explained the stabilization of protein foams in terms of three successive processes: adsorption of the protein at the gas–liquid surface, surface denaturation, and finally coagulation of the protein. The polar groups of a protein surfactant cause the molecules to spread and denature at the surface. Hydration of these polar groups probably contributes to the tenacity of the adsorbed film.

19.1

EGG FOAMS

Egg foams are essential in the preparation of angel cakes, sponge cakes, meringues, soufflés, and fluffy omelets. Egg white forms the most stable foam and is usually separated from the yolk before beating. However, satisfactory sponge cakes can be made by beating whole eggs (Briant and Willman, 1956).

As egg whites are beaten, air bubbles are incorporated. The bubbles gradually become smaller and the color changes from a pale greenish yellow translucency to an opaque white as egg proteins are coagulated. The stiffness and volume increase with continued beating. The surface of the foam is first moist and glossy but gradually becomes dry and dull as beating continues. The amount of air incorporated into the foam may be determined by calculation of *specific gravity* (*weight per unit volume*) or *specific volume* (*volume per unit weight*) (Paul and Palmer, 1972).

Proteins dispersed in egg white are the surface active agents that are responsible for foam formation. (Egg proteins are discussed in Section 23.2.) The proteins not only lower the surface tension of egg white but many of them are easily denatured at the surface. They coagulate at the gas–liquid interface and form a network that gives some rigidity and stability to the foam. Nakamura (1963) found that proteins that foam well are easily surface-denatured. Possible roles in foam formation for the various proteins in egg white were suggested by MacDonnell *et al*. (1955) after fractionating the total protein and using each fraction to make an angel food cake. Globulins appeared to be good foamers, producing small gas bubbles and a large volume. Ovomucin was not a good foamer by itself but stabilized the foam produced by globulins because it was rapidly insolubilized at the bubble surface. All other proteins in the egg white furnished heat denaturable bulk to form a supporting matrix for the baked cake.

Egg white foams may be beaten to various stages. A very soft underbeaten foam has relatively large gas bubbles and is somewhat unstable. Because surface denaturation of the proteins has not been sufficiently extensive, the film around the bubbles of air is not rigid enough to support the foam on standing. Considerable drainage of liquid from the films occurs and some of the bubbles coalesce. On the other hand, in a foam that has been beaten until it appears dry, dull, and curdled, the proteins in the surface films are overcoagulated and the film loses its elasticity. The air bubbles in an overbeaten film tend to coalesce as the films are ruptured. Liquid drains from the foam on standing. Thus underbeating and overbeating both produce unstable foams. Foam stability may be determined by measuring the volume of liquid that drains from a measured amount of foam in a specified time period. Egg white foams should be blended with other ingredients as soon as beating is completed since the foam stiffens and loses its elasticity on standing for more than a few minutes.

FACTORS AFFECTING FOAM QUALITY

The conditions under which the egg whites are beaten and the equipment used affect the rate of beating and the type of foam produced. Egg whips and beaters have wires and blades of varying size and design. Both wire whips and beaters can be satisfactorily used to produce egg white foams. Fine wires and thin blades produce foams with fine air cells. With electric beaters operated at high speed, overbeating may readily occur. Adding sugar at the beginning of beating lengthens the time required to beat a foam and produces a foam of smaller volume. The time of adding sugar and the method of adding it, including how fast it is done and how much is used, influence both volume and stability.

Thin portions of egg white have been reported to beat to a larger foam volume than thick portions (Hunt and St. John, 1931). However, the largest volume is not always the most stable when used in an angel cake. The type of beater may affect the volume of foam produced from thick or thin whites. A good foam volume was reported by Bailey in 1935 to be more easily attained with a power-operated beater than with a hand beater when whipping thick viscous whites. The equipment available for beating has markedly changed since that time. When beating one or two egg whites, a better foam is formed with a hand operated rotary beater than with an electric one. Electric beaters are so forceful that they give a shearing action rather than a folding over motion that is necessary to produce a foam. Electric blenders do not produce good foams for the same reason.

The conditions of storage for eggs affect their foam quality. Meehan et al. (1962) reported that egg whites from shell eggs held seven days at 35°C (95°F) or from two to three weeks at 23.9°C (75°F) gave angel cakes with markedly decreased volumes. It was suggested that alteration of the egg proteins under these conditions of storage was responsible for the decreased cake volume.

Greater foam volume has been reported for egg whites that are beaten at room temperature than for those beaten at refrigerator temperatures (Henry and Barbour, 1933; St. John and Flor, 1931). The surface tension as well as the viscosity of egg whites is lowered by increasing temperature. This may at least partially explain the differences due to the temperature of beating.

Acids or acid salts, such as cream of tartar, citric acid, and acetic acid, increase the stability of egg white foams (Paul and Palmer, 1972). The addition of acid delays foam formation.

Salt is added to egg white foams primarily for flavor. Added salt in the amount of 1 g per 40 g fresh egg whites decreased the stability of the foams when they were beaten for short periods of time. This effect was not observed when foams were beaten for longer periods of time (Hanning, 1945). Sechler et al. (1959) reported that the addition of salt to reconstituted dried egg whites before beating decreased foam stability and increased whipping time.

Sugar delays surface coagulation in egg white proteins and thus delays foam formation. Egg whites beaten with sugar are protected against over-beating. Sugar-containing egg white foams are smoother, more shiny, and more stable than foams made without sugar (Hanning, 1945). Foams made with sugar may stand for a period of time without stiffening and loss of elasticity.

Fat, even in small amounts, has a detrimental effect on egg white foam formation. Egg yolk contains approximately 32 percent fat. The foaming power of egg white was reported to be decreased and leakage from the foam increased by the presence of egg yolk even in concentrations less than 0.1 percent (Bailey, 1935).

MERINGUES

Soft and hard meringues differ in sugar content and in procedures for baking them. Soft, tender meringues contain from 2 to $2\frac{1}{2}$ tbsp of sugar per egg white (Gillis and Fitch, 1956) while hard meringues usually contain about 4 tbsp. Soft meringues are often baked at a moderate to high oven temperature for comparatively short periods of time although recipes include a wide range of recommended temperatures. Heating must be sufficient to destroy any salmonellae organisms that may be present in the eggs. Therefore, relatively low oven temperatures (163°–177°C, or 325°–350°F) for 15–18 minutes are generally recommended. Hard meringues are baked for a long time at a low oven temperature. Their baking is essentially a drying out process. Soft meringues are generally used as toppings for pies, puddings, and baked Alaska while hard meringues are used as foundations or shells for pie fillings, ice cream, etc.

Meringues are prepared by beating egg whites until a foam is started. Sugar is then gradually added, with continued beating after each portion of sugar is incorporated. A soft meringue is beaten after the last addition of sugar until the gas bubbles have been finely distributed, the mixture is thick and rounded peaks form. Stiff peaks are desirable in the preparation of hard meringues.

The problems frequently encountered in preparing satisfactory soft meringues include leaking or weeping and beading. Soft meringues are placed on pie fillings and baked. Fluid *leaking* from the baked meringue collects between the surface of the pie and the base of the meringue. Hester and Personius (1949) found that excessive leakage occurred under conditions that produced undercoagulation of the egg white proteins in the meringue. For example, leakage was high in meringues placed on cold rather than hot pie fillings before they were baked. A short baking time at a high temperature (204°–218°C, or 400°–425°F) also encouraged leakage. A short baking time may produce undercoagulation, particularly if a comparatively large amount of meringue is baked, since more time is required for heat to penetrate to the base of the meringue in this case.

Beading refers to the collection of tiny droplets of syrup on the surface of the baked meringue. It was attributed by Hester and Personius (1949) to overcoagulation of the egg white proteins. For example, placing the meringue on a hot filling and using a long, slow baking period encouraged the development of beading.

Felt *et al.* (1956) found less leakage from pies when meringues were prepared with hot rather than cold syrup. Leakage was decreased when a stabilizer, containing vegetable gum, salt, starch, and citric acid, was added to the meringue. The amount of liquid drained from the pies increased as the temperature decreased for the fillings on which the meringues were placed. The maximum temperature of the interface between the pie filling and the meringue was directly related to the leakage. The baking temperature and time affected leakage indirectly in that they were factors determining the temperature of the pie–meringue interface. These findings supported the theory of Hester and Personius that leakage is related to undercoagulation of egg white proteins. A compromise is apparently necessary in the preparation procedures for soft meringues in order to achieve adequate coagulation of the egg white proteins with a minimum of both leakage and beading while achieving destruction of any salmonellae organisms that may be present.

Addition of a carrageenan stabilizer to soft meringues was found by Morgan *et al.* (1970) to decrease drainage as compared to meringues made without a stabilizer. This hydrocolloid substance may hold liquid in a gel-type structure. The tenderness of meringues with stabilizer was greater than those without, although opposite results were reported by Glabau (1948). Morgan *et al.* also reported that acceptable meringues with no significant differences could be prepared from frozen, foam-spray-dried, freeze-dried, and spray-dried egg whites. Funk *et al.* (1971) found that foam stability, as measured by drainage during an 18 hour period, was significantly less for hard meringues prepared with freeze-dried egg white than for similar meringues prepared with foam-spray-dried and spray-dried egg white. However, sensory evaluations showed no significant differences due to the method of drying egg white for surface appearance, color, texture, moistness, tenderness, or flavor of the meringue.

ANGEL CAKE

Angel cake is made by first preparing a meringue. Flour is then carefully incorporated into the meringue. Desirable characteristics of an angel cake include a slightly rounded surface with a delicate brown color; a large volume in relation to weight; a fine, even texture with thin cell walls; a white, moist, and tender crumb; and a delicate, pleasant flavor. The quality characteristics of an angel cake are affected by the ingredients, the method of preparation, and the baking conditions. A number of studies of the functional properties of eggs have used the quality, and particularly the volume, of angel cakes as an indication of differences in egg whites undergoing various experimental treatments (Paul and Palmer, 1972). Angel cakes from regular recipes are not commonly made in the home since commercial mixes have become popular.

Ingredients Angel cake is made with egg whites, an acid ingredient (usually cream of tartar), sugar, flour, salt, and flavoring. A correct balance of ingredients is important in angel cake production. Egg whites provide the basic foam structure. Heat coagulation of egg proteins during baking sets this structure. Flour contains some protein and starch that, upon partial coagulation and gelatinization, also contribute to permanent cake structure. Sugar is the major tenderizing agent in the cake. No fat is present.

The quality of egg whites used in making angel cake is a very important factor in determining the finished cake quality, particularly the volume. The factors that influence foam quality generally influence angel cake quality. Angel cake volume decreases when eggs of low candled quality are used in its production. Texture, tenderness, and acceptability are also higher with higher quality eggs. In a U. S. Department of Agriculture study involving eggs produced in different parts of the country, graded B and C quality eggs were found to produce cakes with lower volume, tenderness, and sensory panel scores than did those of grade A or AA quality (Dawson et al., 1956).

Freezing, without pasteurization, does not alter the ability of egg whites to produce a good quality angel cake (Clinger et al., 1951; Miller and Vail, 1943). The pasteurization process required to free eggs of salmonellae and other pathogenic organisms before freezing or drying increases the whipping time required for egg whites to produce foams. However, angel cakes with satisfactory volume and texture can be prepared from pasteurized egg products (Cunningham and Lineweaver, 1965).

Although increased whipping times are required for dried egg whites, good quality cakes can be produced with these egg products (Zabik, 1968). Franks et al. (1969) compared angel cakes made with frozen, foam-spray-dried, freeze-dried, and spray-dried egg whites. Cakes made with foam-spray-dried egg whites had the largest volume and those made with spray-dried whites had the smallest volume. Freeze-dried egg whites produced cakes that scored lowest in the quality characteristics of texture, tenderness, and moistness. However, all cakes received good to very good scores for the quality characteristics evaluated. Baldwin et al. (1967) reported that spray-dried egg whites retained their functional properties during 60 days of storage at 54°C (129°F).

The proper degree of beating the egg white foam contributes greatly to the quality of the finished cake. Underbeating limits the amount of air that is enclosed in the foam. Expansion of air and production of steam during baking does not stretch the cell membranes to their full capacity. The result is relatively thick cell walls in a tough cake of low volume. Overbeating the egg white foam produces a loss of extensibility in the films, cell walls break during baking, and a cake of low volume and coarse texture results (Paul and Palmer, 1972).

An acid ingredient, usually cream of tartar, is essential to good cake quality. Acid stabilizes the egg foam structure. It also tenderizes the cake. An angel cake made without cream of tartar is yellowish in color, tough in texture, and low in volume. The acid ingredient lowers the pH of angel cake batter to approximately 5.2–6.0 (Ash and Colmey, 1973). In this pH range the flavonoid pigments in flour are white rather than yellowish as they are at an alkaline pH. The Maillard reaction is also less likely to occur during baking when the batter pH is acid rather than alkaline, thus contributing to a white cake color.

Sugar stabilizes the egg white foam and decreases the danger of overbeating. It is the primary tenderizing agent in the cake batter. It also contributes to flavor by sweetening the batter. Sugar increases the temperature at which egg white proteins coagulate with heating. Excessive amounts of sugar will prevent coagulation during baking. Proportions of sugar, flour, and egg white are important in controlling relationships between cake structure and tenderness.

Cake flour is used in angel cake to provide some structure that supports the basic egg white foam. This is chiefly due to the gelatinization of starch during baking. Cake flour is low in the gluten-forming proteins that contribute to toughness.

Mixing Angel cakes may be mixed in several different ways. All methods, however, involve the preparation of a meringue into which the flour is carefully folded. The egg whites may be beaten with the acid ingredient until soft peaks form and the sugar is then gradually added with continued beating. Alternatively, the egg whites may be beaten until they are stiff, but not dry, and the sugar then folded in. Another method is to cook the sugar with a small amount of water to 116°–117°C (241°–242.6°F) and add the syrup to the stiffly beaten egg whites. Salt and flavoring can be added at the end of the meringue stage. The amount of beating during the meringue stage is critical to the quality of the finished cake.

Flour is folded into the meringue. It should be distributed evenly throughout the meringue to avoid the toughness that may result from the hydration of proteins and damaged starch granules in the flour. At least part of the sugar should always be beaten with the egg whites before they are combined with the flour.

Baking Angel cakes are generally baked in a tube pan. This type of pan provides support for the batter and keeps a large amount of surface area in contact with the pan to allow even heat penetration. The pan is ungreased so that the cake can cling to the sides of the pan during baking and cooling. All sponge-type cake should be thoroughly cooled while inverted before the pan is removed.

Baking time is directly related to temperature. Early workers recommended the use of low temperatures with slow rates of temperature rise. They assumed that baking temperatures above 177°C (351°F) would toughen the egg white proteins (Barmore, 1936). At a later time, high oven temperatures were recommended. Miller and Vail (1943) baked angel cakes at 177°, 191°, 204°, 218°, and 232°C (350°, 375°, 400°, 425°, and 450°F) oven temperatures. The volume and tenderness of the cakes increased up to 218°C. Cakes baked at 204°C were rated highest in palatability but those baked at 218°C were most tender and were still rated high in palatability. A baking temperature of 204° or 218°C was recommended by these workers for angel cakes. Differing results were reported by Elgidaily *et al.* (1969) who baked angel cakes made from commercial mixes at 177°, 191°, 204°, and 218°C oven temperatures. They found that the rate of temperature rise within cakes depended on oven temperature, with the slowest rise recorded at the lowest baking temperature. Maximum internal temperatures reached during baking increased with oven temperature, but the increase was not necessarily proportional to the increased oven temperature. Cakes baked at 177° and 191°C scored higher in all quality characteristics than did those baked at 204° and 218°C. Volume decreased as baking temperature increased.

SPONGE AND CHIFFON CAKE

Sponge cake is made with whole egg, lemon juice, sugar, flour, and salt. The egg whites and yolks are usually beaten separately. However, Briant and Willman (1956) successfully made sponge cake with unseparated eggs if salt was omitted or added with the dry ingredients. The lemon juice was added to the eggs before they were beaten and the eggs were beaten until they formed soft peaks. Sponge cake may be made from yolks alone if some water is added and the yolks are beaten with sugar until they are very light. Sufficient beating of eggs is an important technique in the preparation of sponge cake.

A sponge cake of good quality has high volume in relation to weight, a relatively fine but somewhat open texture, tenderness, and a pleasing flavor. Sponge cakes made from dark-colored yolks were found to be more moist but less preferred by a sensory testing panel than cakes made from light-colored yolks (Deethardt *et al.*, 1965a). The color of yolks can be varied by adjusting the diet of the hens (Deethardt *et al.*, 1965b).

Chiffon cakes are similar to sponge cakes but contain oil and a small amount of baking powder that aids in leavening. More egg whites than yolks are used in these cakes. The yolks are added with the liquid and the whites are beaten into a foam.

19.2

MILK FOAMS

Foams may be produced from evaporated milk, dried milk, or cream. The proteins in milk show surface active properties and are responsible for foam formation. Milk foams are used as toppings or combined with other ingredients in such products as desserts and salads.

EVAPORATED MILK FOAMS

Evaporated milk has been concentrated to approximately double the solids content of whole milk. Increasing the concentration of solids increases the viscosity. Increased viscosity makes it easier for gas bubbles to be retained as the milk is beaten. Evaporated milk whips most satisfactorily when it has been chilled to the point that ice crystals begin to form. The ice crystals increase the concentration of solids by removing water from solution and also increase the viscosity by their presence in the milk. The addition of an acid ingredient, such as lemon juice, increases the stability of the foam by its effect on protein dispersibility.

Evaporated milk whips to a foam of large volume. The milk proteins are concentrated at the air–liquid interface and contribute to the formation of thin films surrounding air bubbles. The increased protein concentration in evaporated milk aids in foam formation. The increased butterfat content also helps to some degree by solidifying in the surface films. However, the fat content is not sufficient to give stability to the foam. The films around the gas bubbles do not become rigid enough to support the foam, liquid drains from the films, and the foam collapses on standing. Therefore, it should be used immediately after whipping.

DRIED MILK FOAMS When dried milk is reconstituted with less water than is required to give the usual concentration of solids, the concentrated milk mixture may be whipped into a foam. The foam is fluffy and of large volume. The increased level of protein and other solids increases the viscosity of the milk and aids in the retention of air bubbles. Some of the protein becomes denatured at the air–liquid surface and stabilizes the foam. The addition of an acid ingredient, such as lemon juice, increases foam stability. Reconstituting the milk with chilled water increases the viscosity of the mixture and therefore aids in foaming. The foam is unstable. On standing, liquid drains from the films and the foam gradually collapses.

WHIPPED CREAM The whipping quality of cream is dependent on its butterfat content. It improves with increasing fat content up to approximately 30 percent. Cream with less than 22 percent fat does not whip satisfactorily. The proteins in cream are adsorbed at the air–liquid interface, lower the surface tension of the water solvent, and are responsible for the formation of a foam when cream is beaten. The stabilization of a whipped cream foam is primarily due to the clumping of solidified fat globules on the surface of the dispersed air bubbles, thus giving rigidity to the system. The mechanical beating of cream removes some of the emulsifier membrane around the butterfat globules dispersed in the cream. As two partially denuded globules contact each other, they tend to adhere, thus producing clumps of fat. The temperature of whipping cream must be low enough to assure that fat globules are solid. If the cream is too warm, it will not whip to a stable foam because the fat is soft or melted. When these fat globules collide, they tend to coalesce rather than adhere to each other and clumping on the air bubble surface does not occur (Babcock, 1922).

Pasteurization impairs the whipping quality of cream to some degree. Homogenization decreases the whipping quality more markedly (Babcock, 1922). The impairment may be due to greater dispersion of fat globules and/or damage to the protein than is necessary for film formation. The whipping ability of cream improves with age, reaching a maximum at about 72 hours. Sugar decreases the stiffness of whipped cream, whether added before or after whipping. When sugar is added before whipping, the volume of the whipped cream is decreased and the whipping time is increased.

SUMMARY

Foams are similar to emulsions except that the dispersed droplets in foams are gaseous. A surfactant lowers the surface tension of a liquid phase and allows the expansion of its surface area. A closely packed film is formed around the dispersed gas bubbles by the surfactant. The film must have strength if the foam is to be stable.

Egg foams are essential in the preparation of angel cakes, sponge cakes, meringues, soufflés, and fluffy omelets. Egg white foams are more stable than egg yolk foams. Proteins are the surface active agents responsible for egg foam formation. Proteins not only lower the surface tension of egg white but many of them are easily denatured at the air–liquid surface. They form a network as they coagulate and give rigidity and stability to the foam. The roles in foaming of each of the egg white proteins have been postulated.

A very soft underbeaten egg white foam has relatively large gas bubbles and is somewhat unstable. Considerable drainage of liquid from the films occurs. A dry overbeaten foam is also unstable. The proteins at the surface are overcoagulated and the films collapse.

Various factors affect the foam quality in egg white. These include the equipment used in beating, the viscosity of the white, the conditions of storage for the eggs, and the temperature of the eggs. The addition of acid and sugar stabilize the foam. Salt may decrease the stability under some conditions. Even small amounts of fat have a detrimental effect on foam formation.

Meringues contain egg whites and sugar. Soft and hard meringues differ in sugar content and in procedures for baking. Problems encountered in preparing satisfactory soft meringues include leaking or weeping and beading. Excessive leakage occurs under conditions producing undercoagulation of the egg white proteins. Beading has been attributed to overcoagulation of the egg white proteins. A compromise is necessary in preparation procedures to achieve adequate coagulation of egg white proteins with a minimum of both leakage and beading while destroying any salmonellae that may be present.

Angel cake is made by first preparing a meringue. Flour is then carefully incorporated into the meringue. Desirable characteristics of an angel cake include high volume, fine texture, tenderness, and pleasant flavor. The quality characteristics are affected by the ingredients, the method of preparation, and the baking conditions. Egg whites provide the basic foam structure for angel cake, although flour also contributes to the cake structure. Angel cake volume decreases when eggs of low candled quality are used in its production. Freezing does not alter the ability of egg white to produce a good quality angel cake. Pasteurization of egg whites increases the whipping time for foam production. The proper degree of beating for the egg white foam is important to cake quality. Both underbeating and overbeating result in cakes of low volume and coarse texture.

Acid in angel cake stabilizes the egg foam structure. It also tenderizes the cake and contributes to the production of a white color by lowering the pH. Sugar stabilizes the egg white foam and decreases the danger of overbeating. It is the primary tenderizing agent in the cake batter. Proportions among sugar, flour, and egg white are important in controlling relationships between cake structure and tenderness. Gelatinization of starch in the flour during baking contributes to cake structure.

Although angel cakes may be mixed by several different methods, all methods involve the preparation of a meringue into which the flour is folded. Stirring, after the flour is added, must be carefully controlled to avoid toughness.

The baking time of an angel cake is directly related to the baking temperature. Conflicting results have been reported on the most satisfactory baking temperature for angel cakes. Both 177°C (350°F) and 204°C (400°F) have been recommended. The rate and extent of temperature rise within the cake apparently depend on oven temperature.

Sponge cake is made with whole egg. The whites and yolks are usually beaten separately but unseparated eggs may be successfully used. The adequate beating of eggs is particularly important to the production of a quality cake.

Foams may be produced from evaporated milk, dried milk, or cream. The milk proteins are surface active agents that are responsible for foam formation. The increased solids content of evaporated milk increases viscosity and makes it easier for gas bubbles to be retained during beating. The presence of ice crystals in the milk also increases viscosity. Evaporated milk whips to a foam of large volume. However, the surface films do not become rigid and the foam is not stable. Liquid drains from the films and the foam collapses on standing for a short time.

Dried milk will whip to a foam when it is reconstituted with less water than is required to give the usual concentration of solids. The viscosity of the concentrated dispersion is relatively high and aids in gas retention during whipping. Addition of acid stabilizes the foam to some degree. However, on standing, liquid drains from the films and the foam gradually collapses.

The whipping quality of cream is dependent on its butterfat content. It improves with increasing fat content up to approximately 30 percent. The cream must have at least 22 percent butterfat to whip satisfactorily. The proteins are responsible for foam formation. The foam is stabilized by the clumping of solidified fat globules on the surface of the dispersed air bubbles. The temperature of whipping cream must be low enough to assure that fat globules are solid. Pasteurization impairs the whipping quality of cream to some degree; homogenization decreases whipping quality more markedly, and the addition of sugar, either before or after whipping, decreases foam stiffness.

STUDY QUESTIONS

The formation and stabilization of a foam is a complex process that requires the presence of a surface active agent.

1. Draw and label a general diagram showing the microscopic structure of a foam. Then for each of the following food foam systems, indicate the surface active agent and discuss how it is oriented at the surface films. Also indicate whether or not the foam is stable and how it is stabilized in each stable foam.

   Food foam systems
   egg whites beaten to form shiny soft peaks
   soft meringue, baked
   hard meringue, unbaked
   meringue for angel cake
   angel cake, baked
   whipped cream
   whipped evaporated milk
   whipped dried milk

The production and stabilization of an egg white foam is affected by various factors.

2. Describe and explain the effects of type of beater, viscosity of the whites, temperature of the whites, addition of acid, addition of salt, addition of sugar, and addition of fat on the production and stability of an egg white foam.
3. Draw and explain diagrams illustrating the foam structure of an underbeaten, an overbeaten, and an optimally beaten egg white foam.

Meringues are egg white foams containing sugar.

4. Describe the differences in procedure and finished product between soft and hard meringues.
5. Describe weeping and beading in soft meringues, explain probable causes for these defects, and suggest procedures to prevent them.

Each ingredient in angel cake plays one or more particular roles in the production of the finished cake.

6. Describe and explain the contributions of egg whites, sugar, cream of tartar, salt, and flour to the characteristics of a finished angel cake.
7. Suggest possible roles for the various egg white proteins in the preparation of an angel cake.

8. Describe several satisfactory methods for mixing angel cake and explain why the various procedures are successful.
9. Suggest appropriate type and preparation of pan, baking temperature, and cooling procedure for angel cake and justify your suggestion.

Foams may be produced from various milk products.

10. Draw, label, and explain a diagram illustrating the probable microscopic structure of whipped cream containing 30 percent butterfat.
11. Explain the effects of butterfat content, temperature, and homogenization on the quality of the whipped cream foam.
12. What is the surface active agent responsible for foam formation in whipped milk products? Why is it effective?
13. Explain the instability of evaporated and of dried milk foams.

REFERENCES

1. Ash, D. J. and J. C. Colmey. 1973. The role of pH in cake baking. *Bakers Digest* 47 (No. 1), 36.

2. Babcock, C. J. 1922. The whipping quality of cream. U. S. Department of Agriculture Bulletin No. 1075.

3. Bailey, M. I. 1935. Foaming of egg whites. *Industrial and Engineering Chemistry* 27, 973.

4. Baldwin, R. E., O. J. Cotterill, M. M. Thompson, and M. Myers. 1967. High temperature storage of spray-dried egg white. 1. Whipping time and quality of angel cake. *Poultry Science* 46, 1421.

5. Barmore, M. A. 1934. The influence of chemical and physical factors on egg white foams. Colorado Agricultural Experiment Station Technical Bulletin No. 9.

6. Briant, A. M. and A. R. Willman. 1956. Whole-egg sponge cakes. *Journal of Home Economics* 48, 418.

7. Clinger, C., A. Young, I. Prudent, and A. R. Winter. 1951. The influence of pasteurization, freezing, and storage on the functional properties of egg white. *Food Technology* 5, 166.

8. Cumper, C. W. N. 1953. The stabilization of foams by proteins. *Transactions of the Farraday Society* 49, 1360.

9. Cunningham, F. E. and H. Lineweaver. 1965. Stabilization of egg-white proteins to pasteurizing temperatures above 60°C. *Food Technology* 19, 1442.

10. Dawson, E. H., C. Miller, and R. A. Redstrom. 1956. Cooking quality and flavor of eggs as related to candled quality, storage conditions, and other factors. U. S. Department of Agriculture Agricultural Information Bulletin No. 164.

11. Deethardt, D. E., L. M. Burrill, and C. W. Carlson. 1965a. Relationship of egg yolk color to the quality of sponge cakes. *Food Technology* 19, 73.

12. Deethardt, D. E., L. M. Burrill, and C. W. Carlson. 1965b. Quality of sponge cakes made with egg yolks of varying color produced by different feed additives. *Food Technology* 19, 75.

13. Elgidaily, D. A., K. Funk, and M. E. Zabik. 1969. Baking temperature and quality of angel cakes. *American Dietetic Association Journal* 54, 401.

14. Felt, S. A., K. Longrée, and A. M. Briant. 1956. Instability of meringued pies. *American Dietetic Association Journal* 32, 710.

15. Franks, O. J., M. E. Zabik, and K. Funk. 1969. Angel cakes using frozen, foam-spray-dried, freeze-dried, and spray-dried albumen. *Cereal Chemistry* 46, 349.

16. Funk, K., M. T. Conklin, and M. E. Zabik. 1971. Hard meringues prepared with foam-spray-, freeze- and spray-dried albumen. *Poultry Science* 50, 374.

17. Gillis, J. N. and N. K. Fitch. 1956. Leakage of baked soft-meringue topping. *Journal of Home Economics* 48, 703.

18. Glabau, C. A. 1948. Stabilizing custard type pie fillings and meringues. Part IV. *Bakers Weekly* 138 (11), 52.

19. Hanning, F. M. 1945. Effect of sugar or salt upon denaturation produced by beating and upon the ease of formation and the stability of egg white foams. Iowa State College *Journal of Science* 20, 10.

20. Henry, W. C. and A. D. Barbour. 1933. Beating properties of egg white. *Industrial and Engineering Chemistry* 25, 1054.

21. Hester, E. E. and C. J. Personius. 1949. Factors affecting the beading and leakage of soft meringues. *Food Technology* 3, 236.

22. Hunt, L. W. and J. L. St. John. 1931. Angel food cake from the thick and thin portions of egg white. *Journal of Home Economics* 23, 1151.

23. MacDonnell, L. R., R. E. Feeney, H. L. Hanson, A. Campbell, and T. F. Sugihara. 1955. The functional properties of the egg white proteins. *Food Technology* 9, 49.

24. Meehan, J. J., T. F. Sugihara, and L. Kline. 1962. Relationships between shell egg handling factors and egg product properties. *Poultry Science* 41, 892.

25. Miller, E. L. and G. E. Vail. 1943. Angel food cake from fresh and frozen egg whites. *Cereal Chemistry* 20, 528.

26. Morgan, K. J., K. Funk, and M. E. Zabik. 1970. Comparison of frozen, foam-spray-dried, freeze-dried, and spray-dried eggs. 7. Soft meringues prepared with a carrageenan stabilizer. *Journal of Food Science* 35, 699.

27. Nakamura, R. 1963. Studies on the foaming property of the chicken egg white. Part VI. Spread monolayer of the protein fraction of the chicken egg white. *Agricultural and Biological Chemistry* 27, 427.

28. Paul, P. C. and H. H. Palmer. 1972. *Food Theory and Applications*. New York: Wiley.

29. Sechler, C., L. G. Maharg, and M. Mangel. 1959. The effect of household table salt on the whipping quality of egg white solids. *Food Research* 24, 198.

30. St. John, J. L. and I. H. Flor. 1931. A study of whipping and coagulation of eggs of varying quality. *Poultry Science* 10, 71.

31. Zabik, M. E. 1968. Foam cakes prepared with dried eggs. *Bakers Digest* 42 (No. 6), 32.

CHAPTER 20

PECTIC SUBSTANCES AND JELLIES

Pectic substances are present within and between the cell walls of plant tissues. They are closely associated with cellulose and hemicelluloses in the cell walls and are one of the substances included in the broad designation of dietary fiber. As a component of the middle lamella, which is a narrow space between plant cells, they play a role in holding the cells together.

Some of the pectic substances have gel-forming properties. Fruit jellies and jams can be made from fruits and fruit juices that naturally contain sufficient quantities of gel-forming pectin. Pectin is commercially produced from such fruit tissues as apple and citrus after the juices have been extracted from them. The availability of purified pectins for both home and industrial use makes possible the preparation of jellies and jams from a wide variety of fruits that lack sufficient quantities of natural pectin for gelation.

20.1

NOMENCLATURE

Historically, researchers used various methods to extract pectic materials from plants for the purpose of studying their chemical structures and characteristics. Different names were applied to describe the heterogeneous groups of pectic substances extracted. As early as 1848 Frémy reported on the occurrence of a water-insoluble *pectose* that was changed to a water-soluble pectin by heating it in dilute acid solutions (Joslyn, 1962). Pectose was later named *protopectin* and was shown to be the parent of the other pectic substances. The American Chemical Society adopted the following nomenclature in 1944 and it has since been widely used to define the pectic substances (Kertesz, 1951).

Pectic substances—A group designation for those complex colloidal carbohydrate derivatives that occur in, or are prepared from, plants and contain a large proportion of anhydrogalacturonic acid units that are thought to exist in a chainlike combination. The carboxyl groups of these polygalacturonic acids may be partly esterified by methyl groups and partly or completely neutralized by one or more bases.

Protopectin—The water-insoluble parent pectic substance that occurs in plants and that, upon restricted hydrolysis, yields pectinic acids.

Pectinic acids—Colloidal polygalacturonic acids containing more than a negligible proportion of methyl ester groups. Pectinic acids, under suitable conditions, are capable of forming gels (jellies) with sugar and acid or, if suitably low in methoxyl content, with certain metallic ions. The salts of pectinic acids are either normal or acid pectinates.

Pectin—The general term pectin designates those water-soluble pectinic acids of varying methyl ester content and degree of neutralization that are capable of forming gels with sugar and acid under suitable conditions.

Pectic acid.—Pectic substances composed primarily of colloidal polygalacturonic acids and essentially free from methyl ester groups. The salts of pectic acid are either normal or acid pectates.

20.2

CHEMICAL STRUCTURE OF PECTIC SUBSTANCES

Chemically the pectic substances are linear polymers of D-galacturonic acid joined in α-(1→4) glycosidic linkages. Part of the carboxyl groups of the galacturonic acid are esterified with methanol. Depending upon the pH and the presence of metallic ions in the dispersion, the carboxyl groups will be variably ionized, giving the polymer a negative charge. The structure for galacturonic acid and for a methyl ester of galacturonic acid are shown in Figure 20.1.

The molecular weights of pectic substances range from 10,000 to

Figure 20.1

Chemical structures for galacturonic acid and its methyl ester.

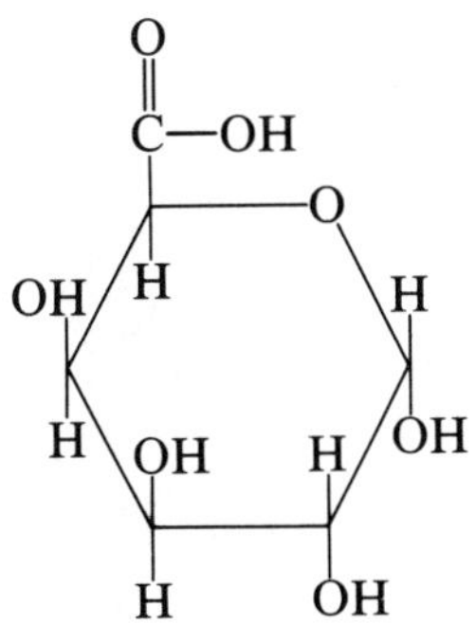

D–galacturonic Acid

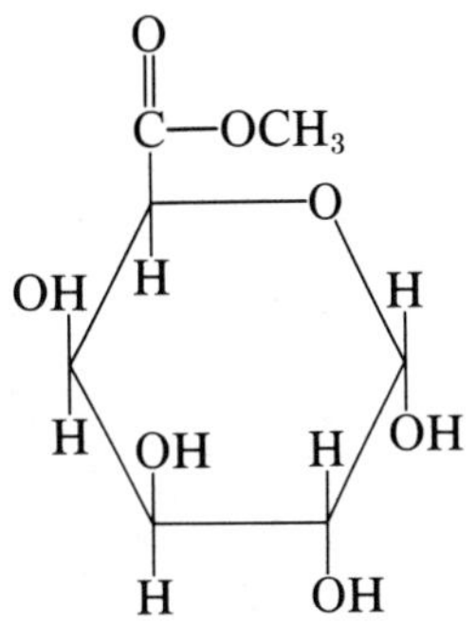

Methyl Ester of D–galacturonic Acid

400,000. Each of the groups defined in Sec. 20.1 differs in size and/or degree of esterification. Degree of methyl esterification is sometimes expressed as a percentage of the polygalacturonic acid present, determined on an ash-and moisture-free basis. Using this method of expression, a pectin with 16.3 percent methoxyl groups would be 100 percent esterified whereas a sample with 8 percent methoxyl would have approximately half of the carboxyl groups esterified. Protopectin, being the parent molecule, is the largest and has the highest degree of esterification. Pectinic acid molecules with approximately half of the carboxyl groups esterified (8 percent methoxyl) usually have excellent gel-forming properties with sugar and acid. Low-methoxyl pectins are pectinic acids with one-eighth to one-fourth of the carboxyl groups methylated (2–4 percent methoxyl). Low-methoxyl pectin is sometimes called *low-sugar pectin* because sugar is not necessary for its gel formation as

Figure 20.2

Pectinic acid and pectic acid are linear polymers.

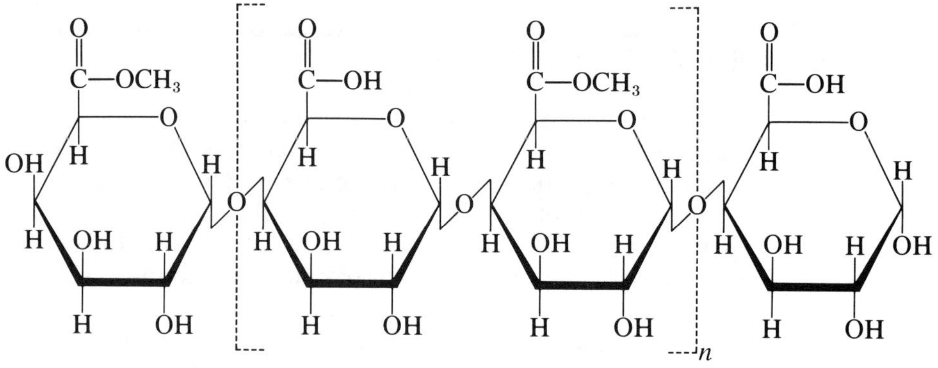

Pectinic acid

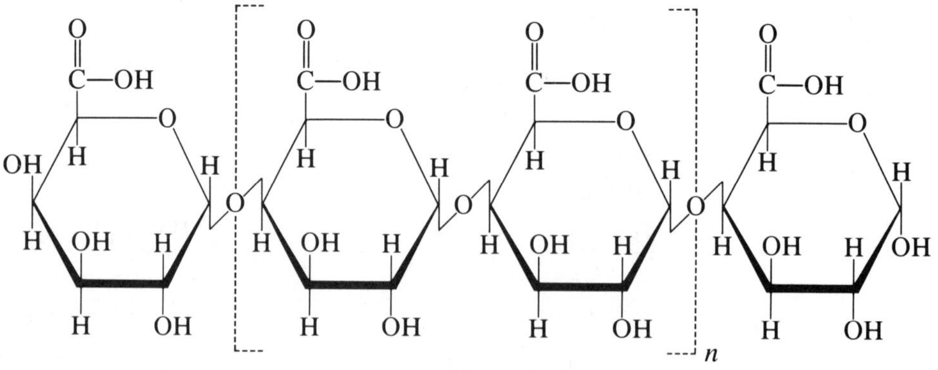

Pectic Acid

it is with regular pectin preparations. A divalent cation, such as Ca^{++}, is needed for gel formation with low-methoxyl pectins, however. Pectic acid molecules have essentially no carboxyl groups esterified with methanol. Pectic acid tends to form insoluble salts with divalent cations and is at least partially responsible for the firming effect of traces of calcium that are commonly added to canned tomatoes or to other canned vegetables. Portions of pectinic acid and pectic acid chains are shown in Figure 20.2.

Commercially produced pectin is a heterogeneous mixture of differently sized molecules with varying degrees of methyl ester formation. The exact molecular composition of these pectins is seldom determined. In a research laboratory, Smit and Bryant (1967) separated a sample of a commercial slow setting citrus pectin into four major fractions on diethylaminoethylcellulose chromatography columns. They reported that the fractions showed progressively lower methoxyl values and equivalent weights as they were eluted from the column with increasing concentrations of NaH_2PO_4. The original pectin sample had 10 percent methoxyl groups (expressed on an ash-and-moisture-free basis). The four fractions varied from 8.9 to 10.6 percent methoxyl groups. The decrease in methoxyl content from one fraction to the next was accompanied by an increase in setting times and pectin grades.

Protopectin is insoluble in water. However, it is soluble in hot acid solution. Pectinic acid or pectin is soluble in water (Joslyn and Deuel, 1963). Both dilute acid and alkali cause removal of the methyl esters. Dilute acid also causes depolymerization of the pectin molecules, especially at high temperatures.

Pectin dispersions exhibit high viscosity. The higher the molecular weight and the greater the degree of esterification, the greater will be the viscosity. The viscosity of fruit juices is an indication of pectin content.

20.3

PECTIC ENZYMES

Two types of enzymes operate in a sequential manner in the hydrolysis of pectic substances. They are pectin esterase and pectinase (polygalacturonase). These enzymes participate in the normal fruit ripening process and, along with other enzymes, are synthesized by plant tissues in increased amounts as ripening begins (Dilley, 1972). Thus during the ripening of fruit, protopectins are hydrolyzed to pectinic acids and on to pectic acids. This is generally associated with softening of fruit tissues. Changes in polygalacturonase activity in dates during ripening was studied by Hasegawa *et al.* (1969). Polygalacturonase activity was virtually absent at the green stage. It began to develop as maturity progressed with maximum activity occurring when the fruit began to soften.

Pectinase catalyzes the breaking of the α-(1→4) linkages between galacturonic acid residues. Pectinase enzymes may be further divided into endoenzymes and exoenzymes (Aurand and Woods, 1973). The *endoenzymes* act within the molecule, whereas the *exoenzymes* catalyze the progressive removal of galacturonic acid molecules from the nonreducing end of the pectin chain. Pectin esterase catalyzes the hydrolysis of the methyl esters, forming free acid groups and methanol. Thus, by the action of these two types of enzymes, pectic substances are decreased in both size and degree of esterification.

Pectic enzymes are utilized commercially for clarification of fruit juices, such as apple juice, so that a clear, sparkling juice results. For this purpose, enzymes produced by fungi such as *Aspergillus niger* are commonly used. Dahodwala *et al.* (1974) reported on the kinetic behavior of fungal pectinase, fungal pectin esterase, and tomato pectin esterase. The pectinase, in this case, appeared to be primarily an endoenzyme, hydrolyzing linkages within the molecule. It had a pH optimum of 4.4. Pectin esterase was found to be essential for depolymerization of pectin by pectinase. Pectinase catalyzed the hydrolysis of the pectin molecule at points where the galacturonide unit had been deesterified.

Pasteurization of citrus juices inactivates native pectic enzymes. This protects the desirable cloudy nature of these juices.

20.4

PECTIC SUBSTANCES IN PLANT TISSUES

Numerous studies have been made to determine the quantity and characteristics of pectic substances in fruits and vegetables. These substances often have a marked effect on the texture of both the fresh and the processed product. For example, Shewfelt *et al.* (1971) reported that changes in pectic substances during ripening were closely related to the textural characteristics of freestone peaches. A decrease in firmness of the tissues occurred as the molecular size and esterification decreased. They measured pectic constituents of the peaches at four stages of ripeness. An increase in the pectinic acid fraction, a decrease in the size of molecules in this fraction, and a decrease in esterification of the pectic substances occurred as ripening advanced.

Van Buren (1974) studied the influence of heating on the pectic substances present in red tart cherries. Heating at temperatures between 55°–70°C (131°–190°F) produced a decrease in water-soluble pectin, lower degrees of esterification, and greater firmness. It was concluded that heating in this temperature range led to increased firmness by initiating a pectin esterase-mediated change of pectins to less esterified forms that are insoluble in cherry tissue.

Luh and Dastur (1966) reported that canned apricots gradually softened during storage. Correlated with the softening were increases in water-soluble pectin in the sirup and decreases in protopectin in the fruit tissue.

Saeed *et al.* (1975a) reported a relationship between the viscosity of mango nectar and its total pectin content. Nectars with high pectin content exhibited high viscosity. The pectic substances in mango were characterized for molecular weight, esterification, and anhydrouronic acid content (Saeed *et al.*, 1975b). The purpose of this characterization was to better understand the textural properties of various mango cultivars.

20.5

FRUIT PECTIN GELS

Several types of fruit mixtures that are gelled by pectin are prepared both commercially and at home. They differ in the kind of fruit used and the way in which it is processed.

Jelly is a translucent gel made from fruit juice. It is firm enough to hold its shape when turned out of a container. Jam is made from crushed or ground fruit. It tends to hold its shape but is less firm than jelly. Conserves are jams made from a mixture of fruits, usually including citrus fruit. Raisins and nuts are often added. Marmalade is a jelly with small pieces of fruit spread evenly throughout. Marmalade is commonly made from citrus fruit. Preserves are whole or large pieces of fruit suspended in a thick sirup. They are often slightly gelled. Detailed instructions for preparing jellies, jams, and preserves at home are given in USDA Home and Garden Bulletin No. 56 (1977).

COMMERCIAL PECTINS

Pectin is available commercially in both liquid and powdered form. It has generally been extracted from either apples or citrus fruits.

Some fruits contain enough natural pectin to form strong gels. Examples of such fruits, that also contain high acid content, include sour apples, crab apples, citrus fruits, grapes, sour cherries, cranberries, and currants. However, it has become standard practice in the preserving industry to add pectin in the preparation of all jellies and jams. This allows flavorful fully ripe fruit to be used, even though the pectin content in these fruits decreases with their increasing ripeness. Many jellies are also made with added pectin in the home. Cooking time is shorter and is standardized so that there is no question as to when the product is done. The yield of product is large because of the short cooking time and the small amount of water that is evaporated. The flavor of natural fruit is sometimes less strong, however, when the jelly is made with added pectin than when made with only that present in the fruit. This is because the short boiling period does not concentrate the fruit flavor.

Pectins are graded for the food industry. Grading is done according to sugar-carrying power. If 1 lb of pectin will carry 100 lbs of sugar in the making of a standard jelly, it is a 100 grade pectin. In other words, as the gel strength and grade of a pectin increase, the amount of sugar to be optimally used also increases. In the grading of pectins, a standard jelly is usually prepared and its gel strength measured. Instruments for testing jellies include a ridgelimeter (Cox and Higby, 1944). This instrument measures the percent of sag in a specified amount of time for an unmolded sample of jelly of a specified shape and size. Other types of instruments measure the force required by various types of instruments to break the surface of a gel.

The molecular weight and degree of esterification of a pectin influence its grade. Smit and Bryant (1968) reported that maximum jelly grades for a pectin extracted from lemon peel were obtained when the pectin was esterified at about 45 percent of total possible ester formation. However, at this ester level the pH at which a high jelly grade was obtained was very low (pH 2.2).

Low-methoxyl pectins are available commercially. They do not require sugar for gel formation and are not as sensitive to pH as are regular pectins. They are particularly useful in the preparation of dessert gels for individuals who must restrict their intake of sugar. Low-sugar pectin gels require refrigeration since high concentrations of sugar are not present to inhibit microbial growth.

About half or more of the methyl ester groups of regular pectin are removed to produce low-methoxyl pectin. Deesterification may be accomplished by use of acid, alkalis, or enzymes. Pectins produced by enzyme demethylation are inferior because the demethylation is not random. Black and Smit (1972b) compared the characteristics of low-methoxyl pectins prepared by acid and by alkali demethylation. In general, the acid samples produced firmer, stronger gels at relatively high methoxyl levels. Low-methoxyl pectins are sensitive to such divalent metal cations as calcium. Gel formation is induced by the divalent ions.

Since high concentrations of sugar are not used in the preparation of low-methoxyl gels, the same grading procedure as that used for regular pectins is not appropriate. Black and Smit (1972a) outlined a possible grading procedure in terms of measuring low-ester gel firmness (indicated by F) by percent sag of a standard unmolded jelly and low-ester gel strength (indicated by S) by breaking pressure.

JELLYMAKING WITHOUT ADDED PECTIN

A successful fruit jelly must be balanced in terms of pectin, acid, and sugar. Sufficient pectin must be present in the finished jelly to provide a framework for gel structure. Although the quantity of pectin required is dependent on its quality, usually from 0.5 to 1.0 percent pectin will produce appropriate gel strength. If a fruit juice is relatively low in pectin, the pectin must be concentrated by boiling the juice mixture during the jellymaking process. The addition of sugar before boiling may aid in minimizing degradation of the pectin. Pectins from different fruits vary in gel-forming characteristics as well as in total quantity of pectin present. For example, the pectin extracted from peaches produced generally weak jellies when compared with pectins derived from such fruits as citrus and apple (Chang and Smit, 1973). Poor gelling characteristics may have been due to the presence of acetyl groups on peach pectins.

A certain degree of active acidity is essential for gel formation in fruit jellies. Acid also contributes to flavor in the finished product. An optimum pH for gel formation is approximately 3.2, although the quality of the pectin and the concentration of sugar affect the optimum pH to some degree. Gel strength gradually decreases at pH values below 3.2. Gel formation will usually not occur at a pH above 3.5. In the home preparation of jellies, lemon juice may be added to fruit juices that are deficient in acid. A rough measure of the desired active acidity of a fruit juice for jellymaking may be made by comparing the tartness with a mixture of 1 volume of lemon juice to 8 volumes of water.

Sugar plays an important role in gel formation. It also acts as a preservative since microorganisms cannot grow at the high osmotic pressure produced by concentrated sugar solutions. The optimum total solids content of most jellies is approximately 65 percent, the solids being primarily sugar. A gel may form with sugar concentrations between 40 and 70 percent. The volume of jellies containing higher percentages of sugar is greater than those with less sugar because less boiling is required to concentrate them. The final cooking temperature for a jelly mixture can be used as an indication of the solids content. A 65 percent sucrose solution boils at approximately 104°C (219°F) at sea level. Some invert sugar is produced from sucrose during the process of boiling the acid mixture. The rate of conversion is influenced by the length of heating time and the pH of the solution. Invert sugar is more soluble than is sucrose and aids in preventing crystallization of sucrose in the finished jelly.

The amount of sugar added to fruit juice as jelly is made is dependent upon the pectin content of the juice. If pectin is present in comparatively large amounts, a lesser degree of concentration of the juice by boiling is necessary to achieve an appropriate concentration of pectin in the final product. A comparatively large amount of sugar per cup of juice must be used with a high pectin juice since the degree of concentration of sugar will also be less in the shorter boiling period. At the end of the cooking period, the concentrations of pectin, sugar, and hydrogen ions must each be in an appropriate range for gel formation.

Theory of Gel Formation   Pectin, acid, and sugar interact in the formation of a gel. Pectin molecules are negatively charged at the pH of fruit juices. The similar negative charges on each molecule cause the molecules to repel each other and thus stabilize their dispersion in the water medium. In addition, the pectin molecules contain many polar groups. There is a particularly large proportion of -OH groups that attract water. This high degree of hydration also stabilizes the pectin dispersion.

The addition of sugar changes the pectin–water equilibrium that has been established. Sugar is a very hygroscopic substance and attracts some of the water that was held by pectin, thus partially dehydrating it. The pectin molecules are less repelled by each other and can conglomerate to form a network of fibers. At the same time, a pH of approximately 3.2 reduces the negative charge on the pectin molecules

that results from ionization of the free carboxyl groups ($-\overset{\overset{\displaystyle O}{\|}}{C}OH \leftrightarrow$

$-\overset{\overset{\displaystyle O}{\|}}{C}O^- + H^+$) to the degree that the pectin molecules may form cross-bonds with each other and establish a brush-heap gel structure. Water is held within the fibrous network and a rigid, moldable product results. Appropriate acid conditions contribute to the formation of a tough gel structure.

Low-methoxyl pectins that do not require sugar for gel formation form gels in a different manner than regular or high-methoxyl pectins. With a comparatively large number of free carboxyl groups on the pectin, strong salt linkages can be formed between pectin molecules by a divalent ion such as Ca^{++} as shown in Figure 20.3. The salt formation establishes sufficient crossbonds between pectin molecules to produce a fibrous network in which the watery portion of the mixture is entrapped.

Figure 20.3

Low-methoxyl pectins may form cross linkages through calcium salts.

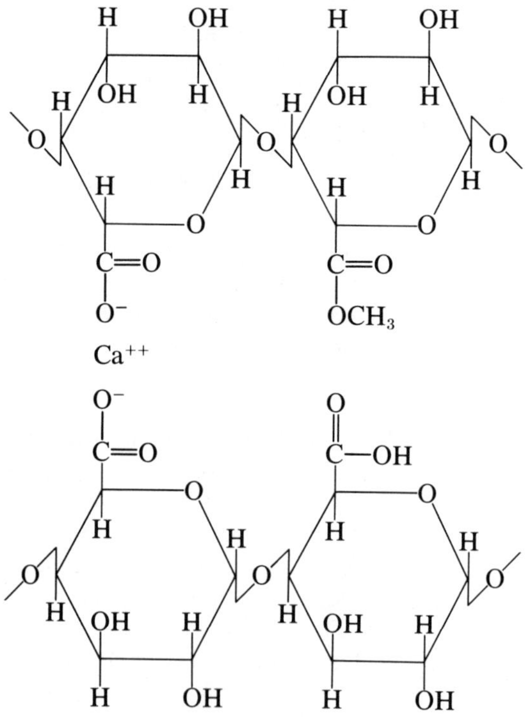

Extraction of Pectin Pectin is extracted from fruit tissues after a short heating period that softens these tissues. Usually some water is added. Firm fruits are sliced or chopped. Juicy berries may be crushed and the juice pressed out without heating, but more pectin can usually be extracted with a short heating period. Fruit that is just ripe or slightly underripe has a higher pectin content than does fully ripe or overripe fruit, although more fruit flavor is developed as the fruit ripens. Specific instructions for preparing different fruits are given in USDA Home and Garden Bulletin No. 56.

The heated fruit is strained to separate the juice from the pulp. The clearest jelly comes from allowing the juice to drip through a bag or a double layer of cheesecloth. However, pressing on the bag increases the yield of juice. Pressed juice should be restrained.

Testing for Pectin Content It is important to test the extracted juice for pectin content in order to add the appropriate amount of sugar. A precise method for evaluating the quantity and quality of pectin in the home is not available. However, if from two to three volumes of alcohol (denatured) are added to one volume of fruit juice, pectin is dehydrated and precipitated. If a relatively large cohesive mass of precipitate is formed, the juice probably contains sufficient pectin to make a firm jelly. The usual amount of sugar added per cup of fruit juice is three-fourths of a cup.

Pectin has a marked effect on the viscosity of fruit juice. When more pectin is present, the viscosity is increased. The large, hydrated pectin molecules delay the flow of fruit juice through a capillary tube. A small glass tube with a fine capillary attached at the bottom, called a *jelmeter,* was previously available for home use. It is a type of *viscometer.*

Tests for Doneness The final cooking temperature may be used as a test of doneness for jelly made in the home. The jelly mixture should be cooked to a temperature 4.4°C (8°F) above the boiling point of water. At this temperature the concentration of sugar will be approximately 65 percent and should be sufficient for most jellies. The boiling point of water will vary with the altitude.

Figure 20.4

The sheet test indicates doneness in jellymaking.

The sheet or spoon test also gives an indication of doneness indicating the consistency of the boiling mixture. A cool metal spoon is dipped in the boiling jelly mixture. It is then raised from the mixture and the sirup allowed to drain off the edge of the spoon. If the sirup forms two drops that flow together and fall off the spoon as one sheet, the jelly should be done (see Figure 20.4). This test may be used in combination with the thermometer test.

SUMMARY

Pectic substances are found within and between the cell walls of plant tissues. They act as cementing substances, holding cells together.

Pectic substances are a group of complex carbohydrates that contain a large proportion of anhydroglacuronic acid units joined in a chain-like combination with α-(1→4) glycosidic linkages. Protopectin is the water-insoluble parent substance and yields pectinic acids on restricted hydrolysis. Both protopectin and pectinic acids contain variable quantities of methyl esters. Pectic acid is essentially free from methyl ester groups. The molecular weights of pectic substances range from 10,000 to 400,000.

Pectinic acid molecules with approximately half of the carboxyl groups esterified with methanol usually have excellent gel-forming properties. The general term pectin designates those water-soluble pectinic acids that are capable of forming gels with sugar and acid under suitable conditions. Low-methoxyl pectins have one-eighth to one-fourth of the carboxyl groups esterified. They form gels in the presence of divalent cations such as calcium. Salt formation links chains of low-methoxyl pectin into a fibrous network during formation of a gel.

Two types of enzymes operate in the hydrolysis of pectic substances. Pectinase (polygalacturonase) catalyzes the breaking of the α-(1→4) linkages between galacturonic acid residues. Pectin esterase catalyzes the hydrolysis of the methyl ester groups.

Since pectic substances often have marked effects on the texture of both fresh and processed fruits and vegetables, these substances have been studied in plant tissues. Generally in fruits the size of pectic molecules and the degree of esterification decrease as ripening advances. Increases in water-soluble pectin in the sirup of canned apricots and decreases in protopectin in the fruit tissue have been reported during storage of this canned product.

Several types of fruit mixtures are gelled by pectin. These include jellies, jams, conserves, marmalades, and preserves. Purified pectin is available commercially and is commonly added in the home preparation of these products. Some fruits contain sufficient pectin and active acidity to make satisfactory jellies without the addition of pectin.

Pectins are graded in terms of sugar-carrying power. The grade is expressed as the number of pounds of sugar that 1 lb of pectin will carry in the making of a standard jelly. Low-methoxyl pectins require a different grading system.

In the making of a fruit jelly without added pectin, care must be exercised to balance the pectin, acid, and sugar. Sufficient pectin (usually from 0.5 to 1 percent) must be present in the finished jelly to provide a framework for gel structure. An optimum pH for gel formation is approximately 3.2. Gel formation will usually not occur at a pH above 3.5. The optimum total solids content, primarily sugar, is approximately 65 percent. The amount of sugar added to fruit juice as jelly is made is dependent upon the pectin content of the juice. High pectin juice requires relatively large proportions of sugar to juice and the boiling period, in which both pectin and sugar are concentrated, is relatively short.

In the formation of a gel with regular pectin, the sugar acts as a dehydrating agent to destabilize the pectin dispersion. Hydrogen ions tend to decrease the magnitude of the negative charge on the pectin molecules. Pectin molecules are thus less repelled by each other and can conglomerate to form a network of fibers.

Pectin is extracted in the juice of fruits after a short heating period that softens the tissues. The heated fruit is strained to separate the juice from the pulp. The extracted juice is tested for pectin content in order to determine the appropriate quantity of sugar to add per cup of juice. Alcohol precipitates pectin and gives an indication of pectin content. The usual amount of sugar added per cup of fruit juice is three-fourths cup.

Doneness of jelly made at home may be tested by measuring the final cooking temperature, which is 4.4°C (8°F) above the boiling point of water. A sheet or spoon test also gives an indication of doneness.

STUDY QUESTIONS

The American Chemical Society in 1944 adopted a standard nomenclature for pectic substances which has been widely used.

1. Describe five major categories in the ACS classification.

The chemical structures of the pectic substances differ in molecular size and degree of esterification.

2. Write the name and the chemical structure of the basic building unit of the pectic substances. Show how a methyl ester is formed on this basic molecule.
3. Describe similarities and differences in chemical structure among protopectin, pectinic acid, and pectic acid.
4. Identify the following as protopectin, pectinic acid, or pectic acid.

Description
Galacturonic acid units linked in chains as:

Approximately 85 to 90 percent of carboxyl groups are esterified with methanol. Molecular weight average is about 300,000.

5. List the approximate percentage of methoxyl groups (on an ash-and-moisture-free basis) in low-methoxyl pectins and in regular or high-methoxyl pectins. List three methods that may be used for demethylating regular pectin to produce low-methoxyl pectin.

Two types of enzymes participate in the hydrolysis of pectic substances in plants.

6. Compare the action of pectinase (polygalacturonase) and pectin esterase on pectic substances.
7. Describe the role of the pectic enzymes in fruit ripening.

Pectin content of fruit juices may be estimated in various ways preparatory to the making of jelly at home.

8. Describe possible procedures for estimating the pectin content of fruit juices. Explain the basis of the tests.
9. Define pectin grade.

Pectin, acid, and sugar must be balanced in a well made fruit jelly.

10. Describe the process usually involved in extracting pectin from fruit for making jelly at home.
11. Explain the roles of pectin, hydrogen ions, and sugar in the making of jelly and describe a current theory of gel formation using regular or high-methoxyl pectin.
12. Describe two tests for doneness in jellymaking and evaluate the basis for each test.

Low-methoxyl pectins require a divalent cation for gel formation.

13. Explain why sugar is not a necessary ingredient in the making of low-methoxyl pectin gels and describe a current theory of gel formation for these pectins.

Practical problems are often encountered in making jelly at home.

14. A homemaker extracted juice from overripe currants, added 1 cup sugar

per cup of juice and boiled the mixture to 99.5°C (at an altitude of 4500 ft above sea level) before pouring it into sterilized glasses. After cooling, the resulting jelly was found to be sirupy with only slight gel formation. The homemaker would like an explanation as to what went wrong and what might be done to correct it. Please diagnose and prescribe.

REFERENCES

1. Aurand, L. W. and A. E. Woods. 1973. *Food Chemistry*. Westport, Conn.: Avi Publishing Co.

2. Black, S. A. and C. J. B. Smit. 1972a. The grading of low-ester pectin for use in dessert gels. *Journal of Food Science* 37, 726.

3. Black, S. A. and C. J. B. Smit. 1972b. The effect of demethylation procedures on the quality of low-ester pectins used in dessert gels. *Journal of Food Science* 37, 730.

4. Chang, Y. S. and C. J. B. Smit. 1973. Characteristics of pectins isolated from soft and firm fleshed peach varieties. *Journal of Food Science* 38, 646.

5. Cox, R. E. and R. H. Higby. 1944. A better way to determine the jelling power of pectins. *Food Industries* (June), p. 441.

6. Dahodwala, S., A. Humphrey, and M. Weibel. 1974. Pectic enzymes: Individual and concerted kinetic behavior of pectinesterase and pectinase. *Journal of Food Science* 39, 920.

7. Dilley, D. R. 1972. Postharvest fruit preservation: Protein synthesis, ripening and senescence. *Journal of Food Science* 37, 518.

8. Hasegawa, S., V. P. Maier, H. P. Kaszycki, and J. K. Crawford. 1969. Polygalacturonase content of dates and its relation to maturity and softness. *Journal of Food Science* 34, 527.

9. Joslyn, M. A. 1962. The chemistry of protopectin: A critical review of historical data and recent developments. *Advances in Food Research* 11, 1.

10. Joslyn, M. A. and H. Deuel. 1963. The extraction of pectins from apple marc preparations. *Journal of Food Science* 28, 65.

11. Kertesz, Z. D. 1951. *The Pectic Substances*. New York: Wiley.

12. Luh, B. S. and K. D. Dastur. 1966. Texture and pectin changes in canned apricots. *Journal of Food Science* 31, 178.

13. Saeed, A. R., A. H. El Tinay, and A. H. Khattab. 1975a. Viscosity of mango nectar as related to pectic substances. *Journal of Food Science* 40, 203.

14. Saeed, A. R., A. H. El Tinay, and A. H. Khattab. 1975b. Characterization of pectic substances in mango marc. *Journal of Food Science* 40, 205.

15. Shewfelt, A. L., V. A. Paynter, and J. J. Jen. 1971. Textural changes and molecular characteristics of pectic constituents in ripening peaches. *Journal of Food Science* 36, 573.

16. Smit, C. J. B. and E. F. Bryant. 1968. Ester content and jelly pH influences on the grade of pectins. *Journal of Food Science* 33, 262.

17. Smit, C. J. B. and E. F. Bryant. 1967. Properties of pectin fractions separated on diethylaminoethyl-cellulose columns. *Journal of Food Science* 32, 197.

18. U. S. Department of Agriculture. 1977. How to make jellies, jams and preserves at home. Home and Garden Bulletin No. 56.

19. Vab Buren, J. P. 1974. Heat treatments and the texture and pectins of red tart cherries. *Journal of Food Science* 39, 1203.

CHAPTER 21

GELATIN

The preparation of gels with gelatin has long been a treasured art of the homemaker. The early methods of processing gelatin in the home for the preparation of clear jellies were vastly different from modern methods that use industrially manufactured gelatin and gelatin mixes. However, the basic principles utilized for gelatin extraction in colonial America were the same as those employed for commercial production today, as illustrated in the following recipe used by Virginia housewives (Carson, 1968).

To Make Jelly from Feet

Boil four calfs' feet, that have been nicely cleaned, and the hoofs taken off; when the feet are boiled to pieces, strain the liquor through a colander, and when cold, take all the grease off, and put the jelly in a skillet, leaving the dregs which will be at the bottom. There should be from four feet, about two quarts of jelly: pour into it one quart of white wine, the juice of six fresh lemons strained from the seeds, one pound and a half of powdered loaf sugar, a little pounded cinnamon and mace, and the rind thinly pared from two of the lemons; wash eight eggs very clean, whip up the whites to a froth, crush the shells and put with them, mix it with the jelly, set it on the fire, stir it occasionally till the jelly is melted, but do not touch it afterwards. When it has boiled till it looks quite clear on one side, and the dross accumulates on the other, take off carefully the thickest part of the dross, and pour the jelly in the bag; put back what runs through, until it becomes quite transparent—then set a pitcher under the bag, and put a cover all over to keep out the dust . . .

21.1

COLLAGEN

Collagen is the major protein constituent of skin, tendon, cartilage, bone, and connective tissue in mammals. It accounts for a third of the protein in the human body and is of great physiological importance.

(General characteristics of proteins are discussed in Chapter 22.) In the industrial world, collagen from bone, cattle hides and pigskins is the basic raw material for the manufacture of glue as well as gelatin. It also accounts for the toughness of leather (Gross, 1961).

The basic collagen molecule is called *tropocollagen*. It has a thin rodlike structure with a molecular weight of about 300,000. It consists of three polypeptide chains of equal length, each in a left handed helix form. The chains include two α_1 and one α_2 polypeptides. These three chains are intertwined about a common axis in a coiled-coil conformation. The amino acid, glycine, constitutes every third amino acid residue throughout much of all the polypeptide chains. The characteristic sequence within the chains is Glycine-Proline-X, where X is often hydroxyproline. This characteristic amino acid sequence contributes to the secondary and tertiary structure of collagen. The rodlike tropocollagen molecules aggregate in a highly specific manner to form fibrils of collagen. Figure 21.1 shows an electron micrograph of collagen fibrils. Cross-links form between tropocollagen molecules and aid in stabilizing the fibril structure (Ward and Courts, 1977). Collagen exhibits distinctive cross-linking characteristics depending upon the tissue from which it originated, that is, skin, tendon, muscle, or bone (McClain *et al.,* 1970).

Native collagen is very resistant to the actions of enzymes and chem-

Figure 21.1

Collagen fibrils carefully pulled away from human skin. (Reprinted with permission from Gross, J. 1961. Collagen. *Scientific American* 204 [No. 5], 120.)

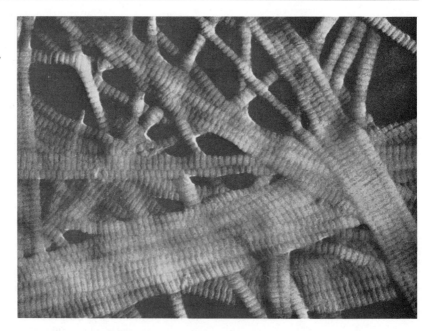

icals. Treatment in alkali causes some swelling and dispersion of collagen and is often the prelude to the conversion of collagen to gelatin. Dilute acids also solubilize varying amounts of collagen. Some swelling and reduced cohesion between fibrils occurs in neutral salt solutions. Complete breakdown of native collagen can only be achieved by the action of a group of bacterial enzymes, the collagenases (Ward and Courts, 1977).

Collagen is denatured when heated in solution between 37°–40°C (98°–104°F). Shrinkage of the fibers occurs about 27°C higher. These temperatures are affected by pH and salt concentration (Ward and Courts, 1977).

21.2

CHEMICAL COMPOSITION OF GELATIN

Gelatin is a derived protein from collagen precursors and is the main product of collagen breakdown when heat is combined with alkali or acid treatment. Gelatin is well defined chemically although it is not homogeneous since the collagen bonds are randomly broken. It is water soluble above 30°C (86°F) and is amphoteric, its charge depending upon the pH of the solution in which it is dispersed. The gelatin obtained from acid treated collagen has a broad isoelectric region between pH 7 and 9. Gelatin made from alkaline treated collagen has an isoelectric region between pH 4.8 and 5.0 (Marks *et al.,* 1968).

Carefully prepared commercial gelatins appear to consist almost entirely of a single family of closely related protein molecules. The molecular weight is probably close to 90,000. The amino acid composition of gelatin is similar to that of the collagen from which it comes. It is, however, affected to some degree by the method of manufacture. For example, alkaline processed gelatins generally have higher hydroxyproline and lower tyrosine content than do acid processed gelatins. Air-dried gelatin has a moisture content of 9–12 percent. Inorganic ash usually accounts for approximately 2 percent of the dry gelatin product. This includes calcium, sodium, magnesium, iron, aluminum, potassium sulphate, and chloride. Small amounts of mucoproteins are present in gelatin (Ward and Courts, 1977).

Air-dried gelatin dissolves readily in warm water once the particles have become thoroughly wetted and have had time to swell. Gelatin dispersed in water is subject to hydrolysis. The degradation rate is a function of pH and temperature. The rate increases with acidity at pH values below 5 and also increases with temperature elevations (Tiemstra, 1968). The degree of gelatin degradation affects its gelling power, decreasing as degradation increases. These effects must be considered when gelatin is used in food products, particularly in heat processed products.

21.3

GELATIN MANUFACTURE

The process of gelatin manufacture involves three basic stages. 1. The raw material is treated to separate collagenous from noncollagenous components; 2. the purified collagen is converted into gelatin; 3. the gelatin is refined and recovered in dry form (Ward and Courts, 1977).

In North America, pigskin is the chief raw material for edible gelatin. The skins are washed, degreased, and chopped. Pigskin is then processed by soaking it in dilute acid solution whereas other types of raw material may receive alkaline treatment in preparation for collagen conversion to gelatin.

Methods for conversion of collagen include the use of water and high temperature at neutral pH or cautious use of acid at moderate temperatures. The cross-linkages of collagen are reduced and some peptide bonds are hydrolyzed. Hydrogen bonds are also broken.

Extracted gelatin liquors are filtered and clarified. They are then evaporated and sterilized. Dry gelatin is usually obtained by cooling a concentrated sol to a solid gelatin gel and then drying the gel. The dried product is ground and screened. Standard methods have been established for the sampling and testing of gelatin by the Gelatin Manufacturers Institute.

21.4

THE GELATIN GEL

Gelatin is a gel-forming agent. It has the ability to form stable gels over a wide pH range without the addition of specific ions or other chemical substances. The gelation phenomena apparently includes a number of events. First, on the cooling of a gelatin solution, partial aggregation of the gelatin molecules occurs, the slower the rate of cooling, the more extensive the aggregation. Next, the aggregates link together to form a weak network. The links are apparently of a secondary nature rather than covalent bonds. Approximately five or six sites per molecule for linking will form the basic network. Links may involve an imino-rich (-NH-) section from each of three peptide chains. Water is entrapped in the network mesh. As the mixture is cooled further, or held for an additional period of time at a constant temperature, the set gel develops increased strength. Additional gelatin molecules become attached to each other to produce thickening of the framework and stiffening of the gel. This is more pronounced in concentrated gels and at low temperatures. The setting of a gelatin sol and subsequent changes in the gel network arise through the partial return of disordered gelatin molecules to the collagen structure. A possible network of gelatin molecules in gelation is shown schematically in Figure 21.2.

When a gel is warmed it eventually melts. The melted mixture con-

Figure 21.2

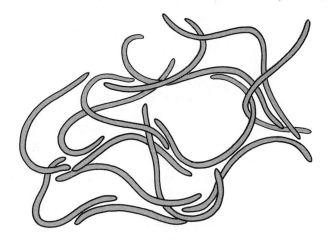

Gelatin molecules form a network during transformation from a sol to a gel.

tains aggregates that disperse, in time and at a high enough temperature, to separate molecules. The least stable short links in the gel network are first to become disordered, or melt. The stronger links persist for longer periods of time (Ward and Courts, 1977). Certain gel-forming polysaccharides are sometimes used in place of gelatin for institutional food service. Gels made from these substances do not melt at warm room temperatures as do gelatin gels. The polysaccharide gels also slide out of a mold without dipping it in warm water.

FACTORS INFLUENCING GELATION

The thermal history of the gel affects its characteristics. The balance between intermolecular reactions and reactions with the solvent is delicate and strongly dependent on temperature. If a gelatin sol is cooled very rapidly, the molecules are disordered and contacts between neighboring molecules occur by chance. Many weak links are formed. In contrast, very slow cooling allows links to form in a more orderly fashion. Stable bonds can form and additional bonds develop in close proximity to these. As either of these gels ages, changes continue to occur as the portions of the molecules between cross-linkages undergo movement and new bonding possibilities arise. However, the changes are less extensive for the gel that is cooled rapidly. The melting point of a gelatin gel may be affected by its thermal history. Gels cooled very rapidly tend to melt at a lower temperature than do those cooled more slowly.

Gel strength increases with increasing molecular weight of the gelatin between about 15,000 and 90,000. Other unidentified factors probably also account for differences in gel strength among various gelatin samples. The pH of the system influences gel strength to some degree. The gel is most rigid at a pH from 5 to 10. A decrease in gel strength occurs at pH values below 4. The rigidity of a gel at a specific pH also varies with the presence of other ions and nonelectrolytes such as sugar. The addition of sugar to gelatin, while maintaining a given gelatin concentration, increases gel strength and melting point to some degree. Small concentrations of sucrose (0.02–0.03 M) increase setting time but concentrations exceeding 0.01 M cause more rapid setting. The presence of various salts affects setting temperature and gel strength in various ways. Gel strength is greater when gelatin is dispersed in milk than in water (Paul and Palmer, 1972).

Proteinases that degrade gelatin molecules prevent gelation. Bromelin, a proteinase present in raw pineapple, will liquify a gelatin mixture if the raw fruit is mixed with a gelatin dispersion. The enzyme is destroyed during heat processing as pineapple is canned. Raw papaya contains the proteinase, papain, and figs contain ficin.

21.5

USES OF GELATIN IN FOOD PRODUCTS

Gelatin for food use must meet certain standards of quality. These include gel strength and microbiological specifications. Satisfactory edible gelatin should have little odor, taste, or color. In foods, gelatin may be used as a gelling agent, stabilizer, emulsifier, thickener, foaming agent, water binder, crystal growth modifier, glaze, adhesive, and binder.

Granular gelatin requires hydration in three to four volumes of cold water before it will disperse readily in hot liquid. The final temperature should reach at least 35°C (95°F) for adequate dispersion. Hydrated gelatin may be heated over hot water to produce a concentrated sol that can be mixed with other ingredients, as long as appropriate precautions are taken. The concentrated sol cannot be readily dispersed in cold liquid. The liquid should be added in small portions to the gelatin sol with constant stirring. Alternatively, granular gelatin may be mixed with sugar and dissolved in hot liquid without hydration.

Dry mixtures to be used in the preparation of gelatin desserts consist of pulverized gelatin, sugar, acid, and other flavoring and coloring agents. The gelatin content varies from about 7 to 14 percent to give from 1.7 to 3 percent gelatin in the prepared gel. The pulverized gelatin–sugar mixture can be dispersed directly in hot water without preliminary hydration.

Gels of satisfactory consistency for salads and desserts will form with 1.5–2.0 percent gelatin. One tablespoon (7 g) granular gelatin dispersed in one pint of water gives a percentage of about 1.5. Increasing the amount of gelatin results in increasing gel strength. Gels may become rubbery and stiff with too much gelatin. The amount of gelatin may need to be increased in a very tart mixture, to compensate for the effect of low pH, or when the gel must support large amounts of coarsely cut pieces of fruits or vegetables.

Gelatin is used in meat products as a jellying agent. The amount required depends on the heat process used. Extra gelatin is needed to allow for breakdown if heat processing is complete.

Gelatin mixtures may be whipped when they have been chilled until the sol is viscous. Air is incorporated in a foam and the setting of the gelatin stabilizes the foam. A *sponge* is a whipped gelatin mixture containing beaten egg whites. Whipped cream may also be added to a gelatin mixture. Gelatin is used as a foaming agent in marshmallows. It also contributes to large foam volumes in chiffon pies that contain an egg white meringue. Gelatin salads and desserts cannot be satisfactorily frozen unless they contain relatively large amounts of whipped cream, cream cheese, etc.

SUMMARY

The preparation of gelatin gels is an old culinary art. Gelatin is a derived protein from collagen precursors. Collagen is the major protein constituent of skin, tendon, cartilage, bone, and connective tissue. The basic collagen molecule is called tropocollagen. It is made up of three polypeptide chains intertwined about a common axis. The rodlike tropocollagen molecules aggregate with cross-linkages to form fibrils of collagen.

Gelatin is well defined chemically although it is not homogeneous since the collagen bonds are randomly broken when gelatin is produced. It is water soluble above 30°C and is amphoteric. Carefully prepared commercial gelatins appear to consist almost entirely of a single family of closely related protein molecules with molecular weights close to 90,000. The amino acid content is similar to that of the collagen from which it is produced. The moisture content of air-dried gelatin is from 9 to 12 percent, and the ash content is about 2 percent. Gelatin in solution is subject to degradation. The rate is a function of pH and temperature.

In North America, pigskin is the chief raw material for the manufacture of edible gelatin. The skins are washed, degreased, and chopped. They are processed by soaking them in dilute acid solution. Collagen is then converted to gelatin by use of water and high temperature at neutral pH or with the cautious use of acid at moderate temperatures. The cross-linkages of collagen are reduced and some peptide bonds hydrolyzed. Hydrogen bonds are also broken.

Extracted gelatin liquors are filtered, clarified, evaporated, and sterilized. Dry gelatin is obtained by cooling a concentrated sol to a solid gelatin gel and drying the gel. The dried product is ground and screened.

Gelatin has the ability to form stable gels over a wide pH range without the addition of specific ions or other chemical substances. On cooling a gelatin solution, partial aggregation of the gelatin molecules occurs. Next, the aggregates link together to form a weak network. The linkages are of a secondary nature rather than covalent bonds. Water is entrapped in the network mesh. With aging, the set gel develops increased strength as additional linkages are formed. In the gelation process the gelatin molecules partially return to the original collagen-type structure. When a gel is warmed it eventually melts as linkages are broken.

Gelation is affected by the thermal history of the gel. If a gelatin sol is cooled very rapidly, the molecules are disordered and many weak links are formed. Very slow cooling allows links to form in a more stable and orderly fashion. The melting point of a gelatin gel is higher for the stable gel. A decrease in gel strength occurs at pH values below 4. Sugar increases gel strength and melting point to some degree. Proteinases such as bromelin, papain, and ficin that degrade gelatin molecules, prevent gelation.

Gelatin may be used in foods as a gelling agent, stabilizer, emulsifier, thickener, foaming agent, water binder, crystal growth modifier, glaze, adhesive, and binder. Granular gelatin requires hydration in cold water before it will disperse readily in hot liquid. Dry mixtures used in the preparation of gelatin desserts consist of pulverized gelatin, sugar, acid, flavoring, and color. They can be dispersed directly in hot water. Gels of satisfactory consistency for salads and desserts will form with from 1.5 to 2.0 percent gelatin.

STUDY QUESTIONS

Gelatin is a derived protein from collagen precursors.

1. Describe the chemical characteristics of collagen and of gelatin.
2. Describe the basic stages in the manufacture of gelatin.

Gelatin dispersions undergo sol-gel transformation.

3. What happens at a molecular level as sol-gel transformation occurs? What are the system requirements for gel formation?
4. Discuss factors that influence the gelation of a gelatin dispersion and explain implications for food preparation.
5. Explain why raw pineapple cannot be used in the preparation of a set gelatin fruit salad.

Gelatin finds wide useage in food products.

6. List various roles that gelatin may play in food processing and preparation.
7. Describe and explain satisfactory procedures for dispersing granular gelatin and dry gelatin dessert mixtures.
8. How much gelatin should generally be used in the preparation of gels for salads and desserts? When should the proportion of gelatin to liquid be increased?

REFERENCES

1. Carson, J. 1968. *Colonial Virginia Cookery*. Williamsburg, Virginia: Colonial Williamsburg, Inc. (distributed by University Press of Virginia, Charlottesville).

2. Gross, J. 1961. Collagen. *Scientific American* (May).

3. Marks, E. M., D. Tourtellotte, and A. Andux. 1968. The phenomenon of gelatin insolubility. *Food Technology* 22, 1433.

4. McClain, P. E., G. J. Creed, E. R. Wiley, and R. J. Gerrits. 1970. Cross-linking characteristics of collagen from porcine intramuscular connective tissue: Variation between muscles. *Biochimica Biophysica Acta* 221, 349.

5. Paul, P. C. and H. H. Palmer. 1972. *Food Theory and Applications*. New York: Wiley.

6. Tiemstra, P. J. 1968. Degradation of gelatin. *Food Technology* 22, 1151.

7. Ward, A. G. and A. Courts, editors. 1977. *The Science and Technology of Gelatin*. New York: Academic Press.

PART VI

PROTEINS IN FOOD SYSTEMS

Proteins are widely distributed in variable amounts in plant and animal tissues used for food. The properties of proteins and the effects of processing and preparing them are of particular importance in food products containing large amounts of protein. This part therefore begins with a general discussion of protein characteristics. Several animal foods that make important contributions to the diet are then discussed in four chapters. The last two chapters in this part are concerned with proteins of plant origin. They include discussions of isolated plant proteins, that are being used increasingly in manufactured foods, and wheat proteins, that play important roles as structural agents in baked products.

CHAPTER 22

CHARACTERISTICS OF FOOD PROTEINS

Proteins are important components of foods because of their nutritional value. A certain amount of protein is necessary for life and growth. Proteins are also important in food products because of their so-called functional properties. Proteins function in food preparation as gel formers, emulsifiers, foaming agents, and enzymes. Their water-binding capacity and ability to coagulate on heating are additional properties that make them useful in the processing and preparation of a variety of foods. Considerable research work is aimed at producing isolated proteins with specific functional properties that have particular application in the manufacture of modern food products. (Isolated vegetable proteins are discussed in Chapter 27.)

All animal and plant tissues contain proteins in either major or minor quantities. Since these tissues are subjected to various processing and preparation procedures, knowledge concerning the properties of proteins under various conditions becomes important to the student of food science. Proteins are complex macromolecules and are difficult to study. However, a variety of laboratory techniques have been applied to gain an understanding of their chemical and physical structure and properties. (Proteins in specific food products, of both animal and vegetable origin, are discussed in the remaining chapters of Part VI.)

22.1

AMINO ACIDS

Proteins are high molecular weight polymers of amino acids. Amino acids are the alphabet of protein chemistry. They are joined together through a peptide linkage to produce long chains that coil or bend into shapes that are characteristic for a particular protein. The molecular weights of proteins may range from about 20,000 to more than 1 million. There are approximately 20 α-amino acids commonly included in the structure of proteins. Amino acids have an asymmetric carbon atom and, therefore, are optically active, rotating the plane of polarized

light. Most of the α-amino acids occurring in nature have the L configuration. The α-amino acids have the following general formula, where
R represents a side chain of variable composition.

$$^+H_3N-\underset{\underset{R}{|}}{\overset{\overset{COO^-}{|}}{C}}-H$$

Amino acids are amphoteric; they can function as acids or bases.
The carboxyl group yields a hydrogen ion (H$^+$) while the amino group
acts as a hydrogen ion (proton) acceptor and becomes positively
charged. In addition to the α-amino and primary carboxyl groups, some
amino acids have acidic or basic groups on their side chains. Proteins,
because of the amphoteric characteristics of the amino acid side chains,
play important roles as buffers in food systems.

The side chains of amino acids, represented by R in the general
formula, vary in nature. Some of these groups are polar and some are
nonpolar. The nonpolar side chains generally contain only carbon and
hydrogen atoms (hydrocarbon) and are hydrophobic. The polar side
chains are hydrophilic. Some of them contain sulfur groups (—SH
or —S—S—). Others have hydroxyl groups (—OH), aromatic groups

(—⬡), carboxyl groups (—$\overset{\overset{O}{\|}}{C}$—OH), or amino groups (—NH$_2$). On

a protein molecule, the side chains are the primary groups that are
available to react with other molecules or with other parts of the same
protein molecule, since the α-amino and carboxyl groups are tied up
in linkage. Table 22.1 gives formulas for some of the amino acids
that are of particular importance in the reactions of food proteins.

Free amino acids contribute to the flavor of many foods. Some
amino acids, including glycine, DL-alanine, and D-tryptophan, elicit a
sweet taste. Yamaguchi *et al.* (1970) found glycine and alanine generally to be somewhat less sweet than sucrose but the sweet amino acids
have a complicated taste in addition to sweetness. The salt of an
amino acid, monosodium glutamate (MSG), is a widely used flavor
substance or flavor enhancer, often added to meat dishes and casseroles. A synergistic effect on flavor is produced when MSG and
5'-nucleotides are used together as flavor enhancers. (MSG and 5'-
nucleotides are discussed in Section 1.3.) Other L-amino acids have
flavor effects similar to that of MSG. These include L-homocysteic acid
and ibotenic acid (Yamaguchi *et al.*, 1971).

Amino acids participate in flavor as well as color development for
several food products through the Maillard reaction, that is described
in Section 10.3. For example, the Maillard reaction plays an important
role in the development of cooked meat flavor.

Table 22-1. Selected Amino Acids that Occur in Food Proteins

General Formula

$$\begin{array}{c} COO^- \\ | \\ + H_3N-C-H \\ | \\ R \end{array}$$

	Name	Abbreviation	R Group
Aliphatic Amino Acids			
	Glycine	Gly	—H
	Alanine	Ala	—CH_3
	Leucine	Leu	—CH_2—CH—CH_3
			$\qquad\quad$	CH_3
Hydroxyl-containing Amino Acids			
	Serine	Ser	—CH_2—OH
	Threonine	Thr	—CH—CH_3
			$\quad$	OH
Sulfur-containing Amino Acids			
	Cysteine	Cys	—CH_2—SH
	Cystine		—CH_2—S
			—CH_2—S
Acidic Amino Acids			
	Aspartic acid	Asp	—CH_2—$\overset{O}{\overset{\|}{C}}$—$O^-$
	Glutamic acid	Glu	—CH_2—CH_2—$\overset{O}{\overset{\|}{C}}$—$O^-$
Basic Amino Acids			
	Lysine	Lys	—CH_2—CH_2—CH_2—CH_2—NH_3^+
	Histidine	His	—CH_2—C=CH
			$\qquad$ $\overset{+}{NH_2}N$
			$\qquad\quad$ CH
Aromatic Amino Acids			
	Phenylalanine	Phe	—CH_2— ⬡
	Tyrosine	Tyr	—CH_2— ⬡ —OH
Imino Acid			
	Proline	Pro	(Complete structure)
			CH_2—CH_2 $\quad$ O
			CH_2 $\quad$ CH—$\overset{\|}{C}$—O^-
			$\qquad$ N
			$\qquad$ H

Amino acids are linked together in proteins through the interaction of the amino group of one amino acid with the carboxyl group of another amino acid. This linkage is called a *peptide bond*.

$$\overset{\text{COO}^-}{\underset{\overset{|}{\text{R}}}{{}^+\text{H}_3\text{N}-\overset{|}{\text{C}}\text{H}}} \quad + \quad \overset{\text{COO}^-}{\underset{\overset{|}{\text{R}'}}{{}^+\text{H}_3\text{N}-\overset{|}{\text{C}}\text{H}}} \quad \rightarrow \quad \overset{\overset{\text{peptide bond}}{\overset{\text{O}}{\underset{}{\|}}}}{{}^+\text{H}_3\text{N}-\overset{|}{\underset{\overset{|}{\text{R}}}{\text{C}}\text{H}}-\overset{\text{COO}^-}{\underset{\overset{|}{\text{R}'}}{\text{C}-\text{NH}-\overset{|}{\text{C}}\text{H}}}} \quad + \quad \text{H}_2\text{O}$$

Amino acid   Amino acid   Dipeptide

The further sequential addition of amino acid residues to the dipeptide creates a polypeptide and finally a protein. The sequence of amino acids in each protein is unique and affects the overall shape of the molecule. The first protein for which the amino acid sequence was determined was the hormone, insulin. In 1954 this major feat was accomplished by Sanger and coworkers and the sequence published (Sanger, 1959). The amino acid sequence for a number of proteins has since been determined.

22.2

STRUCTURE OF PROTEINS

The amino acid sequence of a protein constitutes the primary structure of the molecule. A polypeptide chain consists of a string of amino acids joined in a peptide linkage with a free amino group at one end and a free carboxyl group at the other end. The backbone of this polypeptide chain is usually written in a zigzag manner rather than a straight line because of the angles formed by the bonds.

Each protein has a characteristic three-dimensional shape, called *conformation*. The $\overset{\overset{\text{O}}{\|}}{\text{C}}-\text{N}$ (peptide) bond places some restriction on the shape of the molecule since free rotation does not occur around this bond. As amino acids are joined together in peptides, the most flexible movement would be somewhat equivalent to a chain in which each link can move through a limited angle with respect to the next link (Montgomery *et al.*, 1974). The backbone encourages the polypeptide structure to coil in a random fashion. However, other properties of the chain tend to stabilize its structure in a more rigid form. Hydrogen bonds form between the $>$NH and the $>$C$=$O groups in the chain and hold the structure in a fixed position. A right-handed α-helix (originally proposed by Pauling and Corey) may form if the hydrogen bonds connect different parts of the same chain (intrachain). A pleated sheet may form when hydrogen bonds are interchain and polypeptides line up in a parallel fashion. This bonding of a polypeptide chain in a relatively fixed position, usually through hydrogen bonds, constitutes the secondary structure of a protein. The α-helix and pleated sheet conformations are shown in Figure 22–1. Intrachain hydrogen bonding can be seen in the helix and interchain bonding in the pleated sheet conformation. The R groups of the side chains extend out of the backbone structure.

A number of food proteins have helical shapes in at least part of their total structures. For example, the globin (protein) part of myoglobin, found in the red muscle of meat, is considered to be about 80 percent α-helix while the globulin, lysozyme, of egg white is about 35 percent α-helix (Paul and Palmer, 1972).

The tertiary level of protein structure results from folding of the polypeptide chains, often already formed into helices, as interactions occur between side chains of the various amino acid residues. As the chains fold, the nonpolar hydrocarbon side groups tend to be turned toward the interior of the molecule where they can form hydrophobic bonds with one another. The polar side chains tend to be oriented toward the outside of the molecule and give water-dispersible properties to proteins. The polar side chains are attracted to water molecules and form hydrogen bonds with them. They may also form hydrogen bonds with other parts of the molecule.

Some proteins are composed of aggregates of simple protein units. This level of organization is referred to as the *quaternary structure*. The hemoglobin molecule, for example, is composed of four polypeptide chains.

Most native proteins are either globular or rodlike in shape. Examples of globular food proteins, in addition to hemoglobin, are ovalbumin in egg white, β-lactoglobulin in milk, and myoglobin in red muscle meat. Examples of rodlike proteins include collagen in connective tissue and ovomucin in egg white (Paul and Palmer, 1972).

There are additional levels of organization of proteins in food materials. In animal and plant tissues many proteins are arranged in a specific manner within cells.

Figure 22.1

Basic conformations in protein structure.

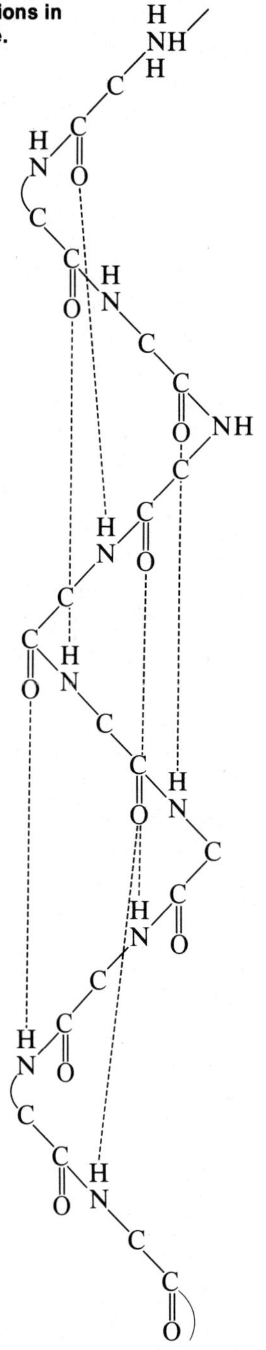

The α–helix Structure of Proteins

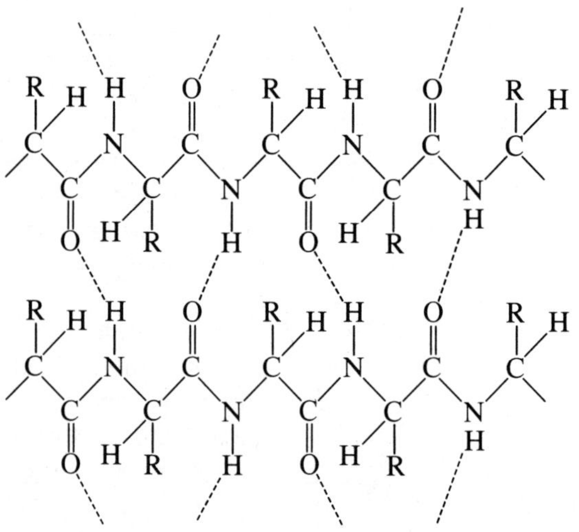

Parallel Pleated Sheet Conformation

PROPERTIES AND REACTIONS

Proteins have a great variety of chemically reactive groups in the side chains of the amino acid residues. In addition, many of the cross-linkages, particularly the hydrogen bonds that hold the protein molecule in its characteristic shape, are relatively weak. Therefore, proteins are subject to a wide range of chemical activity and are sensitive to environmental conditions.

AMPHOTERIC PROPERTIES AND ISOELECTRIC POINT

Proteins carry a charge. In an acid environment that contains excess hydrogen ion, the protein molecules have a net positive charge. In an alkaline medium they have a net negative charge. Between the extremes of acidity and alkalinity, there is a pH at which the net charge is zero because there is an equal number of positive and negative charges. This pH is called the *isoelectric point*. The following diagram illustrates this point.

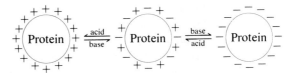

Isoelectric point

A protein is least soluble, and consequently is most easily precipitated, at its isoelectric point. This is especially true for a protein, such as casein in milk, that is poorly stabilized by water of hydration. For example, casein is easily precipitated from milk simply by adding acid until the pH reaches approximately 4.6. Acid-precipitated cottage cheese may be made in this manner. Various proteins differ greatly in their isoelectric points. However, many of them have isoelectric points close to neutrality (pH 7). The isoelectric points of selected proteins are shown in Table 22.2.

Most proteins exist in food products at pH values different from their isoelectric pH values. This causes most protein molecules to have a net charge that is either positive or negative, depending upon the particular isoelectric pH involved. All protein molecules of one kind, such as molecules of ovalbumin in egg white, are charged alike. Since like charges repel each other, the protein dispersion is stabilized (see Section 2.4).

Proteins are *amphoteric*. They can act both as proton donors and as proton acceptors. Proteins are, therefore, good buffers. The terminal amino group and basic groups on the side chains, such as the amino group of lysine, act as proton acceptors when acid is added to a protein dispersion. The terminal carboxyl group and acidic groups on the side

Table 22.2 Isoelectric Points of Selected Proteins

Protein	Source	Isoelectric point pH
Ovalbumin	Chicken eggs	4.55–4.90
Hemoglobin, reduced	Horse blood	6.79–6.83
Hemoglobin, oxy-	Horse blood	6.7
Lactoglobulin	Cow's milk	4.5–5.5
Trypsin	Beef pancreas	5.0–8.0
Casein	Cow's milk	4.6
Gelatin	Calf's skin	4.8–4.85
Gliadin	Wheat flour	6.5
Myosin	Cow muscle	6.2–6.6

Source: From Orten and Neuhaus, 1970.

chains, such as the carboxyl groups on glutamic and aspartic acid, act as proton donors to combine with base when it is added. Proteins thus resist a change in pH over a certain characteristic pH range.

SOLUBILITY

Proteins vary greatly in solubility. The solubility or stability of a protein dispersion is influenced by pH and by the types of ions and small molecules present. Simple proteins, those composed primarily of amino acids, have been classified on the basis of solubility. Albumins, such as ovalbumin in egg white and lactalbumin in milk, are soluble in water. Globulins, such as myosin in meat and edestin in rye, are soluble in dilute salt solutions. Prolamines are soluble in 70 percent alcohol. Examples of these proteins include gliadin of wheat and zein of corn. Glutelins, that include glutenin of wheat and hordenin of barley, are soluble in dilute acid or alkali. Some proteins, such as collagen and elastin of connective tissues and keratin of hair, are insoluble in all ordinary solvents.

Conjugated or compound proteins, that contain other components in addition to amino acids, have variable solubilities. This group of proteins includes glycoproteins, containing carbohydrate; lipoproteins, containing lipids; phosphoproteins, with phosphorus; and metalloproteins, with metals such as iron and zinc.

DENATURATION

Alteration from the naturally ordered conformation of a protein molecule to a randomly structured molecule is called *denaturation* (Orten and Neuhaus, 1970). Most proteins are sensitive to changes in pH, ion concentration, and temperature. The highly ordered structure of a native protein is easily disrupted as weak cross-linkages are broken. The polypeptide chains may unfold and the helix become disordered. The process of denaturation is illustrated in Figure 22.2. Denaturation does not include breaking of the peptide linkage in a hydrolysis process. Hydrolysis of proteins, except when carried out by enzymes, requires extreme conditions of heat and acidity or alkalinity.

Figure 22.2

**The process of dena-
turation involves change
from an ordered struc-
ture to a more random
state.**

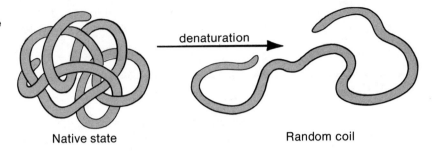

Native state   Random coil

Denaturation is not a very precise term. It has sometimes been used to describe primarily the relatively mild changes that occur with slight uncoiling of the protein structure. Additional changes may also occur as the conditions causing denaturation persist. Other terms have been used to describe the later stages of the process. Coagulation and curdling are two of these terms. For example, when a custard mixture containing egg and milk is heated, the first stage of the process undoubtedly involves mild alterations in the structure or shape of the egg proteins, that could be called denaturation. These changes are followed by additional association reactions between denatured protein molecules, producing gelation or coagulation. If heating of the custard is further continued, curdling occurs. Because of imprecise terminology in this area, it is necessary to carefully consider each of these terms as they are used by various authors to make sure that the meaning is clear (Paul and Palmer, 1972).

Many treatments to which food products are subjected in processing and preparation may cause denaturation of proteins. In addition to heating, proteins are denatured by surface forces created in mechanical beating, by alteration of pH, and by changing concentrations of salts. Freezing may produce some protein denaturation. Proteins participating in the Maillard reaction are also denatured. Enzymes which are proteins lose their biological activity upon denaturation.

Gelation or coagulation of proteins plays an important role in the development of characteristic properties for several food products. (For example, the gelation of egg proteins in the preparation of baked custards is discussed in Section 23.5.) The proteins of meat, fish, and poultry are coagulated or gelled when subjected to heat in usual preparation procedures. Coagulation of wheat proteins occurs during the baking of bread and contributes substantially to the structure of the loaf. In each of these products, denaturation of proteins has been followed by crossbonding between unfolded peptide chains, producing a somewhat rigid structure. (The general structure of gels is discussed in Section 17.4.) Many proteins contain polar groups that are attracted to water, thus giving these molecules considerable water binding capacity. Coagulated proteins may still bind considerable amounts of water and hold it in a gel structure, as in baked custards. However, if over-coagulation occurs, as in an overbaked custard, the strands of protein shrink and squeeze out some water. The leaking of liquid from a gel is called *syneresis*.

SUMMARY

Proteins are important components of foods because of both their nutritional value and their functional properties. They function in food preparation as structural agents, gel formers, emulsifiers, foaming agents, enzymes, and water-binding agents. Their ability to coagulate on heating and participate in gelation extends their useful properties. All animal and plant tissues contain proteins. Many isolated proteins are produced for use in food products.

Proteins are high molecular weight polymers of amino acids joined through a peptide linkage. There are approximately 20 α-amino acids included in proteins. Amino acids are amphoteric since they have both a carboxyl and an amino group. The side chains of amino acids vary in nature. Some groups, including hydroxyl, carboxyl, and amino, are polar. Others, including hydrocarbon chains, are nonpolar.

The sequence of amino acids in a polypeptide or protein is unique and affects the overall shape of the molecule. The amino acid sequence constitutes the primary structure of a protein. The coiling of the long chain, held in a more rigid position by weak bonds (chiefly hydrogen bonds), constitutes the secondary structure. A right-handed α-helix and a pleated sheet are common types of secondary structure resulting from bonding intra- or intermolecularly, respectively. The tertiary level of protein structure results from folding of the polypeptide chains as interactions occur between side chains of the amino acid residues. Nonpolar groups tend to be oriented toward the interior of the molecule and polar groups on the outside. The quaternary structure of proteins results from aggregation of simple protein units to form larger molecules. Most proteins are either globular or rodlike in shape.

Proteins have a variety of chemically reactive groups in the side chains of the amino acid residues. Many of the cross-linkages that hold the molecule in a fixed position are relatively weak and easily broken. Therefore, proteins are subject to a wide range of chemical activity.

Proteins carry a net positive charge in an acid environment and a net negative charge in an alkaline medium. Between these extremes there is a pH at which the net charge is zero. This pH is called the isoelectric point. A protein is least soluble and most easily precipitated at its isoelectric point. Most proteins are present in foods at pH values other than their isoelectric points and are stabilized by the resulting like charges. Proteins are amphoteric; they can act either as proton donors or proton acceptors. They are, therefore, good buffers.

The solubility of proteins is influenced by pH and by the types of ions and small molecules present. Simple proteins have been classified on the basis of solubility. Albumins are soluble in water; globulins in dilute salt solutions; prolamines in 70 percent alcohol; and glutelins in dilute acid or alkali. Conjugated or compound proteins contain other components in addition to amino acids. This group includes glycoproteins, lipoproteins, and phosphoproteins.

Alteration from the naturally ordered conformation of a protein molecule to a randomly structured molecule is called denaturation. Denaturation generally includes relatively mild changes in the protein molecule involving unfolding of the polypeptide chain and loss of biological activity. It does not include breaking of the peptide linkage in hydrolysis. Denaturation is not a very precise term. Distinction should be made between denaturation, coagulation, curdling, etc. Gelation occurs after denaturation and is characterized by crossbonding between unfolded peptide chains.

Many treatments to which food products are subjected in processing and preparation may cause denaturation of proteins. These include heating, surface forces created by mechanical beating, the Maillard reaction, freezing, alteration of pH, and changing concentrations of salts.

STUDY QUESTIONS

Amino acids are building blocks for proteins.

1. Write a formula that will represent any α-amino acid.
2. Write chemical structures for a sulfur-containing amino acid; a hydroxyl-containing amino acid; an aromatic amino acid; an amino acid with two carboxyl groups; an amino acid with two amino groups; and an amino acid with a hydrocarbon side chain.
3. Write the chemical structure for a peptide combining at least three amino acids.
4. Describe primary, secondary, and tertiary structure for protein molecules generally.
5. Give several examples of proteins found in foods.

Proteins have characteristic properties.

6. From the following list of characteristics of chemical substances, identify those that are typical for proteins.

   Characteristics
   Amphoteric
   Forms a true solution
   Always contains carbon, hydrogen, oxygen and nitrogen
   Has a molecular weight less than 5000
   Contains fatty acids as the basic unit
   Is present in all biological cells
   Often contains sulfur

Soluble in fat
Macromolecule
Contains a monosaccharide as the basic building unit
Most stable at its isoelectric point
Forms a sol
May be denatured
Always contains iron or copper
Contains amino acids as the basic building units
Basic units are joined by a peptide linkage
Contains both acid and basic groups
Basic units are joined by an ester linkage
Proline is an example of one basic unit
May be ionized

Proteins are subject to certain changes in secondary or tertiary structure that are called denaturation.

7. Given a list of treatments or procedures, identify those that are likely to cause denaturation of the major proteins present. Also, describe treatments commonly used in food processing or preparation that are likely to cause the denaturation of proteins.

Treatments or procedures
  long heating at a relatively high temperature
  baking bread
  whipping a thickened gelatin sol
  adding raw pineapple to a gelatin mixture
  freezing mayonnaise
  adding rennin to milk
  poaching eggs
  roasting beef ribs to a medium rare stage
  whipping egg whites
  adding vinegar to milk

8. Distinguish between denaturation and coagulation or gelation. Of what significance is gelation to food preparation?

REFERENCES

1. Montgomery, R., R. L. Dryer, T. W. Conway, and A. A. Spector. 1974. *Biochemistry*. St. Louis: Mosby.

2. Orten, J. M. and O. W. Neuhaus. 1970. *Biochemistry*, 8th edition. St. Louis: Mosby.

3. Paul, P. C. and H. H. Palmer. 1972. *Food Theory and Applications*. New York: Wiley.

4. Sanger, F. 1959. Chemistry of insulin. *Science* 129, 1340.

5. Yamaguchi, S., T. Yoshikawa, S. Ikeda, and T. Ninomiya. 1971. Measurement of the relative taste intensity of some L-α-Amino Acids and 5′-Nucleotides. *Journal of Food Science* 36, 846.

6. Yamaguchi, S., T. Yoshikawa, S. Ikeda, and T. Ninomiya. 1970. Studies on the taste of some sweet substances. Part I. Measurement of the relative sweetness. *Agricultural and Biological Chemistry* 34, 181.

CHAPTER 23

EGGS AND EGG PRODUCTS

The natural function of the egg is to provide for the protection and development of the chick embryo. However, eggs have also been used as a staple item in the diet of many peoples for thousands of years. They are now employed in food preparation for many purposes quite different from their natural function. Egg whites, yolks, or whole eggs act as structural components, emulsifiers, foaming agents, clarifying agents, binders, coatings, and gel formers. They also provide a source of high quality dietary protein and other essential nutrients, including iron. (Egg foams are considered in Chapter 19, emulsions in Chapter 18 and the basic structures of gels, foams, and emulsions are included in Chapter 17.)

23.1

STRUCTURE

The egg has a variety of distinct parts that are diagrammed in Figure 23.1. The contents are held within the shell that consists largely of calcium carbonate (94 percent) with some magnesium carbonate and calcium phosphate deposited on an organic matrix. The organic matter is primarily protein. The shell contains pores for exchange of gases. A protein layer of keratin partially seals the pores but does allow loss of carbon dioxide and moisture from the egg contents. The shell makes up from 9 to 12 percent of the total egg weight. Two shell membranes, the outer and the inner, are found immediately within the shell. These are thin keratinlike membranes that act as one of the egg's chief defenses against bacterial invasion. An air space (cell) develops in the large end of the egg in the form of a bubble separating the two shell membranes (Stadelman and Cotterill, 1973).

The white or albumen portion of the egg constitutes about 60 percent of the total egg weight. The white occurs in four concentric layers in most chicken eggs. Immediately inside the inner shell membrane is a layer of white of low viscosity. This envelops a second layer of firm

Figure 23.1

The parts of an egg. (Courtesy U. S. Department of Agriculture.)

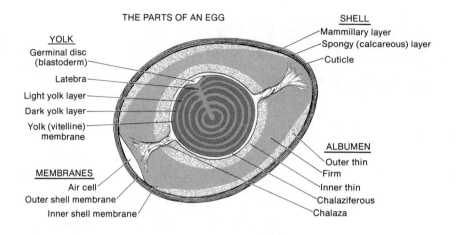

THE PARTS OF AN EGG

white. Inside this is a third layer consisting of low-viscosity white. A *chalaziferous* or inner firm layer of white then envelops the yolk membrane (*vitelline* membrane) and is continuous with the chalazae that anchor the yolk in position. The proportion of firm and thin layers varies widely in different eggs.

The vitelline membrane is composed of several layers that are high in protein (87 percent). The chalaziferous layer on the outside gives support. In fact, the strength of the vitelline membrane appears to be related to the density or quantity of the chalaziferous layer (Fromm, 1964). The vitelline membrane may play some role in controlling diffusion of water from the white to the yolk. However, the structure of the yolk is apparently more important than this membrane in imposing barriers to diffusion (Carter, 1968).

The yolk is made up of concentric layers of light and dark. It comprises from 30 to 33 percent of the weight of the whole egg.

23.2

COMPOSITION

The white and the yolk of the egg are very different from each other in chemical composition, as indicated in Table 23.1. The composition of whole egg, consisting of approximately two-thirds white and one-third yolk, reflects these proportions.

EGG WHITE

Egg white is mainly water and protein with a small amount of sugar and inorganic ions. It is relatively easy, from a biochemical standpoint, to extract the proteins from egg white. They are mostly soluble and less complex than are the proteins of the yolk. Therefore, some of them have been studied in great detail. Most of the proteins of the white are typical globular proteins and many of them are combined with carbohydrate to produce glycoproteins. Egg white contains as many as 40 different proteins. Only about ten have been studied extensively, either because they are present in relatively large amounts or they have particularly interesting properties (Whitaker and Tannenbaum, 1977).

The thick (firm) white of egg is obviously different from the thin (low-viscosity) white. It is very viscous and appears to be structured in layers. These layers are sheared off during the mechanical beating of egg white and coil to give the appearance of fibers. Apparently the quantity of the protein, ovomucin, is the only chemical difference between the thick and the thin egg white. The thick white contains approximately four times as much ovomucin as does the thin white (Feeney *et al.*, 1952; Baliga *et al.*, 1971).

Ovomucin is different from most of the other proteins in egg white. It is a very large glycoprotein containing sulfate esters. It is composed of subunits that are linked together to give a filamentous and fiberlike structure. When eggs are fresh the thick white is firm. As the egg deteriorates its thick white loses firmness. Ovomucin is apparently involved in a major way in the thinning of thick egg whites. Several mechanisms have been proposed to explain the role of ovomucin in the deterioration of the egg. These suggested mechanisms have involved 1. the complexing of ovomucin with another egg white protein, lysozyme; 2. the dissociation of a complex between ovomucin and lysozyme; 3. a breaking of disulfide bonds; 4. a loss of carbohydrate from the ovomucin molecule; and 5. the interaction of glucose with the protein. Although data have been collected to support each of these proposed mechanisms, they are not yet sufficient to determine the exact role of ovomucin in the thinning process (Whitaker and Tannenbaum, 1977). Ovomucin makes up approximately 3.5 percent of the total egg white solids.

Table 23.1 Composition of Albumen, Yolk, and Whole Egg

Component	Water* (%)	Protein (%)	Lipid (%)	Carbohydrate (%)	Ash (%)
Albumen	87.6	9.7–10.6	0.03	0.4–0.9	0.5–0.6
Yolk	51.1	15.7–16.6	31.8–35.5	0.2–1.0	1.1
Whole egg	73.7	12.8–13.4	10.5–11.8	0.3–1.0	0.8–1.0

Source: From Stadelman and Cotterill, 1973.
* Watt and Merrill, 1963.

Lysozyme is a low molecular weight egg white protein enzyme that has been extensively studied and characterized. At least 2600 articles about this protein were published during the period from 1922 to 1972. Its structure has been determined. Lysozyme hydrolyzes a polysaccharide found in the cell walls of certain bacteria. It, therefore, has antibacterial properties that may protect the developing chick. It is a globulin and makes up about 3.4 percent of the total egg white solids.

Ovalbumin accounts for about 54 percent of the total solids in egg white. It, too, has been extensively investigated. It is a nearly spherical globular protein containing phosphorus and a carbohydrate group. This protein is found in various forms that differ in phosphorus content. It is very susceptible to denaturation.

A protein in egg white that has the ability to bind iron was first named *conalbumin*. It is now called *ovotransferrin,* however, because of its similarity to other iron-carrying proteins. This protein inhibits bacterial growth for those bacteria requiring iron. When the protein is complexed with iron, it becomes more stable to heat than it is in the uncomplexed form. Ovotransferrin is more heat sensitive than is ovalbumin but less susceptible to denaturation by mechanical forces (Stadelman and Cotterill, 1973). It comprises approximately 12 percent of the egg white solids.

Ovomucoid is a heat-resistant glycoprotein. It has the ability to inhibit the activity of the proteinase, trypsin. This protein makes up about 11 percent of the egg white proteins. Other proteinase inhibitor proteins are also present in egg white.

Avidin is a protein present in egg white in only minor quantity (0.5 percent). It is of interest from a nutritional standpoint since it binds the vitamin, biotin. It has been called the egg white *injury factor* because of the vitamin deficiency syndrome produced by feeding large amounts of raw egg whites to experimental animals. This type of injury is not produced from cooked egg white because avidin is denatured by heat.

EGG YOLK

Essentially all of the lipid of whole egg is present in the yolk. The fatty materials make up about one-third of the weight of the fresh yolk and include triglycerides (65.5 percent), phospholipids (28.3 percent), and cholesterol (5.2 percent). The fatty acid composition of yolk lipid is influenced by the type of fat in the diets of the hens. The linoleic acid content of yolk increases when the level of polyunsaturated fatty acids in the hen's diet is raised (Stadelman and Cotterill, 1973).

Egg yolk is a very complex system containing particles suspended in a protein solution. Particulate granules can be easily separated from the plasma solution by high-speed processing in a centrifuge. The granules contain about 70 percent α- and β-lipovitellins (high-density lipoproteins); 16 percent phosvitin (a nonlipid phosphoprotein); and 12 percent low-density lipoproteins. Plasma is composed of about 66 percent low-density lipoproteins and 11 percent lipid-free globular proteins called *livetins* (Stadelman and Cotterhill, 1973).

The lipovitellins in the granules of egg yolk contain about 20 percent lipid and small amounts of phosphorus. The lipid includes approximately 60 percent phospholipids and 40 percent triglycerides. The low-density lipoproteins in the plasma contain large amounts of lipid (80–90 percent), made up of 25–28 percent phospholipids and about 65 percent triglycerides. The low-density lipoprotein fraction appears to be present in the egg yolk in the form of tiny micelles. These micelles have a core of triglycerides with phospholipids and proteins radiating toward the surface of the micelle, giving it water-soluble properties. Such a complex system as is found in egg yolk is difficult to study and offers a great challenge to the biochemist.

Proteins have been separated from whole egg and the patterns compared to those obtained from egg yolk and egg white analyzed separately. Mixing yolk with white appears to produce a change in some of the protein components. The main effect is conversion of some insoluble lipoproteins to a more soluble form (Parkinson, 1972).

23.3

EGG QUALITY

Egg quality is compounded of those characteristics of an egg that affect its acceptability to the consumer (Carter, 1968). The U. S. Department of Agriculture (USDA) has developed grade standards which define various quality factors for fresh chicken eggs. The condition of the white and yolk, the size of the air cell, the soundness of the shell, and the cleanliness of the egg are specified in the grade standards. In addition to grading in terms of quality factors, eggs are classified according to weight (or size) into relatively narrow weight classes. The minimum weight in each class is specified. The weight classes of eggs are given in Table 23.2.

Grade standards provide a uniform yardstick against which to measure differences in quality that are important to the consumer. The

Table 23.2 U. S. Weight Classes for Consumer Grades for Shell Eggs

Size or Weight Class	Minimum Net Weight per Dozen (Ounces)	Minimum Weight for Individual Eggs at Rate per Dozen (Ounces)
Jumbo	30	29
Extra Large	27	26
Large	24	23
Medium	21	20
Small	18	17
Peewee	15	—

Source: U. S. Department of Agriculture, 1968.

marketing of eggs is facilitated by grading. As the grade of eggs decreases, a number of desirable characteristics have been shown to change (Dawson *et al.,* 1956). The flavor of soft cooked eggs, baked custard, and angel cake was less desirable when made with lower grades of eggs, particularly those graded B and C. Angel cake volume, tenderness, and acceptability decreased with use of lower grade eggs.

The grading of eggs involves the assessment of both exterior and interior quality. The interior quality of the egg is checked by candling. *Candling,* generally carried out in mass operations with automated equipment, is the process of viewing the egg under a bright light while it is being rotated so that the internal contents are spinning within the shell. The appearance of the yolk as the egg is twirled is one of the best indicators of candled quality. The movement of the yolk is dependent on the condition of the egg white. Thick white permits only limited movement of the yolk and an indistinct shadow is seen in bright light. The size and shape of yolk, germ development, and blood spots and size of air cell are also evaluated during candling (U. S. Department of Agriculture, 1968).

Table 23.3. **Summary of United States Standards for Quality of Individual Shell Eggs**

Quality factor	Specifications for Each Quality Factor			
	AA Quality	**A Quality**	**B Quality**	**C Quality**
Shell	Clean, unbroken; practically normal	Clean, unbroken; practically normal	Clean to very slightly stained, unbroken; may be slightly abnormal	Clean to moderately stained; unbroken; may be abnormal
Air cell	⅛ inch or less in depth	3/16 inch or less in depth	3/8 inch or less in depth	May be over 3/8 inch in depth; may be free or bubbly
White	Clean, firm. (72 Haugh units or higher)	Clear; may be reasonably firm (60 to 72 Haugh units)	Clear; may be slightly weak (31 to 60 Haugh units)	May be weak and watery; small blood clots or spots may be present* (less than 31 Haugh units)
Yolk	Outline slightly defined; practically free from defects	Outline may be fairly well defined; practically free from defects	Outline may be well defined; may be slightly enlarged and flattened; may show definite but not serious defects	Outline may be plainly visible; may be enlarged and flattened; may show clearly visible germ development but no blood; may show other serious defects

Source: U.S. Department of Agriculture, 1968.
* If they are small (aggregating not more than ⅛ inch in diameter).

On the basis of candled appearance, eggs are graded as AA, A, B, and C quality. A summary of the standards applied in the grading process is given in Table 23.3. Egg grading subjectively classifies eggs into categories. The quality factors do not break into sharp divisions but follow a linear or curvilinear change. Egg quality is not stable, even under the most favorable conditions, and deteriorates from the time the egg is laid until it is consumed. Figure 23.2 illustrates graphically the continuously changing nature of egg quality and the range of quality within any one grade. Figure 23.3 shows a range of quality in graded eggs broken out of the shell.

Indices of albumen and yolk quality are available for the egg broken out of the shell. These have been shown to correlate with candled quality in some cases but the correlation is not always significant (Sauter *et al.*, 1953; Baker and Vadehra, 1970). Some indices in broken-out eggs are used in a flock certification grading program. It has been shown that a small sample of eggs randomly selected from flocks of uniform age managed under similar conditions accurately reflects the average quality of the lot. The most widely used measure of albumen condition in the broken-out egg is the *Haugh unit*. This quality determination consists of measuring the height of the thick albumen. A micrometer or height gauge is used as shown in Figure 23.4. This particular instrument gives direct reading in Haugh units. The Haugh unit relates egg weight and height of thick albumen in a mathematical formula, with higher values indicating better quality. An interior egg quality calculator has been developed for rapid conversion of egg weight and albumen height data to Haugh units (Stadelman and Cotterill, 1973). The *albumen index* is the ratio of thick albumen height to mean width. A

Figure 23.2

There is a range of quality within official egg grades. (Courtesy U. S. Department of Agriculture.)

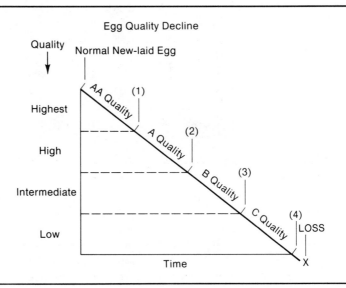

Figure 23.3

Albumen and yolk quality may vary over a limited range in graded eggs. (Courtesy U. S. Department of Agriculture.)

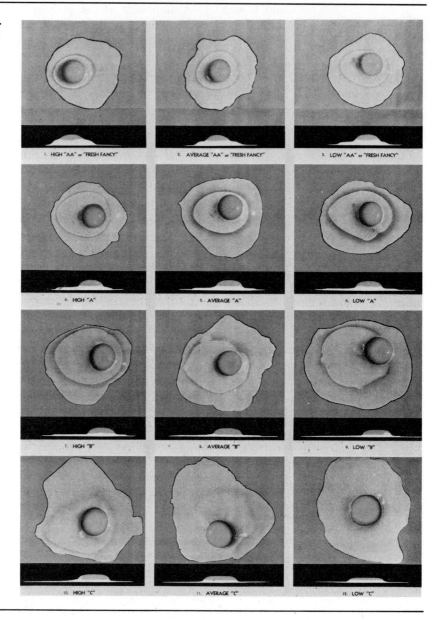

1. HIGH "AA" or "FRESH FANCY"   2. AVERAGE "AA" or "FRESH FANCY"   3. LOW "AA" or "FRESH FANCY"

4. HIGH "A"   5. AVERAGE "A"   6. LOW "A"

7. HIGH "B"   8. AVERAGE "B"   9. LOW "B"

10. HIGH "C"   11. AVERAGE "C"   12. LOW "C"

yolk index is expressed as the ratio of the height to the width of the yolk. It describes the degree of flattening of the yolk, that tends to occur as the vitelline membrane weakens.

Functional properties of egg white offer another check on egg quality. Whipping and angel cake performance tests have been outlined to measure the functional performance of egg white (Stadelman and Cot-

Figure 23.4

Break-out examination of eggs using a microm- eter that gives direct reading in Haugh units. (Courtesy U. S. Depart- ment of Agriculture.)

terill, 1973). (The whipping properties of egg white are discussed in Section 19.1.)

CHANGES IN EGG QUALITY

Changes in the physical characteristics of eggs begin as soon as the eggs are laid. The extent of these changes is affected by the conditions under which the eggs are held. The first change that takes place in the egg after it is laid is loss of weight. This is due chiefly to evaporation of moisture through the shell. There is also a loss of gases such as carbon dioxide. As the egg cools from a laying temperature of approximately 40°C (104°F), contraction of the egg contents produces an air cell be- tween the inner and outer shell membranes at the blunt end of the egg. This air cell increases in size as moisture is lost from the egg. As carbon dioxide is lost, the pH of the white increases. The pH of egg white in freshly laid eggs is approximately 7.6. After a few days of storage without shell treatment it may be anywhere from 8.9 to 9.4. The change occurs more rapidly at higher storage temperatures. The pH of the yolk is 5.9–6.1 in freshly laid eggs and rises to about 6.8 after storage (Paul and Palmer, 1972).

An important change affecting the quality of eggs is the gradual thinning of the thick white. This characteristic is expressed in decreasing values for Haugh units and albumen index. The albumen spreads to cover a relatively wide area when the egg is broken out of the shell. Ovomucin appears to be an important participant in the thinning process and possible roles for this protein are discussed in Section 23.2

The broken-out egg yolk tends to flatten as the egg is stored. The vitelline membrane weakens and stretches. The network of fibers on the surface of the membrane, that are apparently part of the chalaziferous layer, tend to dissipate as the pH of the albumen rises (Fromm, 1967).

23.4

PROCESSING AND PRESERVATION

In the handling of shell eggs, commercial practices are aimed at minimizing the changes in egg characteristics that affect quality. Storage temperature, air movement, and relative humidity are controlled. Fresh eggs are commonly treated by spraying or dipping them in mineral oil before they are placed in cold storage in order to decrease the permeability of the shell. Retention of moisture and carbon dioxide is increased by oiling. Preventing loss of carbon dioxide aids in maintaining a low pH and initial albumen quality. Meehan *et al.* (1962) reported that oiling on the day of lay maintained a relatively low pH that protected the albumen proteins from damage when the eggs were stored at 35°C (95°F) for 7 days or 23.9°C (75°F) for two to three weeks. Damage to the egg whites was evidenced by decreased volume of angel cakes.

It is generally desirable to oil eggs immediately after lay. However, oiling does not change the requirement for low storage temperatures in the maintenance of quality characteristics. Heath and Owens (1978) found that the temperature at which eggs were held prior to oiling was important in maintaining egg quality over a four-week storage period. Untreated eggs held at 12°C (53.6°F) overnight remained grade AA while those held overnight at 22°C (71.6°F) and 32°C (89.6°F) were grade A by the end of this holding period. The storage temperature after oiling was the major factor affecting grade, however. While eggs stored at 12°C in all cases remained grade A for the entire four weeks of storage, regardless of preoiling holding conditions, those stored at 22° and 32°C frequently fell below grade A. The least deterioration occurred in those eggs that were held at 12°C immediately after lay, oiled and then stored at 12°C.

PASTEURIZATION OF EGG PRODUCTS

Salmonellosis is an important enteric disease affecting man in all parts of the world. The *Salmonellae* microorganisms responsible for this disease are commonly harbored in poultry and transmitted to eggs. Eggs and egg products, particularly frozen and dried eggs, have been implicated in a number of salmonellosis outbreaks. Because of the health hazard created by salmonella-infected eggs, pasteurization of egg products produced in bulk has become mandatory for all U. S. egg-breaking plants that participate in the USDA inspection program.

Successful pasteurization of egg products must fulfill two objectives. It must destroy pathogenic microorganisms while still maintaining the functional properties of the eggs. Functional properties include whipping characteristics, performance in heated food products, and emulsifying ability. Laboratory tests designed to measure the functional properties of pasteurized egg whites include the beating rate, meringue stability, and angel cake volume. Similar tests indicate the functional quality of pasteurized whole egg, using layer or sponge cakes in this case rather than angel cakes. The stability of mayonnaise and salad dressings gives an indication of the emulsifying properties of pasteurized egg yolk. The gel structure of baked custards may reflect the coagulating performance of pasteurized whole egg. The impairment of performance in pasteurized egg products is due chiefly to denaturation of the egg proteins. Some of the proteins are more sensitive to heat than are others.

The USDA requires that liquid whole egg be heated to at least 60°C (140°F) in the pasteurization process and be held at this temperature for no less than $3\frac{1}{2}$ minutes. A number of researchers have reported on the performance of pasteurized whole egg in custards and cakes. Denaturation of whole egg proteins, as indicated by change in viscosity, takes place between 56°–66°C (between 133°–151°F). Coagulation occurs rapidly above 73.3°C (164°F) (Payawal *et al.,* 1946). Hanson *et al.* (1947) found that pasteurization at temperatures below 71°C (160°F) had no harmful effect on custard-making properties. Sponge cakes made from whole egg pasteurized in the range of 60°–68.3°C (140°–155°F) had volumes approximately 4 percent less than those made from unpasteurized eggs. Sugihara *et al.* (1966) reported that the performance quality of pasteurized whole egg, as evaluated in layer cakes and sponge cakes, was not significantly damaged until pasteurization temperatures exceeded 63.3°C (146°F) for $3\frac{1}{2}$ minutes or 73.9°C (165°F) for 2–3 seconds. However, pasteurized frozen whole eggs gave true sponge cakes of lower volume than did frozen whole eggs that were not pasteurized. Homogenization of whole eggs before freezing decreased the viscosity of the thawed product and restored the volume loss in sponge cakes. Pasteurization of whole egg at the temperature required for microbiological safety thus does not appear to significantly affect the functional properties of this product.

Egg whites are generally more sensitive to heating than are whole egg mixtures and whipping properties are damaged if the pasteurization temperature is too high. The sensitivity is due primarily to the instability of the proteins *conalbumin* (now called *ovotransferrin*), ovalbumin, and lysozyme to heat. Lineweaver *et al.* (1967) estimated that heating egg white at pH 9 for $3\frac{1}{2}$ minutes at 62°C (143.6°F) will alter from 3 to 5 percent of the ovalbumin, from 90 to 100 percent of the lysozyme, and more than 50 percent of the ovotransferrin. Lowering the pH to 7 reduces greatly the amount of ovalbumin and lysozyme altered. Formation of a metal complex with ovotransferrin greatly reduces the heat-induced alteration of this protein at pH 7. Therefore, lowering the pH and forming a metal (such as aluminum) salt of ovotransferrin increases the stability of egg white to pasteurization by at least twentyfold. Only a slight effect on functional properties of egg white, particularly whipping ability, occurs when it is pasteurized under these conditions at 60°–62°C (140°–143.6°F) for $3\frac{1}{2}$ minutes. A patented commercial pasteurization method uses lactic acid to lower the pH and aluminum sulfate for salt formation with ovotransferrin (Stadelman and Cotterill, 1973).

Other satisfactory methods for pasteurizing egg white may be used. Heating in combination with added hydrogen peroxide allows the necessary microbial destruction at lower temperatures than when hydrogen peroxide is not present. The enzyme catalase is then added to destroy the remaining peroxide. A method involving heating under a vacuum permits lower temperatures to achieve the same destruction of microorganisms that occurs at higher temperatures. Egg whites that are to be dried may be pasteurized at a low temperature if drying is followed by storage for several hours at elevated temperatures (Stadelman and Cotterill, 1973).

Salmonellae organisms are more heat-resistant in egg yolk than in whole egg because of the somewhat lower pH and higher solids content of yolk. A higher temperature must, therefore, be used for the pasteurization of yolk than of whole egg. Addition of sugar or salt in yolks that are to be frozen or dried, increases the thermal resistance of microorganisms in egg yolk. Sugar gives protection to yolk proteins against denaturation, however. The emulsifying properties of salted egg yolk are little affected by pasteurization at 62.2°C–64.4°C (144°–148°F) (Palmer *et al.,* 1969a). Pasteurized egg yolks perform well in doughnuts. Sugared yolks, pasteurized at temperatures from 60° to 64.4°C (from 140° to 148°F), produce satisfactory sponge and layer cakes (Palmer *et al.,* 1969b; Stadelman and Cotterill, 1973).

FREEZING EGG PRODUCTS

Frozen egg products include egg white, yolk, and whole egg as well as a variety of blends of yolk and white. These products are generally marketed as ingredients for use in other foods. Commercially frozen egg products are pasteurized before they are frozen.

Egg white may be frozen with only minor changes. Some thinning of thick white may occur but functional properties are not impaired by the freezing process. Gelation occurs in yolks that have been frozen and stored below -6°C (21.2°F), due to aggregation of low density lipoproteins. The gelation may be controlled by the addition of about one tablespoon of sugar or one teaspoon of salt per cup of yolks. (The freezing of raw eggs is discussed in Section 7.6.)

Cooked egg yolk may be satisfactorily frozen by conventional methods. However, cooked egg white becomes tough and rubbery and water separates from the coagulated mass. This damage is apparently caused by large ice crystal formation during slow freezing. Freezing cooked whites very rapidly at extremely low temperatures improves the quality of the thawed product (Stadelman and Cotterill, 1973).

DEHYDRATION OF EGGS

Dehydration of eggs has been carried out commercially in the United States since the late 1800s. Dried egg products are used in a wide variety of foods, including cake mixes, mayonnaise, salad dressing, noodles, candies, and all types of bakery products. Technological improvements through the years have increased the quality of dried egg products. The use of egg solids has become well established in the food manufacturing industry. They are much less widely used at the consumer level. Tuttle *et al.* (1972) evaluated the acceptability by consumer panels of scrambled eggs prepared from fresh eggs and from three commercial spray-dried whole egg products. Although scrambled fresh eggs were preferred, a dried whole egg product containing nonfat milk solids and vegetable oil was almost as acceptable. The use of dried egg products in volume food service was suggested by Janek and Downs (1969). However, a panel gave higher flavor scores to scrambled eggs prepared from frozen and freeze-dried eggs than to those prepared from foam-spray-dried eggs.

A series of papers has been published comparing functional properties of foam-spray-dried, freeze-dried, and spray-dried egg products. These reports indicate that frozen, freeze-dried, and spray-dried albumen possess similar foaming abilities. Foam-spray-dried albumen gives a slightly less stable foam (Zabik and Brown, 1969). Similar emulsion stabilities were shown by frozen, foam-spray-dried, and freeze-dried whole eggs. Spray-dried whole egg emulsions were less stable. Frozen egg yolks exhibited greater emulsifying abilities than any of the dehydrated yolks (Zabik, 1969). Cream puffs prepared from foam-spray-dried eggs were somewhat tougher than those prepared from frozen, freeze-dried, or spray-dried eggs. However, all cream puffs scored fair to good in shape, exterior appearance, shell thickness, interior appearance, interior moistness, and flavor (Funk *et al.,* 1970b). Yellow layer cakes of similar quality were prepared from frozen, foam-spray-dried, freeze-dried, and spray-dried whole eggs (Funk *et al.,* 1970a).

In the drying of eggs, moisture is removed by evaporation until only the solid portion with a small quantity of moisture remains. Egg white is essentially fat free and may be dried without major changes in the physical structure of its components. Egg yolk, on the other hand, contains lipid substances dispersed in complex micelles. The drying process, in removing water, apparently irreversibly changes the structure of the low-density lipoproteins of the yolk. Free lipid is released from these lipoproteins and the lipid has a foam-inhibiting effect when the dried eggs are reconstituted and whipped (Schultz *et al.*, 1968). When yolk and whole egg are dried with added carbohydrate, often corn syrup, the carbohydrate partially protects the lipoproteins from the irreversible structural change, probably by replacing, during the drying process, the water of hydration at its binding sites on the lipoproteins.

Dehydrated egg products are subject to deteriorative changes during storage. These include loss of solubility, decreased functionality, and the development of off-color and objectionable flavor. The presence of glucose in the egg, although in very small quantities, is responsible for many of these changes. The Maillard reaction, that begins with the interaction of glucose and the amino groups of proteins, eventually results in the formation of brownish-colored compounds as untreated egg products are stored. The interaction of glucose with a phospholipid (cephalin) in egg yolk may also contribute to the development of deteriorative changes in dried egg products.

Glucose must be removed from egg white prior to drying if the dried product is to be stable. The stability of yolk and whole egg products may also be improved by glucose removal. This may be accomplished by controlled fermentation of the glucose, that converts the glucose to acid. A number of different bacterial cultures, including species of *Lactobacillus* as well as yeast, have been utilized in fermentation. An alternative procedure for glucose removal from dehydrated egg products employs the use of the enzyme glucose oxidase. This enzyme catalyzes the oxidation of glucose to gluconic acid, that does not participate in the Maillard reaction. Hydrogen peroxide is also a product of this reaction. An enzyme system was developed that included glucose oxidase and catalase, an enzyme that catalyzes the decomposition of hydrogen peroxide to water and oxygen (Stadelman and Cotterill, 1973).

$$C_6H_{12}O_6 + O_2 + H_2O \xrightarrow{\text{glucose oxidase}} C_6H_{12}O_7 + H_2O_2$$

Glucose   Gluconic   Hydrogen
                        acid   peroxide

$$2H_2O_2 \xrightarrow{\text{catalase}} 2H_2O + O_2$$

The net reaction uses one-half mole of oxygen ($\frac{1}{2}O_2$) as each glucose molecule is oxidized to gluconic acid. In addition to its use in dehydrating egg products, this system has been used as an oxygen scavenger to remove small amounts of oxygen from a sealed product.

23.5

COAGULATION OF EGG PROTEINS

Egg proteins exhibit the ability to undergo sol-gel transformation. The proteins in the native egg are colloidally dispersed in a sol. When heat is applied, the pourable dispersion gradually becomes thicker and gel-like. In addition to heat, mechanical forces, salts, acids, and alkalies may bring about these changes. As the proteins become irreversibly insoluble, coagulation is said to occur. During the process of heating, egg white changes from a clear, transparent fluid to a white, opaque, solid mass as it coagulates. The proteins are denatured, unfolding from their original conformation, and then apparently form new cross-links joining the unfolded molecules together in a coagulated mass. The coagulation or gelation of egg proteins plays an important structural role in the preparation of a variety of egg dishes, custards, puddings, cakes, etc. It also contributes to the function of eggs as binding and coating agents. The time and temperature of heating and the presence of other ingredients influence the course of coagulation.

TEMPERATURE

Coagulation of egg proteins by heat generally does not occur instantaneously at a given temperature. It takes place over a period of time and the process is accelerated with rising temperature. At high temperatures it becomes almost instantaneous. Coagulation of undiluted egg white begins at about 62°C (144°F) and the mass ceases to flow when it reaches about 65°C (149°F). At 70°C (158°F) the coagulum is fairly firm, but tender. It becomes very firm or toughened at higher temperatures. Egg yolk begins to coagulate at 65°C (149°F) and ceases to flow when it reaches a temperature of about 70°C (158°F). Coagulation of both white and yolk is an endothermic process; that is, heat is absorbed as coagulation occurs. Overcoagulation and toughening of egg proteins results from too much heat, either from too high a temperature or too long a time at any temperature (Stadelman and Cotterill, 1973).

DILUTION

As egg proteins are diluted, the coagulation temperature rises. Therefore, the temperature at which custards, or other egg dishes containing added liquid, coagulate is dependent upon the concentration of egg solids in the mixture. The coagulum also becomes less firm as egg is diluted with liquid. When egg white is heated by microwaves the firmness of the coagulum decreases less with increasing dilution than it does when heated in a conventional oven at 163°C (325°F) (Baldwin *et al.*, 1967).

ADDITION OF SUGAR AND SALTS

The coagulation temperature of egg proteins is increased by the addition of sugar. Sugar has a protective effect on the protein structure, decreasing the rate of heat denaturation. The stiffness of the coagulum is also decreased by sugar.

Salts present in egg white contribute to its ability to coagulate. The salts in the milk that is commonly added to egg in the making of custard are also necessary for the production of the typical custard gel. The usual gelation does not occur when water is substituted for milk in the preparation of custard. A number of salts will promote coagulation. A balance of cation and anion activity is important in gelation. Addition of sodium chloride tends to promote the coagulation of egg proteins (Stadelman and Cotterill, 1973).

ACIDITY

Egg proteins generally tend to coagulate more readily as the pH is decreased from that of fresh eggs, although the effect on each protein depends upon the pH of its isoelectric point. Ovalbumin, the protein present in the egg in largest amount, has an isoelectric point of 4.6–4.8. A protein is least stable at its isoelectric pH and is thus more likely to precipitate or coagulate. Egg proteins such as ovalbumin tend to coagulate at lower temperatures when the pH is close to their isoelectric points. However, if enough acid is added to decrease the pH well below the isoelectric point, the coagulation temperature is not lowered. The addition of egg to acid-containing pie fillings, such as lemon, does not create practical problems in terms of the effect on egg protein coagulation. Adding acid to the water in which eggs are poached favors coagulation and improves the shape of the cooked eggs. Coagulated egg whites are more tender when exposed to microwaves or to heating if the albumen is acidified (Baldwin et al., 1967).

COOKING EGGS

Eggs are often cooked in the shell by immersing them in hot water. The length of cooking depends upon the desired consistency of the eggs, the temperature of the water, and the quantity of water used. The candled quality of an egg greatly influences the quality of the hard cooked product. Difficulty in peeling the shell from a hard cooked egg has been attributed to the maintenance of a low pH in the albumen (Meehan et al., 1961). The shell is not easily removed and pieces of cooked white adhere to the shell unless the pH of the white is 8.9 or higher. Eggs that are oiled immediately after laying and stored at low temperatures, maintaining a relatively low pH and high candled quality, tend to peel with difficulty when hard cooked. However, when eggs are hard cooked by placing them in boiling water and holding them at simmering temperature (85°C or 185°F) for 18 minutes they are easier to peel than when they are cooked by placing them in cold water, bringing the water to a boil, removing them from the heat and letting them stand for 25 minutes (Irmiter et al., 1970).

Irmiter et al. (1970) reported that eggs hard cooked by the boiling water method rated higher than those cooked by the cold water method. However, eggs tended to be underdone when cooked for 18 minutes by the boiling water method if they were taken from the refrigerator immediately prior to cooking or if a large number of eggs were cooked at one time.

The dark greenish color that sometimes forms on the surface of the yolk of a hard cooked egg is due to the formation of ferrous sulfide. Hydrogen sulfide gas is evolved during prolonged heating of the white. This diffuses to the yolk and combines with iron to give the dark color. There is enough sulfur and iron in the yolk to form the compound when white is not present as long as the pH is high. Cooling hard cooked eggs quickly in cold water should help to prevent the formation of the ferrous sulfide ring. However, if eggs are heated for 30 minutes in boiling water or if they are of low candled quality with the accompanying high pH, ferrous sulfide will form in spite of rapid cooling (Paul and Palmer, 1972).

CUSTARDS

Custards may be soft and pourable or baked and gelled. A soft custard is stirred while cooking over hot, but not boiling, water. A baked custard is cooked in the oven without stirring so that a moldable gel is produced. It is done when the tip of an inserted knife comes out clean. The custard is usually protected from overheating by placing the custard containers in water during baking. The egg provides heat coagulable protein for the gel structure. Only a small proportion of the milk protein is coagulated by heating under the usual conditions of custard preparation. Salts in the milk contribute to gel formation. The addition of sugar raises the coagulation temperature of the egg proteins. With about 2 tablespoons of sugar to one cup of milk and one egg (48 g), stirred custards will reach serving consistency, at which point they coat the surface of a spoon, at 80°–84°C (176°–183.2°F). Curdling may occur between 85°–87°C (185°–188.6°F). When the custard mixture is heated rapidly, coagulation and curdling occur at slightly higher temperatures (Paul and Palmer, 1972). The quality of a curdled custard may be improved by rapid cooling and beating.

Wolfe and Zabik (1968) baked custards prepared from both frozen and dehydrated eggs to endpoints of 81–83°C (177.8–181.4°F) and 85–87°C (185–188.6°F). They reported that the custards baked to 85–87°C were firmer and received improved flavor ratings over custards baked to 81–83°C. Although custards are commonly baked at oven temperatures of approximately 177°C (350.6°F), higher oven temperatures may be satisfactorily used if the baking time is shortened. Overcoagulation in baked custards results in syneresis or weeping of liquid from the shrunken gel structure.

Custards prepared from dehydrated eggs may be grayer and less yellow than custards prepared from frozen eggs. Differences in gel firmness have been reported for various types of dehydrated egg products prepared in 5-ounce cups (Wolfe and Zabik, 1968). Few subjective differences were reported for custards made from frozen or dehydrated egg products when they were baked in quantity (Funk *et al.,* 1969).

SUMMARY

Eggs play many roles in food preparation. They are used as structural agents, emulsifiers, foaming agents, clarifying agents, binders, coatings, and gel formers. The egg has a number of distinct parts. Within the shell, that consists largely of calcium carbonate, are two shell membranes. These act as the first line of defense against bacterial invasion. The white occurs in layers of thick and thin albumen. The vitelline membrane surrounds the yolk, which is composed of concentric layers of light and dark.

The white and yolk differ in chemical composition. Egg white is mainly water and protein. Essentially all of the lipid of the whole egg is present in the yolk. Most of the proteins of the egg white are typical globular proteins and many of them are glycoproteins. Some of the egg white proteins that have been extensively studied include ovalbumin, lysozyme, ovomucoid, ovotransferrin (conalbumin), and ovomucin. The thick white contains approximately four times as much ovomucin as does the thin white.

Egg yolk is a very complex system containing particles suspended in protein solution. The particulate granules contain about 70 percent high-density lipoproteins which have about 20 percent lipid. The plasma solution is composed of about 66 percent low-density lipoproteins which contain 80 to 90 percent lipid. The low-density lipoproteins are present in the egg yolk in the form of tiny micelles with a triglyceride core. Phospholipids and proteins solubilize the core.

Egg quality is compounded of those characteristics of an egg that affect its acceptability to the consumer. The USDA has developed grade standards that define various quality factors for eggs. Both exterior and interior quality is assessed in grading. The shell is inspected for shape, soundness, and cleanliness. The interior quality is determined by candling. The movement of the yolk is dependent upon the thickness of the white. Germ development and blood spots are also evaluated during candling. Eggs are graded as AA, A, B, and C quality.

Indices of albumen and yolk quality are available for the egg broken out of the shell. They include the Haugh unit, that relates egg weight and height of thick albumen in a mathematical formula; albumen index, that is the ratio of thick albumen height to mean width; and yolk index, that is the ratio of the height to the width of the yolk. Functional properties of egg white, particularly whipping and angel cake performance, offer another check on egg quality.

Changes in the physical characteristics of eggs begin as soon as the eggs are laid, the extent depending upon the conditions of holding. The thick white gradually thins. Ovomucin appears to be an important participant in the thinning process although its precise role has not been determined. Evaporation of moisture through the shell produces a loss of weight. There is also loss of carbon dioxide through the shell with a consequent increase in pH. The broken-out egg yolk tends to flatten as the vitelline membrane weakens.

Commercial practices in the handling of shell eggs are aimed at minimizing the changes in quality. Fresh eggs are commonly sprayed or dipped in mineral oil to decrease the permeability of the shell before they are placed in cold storage. Retention of moisture, carbon dioxide, and a low pH is increased by oiling.

Because the salmonella-infection rate of eggs is relatively high, egg products are pasteurized before freezing or dehydration. Successful pasteurization must fulfill two objectives, destroying pathogenic microorganisms while still maintaining the functional properties of the eggs. The USDA requires that liquid whole egg be heated to at least 60°C in the pasteurization process and be held at this temperature for no less than 3½ minutes. These temperatures do not affect the custard-making properties and layer cake performance of whole egg but they may have a slight effect in decreasing the volume of sponge cakes made from the pasteurized eggs. Egg whites are more sensitive to heating than are whole eggs and require special treatment to avoid loss of whipping properties. Egg whites may be satisfactorily pasteurized after acidification to pH 7 and the addition of aluminum sulfate, that forms a salt with ovotransferrin and makes it less sensitive to heat. Other approved methods of pasteurizing whites are also available. Egg yolks require a higher pasteurizing temperature than do other egg products because salmonellae are more heat-resistant in yolks.

Egg whites may be frozen with only minor changes. Yolks require the addition of one percent or more of sugar, corn syrup, or salt before freezing to avoid gelation that results from the denaturation and aggregation of low-density lipoproteins on freezing and storage below−6°C.

Dehydrated egg products find wide useage and generally perform well in foods, but consumer acceptability may be somewhat less with dehydrated than with fresh or frozen egg products. Egg white is essentially fat free and may be dried without major changes in its physical structure. However, the drying process produces irreversible changes in the structure of the low-density lipoproteins of egg yolk. Free lipid is released and has a foam-inhibiting effect when the dried eggs are reconstituted and whipped. The addition of sugars before drying protects the lipoproteins from this change. The removal of glucose from egg whites before drying is necessary to avoid the undesirable changes resulting from the Maillard reaction. Dehydrated whole eggs and yolks may also be improved by glucose removal. This may be done by bacterial or yeast fermentation or by use of the enzyme glucose oxidase.

Egg proteins undergo sol-gel transformation when heated. As the proteins become irreversibly insoluble, coagulation occurs. The proteins are denatured, unfolding from their original conformation, and then form new cross-links joining the unfolded molecules together in a coagulated mass. Coagulation by heating is important in the preparation of custards and other egg dishes. Egg white begins to coagulate at a slightly lower temperature than does yolk. Coagulation is a gradual process but the rate is increased with increasing temperature. Over-coagulation and toughening result from too high a temperature or too long a period of heating. Both dilution and the addition of sugar increase the temperature at which egg proteins coagulate. The addition of acid generally decreases it. Salts are necessary for gel formation.

The egg in custards provides heat coagulable protein for the gel structure. The sugar raises the temperature at which coagulation occurs and, therefore, the curdling temperature. Satisfactory custards may be prepared using dehydrated egg products although differences in color have been reported.

STUDY QUESTIONS

The gross composition and structure of egg white differs markedly from that of yolk.

1. Compare the gross composition of egg white, egg yolk, and whole egg.
2. Draw a diagram representing a longitudinal cross section of an egg and label the major parts. Describe major characteristics of each part.
3. List and give a distinguishing characteristic for each of five egg white proteins and two egg yolk proteins.
4. Describe how lipids and proteins are possibly combined to produce solubility in egg yolk. In terms of this structure, explain why dehydration of egg yolk and whole egg may decrease their whipping abilities.
5. Compare the pH of egg white and yolk in both newly laid eggs and after storage.

Various egg quality factors have been defined by USDA in grade standards.

6. List four USDA grades for eggs and describe distinguishing characteristics of each grade that may be noted when the egg is candled and when it is broken out of the shell.
7. From the following list, select those products that would require high grade eggs (AA or A) for best results and explain why in each case.

   Egg-containing food products
     scrambled eggs
     angel cake
     poached eggs on toast
     chocolate cake
     baked custard
     creamed eggs on rice
     cheese fondue
     butterscotch pudding
     puffy omelet

8. List six official USDA weight classes and weights based on minimum weight for a dozen eggs.

Changes occur during storage of eggs and are especially pronounced at high storage temperatures.

9. Describe changes that commonly occur in eggs as they are stored and give a possible explanation for each change.
10. Suggest procedures that might be followed to effectively retard deteriorative changes in eggs as they are held.

Eggs are commonly preserved by freezing and by dehydration and pasteurization is required in each case.

11. What is the major reason for requiring pasteurization of egg products?
12. What problems in the use of egg products may be created by the need for pasteurization? Explain.
13. Describe and explain the special problem that makes the freezing of yolks difficult and suggest a satisfactory solution to this problem.
14. Why is glucose removed from egg products, especially egg whites, before they are dried? Explain. Describe two methods that may be satisfactorily used for this process.

Egg proteins are denatured and coagulated by heat.

15. Define denaturation. Define coagulation.
16. Describe the changes that probably occur in egg proteins as they are coagulated and relate these changes to their role in thickening and gel formation.
17. List coagulation temperatures for egg white and egg yolk. Describe the effect on egg white of heating well above the coagulation temperature for a prolonged period of time.
18. Describe the effect of dilution, of a rapid rate of heating, of sugar, and of acid on the coagulation temperature of egg proteins. Give examples of products in which each of these factors may be of practical importance.
19. Give examples of food products where the heat coagulability of eggs participates importantly in their preparation.
20. List the usual coagulation and curdling temperatures for stirred custards. Describe and explain curdling.
21. Describe what probably happens to the structure of a baked custard when it is heated too long or at too high a temperature.
22. George prepared a soft custard in a small saucepan and quickly brought the milk, sugar, and egg mixture to a boil, stirred the mixture constantly, and boiled it for exactly one minute. He then placed the pan in cold water and continued to stir the custard so that it cooled quickly. He noticed that curds had formed and there was a separation of liquid from the curds. Explain to him what might have happened and suggest how he might prepare a smooth custard sauce next time.

Hard cooking eggs in the shell may present special problems in maintaining desirable texture and appearance.

23. Why should hard cooked eggs be prepared at below boiling temperatures? Explain.
24. Mrs. Harris prepared hard cooked eggs for a picnic. When the eggs were peeled, there was a dark green color around the yolks that were not centered in the whites. The children made fun of the eggs and the little ones refused to eat any. Mrs. Harris would like to avoid this in the future. Please give her some explanations and advice.

REFERENCES

1. Baker, R. C. and D. V. Vadehra. 1970. The influence of quantity of thick albumen on internal egg quality measurements. *Poultry Science* 49, 493.

2. Baldwin, R. E., J. C. Matter, R. Upchurch, and D. M. Breidenstein. 1967. Effects of microwaves on egg whites. I. Characteristics of coagulation. *Journal of Food Science* 32, 305.

3. Baliga, B. R., S. B. Kadkol, and N. L. Lahiry. 1971. Thinning of thick albumen in shell eggs—changes in ovomucin. *Poultry Science* 50, 466.

4. Carter, T. C., editor. 1968. *Egg Quality. A Study of the Hen's Egg.* Edinburgh: Oliver & Boyd.

5. Dawson, E. H., C. Miller, and R. A. Redstrom. 1956. Cooking quality and flavor of eggs as related to candled quality, storage conditions, and other factors. U. S. Department of Agriculture, Agriculture Information Bulletin No. 164.

6. Feeney, R. E., E. D. Ducay, R. B. Silva, and L. R. MacDonnell. 1952. Chemistry of shell egg deteriorations: The egg white proteins. *Poultry Science* 31, 639.

7. Fromm, D. 1967. Some physical and chemical changes in the vitelline membrane of the hen's egg during storage. *Journal of Food Science* 32, 52.

8. Fromm, D. 1964. Strength distribution, weight and some histological aspects of the vitelline membrane of the hen's egg yolk. *Poultry Science* 43, 1240.

9. Funk, K., M. A. Boyle, D. M. Downs, and M. E. Zabik. 1969. Custards made in quantity with processed eggs. *American Dietetic Association Journal* 55, 572.

10. Funk, K., M. T. Conklin, and M. E. Zabik. 1970a. Use of frozen, foam-spray-dried, freeze-dried, and spray-dried, whole eggs in yellow layer cakes. *Cereal Chemistry* 47, 732.

11. Funk, K., M. E. Zabik, G. Charlegois, and D. M. Downs. 1970b. Cream puffs prepared with frozen, foam-spray-dried, freeze-dried, and spray-dried eggs. *Cereal Chemistry* 47, 324.

12. Hanson, H., B. Lowe, and G. F. Stewart. 1947. Pasteurization of liquid egg products. 5. The effect on performance in custards and sponge cakes. *Poultry Science* 26, 277.

13. Heath, J. L. and S. L. Owens. 1978. Effect of oiling variables on storage of shell eggs at elevated temperatures. *Poultry Science* 57, 930.

14. Irmiter, T. F., L. E. Dawson, and J. G. Reagan. 1970. Methods of preparing hard cooked eggs. *Poultry Science* 49, 1232.

15. Janek, D. A. and D. M. Downs. 1969. Scrambled eggs prepared from three types of dried whole eggs. *American Dietetic Association Journal* 55, 578.

16. Lineweaver, H., F. E. Cunningham, J. A. Garibaldi, and K. Ijichi. 1967. Heat stability of egg white proteins under minimal conditions that kill Salmonellae. U. S. Department of Agriculture, Agricultural Research Service, Report ARS 74-39.

17. Meehan, J. J., T. F. Sugihara, and L. Kline. 1961. Relation between internal egg quality stabilization methods and the peeling difficulty. *Poultry Science* 40, 1430.

18. Meehan, J. J., T. F. Sugihara, and L. Kline. 1962. Relationships between shell handling factors and egg product properties. *Poultry Science* 41, 892.

19. Palmer, H. H., K. Ijichi, S. L. Cimino, and H. Roff. 1969a. Salted egg yolks. 1. Viscosity and performance of pasteurized and frozen samples. *Food Technology* 23 (No. 11), 148.

20. Palmer, H. H., K. Ijichi, H. Roff, and S. Redfern. 1969b. Sugared egg yolks. Effects of pasteurization and freezing on performance and viscosity. *Food Technology* 23, 85.

21. Parkinson, T. L. 1972. Separation of the proteins of egg white and egg yolk and a study of their interactions in whole egg. I. Quantitative fractionation of proteins. *Journal of the Science of Food and Agriculture* 23, 649.

22. Paul, P. C. and H. H. Palmer, editors. 1972. *Food Theory and Applications.* New York: Wiley.

23. Payawal, S. R., B. Lowe, and G. F. Stewart. 1946. Pasteurization of liquid-egg products. 2. Effect of heat treatment on appearance and viscosity. *Food Research* 11, 246.

24. Sauter, E. A., J. V. Harns, and W. J. Stadelman. 1953. Relationship of candled quality of eggs to other quality measurements. *Poultry Science* 32, 850.

25. Schultz, J. R., H. E. Snyder, and R. H. Forsythe. 1968. Co-dried carbohydrates effect on the performance of egg yolk solids. *Journal of Food Science* 33, 507.

26. Stadelman, W. J. and O. J. Cotterill, editors. 1973. *Egg Science and Technology.* Westport, Conn.: Avi Publishing Company.

27. Sugihara, T. F., K. Ijichi, and L. Kline. 1966. Heat pasteurization of liquid whole egg. *Food Technology* 20 (No. 8), 100.

28. Tuttle, J. W., J. H. Wolford, H. E. Larzelere, and L. E. Dawson. 1972. Acceptability of scrambled eggs from egg solids product. *Poultry Science* 51, 56.

29. U. S. Department of Agriculture. 1968. Egg grading manual. Agriculture Handbook No. 75.

30. Watt, B. K. and A. L. Merrill. 1963. Composition of foods. U. S. Department of Agriculture, Agriculture Handbook No. 8.

31. Whitaker, J. R. and S. R. Tannenbaum, editors. 1977. *Food Proteins.* Westport, Conn.: Avi Publishing Company.

32. Wolfe, N. J. and M. E. Zabik. 1968. Comparison of frozen, foam-spray-dried, freeze-dried, and spray-dried eggs. 3. Baked custards prepared from eggs with added corn syrup solids. *Food Technology* 22, 1470.

33. Zabik, M. E. 1969. Comparison of frozen, foam-spray-dried, freeze-dried, and spray-dried eggs. 6. Emulsifying properties at three pH levels. *Food Technology* 23 (No. 6), 130.

34. Zabik, M. E. and S. L. Brown. 1969. Comparison of frozen, foam-spray-dried, freeze-dried, and spray-dried eggs. 4. Foaming ability of whole eggs and yolks with corn sirup solids and albumen. *Food Technology* 23 (No. 2), 128.

CHAPTER 24

MILK AND MILK PRODUCTS

The milk of animals has been used as food since prehistoric times. Although much of it is consumed with minimal processing, highly processed milk products and components also find wide usage in foods. Protein, carbohydrate, and fat, isolated from whole milk, are used as ingredients in a variety of manufactured food products (National Dairy Council, 1977). In food preparation, milk is combined with many other foods. It is an excellent source of high quality protein, calcium, and riboflavin for individuals of all ages.

The term milk, when used in the United States, implies cow's milk. As critical demands continue to be placed on world food production resources, the conversion of forages and fibrous feeds to milk by the dairy cow appears to offer a reasonably efficient system for conservation. Mechanization in the dairy industry is increasing productivity (Harshbarger, 1975). (Milk foams were treated in Section 19.2.)

24.1

CHEMICAL AND PHYSICAL COMPOSITION OF MILK

Milk is a remarkable blend of complex biological molecules. It is secreted by the mammary gland primarily as sustenance for the young of the species. The precise composition of cow's milk varies somewhat from one breed to another and from one cow to another. However, an average gross composition is as follows:

Water	87.0%
Protein	3.5%
Fat	3.5–3.7%
Carbohydrate (primarily lactose)	4.9%
Minerals	0.7%

The chemical composition of milk is much more complex than the gross composition may indicate. It contains at least small amounts of most essential nutrients. Therefore, the list of vitamins and minerals present in milk is long. Calcium and phosphorus are found in relatively large amounts. About one-third of the calcium in milk is in true solution, some of it as calcium ion (Ca^{++}). Much of the remainder is in colloidal dispersion combined with the casein proteins, phosphorus, and citrate (Lampert, 1970). Milk calcium exerts an important influence upon certain processing operations. It participates in the coagulation of milk by rennin and affects the thickness of evaporated milk since the balance of salts in concentrated milk influences the coagulation of the proteins. Although the carbohydrate of milk is chiefly lactose, small quantities of the monosaccharides glucose and galactose are also present. A variety of oligosaccharides have been found in small amounts in milk by newer chromatographic methods of analysis. These sugars are dissolved in the aqueous portion of milk. Milk fat contains at least 142 fatty acids, both straight and branched chain. Saturated, monounsaturated, and polyunsaturated fatty acids are all present. Although a large proportion of the fatty acids are of relatively short chain length, they vary from four to twenty-two carbons (National Dairy Council, 1971). Milk also contains many enzymes and metabolites that participate in cellular reactions. The enzymes include lipase, that catalyzes the hydrolysis of triglycerides; protease, that hydrolyzes protein; alkaline phosphatase, that catalyzes the hydrolysis of organic phosphate esters; xanthine oxidase, that oxidizes the purine base xanthine to uric acid; and peroxidase, that catalyzes the transfer of oxygen from peroxides to other substances.

Federal and state standards have been developed for the composition of most milk products (U. S. Department of Agriculture, 1971). The federal standards apply to products entering interstate commerce. If there are no federal standards for a particular item, the state standard applies.

Milk, unless sterilized, contains living microorganisms. If it is obtained from healthy cows and produced under sanitary conditions, the bacterial count will be low. Handling conditions are geared to maintaining good sanitary quality. *Lactobacilli* and *Streptococcus lactis* bacteria ferment lactose and produce lactic acid which eventually sours and clots the milk. Certain desirable lactic acid-producing organisms are purposefully added in the preparation of fermented milk products such as yogurt and buttermilk. Some harmless bacteria survive pasteurization.

The chemical substances present in milk are dispersed in a variety of ways, increasing the complexity of this fluid. Physically, milk is a true solution, a colloidal dispersion, and a dilute emulsion. In true solution are found the sugars, water-soluble vitamins, and many of the mineral salts. Proteins and some calcium phosphate are colloidally dispersed. Fat globules are emulsified and suspended in the aqueous phase of milk. A complex fat globule membrane acts as an emulsifier. Fat-soluble vitamins are dispersed in the fat.

PROTEINS

The pH of fresh milk is usually about 6.6. The addition of acid to skim milk with stirring until the pH reaches 5.2–4.6 causes precipitation of the casein proteins, that make up the largest proportion of milk proteins. Remaining in the whey (milk serum) after the casein precipitate has been separated are lactalbumins and lactoglobulins. The whey proteins may be precipitated by *salting-out* methods. This classical procedure for fractionating milk proteins has been greatly expanded by modern laboratory analyses that include electrophoresis and ultracentrifugation. Each traditional protein fraction (casein, lactalbumin, and lactoglobulin) has been shown to be composed of many components.

Casein is an extraordinarily complicated chemical mixture. It has been called a *phosphoprotein* because it contains phosphorus. Several casein components, including alpha$_{s1}$-, beta-, and kappa-caseins, are combined in an orderly fashion to form approximately spherical micelles that are colloidally dispersed in the aqueous medium. Calcium is associated with the casein micelles. In fact, the integrity of the micellar structure is apparently maintained by colloidal calcium phosphate. Kappa-casein also plays an important role in micelle stabilization. It is acted upon by the enzyme rennin, causing eventual destabilization of the micelle, when milk is clotted. Commercial casein is made either by coagulation with rennin or precipitation with acid. Casein preparations find wide usage in both manufactured foods and nonfood products (Rose *et al.*, 1970; Webb *et al.*, 1974).

The *whey* (or *serum*) proteins (lactalbumins and lactoglobulins) constitute about one-fifth of the total milk proteins. As with casein, several proteins have been isolated from each of the traditional fractions. To add to the complexity, one of the proteins isolated from the lactalbumin fraction was found to have the characteristics of a globulin and is named *beta-lactoglobulin*. The whey proteins are not precipitated by acid, as is the casein fraction. They are generally more highly hydrated than is casein and are, therefore, less sensitive to precipitation by ions. Unlike casein, the whey proteins are relatively easily denatured by heat.

LIPIDS

Triglycerides (triacylglycerols) make up 95–96 percent of total milk lipids. Small quantities of other lipid substances present include mono- and diglycerides, phospholipids (chiefly phosphoglycerides), free fatty acids, sterols, and fat-soluble vitamins.

The milk fat of ruminants contains a relatively low concentration of polyunsaturated fatty acids since these fatty acids in the feed are mostly hydrogenated by bacteria in the rumen. Recently a procedure for producing milk of higher polyunsaturated fat content was devised. Cows are fed oils that are encapsulated in sodium caseinate and then treated with formaldehyde. This treatment denatures the protein on the surface of the fat globules and protects it from hydrolysis in the rumen. The polyunsaturated fatty acids thus escape hydrogenation and are eventually absorbed (Jensen, 1973).

Milk fat is secreted and exists in milk in the form of microscopic, emulsified globules. The fat globules are stabilized in this emulsion by a surface covering called the *fat globule membrane*. This membrane consists of a mixture of proteins and lipids that seem to exist in some type of ordered complex. A number of enzymes have been found to be associated with the fat globule membrane. The membrane has been isolated and studied. It contains from 30 to 60 percent protein. The remaining material consists principally of phospholipids and other associated lipids (Webb *et al.*, 1974).

Although the chemical composition of the fat globule membrane has been reasonably well elucidated, the organization of these components in the membrane is not completely understood. From electron microscopy it has been suggested that the fat globule membrane consists of a relatively continuous basic protein-rich structure on which lipoprotein particles are adsorbed (Webb *et al.*, 1974). The lipoproteins contain both polar and nonpolar groups and effectively act as emulsifiers.

The emulsion in unprocessed milk does not remain homogeneous. As milk stands, a phenomenon known as *creaming* occurs. The fat globules, being lighter than the aqueous phase of the milk, rise in clusters to form a creamy layer. With the widespread use of homogenization, the creaming phenomenon is no longer of practical importance. Homogenization reduces the size of the fat globules to the degree that they remain homogeneously distributed throughout the milk.

24.2

PROCESSING

PASTEURIZATION

Pasteurization is the process of heating a food at a definite temperature for a definite time, sufficient to destroy pathogenic microorganisms but not sufficient to achieve sterilization. The product is cooled immediately. Pasteurization as applied to milk by the U. S. Public Health Service milk ordinance means that every particle of milk is heated to at least 62.8°C (145°F) and held continuously at or above this temperature for at least 30 minutes. All yeasts and molds are generally destroyed by this process. Pathogenic bacteria are destroyed as are about 95–99 percent of nonpathogens.

Pasteurization of milk may also be done by heating to at least 71.7°C (161°F) and held for at least 15 seconds. This is called *high-temperature short-time* (HTST) *pasteurization*. When temperatures well above 72°C are used with the heating time lasting only a few seconds, the process may be called *ultra-high temperature pasteurization*. Careful control of equipment is required to avoid a scorched flavor in the milk. Keeping quality is similar for all methods (Glazier, 1963). Ultra-high temperature treatment may also be used for milk sterilization coupled with aseptic packaging. This method produces a product that will remain in good condition for several months of storage without the necessity of refrigeration (Andrews and Cheeseman, 1971).

Since pasteurized milk products are not sterile, they require cold storage temperatures, 10°C (50°F) or below, to retard the growth of surviving organisms. Recontamination must also be avoided. Pasteurization of milk and milk products is a public health measure necessary to control the spread of disease-producing microorganisms.

The adequacy of pasteurization may be monitored by testing for the presence of certain enzymes. For example, no phosphatase activity will be found in properly pasteurized milk.

HOMOGENIZATION

Homogenization is an important step in the processing of many milk products. This process breaks up the already small fat globules (averaging about 2 μm in diameter) in milk to even smaller globules (see Figure 24.1). The fat-in-water emulsion is stabilized to the extent that there is no noticeable rising of fat to form a cream layer. Milk is homogenized by pumping it under high pressure, generally from 2000 to 3000 lb per sq in, through very small openings. In some cases this is a two-stage process with the pressure on the second stage usually less than that used on the first stage. The second stage disrupts clumps of the small fat globules that may form after the first stage of pasteurization (Lampert, 1970).

The fat globule membrane is disrupted during homogenization as new surfaces are created. Apparently casein and whey proteins both participate, along with the fat globule membrane material, in emulsifying the newly formed fat globules (Brunner *et al.*, 1953; Jackson and Brunner, 1960). Therefore, significant changes occur in the properties of these proteins and these changes seem to contribute materially to the overall characteristics of homogenized milk.

Figure 24.1

In homogenization of milk, the fat globules are markedly reduced in size. (Courtesy of Evaporated Milk Association.)

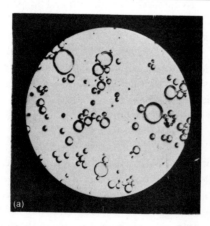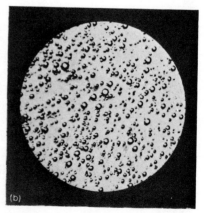

Homogenized milk, as compared with the nonhomogenized product, is whiter in appearance, more viscous, more bland in flavor, and foams more easily. It is less stable to heat and may curdle more readily when heated in such products as cream soups, cereals, and scalloped potatoes. It produces a softer curd when clotted. Starchy puddings made with homogenized milk are slightly thicker than those made with nonhomogenized milk (Jordan *et al.*, 1953). Cocoa beverages are also thicker. Homogenized milk is more sensitive to light-induced flavor deterioration. The fine state of dispersion of the fat accounts for the whiter appearance because of a greater opportunity for both the absorption and reflection of light. The small fat globules also affect flavor, making it more like the skim milk phase. The soft curd probably results from the finer fat globules that break up the gel and change the protein distribution. Because of the greater fat surface in homogenized milk, it is susceptible to the action of lipase and the production of "off-flavors" from hydrolytic rancidity (see Section 18.4). For this reason homogenized milk is always pasteurized. This process destroys lipase. The change in proteins and their distribution on the surface of the fat globules probably increases the likelihood of light-induced "off-flavor." This flavor apparently results from a reaction involving amino acids such as methionine and the vitamin riboflavin (Webb *et al.*, 1974).

FERMENTATION

Fermentation is a process in which chemical changes are brought about in an organic substrate through the action of enzymes elaborated by specific types of living microorganisms. Milk is generally a good medium for the culture of microorganisms. Some of the results are undesirable, leading to spoiled products, while others are desirable, producing such flavorful foods as buttermilk, yogurt, and cheese. Fermented milks are usually fluid or semi-fluid in consistency and all contain lactic acid in varying proportions.

Cultured buttermilk is produced from a skimmed or partly skimmed milk. A starter usually contains several strains of bacteria, including lactic acid-producing streptococci and leuconostocs. About 0.1 percent salt is usually added. The lactic acid is present in amounts up to 0.9 percent, being produced by fermentation of lactose.

Yogurt is a coagulated milk resulting from the fermentation of milk sugars by two microorganisms, *Lactobacillus bulgaris* and *Streptococcus thermophilus*. Growing together, they are responsible for the lactic acid production and typical yogurt flavor. The basic culture medium may contain whole milk, partly skimmed, skimmed evaporated, or dried milk. Although the bacteria in yogurt ferment lactose, appreciable amounts of lactose may remain in commercial yogurts made in the United States because of the common practice of fortifying the yogurt mix with nonfat milk solids. O'Leary and Woychik (1976) reported that satisfactory yogurt could be made from lactase-treated milks although the flavor may differ somewhat from yogurt made with untreated milks. The lactase-treated yogurts contain substantially less lactose and may be used by individuals who have an intolerance for this sugar.

Yogurt consumption in North America has increased spectacularly over the past several years. U. S. consumption rose from 172 million lb in 1970 to 362 million lb in 1974. During a survey in Pennsylvania to determine consumer attitudes toward yogurt, it was found that 10 percent of the yogurt eaters interviewed make their own yogurt regularly at home. They generally use commercial plain yogurt as a starter culture (Kroger and Fram, 1975). Innoculated milk, covered and held at room temperature, will reach yogurt consistency in five to ten hours.

Sour cream is cultured with lactic acid-producing bacteria similar to those used in making buttermilk. It contains about 18 percent milk fat. Nonfat dry milk solids may be added to the cream to obtain a thick body.

DRYING

A variety of milk products are dried commercially. These include non-fat dry milk (NDM), dried whole milk, dried whey, dry buttermilk, dry cream, and malted milk powder. Dried whole milk, because of its fat content, is less stable to storage than is NDM. In 1970, about 20 percent of the total U. S. milk supply was converted to NDM. This product is produced by condensing skim milk under reduced pressure to avoid scorching and then drying the concentrated liquid by spraying it into a heated vacuum chamber. An instant NDM, that disperses more readily than the regular product, is made by carefully moistening the surface of NDM particles and allowing them to agglomerate before redrying. The particle aggregates are loose and spongy and lactose crystallizes at the surface. Water is attracted to the lactose crystals and quickly penetrates the loose structure as the milk is reconstituted (Webb et al., 1974).

Whey is a byproduct in the manufacture of cheese, varying in characteristics with the type of cheese from which it originates. A considerable effort is being made to improve the utilization of this product. Dried whey generally has a composition similar to that of NDM but with somewhat more lactose and about half as much protein. The proteins in whey are lactalbumin and lactoglobulin and have high biological value. Undenatured whey protein concentrates have been produced containing up to 82 percent protein. The potential for use of whey concentrate in fortifying soft drinks has been demonstrated (Holsinger et al., 1973). It may also be valuable as an emulsifier and foaming agent in manufactured foods (Morr, 1976). However, undenatured whey foams tend to collapse when subjected to high heat, such as during cake baking (DeVilbiss et al., 1974).

Whey products are sometimes used in baked products as substitutes for NDM. Zaehringer (1972) studied the effect of whey on the properties of doughs and gluten. She reported that dried whey decreased the extensibility and the volume of gluten extracted from all purpose flour but increased the tenderness and the lightness of color.

Evaporated milk is whole milk from which about 60 percent of the water has been removed by heating under a vacuum. The U. S. standard of identity for evaporated milk requires that it contain not less than 7.9 percent milk fat and not less than 25.9 percent total milk solids. The addition of not over 0.1 percent of stabilizer salts is permitted as well as fortification with vitamin D. The vegetable gum, carrageenan, is also allowed as a stabilizer in amounts up to 0.015 percent. The concentrated milk is homogenized and canned, then sterilized in a pressure canner (Lampert, 1970).

Milk proteins are susceptible to coagulation when heated to high temperatures such as those required for the sterilization of canned evaporated milk. This is especially true when the milk solids are concentrated. A forewarming treatment to which the milk is subjected before concentration aids in stabilizing the proteins so that they do not coagulate. The forewarming period is usually from 10 to 20 minutes at 95°C (203°F), but varies with the lot of milk being processed. The balance of salts in milk also has an important influence on the coagulation of the proteins with heating. Calcium chloride, phosphates, and citrates may be added as stabilizer salts in amounts indicated by testing various lots of milk.

Sweetened condensed milk is produced by concentrating, through evaporation, whole milk to which about 15 percent sugar has been added. The finished product contains about 40–42 percent sugar, which is sufficient to prevent spoilage by microorganisms. Federal standards require a minimum of 8.5 percent milkfat and 28.0 percent total milk solids.

24.3

FLAVOR OF MILK

The natural flavor of milk is difficult to describe because it is basically a bland product. It has a slightly sweet taste as a result of its lactose content and a slightly salty taste due to the presence of chloride salts. There is also a low intensity olfactory sensation. This is attributed to such low-molecular-weight compounds as acetone, acetaldehyde, dimethyl sulfide, traces of short chain fatty acids, methyl ketones, and delta-lactones. Modern analytical methods have made relatively easy the analysis of volatile compounds from dairy products. One of the major flavor sensations of milk is its pleasant "mouth-feel." This is due to the fat emulsion and the colloidal structure of milk (Forss, 1969). Milk fat contains both volatile and nonvolatile compounds that probably are unique to this fat and contribute to milk flavor (Tamsma *et al.*, 1969). Important contributors to the flavor of butterfat are dimethyl sulfide, the $C_{2,4,6,8,10}$ n-alkanoic acids, and the $C_{8,10,12}$ delta-lactones. Lactones are formed from hydroxyacids and increase from two to four times when butter or butteroil is heated (Forss, 1969).

"Off-flavors" may appear in milk for a variety of reasons (Shipe *et al.*, 1978). Environmental influences are often responsible for variations in flavor. The stage of lactation has significant effects on flavor and apparently interacts with other types of "off-flavor." Different flavor effects also result from winter and summer management practices (Kratzer *et al.*, 1957). Feed consumed by the cow may be a contributing cause of abnormal flavors in milk. Weeds such as ragweed and wild onion are examples of green plants that when eaten by the cow, produce "off-flavors" in milk.

All raw milks are susceptible to the development of rancid flavors that result from the liberation of short chain fatty acids by the action of the enzyme lipase. Butyric acid, and possibly other short chain fatty acids, exhibit particularly unpleasant odors that contribute to "off-flavor."

Oxidized flavor may develop in milk, with milk from some cows being much more susceptible to this "off-flavor" than that from others. The presence of trace amounts of copper or iron hastens its development. This "off-flavor" has been described as cardboardlike or tallowy. The "off-flavor" apparently has its origin in oxidative change that involves the phospholipids present in the fat globule membrane. Homogenization, which physically alters the membrane, inhibits the oxidation (Schultz *et al.*, 1967).

An "off-flavor" very similar to oxidized flavor may be produced by exposure of milk for even short periods of time to direct sunlight. Incandescent or fluorescent light to which milk may be exposed during handling, processing, and storage can also contribute to light-induced "off-flavor." The sunlight flavor develops rapidly and originates in the proteins of milk. The vitamin riboflavin apparently acts as a photosensitizer as particular amino acid residues of the protein, including methionine, are destroyed. Sunlight, therefore, decreases the riboflavin content of milk at the same time as the protein-derived "off-flavored" substances develop (Webb *et al.*, 1974).

A cooked flavor may develop in milk heated to approximately 74°C (165°F). The intensity of the flavor is affected by the specific length of time and the temperature of heating. The flavor is the result of volatile sulfides and sulfhydryl compounds, particularly hydrogen sulfide, that are liberated from beta-lactoglobulin and from the proteins of the fat globule membrane. When the heat treatment is prolonged at 74°C or increased to higher temperatures, the cooked flavor gives way to a carmelized flavor as the Maillard or browning reaction takes place (Schultz *et al.*, 1967). The mechanism for production of sulfur compounds in heated milk has not been clarified (Ferretti, 1973).

24.4

MILK IN FOOD PREPARATION

Milk is used as a major ingredient in a variety of puddings, sauces, and soups. It is also widely used as the liquid that hydrates many baked flour mixtures. In most of these products, the milk is heated to some degree. In addition, a number of processing treatments in the production of dairy products involve heating. These include pasteurization, sterilization, forewarming, evaporating, and drying. Heating may, under certain conditions, cause coagulation of milk proteins. Coagulation may also be brought about by action of the enzyme rennin and by acid.

EFFECTS OF HEAT   The effects of heat on milk are complex and involve several components. Heating may affect serum proteins, casein, and various salts including calcium phosphates and citrates. In addition, these components may interact with each other and with the lactose in milk. The stability of the milk dispersion is affected in various ways by heating.

Salt equilibria shift with heat. Calcium and phosphorus salts become less soluble upon heating in milk, with a consequent decrease in soluble and ionic calcium concentration and an increase in colloidal calcium phosphate. The levels of colloidal and soluble salts affect the stability of casein micelles. Many of these changes revert on cooling the milk at 5°C (41°F). The buffer capacity of the milk salts changes on heating and slightly increases the acidity. This more than balances the slight decrease in acidity resulting from loss of carbon dioxide on heating (Webb *et al.*, 1974).

Mild heat treatments have little effect on the coagulation of casein. However, elevated temperatures (100°C and above) produce a release of phosphate, that is esterified to the casein molecules, and the breaking of some peptide bonds. Changes of these types are probably related to the coagulation of milk subjected to high temperatures or long periods of heating. The stability of casein to heat decreases with increasing milk solids concentration as occurs in the production of evaporated milk. Casein, being poorly hydrated, is more susceptible to precipitation by change in pH than it is by heating.

The serum proteins are more subject to heat denaturation than is casein. Heat treatment of skim milk at 70°C (158°F) for 30 minutes denatures about 30 percent of the total serum proteins. The extent of denaturation increases with increasing temperature. Sulfhydryl groups are activated by the denaturation of serum proteins. This has been associated with the development of a cooked flavor in heated milk. Serum proteins precipitated on the bottom of a pan in which milk is heated cause scorching to occur. The denaturation of serum proteins, along with changes in salt equilibria, are thought to be responsible for the effect of forewarming in increasing the stability of evaporated milk (Webb *et al.*, 1974). When unheated milk is used in breadmaking, the dough may become too soft, slack and sticky. This defect does not occur with heat-treated milk. The improvement resulting from heating approximately parallels the denaturation of serum or whey proteins. (The dough-softening effect is discussed in Section 32.1.)

EFFECT OF RENNIN Rennet is a crude extract from the stomach of milk-fed calves that contains the enzyme rennin. This enzyme is used in the making of puddings and ice creams and in the clotting of milk for cheese making. Rennin also has a proteolytic effect that may influence the process of cheese ripening. Since the quantity of rennet available in the United States is insufficient for the demands of the cheese industry, other milk-clotting enzymes are also used. Nonrennet clotting enzymes used in cheese making include proteases from several fungi and pepsin from the pig stomach (Webb *et al.,* 1974). Enzymes from some plant sources, such as papain from papaya and ficin from figs, are capable of clotting milk but may be unsatisfactory for cheese making because they also digest the clot. Additional plant sources are being studied (Gupta and Eskin, 1977).

The action of rennin has both an industrial interest, particularly for the cheesemaker, and a theoretical interest for the physiology scientist. It has, therefore, been widely studied. Milk clotting occurs in two separate phases. A *primary phase* involves the enzyme's attack on kappa-casein with the release of a macropeptide having a molecular weight of about 6000–8000. The macropeptide is heterogeneous and some components of this peptide contain carbohydrate groups. Kappa-casein functions to stabilize the casein micelles in milk. The primary phase of rennin action destroys this stabilizing effect by hydrolyzing a specific peptide bond in the molecule. The primary phase may be represented as follows (Webb *et al.,* 1974):

$$\text{kappa-casein} \xrightarrow{\quad\text{Rennin}\quad} \underset{\text{(insoluble)}}{\text{para-kappa-casein}} + \underset{\text{(soluble)}}{\text{macropeptide}}$$

A *secondary phase* of milk clotting is nonenzymatic in character. The mechanism of action for this phase is less well understood. Gelling apparently takes place because certain chemical groups exposed by the removal of the macropeptide can participate in a polymerization reaction. Calcium ions (Ca^{++}) are required for the gelation to occur. Its specific role in gel formation has not been clarified. Electron microscopy was used to study the sequence of physical changes occuring during the clotting of milk. Initially, short threadlike structures appeared to join the casein micelles. Later these formed into large fibrils and the particles tended to agglomerate. They eventually changed into a cross-linked network of fibrous structures. The milk fat globules and whey were trapped within the paracasein structure (Webb *et al.,* 1974).

Milk that has been heated to 65°–100°C (149°–212°F) for 30 minutes and then immediately cooled shows an increase in rennet coagulation time. On standing, there is a further increase in the coagulation time. The clotting by rennin is inhibited and the clot that is formed is weak in evaporated milk, that has previously been subjected to sterilizing temperatures. Although changes in the proportions of colloidal and soluble calcium may play some role in this effect, alterations in the milk proteins are probably of more importance. It has been suggested that heat-induced interactions between beta-lactoglobulin and kappa-casein may interfere with the primary phase of rennin action on casein (Webb *et al.*, 1974).

Optimum conditions for the action of rennin include a temperature of about 40°–42°C (104°–107.6°F). Clotting does not occur below 10°C (50°F) or above 65°C (149°F). Coagulation is influenced by the pH of the milk. The reaction is stronger as the pH is lowered from about 6.6 to about 5.8. Clotting does not occur at a strongly alkaline pH. As the clot is stirred or cut, liquid seeps out and two phases are formed—the curd and the whey.

EFFECT OF ACID

The addition of acid sufficient to lower the pH of milk to approximately 5.2 causes the coagulation of the casein micelles to begin. Casein is sensitive to acid because it is stabilized primarily by a negative charge on the particles that is neutralized by hydrogen ion (H^+). Acid may accumulate in the milk by action of lactic acid-producing bacteria. Production of acid is largely responsible for the increased viscosity in cultured buttermilk and the gelation in yogurt.

Combination of milk or cream with acid-containing fruits may cause thickening and even curdling. The casein in milk becomes unstable to heating when the pH is lowered even though the degree of acidity is insufficient to produce coagulation at room temperature. In the making of tomato soup the combination of acid tomato juice with milk makes it necessary to carefully control the heat applied in order to avoid curdling. Thickening the milk by making a white sauce aids in protecting the casein against precipitation, probably due to the effect of the gelatinized starch on protein dispersal.

Curdling may occur when milk is combined with foods containing *polyphenolic compounds,* previously called *tannins.* Curdling of scalloped potatoes may be influenced by these substances.

24.5

CHEESE

People have been eating cheese for thousands of years although its origin is the subject of some speculation. Pilgrims coming to the new world included cheese in the food supplies they brought aboard their ship, the Mayflower. The first cheese factory in the United States was built in Rome, New York in 1851. Making cheese is an art that is centuries old. The science of cheese was developed more recently.

TYPES OF CHEESE

Cheese represents a concentrated food. It is made from milk and consists of the casein, variable amounts of the fat, mineral salts, and part of the milk serum. In the small amount of serum present are dissolved lactose, whey proteins, and vitamins. The cheese curd may be formed by addition of rennin or by acidification of the milk. The cheese may be unripened, ripened by bacteria, or ripened by molds.

Although more than 400 varieties of cheese have been described, many of them are similar and there are only about 14 distinct types. Cheese may be classified according to texture, moisture, ripening agent, and method of manufacture. Table 24.1 describes characteristics of a number of cheeses that are typical of the different processes by which these products are made. Several cheese varieties are shown in Figure 24.2.

COMPOSITION

The protein in cheese is mainly casein. Only about one-fifth of the total protein in hard cheeses is accounted for by whey proteins since these proteins do not coagulate at the pH and temperature used to make most cheeses. About four-fifths of the milk calcium, two-thirds of the phosphorus, and five-sixths of the vitamin A remain in a Cheddar-type cheese. Varying amounts of lactose are found in freshly prepared cheeses but lactose decreases during ripening and may completely disappear after four to six weeks. Some of the protein and fat is digested during ripening (Webb *et al.*, 1974). The typical composition of selected cheeses is given in Table 24.2.

MANUFACTURE OF CHEESE

Similar steps are followed in the manufacture of most cheeses. These include formation of curd; cutting the curd; cooking the curd; draining, salting, and pressing; and ripening (Paul and Palmer, 1972).

The curd is usually formed by addition of rennin or another milk-clotting enzyme. (The action of rennin is discussed in Section 24.4.) In cheeses that are to be ripened, a starter culture is first added. The culture will vary with the type of cheese desired. The formation of the curd is affected by the temperature, the acidity developed, and the amount of rennet added. These conditions are carefully controlled.

The curd is cut in small cubes to permit a large proportion of the whey to escape from the curd. A thin coating forms quickly on the surface of each curd particle after cutting and aids in retaining fat and moisture within the particle. After the curd settles, it is occasionally stirred slowly.

Heating or cooking is used in making many kinds of cheese. Heating hastens expulsion of the whey from the curd, increases elasticity, produces a more compact texture, and alters the bacterial flora. After cooking, the whey is drained from the curd and the curd is salted and pressed in its characteristic shape. Salt improves the flavor and retards microbiological activity.

Cheese may be held under controlled conditions of temperature and humidity for variable periods of time while a number of chemical and physical changes take place in a ripening process. The temperatures for most varieties are between 4.4°–12.8°C (40°–55°F). During the early stages of ripening, lactose continues to be fermented to lactic acid with small amounts of acetic and propionic acids and carbon dioxide also

Table 24.1 Characteristics of Some Popular Varieties of Natural Cheeses

Kind or name Place of origin	Kind of milk used in manufacture	Ripening or curing time	Flavor	Body and texture	Color	Retail packaging	Uses
Soft, Unripened Varieties							
Cottage, plain or creamed. (Unknown)	Cow's milk skimmed; plain curd, or plain curd with cream added.	Unripened	Mild, acid	Soft, curd particles of varying size.	White to creamy white.	Cup-shaped containers, tumblers, dishes.	Salads, with fruits, vegetables, sandwiches, dips, cheese cake.
Cream, plain (U.S.A.)	Cream from cow's milk.	Unripened	Mild, acid	Soft and smooth	White	3- to 8-oz packages	Salads, dips, sandwiches, snacks, cheese cake, desserts.
Neufchatel (Nū-shä-těl'). (France)	Cow's milk	Unripened	Milk, acid	Soft, smooth similar to cream cheese but lower in milkfat.	White	4- to 8-oz. packages.	Salads, dips, sandwiches, snacks. cheese cake, desserts.
Ricotta (Ri-co´-ta) (Italy)	Cow's milk, whole or partly skimmed or whey from cow's milk with whole or skim milk added. In Italy, whey from sheep's milk.	Unripened	Sweet, nut-like.	Soft, moist or dry	White	Pint and quart paper and plastic containers, 3 lb. metal cans.	Appetizers, salads, snacks, lasagne, ravioli, noodles and other cooked dishes, grating, desserts.

Table 24.1 (continued)

Kind or name Place of origin	Kind of milk used in manufacture	Ripening or curing time	Flavor	Body and texture	Color	Retail packaging	Uses
Firm, Unripened Varieties							
Gjetost, (Yĕt´ŏst) (Norway)	Whey from goat's milk or a mixture of whey from goat's and cow's milk.	Unripened	Sweetish, caramel.	Firm, buttery consistency.	Golden brown	Cubical and rectangular.	Snacks, desserts, served with dark breads, crackers, biscuits or muffins.
Mysost (Mŭs-ŏst) also called Primost (Prēm´-ŏst). (Norway)	Whey from cow's milk.	Unripened	Sweetish, caramel.	Firm, buttery consistency.	Light brown	Cubical, cylindrical, pie-shaped wedges	Snacks, desserts, served with dark breads.
Mozzarella (Mŏ-tsa-rĕl´la) also called Scamorza. (Italy)	Whole or partly skimmed cow's milk. In Italy, originally made from buffalo's milk.	Unripened	Delicate, mild.	Slightly firm, plastic.	Creamy white	Small round or braided form, shredded, sliced.	Snacks, toasted sandwiches, cheeseburgers, cooking, as in meat loaf, or topping for lasagne, pizza, and casseroles.
Soft, Ripened Varieties							
Brie (Brē) (France)	Cow's milk	4 to 8 weeks.	Mild to pungent.	Soft, smooth when ripened.	Creamy yellow interior; edible thin brown and white crust.	Circular, pie-shaped wedges.	Appetizers, sandwiches, snacks, good with crackers and fruit, dessert.

Kind	Kind of milk	Ripening time	Flavor	Body and texture	Color	How marketed	Uses
Camembert (Kăm'ĕm-bâr). (France)	Cow's milk	4 to 8 weeks.	Mild to pungent.	Soft, smooth; very soft when fully ripened.	Creamy yellow interior; edible thin white, or gray-white crust.	Small circular cakes and pie-shaped portions.	Appetizers, sandwiches, snacks, good with crackers, and fruit such as pears and apples, dessert.
Limburger (Belgium)	Cow's milk	4 to 8 weeks.	Highly pungent, very strong.	Soft, smooth when ripened; usually contains small irregular openings.	Creamy white interior; reddish yellow surface.	Cubical, rectangular.	Appetizers, snacks, good with crackers, rye or other dark breads, dessert.
Semisoft, Ripened Varieties							
Bel Paese (Bĕl Pä-ā-zĕ). (Italy)	Cow's milk	6 to 8 weeks.	Mild to moderately robust.	Soft to medium firm, creamy.	Creamy yellow interior; slightly gray or brownish surface sometimes covered with yellow wax coating.	Small wheels, wedges, segments.	Appetizers, good with crackers, snacks, sandwiches, dessert.
(Brick) (U.S.A.)	Cow's milk	2 to 4 months.	Mild to moderately sharp.	Semisoft to medium firm, elastic, numerous small mechanical openings.	Creamy yellow	Loaf, brick, slices, cut portions.	Appetizers, sandwiches, snacks, dessert.
Muenster (Mün'stĕr). (Germany)	Cow's milk	1 to 8 weeks.	Mild to mellow.	Semisoft, numerous small mechanical openings. Contains more moisture than brick.	Creamy white interior; yellow tan surface.	Circular cake, blocks, wedges, segments, slices.	Appetizers, sandwiches, snacks, dessert.

Table 24.1 (continued)

Kind or name Place of origin	Kind of milk used in manufacture	Ripening or curing time	Flavor	Body and texture	Color	Retail packaging	Uses
Semisoft, Ripened Varieties (continued)							
Port du Salut (Por dü Sa-lü') (France)	Cow's milk	6 to 8 weeks.	Mellow to robust.	Semisoft, smooth, buttery, small openings.	Creamy yellow ...	Wheels and wedges.	Appetizers, snacks, served with raw fruit, dessert.
Firm Ripened Varieties							
Cheddar (England)	Cow's milk	1 to 12 months or more.	Mild to very sharp.	Firm, smooth, some mechanical openings.	White to medium-yellow-orange.	Circular, cylindrical loaf, pie-shaped wedges, oblongs, slices, cubes, shredded, grated.	Appetizers, sandwiches, sauces, on vegetables, in hot dishes, toasted sandwiches, grating, cheeseburgers, dessert.
Colby (U.S.A.)	Cow's milk	1 to 3 months.	Mild to mellow.	Softer and more open than Cheddar.	White to medium-yellow-orange.	Cylindrical, pie-shaped wedges.	Sandwiches, snacks cheeseburgers.
Caciocavallo (Kä' chô-kä-val'lô). (Italy)	Cow's milk. In Italy, cow's milk or mixtures of sheep's, goat's, and cow's milk.	3 to 12 months.	Piquant, similar to Provolone but not smoked.	Firm, lower in milkfat and moisture than Provolone.	Light or white interior; clay or tan colored surface.	Spindle or tenpin shaped, bound with cord, cut pieces.	Snacks, sandwiches, cooking, dessert; suitable for grating after prolonged curing.

Name (origin)	Kind of milk	Ripening time	Flavor	Body and texture	Color	Retail packaging	Uses
Edam (Ē'dăm) (Netherlands).	Cow's milk, partly skimmed.	2 to 3 months.	Mellow, nut-like.	Semisoft to firm, smooth; small irregularly shaped or round holes; lower milkfat than Gouda.	Creamy yellow or medium yellow-orange interior; surface coated with red wax.	Cannon ball shaped loaf, cut pieces, oblongs.	Appetizers, snacks, salads, sandwiches, seafood sauces, dessert.
Gouda (Gou'-dä) (Netherlands)	Cow's milk, whole or partly skimmed.	2 to 6 months.	Mellow, nut-like.	Semisoft to firm, smooth; small irregularly shaped or round holes; higher milkfat than Edam.	Creamy yellow or medium yellow-orange interior; may or may not have red wax coating.	Ball shaped with flattened top and bottom.	Appetizers, snacks, salads, sandwiches, seafood sauces, dessert.
Provolone (Prō-vō-lō'-nē) also smaller sizes and shapes called Provolette, Provoloncini (Italy)	Cow's milk	2 to 12 months or more	Mellow to sharp, smoky, salty.	Firm, smooth	Light creamy interior; light brown or golden yellow surface.	Pear shaped, sausage and salami shaped, wedges, slices.	Appetizers, sandwiches, snacks, souffle, macaroni and spaghetti dishes, pizza, suitable for grating when fully cured and dried.
Swiss, also called Emmentaler. (Switzerland)	Cow's milk	3 to 9 months.	Sweet, nut-like.	Firm, smooth with large round eyes.	Light yellow	Segments, pieces, slices.	Sandwiches, snacks, sauces, fondue, cheeseburgers.

Table 24.1 (continued)

Very Hard Ripened Varieties

Kind or name Place of origin	Kind of milk used in manufacture	Ripening or curing time	Flavor	Body and texture	Color	Retail packaging	Uses
Parmesan (Pär´mĕ-zän´) also called Reggiano. (Italy)	Partly skimmed cow's milk.	14 months to 2 years.	Sharp, piquant.	Very hard, granular, lower moisture and milkfat than Romano.	Creamy white	Cylindrical, wedges, shredded, grated.	Grated for seasoning in soups, or vegetables, spaghetti, ravioli, breads, popcorn, used extensively in pizza and lasagne.
Romano (Rô-mä´-nō) also called Sardo Romano Pecorino Romano. (Italy)	Cow's milk. In Italy, sheep's milk (Italian law).	5 to 12 months.	Sharp, piquant.	Very hard granular.	Yellowish-white interior, greenish-black surface.	Round with flat ends, wedges, shredded, grated.	Seasoning in soups, casserole dishes, ravioli, sauces, breads, suitable for grating when cured for about one year.
Sap Sago (Săp´-să-gō). (Switzerland)	Skimmed cow's milk.	5 months or more.	Sharp, pungent clover-like.	Very hard	Light green by addition of dried, powdered clover leaves.	Conical, shakers	Grated to flavor soups, meats, macaroni, spaghetti, hot vegetables; mixed with butter makes a good spread on crackers or bread.

Blue-Vein Mold Ripened Varieties

Kind of cheese	Kind of milk used	Ripening period	Flavor	Body and texture	Color	Shape and style of packaging	Uses
Blue, spelled Bleu on imported cheese. (France)	Cow's milk	2 to 6 months.	Tangy, peppery.	Semisoft, pasty, sometimes crumbly.	White interior, marbled or streaked with blue veins of mold.	Cylindrical, wedges, oblongs, squares, cut portions.	Appetizers, salads, dips, sandwich spreads, good with crackers, dessert.
Gorgonzola (Gôr-gŏn-zō´-lä). (Italy)	Cow's milk. In Italy, cow's milk or goat's milk or mixtures of these.	3 to 12 months.	Tangy, peppery.	Semisoft, pasty, sometimes crumbly, lower moisture than Blue.	Creamy white interior, mottled or streaked with blue-green veins of mold. Clay colored surface.	Cylindrical, wedges, oblongs.	Appetizers, snacks, salads, dips, sandwich spread, good with crackers, dessert.
Roquefort (Rōk´-fĕrt) or (Rŏk-fôr´). (France)	Sheep's milk	2 to 5 months or more.	Sharp, slightly peppery.	Semisoft, pasty, sometimes crumbly.	White or creamy white interior, marbled or streaked with blue veins of mold.	Cylindrical, wedges, oblongs.	Appetizers, snacks, salads, dips, sandwich spreads, good with crackers, dessert.
Stilton (England).	Cow's milk	2 to 6 months	Piquant, milder than Gorgonzola or Roquefort.	Semisoft, flaky; slightly more crumbly than Blue.	Creamy white interior, marbled or streaked with blue-green veins of mold.	Circular, wedges, oblongs.	Appetizers, snacks, salads, dessert.

Source: U.S. Department of Agriculture.

425

Figure 24.2

Many varieties of cheese are produced. (Courtesy U. S. Department of Agriculture.)

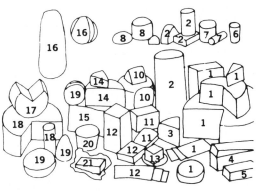

1. Cheddar
2. Colby
3. Monterey or Jack
4. Pasteurized Process Cheese
5. Cheese Foods
6. Cheese Spreads
7. Cold Pack Cheese Food or Club Cheese
8. Gouda and Edam
9. Camembert
10. Muenster
11. Brick
12. Swiss
13. Limburger
14. Blue
15. Gorgonzola
16. Provolone
17. Romano
18. Parmesan
19. Mozzarella and Scamorze
20. Cottage Cheese
21. Cream Cheese

being formed. The lactic acid formed depresses the growth of undesirable microorganisms.

The chemical changes occurring in cheeses during ripening are induced chiefly by enzymes. The enzymes come from microorganisms added as starters, from various microorganisms already present in the milk, and from the milk itself. Protein hydrolysis by proteases causes

Table 24.2 Typical Composition of Cheese

Type	Cheese	Moisture (%)	Fat (%)	Protein (%)	Ash (%)	Salt (%)	Calcium (%)	Lactose (%)
Soft, unripened								
Low-fat	Cottage	79.0	0.4	16.9	0.8	1.0	0.09	2.7
	Creamed cottage	78.3	4.2	13.6	0.8	1.0	0.09	3.3
High-fat	Cream	51.0	37.0	8.8	1.2	1.0	0.08	1.5–2.1
Soft, ripened by surface bacteria	Limburger	46.0	27.0	21.5	3.6	2.0	0.5	0–2.2
Soft, ripened by external molds	Camembert	51.0	26.0	20.0	3.8	2.5	0.6	0–1.8
Semi-soft, ripened by internal molds	Blue	41.5	30.5	21.5	6.0	4.0	0.7	0–2.0
Hard, ripened by bacteria	Cheddar	37.0	32.0	22.0	3.7	1.6	0.7	0–2.1
Hard, ripened by eye-forming bacteria	Swiss	37.0	28.0	27.5	3.8	1.3	1.0	0–1.7
Very hard, ripened by bacteria	Parmesan	30.0	26.0	36.0	5.1	1.8	1.1	0–2.9

Source: From Webb et al., 1974.

the body of the cheese to lose its firm, tough, curdy properties and become soft and mellow. Proteins are converted to proteoses, peptones, amino acids, and ammonia. The casein proteins are apparently degraded preferentially in the order of kappa-casein first, followed by beta- and alpha$_s$-caseins. The rate and extent of characteristic flavor development appears to be related directly to beta-casein degradation (Harper et al., 1971). Breakdown of fat with liberation of fatty acids contributes a great deal to the development of flavor in ripened cheese. Typical cheddar cheese flavor was reported to be related to a balance of free fatty acids and acetate. Cheese made from skim milk did not acquire either cheddar cheese flavor or body characteristics during ripening (Ohren and Tuckey, 1969). Both volatile and nonvolatile compounds are responsible for the flavor of ripened cheese. Volatile substances include short chain fatty acids, aldehydes, ketones, alcohols, amines, esters, and sulfides. Each different variety of cheese is characterized by a specific type of ripening that depends on the microorganisms present, the composition of the milk, the rennet, the amount of salt, and the conditions of manufacture and curing. Although many flavor-producing substances have been isolated from cheese, no single one or combination represent typical cheese flavor. Apparently cheese flavor results from a balanced blending of many specific flavor substances (Webb et al., 1974).

Processed Cheese Natural cheese is made directly from milk. *Processed* (or *process*) *cheese* is made from natural cheese by grinding and mixing together, with heating and stirring, several lots of cheese of the same variety or two or more varieties. An emulsifying agent and certain optional ingredients are also blended with the mixture. The final product has about the same moisture content as the natural cheese. It is packed in a mold while hot. Heating destroys microorganisms and stops the ripening process. The cheese slices without crumbling and melts smoothly. It blends more evenly with cooked foods than do most natural cheeses and is not adversely affected by high temperatures. Therefore, sauces made with processed cheese are very smooth in texture and do not become grainy when heated to relatively high temperatures or upon prolonged heating. Its flavor is usually more mild.

Process cheese food may contain skim milk or whey as well as some other optional ingredients. However, at least 51 percent of the weight of the cheese food must consist of the cheese ingredient. *Process cheese spread* is softer than *process cheese food*. It contains a higher percentage of moisture and a lower percentage of fat.

CHEESE IN COOKED PRODUCTS

Cheddar cheese is most commonly used in cooked dishes. When the cheese is heated, it softens as the fat melts. When the temperature is increased or as heating continues, moisture is lost, the proteins coagulate, toughen, and shrink and the emulsion breaks. Fat separates from the mass.

Cheese is often blended with liquid sauces in food preparation. Cheeses with relatively high moisture and fat contents blend most readily with liquid. Ripened cheese blends with increasing ease as the ripening period continues, due in part to the hydrolysis of protein. The cheese disperses well at pH 5.8 to 8.0 (Personius *et al.,* 1944). The temperature of the liquid into which cheese is blended should be hot enough to melt the cheese but not so hot as to cause toughening and stringiness.

SUMMARY

Although much milk is consumed with minimal processing, highly processed milk products and components also find wide usage in foods. In the United States, milk implies cow's milk.

Milk is a remarkable blend of complex biological molecules. An average composition is: 87.0 percent water, 3.5 percent protein, 3.6 percent fat, 4.9 percent carbohydrate, and 0.7 percent minerals. The chemical composition is more complex than the gross composition indicates, however. It contains at least small amounts of most essential nutrients. It contains calcium in true solution and in colloidal dispersion combined with casein, phosphorus, and citrate. Many enzymes and metabolites are also present. Milk, unless sterilized, contains living microorganisms. Handling conditions are geared to maintaining good sanitary quality in milk.

Physically, milk is a true solution, a colloidal dispersion, and a dilute emulsion. Sugars, vitamins, and many mineral salts are in true solution. Proteins and some calcium phosphate are colloidally dispersed. Fat globules are emulsified and suspended in the aqueous phase of milk.

Milk was traditionally fractionated to yield the proteins casein, lactalbumin, and lactoglobulins. Each of these proteins has since been found to contain several components. Casein includes alpha$_{s1}$-, beta-, and kappa-caseins. It is present in milk as minute micelles, stabilized by kappa-casein and by colloidal calcium phosphate. Casein is easily precipitated by adding acid to a pH of 5.2–4.6. The whey or serum proteins, lactalbumin and lactoglobulin, are not precipitated by acid but are readily heat denatured.

Milk fat exists in milk as microscopic, emulsified globules stabilized by a surface covering called the fat globule membrane. The membrane consists of a mixture of proteins and lipids in an ordered arrangement.

Milk commonly undergoes various processing treatments. Pasteurization involves heating the milk to 62.8°C for at least 30 minutes or to 71.7°C for at least 15 seconds. Pathogenic bacteria are destroyed but the milk is not sterile. Homogenization forces the milk through small openings and breaks up the fat globules. The fat globule membrane is disrupted as new surfaces are created. Casein and whey proteins participate in emulsifying the newly formed fat globules. Significant changes occur in these proteins and affect the stability of homogenized milk to heating.

Fermentation brings about chemical changes through the action of enzymes liberated by microorganisms. Cultured buttermilk, sour cream, and yogurt are fermented milk products. Fermentation also occurs in cheese during manufacture and ripening.

Nonfat dry milk (NDM) has superior storage quality to dried whole milk. The milk is condensed under reduced pressure and dried by spraying into a heated vacuum chamber. An instant NDM is made by remoistening and agglomerating the NDM particles. Dried whey has a composition similar to that of NDM. Evaporated milk is whole milk from which about 60 percent of the water has been removed by heating under a vacuum. Milk proteins are susceptible to coagulation when the concentrated mixture is heated to sterilizing temperatures. Forewarming the milk and the addition of stabilizer salts aid in preventing coagulation.

Milk has a slightly sweet taste due to its lactose content and a slightly salty taste due to the presence of chloride salts. Odor and flavor are also attributed to a variety of low-molecular-weight compounds such as acetone, acetaldehyde, fatty acids, and lactones. Rancid flavor may come from the action of lipase with the release of volatile short chain fatty acids. Oxidized flavor apparently originates with the phospholipids present in the fat globule membrane. An "off-flavor" may be induced by exposure of the milk to direct sunlight, originating in the proteins with riboflavin acting as a photosensitizer. A cooked flavor may be due to liberation of sulfides from the heated beta-lactoglobulin.

Milk is a major ingredient in a variety of puddings, sauces, and soups. Mild heat treatment has little effect on the coagulation of casein. However, elevated temperatures may produce coagulation, especially when milk solids are concentrated.

Rennin is used to clot milk in the making of puddings and ice creams and in cheese production. Coagulation occurs in two phases. A primary phase involves the enzyme's hydrolysis of a glycopeptide from kappa-casein, thereby destabilizing the casein micelle. A secondary phase requires calcium ion in a nonenzymatic gelling reation. Action of rennin requires optimum conditions of temperature and pH.

Acid may be produced in milk by fermenting microorganisms and readily coagulates casein. Combination of milk or cream with acid-containing fruits or polyphenol-containing vegetables may cause thickening and curdling. Casein may coagulate when tomato soup is heated.

Cheese is a concentrated milk product. Many varieties are produced from coagulated milk. Cheese may be ripened by bacteria or molds. The protein in cheese is mainly casein and the fat content is often between 25 and 30 percent.

Cheese is manufactured by forming a curd with milk; cutting the curd; cooking the curd; draining, salting, and pressing; and ripening. Rennin is usually used to form the curd. In cheeses that are to be ripened, a starter culture is first added. The finished cheese is then held for varying periods under carefully controlled conditions for ripening to occur. During ripening, lactic acid fermentation is completed. Protein and fat hydrolysis by enzymes produce changes in flavor and texture.

Cheddar cheese is most commonly used in cooked dishes. It softens as it is heated. At elevated temperatures or long periods of heating, the proteins toughen and shrink and the fat emulsion breaks. Cheeses with relatively high moisture and fat contents blend most readily with liquids in such products as sauces. Process cheese contains an emulsifier that is responsible for its excellent blending properties. Ripened cheese blends with increasing ease as the ripening period continues.

STUDY QUESTIONS

Whole milk contains substances in true solution, in colloidal dispersion, and in suspension.

1. List the average gross composition of whole milk.
2. For each of the following components of whole milk, describe the usual state of dispersion. Describe and explain any changes in dispersion produced by homogenization.

   a. Lactose

b. Casein
c. Lactalbumins
d. Lactoglobulins
e. Fat
f. Calcium phosphate
g. Vitamins
h. Mineral ions

3. Why is whole milk classified as an emulsion? What is the fat globule membrane in milk? Describe its composition and possible structure.

Many milk proteins have been isolated and studied.

4. Name three major groups of proteins in milk. Which one is present in largest amount?
5. Describe at least two distinguishing characteristics of casein and of the whey proteins. How are these proteins stabilized in their dispersion in milk?
6. List the usual pH of fresh milk and the pH at which casein usually precipitates. Explain why casein precipitates readily at this particular pH.

Milk commonly undergoes a variety of processing treatments.

7. Describe the usual time-temperature relationships used in pasteurizing milk. Explain the reason for pasteurization.
8. Describe the process of homogenization of whole milk. Explain why homogenized milk must always be pasteurized.
9. Compare the physical characteristics of homogenized and nonhomogenized milk. Describe several effects of homogenization on the cooking characteristics of milk.
10. How is evaporated milk produced? What is the purpose of forewarming? Why are stabilizers commonly added? Explain.
11. Account for the gelled character and the particular flavor of yogurt.
12. Explain how instant NDM is made and why it is more readily dispersible in water than the noninstant product.
13. Describe some possible uses of whey and whey protein concentrate in the food industry.
14. Account for the natural flavor of milk.
15. Explain the probable cause of each of the following ''off-flavors'' in milk: rancid, oxidized, light-induced, and cooked.

Milk proteins may be denatured and coagulated during food processing and preparation.

16. Describe the effects of heat treatment on milk proteins and on calcium salts.
17. Give examples from food preparation that illustrate the coagulation of milk by: heat, acid, heat and acid, and rennin.
18. Write and explain a two-phase reaction that describes the clotting of milk by rennin. List optimal conditions for the action of this enzyme.

Cheese may be classified in terms of moisture or texture and on the basis of the kind and extent of ripening.

19. From the list of cheeses given below identify those that are classified as

soft, unripened; as firm, unripened; as soft, ripened; as firm, ripened; and as very hard, ripened.

Cheeses
    Colby
    Parmesan
    Cottage
    Gouda
    Neufchatel
    Mozzarella
    Cream
    Limburger
    Swiss
    Camembert
    Cheddar
    Edam

20. Describe and explain changes that occur during the ripening of cheese.

Cheddar cheese requires low temperature and short heating periods when used in cooking.

21. Describe and explain the changes occurring as cheddar cheese is heated to relatively high temperatures. What precautions might be observed in order to avoid the undesirable changes?
22. Explain why processed cheese blends more easily in sauces than does natural cheese.

REFERENCES

1. Andrews, A. T. and G. C. Cheeseman. 1971. Properties of aseptically packed UHT milk: casein modification during storage and studies with model systems. *Journal of Dairy Research* 38, 193.

2. Brunner, J. R., C. W. Duncan, and G. M. Trout. 1953. The fat globule membrane of nonhomogenized and homogenized milk. III. Differences in the sedimentation diagram of the fat globule membrane protein. *Food Research* 18, 469.

3. DeVilbiss, E. D., V. H. Holsinger, L. P. Posati, and M. J. Pallansch. 1974. Properties of whey protein concentrate foams. *Food Technology* 28 (No. 3), 40.

4. Ferretti, A. 1973. Inhibition of cooked flavor in heated milk by use of additives. *Agricultural and Food Chemistry* 21, 939.

5. Forss, D. A. 1969. Flavors of dairy products: A review of recent advances. *Journal of Dairy Science* 52, 832.

6. Glazier, L. R. 1963. Quality comparisons of high-temperature, short-time and ultra-high-temperature pasteurized milk. *Journal of Milk and Food Technology* 26, 347.

7. Gupta, C. B. and N. A. M. Eskin. 1977. Potential use of vegetable rennet in the production of cheese. *Food Technology* 31 (No. 5), 62.

8. Harper, W. J., A. Carmona, and T. Kristoffersen. 1971. Protein degradation in cheddar cheese slurries. *Journal of Food Science* 36, 503.

9. Harshbarger, K. E. 1975. The role of the dairy cow in meeting world food needs. *Nutrition News,* National Dairy Council 38 (No. 3), 9.

10. Holsinger, V. H., L. P. Posati, E. D. DeVilbiss, and M. J. Pallansch. 1973. Fortifying soft drinks with cheese whey protein. *Food Technology* 27 (No. 2), 59.

11. Jackson, R. H. and J. R. Brunner. 1960. Characteristics of protein fractions isolated from the fat/plasma interface of homogenized milk. *Journal of Dairy Science* 43, 912.

12. Jensen, R. G. 1973. Composition of bovine milk lipids. *Journal of the American Oil Chemists Society* 50, 186.

13. Jordan, R., E. S. Wegner, and H. A. Hollender. 1953. The effect of homogenized milk upon the viscosity of cornstarch puddings. *Food Research* 18, 649.

14. Kratzer, D. D., C. F. Foreman, A. E. Freeman, E. E. Bird, W. S. Rosenberger, and F. E. Nelson. 1967. Important sources of variation in milk flavor. *Journal of Dairy Science* 50, 1384.

15. Kroger, M. and S. R. Fram. 1975. Consumer attitudes toward yogurt. *Food Technology* 29 (No. 11), 52.

16. Lampert, L. M. 1970. *Modern Dairy Products.* New York: Chemical Publishing Company.

17. Morr, C. V. 1976. Whey protein concentrates: An update. *Food Technology* 30 (No. 3), 18.

18. National Dairy Council. 1977. Utilization of milk components by the food industry. *Dairy Council Digest* 48 (No. 5), 25.

19. National Dairy Council. 1971. Composition and nutritive value of dairy foods. *Dairy Council Digest* 42 (No. 1), 1.

20. Ohren, J. A. and S. L. Tuckey. 1969. Relation of flavor development in cheddar cheese to chemical changes in the fat of the cheese. *Journal of Dairy Science* 52, 598.

21. O'Leary, V. S. and J. H. Woychik. 1976. A comparison of some chemical properties of yogurts made from control and lactase-treated milks. *Journal of Food Science* 41, 791.

22. Paul, P. C. and H. H. Palmer. 1972. *Food Theory and Applications.* New York: Wiley.

23. Personius, C., E. Boardman, and A. R. Ausherman. 1944. Some factors affecting the behavior of Cheddar cheese in cooking. *Food Research* 9, 304.

24. Rose, D., J. R. Brunner, E. B. Kalan, B. L. Larson, P. Melnychyn, H. E. Swaisgood, and D. F. Waugh. 1970. *Nomenclature of the Proteins of Cow's Milk:* Third Revision. *Journal of Dairy Science* 53, 1.

25. Schultz, H. W., E. A. Day, and L. M. Libbey, editors. 1967. *The Chemistry and Physiology of Flavors.* Westport, Conn.: Avi Publishing Company.

26. Shipe, W. F., R. Bassette, D. D. Dean, W. L. Dunkley, E. G. Hammond, W. J. Harper, D. H. Kleyn, M. E. Morgan, J. H. Nelson, and R. A. Scanlan. 1978. Off flavors of milk: Nomenclature, standards and bibliography. *Journal of Dairy Science* 61, 855.

27. U. S. Department of Agriculture. 1974. How to buy cheese. Home and Garden Bulletin No. 193.

28. U. S. Department of Agriculture. 1971. Federal and state standards for the composition of milk products. Agriculture Handbook No. 51.

29. Webb, B. H., A. H. Johnson, and J. A. Alford, editors. 1974. *Fundamentals of Dairy Chemistry,* 2nd edition. Westport, Conn.: Avi Publishing Company.

30. Zaehringer, M. W. 1972. Properties of glutens from dough containing components of cheddar-cheese whey. *Cereal Chemistry* 49, 307.

CHAPTER 25

MEAT

Meat is commonly the major item around which a menu is planned and is likely to be the most costly portion of a meal. Therefore, knowledge of meat's chemical composition, physical properties, storage life, preparation, and nutritive value is of great importance to the consumer and producer alike.

Meat has been defined as the flesh of animals used for food. This definition includes both fresh and processed tissues. Beef, pork, veal, lamb or mutton, poultry, and fish are the predominant meats consumed in the United States. Beef comprises nearly half of the meat eaten, with an average consumption of 109 lb per person in 1973. Pork accounts for approximately 30 percent of the total meat eaten in the United States (U. S. Department of Agriculture, 1975). In some other countries of the world meat may more commonly include goat, horse, llama, camel, deer, or rabbit. (Poultry and fish are discussed in Chapter 26.)

25.1

COMPOSITION AND STRUCTURE

Meat is derived primarily from muscle tissue. The muscle is composed of various types of connective tissue, including fibrous connective tissue, adipose tissue, cartilage, and bone (Forrest *et al.,* 1975). The composition of a typical skeletal muscle with all of the visible fat removed is approximately (Cole and Lawrie, 1975):

Water	75.0%
Protein	19.0%
Lipid	2.5%
Miscellaneous soluble nonprotein substances	2.3%

The gross composition of market meat cuts varies greatly, depending upon the amount of adipose tissue that accompanies the muscle tissue.

The amount of fat on the carcass varies with the grade as well as with the particular cut of meat. Table 25.1 gives the composition for selected cuts of raw meat. An extensive study of the composition of cooked meat was done by Leverton and Odell (1958). They divided cooked meat into categories: 1. The *extremely lean* portion that had no visible fat; 2. the *lean-marbled-with fat* portion that had streaks of visible *intermuscular fat* (*marbling*); 3. the obviously *fat* portion that had no visible lean or marbled areas. When they referred to *lean-plus-marble,* they included the *extremely lean* portion plus *the lean-marbled-with-fat* portion. This has been reported as *separable lean* by other researchers. Table 25.2 gives data from this study on selected cuts of cooked meat.

STRUCTURE OF MUSCLE TISSUE

Muscle is a complex system in terms of structure and function. In the living animal, muscles allow for voluntary locomotion as they convert chemical energy into mechanical energy through the process of contraction. The mechanism of muscle contraction has been extensively studied since it is of great interest to the biologist and to the medical researcher. The meat scientist studies the muscles of the slaughtered animal. However, some aspects of contraction and relaxation in the living muscle are similar to postmortem changes that cause shortening of fibers and changes in tenderness of the meat. Since the structure and function of muscle tissue do affect the quality of meat as it is prepared for consumption, knowledge of these aspects is important to the student of food science.

A basic unit of muscle tissue is the fiber or muscle cell. This is a long, threadlike cell that tapers slightly at both ends, as shown in Figure 25.1. One cell may be many centimeters in length and from 10 μm to more than 100 μm in diameter. Many muscle fibers are bound together by

Table 25.1 Composition of Selected Cuts of Raw Meat, 100 Grams, Edible Portion

Cut of meat	Water (%)	Kcal	Protein (g)	Fat (g)	Ash (g)
Beef, retail cuts					
Arm (chuck), choice grade	64.2	223	19.4	15.5	0.9
Arm, good grade	67.3	191	20.3	11.6	0.9
Flank, choice grade	71.7	144	21.6	5.7	1.0
Flank, good grade	72.1	139	21.8	5.1	1.0
T-bone, choice grade	47.5	397	14.7	37.1	0.7
T-bone, good grade	50.6	366	15.4	33.3	0.7
Rib, 11th–12th, choice grade	43.0	444	13.8	42.7	0.6
Rib, 11th–12th, good grade	49.5	376	15.5	34.3	0.7
Round, choice grade	66.6	197	20.2	12.3	0.9
Port, retail cuts					
Loin, medium-fat class	57.2	298	17.1	24.9	0.9
Ham, fresh, medium-fat class	56.5	308	15.9	26.6	0.7

Source: From Watt and Merrill, 1963.

Table 25.2 Composition of Selected Cuts of Cooked Meat, 100 Gram Portions

Cut of meat	Water (g)	Kcal	Protein (g)	Fat (g)	Ash (g)
Beef					
Arm pot roast,					
lean-plus-marble	52.6	263	33.0	13.5	1.07
lean-plus-marble-plus-fat	44.5	367	26.8	28.0	0.92
Flank					
lean-plus-marble	55.7	235	33.4	10.2	1.23
T-bone					
lean-plus-marble	58.0	247	25.3	15.5	1.03
lean-plus-marble-plus-fat	46.2	378	20.3	32.3	0.87
Rib					
lean-plus-marble	56.6	262	25.5	17.0	1.07
lean-plus-marble-plus-fat	45.2	391	20.4	33.7	0.93
Round, bottom					
lean-plus-marble	53.1	238	35.5	9.5	1.18
lean-plus-marble-plus-fat	47.5	306	31.3	19.1	1.09
Pork					
Loin, center cut					
lean-plus-fat	43.7	357	29.4	25.6	1.15
Ham, fresh					
lean-plus-marble	52.6	237	37.0	8.8	1.47
lean-plus-marble-plus-fat	47.3	306	32.9	18.3	1.37

Source: From Leverton and Odell, 1958.

thin sheets of connective tissue to form a muscle as illustrated in Figure 25.2. The muscle fiber is immediately surrounded by a thin membrane called the *sarcolemma*. Located periodically along the length of the fiber and around its entire circumference are invaginations of the sarcolemma that form a network of tubules within the cell that play key roles in initiating the contraction process. Motor nerve fiber endings terminate on the sarcolemma.

Inside the muscle fiber or cell is the *cytoplasm* which, in this case, is called *sarcoplasm*. Suspended in the sarcoplasm are tiny cylindrical

Figure 25.1

Muscle fibers are long, threadlike cells.

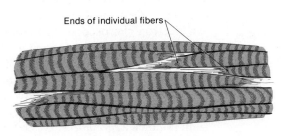

Ends of individual fibers

Figure 25.2

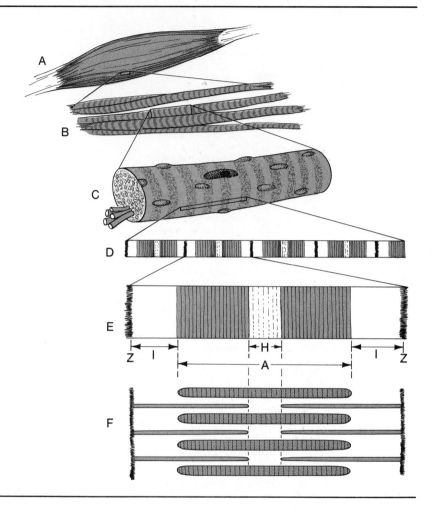

Striated muscle is dissected in these schematic drawings. A muscle (A) is made up of muscle fibers (B) that appear striated in the light microscope. The small branching structures at the surface of the fibers are the end-plates of motor nerves, that signal the fibers to contract. A single muscle fiber (C) is made up of myofibrils, beside which lie cell nuclei and mitochondria. In a single myofibril (D) the striations are resolved into a repeating pattern of light and dark bands. A single unit of this pattern (E) consists of a Z-line, then an I-band, then an A-band which is interrupted by an H-zone, then the next I-band and finally the next Z-line. Electron micrographs have shown that the repeating band pattern is due to the overlapping of thick and thin filaments (F). (Reprinted with permission from Huxley, H. E. 1958. The contraction of muscle. *Scientific American* 206 [No. 11].)

rods called *myofibrils*. The *myofibril* is an *organelle* that is unique to muscle tissue. It consists of an ordered array of protein molecules. Some of the proteins form thick filaments while others form thin filaments. Because of the arrangement of the filaments, a distinct repeating pattern of light and dark bands appears when muscle is viewed through an electron microscope. In Figure 25.3 is seen a striated muscle with light and dark bands appearing on the myofibrils. For purposes of study and comparison, the bands and lines on the repeating pattern of the myofibril have been identified with letters. Figure 25.4 shows parts of two myofibrils and indicates how the thick and thin protein filaments in the myofibril relate to the density of the various parts. One repeating unit is called a *sarcomere*. It is bounded by *Z lines* on each end. Next to the Z line is a light segment named the *I band*. The dark center zone is called the *A band*. However, the A band has a somewhat lighter *H zone*

Figure 25.3

Electron micrograph of striated muscle from a rabbit showing light and dark bands on the myofibrils. (Enlarged 24,000 diameters.) (Reprinted with permission from Huxley, H. E. 1958. The contraction of muscle. *Scientific American* **206 [No. 11].)**

in the center and the H zone is also dissected by an *M line*. The arrangement of thick and thin filaments can be seen in Figure 25.4 and also in Figure 25.2.

The thick and the thin filaments are composed of different proteins with differing functions in the contraction process. The thick filaments, that constitute the A band of the sarcomere, consist almost entirely of the protein myosin. Myosin molecules each have a head and a tail. They are grouped together in an organized manner to form the thick myosin filaments as shown in Figure 25.5. The myosin molecules are held together in the thick filaments by placement of C proteins at periodic intervals. Myosin filaments are held in alignment by cross connections of another protein at the M line. The heads of the myosin

Figure 25.4

Electron micrograph of parts of two myofibrils and a diagram showing the relationship of protein filaments to the bands in the myofibril. (Reprinted with permission from Huxley, H. E. 1965. The mechanism of muscular contraction. *Scientific American* 213 [No. 6], 18.)

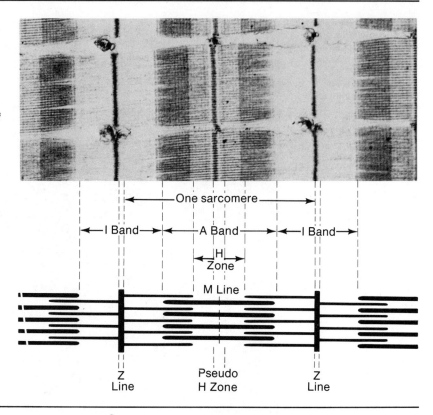

Figure 25.5

The thick filament is an assembly of myosin molecules, long rods with a double head at one end. The head has an active site where the chemical events involved in muscle contraction take place. In thick filaments myosins are bundled into a sheaf with heads projecting in groups of three. (From Murray, J. M. and A. Weber. 1974. The cooperative action of muscle proteins. *Scientific American* 230 [No. 2], 58. With permission.)

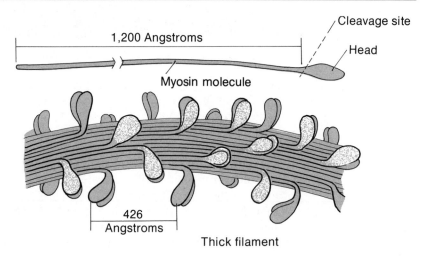

molecules are the active sites that form cross-bridges during muscle contraction.

The thin filaments, that constitute the I band and proceed on into the darkest section of the A band, are composed primarily of the protein actin. Individual actin units are globular proteins, as shown in Figure 25.6, and are called *G-actin*. These globular molecules polymerize into a fibrous strand called *F-actin*. Two strands of F-actin coil around each other and are bound together by strands of tropomyosin (see Figure 25.6). Thin actin filaments are connected to Z filaments at the Z line.

Each myofibril, that is made up of orderly arrays of many thick and thin filaments, is surrounded by the *sarcoplasmic reticulum* (SR). The SR is a membranous system of tubules and cisternae (flattened reservoirs for holding Ca^{++}), forming a closely meshed network. Transverse tubules cross the SR at regular intervals and are connected with the sarcolemma that surrounds the entire muscle fiber (Forrest *et al.*, 1975). The structure of a muscle fiber with its many myofibrils is shown by a cut-away diagram in Figure 25.7.

Groups of individual muscle fibers are joined together into bundles of varying sizes. The sarcolemma of individual fibers is surrounded by a very thin sheath of connective tissue called the *endomysium*. Even though these two membranes, the sarcolemma and the endomysium, both encase the muscle fiber, they are two separate and distinct structures. Approximately 20–40 muscle fibers are grouped into *primary bundles*. A number of primary bundles are grouped together to form larger *secondary bundles*. The primary and secondary bundles are each surrounded by sheaths of connective tissue called the *perimysium*. Finally, a number of secondary bundles are grouped together and ensheathed in the *epimysial connective tissue* to form a muscle. Associated nerves and blood vessels are bound together in the *organized muscle structure* (For-

Figure 25.6

The thin filament is an assembly of actin, tropomyosin and troponin molecules. The actins are small spheroidal molecules that are linked to form a double helix. Tropomyosin forms a continuous strand that sits on the string of actins. Troponin is affixed near one end of each tropomyosin. (From Murray, J. M. and A. Weber. 1974. The cooperative action of muscle proteins. *Scientific American* 230 [No. 2], 58. With permission.)

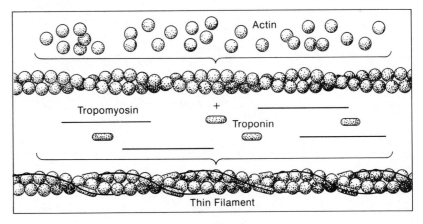

Figure 25.7

Structure of muscle fiber consists of a number of fibrils, which in turn are made up of orderly arrays of thick and thin filaments of protein. A system of transverse tubules opens to the exterior of the fiber. The sarcoplasmic reticulum is a system of tubules that does not open to the exterior. The two systems meet at a number of junctions called dyads or triads. (From Hoyle, G. 1970. How is muscle turned on and off? *Scientific American* 222 [No. 4], 84. With permission.)

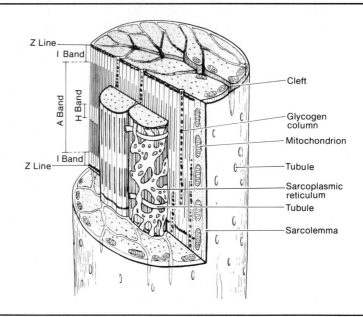

Figure 25.8

Groups of individual muscle fibers are joined together in bundles of varying sizes.

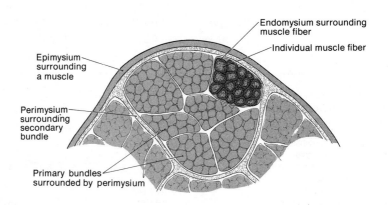

rest *et al.,* 1975). Figure 25.8 illustrates the grouping of muscle fiber bundles in a cross section of muscle. The primary bundles make up the grain of a cut of meat. The various muscles of an animal differ in cooking characteristics. Several muscles of beef cuts are identified in Figure 25.9.

Figure 25.9

**Beef muscles in se-
lected retail cuts.**

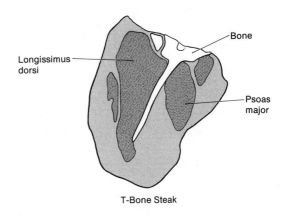

Longissimus
dorsi

Bone

Psoas
major

T-Bone Steak

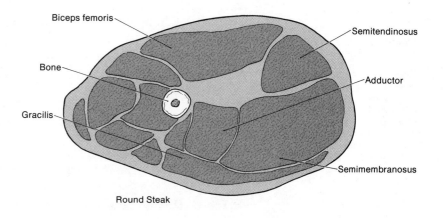

Biceps femoris

Semitendinosus

Bone

Adductor

Gracilis

Semimembranosus

Round Steak

Muscles are usually classified as *red* or *white*, based primarily on their color intensity. Most muscles contain a mixture of red and white muscle fibers. Those with a high proportion of red fibers appear red while those with a high proportion of white fibers appear white. Red and white fibers differ not only in their color but also in their function and metabolism. Red fibers contain larger amounts of the oxygen-carrying pigment, *myoglobin,* are smaller in diameter, contain a lower amount of glycogen, and contract more slowly than do white fibers. Red fibers have a high capacity for *oxidative energy metabolism,* that occurs in the tiny powerhouses called *mitochondria,* while the white fibers have a greater capacity for *anaerobic (glycolytic) metabolism* that allows them to contract rapidly in short bursts (Forrest *et al.,* 1975).

Contraction of Skeletal Muscle   The intricate structure of muscle components that has been described previously is necessary for contraction to occur in a smooth and organized manner. During contraction, the muscle shortens as the thick and thin filaments slide past each other. Figure 25.10 illustrates this event. This process of *sliding contraction* requires energy. The head of each of the myosin molecules in the thick filaments possesses enzyme activity, functioning as an ATPase. The high energy compound, adenosine triphosphate (ATP), is hydrolyzed to adenosine diphosphate (ADP) and inorganic phosphate by the action of the ATPase with the release of energy for contraction (Huxley, 1965). Cross-bridges are formed between the heads of the myosin molecules in the thick filament and the actin in the thin filament. The protein complex formed when these substances interact is called *actomyosin.* Each cross-bridge formed generates enough force to slide the actin component a little farther toward the center of the thick filament. Filament sliding requires a cyclic making and breaking of cross-bridges as contraction proceeds (Forrest *et al.,* 1975).

A question only recently answered asks how muscle is turned on or off in the contraction process. The answer involves a flow of calcium

Figure 25.10

Contraction of muscle entails change in relative position of the thick and thin filaments. The effect of contraction on the band pattern of muscle is indicated by four electron micrographs and accompanying schematic illustrations of muscle in longitudinal section, fixed at consecutive stages of contraction. First the H zone closes (*1*), then a new dense zone develops in the center of the A band (*2, 3* and *4*) as thin filaments from each end of the sarcomere overlap. (Reprinted with permission from Huxley, H. E. 1965. The mechanism of muscular contraction. *Scientific American* 213 [No. 6], 18.)

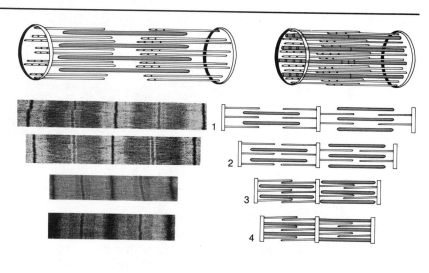

ions that occurs in response to a nerve signal (Hoyle, 1970). In the relaxed state there are no cross-bridges between myosin and actin molecules in the thick and thin filaments. There is a very low level of calcium ions (Ca^{++}) in the sarcoplasm that bathes the myofibrils. Most of the calcium in the muscle fiber, during the relaxed state, is bound in the SR. A relatively high concentration of ATP is also maintained in the myofibril during relaxation to prevent the interaction of myosin and actin. A nerve impulse depolarizes the sarcolemma membrane at the surface of the muscle fiber as the contraction process is initiated. This impulse is transmitted to the myofibrils within the muscle fiber through the transverse tubules and causes the release of bound Ca^{++} from the SR to the sarcoplasm bathing the myofibrils. The increased amount of Ca^{++} in the sarcoplasm triggers the contraction mechanism in the myofibril. Calcium ions are bound by troponin, a small protein that is attached to the actin filament and helps to inhibit the formation of cross-bridges. With this inhibition removed by calcium binding, myosin is freed to form cross-linkages between the filaments and the sliding mechanism proceeds. Calcium is again returned to the SR as the fibril relaxes (Forrest *et al.*, 1975; Hoyle, 1970).

CONNECTIVE TISSUE

As previously discussed, connective tissue binds muscle fibers in bundles to form muscles. Connective tissue also functions in other areas of the animal body to connect and hold various parts together. The skin or hide is attached to the body by connective tissue. Connective tissue generally has few cells and a considerable amount of extracellular substance. Fibers are characteristically embedded in the extracellular material (Forrest *et al.*, 1975). The amount of and character of connective tissue affects tenderness in meat (Hiner, 1955).

Connective tissue proper consists of a structureless ground substance through which are distributed extracellular fibers. A few cells, particularly fibroblasts, are also present. The fibers of connective tissue include reticulin, collagen, and elastin. *Reticulin* consists of small fibers that form delicate networks around cells, blood vessels, neural structures, and epithelium holding them in place. *Elastin* fibers are rubbery and elastic. Aggregations of these fibers have a yellow color and are resistant to solubilization by either digestive enzymes or heat in cooking. Elastin is much less abundant in the connective tissue of meat than is collagen. *Collagen* is the principal structural protein of connective tissue (Forrest *et al.*, 1975). The basic structural molecule from which collagen fibers are built is called *tropocollagen*. Since collagen is the raw material from which gelatin is produced, it is discussed in Section 21.2.

ADIPOSE TISSUE

Adipose tissue consists of accumulations of cells called *adipocytes* in which fat is stored. The adipocytes are deposited in connective tissue in various body sites. Fat deposited in the connective tissue beneath the skin is called *subcutaneous fat*. This fat becomes the outer covering on the meat carcass after slaughter. Fat deposited between the muscles, called *intermuscular fat,* is usually in the *epimysium.* Intramuscular fat lies in the *perimysium* and *endomysium.* Inter- and intramuscular fat distribution is called *marbling.* Intramuscular fat is usually laid down only after the subcutaneous and intermuscular depots are reasonably well supplied. The fatness of an animal is dependent upon age, feed, and management.

25.2

POSTMORTEM CHANGES IN MUSCLE

A distinction is generally made between the terms *muscle* and *meat.* Meat has, of course, most of the chemical and structural characteristics of muscle. However, there are a number of differences. With the death of the animal, a series of complex biochemical reactions initiates some important changes that bring about the transformation of muscle into meat. The magnitude of these changes affects meat quality. In fact, during the first 24–48 hours postmortem, almost all quality attributes of meat are established.

At slaughter, the animal is generally *exsanguinated;* that is, as much blood as possible is removed from its body. Therefore, the blood no longer carries nutrients and oxygen to the muscles of the animal nor carries waste products away. As the oxygen supply of the muscle is depleted, the *aerobic* (oxidative) pathway for energy metabolism can no longer function. For a time, an anaerobic pathway takes over the metabolism of glucose to yield the high energy compound, adenosine triphosphate (ATP). Glucose is derived from the glycogen that is stored in the muscle. The anaerobic pathway for glucose metabolism produces lactic acid. Normally, in the living animal, lactic acid is transported in the blood to the liver where it is used for the synthesis of more glucose and glycogen. Since this can no longer occur, lactic acid accumulates in the muscle and causes a decrease in pH. The ultimate pH reached in muscle postmortem depends to a great degree on the amount of glycogen that was stored in the muscle at the time of exsanguination.

The rate of pH decrease and the ultimate pH achieved vary widely from one animal to another and vary slightly among the muscles from a single animal (Khan and Ballantyne, 1973). The changes in pH affect meat quality. If the pH decreases too rapidly before body heat has been dissipated through carcass chilling, the muscle proteins are denatured with an accompanying loss of water holding capacity. The myoglobin pigment also appears pale in color. If the pH remains high, the color of the meat will be dark and the surface will be dry because water is tightly bound to the proteins (Forrest *et al.,* 1975). The average initial pH of the *loin muscle (longissimus dorsi)* of five beef animals was reported by Bodwell *et al.* (1965) to be 6.99. This declined to 5.46 at 48 hours postmortem. The mean initial pH of an *arm muscle (triceps brachii)* of eight steers was reported to be 7.1 and dropped to 5.6 after

48 hours (Ashmore *et al.*, 1972). Beef muscle with an ultimate pH above 6 is dark and dry in appearance. Antemortem stress to the animal, such as prolonged struggling before slaughter, might deplete muscle glycogen and therefore produce a relatively high muscle pH.

The general stiffening phenomenon that occurs in the animal carcass a short time after death as a result of metabolic changes is called *rigor mortis*. At the moment of death, energy in the form of ATP is used to maintain the integrity of the muscle cells. The muscles are soft and pliable. ATP is necessary to keep the myofibrils in a relaxed state. As metabolism in the muscle cell gradually slows down and stops and the supply of ATP is depleted, the muscle stiffens. Cross-bridges form between actin and myosin in the myofibrils and these bridges generally cannot be broken. The muscle assumes a contracted state, similar to the one existing in the living animal except that this contracted state is permanent. Accompanying the rigor mortis are loss of muscle elasticity and extensibility, increase in tension, and shortening. Meat cooked while in rigor tends to be tough.

AGING

As meat is held after the development of rigor mortis, a gradual softening takes place. The decreased tenderness that is associated with the onset of rigor is reversed. Tenderness increases with the increasing length of the holding period up to an optimum time. The process of holding meat after the resolution of rigor mortis is called *aging*.

Resolution of rigor mortis or *softening* of the meat is thought to result from alterations in the structure of the myofibrils. The appearance of the sarcomere changes, and can be observed under the microscope. Actin filaments may become dissociated from their attachments at the Z line and the Z line becomes less distinct when the myofibril is examined histologically. Sarcomere length increases somewhat during aging, probably as a result of changes in the amount of cross-bonding. Muscle proteins increase their water holding capacity. These changes are related to increased tenderness (Lawrie, 1974). Muscles contain proteolytic enzymes, called *cathepsins*. It is possible that the action of these proteases has some effect on the structural changes related to the resolution of rigor mortis. The extent of their influence is not known (Forrest *et al.*, 1975).

Aging does not have the same effect on the palatability of meat from all species. Beef is generally improved by aging. Smith *et al.* (1978) aged beef carcasses in a cooler at 1°C (34°F) for varying periods of time, up to 28 days. These researchers found that aging for 11 days optimized tenderness in broiled or roasted cuts of Choice grade meat from loin, chuck, rib, and round portions. Aging for longer periods did not improve tenderness further. Overall palatability was also optimal after 11 days of aging for most of the cuts. In contrast to the improvement reported for beef, the aging of pork loins for longer than one day was reported by Harrison *et al.* (1970) to be of little benefit in terms of the characteristics of pork that affect consumer acceptance, although tenderness was increased slightly after 12 days of aging. However, Ramsey *et al.* (1973) reported that aging pork loins for about one week resulted in a product that was judged superior in terms of palatability to that not aged or aged longer than a week. Flavor was not generally improved by one week of aging and flavor scores actually decreased with aging periods longer than one week. Pork fat is particularly susceptible to the development of "off-odors" resulting from oxidation.

Primal (*wholesale*) and *subprimal* cuts of meat are sometimes vacuum packaged in a centralized location as an aid in marketing. The major purposes of vacuum packaging are to improve sanitation and reduce meat shrinkage. Minks and Stringer (1972) studied the effect of vacuum packaging on the aging of beef loins and ribs. They reported that this treatment had no significant influence on changes in tenderness, flavor, and juiciness produced by aging but that there was a highly significant reduction in weight loss during the aging period. Ramsey *et al.* (1973) also found that vacuum packaging reduced the shrinkage of pork loins during aging.

The temperature at which aging is done affects the rate of changes occurring in the meat, aging being more rapid at a higher temperature. Beef rib steaks from sides aged at 16°C (61°F) for one day postmortem were as tender as steaks from sides aged at 2°C (35.6°F) for seven days postmortem. Flavor development of the steaks was also more rapid at 16°C. The differences due to temperature during aging were not as great in the semitendinosus muscle as they were in the rib (Parrish *et al.*, 1973).

25.3

INSPECTION AND GRADING

INSPECTION

Inspection of meat by qualified personnel is required in the United States to assure that the animal is free from disease and that the meat is fit for human consumption at the time of slaughter. The Federal Meat Inspection Act of 1906, applying to all meat entering interstate commerce, was passed in response to a need for the curtailment of unsanitary and unsafe practices in the packing industry. This act regulates the inspection of live animals before slaughter, their carcasses following slaughter, and all meat products produced from these carcasses. To assure similar standards for meat processed within the various states, the Wholesome Meat Act of 1967 was passed. This law provides for a State-Federal cooperative program to set up state meat inspection programs that are equivalent to the federal procedures. With the passage of the Wholesome Meat Act, the provisions of this act and those of the Federal Meat Inspection Act of 1906 were consolidated into one Federal Meat Inspection Act. The U. S. Department of Agriculture (USDA) administers the law.

The inspection of animals by a qualified inspector immediately prior to slaughter is mandatory under the provisions of the meat inspection

Figure 25.11

This stamp is similar to those placed on meat carcasses that have passed official inspection. (Courtesy U. S. Department of Agriculture.)

law. After slaughter, each carcass and its organs are examined. Meat carcasses that pass this examination are stamped, using a safe purple ink, with the official mark similar to that shown in Figure 25.11. The stamp shown in Figure 25.12 is similar to those used for inspected meat products. During the actual processing, all ingredients and processing procedures are continually checked to insure wholesomeness. Establishments in which inspectors operate must meet prescribed standards for sanitation. Meat products must also be labeled according to established regulations.

GRADING

A voluntary program that is related to inspection but separate from it is the USDAs program of grading meats for quality characteristics. Meat grading is a procedure whereby meats or meat products with common characteristics are segregated into standardized groups. Each grade has a specified minimum level for each of the characteristics designated (Forrest *et al.*, 1975).

The major purpose behind meat grading is to facilitate the marketing and merchandising of meat products. Grades provide uniform stan-

Figure 25.12

This stamp is similar to those used for officially inspected meat products. (Courtesy U. S. Department of Agriculture.)

dards for classification and terminology that can be used by the producer and the consumer alike. There are two general types of federal grades for meat; they are grades for *quality* and grades for *quantity* (*yield grades*). *Quality grades* categorize meat on the basis of palatability traits. *Yield grades* classify carcasses in terms of an expected yield of trimmed retail cuts. The USDA administers the grading program through its Consumer and Marketing Service.

Several factors, all having to do with palatability, are used to establish quality grades. These include the maturity of the animal, the marbling of fat within muscles, and the color and texture of the lean. Quality grades for beef, veal and calf, lamb, mutton, and pork are given in Table 25.3. USDA grades for pork are not intended to identify differences in quality to consumers since much of the pork is processed before reaching the retail market. These grades are more concerned with yield than with quality. Brand names may be used by the meat processor to designate grades. A purple shield-shaped grademark (see Figure 25.13) is applied to the carcass with a roller stamp.

Yield grades are designated in terms of *cutability* and are used along with quality grades for beef and lamb. They indicate the proportionate amount of salable retail cuts that can be obtained from a carcass. Yield grades are indicated by the numbers 1, 2, 3, 4, and 5, with number 1 indicating the highest yield.

Not all of the factors used to establish quality grades are closely related to palatability. The maturity of the animal affects the lean meat texture, with the grain generally becoming more coarse with increasing maturity. Fine textured lean is usually slightly more tender than lean with a very coarse texture. A very mature animal usually develops changes in connective tissue that contribute to decreased tenderness. However, tenderness scores may increase with the increasing maturity of some cuts of beef up to an optimum stage (Hoke and Hedrick, 1969). Although the grading system does not directly determine tenderness, some studies have indicated that Choice grade beef is generally more tender than Commercial grade (Moore, 1966) and possibly more tender

Table 25.3 USDA Quality Grades for Meat

Beef	Veal and Calf	Lamb and Yearling Mutton	Mutton	Pork Carcasses
Prime	Prime	Prime		U. S. No. 1
Choice	Choice	Choice	Choice	U. S. No. 2
Good	Good	Good	Good	U. S. No. 3
Standard	Standard	Utility	Utility	U. S. No. 4
Commercial	Utility	Cull	Cull	U. S. Utility
Utility	Cull			
Cutter				
Canner				

Figure 25.13

Shield-shaped grade marks are applied to carcasses by USDA personnel. (Courtesy U. S. Department of Agriculture.)

than Good grade (Hoke and Hedrick, 1969). Higher flavor scores have also been reported for Choice than for Good grade beef cuts. The marbling of fat in beef cuts has been found by some researchers but not by others, to contribute to juiciness and tenderness (Jennings *et al.*, 1978).

25.4

MEAT IDENTIFICATION

Meat carcasses are commonly divided into *primal* (*wholesale*) cuts and these are further divided into *subprimal* or *retail* cuts. Figures 25.14 through 25.17 show the usual divisions of carcasses for beef, pork, lamb, and veal. In order to make the wisest decisions when purchasing meat, the consumer should be able to identify cuts of meat and have knowledge of their distinguishing characteristics. Division into cuts is made in relation to bone and muscle structure. Muscles contained within one retail cut generally have similar characteristics of tenderness and texture. The shapes and sizes of bones and muscles in retail cuts are guides to identification.

A standardized nomenclature for meat cuts is essential for effective merchandising. The meat industry realized the importance of uniform identity standards and appointed an Industrywide Cooperative Meat Identification Standards Committee. This committee was assigned the responsibility of developing standards for the retail meat trade. Their report was published in 1973 by the National Live Stock and Meat Board. A master list of recommended names totaling 314 identifications for retail cuts of beef, pork, lamb, and veal is included in their report. This list serves all regions of the United States. The recommended retail package label information includes the species or kind of meat, the primal or wholesale cut name, and the specific retail name from the master list. A typical label would be:

BEEF CHUCK
BLADE ROAST

Figure 25.14

Retail cuts and primal cuts of beef. (Adapted from Uniform Retail Meat Identity Standards, National Live Stock and Meat Board, Chicago, Ill., 1973.)

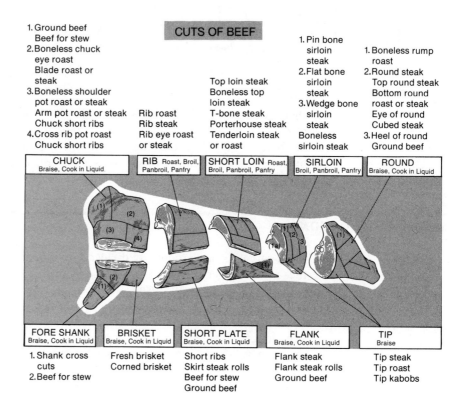

CUTS OF BEEF

1. Ground beef
   Beef for stew
2. Boneless chuck
   eye roast
   Blade roast or
   steak
3. Boneless shoulder
   pot roast or steak
   Arm pot roast or steak
   Chuck short ribs
4. Cross rib pot roast
   Chuck short ribs

Rib roast
Rib steak
Rib eye roast
or steak

Top loin steak
Boneless top
loin steak
T-bone steak
Porterhouse steak
Tenderloin steak
or roast

1. Pin bone
   sirloin
   steak
2. Flat bone
   sirloin
   steak
3. Wedge bone
   sirloin
   steak
   Boneless
   sirloin steak

1. Boneless rump
   roast
2. Round steak
   Top round steak
   Bottom round
   roast or steak
   Eye of round
   Cubed steak
3. Heel of round
   Ground beef

CHUCK Braise, Cook in Liquid	RIB Roast, Broil, Panbroil, Panfry	SHORT LOIN Roast, Broil, Panbroil, Panfry	SIRLOIN Broil, Panbroil, Panfry	ROUND Braise, Cook in Liquid

FORE SHANK Braise, Cook in Liquid	BRISKET Braise, Cook in Liquid	SHORT PLATE Braise, Cook in Liquid	FLANK Braise, Cook in Liquid	TIP Braise

1. Shank cross
   cuts
2. Beef for stew

Fresh brisket
Corned brisket

Short ribs
Skirt steak rolls
Beef for stew
Ground beef

Flank steak
Flank steak rolls
Ground beef

Tip steak
Tip roast
Tip kabobs

25.5

MEAT TENDERNESS

One of the most highly valued palatability traits for meat is tenderness. Because of this, no aspect of meat acceptability has received more research study than has this characteristic. Many factors that influence tenderness have been identified, but much of the variation that occurs from one animal to another still remains unexplained.

Figure 25.15

Retail cuts and primal cuts of pork. (Adapted from Uniform Retail Meat Identity Standards, National Live Stock and Meat Board, Chicago, Ill., 1973.)

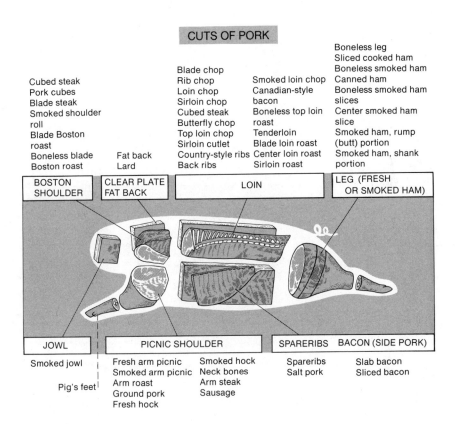

CUTS OF PORK

| Cubed steak
Pork cubes
Blade steak
Smoked shoulder
roll
Blade Boston
roast
Boneless blade
Boston roast | Fat back
Lard | Blade chop
Rib chop
Loin chop
Sirloin chop
Cubed steak
Butterfly chop
Top loin chop
Sirloin cutlet
Country-style ribs
Back ribs | Smoked loin chop
Canadian-style
bacon
Boneless top loin
roast
Tenderloin
Blade loin roast
Center loin roast
Sirloin roast | Boneless leg
Sliced cooked ham
Boneless smoked ham
Canned ham
Boneless smoked ham
slices
Center smoked ham
slice
Smoked ham, rump
(butt) portion
Smoked ham, shank
portion |

| BOSTON
SHOULDER | CLEAR PLATE
FAT BACK | LOIN | LEG (FRESH
OR SMOKED HAM) |

| JOWL | PICNIC SHOULDER | SPARERIBS | BACON (SIDE PORK) |

| Smoked jowl

Pig's feet | Fresh arm picnic
Smoked arm picnic
Arm roast
Ground pork
Fresh hock | Smoked hock
Neck bones
Arm steak
Sausage | Spareribs
Salt pork | Slab bacon
Sliced bacon |

MEASUREMENT OF TENDERNESS

The consumer perceives tenderness as a part of texture as the meat is being eaten. Therefore, when tenderness is measured in research studies, judging panels are commonly used in a sensory or subjective evaluation of the meat products being studied. Various mechanical devices have been constructed for measuring tenderness objectively. Although these instruments are useful, none of them can adequately duplicate the human sensory analysis.

Even with the use of human sense organs in a judging panel, the

Figure 25.16

Retail cuts and primal cuts of lamb. (Adapted from Uniform Retail Meat Identity Standards, National Live Stock and Meat Board, Chicago, Ill., 1973.)

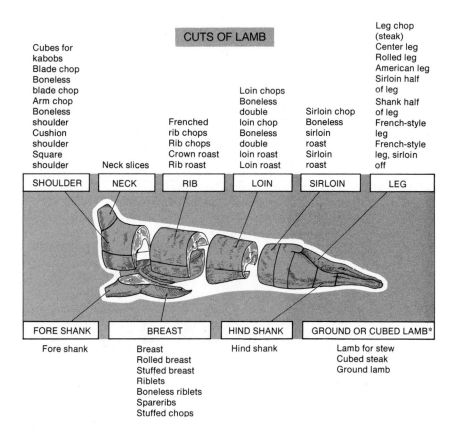

description of meat tenderness is not a simple matter. The perception of tenderness involves stimuli from both muscle fibers and connective tissue. The juiciness of the meat sample also influences the perception of tenderness. A single score for the tenderness of meat being judged has thus been found by many research workers to be inadequate. Cover and Hostetler (1960) described the perception of tenderness in terms of several components.

Figure 25.17

Retail cuts and primal cuts of veal. (Adapted from Uniform Retail Meat Identity Standards, National Live Stock and Meat Board, Chicago, Ill., 1973.)

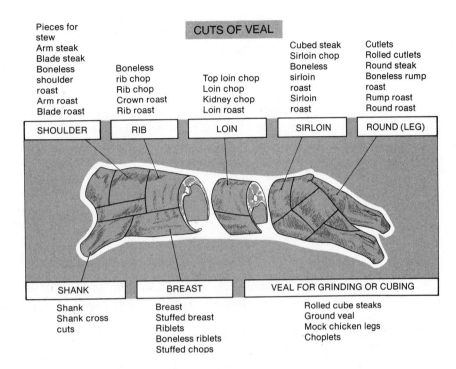

1. Softness
   a. Resistance to tooth pressure (force needed to sink teeth into meat).
   b. Feel on tongue and cheek (tactile sensation).
2. Muscle fiber components
   a. Ease of fragmentation (ability of the teeth to cut across the fibers).

b. Adhesion (degree to which fibers are held together).

c. Mealiness (fragmentation of fibers into small, hard, dry particles).

3. Connective tissue

a. Ease of mastication of connective tissue or residue remaining after most of the sample has been masticated.

The Warner-Bratzler shear device is used by many investigators for the objective measurement of meat tenderness. With this instrument, a cylindrical sample of meat, cut lengthwise with the grain, is inserted through a triangular opening in a metal plate. The plate, with the sample, is pulled upward through two cutting bars. The cutting bars are thus forced against the meat as the plate rises and they shear the sample into two parts against the edge of the metal plate. The plate is attached to a spring scale that measures the force required for a motor to pull the plate until the sample is sheared (Paul and Palmer, 1972). Other instruments used to measure shear force, including the meat shear cell of the Texture Test System and specialized attachments for the Instron Universal Testing Machine, have been developed. Correlations among values obtained with these various instruments are not always high. Correlations of individual instrument readings with judging panel scores are variable. The shear presses apparently measure some different parameters than do judging panels. However, useful information on the comparative tenderness of various muscle tissues and meat cuts is obtained with the use of instruments such as the Warner-Bratzler shear device (Khan *et al.,* 1973; Sharrah *et al.,* 1965).

FACTORS INFLUENCING TENDERNESS

Connective tissue Differences in the amount of and nature of connective tissue present account for much of the variation in tenderness from muscle to muscle within the same animal. Hiner *et al.* (1955) reported that the amount of connective tissue in beef muscles from animals varying in age was related to tenderness, as measured objectively. More connective tissue was found in the muscles of older animals than was found in younger ones. More connective tissue was also reported in muscles of the same animal that were used for locomotion, such as the muscles in the round and the chuck, than was reported in muscles of support, such as the *longissimus dorsi* of the loin. The connective tissue in well-used muscles contains extensively cross-linked collagen fibrils. Hill (1966) suggested that an increase in the number or the strength of cross-links was a more important factor affecting tenderness as it decreases with the age of animal than was the amount of collagen present. Ritchey *et al.* (1963) found less collagen in beef *longissimus dorsi* muscle than in the *biceps femoris* muscle of the round when it was measured in both raw and cooked samples. The collagen in raw steaks was related to subjective panel scores for tenderness of connective tissue in steaks cooked to 61°C (142°F) (Kim *et al.,* 1967).

In the very young animal, such as the veal, the relatively large amount of connective tissue in relation to the immature muscle structure affects less tenderness than might be expected in the muscle of an animal so young. As the calf matures, the muscle development may actually dilute the existing connective tissue and produce a temporary increase in tenderness (Forrest *et al.*, 1975).

Collagen is the connective tissue protein present in largest amount in muscle tissue. However, some elastin is also present in certain muscles. Bendall (1967) reported that most of the cuts of meat from the hindquarter and loin of beef contained less than 5 percent of the total connective tissue as elastin. The chief exception was the semitendinosus muscle of the round that contained about 40 percent of total connective tissue as elastin. Elastin appeared to contribute toughness to the cooked muscle to about the same extent as did collagen. Considerable variation in the collagen and elastin content of beef and veal muscles has been found within grades, however, differences between grades have not been found to be significant (Wilson *et al.*, 1954). Although connective tissue is an important factor in determining the tenderness of meat, other factors also contribute (Cross *et al.*, 1973).

Muscle Fiber Characteristics   The contraction state of the muscle after rigor mortis has developed affects meat tenderness. The hanging of an animal carcass during the chilling process after slaughter places tension on muscles. The tension is not the same for all muscles in the animal. In some cases the sarcomeres and connective tissue (Buck and Black, 1968) are stretched more than in others. If muscles are free to shorten during the onset of rigor mortis, they are often lacking in tenderness. Longer sarcomeres are related to increased tenderness (Hostetler *et al.*, 1970). Differences in the tenderness of various muscles have been reported for carcasses suspended in different positions (Bouton *et al.*, 1973; Hostetler *et al.*, 1972). The practice of hanging a carcass vertically probably stretches the tenderloin (*psoas major*) muscle to about 160 percent of its resting length and may contribute in large measure to the tenderness for which this fillet is noted (Weidemann *et al.*, 1967).

The forming of cross-bridges between actin and myosin molecules during rigor mortis continues, in spite of the position of the carcass and control of shortening during chilling. These cross-bridges, which produce a contracted state for the muscle, contribute to toughness in meat. During the aging process, disruption of the actin filaments and breaking down of linkages between actin and myosin occurs and apparently contributes to the increase in tenderness noted during this process (Weidemann *et al.*, 1967). (Aging is discussed in Section 25.2.)

Water holding capacity and muscle tenderness are well correlated. Tenderness increases with increased water holding capacity. The characteristic toughness found in meat cooked immediately after the completion of rigor mortis may be at least partially due to the fact that the water is free to escape from the cell during the cooking process. Cells shrunken by water loss do not rupture easily when chewed and may give an impression of toughness (Forrest et al., 1975). Other factors that affect the water holding capacity of meat, in addition to the decrease in bound water that occurs on heating, are changes in pH, salt concentration, cross-bonding between muscle fibers, and hydrolysis of meat protein molecules (Paul and Palmer, 1972).

Other Factors The temperature at which a carcass is held immediately after slaughter affects tenderness. Holding beef carcasses for the first 16–20 hours postmortem in a 16°C (61°F) cooler enhanced tenderness by 28–47 percent in comparison to a holding temperature of 2°C (35.6°F) (Smith et al., 1971).

Differences in tenderness have been noted among breeds of cattle (Purchas, 1972). The management regime as the animal is developing may also affect tenderness.

Enzyme treatment is sometimes applied to meat in an effort to increase tenderness. Proteases of plant origin, such as papain from papaya, ficin from figs, and bromelin from pineapple, are commonly employed. Injection into the vascular system immediately prior to slaughter allows distribution of the enzyme preparation to all parts of the animal body. Alternatively, the enzyme mixture is applied directly to the surface of meat cuts (Kang and Warner, 1974; Smith et al., 1973). The enzymes do not degrade proteins at the usual temperatures of storage. As the temperature rises during cooking, the enzymes are activated. Papain is active between 55°–75°C (between 131°–167°F) and is inactivated at approximately 85°C (185°F). These enzymes degrade both connective tissue and muscle proteins. Kang and Rice (1970) reported that bromelin degraded the connective tissue fraction of beef more strongly than the myofibril fraction while the reverse was true for papain and ficin.

Mechanical tenderization by passing pieces of meat through cutting blades has a softening effect on less tender cuts of meat. The amount of organoleptically detectable connective tissue, as well as shear force values, are decreased by blade tenderization. Although improvement in tenderness has been noted, it is doubtful that beef from mature cow and bull carcasses can be improved enough by blade tenderization to make it comparable to beef from steer carcasses (Tatum et al., 1978; Seideman et al., 1977).

Changing the pH may increase the water binding capacity and possibly the tenderness of meat. The preparation of sauerbraten involves the soaking of beef muscle in vinegar before it is cooked, producing a variable decrease in pH. Solutions do not penetrate readily into intact muscle tissue. The strong buffering effect that occurs in meat also contributes to the difficulty of markedly changing the pH of the tissues. Lind et al. (1971) reported that soaking a low grade top round steak in a wine vinegar solution for 48 hours before cooking it by braising increased the tenderness and juiciness but decreased the flavor and overall acceptability scores. However, Griswold (1955) did not find an increase in tenderness when beef was soaked in diluted vinegar for 48 hours before cooking.

The electrical stimulation of animals or carcasses on the kill floor has been suggested as a means of tenderizing meat. Electrical stimulation (100 volts, 5 amps) has been reported to increase tenderness by 12–55 percent and to decrease variability in tenderness among animal groups (Smith et al., 1977).

25.6

MEAT PIGMENTS AND CURING

The most important contributor to meat color is the pigment, myoglobin. Hemoglobin also makes a contribution, although it constitutes only about 10–20 percent of the total pigment in the well-bled animal. Other factors influence the perception of color in meat. These include the texture of the cut meat surface and the lighting conditions. The changing color of both fresh and cured meat products is due primarily to chemical changes in myoglobin and in hemoglobin.

HEME PIGMENTS

Hemoglobin and myoglobin are similar in chemical structure, but the myoglobin molecule is only one-fourth as large as hemoglobin. Myoglobin contains a globular protein portion, called *globin*, and a nonprotein pigment portion, *heme*. Figure 25.18 shows the flat disclike nature of the heme portion of myoglobin and its point of attachment to the globin molecule. Iron (Fe) is coordinated in the center of the heme molecule.

The quantity of myoglobin in meat varies with species, age, sex, muscle, and physical activity. Veal contains less myoglobin than beef because of the difference in age. Pork contains approximately the same

Figure 25.18

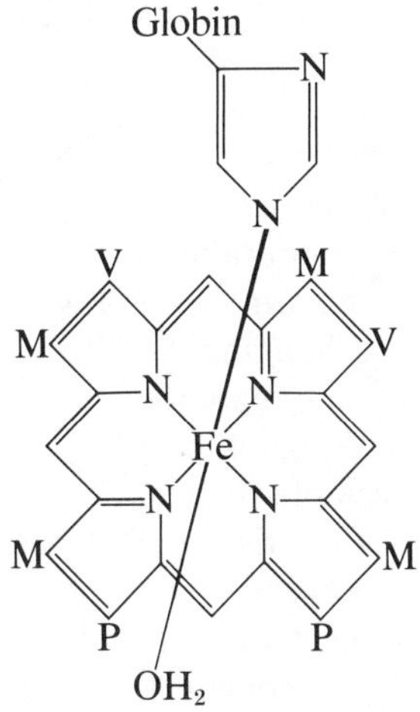

Schematic representation of the heme complex of myoglobin. The globin and water are not part of the planar heme complex. M, V, and P stand for methyl, vinyl, and propyl radicals attached to the porphyrin ring that surrounds the iron atom. (From Bodwell, C. E. and P. E. McClain, Chemistry of animal tissues—proteins. In: *The Science of Meat and Meat Products,* 2nd edition. J. F. Price and B. S. Schweigert, editors. San Francisco: W. H. Freeman and Company, 1971. With permission.)

amount of myoglobin as veal, while mutton averages somewhat higher quantities than does pork. In well-used muscles with a comparatively large blood supply and therefore a high requirement for oxygen, the myoglobin content is relatively high. Red muscle fibers are rich in myoglobin.

The iron of heme is able to combine with several other substances, each with a characteristic effect on the color of the pigment. The *oxidation state* or *valence* of the iron atom also changes under different environmental conditions and affects the color. In uncut meat, iron is generally in the reduced ferrous state (Fe^{++}) and can readily combine with water. In this state myoglobin is a purplish red color. When meat is cut and its surface exposed to air, the reduced myoglobin combines with oxygen instead of water and forms *oxymyoglobin*. The iron in oxymyoglobin is still in the ferrous state but this pigment is bright red in color. These changes are illustrated in Figure 25.19.

Reducing substances in meat tissue maintain the iron of myoglobin and oxymyoglobin in the ferrous state. When these reducing substances are depleted, as occurs more rapidly at relatively high storage temperatures and when microbial activity uses available oxygen, the iron is oxidized to the ferric state and the brownish-red metmyoglobin pigment is formed. Metmyoglobin formation is also accelerated in the presence of fluorescent light and incandescent light of certain intensity. Meat is palatable after cooking, even though metmyoglobin formation has occurred. However, if further oxidative changes take place in the fresh meat, a number of greenish compounds may be produced from the degradation of the heme pigments.

The color of meat in the retail market is important to many consumers. It has been suggested that consumers want a bright red color in the

Figure 25.19

Changes may occur in fresh meat pigments.

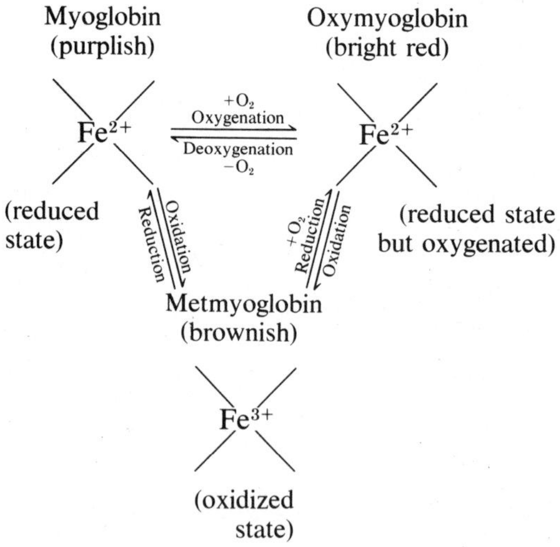

packaged meat that they buy in a supermarket. However, from a study concerned with consumer acceptance of beef steaks that varied in color, Jeremiah *et al.* (1972) reported that consumers preferred steaks that were somewhat paler than the cherry red color formerly suggested as ideal. The consumers sampled in this study preferred steaks that were neither very dark nor very pale. In another study carried out by Wachholz *et al.* (1978), pork chops representing pale, normal, or dark appearances were displayed in a supermarket at equal prices. Over half of the purchasers of pork chops chose those of normal color. The remaining purchases were almost equally divided between the pale and the dark pork. These findings suggest that some consumers may be aware of and actively select for normal pork color while others are either unaware of differences or actually prefer the pale or dark pork. Pale pork muscles are also soft and very moist because of rapid changes in pH occurring in the pork carcass immediately after the animal's death. These muscles have decreased water binding capacity and are referred to as pale, soft, exudative, or PSE. The opposite is true of dark pork muscle that is firm and dry. Neither of these types of pork produces as palatable a product when processed or cooked as does pork muscle of normal color.

Transparent materials used to wrap fresh meat for market display are usually highly permeable to oxygen to allow oxymyoglobin to persist as the meat is displayed. These films also have low water permeabilities. Meat should not be held on the retail display counters under conditions and time periods that will encourage the formation of the brownish metmyoglobin pigment.

CURING OF MEAT

Meat curing involves the application of salt, color fixing ingredients, and seasonings to meat in order to impart unique properties to the end product. In early times, enough salt was added to preserve the meat from microbial spoilage (Forrest *et al.*, 1975). Many cured meat products on the market today are only lightly cured and require refrigeration. Cured meat products include ham, bacon, corned beef, frankfurters, many types of sausage items, and smoked tongue.

The major color fixing ingredient in cured meats is nitrite, used either as a potassium or sodium salt. In the process of curing, nitrite first oxidizes myoglobin and oxymyoglobin to metmyoglobin. The meat thus turns a brownish color. The metmyoglobin then combines with nitric oxide (NO) that is produced from nitrite. The metmyoglobin is also reduced to myoglobin and the resulting product is nitric oxide myoglobin, a red pigment. Reducing agents, such as ascorbic acid salts, are commonly added in curing mixtures to accelerate this reduction process. The final reaction in the production of typical cured meat color is the formation of nitrosyl hemochrome. A heating process that accompanies curing denatures the globin protein that is attached to the heme portion of myoglobin but leaves the heme intact with the nitric oxide attached. This compound, called *nitrosyl hemochrome,* is responsible for the typical pink color of cured meat and is a heat stable pigment. It does not undergo further change with cooking (Forrest *et al.*, 1975). The color changes involved in cured meat products are outlined in Figure 25.20.

Since nitrite is toxic if consumed in excessive amounts, the level in cured meat products is controlled by the U. S. Food and Drug Administration. Under certain conditions, cancer-producing substances called *nitrosamines* can be formed in food products by reactions between nitrite and secondary amines. Nitrosamines have been isolated from some cured meat products such as home-cooked bacon (Wasserman *et al.*, 1978). It appears, however, that frying bacon at low or medium heat for less than ten minutes results in the formation of only small amounts, less than 10 μg/kg, of nitrosamine. The precursor for nitrosamine formation is apparently in the adipose tissue rather than the lean portion of bacon (Fiddler *et al.*, 1974).

Nitrite performs additional functions in a curing mixture besides fixation of color and thus its complete elimination becomes difficult. Nitrite inhibits the germination of *Clostridium botulinum* spores and

Figure 25.20

The chemistry of cured meat color.

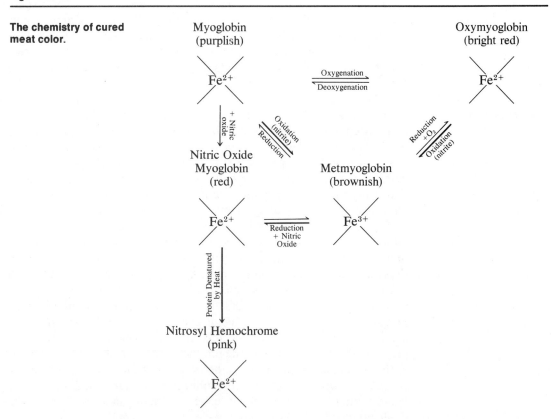

thus prevents toxin production in cured meat products that are only heat-pasteurized during processing and require refrigeration thereafter. Approximately 150 ppm of nitrite is the minimum level required to inhibit the germination of this organism. Without nitrite, the manufacturing process for frankfurters, bologna, bacon, ham, and other such products would have to be substantially changed (Forrest *et al.*, 1975). In addition, nitrite contributes to the characteristic flavor of cured products such as frankfurters (Wasserman and Talley, 1972) and cured pork (Cho and Bratzler, 1970).

25.7

COOKING MEAT

Since meat is a very complex system, heating or cooking meat may be expected to produce varied biochemical and physical reactions. Both time and temperature are important in all of these reactions. A well-cooked piece of meat apparently represents well balanced harmony among the many reactions occurring. Factors affecting the characteristics of cooked meat are also many and varied. They include the maturity of the animal, the fat content, postmortem changes and contraction state, aging, moisture binding ability, the characteristic behavior of the different proteins during heating, the rate of temperature rise, and the method of cooking (Laakkonen, 1973).

MAJOR CHANGES PRODUCED BY HEATING

The heating of meat causes shrinkage, thus weight and volume losses occur. These effects are due to changes in both muscle and collagen fibers. It has been suggested that, in general, changes in the myofibrils contribute to the hardening or toughening of meat during heating while changes in connective tissue contribute to the softening or tenderizing (Paul and Palmer, 1972). Results from a number of studies lend support to this suggestion. For example, from the heating of one-half inch cylinders of meat in tubes immersed in a thermally controlled water bath, Machlik and Draudt (1963) concluded that there was little change in tenderness (shear force) up to 50°C (122°F), a marked increase in tenderness between 50° and 60°C (between 122° and 140°F), a decrease in tenderness from 60° to 70°C (from 140° to 158°F) and some increase in tenderness at about 75°C (167°F). The initial increase in tenderness (between 50° and 60°C) was attributed to a shrinkage of collagen and the following decrease to a hardening of the muscle fibers. The final increase in tenderness was attributed to the hydrolysis of collagen to gelatin.

Hearne *et al.* (1978a) heated cylinders of beef semitendinosus muscle at two different rates to endpoints of 40°, 50°, 60°, and 70°C. Tenderness increased, as indicated by Warner-Bratzler shear values, from 40° to 50° to 60°C. Muscle fiber diameters decreased during this period. Sarcomere length in muscle fibers also decreased and muscle fibers disintegrated from 60° to 70°C. Fiber disintegration, viewed by electron microscopy (Hearne *et al.*, 1978b), might be expected to be indicative of an increase in tenderness. However, shear values did not show a change at 60°–70°C. Apparently other factors oppose the tenderizing effect of muscle fiber disintegration. Connective tissue changes were not documented in this study.

Water holding capacity of meat decreases with cooking. This decrease appears to be related to the denaturation of muscle fiber proteins and a decrease in diameter of the fibers (Laakkonen, 1973). As myofibril proteins are denatured and coagulate, water is squeezed out of the tissue. The water contains water-soluble substances such as salts, sarcoplasmic proteins, and nonprotein compounds. Most of the water evaporates if cooking is done with dry heat (Paul and Palmer, 1972). Fat melts during heating. Drippings consist largely of fat that is melted out of the meat during cooking. The lean tissue may increase in fat content during the cooking period.

Heating denatures the globin portion of the myoglobin molecule. In addition, the iron coordinated in the center of the heme ring is usually oxidized to the ferric state (Fe^{+++}). The resulting pigment is tan-brown in color and is generally called *denatured globin hemichrome*. Tarladgis (1962) reported that the pigment of cooked meat is similar to methemoglobin or metmyoglobin. He suggested naming it "metmyochromogen." The Maillard or carbonyl-amine browning reaction also occurs in cooking meats, especially when the surface of the meat is dry and high temperatures are achieved.

COOKING BY DRY OR MOIST HEAT

The terms dry and moist heat in relation to the cooking of meat refer to the atmosphere that surrounds the piece of meat during cooking. Heat penetration is usually more rapid with moist heat than with dry heat. The surface of the meat reaches a higher temperature with dry heat. In moist heating, the surface does not rise above the boiling point of water. *Dry heat* methods of meat cookery include roasting and broiling. *Moist heat* methods are braising and potroasting. Frying is classified as a dry heat method of cookery because the meat is not surrounded by a moist atmosphere. However, the liquid fat used in frying is a better heat conductor than is the dry air and, therefore, heat is applied more rapidly during frying than during roasting. The microwave oven cooks by dry heat also but in a different manner than does a conventional oven. Electromagnetic energy is absorbed by the meat and this energy is converted to heat inside the product being cooked.

Traditionally, moist heat methods of cookery were recommended for less tender cuts of meat that contain more connective tissue requiring tenderization. Cuts of beef that are relatively high in collagen content usually come from the chuck, round, plate, brisket, and flank while cuts from the rib, loin, and sirloin are generally low in collagen. Pork usually comes from young animals and is tender. However, pork chops have often been cooked by moist heat which extends cooking time and endpoint temperature in order to assure the destruction of any trichina larvae that may be present and cause trichinosis if the meat is eaten. Lamb legs and chops are tender cuts. Roasting to an internal temperature of 82°C (180°F) is satisfactory for leg of lamb. Veal comes from a young animal and is generally tender. However, because of the immature muscle structure, the connective tissue may be proportionately great enough that some veal cuts may be improved by moist heat cookery. Because of the mild flavor of veal, the liquid used in cooking is generally a flavorful sauce in which the meat is served.

In spite of traditional recommendations for cooking less tender cuts of meat with moist heat several studies have shown that dry heat may be satisfactorily used. Long cooking periods at low oven temperatures give tender, palatable beef roasts even though the meat comes from the chuck or round. Bramblett and Vail (1964) reported that beef muscles from the round cooked to an internal temperature of 65°C (149°F) at an oven temperature of 68°C (155°F) were more tender and had a slightly better appearance and flavor than similar muscles cooked at an oven temperature of 93°C (200°F). However, the muscles cooked at 68°C exhibited greater cooking losses and were less juicy. In either case, these less tender cuts were very acceptable when roasted by dry heat. Nielsen and Hall (1965) found that Choice grade beef blade roasts could be successfully oven-roasted to an internal temperature of 71°C (160°F) at either 107°C (225°F) or 163°C (325°F). Those roasted at 107°C were more tender than those roasted at 163°C and equally as tender as a similar cut that was braised. The beef that was dry-roasted at either temperature was more juicy than were braised blade roasts.

Laakkonen et al. (1970) studied the changes in tenderness occurring during the low-temperature, long-time heating of beef muscles. They concluded that the final internal temperature of the meat is extremely critical in affecting tenderness and weight loss. If the final temperature is below the temperature at which collagen shrinks (from 50° to 60°C), a major decrease in tenderness does not occur. At higher temperatures than this, the more severe coagulation of muscle proteins causes less tender tissue and higher weight loss. At about 60°C the weight loss is reasonably low and yet the major increase in tenderness has occurred. If the meat is to be well done, Laakkonen et al. recommended holding it at this temperature for a longer period of time rather than heating it to a higher temperature. Slow heating with a slow rate of heat penetration may be essential in order to obtain the benefits of heating meat no higher than 60°C. Penfield and Meyer (1975) found prolonged proteolytic activity in slowly heated meat and suggested that this might promote increased tenderness.

All muscles do not respond alike to moist and dry heat methods of cooking. Cover et al. (1957) found that the beef longissimus dorsi muscle from the loin was most tender when it was broiled rare to an internal temperature of 61°C but that the biceps femoris muscle from the round was most tender when it was braised well done (100°C) and held there for 25 minutes. Loin steaks became tougher as they were cooked thoroughly and moist heat did not seem to tenderize them as it did cuts from the round (Cover and Hostetler, 1960).

Shaffer *et al.* (1973) reported that moist heat, produced by cooking in oven film bags, required less time than did dry heating in open pans for top round beef roasts when the final internal temperature of the meat was 80°C (176°F). However, greater weight loss occurred with the moist heat cooking. Generally the palatability of meat was similar for roasts cooked by dry and moist heat to the same end point temperature, although beef cooked by moist heat appeared more well done.

ROASTING

Roasting is a dry heat method of cooking that involves placing the meat on a rack in an uncovered pan and heating it in an oven to a desired degree of doneness. A rack is not necessary when the bone supports the meat above the drippings. Convection currents, which are created as heated air circulates in the oven, are the principal means of transmitting heat energy to the surface of the roast. Heat moves from the surface to the interior of the meat by conduction. Seasoning the meat is not necessary prior to roasting.

Oven temperatures most frequently used for roasting tender cuts of meat at home are between 149° and 204°C (between 300° and 400°F). Increasing the oven temperature used in the roasting of beef, through the range of 149°–232°C (300°–450°F), has been shown to decrease the cooking time, increase the cooking losses, and decrease the uniformity of doneness and the amount of pink-colored interior remaining at the rare stage (Paul and Palmer, 1972). Carlin *et al.* (1965) roasted rib and loin pork cuts at oven temperatures of 149°, 163°, 177°, and 191°C (300°, 325°, 350°, and 375°F). They found that cooking rates increased significantly as oven temperatures increased. Roasts cooked at 191°C appeared overcooked at the same internal temperature as those cooked at lower oven temperatures. The highest oven temperature (191°C) caused the drippings to char on the roasting pan and the inside of the oven to be spattered with fat. The generally recommended oven temperatures for roasting tender cuts of meat are 149° or 163°C. Initial browning or searing of the meat before roasting is not recommended since it does not aid in the retention of juices.

The degree of doneness for roasts may vary from one type of meat to another and according to individual preference. Beef may be roasted until it is cooked rare, medium-rare, medium, or well done. The usual final internal temperature for rare beef is from 58° to 60°C (from 136° to 140°F). For medium-rare beef it is from 66° to 68°C (from 151° to 154°F). Medium and well done beef are cooked to 73°–75°C (163°–167°F) and 80°–82°C (176°–180°F), respectively (Paul and Palmer, 1972). As the internal temperature increases, the cooking losses increase, juiciness decreases, and the meat becomes dry in appearance (Visser *et al.,* 1960). The color changes from a bright reddish pink to a brownish gray color. The degree of tenderness in normally tender cuts of beef may not change with increasing internal temperature. However, the texture of the meat changes. Well done beef may be crumbly and fragmented.

Traditionally it has been recommended that pork always be cooked to an internal temperature of 84°C (185°F) in order to assure the destruction of trichina larvae which may be present. However, the thermal death point of *trichinae* has been reported to be between 54.4° and 60°C (between 130° and 140°F) (Carlin *et al.*, 1969). Recommendations for somewhat lower internal temperatures in pork roasts have therefore been made. Carlin *et al.* (1965) reported that rib and loin pork roasts cooked to internal temperatures of 76.7°C (170°F) required less cooking time, had greater cooked meat yields, were higher in juiciness, and were comparable in flavor and tenderness to roasts cooked to 84°C (185°F). Bramblett *et al.* (1970) found an internal temperature of 76.7°C to be satisfactory for roasting boned and tied fresh pork hams and shoulders at an oven temperature of 163°C (325°F).

BROILING

Oven broiling and pan broiling are rapid methods of cooking meats that are low in collagen. Broiled meat is heated primarily by radiant heat. The distribution of heated air by convection currents plays a minor role. Heat is conducted from the surface of the meat to the interior. Thin cuts, such as steaks and chops, are generally broiled so that heat can penetrate to the center of the cut before the surface of the meat is overcooked. Steaks or chops that are less than one inch thick are usually pan broiled while those greater than one inch are often oven broiled. Since broiling is a rapid method of cooking, the temperature of the heat source at the meat surface is often difficult to control. Only low collagen cuts of meat are cooked by this method because tenderization of high collagen cuts is not likely to occur during broiling.

Gilpin *et al.* (1965) broiled steaks from beef rib and round to three internal temperatures. The rib steaks scored higher in tenderness, juiciness, and flavor than did steaks from the round. As steaks were broiled to higher internal temperatures, they were usually less tender, less juicy, and less flavorful. The effects of marbling on palatability characteristics were inconsistent.

COOKING BY MICROWAVES

Energy is supplied in the microwave oven by high frequency electromagnetic waves. Frequencies of 915 and 2450 megahertz (millions of cycles per second) have been approved in the United States for use in electronic cookery. Food absorbs the electromagnetic waves. They penetrate two to three inches into the food product and the rapidly fluctuating electromagnetic field causes oscillation of the polar molecules that make up the food. The moving molecules produce heat. Heat is conducted to the center of the food product if it is so large that the electromagnetic waves cannot penetrate to the center.

The cooking time is significantly shorter for cooking meat in the microwave oven as compared to conventional heating methods. However, in some studies the cooking losses have been reported to be higher with microwave cooking. For example, Korschgen *et al.* (1976) found significantly greater cooking losses for microwave cooking than for conventional roasting of the *longissimus dorsi* muscle of beef and of pork and the deboned leg of lamb. Their cooking treatments included intermittent energy application (three minute cycle) with a microwave range operated at 220V and intermittent energy application (six minute cycle) with a microwave range operated at 115V and a conventional gas oven at 163°C (325°F). Although some flavor differences in samples taken from the edge of slices of lamb and pork were related to the method of cooking, the authors concluded that there was no major advantage of one method of cooking over another.

Deethardt *et al.* (1973) reported similar total cooking loss for pork loin roasts oven roasted or cooked in the electronic oven. However there was significantly more drip loss in the electronically cooked roasts. Although the overall appearance of the roast from the electronic oven was not as acceptable as the conventionally prepared roasts, no significant differences were found in panel evaluations of texture, tenderness, juiciness, and flavor. In a study of the aroma of beef cooked conventionally and by microwaves, MacLeod and Coppock (1978) reported that microwave cooked beef had a "meaty, boiled" aroma. Penner and Bowers (1973) compared freshly cooked (conventionally heated), conventionally reheated after frozen storage, and microwave reheated pork loin muscle. The freshly cooked and microwave reheated pork had sweeter aromas and less metallic flavor than did the conventionally reheated pork. Microwave reheated pork, however, was less juicy than pork heated conventionally. Ground beef patties cooked by microwaves were found by Janicki and Appledorf (1974) to be lower in moisture and crude fat than patties cooked by broiling or grill frying.

Since the cooking time is short in a microwave range, the tenderization of less tender cuts of meat does not generally occur. Ream *et al.* (1974) recommended that beef arm roasts not be cooked by microwaves. The arm roasts cooked in a microwave oven were less tender, juicy, and flavorful than similar cuts cooked in a conventional oven at 121°C (250°F). Marshall (1960) found that top round of beef could not be satisfactorily cooked in a microwave oven. Portions of the roast became very hard and dry and were unpalatable. An acceptable product was obtained by variations in the method of electronic cooking, such as covering the meat, protecting portions with aluminum foil, or preparing a stew with the meat. However, decrease in quality was still observed, when compared with beef round cooked by conventional means.

BRAISING

Braising usually includes browning the surface of meat cuts, covering them and cooking them at a low temperature until they are tender. Liquid may or may not be added. Sufficient water is present within the meat to provide a moist atmosphere and hydrolyze the connective tissue to gelatin. Convection currents in the moist atmosphere aid in distributing the heat. Heat is also conducted from the surface of the pan or rack on which the meat is placed. Braising may be accomplished on a surface burner or in the oven. Heat is transferred more rapidly to the surface of the meat in a moist than in a dry atmosphere. The temperature of the meat, however, does not rise above the boiling point of water, unless cooking is done in a pressurized container. Cooking in a pressure cooker shortens the cooking time because of the elevated temperature that is produced. Griswold (1955) found that braising beef round in a covered pan in the oven to an internal temperature of 85°C (185°F) produced a more palatable product than was produced by similar cuts cooked to the same internal temperature under 5, 10, or 15 pounds of pressure.

Bowers and Goertz (1966) studied the skillet- and oven-braising of pork chops. Generally, cooking losses tended to increase and juiciness decrease with increasing internal temperatures for both oven- and skillet-braised chops. The chops braised to an internal temperature of 77°C (170°F) were more acceptable than those braised to 85°C (185°F). Adding water in the skillet-braising had little effect on eating quality, cooking loss, or time of cooking, but it did decrease browning.

Both small and large cuts of meat may be cooked by braising. In the case of relatively large cuts, the process is commonly called pot-roasting. Stewing involves cooking very small pieces of meat in enough liquid to cover them.

COOKING IN FOIL

Aluminum foil is sometimes used as a wrap for meat while the meat is cooking in an oven. Foil-wrapped meat cooks by moist heat, since a moist atmosphere is maintained at the surface of the meat. Blaker *et al.* (1959) cooked ready-to-eat hams and top round beef roasts, some wrapped tightly in foil and some unwrapped, at an oven temperature of 177°C (350°F) to an internal temperature of 62.8°C (145°F). They found that the foil cooking produced increased weight loss and a steamed flavor. Greater fuel consumption was used for cooking the meat in foil. Similar findings were reported by Hood (1960) for beef chuck roasts from the *triceps brachii* muscle tightly wrapped in foil. Hood used an oven temperature of 149°C (300°F) and reported that tenderness scores were less for roasts that were foil wrapped than for those cooked by dry heat. If cooking time had been extended for the foil wrapped meat, tenderness would probably have been increased.

Baity *et al.* (1969) reported that the cooking time was significantly more for ground beef loaves baked unwrapped at an oven temperature of 93°C (200°F) than for those tightly wrapped in foil. The temperature in the unwrapped loaves reached a plateau and stayed there for a long period of time. It was suggested that this was due to the balance created between the heat energy absorbed and that used to vaporize water from the surface of the loaf. Less evaporation occurred with foil wrapped loaves and the heating curve did not plateau in this case. At an oven temperature of 232°C (450°F) no plateau occurred in the unwrapped loaves and they cooked rapidly. The foil wrapped loaves cooked at 232°C actually took longer to cook than did the unwrapped ones because the foil, in this case, acted as an insulating shield to decrease heat transfer.

25.8

FLAVOR OF MEAT

Crocker reported on the flavor of meat in 1948. He stated that "the flavor of raw meat resides mostly in the juice. It is apparently due to the sweetness and saltiness of actual blood and only incidentally and unimportantly to the presence of the bases creatine and creatinine which have but weak tastes." He further suggested that the cooked beef flavor came from the meat fiber. It was sweet, salty, fatty, and somewhat livery.

Since 1948, much information has been reported on meat flavor. The flavor of cooked meat comes from water- or fat-soluble precursor substances present in the raw meat. Heating in air promotes reactions among these precursors to produce the characteristic taste and aroma of cooked meat (Paul and Palmer, 1972). The Maillard reaction between amino groups and sugars (aldehyde groups) apparently plays an important role in the development of meat flavor but other mechanisms are also operating.

The aroma of cooked meat exerts a major influence on overall flavor. Chromatography has provided a valuable tool for isolating and identifying the volatile flavor compounds from meat. Hirai *et al.* (1973) identified 54 volatile compounds that were isolated from boiled beef. These included hydrocarbons, alcohols, esters, ethers, lactones, aldehydes, ketones, acids, sulfides, aromatic compounds, and heterocyclic compounds.

Hornstein and Crowe (1960 and 1961) conducted an extensive study of water- and fat-soluble components of muscle tissue from several species. They suggested that the *lean portion* contributes a *basic meaty flavor* that is practically identical in beef, pork, and lamb. The *fat portion* contributes the *unique flavor* that characterizes the meat from these species. Wasserman and Talley (1967) studied the ability of taste panel members to identify roasted beef, pork, lamb, and veal by flavor alone. Only about one-third of the panel could do this. Beef and lamb were identified correctly by the panel more often when the ground roasts contained fat in usual amounts than when very lean meats were tested. This was not the case, however, with pork and veal. When pork fat was added to veal, the identification of this veal sample as pork occurred with increased frequency. The factor that was responsible for the identification of pork fat was water soluble and could be removed from the fat. Lamb fat contained a fat-soluble component that significantly increased the identification of veal as lamb when lamb fat was added to the veal. Addition of beef fat did not increase recognition by the panel of veal as beef. These studies and others suggest that both *adipose tissue* and *muscle tissue* are important in the development of *cooked meat flavor* (Pepper and Pearson, 1971; Yamato *et al.,* 1970).

An "off-flavor" frequently develops in cooked meats. It is described as rancid, stale, or "warmed-over" and usually develops rapidly as cooked meat is stored. This is an oxidative reaction involving lipids in the meat. Both heme iron and nonheme iron in the cooked meat appear to act as prooxidants in the reaction (Pearson *et al.,* 1977).

SUMMARY

Meat is defined as the flesh of animals used for food. It is derived primarily from muscle tissue. Typical skeletal muscle contains 75 percent water, 19 percent protein, and 2.5 percent lipid. The gross composition of marketed cuts varies greatly, depending upon the amount of adipose tissue that accompanies the muscle.

Muscle is a complex system in terms of structure and function. The basic muscle cell or fiber is long and threadlike. The cell is surrounded by a thin membrane called the sarcolemma. Inside the cell are tiny myofibrils suspended in the sarcoplasm. The myofibril consists of an ordered array of protein molecules that form thick and thin filaments. The repeating pattern is a system of dark and light bands called a sarcomere. The thick filaments consist almost entirely of the protein myosin while the thin filaments are composed mostly of actin. Each myofibril is surrounded by a system of tubules in the form of the sarcoplasmic reticulum (SR). Transverse tubules crossing the SR are connected with the sarcolemma.

The sarcolemma is surrounded by a thin sheath of connective tissue called the endomysium. Groups of muscle fibers are tied together by the perimysium. These primary and secondary bundles that are thus formed are finally bound together by the epimysium to form a muscle. The various muscles of an animal differ in cooking characteristics. Muscles are classified as red or white on the basis of their color intensity.

During contraction, the muscle shortens as the thick and thin filaments slide past each other. Cross-bridges are formed between actin and myosin molecules. Myosin is an ATPase that hydrolyzes ATP for energy to support the process of contraction. The release of Ca^{++} from the SR, initiated by a nerve impulse to the sarcolemma, starts the contraction process.

Connective tissue has few cells and a considerable amount of extracellular substance. Fibers of reticulin, elastin, or collagen are embedded in the extracellular material. Adipose tissue is an accumulation of fat-containing cells deposited in connective tissue.

A series of complex changes occurring after death of the animal transforms muscle to meat. As the animal is bled and the tissues are depleted of oxygen, only anaerobic metabolism continues in the muscle. Lactic acid accumulates and causes a decrease in pH. A rapid pH decrease to an ultimately low level may denature muscle proteins and decrease water holding capacity. A high pH produces a dry, dark colored meat. As ATP disappears from the muscle, rigor mortis develops. The muscle becomes stiff, short, inextensible, and inelastic.

As meat is held, rigor passes, and the muscle softens. Tenderness increases during this holding or aging period. The effect is probably due to changes in the myofibrils. Aging improves the quality of beef but has little effect on pork. It occurs more rapidly at 16°C than at 2°C.

Inspection of animals for possible disease immediately before slaughter and of the carcass afterward is mandatory by federal law. A USDA grading program implemented to facilitate marketing is voluntary. Two general types of grades are those for quality and those for expected yield. Quality grades consider maturity of the animal, amount and distribution of fat, color, and muscling of tissues.

Meat carcasses are divided into wholesale cuts that are then subdivided into retail cuts. Industrywide standards have been determined as a guide to the naming of meat cuts.

Tenderness is one of the most highly valued characteristics of meat. Tenderness, as evaluated by a taste panel, apparently consists of several sensory impressions created by both muscle fibers and connective tissue. Objective measurement of meat tenderness commonly involves an apparatus that shears across the meat fibers. Several factors affect tenderness. Differences in the amount and nature of connective tissue are found among muscles of the same animal and are also found when the muscles of different animals are compared. Connective tissue increases in amount and firmness with increasing age. Muscles used for locomotion have more connective tissue than those used for support. The contraction state of muscle fibers also affects tenderness. Longer sarcomeres are related to increased tenderness. The disruption of cross-bridges between actin and myosin on aging is a contributing factor. High water holding capacity of meat is also associated with increased tenderness. And treatment of meat with proteases and cutting meat mechanically are sometimes used to increase tenderness.

Meat color is due primarily to the presence of the heme pigment, myoglobin. The amount of myoglobin increases with the age of the animal and differs among the species from which the meat comes. Myoglobin is a purplish red. When the iron in the center of the heme portion of the molecule is combined with oxygen, it forms oxymyoglobin which is bright red in color. When the iron is oxidized to a ferric state, metmyoglobin is formed. It is brownish in color. The characteristic cured meat pigment is produced by the addition of nitrite to the meat. It is called nitrosyl hemochrome. In cured meats, nitrite also inhibits germination of *Clostridium botulinum* spores and contributes to flavor. Nitrite may have toxic effects if used in excessive amounts.

Heating produces varied biochemical and physical reactions in meat. Weight and volume losses occur as meat shrinks. In general, the myofibrils tend to toughen and the connective tissue softens with continued heating. Collagen begins to shrink between 50° and 60°C. Water holding capacity decreases with cooking as muscle fiber proteins denature. Fat melts. Myoglobin is changed to denatured globin hemichrome which is tan-brown in color.

Traditionally, moist heat cookery has been used for less tender cuts of meat and dry heat methods for tender cuts. However, less tender cuts of beef can be satisfactorily cooked by roasting them at very low oven temperatures (65°–107°C) for long periods of time. A final internal temperature of about 60°C has been recommended for maximum tenderness. All muscles do not respond alike to moist and dry heat.

Roasting is a dry heat method that involves placing the meat on a rack in an uncovered pan and heating in an oven to a desired degree of doneness. Cooking rates increase as oven temperatures increase. As the internal temperature of the meat increases, the cooking losses increase, juiciness decreases, and the meat becomes dry in appearance.

Thin cuts of tender meat may be broiled. Broiling to high internal temperatures decreases tenderness and juiciness.

Cooking time is shortened by cooking meat in a microwave oven. However, the cooking losses may be greater with microwaves than with conventional cooking. The cooking period is too short to allow time for the tenderization of less tender cuts by microwave heating.

Braising involves cooking in moist heat. Heat is transferred more rapidly by moist than by dry heat. Wrapping meat in foil and heating it in an oven cooks by moist heat. At high oven temperatures the foil may act as an insulator and increase the cooking time.

The flavor of cooked meat comes from water- and fat-soluble precursor substances present in the raw meat. The Maillard reaction contributes to flavor. Many volatile substances contribute to aroma. The fat portion of meat contributes to the unique flavor that characterizes a species. A stale "off-flavor" may develop in cooked meats.

STUDY QUESTIONS

Muscle tissue is a complex organized system of fibers held together by sheaths of connective tissue.

1. Describe, with the use of diagrams, the structure of a muscle cell or fiber and its myofibril components.
2. How is a muscle, such as *longissimus dorsi,* built up from muscle fibers? Show by diagrams.
3. What is a sarcomere? Draw and label one.

4. How are thick and thin filaments structured? What proteins do they contain?
5. Describe what initiates muscle contraction and what happens in the muscle as contraction takes place.
6. Describe the structure of connective tissue proper.

Many chemical and physical changes occur after death of an animal as muscle becomes meat.

7. What is rigor mortis? What effect does it have on the tenderness of meat?
8. Explain and describe pH changes that generally occur in muscle postmortem.
9. Explain differences in water holding capacity among normal colored, dark, and pale meat.
10. What is meant by aging meat? What advantages does it have for beef and for pork? Explain.
11. Describe the general effect of holding temperature on the aging process.

Meat inspection is mandatory while meat grading is voluntary.

12. Explain the purpose and the general process involved in meat inspection.
13. What is the basic function of the Wholesome Meat Act of 1967?
14. List two general types of meat grades and describe the major purpose of grading.
15. What criteria are used in meat grading for quality?
16. List USDA quality and yield grades for beef and lamb. List quality grades for veal and mutton.

Many factors appear to influence tenderness in meat.

17. Discuss the relationship between meat grading and tenderness of the meat cuts.
18. How is tenderness generally measured in meat? Which methods are objective? Which methods are subjective?
19. Describe several components of tenderness that have been separately identified and evaluated by taste panel members.
20. From the following list, identify those factors that are likely to influence tenderness in meat. Indicate whether each factor generally increases or decreases tenderness and explain its action in doing so.

Factors
Small diameter of muscle fiber or fine grain of meat
Marbling of fat
Large amount of connective tissue
Cooking to a well done stage
Content of glycogen
High fat content
Addition of papain
Hanging an animal carcass during chilling
Aging
Very low roasting temperatures for long periods of time
Grinding meat

Characteristic changes in color occur during the handling and curing of meat.

21. For each of the pigments listed below, describe (a) color, (b) chemical group coordinated with iron, (c) the valence state of iron (ferrous or ferric), and (d) the conditions under which you would expect to find the pigment present in meat.

    Pigments
    Myoglobin
    Metmyoglobin
    Oxymyoglobin
    Nitric oxide myoglobin
    Nitrosyl hemochrome
    Denatured globin hemichrome

22. List several cured meat products.
23. Name the color fixing ingredient in curing mixtures and explain its role(s) in the curing process.
    Explain why levels of this agent are controlled by the U. S. Food and Drug Administration.

Heat has various effects on muscle fibers and connective tissue.

24. Describe the major changes in muscle fibers and in connective tissue that occur when meat is subjected to continuous heating. Explain the possible significance of this knowledge in suggesting practical cooking methods for tender and less tender cuts of meat.
25. Describe the traditional recommendations for cooking tender and less tender cuts of beef and evaluate these recommendations in light of more recent research involving very low temperatures for roasting.
26. What are the major steps involved in each of the following methods of meat cookery? What meat cuts may be satisfactorily cooked by each method?

    Roasting
    Broiling
    Braising

27. Recommend an oven temperature for roasting and a final internal temperature for a beef rib roast and justify your recommendation.
28. What are advantages and disadvantages of cooking meat by microwaves and of cooking meat wrapped in aluminum foil?

REFERENCES

1. Ashmore, C. R., W. Parker, and L. Doerr. 1972. Respiration of mitochondria isolated from dark-cutting beef: Postmortem changes. *Journal of Animal Science* 34, 46.

2. Baity, M. R., A. E. Ellington, and M. Woodburn. 1969. Foil wrap in oven cooking. *Journal of Home Economics* 61, 174.

3. Blaker, G. G., J. L. Newcomer, and W. D. Stafford. 1959. Conventional roasting vs. high-temperature foil cookery. Effect on cooking time, palatability, weight loss and fuel consumption. *American Dietetic Association Journal* 35, 1255.

4. Bendall, J. R. 1967. The elastin content of various muscles of beef animals. *Journal of the Science of Food and Agriculture* 18, 553.

5. Bodwell, C. E., A. M. Pearson, and M. E. Spooner. 1965. Post-mortem changes in muscle. I. Chemical changes in beef. *Journal of Food Science* 30, 766.

6. Bouton, P. E., P. V. Harris, W. R. Shorthose, and R. I. Baxter. 1973. A comparison of the effects of aging, conditioning and skeletal restraint on the tenderness of mutton. *Journal of Food Science* 38, 932.

7. Bowers, J. R. and G. E. Goertz. 1966. Effect of internal temperature on eating quality of pork chops. I. Skillet- and oven-braising. *American Dietetic Association Journal* 48, 116.

8. Bramblett, V. D., M. D. Judge, and R. B. Harrington. 1970. Effect of temperature and cut on quality of pork roast. *American Dietetic Association Journal* 57, 132.

9. Bramblett, V. D. and G. E. Vail. 1964. Further studies on the qualities of beef as affected by cooking at very low temperatures for long periods. *Food Technology* 18, 245.

10. Buck, E. M. and D. L. Black. 1968. Microscopic characteristics of cooked muscles subjected to stretch-tension during rigor. *Journal of Food Science* 33, 464.

11. Carlin, A. F., D. M. Bloemer, and D. K. Hotchkiss. 1965. Relation of oven temperature and final internal temperature to quality of pork loin roasts. *Journal of Home Economics* 57, 442.

12. Carlin, A. F., C. Mott, D. Cash, and W. Zimmermann. 1969. Destruction of trichina larvae in cooked pork roasts. *Journal of Food Science* 34, 210.

13. Cho, I. C. and L. J. Bratzler. 1970. Effect of sodium nitrite on flavor of cured pork. *Journal of Food Science* 35, 668.

14. Cole, D. J. A. and R. A. Lawrie, editors. 1975. *Meat.* Westport, Conn.: Avi Publishing Company.

15. Cover, S., J. A. Bannister, and E. Kehlenbrink. 1957. Effect of four conditions of cooking on the eating quality of two cuts of beef. *Food Research* 22, 635.

16. Cover, S. and R. L. Hostetler. 1960. An examination of some theories about beef tenderness by using new methods. Texas Agricultural Experiment Station Bulletin No. 947.

17. Crocker, E. C. 1948. Flavor of meat. *Food Research* 13, 179.

18. Cross, H. R., Z. L. Carpenter, and G. C. Smith. 1973. Effects of intramuscular collagen and elastin on bovine muscle tenderness. *Journal of Food Science* 38, 998.

19. Deethardt, D., W. Costello, and K. C. Schneider. 1973. Effect of electronic, convection and conventional oven roasting on the acceptability of pork loin roasts. *Journal of Food Science* 38, 1076.

20. Fiddler, W., J. W. Pensabene, J. C. Fagan, E. J. Thorne, E. G. Piotrowski, and A. E. Wasserman. 1974. The role of lean and adipose tissue on the formation of nitrosopyrrolidine in fried bacon. *Journal of Food Science* 39, 1070.

21. Forrest, J. C., E. D. Aberle, H. B. Hedrick, M. D. Judge, and R. A.

Merkel. 1975. *Principles of Meat Science.* San Francisco: W. H. Freeman and Company.

22. Gilpin, G. L., O. M. Batcher, and P. A. Deary. 1965. Influence of marbling and final internal temperature on quality characteristics of broiled rib and eye of round steaks. *Food Technology* 19, 834.

23. Griswold, R. M. 1955. The effect of different methods of cooking beef round of commercial and prime grades. I. Palatability and shear values. *Food Research* 20, 160.

24. Harrison, D. L., J. A. Bowers, L. L. Anderson, H. J. Tuma, and D. H. Kropf. 1970. Effect of aging on palatability and selected related characteristics of pork loin. *Journal of Food Science* 35, 292.

25. Hearne, L. E., M. P. Penfield, and G. E. Goertz. 1978a. Heating effects on bovine semitendinosus: Shear, muscle fiber measurements and cooking losses. *Journal of Food Science* 43, 10.

26. Hearne, L. E., M. P. Penfield, and G. E. Goertz. 1978b. Heating effects on bovine semitendinosus: Phase contrast microscopy and scanning electron microscopy. *Journal of Food Science* 43, 13.

27. Hill, F. 1966. The solubility of intramuscular collagen in meat animals of various ages. *Journal of Food Science* 31, 161.

28. Hiner, R. L. 1955. Amount and character of connective tissue as it relates to tenderness in beef muscle. *Food Technology* 9, 80.

29. Hirai, C., K. O. Herz, J. Pokorny, and S. S. Chang. 1973. Isolation and identification of volatile flavor coupounds in boiled beef. *Journal of Food Science* 38, 393.

30. Hoke, K. E. and H. B. Hedrick. 1969. Maturity and carcass grade effects on palatability of beef. *Food Technology* 23, 330.

31. Hood, M. P. 1960. Effect of cooking method and grade on beef roasts. *American Dietetic Association Journal* 37, 363.

32. Hornstein, I. and P. F. Crowe. 1960. Flavor studies on beef and pork. *Journal of Agricultural and Food Chemistry* 8, 494.

33. Hornstein, I. and P. F. Crowe. 1961. Meat flavors from fat—not lean. *Agricultural Research* 9 (No. 7), 14.

34. Hostetler, R. L., W. A. Landmann, B. A. Link, and H. A. Fitzhugh, Jr. 1970. Influence of carcass position during rigor mortis on tenderness of beef muscles: Comparison of two treatments. *Journal of Animal Science* 31, 47.

35. Hostetler, R. L., B. A. Link, W. A. Landmann, and H. A. Fitzhugh, Jr. 1972. Effect of carcass suspension on sarcomere length and shear force of some major bovine muscles. *Journal of Food Science* 37, 132.

36. Hoyle, G. 1970. How is muscle turned on and off? *Scientific American* 222 (No. 4), 84.

37. Huxley, H. E. 1965. The mechanism of muscular contraction. *Scientific American* 213 (No. 6), 18.

38. Janicki, L. J. and H. Appledorf, 1974. Effect of broiling, grill frying and microwave cooking on moisture, some lipid components and total fatty acids of ground beef. *Journal of Food Science* 39, 715.

39. Jennings, T. G., B. W. Berry, and A. L. Joseph. 1978. Influence of fat thickness, marbling and length of aging on beef palatability and shelf-life characteristics. *Journal of Animal Science* 46, 658.

40. Jeremiah, L. E., Z. L. Carpenter, and G. C. Smith, 1972. Beef color as related to consumer acceptance and palatability. *Journal of Food Science* 37, 476.

41. Kang, C. K. and E. E. Rice. 1970. Degradation of various meat fractions by tenderizing enzymes. *Journal of Food Science* 35, 563.

42. Kang, C. K. and W. D. Warner. 1974. Tenderization of meat with papaya latex proteases. *Journal of Food Science* 39, 812.

43. Khan, A. W. and W. W. Ballantyne. 1973. Post-slaughter pH variation in beef. *Journal of Food Science* 38, 710.

44. Khan, A. W., C. P. Lentz, and L. van den Berg. 1973. Relation between shear force and tenderness of beef. *Journal of Food Science* 38, 1258.

45. Kim, C. W., G. P. Ho, and S. J. Ritchey. 1967. Collagen content and subjective scores for tenderness of connective tissue in animals of different ages. *Journal of Food Science* 32, 586.

46. Korschgen, B. M., R. E. Baldwin, and S. Snider. 1976. Quality factors in beef, pork and lamb cooked by microwaves. *American Dietetic Association Journal* 69, 635.

47. Laakkonen, E. 1973. Factors affecting tenderness during heating of meat. *Advances in Food Research* 20, 257.

48. Laakkonen, E., G. H. Wellington, and J. W. Sherbon. 1970. Low-temperature, long-time heating of bovine muscle. 1. Changes in tenderness, water-binding capacity, pH and amount of water-soluble components. *Journal of Food Science* 35, 175.

49. Lawrie, R. A. 1974. *Meat Science,* 2nd edition. New York: Pergamon Press.

50. Leverton, R. M. and G. V. Odell, 1958. The nutritive value of cooked meat. Oklahoma Agricultural Experiment Station Miscellaneous Publication MP-49.

51. Lind, J. M., R. M. Griswold, and V. D. Bramblett. 1971. Tenderizing effect of wine vinegar marinade on beef round. *American Dietetics Association Journal* 58, 133.

52. Machlik, S. M. and H. N. Draudt. 1963. The effect of heating time and temperature on the shear of beef semitendenosus muscle. *Journal of Food Science* 28, 711.

53. MacLeod, G. and B. M. Coppock. 1978. Sensory properties of the aroma of beef cooked conventionally and by microwave radiation. *Journal of Food Science* 43, 145.

54. Marshall, N. 1960. Electronic cookery of top round of beef. *Journal of Home Economics* 52, 31.

55. Minks, D. and W. C. Stringer. 1972. The influence of aging beef in vacuum. *Journal of Food Science* 37, 736.

56. Moore, A. J. 1966. The differential response of choice, good, and commercial grades of the longissimus dorsi of beef to controlled aging. *Journal of Home Economics* 58, 171.

57. Nielsen, M. M. and F. T. Hall. 1965. Dry-roasting of less tender beef cuts. *Journal of Home Economics* 57, 353.

58. Parrish, F. C., Jr., R. B. Young, B. E. Miner, and L. D. Andersen. 1973. Effect of postmortem conditions on certain chemical, morphological and organoleptic properties of bovine muscle. *Journal of Food Science* 38, 690.

59. Paul, P. C. and H. H. Palmer. 1972. *Food Theory and Applications*. New York: Wiley.

60. Pearson, A. M., J. D. Love, and F. B. Skorland. 1977. ''Warmed-over'' flavor in meat, poultry, and fish. *Advances in Food Research* 23, 1.

61. Penfield, M. P. and B. H. Meyer. 1975. Changes in tenderness and collagen of beef semitendinosus muscle heated at two rates. *Journal of Food Science* 40, 150.

62. Penner, K. K. and J. A. Bowers. 1973. Flavor and chemical characteristics of conventionally and microwave reheated pork. *Journal of Food Science* 38, 553.

63. Pepper, F. H. and A. M. Pearson. 1971. Possible role of adipose tissue in meat flavor—the nondialyzable aqueous extract. *Journal of Agricultural and Food Chemistry* 19, 164.

64. Purchas, R. W. 1972. The relative importance of some determinants of beef tenderness. *Journal of Food Science* 37, 341.

65. Ramsey, C. B., K. D. Lind, L. F. Tribble, and C. T. Gaskins, Jr. 1973. Diet, sex and vacuum packaging effects on pork aging. *Journal of Animal Science* 37, 40.

66. Ream, E. E., E. B. Wilcox , F. G. Taylor, and J. A. Bennett. 1974. Tenderness of beef roasts. *American Dietetic Association Journal* 65, 155.

67. Ritchey, S. J., S. Cover, and R. L. Hostetler. 1963. Collagen content and its relation to tenderness of connective tissue in two beef muscles. *Food Technology* 17, 194.

68. Seideman, S. C., G. C. Smith, Z. L. Carpenter, and W. H. Marshall. 1977. Blade tenderization of beef psoas major and semitendinosus muscles. *Journal of Food Science* 42, 1510.

69. Shaffer, T. A., D. L. Harrison, and L. L. Anderson. 1973. Effects of end point and oven temperatures on beef roasts cooked in oven film bags and open pans. *Journal of Food Science* 38, 1205.

70. Sharrah, N., M. S. Kunze, and R. M. Pangborn. 1965. Beef tenderness: Comparison of sensory methods with the Warner-Bratzler and L.E.E.-Kramer shear presses. *Food Technology* 19, 238.

71. Smith, G. C., G. R. Culp, and Z. L. Carpenter. 1978. Postmortem aging of beef carcasses. *Journal of Food Science* 43, 823.

72. Smith, G. C., T. R. Dutson, Z. L. Carpenter, and R. L. Hostetler. 1977. Using electrical stimulation to tenderize meat. *Proceedings of the Meat Industry Research Conference,* p. 147.

73. Smith, G. C., T. C. Arango, and Z. L. Carpenter. 1971. Effects of physical and mechanical treatments on the tenderness of the beef longissimus. *Journal of Food Science* 36, 445.

74. Smith, G. C., R. L. West, R. H. Rea, and Z. L. Carpenter. 1973. Increasing

the tenderness of bullock beef by use of antemorten enzyme injection. *Journal of Food Science* 38, 182.

75. Tarladgis, B. G. 1962. Interpretation of the spectra of meat pigments. I. Cooked meats. *Journal of the Science of Food and Agriculture* 13, 481.

76. Tatum, J. D., G. C. Smith, and Z. L. Carpenter. 1978. Blade tenderization of steer, cow and bull beef. *Journal of Food Science,* 43, 819.

77. U. S. Department of Agriculture. 1975. Meat research, an ARS progress report. Agriculture Information Bulletin No. 375.

78. Viser, R. Y., D. L. Harrison, G. E. Goertz, M. Bunyan, M. M. Skelton, and D. L. Mackintosh. 1960. The effect of degree of doneness on the tenderness and juiciness of beef cooked in the oven and in deep fat. *Food Technology* 14, 193.

79. Wachholz, D., R. G. Kauffman, D. Henderson, and J. V. Lochner. 1978. Consumer discrimination of pork color at the market place. *Journal of Food Science* 43, 1150.

80. Wasserman, A. E., J. W. Pensabene, and E. G. Piotrowski. 1978. Nitrosamine formation in home-cooked bacon. *Journal of Food Science* 43, 276.

81. Wasserman, A. E. and F. Talley. 1972. The effect of sodium nitrite on the flavor of frankfurters. *Journal of Food Science* 37, 536.

82. Wasserman, A. E. and F. Talley. 1967. Organoleptic identification of roasted beef, veal, lamb and pork as affected by fat. *Journal of Food Science* 33, 219.

83. Watt, B. K. and A. L. Merrill. 1963. *Composition of Foods.* U. S. Department of Agriculture. Agriculture Handbook No. 8.

84. Weidemann, J. F., G. Kaess, and L. D. Carruthers. 1967. The histology of pre-rigor and post-rigor ox muscle before and after cooking and its relation to tenderness. *Journal of Food Science* 32, 7.

85. Wilson, G. D., R. W. Bray, and P. H. Phillips. 1954. The effect of age and grade on the collagen and elastin content of beef and veal. *Journal of Animal Science* 13, 826.

86. Yamato, T., T. Kurata, H. Kato, and M. Fujimaki. 1970. Volatile carbonyl compounds from heated beef fat. *Agricultural and Biological Chemistry* 34, 88.

CHAPTER 26

POULTRY AND FISH

26.1

POULTRY

Poultry represents a widely used source of dietary protein. It has been estimated that chicken appears in the diet of more people throughout the world as a source of meat than does the meat from any other animal or bird. With the exception of strict vegetarians, there are few social or religious stigmas attached to the use of poultry as food (Mountney, 1976). In the American diet, poultry constitutes over 20 percent of the total meat supply (Stadelman, 1978).

MARKET CLASS

Poultry are divided into market classes according to their species, age, and sex. Sex may not be specified when it has no effect on the market quality. The market classes of chickens and turkeys are given in Table 26.1. Ducks, geese, guineas, and pigeons are also marketed.

COMPOSITION

The composition of any type of poultry changes with the age and nutriture of the bird. The carcasses of young birds contain more moisture than those of older fowl. For example, the edible portion of chicken broilers contains approximately 71 percent moisture. Roasters contain about 66 percent and hens about 56 percent moisture (Mountney, 1976). The caloric content of a specified quantity of poultry meat increases with decreasing moisture.

The fat content of poultry varies with age, sex, and species. Fat content will also vary from one part of the bird to another. For example, turkey skin has been reported to contain 33.8 percent fat and breast meat only from 6.7 to 8.3 percent (Scott, 1956). The type of fat in the diet of the bird affects the composition of its body fat. Diets containing oils, such as corn oil and rapeseed oil, produce tissue fat that is more unsaturated than do diets containing saturated fats such as beef tallow, lard, or coconut oil. The body tissues tend to assume the fatty acid

Table 26.1   Market Classes of Poultry

	Class	Sex	Age
Chicken:	Cornish game hen	Either	5–7 weeks
	Broiler	Either	9–12 weeks
	Roaster	Either	3–5 months
	Capon	Unsexed male	under 8 months
	Stag	Male	under 10 months
	Hen or stewing chicken or fowl	Female	over 10 months
	Cock	Male	over 10 months
Turkey:	Fryer-roaster	Either	under 16 weeks
	Young hen	Female	5–7 months
	Young tom	Male	5–7 months
	Yearling hen	Female	under 15 months
	Yearling tom	Male	under 15 months
	Mature or old	Either	over 15 months

Source: U. S. Department of Agriculture, 1961.

composition of the fat in the diet (Salmon and O'Neil, 1973; Mickelberry et al., 1966; Mickelberry et al., 1964; Marion and Woodroof, 1963).

Poultry is a good source of high quality protein. Cooked poultry meat contains from 25 to 35 percent protein, depending on the part of the carcass being considered and the method of preparation used (Scott, 1956). Stadelman (1978) reported that the mean protein content of cooked chicken breast was 32.6 percent and that of thigh was 29.4 percent. The moisture, fat, protein, and ash content of several broiler chicken parts, raw and cooked by oven frying are given in Table 26.2. Stadelman pointed out that the moisture content of cooked chicken parts varied considerably. Factors affecting moisture loss probably include size and shape of the piece and protection by skin. The size of the

Table 26.2   Composition of Meat and Skin from Selected Chicken Parts

Anatomical Part	% Moisture		% Fat		% Protein		% Ash	
	Raw	Cooked*	Raw	Cooked*	Raw	Cooked*	Raw	Cooked*
Breast	77.6	61.8	0.7	4.0	21.3	32.6	0.87	1.15
Thigh	77.4	59.7	3.8	8.6	18.1	29.4	0.82	1.24
Leg	78.2	60.1	2.7	7.0	18.8	32.6	0.83	1.16
Back	76.7	46.3	5.9	15.1	17.5	31.3	0.68	1.56
Wing	78.2	62.2	2.7	6.5	19.4	30.6	0.58	0.82
Neck	78.7	58.0	4.0	10.4	16.8	28.7	0.71	1.19

Source: From Stadelman, 1978.
* Oven fried.

piece has a considerable effect on the composition and yield of edible meat. In general, a higher percentage of meat from each part is found as the birds become larger.

PROCESSING, INSPECTION, AND GRADING

Poultry is scalded by immersion in hot water in order to facilitate the removal of feathers. Semi- or soft-scalding is most commonly used in commercial processing. This method is carried out at 50.6°–54.4°C (123°–130°F) for 90–120 seconds. This leaves the skin intact, whereas scalding at higher temperatures will break down the outer layer of skin. The feathers are then removed as the birds, hanging by the feet, are conveyed through a system of rubber-fingered picking devices which serve to beat and rub the feathers from the carcasses. A steady stream of water washes the feathers away. After the carcasses are eviscerated and inspected for signs of disease, they are sorted according to weight and chilled to at least 4.4°C (40°F) internal temperature (Mountney, 1976). Chilling is commonly accomplished by immersing the carcasses in cold running water or slush ice. A possible alternative to immersion chilling was tested by Arafa and Chen (1978a). They chilled individually packaged broiler carcasses by passing them through a commercial liquid nitrogen spraying tunnel. The muscles of the liquid nitrogen chilled birds had sarcomeres of longer length and were more tender than those of birds undergoing immersion chilling.

Most processors supply carcasses packed in boxes and iced or packed dry with carbon dioxide snow. Some whole poultry carcasses are marketed in a frozen state. Chickens are generally individually packaged and cut into portions at the retail unit. Loss of moisture is rapid from cut-up parts. However, well packaged cut-up parts have been held at temperatures just above freezing for several weeks. Arafa and Chen (1978b) reported that dipping cut-up broiler parts in one percent ascorbic acid solution for 3 minutes retarded microbial growth and increased the refrigerated shelf life for six to seven days when compared with water dipping. The ascorbic acid had no adverse effect on palatability.

Inspection The Poultry Products Inspection Act of 1959 makes inspection of poultry and poultry products mandatory not only for products entering interstate commerce but also for those in designated major consuming areas. Therefore, most of the poultry marketed in the United States is now inspected for wholesomeness by agents of the U. S. Department of Agriculture (USDA). Under the law, the poultry inspection service is responsible for inspecting poultry and poultry products to assure that they are wholesome, free from disease and adulteration, and accurately labeled. It is also responsible for approving the facilities and processing procedures to insure sanitary operations in each processing plant for which inspection is mandatory (U. S. Department of Agriculture, 1961). In the inspection procedure, the inspector examines each carcass along with its viscera. The inspection

Figure 26.1

This stamp is similar to those placed on officially inspected poultry. (Courtesy U. S. Department of Agriculture.)

mark placed on birds that have passed inspection is similar to that shown in Figure 26.1.

Grading The USDA has established standards for grades of poultry. These provide a reasonably accurate and objective method of identifying quality and are uniform for all areas of the country. As with grades for other commodities, they are a merchandising aid.

U. S. grades apply to five kinds of poultry: chicken, turkey, duck, goose, and guinea. Dressed and ready-to-cook poultry are graded first for class (age) and then for condition and quality. Official grades for individually graded carcasses are A, B, and C. Carcasses graded A and B are pictured in Figure 26.2. Quality factors applied in grading include conformation, fleshing, fat distribution, freedom from pinfeathers, and

Figure 26.2

Young turkeys, U. S. Grade A (*left*) and U. S. Grade B (*right*). (Courtesy U. S. Department of Agriculture.)

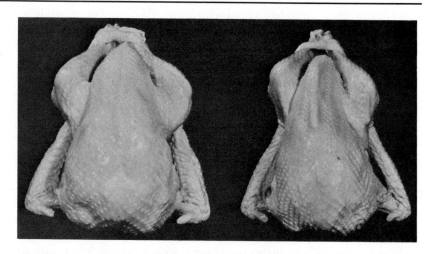

freedom from defects. An A grade carcass has a normal conformation, is well fleshed with a deep and rounded breast, well covered with fat, and free from pinfeathers. A mark for U. S. grade A is shown in Figure 26.3. The inspection and grade marks may be included together on the wing-tag as illustrated in Figure 26.3.

Effect of Processing on Tenderness   Some of the procedures employed in the processing of poultry may affect the tenderness of the bird. In general, increasing the severity of the scalding procedure, either by raising the temperature of the scald water or prolonging the time of immersion, will decrease the tenderness of the poultry. The severity of the feather-plucking operation also contributes to toughness. The rate of onset for rigor mortis is more rapid with severe scalding and plucking operations than with normal procedures (de Fremery, 1963). A rapid onset of rigor, a low level of muscle ATP, and a high level of muscle lactic acid are associated with tough meat (Stadelman, 1978; de Fremery and Pool, 1960).

An aging period to allow the passing of rigor mortis is necessary to avoid toughening of poultry meat. However, this period is much shorter than that required for large animals such as beef. Cantrell and Hale (1974) found that both thigh and breast chicken muscles that had aged at least 20 hours were significantly more tender than those cooked immediately after processing. If poultry is frozen immediately after processing, development of rigor will be inhibited. As the frozen muscles are then thawed, a very rapid "thaw rigor" is induced. After the thawed poultry is cooked, it is less tender than a similar piece that has been aged until rigor mortis has passed before it is frozen or cooked. The passing of rigor should occur in from 12 to 24 hours, depending upon the size of the bird (de Fremery, 1963).

COOKING POULTRY   Poultry muscle responds to heat in a similar manner as does meat. Older poultry are generally less tender than young birds and require

Figure 26.3

The inspection and grade marks may be placed on the wing-tag. (Courtesy U. S. Department of Agriculture.)

cookery methods adapted to their less tender state as do less tender cuts of meat.

Chickens Many poultry parts are cooked and cooled in water before being further processed as precooked poultry products. Determination of doneness in this poultry is often difficult. End-point temperature is not always an adequate determinant. Lyon *et al.* (1973) reported that adequate doneness appeared to vary with the placement of the thermocouple for temperature measurement, the size and shape of the piece of poultry, and the method of cooking.

Lyon *et al.* (1975) investigated a subjective method and an objective method of determining doneness in water-cooked broiler thighs. The subjective method involved sensory panels using a modified descriptive analysis technique. The objective method measured color with a Hunter Color and Color Difference Meter. From this study, it appeared that measurement of *Hunter a_L values (measure of redness)* offered the potential to provide an objective method to monitor standards of doneness in precooked poultry products. However, the panels failed to establish an absolute level of doneness since the definition of doneness involves individual preference.

Temperatures and times of cooking have been shown to affect the color of broiler thighs cooked in water, as indicated by Hunter a_L values. In general, the redness color values decrease as end point temperatures and holding times increase (Lyon *et al.*, 1975a).

Some problems with lack of adhesion of breading material have been encountered in the merchandizing of precooked fried chicken. Various methods have been employed in the preparation of this product. These have included precooking by steaming, simmering, or boiling followed by breading and frying; pressurized deep fat frying; and microwave cooking followed by deep fat frying. Baker *et al.* (1972a) recommended breading, battering, and breading; frying for 20 seconds; steaming until done; and then refrying for 20 seconds. Adhesion of the batter was improved by dusting the chicken with dried egg albumen or vital wheat gluten before battering and breading (Baker *et al.*, 1972b).

Fowl are less tender than fryers and are less in demand in the consumer market. Baker and Darfler (1968) suggested that Leghorn fowl could be satisfactorily used for precooked battered fried chicken if they were cooked until tender before battering. They reported that Leghorn fowl compared favorably with fryers when evaluated as precooked fried chicken by a taste panel.

Goertz *et al.* (1964) cooked broilers in the broiling compartments of gas ranges at temperatures of 177°C (350°F), 191°C (375°F), or 204°C (400°F) on the surface of the broilers. The end point temperature in the breast muscle was 95°C (203°F). Broilers cooked at 177°C were nearer optimal doneness than the other birds, as judged by general appearance. However, no differences in cooking time, cooking losses, juiciness, and tenderness scores were apparent as a result of cooking temperature.

The yield of cooked chicken meat varies with age of bird and the cooking method. Jacobson *et al.* (1969) reported that chickens that were 9 weeks or older had a significantly higher percentage of lean cooked meat, based on ready-to-cook weight, than did younger birds. The percentage of bone decreased regularly with each increase in age studied. The oven frying of chicken parts resulted in less cooked lean meat than did the roasting of whole chickens. The yield of lean meat for roasted birds averaged 39.6 percent while that of oven-fried parts was 38.4 percent. Roasting was done at an oven temperature of 163°C (325°F) to an internal temperature in the thigh muscle of 88°C (190°F). Oven frying was done at an oven temperature of 163°C to an internal temperature of 91°C (195°F). Hoke (1968) reported a greater yield of cooked meat, 44.0 vs. 41.6 percent, from chickens roasted at 163°C (325°F) than at 191°C (375°F). The eating quality was not significantly different. Dawson *et al.* (1960) reported a yield of 41 percent lean meat when chickens were roasted whole at 163°C.

Unstuffed Turkeys Turkeys may be cooked by a variety of methods including roasting, frying, broiling, braising, and microwave cooking. Roasting is one of the most commonly used methods.

Turkeys are usually marketed in the frozen state. Frozen tom turkeys were thawed four days in a refrigerator, thawed ten hours in cold running water, or roasted directly from the frozen state by Brodine and Carlin (1968). Cooking time for the frozen turkeys was approximately twice that required for the thawed birds. However, thawing methods had no effect on flavor, juiciness, and tenderness. Fulton *et al.* (1967) found that the palatability and yield were not significantly different when turkeys were roasted from the frozen state or thawed in the refrigerator before roasting. Similar findings were reported by Fulton and Davis (1974) when turkeys were roasted, braised, or fried. In order to achieve optimal tenderness, turkeys must be held for a sufficient period before they are frozen to allow the passing of rigor mortis.

Klose *et al.* (1968) thawed frozen ready-to-cook turkeys in commercial plastic bags at air temperatures of 12.8°C (55°F), 21°C (70°F), or 28.9°C (84°F). With the exception of the largest bird at the highest temperature, all carcasses were thawed before bacterial growth would have doubled four times. An important increase in the time between thawing and potential bacterial growth was produced by enclosing the plastic-bagged turkey in a double-walled paper bag for the thawing process. It was concluded that ambient air temperature thawing is a satisfactory alternative to refrigerator thawing providing exposure times are not too long and the birds are cooked or refrigerated within a few hours after thawing.

The effect of time in frozen storage on muscle protein composition and eating quality of turkeys was studied by Hoke *et al.* (1968). There was a decrease in the actomyosin nitrogen of muscle and some indication of proteolytic changes when the turkey was stored up to ten months.

The magnitude of these changes was not large. Total cooking losses were greater for the birds frozen five or ten months than for the unfrozen turkeys. However, a taste panel could not detect differences in juiciness due to frozen storage. Cooked thigh muscles were more tender and mealy from frozen-stored than fresh turkeys. There was some indication that an undesirable flavor developed in the thigh meat of turkeys stored ten months. Goertz et al. (1960b) found dripping losses to be lower and light meat flavor scores and dark meat tenderness scores to be higher for frozen turkeys stored one and three months than for fresh-unfrozen or fresh-frozen birds.

A number of studies have been reported concerned with the doneness of turkeys roasted to several internal temperatures. End point temperatures in both thigh and breast muscles have been used. Hoke *et al.* (1967) reported that as internal temperatures of light and dark meat turkey roasts increased from 73.9°C (165°F) to 90.6°C (195°F), yields and juiciness of cooked meat decreased while scores for odor, flavor, mealiness, and doneness increased. Fresh turkeys apparently require a higher end point temperature for comparable doneness than do frozen-stored turkeys (Hoke *et al.*, 1968).

Goertz *et al.* (1960a) found that frozen turkey halves roasted to either 90°C (194°F) in the *pectoralis major* (breast) muscle or 95°C (203°F) in the thigh were satisfactorily done. Turkey halves cooked to end point temperatures of 85°C (185°F) in the thigh were thought to be underdone.

The effect of oven temperature on the quality of roasted turkeys was studied by Goertz and Stacy (1960). Temperatures of 149°C (300°F), 163°C (325°F), and 177°C (350°F) were used. Total cooking and drip losses, press fluid yields, and shear values were similar when birds were roasted at any of the oven temperatures. Palatability scores for tenderness and juiciness of light and dark meat were also similar. Cooking time was less at 163° and 177°C than at 149°C. Generally turkeys cooked to 90°C in the breast muscle were considered done at any of the oven temperatures used.

Turkeys are sometimes wrapped in foil before roasting in an oven. Martinsen and Carlin (1968) found that, although total cooking losses were similar for unwrapped and foil-wrapped turkey roasts, the proportion of drip to volatile losses was greater with foil wrapping. Deethardt *et al.* (1971) reported that taste panel members preferred turkeys prepared by open-pan roasting in a 163°C (325°F) oven over those tightly wrapped in foil and roasted in a 233°C (451°F) oven. The foil-wrapped product was significantly less juicy.

Stuffed Turkeys Hoke *et al.* (1965) reported that heat penetration into the stuffing of stuffed turkeys was adequate to destroy spoilage organisms when the birds were roasted to 90.6°C (195°F) in the breast muscle. The temperature rise of the stuffing during a 20 minute holding period following roasting was included, however. The birds were roasted at an oven temperature of 163°C (325°F). Hoke and Kleve (1966) found that turkeys roasted at an oven temperature of 163°C to an end point of 85°C (185°F) or higher in the thigh usually had temperatures in the stuffing high enough to assure destruction of food-poisoning bacteria that are likely to be a problem in turkeys.

Bramblett and Fugate (1967) reported that conditions of stuffing turkeys, including the temperature of the stuffing, had little or no effect on the cooking time. Turkeys roasted at 163°C (325°F) to a temperature of 82.2°C (180°F) in the inner thigh muscle were considered to be more desirable than turkeys cooked in foil at either a low or high oven temperature.

Time–temperature relations in cooking stuffed turkeys, as well as the end point temperature, should be considered in evaluating the microbiological safety of this product. In foil-wrapped turkeys cooked in a 232°C (450°F) oven, inadequate heating of stuffing was observed in 20 out of 24 turkeys tested at the end of the cooking (Woodburn and Ellington, 1967). Warm stuffing may generally be safely placed in a chilled bird if the stuffed bird is immediately roasted or refrigerated. However, the size of the bird and the temperature of the refrigerator should be considered.

Based on reported research, general recommendations for roasting turkeys include placing the birds on a rack in an uncovered pan and roasting them in the oven at 149°–163°C (300°–325°F). The lower temperature is suggested for larger birds. Roasting to an end point temperature of 85°–89°C (185°–192°F) is usually satisfactory. Higher temperatures decrease juiciness. Partial covering with foil or cheese cloth may prevent drying and overcooking of the smaller parts of the bird. Heating must be adequate to destroy potentially harmful bacteria, particularly salmonellae, that may be present in the poultry flesh.

26.2

FISH

The sea is a vast resource for food production. In the past hundred years, the amount of food taken from the sea has multiplied more than tenfold. However, the annual catch cannot continue to grow indefinitely and some species are already dwindling. Fish farming both in salt water (mariculture) and fresh water (aquaculture) is providing a supplementary source of fish. The retail prices of farmed fish can be expected to be from three to five times higher than the retail prices of fish gathered by net or traps. Nevertheless, there are a number of reasons why interest in fish culture is expanding (Weatherley and Cogger, 1977; Brown, 1973).

There are thousands of species of fish. Only about 200 of these are of commercial importance. The per capita consumption of fish in the United States is about 11 lb per year, while that of beef is about 109 lb and pork is about 68 lb. By contrast, in Japan fish accounts for 55 percent of the animal protein consumed. More than half of the human population of the world depends on fish for a large part of their animal protein requirements (Brown, 1973).

TYPES OF FISH

Seafoods are usually classified, on the basis of anatomy, as vertebrate (fish) and invertebrate (shellfish). Fish may be further grouped into categories related to composition as lean or fat. *Lean fish* contain less than 5 percent fat while *fat fish* may have up to 22 percent fat. Examples of lean fish include cod, flounder, haddock, halibut, red snapper, sea trout, grouper, and hake. Examples of fat fish include butterfish, herring, mackerel, shad, lake trout, and whitefish. The various types of salmon vary from lean to fat.

Shellfish may be further classified as mollusks and crustaceans. *Mollusks* have a soft body inside a very hard outer shell. Examples of mollusks include abalone, clams, mussels, oysters, and scallops. *Crustaceans* have a crusty, segmented outer shell. Crabs, crayfish, lobsters, and shrimp belong in this category. Shellfish are generally low in fat content.

COMPOSITION

The gross composition of seafood is similar to that of land animals. Fish generally contain 66–84 percent water, 15–24 percent protein, 0.1–22 percent lipid, and 0.8–2 percent mineral substances (Borgstrom, 1961). The protein of fish is of high biological value. The composition of fish is influenced by feeding, locality, size, age, and season as well as by species. The proximate composition of selected cooked fish products is given in Table 26.3.

STRUCTURE OF FISH MUSCLE

Skeletal muscle makes up the major portion of fish fillets. Although fish muscle is similar to that of land animals, there are enough differences to warrant special research attention to fish.

The muscle fiber cells of fish present the usual features of skeletal muscle cells, including myofibrils, sarcoplasm, and sarcoplasmic reticulum. However, the fibers of fish muscle are short (up to about 3 cm in length) and their ends are inserted into sheets of connective tissue called *myocommata*. Small blocks or segments of such cells are called *myotomes*. During cooking the collagen in the connective tissue sheets of fish is hydrolyzed to gelatin and the muscle segments are freed. They separate as flakes. Fish muscle contains small amounts of connective tissue in comparison with meat. The collagen of fish connective tissue also appears to be degraded at a lower temperature than that of mammalian collagen (Schultz and Anglemier, 1964). The tenderness of fish can, therefore, be attributed to both its low content of connective tissue and the soft and easily degraded nature of this component.

The main muscle of most vertebrate fish is without pigment and

Table 26.3 Proximate Composition of Selected Cooked Fish Dishes (all products prepared with added fat)

Fish Product	Mois- ture (g)	Kcal.	Protein (g)	Fat (g)	Carbo- hydrate (g)	Ash (g)
Fish						
Baked flounder fillets	58.1	195	30.0	8.2		2.2
Oven-fried haddock fillets*	66.1	155	17.2	5.0	9.8	1.9
Broiled halibut steaks	66.6	165	25.2	7.0		1.7
Baked salmon steaks	67.6	140	26.1	3.8		1.6
Baked shad	64.0	195	23.2	11.3		1.4
Broiled mackerel fillets	61.6	230	21.8	15.8		1.6
Shellfish						
Baked crab meat**	69.6	165	12.8	10.6	4.7	2.3
Fried Oysters*	54.7	235	8.6	13.9	18.6	1.5
French fried shrimp*	54.2	240	20.4	12.5	11.1	1.8

Source: From Lee, 1961.
* Contains breading mixture.
** Contains milk, egg yolks, and flour

essentially colorless. Underneath the skin of many fish, however, making up about 10 percent of total body muscle, is a layer of heavily pigmented, reddish-brown muscle. This muscle is rich in myoglobin and lipid material and may function in providing sustained muscular activity. The heme pigments may act as pro-oxidants for the lipid. This helps to explain the tendency toward the development of rancidity that has been noted for the dark muscles (Schultz and Anglemier, 1964).

FRESH FISH

Fish are more perishable than red meat. Freshly caught fish have a shining, iridescent surface, protruding bright eyes, bright gills, and soft flesh. Rigor mortis sets in soon after death and the flesh becomes firm until the passing of rigor is completed. The duration of rigor is generally shorter in fish than in mammals.

As fish deteriorate in quality and spoil, the surface loses its bright sheen and becomes covered with a thick slime. The eyes shrink and sink, the gills become greyish brown and slime-covered, the flesh becomes very soft and inelastic, and the odor becomes very fishy, ammonialike, and eventually putrid. The changes are caused by bacteria, by digestive enzymes present in the fish, and by reactions such as oxidation of lipids. The digestive enzymes produce spoilage rapidly in fish that are not drawn (Borgstrom, 1965). Proteases are also present in the lysosomes of fish skeletal muscle cells (Reddi *et al.*, 1972) and may degrade proteins in the flesh.

The keeping quality of fresh fish is greatly influenced by the temperature at which it is held. Hydrolytic enzymes bring about deteriorative changes at higher temperatures. Fish are usually iced in bulk after catching and while in route to the market. The fish may also be displayed in ice at the fish market.

A condition of fish muscle called *chalkiness* has been described. The flesh is dull, white, opaque, soft, and flabby, somewhat similar to pale, soft, exudative (PSE) pork. Chalkiness appears to be related to the pH of fish muscle, occurring when the pH falls to about 6.0 or lower. During storage of fish with this defect, there is increased drip (Paul and Palmer, 1972).

Fresh fish may be marketed in several different forms. These include whole or round fish, drawn fish, dressed or pan-dressed, steaks, single fillet, butterfly fillet, and sticks. These market forms are shown in Figure 26.4.

Federal inspection and grading is done for some fish and fish products. This is a voluntary service. When inspection and grade marks appear on the labels of fish products they indicate that the products have been produced in accordance with official U. S. grade standards or approved specifications.

FREEZING FISH

Fish has been frozen as a means of preservation for over 100 years. A number of changes occur in fish muscle during freezing and frozen storage. Ice crystals form and the volume of the muscle expands. A slow rate of freezing produces larger ice crystals than does a rapid rate. With large ice crystals there is greater tissue damage. They penetrate cell walls, resulting in a larger loss of drip when the fish thaws (Borgstrom, 1965). Desiccation of the surface of frozen fish during storage may occur because of sublimation of ice crystals in the frozen product. Tight wrapping in moisture-vapor-proof materials helps to control the desiccation.

Frozen storage increases toughness of fish muscle. The toughness has been described as stringiness, chewiness, or rubberiness. This is particularly apparent when frozen fish is stored at a temperature greater than $-5°C$ ($23°F$). The amount of myofibrillar proteins that can be extracted from fish muscle decreases with frozen storage. Changes in these proteins are thought to influence the texture deterioration that occurs (Schultz and Anglemier, 1964). As water is frozen and ice crystals form, the concentration of salts in the remaining unfrozen water increases and protein dehydration occurs (Paul and Palmer, 1972). At storage temperatures below about $-30°C$ ($-22°F$), alterations in the myofibrillar proteins of fish muscle are slow and may take a year or more to become apparent (Schultz and Anglemier, 1964).

Changes may occur in lipid materials during the frozen storage of fish. The highly unsaturated fatty acids of fatty fish are sensitive to oxidative deterioration and rancidity. The basic reaction is apparently the process of autoxidation. However, enzyme systems in the tissue play a role in oxidation by acting as pro-oxidants. Metal ions also act as pro-oxidants. The reddish-brown muscle of fish is the tissue most sensi-

Figure 26.4

Market forms of fish (a) Whole or round fish (b) Drawn fish (c) Dressed or pan-dressed (d) Steaks (e) Single fillet (f) Butterfly fillet (g) Sticks (Courtesy of National Marine Fisheries Service, U.S. Department of Commerce.)

PURCHASING FISH

MARKET FORMS

Fish is marketed in various forms for different uses. Knowing these forms or "cuts" is important in buying fish. The best known market forms of fish are:

(a)

WHOLE OR ROUND fish are those marketed just as they come from the water. Before cooking, they must be scaled and eviscerated (which means removing the entrails). The head, tail, and fins may be removed if desired, and the fish either split or cut into serving-size portions, except in fish intended for baking. Some small fish, like smelt, are frequently cooked with only the entrails removed.

(b)

DRAWN fish are marketed with only the entrails removed. In preparation for cooking, they generally are scaled. Head, tail, and fins are removed, if desired, and the fish split or cut into serving-size portions. Small drawn fish, or larger sizes intended for baking, may be cooked in the form purchased after being scaled.

(c)

DRESSED fish are scaled and eviscerated, usually with the head, tail, and fins removed. The smaller sizes are ready for cooking as purchased (pan-dressed). The larger sizes of dressed fish may be baked as purchased but frequently are cut into steaks or serving-size portions. A cross section of the backbone is usually the only bone in the steak.

(d)

STEAKS are cross section slices of the larger sizes of dressed fish. They are ready to cook as purchased, except for dividing the very largest into serving-size portions. A cross section of the backbone is usually the only bone in the steak.

(e)

The sides of the fish, cut lengthwise away from the backbone, are called FILLETS. They are practically boneless and require no preparation for cooking. Sometimes the skin, with the scales removed, is left on the fillets;others are skinned. A fillet cut from one side of a fish is called a single fillet. This is the type of fillet most generally seen in the market.

(f)

BUTTERFLY FILLETS are the two sides of the fish corresponding to two single fillets held together by uncut flesh and the skin.

(g)

STICKS are pieces of fish cut lengthwise or crosswise from fillets or steaks into portions of uniform width and length.

tive to oxidation (Borgstrom, 1965). Lean fish muscle contains from 0.5 to 1.0 percent unsaturated lipid which oxidizes. However, rancidity does not commonly develop in these fish on frozen storage. Castell (1971) suggested that the oxidized lipids become bound up in lipid–protein complexes instead of forming carbonyl compounds that are usually associated with rancidity. The lipid–protein complexes may contribute to the toughened texture of over-stored or poorly stored frozen fish. Anderson and Ravesi (1970) found a relationship between a decrease in the readily extractable protein of frozen-stored cod muscle and free fatty acid formation.

COOKING FISH

Little scientific research has been reported on the cooking of fish and shellfish. Armstrong *et al.* (1960) compared codfish fillets cooked at 149°C (300°F) or 260°C (500°F). Cooking losses and acceptability were similar at both temperatures. However the fish that was cooked uncovered was found to be more attractive and palatable than that cooked covered. Dyer and Fraser (1964) reported that palatability of frozen fish stored at relatively high freezing temperatures was higher when the fish was cooked by frying than when it was cooked by baking or steaming.

The baking of 1-in. salmon steaks was reported by Charley (1952). Scores for moistness and the amount of fluid that could be pressed from the tissues decreased and cooking losses increased as the internal temperature increased from 70°C (158°F) to 75°C (167°F) to 80°C (176°F) and to 85°C (185°F). No significant difference in tenderness was found among the steaks cooked to various internal temperatures. Those cooked to 80° or 85°C were generally more acceptable. Salmon steaks were also baked at four different oven temperatures to an internal temperature of 75°C. No differences in palatability due to oven temperature were found.

Two-pound salmon cuts were baked at various oven temperatures by Charley and Goertz (1958). The baking temperature had no effect on the appearance of the muscle as seen under the microscope. A difference of 100°F in the baking temperature caused a significant increase in total cooking loss but oven temperature did not affect palatability. The cut nearest the head was most flaky and least tender while the section from the tail was the least flaky and the most tender.

Fish generally does not require the tenderization of connective tissue by cooking. Smaller amounts of connective tissue are present in fish muscle than in mammalian meat. The connective tissue in fish is also more easily degraded than is that in meat. Therefore, the cooking method for fish may be chosen to provide variety. Fish may be satisfactorily cooked by broiling, baking, frying, steaming, and poaching in milk or water. Lean fish may be more palatable with the addition of fat when broiled or baked.

Fish is done when flakes of cooked fish separate readily from each other. This occurs when the muscle fiber proteins have coagulated and the connective tissue holding them has been solubilized. The tissue also loses translucency when fish is considered done. Overcooking fish causes dryness and excessive shrinkage. Overcooking may toughen shellfish such as oysters.

Antithiamin activity has been reported in the tissues of many fishes throughout the world. This is usually due to a thiaminase enzyme which destroys the vitamin, thiamin. Cooking destroys the thiaminase. A nonenzymatic anti-thiamin factor has been reported in skipjack tuna. Its activity decreases with refrigerated and frozen storage (Tang and Hilker, 1970).

SUMMARY

Poultry represents a widely used source of dietary protein. Poultry are divided into market classes according to their species, age, and sex. For chickens, these include broiler or fryer, roaster, capon, and fowl.

The fat content of poultry varies with age, sex, and species. It also varies from one part of the body to another. Poultry is a good source of high quality protein. Cooked poultry meat contains from 25 to 35 percent protein.

Poultry are scalded to facilitate the removal of feathers. Using a water temperature of 50.6°–54.4°C for 90–120 seconds leaves the skin intact. The plucked, eviscerated carcasses are inspected for signs of disease and are then chilled. Some poultry is marketed in a frozen state. USDA has established standards for grades of poultry. Official grades are A, B, and C. Quality factors used in grading include conformation, fleshing, fat distribution, freedom from pinfeathers, and freedom from defects.

Some of the procedures employed in the processing of poultry may affect the tenderness of the bird. Severe scalding and plucking conditions decrease tenderness. Rigor must pass before the bird is frozen if tenderness is to be maintained.

Poultry responds to heat in a similar manner as does meat. Older poultry are generally less tender than young birds and require tenderization on cooking. Determination of doneness in poultry is often difficult. Subjective panel appraisal has been used. The objective measurement of color offers potential for monitoring standards of doneness when they are established. Broilers cooked in a gas broiler at 177°C on the surface of the meat to an internal breast temperature of 95°C were nearer optimal doneness than broilers cooked at higher temperatures.

The yield of cooked chicken meat varies with age of bird and cooking method. Birds over nine weeks of age have greater yields than those of younger age. Yield was reported to be higher for roasting than for oven frying. Chickens roasted at an oven temperature of 163°C had higher yields than those roasted at 191°C.

Turkeys are usually marketed in the frozen state. They may be cooked after thawing or cooked directly from the frozen state. Thawing methods have little effect on flavor, juiciness, and tenderness. Cooking time is greater from the frozen state. Some changes in proteins occur in turkey muscle after frozen storage of up to ten months. However, the magnitude of these changes is small.

As the internal temperature of roasted turkeys increases, yields and juiciness of cooked meat decrease. Poultry are most acceptable when cooked well done. Heating must be adequate to destroy harmful bacteria, particularly salmonellae, that may be in the poultry flesh. The oven temperature for roasting has little effect on palatability. When roasting stuffed turkeys, heating must be adequate to destroy potentially harmful bacteria present in the stuffing.

General recommendations for roasting turkeys include placing the birds on a rack in an uncovered pan and roasting them in the oven at 149°–163°C. Roasting to an end point temperature of 85°–89°C is usually satisfactory.

About 200 species of fish are of commercial importance. The per capita consumption of fish in the United States is about 10 percent of beef consumption.

Seafoods are usually classified as vertebrate (fish) and invertebrate (shellfish). Fish may be further grouped into categories as lean or fat. Shellfish may be classified as mollusks, which have a soft body inside a very hard shell, and crustaceans, which have a crusty, segmented outer shell. The gross composition of seafood is similar to that of land animals.

The muscle fiber cells of fish present the usual features of animal skeletal muscle. However, they are short and their ends are inserted into sheets of connective tissue called myocommata. Small blocks of such cells are called myotomes. During cooking the segments separate as flakes after the collagen of connective tissue is hydrolyzed. Fish muscle contains smaller amounts of connective than does meat and it is degraded at a lower temperature.

Fish are more perishable than red meat. As fresh fish deteriorate in quality and spoil, the surface loses its bright sheen and becomes covered with a thick slime. The eyes shrink and sink, the gills become greyish brown, the flesh becomes soft and inelastic, and the odor becomes very "fishy." The changes are caused by bacteria, by digestive enzymes, and by reactions such as oxidation of lipids. Fresh fish may be marketed as whole fish, drawn, dressed, steaks, single fillet, butterfly fillet, and sticks.

A number of changes occur in fish muscle during freezing and frozen storage. Ice crystals form and may penetrate cell walls, especially when the fish is frozen slowly. Frozen storage increases toughness in fish muscle, particularly when storage is at a temperature greater than −5°C. The solubility of the myofibrillar proteins decreases, possibly due to dehydration. Oxidation of lipids in fish muscle may also occur during frozen storage. In lean fish, a lipid–protein complex may contribute to the toughening that accompanies frozen storage.

Little scientific research has been reported on the cooking of seafood. Baked salmon steaks were reported to decrease in moistness and press fluid and cooking losses increased as the final internal temperature increased up to 85°C. However, steaks cooked from 80° to 85°C were generally more acceptable than those cooked to lower temperatures. The baking temperature did not affect palatability. Fish generally does not require the tenderization of connective tissue by cooking. Therefore, the cooking method may be chosen to provide variety. Fish is done when flakes of cooked fish separate readily from each other.

STUDY QUESTIONS

Poultry may be classified on the basis of age and weight.

1. List common market classes of chickens and turkeys, giving age and sex differences. Suggest satisfactory methods for cooking each class.

USDA inspection of poultry is mandatory but grading is voluntary.

2. Explain the major purpose of federal inspection for poultry.
3. List USDA grades for poultry and describe quality factors applied in grading.
4. How may processing procedures affect the tenderness of processed poultry? Explain.

Poultry may be cooked in a variety of ways.

5. Discuss the possible value of a Hunter Color Difference Meter in assessing the doneness of chicken.
6. Suggest acceptable methods for thawing turkeys before cooking. What precautions must be taken and why?
7. Recommend an appropriate procedure for assessing the doneness of roasted turkey cooked in the home.
8. Outline an appropriate step-by-step procedure for roasting a turkey and explain why this procedure should be followed.

Seafoods are commonly classified on the basis of anatomy and composition.

9. What is the basis for the classification of seafood as fish and shellfish? Describe a subclassification for each of these types of seafood.
10. Describe differences in structure between fish muscle and beef muscle.
11. Describe the characteristics of fresh fish. How do these change as fish deteriorates and spoils?
12. Under what storage conditions does frozen fish increase in toughness and why?

Fish may be satisfactorily cooked by a variety of methods.

13. Explain why cooked fish flakes when it is done.
14. Explain why a cooking method for fish does not need to be chosen in terms of its ability to tenderize.

REFERENCES

1. Anderson, M. L. and E. M. Ravesi. 1970. On the nature of the association of protein in frozen-stored cod muscle. *Journal of Food Science* 35, 551.

2. Arafa, A. S. and T. C. Chen. 1978a. Liquid nitrogen exposure as an alternative means of chilling poultry. *Journal of Food Science* 43, 1036.

3. Arafa, A. S. and T. C. Chen. 1978b. Ascorbic acid dipping as a means of extending shelf life and improving microbial quality of cut-up broiler parts. *Poultry Science* 57, 99.

4. Armstrong, I. L., E. W. Park, and B. A. McLaren. 1960. The effect of time and temperature of cooking on the palatability and cooking losses of frozen Atlantic codfish fillets. *Journal of the Fishery Research Board of Canada* 17, 1.

5. Baker, R. C. and J. Darfler. 1968. A comparison of leghorn fowl and fryers for precooked battered fried chicken. *Poultry Science* 47, 1590.

6. Baker, R. C., J. M. Darfler, and D. V. Vadehra. 1972a. Prebrowned fried chicken. 1. Evaluation of cooking methods. *Poultry Science* 51, 1215.

7. Baker, R. C., J. M. Darfler, and D. V. Vadehra. 1972b. Prebrowned fried chicken. 2. Evaluation of predust materials. *Poultry Science* 51, 1220.

8. Borgstrom, G., editor. 1961. *Fish as Food,* Vol. I. New York: Academic Press.

9. Borgstrom, G., editor. 1965. *Fish as Food,* Vol. IV. New York: Academic Press.

10. Bramblett, V. D. and K. W. Fugate. 1967. Choice of cooking temperature for stuffed turkeys. Part I. Palatability factors. *Journal of Home Economics* 59, 180.

11. Brodine, M. V. and A. F. Carlin. 1968. Chilling and thawing methods and their effect on quality of cooked whole turkeys. *Food Technology* 22, 607.

12. Brown, E. E. 1973. Mariculture and aquaculture. *Food Technology* 27 (Dec.), 60.

13. Cantrell, D. F. and K. K. Hale, Jr. 1974. Influence of chilling methods and aging time on yield and tenderness of fowl. *Poultry Science* 53, 1725.

14. Castrell, C. H. 1971. Metal-catalyzed lipid oxidation and changes of proteins in fish. *Journal of the American Oil Chemists Society* 48, 645.

15. Charley, H. 1952. Effects of internal temperature and of oven temperature on the cooking losses and the palatability of baked salmon steaks. *Food Research* 17, 136.

16. Charley, H. and G. E. Goertz. 1958. The effects of oven temperature on certain characteristics of baked salmon. *Food Research* 23, 17.

17. Dawson, E. H., G. L. Gilpin, and A. M. Harkin. 1960. Yield of cooked meat from different types of poultry. *Journal of Home Economics* 52, 445.

18. Deethardt, D., L. M. Burrill, K. Schneider, and C. W. Carlson. 1971. Foil-covered versus open-pan procedures for roasting turkey. *Journal of Food Science* 36, 624.

19. Dyer, W. J. and D. I. Fraser. 1964. Cooking method and palatability of frozen cod fillets of various qualities. *Journal of the Fishery Research Board of Canada* 21, 577.

20. de Fremery, D. 1963. Relation between biochemical properties and tenderness of poultry. Proceedings of the Meat Tenderness Symposium, Campbell Soup Company, p. 99.

21. de Fremery, D. and M. F. Pool. 1960. Biochemistry of chicken muscle as related to rigor mortis and tenderization. *Food Research* 25, 73.

22. Fulton, L. and C. Davis. 1974. Cooking chicken and turkey from the frozen and thawed states. *American Dietetic Association Journal* 64, 505.

23. Fulton, L. H., G. L. Gilpin, and E. H. Dawson. 1967. Turkeys roasted from frozen and thawed states. *Journal of Home Economics* 59, 728.

24. Goertz, G. E., K. Cooley, M. C. Ferguson, and D. L. Harrison. 1960a. Doneness of frozen, defrosted turkey halves roasted to several end point temperatures. *Food Technology* 14, 135.

25. Goertz, G. E., A. S. Hooper, and D. L. Harrison. 1960b. Comparison of rate of cooking and doneness of fresh-unfrozen and frozen, defrosted turkey hens. *Food Technology* 14, 458.

26. Goertz, G. E., D. Meyer, B. Weathers, and A. S. Hooper. 1964. Effects of cooking temperatures on broiler acceptability. *American Dietetic Association Journal* 45, 526.

27. Goertz, G. E. and S. Stacy. 1960. Roasting half and whole turkey hens. *American Dietetic Association Journal* 37, 458.

28. Hoke, I. M. 1968. Roasting chickens. *Journal of Home Economics* 60, 661.

29. Hoke, I. M. and M. K. Kleve. 1966. Heat penetration, quality, and yield of turkeys roasted to different internal thigh temperatures. *Journal of Home Economics* 58, 381.

30. Hoke, I. M., G. L. Gilpin, and E. H. Dawson. 1965. Heat penetration, quality, and yield of turkeys roasted to an internal breast temperature of 195°F. *Journal of Home Economics* 57, 188.

31. Hoke, I. M., B. K. McGeary, and F. Lakshmanan. 1968. Muscle protein composition and eating quality of fresh and frozen turkeys. *Journal of Food Science* 33, 566.

32. Hoke, I. M., B. K. McGeary, and M. K. Kleve. 1967. Effect of internal and oven temperatures on eating quality of light and dark meat turkey roasts. *Food Technology* 21 (No. 5), 89.

33. Jacobson, M., J. V. Spencer, and D. B. Halvorson. 1969. Yields from meat-type chickens at five ages. *American Dietetic Association Journal* 54, 308.

34. Klose, A. A., H. Lineweaver, and H. H. Palmer. 1968. Thawing turkeys at ambient air temperatures. *Food Technology* 22, 1310.

35. Lee, C. F. 1961. Composition of cooked fish dishes. U. S. Department of the Interior, Circular 29.

36. Lyon, C. E., B. G. Lyon, A. A. Klose, and J. P. Hudspeth. 1975a. Effects of temperature-time combinations on doneness and yields of water-cooked broiler thighs. *Journal of Food Science* 40, 129.

37. Lyon, B. G., C. E. Lyon, and A. A. Klose. 1975b. Subjective and objective methods for estimating doneness in water-cooked broiler thighs. *Journal of Food Science* 40, 133.

38. Lyon, C. E., B. G. Lyon, and J. P. Hudspeth. 1973. The effect of different

cutting procedures on the cooked yield and tenderness of cut-up broiler parts. *Poultry Science* 52, 1103.

39. Marion, J. E. and J. G. Woodroof. 1963. The fatty acid composition of breast, thigh, and skin tissues of chicken broilers as influenced by dietary fats. *Poultry Science* 42, 1202.

40. Martinsen, C. S. and A. F. Carlin. 1968. Rate of heating during pre-cooking in foil and quality of boneless turkey roasts stored at 0°F. *Food Technology* 22 (No. 2), 109.

41. Mickelberry, W. C., J. C. Rogler, and W. J. Stadelman. 1964. Effect of dietary fats on broiler tissues. *American Dietetic Association Journal* 45, 234.

42. Mickelberry, W. C., J. C. Rogler, and W. J. Stadelman. 1966. The influence of dietary fat and environmental temperature upon chick growth and carcass composition. *Poultry Science* 45, 313.

43. Mountney, G. J. 1976. *Poultry Products Technology,* 2nd edition. Westport, Conn.: Avi Publishing Company.

44. Paul, P. C. and H. H. Palmer. 1972. *Food Theory and Applications.* New York: Wiley.

45. Reddi, P. K., S. M. Constantinides, and H. A. Dymsza. 1972. Catheptic activity of fish muscle. *Journal of Food Science* 37, 643.

46. Salmon, R. E. and J. B. O'Neil. 1973. The effect of the level and source and a change of source of dietary fat on the fatty acid composition of the depot fat and the thigh and breast meat of turkeys as related to age. *Poultry Science* 52, 302.

47. Schultz, H. W. and A. F. Anglemier, editors. 1964. *Proteins and Their Reactions.* Westport, Conn.: Avi Publishing Company.

48. Scott, M. L. 1956. Composition of turkey meat. *American Dietetic Association Journal* 32, 941.

49. Stadelman, W. J. 1978. Tenderness, flavor, and nutritive value of chickens. *Food Technology* 32 (No. 5), 80.

50. Tang, N. Y. and D. M. Hilker. 1970. Effect of heating and cold storage on antithiamine activity on skipjack tuna. *Journal of Food Science* 35, 676.

51. U. S. Department of Agriculture. 1961. Poultry grading and inspection. Agriculture Information Bulletin No. 173.

52. Weatherley, A. H. and B. M. G. Cogger. 1977. Fish culture: Problems and prospects. *Science* 197, 427.

53. Woodburn, M. and A. E. Ellington. 1967. Choice of cooking temperature for stuffed turkeys. Part II. Microbiological safety of stuffing. *Journal of Home Economics* 59, 186.

CHAPTER 27

PLANT PROTEINS IN FOOD SYSTEMS

High protein mixtures and isolated proteins from both plant and animal sources are now being used extensively in the food industry. These ingredients have become important for many fabricated foods. Sources of animal protein have always been relatively plentiful in the United States as compared to other countries of the world. The consumption of animal protein is, therefore, relatively high in this country. However, the demand for animal products abroad is now increasing and the total supply is limited. As this trend continues, a transition is likely from a primarily animal protein food economy to one in which plant proteins attain a greater degree of importance (Bird, 1974).

Concentrated plant protein is available from several sources. These include cereal grains, leafy green plants, and residues from oilseeds, such as soybean, sunflower, and cottonseed, after extraction of the oil. The soy processing industry has been a leader in the area of developing a variety of high protein products for human use. Soy, therefore, accounts for the largest volume of marketed oilseed protein products. Cereal flours have been used in a number of nutritious high protein foods produced for various developing countries. Protein is present in cereal grains in relatively small amounts but cereal protein concentrates, including vital wheat gluten, are used to some extent by the food industry. The potential for leafy plants as a source of concentrated protein is great. However, much developmental work must be done before leaf protein concentrates are available and acceptable for widespread human consumption.

27.1

SOY PROCESSING

Although soybeans have been used as foods in the oriental cultures for centuries, it was not until the beginning of the 1900s that the western world recognized soybeans for their human food value. They were first used as a source of oil. Later, as special soy processing techniques were developed, the high protein containing product remaining after oil extraction was utilized. The basic high protein soy products are relatively inexpensive and offer an excellent source of nutrients (Rakosky, 1975).

The dry mature soybean contains about 34 percent protein, 18 percent oil, and 34 percent carbohydrate. Soybeans contain little or no starch. The carbohydrates in soybeans are primarily cell wall polysaccharides plus the oligosaccharides sucrose, raffinose, and stachyose (Whitaker and Tannenbaum, 1977). The oil is contained in numerous cell inclusions called *spherosomes*. Most of the protein is in storage sites called *aleurone grains* or *protein bodies* (see Figure 27.1) (Wolf, 1972).

The two major products from the soybean are oil and meal or flour. The cleaned beans are cracked into small pieces between pairs of sequential rollers. The hulls are separated by air streams. The dehulled cracked beans are heated with steam to soften the structure and are then pressed into flakes as they pass through a pair of rollers. The full-fat flakes may then be heated, to destroy enzymes and anti-nutritional substances, and ground into full-fat flour. This flour finds some uses in bakery production. Most of the full-fat flakes, however, are extracted for the production of soybean oil.

In the extraction process, the organic solvent hexane is percolated through the flakes and dissolves the crude oil. The oil and hexane mixture is then heated to evaporate the hexane, which is condensed and reused. The extracted oil is refined and bleached. The phospholipid

Figure 27.1

Electron micrograph of a section of mature soybean cotyledon. Protein bodies (*PB*), spherosomes (*S*) and cell wall (*CW*) are identified. (Reprinted with permission from Saio, K. and T. Watanabe. 1968. Observations of soybean foods under electron microscope. *Nippon Shokuhin Kogyo Gakkaishi* (Journal of Food Science and Technology) 15, 290. Photograph supplied by W. J. Wolf, Northern Regional Research Center, U. S. Department of Agriculture.)

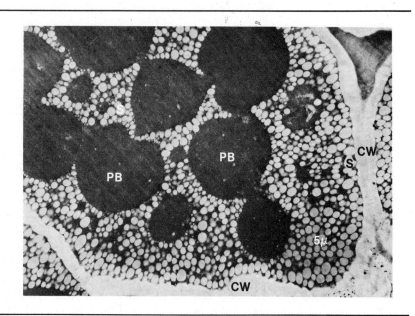

lecithin may also be separated from the oil and hexane mixture and used as a food additive. The flakes may have the residual hexane removed from them by evaporation under vacuum, producing white defatted flakes (Alden, 1975). Alternatively, the flakes may be toasted.

When the defatted flakes are ground to a relatively large particle size, soy grits are produced. Grits are used as a functional ingredient in such products as ground meats, baby foods, and cereal products. When the flakes are ground to a fine powder, soy flour results. The solubility of the protein in different soy flours varies depending upon the amount of heat to which the flakes have been subjected. Defatted soy flour contains from 47 to 53 percent protein, from 0.6 to 9.9 percent fat, from 6 to 8 percent moisture, and about 38 percent carbohydrate.

Soy flour is used in a variety of bakery products. It may be added to bread at levels of 3 percent of the wheat flour weight with no major changes in formulation. Soy flour may also be blended with sweet dairy whey to produce a nutritious milk substitute for use in bread products. Cake doughnuts often contain soy flour at levels of 4–10 percent of the weight of the wheat flour in the product. Soy flour can also be used to advantage in many other sweet bakery items. It improves crust color and tenderness, in many cases. Soy flour with added lecithin is used in high fat pastry items (French, 1977). Soybeans do not contain proteins similar to those of wheat gluten. They therefore lack the unique dough-forming properties of wheat flour and cannot be a direct substitute.

The ground defatted flakes or soy flour serve as the raw material for several additional soy products, as indicated in Figure 27.2. A "meaty"

Figure 27.2

A variety of high protein soy products can be produced from defatted soy flakes. (Reprinted with permission from Alden, D. E. 1975. Soy processing: From beans to ingredients. *Journal of the American Oil Chemists Society* 52, 244A.)

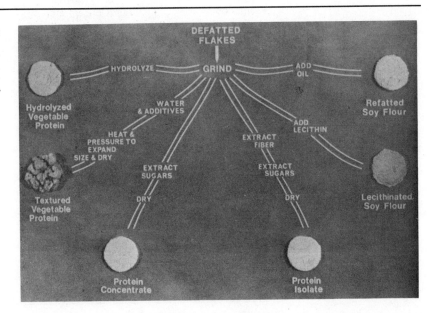

tasting flavor ingredient called *hydrolyzed vegetable protein* is produced by making a slurry of the flour and water and treating it with a protease enzyme or acid. The versatility of soy flour for bakery use is expanded by blending the defatted flour with oil or lecithin at various levels. The oligosaccharides or sugars may be extracted from soy flour, resulting in a more concentrated protein product, called *soy protein concentrate* (Alden, 1975). Concentrates contain 70 percent or more protein. Another soy product, which contains 90 percent or more protein, is called *soy protein isolate*. The production of this product is based on the solubility of the proteins, the majority of which are classified as globulins. The flakes or flours may be extracted with dilute alkali at pH 8–9 and the clarified extract acidified to pH 4.5 to precipitate the globulins.

Table 27.1   Functional Properties of Soybean Products in Food Systems

Functional property	Form of soy protein used	Food system
Emulsification		
Formation	Flour, Concentrate, Isolate	Frankfurters, bologna, sausages Breads, cakes, soups Whipped toppings, frozen desserts
Stabilization	Flour, Concentrate, Isolate	Frankfurters, bologna, sausages Soups
Fat absorption		
Promotion	Flour, Concentrate, Isolate	Frankfurters, bologna, sausages, meat patties
Prevention	Flour, Isolate	Doughnuts, pancakes
Water absorption		
Uptake	Flour, Concentrate	Breads, cakes Macaroni Confections
Retention	Flour, Concentrate	Breads, cakes
Texture		
Viscosity	Flour, Concentrate, Isolate	Soups, gravies, chili
Gelation	Isolate	Simulated ground meats
Shred formation	Flour, Isolate	Simulated meats
Fiber formation	Isolate	Simulated meats
Cohesion	Flour, Isolate	Baked goods Macaroni Simulated meats
Elasticity	Isolate	Simulated meats
Aeration	Isolate	Whipped toppings, chiffon mixes, confections

Source: From Wolf, 1970.

These proteins are then washed, neutralized, and spray-dried to produce the soy protein isolate (Wolf, 1972).

Soy proteins in all forms, as flour, concentrates, or isolates, have functional properties that make them useful in food systems. In soy flour and concentrates, the other components present also contribute to the overall effects produced. Table 27.1 gives some examples of food systems in which the various soy mixtures may function in specific ways to improve the product.

27.2

TEXTURIZING PROTEINS

Textured vegetable proteins are food products made from high protein flours, protein concentrates, and isolated proteins. They are characterized by having structural integrity and identifiable texture such that each unit will withstand hydration in cooking and other procedures used in preparing the food for consumption (Lockmiller, 1972). During the process of texturization, a powdery protein material (a flour) is transformed into one which has texture, described as chewy and fibrous in nature.

In America, the technology of textured vegetable protein products probably had its beginning with groups of vegetarians. One of the early patents in the field was issued to Kellogg in 1907. Dr. Kellogg and his brother originated the breakfast cereal industry. The object of the patent was to provide a palatable and nourishing food product that could be used as a meat substitute. The process consisted essentially of mixing wet wheat gluten, casein, and vegetable oil in a shredding machine and then cooking the mix in a can under pressure. Early textured protein products had wheat gluten as the primary ingredient and generally took the form of patties or small cutlets. They were often canned in a broth.

The textured products designed for the vegetarian market were for the most part unknown to the majority of the U. S. population for many years (Whitaker and Tannenbaum, 1977). During the 1950s, a trend developed toward the use of soy protein products in simulated meats. In 1954, a patent was issued describing a method of processing edible soy protein isolates which utilized textile spinning techniques with the production of continuous filaments. This product is called *spun vegetable protein* (Whitaker and Tannenbaum, 1977). The major steps in the spinning process are outlined in Figure 27.3. The isolated protein is slurried with water and alkali to raise the pH to about 10. This results in a mixture called a *protein dope*. After mixing and filtering out any larger particles, the protein dope is forced through spinnerettes into a coagulating bath, much like the spinning mechanism used in the making of nylon. The fibers are coagulated or set up by the low pH and salt concentration in the bath. They are then gathered into a bundle called a *tow* or *rope*. The fibers are stretched and heated. They are then neutral-

Figure 27.3

Texturizing processes. (Reprinted with permission from Alden, D. E. 1975. Soy processing: From beans to ingredients. *Journal of the American Oil Chemists Society* 52, 244A.)

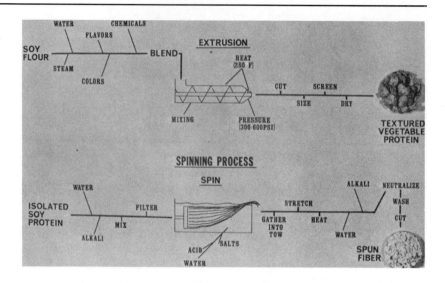

ized, washed, cut, and frozen for shipping (Alden, 1975). In the process of spinning, the globular soy protein chains are apparently first unfolded. Then new bonds, including disulfide and hydrogen bonds, seem to bind the stretched molecules together (Whitaker and Tannenbaum, 1977). The fibers are used as a flavorless textured foundation for the fabrication of meat analogs (Alden, 1975).

For the finished product fabrication, the spun fibrils are blended with fat, flavorings, coloring, supplemental nutrients, and stabilizers and are bound together with a heat-coagulable protein. Egg albumen is the most widely used binding protein. The fiber typically makes up about 40 percent of the dry components of a meat analog, the protein binding system accounts for about 10 percent, and fat comprises about 20 percent. However, fat content may be varied from essentially zero to 50 percent. The balance of the product is composed of other nutrients, flavors, and coloring agents (Thulin and Kuramoto, 1967). Among other meat analogs, a bacon-slice product has been marketed. It contains both red and white parallel strips resembling the lean and fatty portions of typical bacon. The red and white mixtures are prepared separately and layered together before being subjected to treatment which sets the protein binders. A typical formulation is given in Table 27.2.

There is a second type of texturizing process, in addition to spinning, that produces textured protein products. It involves *extrusion*. The major steps in the preparation of this type of textured vegetable protein are shown in Figure 27.3. The flour is blended with steam and water, flavors, colors, and chemical additives to control density or structure. While mixing in an extruder, mechanical heat is developed and steam heat is applied. Most cooking extruders use a single screw system to

Table 27.2 Typical Composition of Bacon Analog

Ingredient	Red Portion (%)	White Portion (%)
Spun fiber	18.0	1.5
Egg albumen	10.0	8.2
Tapioca starch	7.5	5.8
Water	42.5	42.3
Corn oil	6.7	25.7
Soy isolate	3.4	2.6
Carrageenan	0.5	0.2
Sodium caseinate	none	5.2
Colors, flavorings, seasonings	11.4	8.5

Source: From Whitaker and Tannenbaum, 1977.

feed, cook, and meter or pump the high protein material through the apparatus. As the mixture is conveyed down the extruder channel, it is worked into a homogeneous dough. Partial cooking occurs. At the exit point the pressure, which builds up in the extruder, is rapidly released. The material expands as it is extruded and tiny air pockets form uniformly throughout the mass, creating texture. The product is then cut, screened, and dried. Extruded protein mixtures are used primarily as meat extenders (Alden, 1975; Whitaker and Tannenbaum, 1977).

The U. S. Food and Drug Administration has established definitions and standards for labeling vegetable protein products. The regulations establish protein content and the content of some vitamins and minerals that must be included if the food is to be considered to be nutritionally equivalent to the major protein foods, such as meat or fish, for which it is a substitute. The U. S. Department of Agriculture authorized, in 1971, the use of textured vegetable protein fortified with minerals and vitamins in child feeding programs. Standards have been set for its use. It may be added in hydrated form to ground beef up to a maximum of 30 percent by weight, which is the usual maximum level of acceptability (Rakosky, 1975).

27.3

USES FOR SOY PROTEIN PRODUCTS

For textured vegetable protein products to succeed in the marketplace, they must be acceptable to the consumer and offer something of real value over the conventional types of foods that they are replacing. The advantage may be convenience, cost, or a benefit to health due to the absence of cholesterol and saturated fat. A number of the meat analogs produced from spun fiber require only heating before they are ready to be served. This spun fiber type of product is marketed for convenience and is not necessarily less expensive than the meat products that it replaces. However, the extruded protein substances do offer substantial cost savings. Extruded products are usually hydrated with approximately two parts of water per part of textured vegetable matter when they are used as meat extenders. This should be taken into consideration when comparing the prices of fresh meat to the dry protein product (Whitaker and Tannenbaum, 1977).

Extruded soy protein products have been used chiefly as meat extenders in many different foods. These include meat patties and loaves, chili, tacos, pizza, lasagne, stews, casseroles, omelets, chicken salad, stuffed peppers, and frankfurters. Shelef and Morton (1976) surveyed 100 institutional food services in the Metropolitan Detroit area to determine whether or not soy protein was used. Included were 12 schools, 38 hospitals, 11 nursing and convalescent centers, 30 restaurants and caterers, and 9 industrial services. Only 15 institutions out of the 100 surveyed indicated that they used soy protein in their feeding programs. These 15 represented 50 percent of the school lunch programs, 27.3 percent of the nursing centers, 22.2 percent of the industrial services, and 10.5 percent of the hospitals surveyed. The most common use was as extenders of ground meats. A common view among participants in the study appeared to be that soybean products are substitute foods that are inferior to natural meat products. This view may also be widespread among consumer groups. More education concerning the merits of textured vegetable protein will be necessary before wide acceptance of these products occurs.

Nielsen and Carlin (1974) compared frozen, precooked beef and beef-soy loaves. They reported that the use of hydrated textured vegetable protein in the beef-soy loaves at a level of 30 percent by weight reduced cooking losses by 50 percent. However, the beef-soy loaves stored at $-20°C$ ($-4°F$) for six months had a less intense beef flavor and were drier than all-beef loaves that were similarly stored. Judges' scores indicated that soy flavor was pronounced in the beef-soy loaves. Carlin *et al.* (1978) reported that, when textured soy flour was added to beef loaves at 15 or 30 percent levels, the higher amount of soy product produced decreased total and drip losses and increased soy flavor. Williams and Zabik (1975) found that a 30 percent substitution of textured soy product for ground beef and turkey in beef and turkey meat loaves did not adversely affect the quality characteristics of either the beef or turkey loaves. However, soy substitution did lower the flavor, juiciness, and overall acceptability scores of a loaf containing a 50:50 mixture of ham and pork. Nollman and Pratt (1972) found that meat loaves containing 10 g of dry textured soy protein per pound of ground beef were well accepted by a panel for both flavor and texture.

Adding a soy product to beef patties at 15 and 30 percent levels decreased cooking losses as compared to all-beef patties, according to the results of a study completed by Bowers and Engler (1975). The beef patties were less firm and their meaty flavor and aroma were more intense than those of beef-soy patties. Reheated beef-soy patties had less stale flavor and aroma than reheated beef patties. The addition of flavored textured soy protein to beef patties before freeze-drying improved rehydratability and acceptability (Drake *et al.*, 1977).

The protein quality of textured soy products has been studied using human as well as animal subjects. Koury and Hodges (1968) fed isolated soy protein foods to 12 hospitalized patients for 24 weeks. All subjects remained in good health. Turk *et al.* (1973) concluded, from a study of nitrogen balance, that a spun soy protein product containing egg albumen as a binder was a high quality protein food for teenagers and adults. Methionine is the first limiting amino acid in soybean products. Korslund *et al.* (1973) found that the addition of this amino acid to an extruded soybean product significantly increased the quality of the protein when the fortified soybean product was fed to adolescent boys.

27.4

COOKING SOYBEANS

Fresh green vegetable-type soybeans are available in some areas in the late summer or fall. They may be shelled from the pods and boiled until they are tender in about half their volume of salted water. They are similar to cooked green peas or lima beans but have a firmer texture (U. S. Department of Agriculture, 1974).

Dry whole soybeans may be stored for relatively long periods of time. Storage should be in a cool, dry place. As with other dried legumes, soaking is required for proper rehydration. Using 4 cups of water for each cup of dry soybeans, a rapid hot soaking procedure may be followed. The beans may be boiled for two minutes, removed from the heat, and let stand for one hour. The soaked beans may then be simmered in the soaking water, in a covered pan, for two to three hours until they are tender. However, they will remain somewhat firm and will not become mealy. This reflects their lack of starch. Alternatively, the soaked beans may be cooked in a pressure cooker for about 30 minutes at 15 lb pressure. The cooked soybeans may be used in a variety of casserole and chili dishes. Soy milk may also be prepared at home using soaked beans (U. S. Department of Agriculture, 1974).

SUMMARY

High protein mixtures and isolated proteins are finding wide use in the food industry. Several sources of concentrated plant protein are utilized including oilseed meals, cereal grains, and leafy green plants. By far the largest volume of marketed oilseed protein products comes from soybeans.

Soybeans were first used as a source of oil. Later, as technology developed, the protein-containing residue was utilized.

The dry mature soybean contains about 34 percent protein, 18 percent oil, and 34 percent carbohydrate. It has essentially no starch. During processing for oil and meal, the cleaned beans are cracked and the hulls are separated. The cracked beans are heated to soften them and are then pressed into flakes. The oil in the flakes is extracted by use of the solvent hexane, which is then evaporated from the oil. The defatted flakes are ground to make flour which contains from 47 to 53 percent protein. Soy flour is used in a variety of bakery products.

Defatted soy flour may be treated with acid or enzymes to produce hydrolyzed vegetable protein. This ingredient is used to produce a "meaty" flavor. Extraction of sugars from soy flour results in a soy protein concentrate containing 70 percent or more protein. Soy protein isolates with over 90 percent protein are also produced from soy flour. Soy protein mixtures in all these forms have functional properties that are important in food manufacturing. These include emulsification, fat and water absorption, texture development, cohesion, elasticity, and aeration.

High protein mixtures may be given texture by two different treatments. One method involves a spinning process similar to that used in the textile industry. The slurried isolated protein at a pH of about 10 is forced through spinnerettes into a coagulating bath with a low pH where it is set. The filaments formed are gathered into a bundle or rope. The fibers are used as a flavorless textured foundation for the fabrication of meat analogs. In this process they are bound together with another protein substance and are blended with fat, flavorings, coloring, supplemental nutrients, and stabilizers.

A second method of texturizing high protein flours and concentrates involves extrusion. Heat is applied to a flour and water mixture while it is mixed in a cooking extruder. As the mixture is conveyed down the extruder channel, it is worked into a homogeneous dough. At the exit point, pressure is rapidly released and the material expands, creating texture with a uniform distribution of tiny air pockets throughout the mass. Extruded vegetable protein mixtures are employed primarily as meat extenders. They have been used in meat patties and loaves, chili, tacos, pizza, lasagne, stews, frankfurters, etc. However, a survey of 100 institutional food services in Detroit indicated that only 15 were using textured soy protein in their feeding operations. A common view among participants in the survey was that soybean products are substitute foods that are inferior to natural meat products. Advantages offered by vegetable protein mixture may include convenience, cost, and benefit to health due to the absence of cholesterol and saturated fat.

Several reports have been published concerning the performance of textured soy protein in meat loaves and patties. In general, the addition of the protein mixture decreases cooking losses. The meat flavor is diluted and a soy flavor is sometimes apparent. The soy-meat products are usually acceptable, however. The nutritional quality of textured soy protein is relatively high.

Whole soybeans may also be used in home food preparation. Green soybeans are cooked similarly to green peas. Dry, mature soybeans require soaking for rehydration before cooking for 2–3 hours. The cooked product may be utilized in a variety of casserole and chili dishes. Soy milk may be prepared using soaked beans.

STUDY QUESTIONS

Soy processing technology allows the production of a variety of soy protein products.

1. Describe the major steps involved in the production of soybean oil, soy flour, soy concentrate, soy isolate, hydrolyzed soy protein, spun soy protein, and extruded soy protein.
2. How do the various soy products differ in composition? Explain.
3. How is spun soy protein used in the manufacture of meat analogs?
4. How might extruded soy protein be satisfactorily used in food preparation?
5. Discuss advantages and disadvantages for the use of textured vegetable proteins in food preparation.

Dry, mature soybeans may be used in home food preparation.

6. What is the gross composition of dry, mature soybeans?
7. Recommend a satisfactory method for cooking whole soybeans and suggest possible uses for the cooked beans.

REFERENCES

1. Alden, D. E. 1975. Soy processing: from beans to ingredients. *Journal of the American Oil Chemists Society* 52, 244A.

2. Bird, K. M. 1974. Plant proteins: Progress and problems. *Food Technology* 28 (No. 3), 31.

3. Bowers, J. A. and P. P. Engler. 1975. Freshly cooked and cooked, frozen, reheated beef and beef-soy patties. *Journal of Food Science* 40, 624.

4. Carlin, F., Y. Ziprin, M. E. Zabik, L. Kragt, A. Polsiri, J. Bowers, B. Rainey, F. Van Duyne, and A. K. Perry. 1978. Texturized soy protein in beef loaves: Cooking losses, flavor, juiciness and chemical composition. *Journal of Food Science* 43, 830.

5. Drake, S. R., R. A. Kluter, and L. C. Hinnergardt. 1977. Textured soy protein improves quality of freeze-dried beef patties. *Food Technology* 31 (No. 11), 24.

6. French, F. 1977. Bakery uses of soy products. *Bakers Digest* 51 (No. 5), 98.

7. Korslund, M., C. Kies, and H. M. Fox. 1973. Comparison of the protein nutritional value of TVP, methionine-enriched TVP and beef for adolescent boys. *Journal of Food Science* 38, 637.

8. Koury, S. D. and R. E. Hodges. 1968. Soybean proteins for human diets? *American Dietetic Association Journal* 52, 480.

9. Lockmiller, N. R. 1972. What are textured protein products? *Food Technology* 26 (No. 5), 56.

10. Nielsen, L. M. and A. F. Carlin. 1974. Frozen, precooked beef and beef-soy loaves. *American Dietetic Association Journal* 65, 35.

11. Nollman, D. S. and D. E. Pratt. 1972. Protein concentrates and cellulose as additives in meat loaves. *American Dietetic Association Journal* 61, 658.

12. Rakosky, J. 1975. Soy protein in foods: Their use and regulations in the U. S. *Journal of the American Oil Chemists Society* 52, 272A.

13. Shelef, L. A. and L. R. Morton. 1976. Soybean protein foods. *Food Technology* 30 (No. 4), 44.

14. Thulin, W. W. and S. Kuramoto. 1967. "Bontrae—A new meat-like ingredient for convenience foods. *Food Technology* 21, 168.

15. Turk, R. E., P. E. Cornwell, M. D. Brooks, and C. E. Butterworth, Jr. 1973. Adequacy of spun-soy protein containing egg albumin for human nutrition. *American Dietetic Association Journal* 63, 519.

16. U. S. Department of Agriculture. 1974. Soybeans in family meals. Home and Garden Bulletin No. 208.

17. Whitaker, J. R. and S. R. Tannenbaum. 1977. *Food Proteins*. Westport, Conn.: Avi Publishing Company.

18. Williams, C. W. and M. E. Zabik. 1975. Quality characteristics of soy-substituted ground beef, pork and turkey meat loaves. *Journal of Food Science* 40, 502.

19. Wolf, W. J. 1972. What is soy protein? *Food Technology* 26 (No. 5), 44.

20. Wolf, W. J. 1970. Soybean proteins: Their functional, chemical, and physical properties. *Journal of Agricultural and Food Chemistry* 18, 969.

CHAPTER 28

WHEAT PROTEINS AND BAKED PRODUCTS

The protein content of wheat is usually about 12 percent. However, both seed characteristics and plant growing conditions exert a strong influence on protein production. Extensive research has recently been undertaken to increase both the quantity and the quality of protein in wheat. The composition of wheat flour and its performance in baking vary greatly, depending upon the heredity of the seed and the environmental conditions of culture and harvest for the wheat from which the flour is milled (Whitaker and Tannenbaum, 1977). Attempts have been made to relate the composition of flour, particularly its protein content, to its ability to produce a good quality loaf of bread. If these relationships can be determined the baking performance of flour may be improved by the intelligent use of additives to overcome any deficiencies that may be present. (A more specific discussion of the preparation of baked products is included in Chapters 30, 31, and 32.)

28.1

PROTEINS IN WHEAT FLOUR

White flour is milled from the endosperm of wheat. The endosperm makes up approximately 85 percent of the wheat kernel and contains about 70 percent of the total protein of the grain. Although some whole wheat flour, which contains essentially the entire wheat kernel, is used in the preparation of baked products, a much greater amount of white flour is used by the modern baking industry. The viscoelastic properties of wheat flour doughs are primarily due to the gluten-forming proteins that develop most effectively in the absence of wheat bran and germ. Therefore, white flour generally produces bread with a higher volume and finer texture than does whole wheat flour. The vast majority of research in the area of wheat flour and baking is concerned with the proteins and baking performance of white wheat flour. The nutritive content of white and whole wheat flours differs. Although most white flour is enriched with at least three B vitamins (thiamin, niacin, and riboflavin) and iron, all of the vitamins and minerals that are removed from white flour during milling are not generally replaced.

Wheat proteins have been the subject of study for many years. In fact, the separation of gluten proteins from flour by washing a dough with water was first reported by Beccari in the early 1700s. This predates the time when proteins were first named. Wheat and gluten proteins were fractionated on the basis of solubility in comprehensive studies by Osborne (1907). He divided the proteins of wheat into four solubility classes: albumins, that are soluble in water; globulins, that are soluble in salt solutions but insoluble in water; gliadins, that are soluble in 70–90 percent alcohol; and glutenins, that are insoluble in neutral aqueous solutions, saline solutions, or alcohol. Glutenins are soluble in dilute acid.

Separation of wheat proteins on the basis of solubility is still important at the present time. The solubility fractions represent groups of proteins in wheat that differ in overall composition and properties. Discussions of wheat proteins are often organized in terms of the soluble proteins—albumins and globulins; gliadins; and glutenin. The use of many modern laboratory techniques for separation of proteins has been employed in the study of wheat proteins in more recent years. It has been demonstrated that each of the solubility fractions is composed of numerous protein components. As newer techniques are applied, the complexity of each solubility group becomes more apparent. Research studies are being conducted to unravel the mysteries and relate specific components of dough to its baking properties (Pomeranz, 1976).

28.2

THE GLUTEN COMPLEX

Gluten as such is not present in wheat flour. It is produced from gliadins and glutenin by the processes of hydration and mixing. The traditional method of preparing gluten involves gentle washing of a kneaded flour-water dough in an excess of water. This removes most of the starch and much of the other soluble material. The remaining gluten is a moist rubbery mass with an outward appearance something like chewing gum. Figure 28.1 shows the elastic properties of gluten. About two-thirds of the moist gluten consists of absorbed water. The dry solids of gluten contain 75–85 percent protein, depending on how thoroughly the gluten was washed. Approximately 5–10 percent lipid is also present. The fatty substances, for the most part, are bound to the protein during formation of the dough and are not naturally associated with protein in flour. Some of the soluble proteins, the albumins and globulins, are trapped in the crude gluten. Soluble protein content of gluten may comprise about 7 percent of the total protein. Starch is occluded in the gluten to some extent and makes up most of the remainder of the dry matter (Pomeranz, 1971).

Crude gluten may be dried with little loss of its original hydration

Figure 28.1

Gluten (*left*) and gliadin
(*center*) have different
properties which are
blended in gluten (*right*).
(Reprinted with permis-
sion from Dimler, R. J.
1963. Gluten. The key to
wheat's utility. *Bakers
Digest* 37 [Feb.], 52.
Courtesy of Northern
Regional Research
Center, U. S. Department
of Agriculture.)

capacity and baking properties. This product, called *vital wheat gluten,*
has become an increasingly important product of commerce. Today's
estimated annual U. S. consumption is about 100 million lb. In addition
to its use in baked goods, which accounts for approximately 60 percent
of the consumption, gluten is a component of many prepared cereals,
pet foods, pasta, and meat analog products. Vital wheat gluten is valuable in adjusting the protein content of flour for specific uses. The loaf
volume of bread is increased and the structure strengthened by the
addition of gluten (Magnuson, 1977).

Dough is a highly complex system, made up of starch, sugars, proteins, yeast, salts, acids, gases, volatile flavoring substances, and fats.
This system is subject to change throughout the processes of fermentation, proofing, and baking, as yeast bread is prepared. Gluten proteins
play a very important role in this structure, even though they are present in much smaller quantities than is starch. Gluten controls the
rheological or flow properties of the dough. It forms a continuous,
three-dimensional network in which are embedded the starch granules
(Sternberg, 1973). In Figure 28.2 is a scanning electron photomicrograph
of a dough sample showing a well developed gluten film enveloping
starch granules. Gluten is capable of retaining tiny cells of occluded
gases, primarily air incorporated in mixing and carbon dioxide gener-
ated by yeast cells. Various roles in the gluten structure have been
postulated for the gliadin and glutenin components.

GLIADINS

The *gliadins* are a heterogeneous mixture of proteins soluble in 70
percent alcohol. Individual gliadin proteins have been isolated and
characterized. Using various techniques with electrophoresis and
chromatography, as many as 40–46 components of the gliadin fraction

Figure 28.2

Scanning electron
photomicrograph of a
dough sample showing
a developed gluten film
covering starch
granules of variable
sizes. (Reprinted from
Varriano-Marston, E.
A comparison of dough
preparation procedures
for scanning electron
microscopy. *Food Tech-
nology* Vol. 31, No. 10, p.
34, 1977. Copyright © by
Institute of Food
Technologists.)

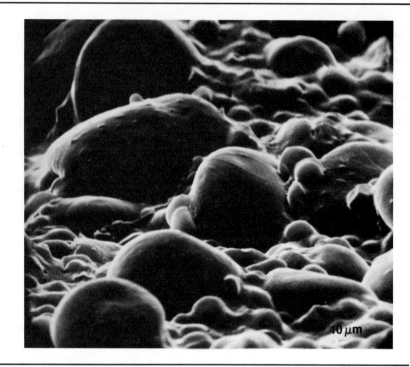

10 μm

in one variety of wheat have been reported (Pomeranz, 1976). Most gliadins have very similar amino acid composition and molecular weights. They are rich in glutamine, which is an amide ($-\overset{\overset{\displaystyle O}{\|}}{C}-NH_2$) of glutamic acid, and they are also rich in proline, but they contain little lysine. Molecular weights range in the 30,000 area, although some gliadins have molecular weights around 70,000. The glutamine residues appear to be concentrated in certain regions of the gliadin molecule and may play important roles in cross-linking molecules by formation of hydrogen bonds (Huebner, 1977). Gliadin molecules generally appear to be single polypeptide chains. They are often represented as spherical molecules (see Figure 28.3). Aggregation of single isolated molecules of α-gliadin to form microfibrils has been reported (Pomeranz, 1976, p. 170).

GLUTENIN

Glutenin is the least soluble component of the gluten proteins. It is also the high molecular weight protein fraction. A number of different techniques have been used in extracting glutenin from flour and therefore several differences in what is called glutenin have been reported. Glutenin is often extracted from flour with dilute acetic acid. However, extraction of protein is not complete with this solvent and considerable

Figure 28.3

Proposed structure of insoluble wheat proteins and possible relationships to viscoelastic properties. (From Huebner, F. R. 1977. Wheat flour proteins and their functionality in baking. *Bakers Digest* 51 [Oct.], 25. Courtesy of Northern Regional Research Center, U. S. Department of Agriculture.)

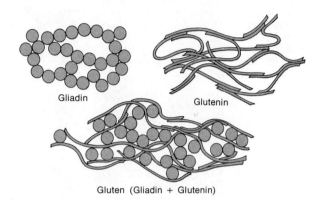

Gliadin

Glutenin

Gluten (Gliadin + Glutenin)

protein remains in the residue (Huebner, 1977). The residue protein has been called *insoluble glutenin* (Khan and Bushuk, 1978).

Glutenin has been fractionated into two or three components. One component was reported to have a molecular weight as high as 20 million. Another component had a molecular weight ranging from 100,000 to 15 million (Huebner, 1977). Reported average molecular weights for glutenin range from 150,000 to 3 million. The major part of glutenin is made up of subunits with varying molecular weights. The subunits are evidently joined together by disulfide (—S—S—) bonds. Disulfide bonds, therefore, govern the molecular size of glutenin in wheat flour (Pomeranz, 1971). These bonds may occur within, intra-, as well as between, inter-, protein chains. It has been known for many years that the physical characteristics of wheat flour doughs could be changed by adding small amounts of oxidizing or reducing agents. These agents may reduce disulfide linkages to sulfhydryl groups or oxidize sulfhydryl groups to disulfides.

The subunits of glutenin are apparently not all alike and they are also different from gliadin. Glutenin evidently exists as a distinct protein entity in the wheat kernel endosperm (Huebner, 1977). These macromolecules have been represented as large linear molecules (see Figure 28.3). Figure 28.4 gives a scanning electron micrograph of a glutelin (glutenin) from common wheat.

LIPID–PROTEIN INTERACTION

Wheat flour contains about 0.8 percent free lipids and an additional 0.6 percent bound lipids, for a total of 1.4 percent. The free lipids can be extracted from flour with petroleum ether, but the bound lipids must be removed from the wheat proteins by extraction with water-saturated

Figure 28.4

Scanning electron photomicrograph of a glutelin from common wheat. (Reprinted with permission from Bushuk, W. 1974. Glutenin functions, properties and genetics. *Bakers Digest* **48 [Aug.], 14.)**

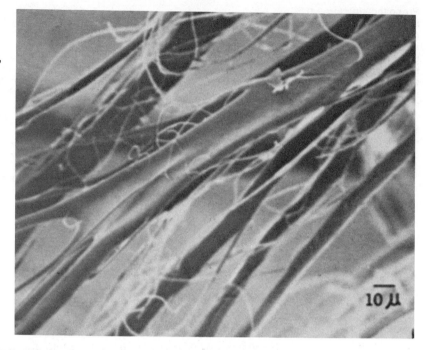

butanol. The bound lipids are polar *glycolipids* (*carbohydrate-containing fats*) and phospholipids. This is also true for about one-fourth of the free lipids. When flour is hydrated and mixed into a dough, some of the free lipids become bound. It is presumed that they form lipoprotein complexes with the glutenin molecules (Hoseney *et al.,* 1970).

The ability of gluten to produce a good quality loaf of bread is impaired if the flour lipids are not present. This has been demonstrated by making loaves from a gluten and starch mixture using gluten from both untreated and defatted flours. Loaf volume was higher in bread baked from lipid-containing flour than from defatted flour components. Glycolipids are apparently bound to the gluten proteins—to glutenin by hydrophobic bonds and to gliadin by hydrogen bonds. They also bind to starch in a complex dough system. Glycolipids appear to be essential for the functioning of gluten in producing a loaf of bread of good quality (Pomeranz, 1973).

MODELS FOR GLUTEN STRUCTURE

Several models to explain the structure of gluten have been proposed. In 1961, Grosskreutz suggested a lipoprotein model of gluten structure, as shown in Figure 28.5. This model includes a continuous protein sheet formed mostly by linkage of one protein platelet with another, probably by hydrogen bonding through an aqueous phase. A leaflet that contains two layers of phospholipids is also bonded to the protein

Figure 28.5

Proposed gluten sheet structure. (From Grosskreutz, J. C. 1961. A lipoprotein model of wheat gluten structure. *Cereal Chemistry* **38, 336. With permission.)**

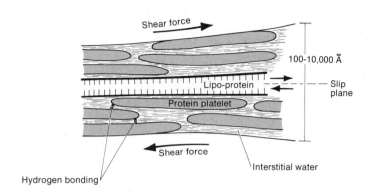

platelets through hydrogen or salt-like linkages. The lipoprotein leaflet acts as a slip-plate when the stress of mixing is applied to this system and the gluten sheet does not generally rupture. The system has plasticity and elasticity as the protein sheet tends to retain its form.

Another model for gluten structure is shown in Figure 28.3. Glutenin is pictured as a mass of long entangled strands in dough that gradually become aligned and associated in the direction of mixing as the dough is developed. Gliadin molecules are smaller and more symmetrical and are dispersed among the glutenin strands. A strong elastic uniform film of glutenin and gliadin forms and envelops the starch granules. The ratio of glutenin to gliadin is important to baking properties. Glutenin gives strength and elasticity to the dough. However, too much glutenin may prevent expansion of gas cells during fermentation of yeast dough. Gliadin molecules, being smaller and more dissociated with less surface area, give extensibility to the mixture. Each protein interacts with and modifies the properties of the other (Huebner, 1977; Bietz *et al.,* 1973).

The electron microscope was used by Bernardin and Kasarda (1973) to study wheat endosperm protein as flour was being hydrated. Sheets of protein material were observed that separated into strands or fibrils when the sheets became very thin. The fibrils formed bundles and a network resulted when one bundle connected with another. Some of these fibrils are shown in Figure 28.4. Bernardin and Kasarda (1973) suggested that the sheets of protein observed result from a laminar deposition of storage protein in the protein bodies of the developing wheat kernel. The sheets of endosperm protein rupture under stress forming webs of protein that are composed of fibrils. Smaller fibrils aggregate to form larger fibrils.

The wheat protein fibrils may have both elastic and viscous properties as soon as they are rehydrated. Because of the web structure, small deformations of bonds between pairs of fibrils could allow relatively large deformations of the protein web, with complete recovery from deformation (elasticity) occurring by restoration of the bonds to their minimum energy positions. Viscous flow could be possible by slippage of one fiber along another, with new bonding interactions occurring once the force causing slippage is removed. Disulfide cross-links between fibrils are not an essential feature of this model. Effects on disulfide linkages occurring within the protein molecules could explain the observed effects of disulfide bond-breaking agents on doughs (Mecham, 1973).

28.3

SOLUBLE FLOUR PROTEINS

The term soluble proteins is generally used to refer to flour proteins that are soluble in dilute salt solutions. This includes albumins and globulins, together with glycoproteins, nucleoproteins, and some lipid–protein complexes. Many of the soluble proteins are enzymes.

The soluble proteins of flour have been much less extensively studied than have the insoluble proteins, gliadin and glutenin. The albumins and globulins do not appear to affect the development of dough in a significant way. In some studies involving reconstituted flours, it appeared that the water soluble proteins were necessary for normal baking characteristics. For example, Pence (1962) suggested that albumins were implicated in the baking performance of flours. However, recent work on wheat flour doughs has not assigned an important functional role to the soluble proteins (Pomeranz, 1971).

Many enzymatic activities have been identified in extracts of wheat and flour. However, most of these have not been studied extensively. The amylases are of some importance in the baking of bread. Beta-amylase is found in milled wheat flour. However, it is unable to attack native, undamaged starch granules and hydrolyzes damaged starch slowly. Only small amounts of maltose are produced by β-amylase during the usual procedures for making yeast bread. This enzyme is relatively easily denatured by heat and its activity is destroyed in the early stages of baking bread. At 57–70°C (134.6–158°F) β-amylase is likely to be denatured. Alpha-amylase is not found in significant amounts in flour from ungerminated grain. It is produced as the grain begins to sprout. Malted grain, which contains α-amylase, is sometimes added in small amounts during commercial breadmaking as a source of this enzyme. Alpha-amylase is more stable to heating than is β-amylase and is not rapidly denatured until the temperature reaches about 75°C (167°F). Therefore this enzyme may hydrolyze some gelatinized starch to dextrins during the baking of bread and contribute to softness of the crumb.

Limited protease activity is present in flour. Proteases increase markedly in germinated wheat and are detrimental to breadmaking at excessive levels. On a practical basis, proteases seem to be of little significance in baking. However, Redman (1971) hypothesized that softening of gluten during the fermentation of doughs is a result of peptide bond hydrolysis catalyzed by proteolytic enzymes in the dough. Proteases are sometimes added in carefully controlled amounts as supplements in commercial bread making and cause a mellowing effect on dough (Kruger, 1971).

28.4

PROTEINS AND BAKING QUALITY

The mixing and baking properties of wheat flour batters and doughs depend ultimately on the interactions among all of the components in this complex mixture. Water, starch, lipids, pentosans, leavening agents, and other substances are present and active, in addition to protein. Protein is an extremely important factor in determining baking quality. (Other ingredients are discussed in Part VII.)

It has been recognized, probably since baking began, that there are differences in baking quality among flours from different types of wheat. Flour from hard wheats with relatively high protein content is generally used to produce bread with large loaf volume and fine, even texture. Flour from soft wheats, which are lower in protein content, is used to make cakes, pastry, and crackers.

Finney (1943) separated flours from different wheat varieties into starch, gluten, and water-soluble fractions. He then recombined these fractions in different proportions and baked breads from both the fractionated and original flours. This research demonstrated that fractionation and recombination of the fractions did not change the original baking properties of the flour. It also demonstrated that the relationship between protein or gluten content and the volume of bread loaves was linear between 7 and 20 percent flour protein. In other words, as the protein content of the flour increased, the loaf volume also increased. Other studies have since confirmed this relationship (Bell and Simmonds, 1963; Pomeranz, 1968).

A standardized bread baking test is commonly used to measure the baking quality of a flour. In this test, important factors that affect performance of the flour, including mixing time, fermentation time, and yeast activity, are all optimized so that they will not limit the results in any way. Loaves of bread may be made either with 100 g of flour or with only 10 g of flour. The volume of the loaves is often determined by measuring the volume of rape seeds that they displace. This test, performed on white wheat flour, has the precision of most generally accepted biological assays (Pomeranz *et al.*, 1970), and is useful in research studies.

The modern baking industry is automated to a large degree.

Mechanized systems using automatic equipment for measuring and mixing make it essential that ingredients for baked products are uniform in composition and properties. Therefore, a reasonably simple test for baking quality that could be used in commercial practice would be very useful. Many researchers have tried to establish the basis for such a test by finding a component of wheat flour that is directly related to its baking quality. Although total protein content is related to loaf volume, there are additional factors that influence the role of protein in baking. A number of studies have involved fractionation of the gluten proteins into various components and attempts to relate the proportions of each to baking strength and quality. Huebner and Rothfus (1968) studied various gliadin fractions from several varieties of wheat. They did not find significant differences in gliadins that were related to baking quality. In fact, the patterns of gliadin components for Red Chief, a poor-baking-quality wheat, were similar to those of Ponca, a good-baking-quality wheat in the same class.

Orth and Bushuk (1973) studied glutenin and its relationship to baking quality. They reported that the number and characteristics of subunits obtained by reduction of glutenin cannot be used to characterize the baking potential of wheat. However, these workers in 1972 reported some correlations between breadmaking quality and the proportion of both glutenin and residue protein. *Residue protein* is the protein remaining after separation of albumins, globulins, gliadin, and glutenin and has been called *insoluble glutenin*. In this study of 26 wheat varieties, the proportion of glutenin in the total flour protein was negatively correlated with loaf volume per unit of protein whereas residue protein and loaf volume were positively correlated.

Cereal chemists continue to search for more knowledge of the relationships between flour components and baking quality. As additional advances are made in protein chemistry, the secret may be revealed.

SUMMARY

The protein content of wheat is usually around 12 percent. White flour is milled from the endosperm of wheat, which contains about 70 percent of the total protein of the grain. These proteins play important roles in determining the baking quality of flours.

The separation of gluten proteins from flour by washing a dough with water was first reported in the early 1700s. In 1907, Osborne reported on the fractionation of flour proteins on the basis of solubility. The groups of proteins were albumins (water soluble), globulins (salt soluble), gliadins (70 percent alcohol soluble), and glutenins (dilute acid soluble). These groupings are still important today.

Gluten is produced from gliadins and glutenin in wheat flour by the processes of hydration and mixing. The traditional method of preparing gluten involves gentle washing of a kneaded flour-water dough in an excess of water. Starch is removed. The remaining gluten mass contains about 66 percent water. The dry gluten solids contain 75–85 percent protein along with 5–10 percent lipid. Crude gluten is dried commercially to produce vital wheat gluten which is used extensively in the baking industry.

Gluten controls the rheological or flow properties of a dough. It forms a continuous, three-dimensional network in which are embedded the starch granules. Various roles in this structure have been postulated for the components, gliadins and glutenin.

As many as 40–46 components of the gliadin fraction have been reported. Most gliadins have similar amino acid composition and molecular weights. They are rich in the amino acids, glutamine and proline, and are often represented as spherical molecules. Aggregation of single isolated molecules of α-gliadin to form microfibrils has been reported.

Glutenin is the least soluble and the largest component of the gluten proteins. It has been fractionated into two or three components. One component was reported to have a molecular weight as high as 20 million. The major part of glutenin is made up of subunits with molecular weights which vary. The subunits are evidently joined together by disulfide bonds.

Wheat flour contains about 1.4 percent total lipids. Some of these are free and some are bound. Polar glycolipids appear to be essential for the functioning of gluten in producing a loaf of bread of good quality. They are apparently bound to the gluten proteins during mixing.

Several models to explain the structure of gluten have been proposed. Grosskreutz suggested a lipoprotein model of gluten structure. This model includes a continuous protein sheet formed mostly by linkage of one protein platelet with another through hydrogen bonds. A phospholipid bimolecular leaflet is also bonded to the protein platelets and acts as a slip-plate during the stress of mixing to avoid rupturing of the gluten sheets. The system has plasticity and elasticity as the protein sheet tends to retain its form.

Another model pictures glutenin as a mass of long entangled strands in dough that gradually become aligned and associated in the direction of mixing as the dough is developed. The smaller, spherical gliadin molecules are dispersed among the glutenin strands and a strong elastic film is formed.

Other researchers have proposed that the wheat plant deposits storage protein in a laminar fashion in the protein bodies of the endosperm. These laminar sheets of protein rupture under stress as they are hydrated and form webs of protein composed of fibrils. Smaller fibrils aggregate to form larger fibrils in the web. The fibrils have both elastic and viscous properties.

Some roles of albumins and globulins in baking have been postulated. However, they do not appear to affect the development of dough in a significant way. Many enzymes are albumins or globulins. Enzymes such as the amylases are of importance in the production of maltose and/or dextrins during the fermentation and the baking of bread.

The quantity and quality of proteins in flour affect its baking quality. As the protein content of flour increases, the loaf volume of bread baked from it generally increases. Standardized bread baking tests are commonly employed to measure the baking performance of flours. A specific protein component of flour that is directly related to its baking quality has not yet been identifed. Studies on gliadin and glutenin components have generally not provided significant information on relationships.

STUDY QUESTIONS

Several proteins of wheat flour have been isolated and studied.

1. Give a classification of wheat flour proteins on the basis of solubility as first suggested by Osborne.
2. Describe unique characteristics of the gliadins, glutenins, and soluble wheat proteins.

Gluten is produced from gliadins and glutenin during the hydration and mixing of wheat flour doughs.

3. Describe the traditional method of preparing crude gluten and explain what is happening during this procedure. What is the composition of the moist gluten product?
4. What is vital wheat gluten and how might it be used?
5. Discuss possible relationships between glycolipids and gluten.
6. Compare three different models that have been suggested to explain the structure of gluten.
7. Explain the need for the proper amount of hydration and for mixing in the development of gluten in dough.
8. Write chemical structures for the amino acids, cystine and cysteine, and explain a possible role for sulfhydryl and disulfide groups in the development of gluten structure.

Flours vary in baking quality.

9. How may the baking quality of a flour be precisely measured? Describe the general procedure.
10. Describe some research that has helped to establish a relationship between flour protein content and baking quality.
11. Suggest possible reasons why a knowledge of how specific flour components are related to baking quality would be very useful to the baking industry. Describe some research attempts to find such a relationship.

REFERENCES

1. Bell, P. M. and D. H. Simmonds. 1963. The protein composition of different flours and its relationship to nitrogen content and baking performance. *Cereal Chemistry* 40, 121.

2. Bernardin, J. E. and D. D. Kasarda. 1973. The microstructure of wheat protein fibrils. *Cereal Chemistry* 50, 735.

3. Bietz, J. A., F. R. Huebner, and J. S. Wall. 1973. Glutenin. *Bakers Digest* 47 (No. 1), 26.

4. Finney, K. F. 1943. Fractionating and reconstituting techniques as tools in wheat flour research. *Cereal Chemistry* 20, 381.

5. Grosskreutz, J. C. 1961. A lipoprotein model of wheat gluten structure. *Cereal Chemistry* 38, 336.

6. Hoseney, R. C., K. R. Finney, and Y. Pomeranz. 1970. Functional (breadmaking) and biochemical properties of wheat flour components. VI. Gliadin-lipid-glutenin interaction in wheat gluten. *Cereal Chemistry* 47, 135.

7. Huebner, F. R. 1977. Wheat flour proteins and their functionality in baking. *Bakers Digest* 51 (No. 5), 25.

8. Huebner, F. R. and J. A. Rothfus. 1968. Gliadin proteins from different varieties of wheats. *Cereal Chemistry* 45, 242.

9. Khan, K. and W. Bushuk. 1978. Glutenin: Structure and functionality in breadmaking. *Bakers Digest* 52 (No. 2), 14.

10. Kruger, J. E. 1971. Effects of proteolytic enzymes on gluten as measured by a stretching test. *Cereal Chemistry* 48, 121.

11. Magnuson, K. 1977. Vital wheat gluten update '77. *Bakers Digest* 51 (Oct.), 108.

12. Mecham, D. K. 1973. Wheat and flour proteins. *Bakers Digest* 47 (Oct.), 24.

13. Orth, R. A. and W. Bushuk. 1973. Studies of glutenin. II. Relation of variety, location of growth, and baking quality to molecular weight distribution of subunits. *Cereal Chemistry* 50, 191.

14. Orth, R. A. and W. Bushuk. 1972. A comparative study of the proteins of wheats of diverse baking qualities. *Cereal Chemistry* 49, 268.

15. Osborne, T. B. 1907. The protein of the wheat kernel. Washington, D. C.: Carnegie Institute Washington.

16. Pence, J. W. 1962. The flour proteins. *Cereal Science Today* 7, 178.

17. Pomeranz, Y., editor. 1976. *Advances in Cereal Science and Technology.* St. Paul, Minn.: American Association of Cereal Chemists.

18. Pomeranz, Y. 1973. From wheat to bread: A biochemical study. *American Scientist* 61, 683.

19. Pomeranz, Y., editor. 1971. *Wheat Chemistry and Technology.* St. Paul, Minn.: American Association of Cereal Chemists.

20. Pomeranz, Y. 1968. Relation between chemical composition and breadmaking potentialities of wheat flour. *Advances in Food Research* 16, 335.

21. Pomeranz, Y., K. F. Finney, and R. C. Hoseney. 1970. Molecular approach to breadmaking. *Science* 167, 944.

22. Redman, D. G. 1971. Softening of gluten by wheat proteases. *Journal of the Science of Food and Agriculture* 22, 75.

23. Sternberg, G. 1973. Practical gluten structure control. *Bakers Digest* 47 (Apr.), 34.

24. Whitaker, J. R. and S. R. Tannenbaum. 1977. *Food Proteins*. Westport, Conn.: Avi Publishing Company.

PART VII

BAKED FLOUR PRODUCTS

Baked flour products often contain similar ingredients but in varying proportions. They are generally leavened and contain at least some wheat flour. (The unique characteristics of wheat flour proteins and the development of gluten were presented in Part VI.) Leavening agents in general are discussed in the first chapter of this unit. The remaining three chapters discuss specific flour mixtures—quick breads, pastry, shortened cakes, and yeast breads. The chapter on yeast breads includes a discussion of yeast as a leavening agent. (Unshortened cakes were included with the discussion of egg foams in Chapter 19.)

CHAPTER 29

LEAVENING AGENTS

Leavening means to make light; to raise. The palatability of most baked products is at least partially dependent upon the development of a light, porous texture. A leavening agent that provides a source of gas and a batter or dough structure that is elastic and capable of retaining gas bubbles are both essential components of a high quality baked product. Small gaseous bubbles are entrapped in a structural framework that becomes set or rigid on baking.

The three basic leavening gases commonly used in baked products are air, water vapor or steam, and carbon dioxide. In many baked items, all three of these agents participate in the leavening process. (Carbon dioxide may be produced biologically by the fermentation of yeast cells. This process is discussed in Section 31.1)

29.1

AIR AND WATER VAPOR LEAVENING

Air is present in all baked products. During mixing, some air is always incorporated. Although it is usually not the major leaven, it plays an important role. For example, Dunn and White (1939) prepared pound cake in such a way that little air was incorporated into a batter containing no baking powder. The volume of the baked cake was approximately half that of a pound cake made by creaming fat and sugar together in the usual way. When part of the batter that had been mixed with incorporation of a minimum of air was then subjected to a vacuum to remove all of the residual air, the volume of this baked cake was decreased by about one-third. Apparently the presence of air bubbles is necessary for the proper functioning of water vapor as a leaven in pound cake.

Hood and Lowe (1948) studied the roles of air, water vapor, and carbon dioxide as leavens in cakes made with several different types of fat. They prepared cakes with all three agents, cakes with water and air only, and cakes containing water but with the air evacuated. When all three leaving agents were present in a cake batter, the largest increase in volume was attributed to carbon dioxide. Water vapor contributed a somewhat lesser amount of gas, its effect being less when the cake was made with butter than when it was made with oil and still less when it was made with lard. In this study, air apparently contributed a small constant amount of leaven, regardless of the type of fat used. Other studies have shown that shortened cake batters contain tiny bubbles of air dispersed in fat globules that are separated as "lakes" throughout the watery batter (Carlin, 1944). The crystalline structure of the fat apparently affects the number and size of incorporated air bubbles. Shortenings with small crystals are more effective in trapping air in shortened cake batters than are fats with large crystal size (Hoerr, 1967). (The structure of cake batters is discussed in Section 30.2.)

The beating of egg whites in the formation of a meringue that is added to a cake batter is a deliberate attempt to incorporate air. Incorporated air expands on heating, increasing the volume even more. Air is an important leavening agent in angel food and sponge cakes which have eggs as a major ingredient. However, water vapor has also been shown to be responsible for a large proportion of leavening in angel cake (Barmore, 1936).

Water vapor or steam is considered to be the primary leavening agent in popovers and cream puffs. Water vapor may have a powerful effect on the expansion of a baked product, as illustrated by the fact that one volume of water vaporized at atmospheric pressure produces approximately 1600 volumes of steam. In popovers and cream puffs the proportion of water to flour is high enough to provide water that is free to vaporize. Some water is bound in flour mixtures by protein and starch. A hot oven temperature, particularly during the first few minutes of baking, converts water to steam. A relatively high proportion of eggs in popovers and cream puffs provides heat coagulable protein for the development of a rigid structure after expansion of the product has occurred.

29.2

CHEMICAL PRODUCTION OF CARBON DIOXIDE

Sodium bicarbonate (baking soda) provides the most commonly used source of chemically released carbon dioxide in baked products. Some carbon dioxide is produced by simply heating soda. The reaction is:

$$\underset{\text{Sodium bicarbonate}}{2NaHCO_3} \xrightarrow{\text{Heat}} \underset{\text{Sodium carbonate}}{Na_2CO_3} + \underset{\text{Carbon dioxide}}{CO_2} + \underset{\text{Water}}{H_2O}$$

The reaction is relatively slow, requiring heat to penetrate throughout the batter. The residue salt from this reaction, sodium carbonate, is bitter tasting. A soapy taste may also develop due to a combination of sodium with fatty acids in the baked product. Sodium carbonate is an alkaline salt, releasing an excess of hydroxyl ions (OH^-) in solution. The production of sodium carbonate occurs whenever an excess of soda over acid ingredients is used in a baked product such as buttermilk biscuits. The excess alkalinity is responsible for development of a yellowish color in white flour products. In an alkaline environment, the flavonoid pigments in flour tend to be yellow in color. In addition, the Maillard reaction occurs more readily in an alkaline medium. Soda, therefore, is not generally used alone for the production of carbon dioxide in baked products.

When sodium bicarbonate is combined with an acid in solution the following reaction takes place:

$$\underset{\text{Acid}}{HX} + \underset{\text{Sodium bicarbonate}}{NaHCO_3} \longrightarrow \underset{\text{Carbon dioxide}}{CO_2} + \underset{\text{Water}}{H_2O} + \underset{\text{Sodium salt}}{NaX}$$

A number of acids may participate in this reaction. Ingredients in baked products may include sour milk or buttermilk that contain lactic acid. Fruit juices or fruits such as applesauce contain a variety of organic acids that may include citric and acetic acids. Molasses and brown sugar contain organic acids. (The chemical structures for a number of organic acids are given in Section 3.1.) The acidity of sour milk, fruits, and molasses is variable. It is, therefore, difficult to add precisely enough soda to combine with the acid present. Generally, $\frac{1}{4}$ teaspoon of baking soda is used with $\frac{1}{2}$ cup sour milk or buttermilk or with $\frac{1}{4}$–$\frac{1}{2}$ cup molasses (American Home Economics Association, 1975). Sweet milk may be made sour by substituting 1 tbsp of vinegar or lemon juice for 1 tbsp of the milk in one cup. When sour milk or molasses is used with baking soda for leavening, the soda should be mixed with the dry ingredients since carbon dioxide is produced immediately when soda is added to an acid in liquid media. Loss of carbon dioxide may result.

The salt produced by the reaction of sodium bicarbonate with lactic acid is sodium lactate. When soda combines with citric or acetic acids, the resulting salts are sodium citrate and sodium acetate, respectively. These salts do not create undesirable flavors in baked products. Carbon dioxide gas is produced during the mixing process as soon as the acid and soda are combined in a moist medium. Therefore, these combinations may be satisfactorily used in leavening.

BAKING POWDER

A dry acid salt that may be effectively combined with soda for leavening has long been available for use in the home. It is potassium acid tartrate or cream of tartar. The chemical structure of this acid salt of tartaric acid is:

$$
\begin{array}{c}
\quad\quad\ \ \overset{\textstyle H}{|}\quad \overset{\textstyle O}{\parallel} \\
HO-\underset{\underset{\textstyle |}{|}}{C}-C-O^-K^+ \\
\quad\quad\ \ \overset{\textstyle O}{\parallel} \\
HO-\underset{\underset{\textstyle H}{|}}{C}-C-OH
\end{array}
$$

The salt residue produced when cream of tartar and soda are combined in a moist medium is sodium potassium tartrate. One-half teaspoon of soda reacts with approximately $1\frac{1}{4}$ tsp cream of tartar. These two agents were mixed separately by homemakers for use in leavening before baking powders were prepared commercially.

The first formulas for baking powder were developed in the United States in 1850. At this time a cream of tartar baking powder was marketed in Boston. It was a number of years after this before baking powder was generally available in American communities (Bailey, 1940).

Baking powder is produced by mixing an acid-reactant with sodium bicarbonate. It generally contains starch as a diluent and an absorbant of moisture. This allows standardization of the baking powder in terms of yield of available carbon dioxide. A baking powder must yield carbon dioxide equal to at least 12 percent of its weight. There is a margin of safety in the preparation of most baking powders and the actual yield is about 14 percent (Paul and Palmer, 1972).

All baking powders have as a common ingredient, sodium bicarbonate. It is the source of carbon dioxide. The distinguishing feature that determines the type of baking powder is the acid substance present. An acid salt, rather than the acid itself, is usually used in the interest of stability. However, a combination of acid and acid salt, tartaric acid and cream of tartar, is used in tartrate baking powder because a faster and more efficient reaction is promoted by the combination. Baking powders are formulated so that neither an excess of soda nor of the acid salt remains in the residue after the action of the baking powder is complete. Since all of the reactions that occur as a baking powder is used for leavening are not known, the amounts of ingredients to use may need to be determined experimentally (Paul and Palmer, 1972). Sodium bicarbonate is readily soluble in water. The solubility of the leavening acid, therefore, determines the rates at which carbon dioxide is released.

Three types of baking powder have been available to the homemaker. These have included single acting baking powders, which release carbon dioxide gas as soon as the dry ingredients are moistened, and double acting baking powders, which release some carbon dioxide when the dry ingredients are moistened and release additional carbon dioxide when heat is applied in baking. At the present time, however, only one type is commonly marketed for home use. This is a double acting baking powder that contains sodium aluminum sulfate (SAS) and monocalcium phosphate monohydrate as acid-producing substances. Tartrate and phosphate baking powders are not generally available in most American communities. A number of different phosphate baking powders are used by commercial bakers and manufacturers of dry flour mixes.

Tartrate baking powder contains tartaric acid and potassium acid tartrate (cream of tartar) as acid ingredients. Tartaric acid dissolves more readily in water than does cream of tartar. Action is rapid, carbon dioxide being liberated as soon as the dry ingredients are moistened. Some gas evolution during mixing is desirable so that gas cell nuclei may be formed in the batter or dough. The reactions that are involved with tartrate baking powder are:

$$2NaHCO_3 \; + \; H_2C_4H_4O_6 \; \longrightarrow \; Na_2C_4H_4O_6 \; + \; 2CO_2 \; + \; 2H_2O$$

| Sodium bicarbonate | Tartaric acid | Sodium tartrate | Carbon dioxide | Water |

$$NaHCO_3 \; + \; KHC_4H_4O_6 \; \longrightarrow \; KNaC_4H_4O_6 \; + \; CO_2 \; + \; H_2O$$

| Sodium bicarbonate | Potassium acid tartrate | Sodium potassium tartrate | Carbon dioxide | Water |

Sodium acid pyrophosphate ($Na_2H_2P_2O_7$) has a slower reaction rate than does monocalcium phosphate. A number of different samples of this compound are available for the commercial baker and have reaction rates ranging from very slow (22 percent gas release by two minutes after mixing) to quite rapid (40 percent gas release by two minutes after mixing). These products release 8–10 percent carbon dioxide between mixing and baking and release the remainder during baking. Sodium aluminum phosphate ($NaAl_3H_{14}(PO_4)_8$) has a slow reaction rate and retains maximum reaction potential for the baking period. The combination of sodium acid pyrophosphate and sodium aluminum phosphate has proved advantageous for such products as refrigerated canned biscuit doughs and chocolate cake mixes (Reiman, 1977).

SAS-phosphate baking powder contains sodium aluminum sulfate along with monocalcium phosphate monohydrate. This is a double acting type of baking powder. The production of carbon dioxide occurs in a series of reactions. The first reaction that produces carbon dioxide involves monocalcium phosphate monohydrate and soda. This reaction is similar to that of the phosphate baking powder described above. It is rapid and occurs as soon as the dry ingredients are moistened. The second reaction involves sodium aluminum sulfate. This compound is not an acid but yields sulfuric acid when it is reacted with water in the presence of heat.

$$\text{Na}_2\text{Al}_2(\text{SO}_4)_4 \; + \; 6\text{H}_2\text{O} \; \xrightarrow{\text{Heat}} \; 2\text{Al(OH)}_3 \; + \; \text{Na}_2\text{SO}_4 \; + \; 3\text{H}_2\text{SO}_4$$

Sodium aluminum sulfate — Water — Aluminum hydroxide — Sodium sulfate — Sulfuric acid

The liberated sulfuric acid then reacts with additional soda during the period of baking.

$$3\text{H}_2\text{SO}_4 \; + \; 6\text{NaHCO}_3 \; \longrightarrow \; 3\text{Na}_2\text{SO}_4 \; + \; 6\text{CO}_2 \; + \; 6\text{H}_2\text{O}$$

Sulfuric acid — Sodium bicarbonate — Sodium sulfate — Carbon dioxide — Water

A double acting baking powder such as SAS-phosphate releases gas rapidly at room temperature during the mixing process. A second release of carbon dioxide occurs when heat is applied during baking. This is the type of baking powder most frequently used by homemakers. The residue remaining after the release of carbon dioxide has a somewhat bitter flavor. SAS-phosphate accelerates the development of rancidity in dry flour mixes containing fat. It, therefore, is not used in the production of cake and other mixes. Various combinations of the phosphate baking powders are generally used for these purposes.

29.3

USE OF BAKING POWDER

Baking powder is used as a leavening agent in a variety of baked products. These include muffins, biscuits, coffee cakes, nut breads, shortened cakes, and cookies. Rapid gas production during mixing affects the physical condition of the batter. In addition to increasing the lightness and porous character of the batter, the baking powder residue salts may affect the gluten structure. Briant and Klosterman (1950) reported that muffin batters made with SAS-phosphate baking powders were heavier than those made with tartrate and phosphate powders and did not readily absorb the liquid. The optimum amount of liquid was, therefore, less for the SAS-phosphate batters. The final structure of the muffins reflected the differences in the batters.

Ingredients vary in number and proportion from one baked product to another. Many interactions occur among the specific ingredients in a product and with baking powder. Mixing methods and baking temperatures also vary. Therefore, many factors affect the optimal amount of baking powder to be used. Too little baking powder in any baked item results in a product that is low in volume and compact in texture. Too much baking powder causes overexpansion of the structure with an open, coarse texture. The product may expand beyond the capacity of the structure to support it. As a result, the baked product collapses. Suggested ranges for amounts of baking powder are from $1\frac{1}{4}$ to 2 tsp per cup of flour for quick breads and from 1 to 2 tsp per cup of flour for shortened cakes (American Home Economics Association, 1975).

The pH of the batter or dough is affected by the type of baking powder used. The residual salts from SAS-phosphate baking powder are less acid than those from tartrate or phosphate powders. The pH is therefore higher when SAS-phosphate baking powder is used (McKim and Moss, 1943). At an alkaline pH, the flavonoid pigments of flour, become yellowish in color.

SUMMARY

The palatability of most baked products is at least partially dependent upon the development of a light, porous texture. A leavening agent provides a source of gas for this purpose. The three basic leavening gases commonly used are air, water vapor, and carbon dioxide.

Air is present in all baked products and plays an important role in leavening, although it is not usually the major factor. In cakes containing baking powder, carbon dioxide contributes the most leavening gas, water vapor an intermediate amount, and air a small constant quantity. Air is beaten into egg whites when a meringue is formed. This adds leaven to cake batter when it is combined with it. Air is, therefore, an important leavening in angel and sponge cakes. However, water vapor has also been shown to be responsible for a large proportion of leavening in angel cake.

Water vapor is the primary leavening agent in popovers and cream puffs. The proportion of water to flour is high in these products and a hot oven temperature quickly converts water to steam.

Some carbon dioxide is produced by simply heating soda (sodium bicarbonate). However, the residue salt from this reaction, sodium carbonate, is bitter tasting and alkaline. When soda is combined with an acid in solution, carbon dioxide is released. A number of acids may satisfactorily participate in this reaction for the leavening of baked products. Lactic acid is present in sour milk or buttermilk. Various organic acids are present in fruit juices and molasses. Cream of tartar, a dry acid salt, may be effectively combined with soda for leavening. One-half teaspoon of soda reacts with approximately $1\frac{1}{4}$ tsp cream of tartar.

Baking powder is produced by mixing an acid-reacting material with sodium bicarbonate along with starch as a diluent and an absorbant of moisture. It is standardized to yield at least 12 percent carbon dioxide. All baking powders, therefore, contain soda, the source of carbon dioxide, and an acid, usually an acid salt.

Although three types of baking powder, differing in the type of acid ingredient, have been available to the homemaker, only one type is now commonly marketed. This is a double acting baking powder that contains sodium aluminum sulfate (SAS) and monocalcium phosphate monohydrate as acid-producing substances. The production of carbon dioxide occurs in a series of reactions. The first reaction with SAS-phosphate baking powder occurs when the dry ingredients are moistened and involves monocalcium phosphate monohydrate and soda, with the release of carbon dioxide. The second reaction involves SAS. This compound is not an acid but yields sulfuric acid when it is heated with water. The liberated sulfuric acid then reacts with additional soda to produce more carbon dioxide during the period of baking. The residue remaining after the release of carbon dioxide has a somewhat bitter flavor.

Tartrate baking powder contains tartaric acid and cream of tartar as acid ingredients. It is a single acting baking powder, with carbon dioxide being rapidly liberated as soon as the dry ingredients are moistened. Phosphate baking powders contain a phosphate leavening acid. These may include calcium phosphates, sodium acid pyrophosphates, or sodium aluminum phosphates. Monocalcium phosphate monohydrate reacts very rapidly with soda. Anhydrous monocalcium phosphate is a coated product with a slower reaction rate. The commercial baker and cake mix manufacterer may use sodium acid pyrophosphate, which has a relatively slow reaction rate, or sodium aluminum phosphate, which reacts to a large extent during baking. These substances are often used in combination with monocalcium phosphate.

Baking powder is used as a leavening agent in a variety of baked products. Gas production during mixing affects the physical condition of the batter. In addition, the residue salts may affect the gluten structure. Many interactions occur among ingredients and with baking powder. Thus, the optimal amount of baking powder to use varies.

STUDY QUESTIONS

Three commonly used leavening gases are air, water vapor, and carbon dioxide.

1. Discuss the relative importance of air and steam in the leavening of baked products generally.
2. Give examples of baked products in which air plays a very important role as a leavening agent. What products are leavened chiefly by steam?

The reaction of baking soda with an acid occurs in many baked products.

3. Write a balanced equation for the reaction of sodium bicarbonate with an acid and explain its significance in food preparation.
4. Name ingredients commonly used in baked products that are sources of acid to combine with added soda. Give examples of acids that may be present in these ingredients.

Excess soda produces undesirable flavor and color effects in baked products.

5. Describe the effects of excess soda in baked products and explain why they are produced.

Baking powder contains soda plus an acid ingredient.

6. Outline and explain the major reactions involved as the following types of baking powder are employed in leavening: tartrate, monocalcium phosphate, and SAS-phosphate.

7. Why is SAS-phosphate baking powder not usually used in commercial flour mixes? What types are used for this purpose?

8. Explain the terminology, "double-acting baking powder," as applied to SAS-phosphate.

9. A cook has started to prepare a quick bread recipe that calls for 3 cups all purpose flour, $\frac{1}{2}$ tsp soda, and 1 cup buttermilk (among other ingredients); however, there is sweet milk but no buttermilk in the kitchen. Suggest several alternatives to follow in order to complete the product immediately.

REFERENCES

1. American Home Economics Association. 1975. *Handbook of Food Preparation*, 7th edition. Washington, D. C.

2. Bailey, L. H. 1940. Development and use of baking powder and baking chemicals. U. S. Department of Agriculture, Circular No. 138.

3. Barmore, M. A. 1936. The influence of various factors, including altitude, in the production of angel food cake. Colorado Agricultural Experiment Station Technical Bulletin No. 15.

4. Briant, A. M. and A. M. Klosterman. 1950. Influence of ingredients on thiamine and riboflavin retention and quality of plain muffins. *Transactions of the American Association of Cereal Chemists* 8, 69.

5. Carlin, G. T. 1944. A microscopic study of the behavior of fats in cake batters. *Cereal Chemistry* 21, 189.

6. Dunn, J. A. and J. R. White. 1939. The leavening action of air included in cake batter. *Cereal Chemistry* 16, 93.

7. Hoerr, C. W. 1967. Changing the physical properties of fats and oils for specific uses. *Bakers Digest* 41 (Dec.), 42.

8. Hood, M. P. and B. Lowe. 1948. Air, water vapor, and carbon dioxide as leavening gases in cakes made with different types of fats. *Cereal Chemistry* 25, 244.

9. McKim, E. and H. V. Moss. 1943. Observations on the pH of chemically leavened products. *Cereal Chemistry* 20, 250.

10. Paul, P. C. and H. H. Palmer. 1972. *Food Theory and Applications*. New York: Wiley.

11. Reiman, H. M. 1977. Chemical leavening systems. *Bakers Digest* 51 (Aug.), 33.

CHAPTER 30

QUICK BREADS AND PASTRY

A variety of flour mixtures is produced, differing in consistency and proportion of ingredients. Flour is the basic component of each. Other ingredients generally used in varying amounts are milk or water, fat, sugar, eggs, salt, and leavening agent.

The term *quick breads* is commonly used to distinguish from *yeast breads* this group of relatively quickly prepared flour mixtures that is leavened primarily by chemical agents, steam, and/or air. It includes muffins, biscuits, popovers, griddle cakes, waffles, fritters, dumplings, and a variety of coffee cakes and nut or fruit breads. The volume of published research on quick breads is small in comparison to that concerned with yeast breads (which are discussed in Chapter 32).

30.1

ROLES OF INGREDIENTS IN QUICK BREADS

LIQUID

The proportion of liquid to flour determines the consistency of a flour mixture. A pour batter is quite fluid in consistency and has a ratio of liquid to flour of approximately 1 : 1. A popover batter is an example of this type. A drop batter has a thicker consistency with a ratio of about 1 : 2 for liquid to flour. Muffin batter and many cookies are examples of drop batters. Soft doughs, such as baking powder biscuits, contain one part of liquid to about three parts of flour (1 : 3). Stiff doughs include an even higher proportion of flour to liquid. Pastry, noodles, and some cookies are examples of stiff doughs. Table 30.1 gives basic proportions of liquid to flour and other ingredients in some quick breads.

The liquid used in quick breads is usually milk, which adds important nutrients and aids in browning. Liquid acts as a dispersing medium for other substances in the mixture. Sugar, salt, and baking powder are in true solution. The action of baking powder to release carbon dioxide begins as the soda and acid salt are dissolved. The proteins of flour absorb water as the batter is mixed and some development of gluten occurs. Starch granules also absorb some moisture, although the

Table 30.1 Basic Proportions of Ingredients for Quick Breads

	All Purpose Flour (cups)	Milk (cups)	Fat (Tbsp.)	Sugar (Tbsp.)	Eggs	Baking Powder (tsp.)	Salt (tsp.)
Biscuits	1	$\frac{1}{3}-\frac{1}{2}$	2–4			$1\frac{1}{2}-2$	$\frac{1}{2}$
Griddle cakes	1	$\frac{3}{4}-\frac{7}{8}$	1	0–1	$\frac{1}{2}$	$1\frac{1}{2}-2$	$\frac{1}{2}$
Muffins	1	$\frac{1}{2}$	2–3	1–2	$\frac{1}{2}$	$1\frac{1}{4}-2$	$\frac{1}{2}$
Popovers	1	1	1–2		2–3		$\frac{1}{4}-\frac{1}{2}$
Waffles	1	$\frac{3}{4}-1$	1–3		1–2	$1\frac{1}{4}-2$	$\frac{1}{2}$

Source: From the American Home Economics Association, 1975.

amount is limited until heat is applied. Since starch is present in flour in much larger amounts than is protein, about half of the bound water in a batter or dough may be held by the starch. Water is necessary for the gelatinization of starch as the product is heated. The formation of steam from water occurs during baking.

FLOUR

Flour provides the basic structure for quick breads. The relatively high proportion of liquid to flour in many batters limits the development of gluten during mixing. The structure of the finished product is, therefore, more dependent upon the gelatinization of starch than on gluten formation. However, overmixing may contribute to toughness in batters such as those used for muffins because the consistency is conducive to gluten development. The texture of quick breads is generally more crumbly than is that of yeast breads because gluten is not developed into cohesive, elastic strands. All purpose flour is commonly used in the preparation of quick breads. Some cake-type muffin formulas call for pastry or cake flour.

FAT

Fat is a tenderizing agent. Products containing fat break apart more easily than those with no fat. Fat is insoluble in water and spreads over the moistened flour particles. It has been suggested that the greater the spreading power of a fat, the greater its shortening power. It interferes with the development of strands or masses of gluten.

Fat is differently dispersed in various baked products. Quick breads generally contain relatively small amounts of fat. The small amount present has little effect on griddle cakes. In rolled biscuits, fat is distributed in small pieces that melt on baking. This leaves spaces between layers of dough that contribute to flakiness. Fat generally softens the crumb of a quick bread and inhibits staling.

SUGAR

Sugar is present in many quick breads in minimal quantities. It contributes sweetness and it tenderizes. When sugar is present in relatively large amounts, it interferes with the development of gluten. This is probably due to a competition for water. It also competes with starch for water and thus interferes with gelatinization. Sucrose or table sugar does not participate in the Maillard reaction because the aldehyde group of the glucose component and the ketone group of the fructose are both tied up in linkage. Sucrose is not a reducing sugar and, therefore, does not react with amino groups in the Maillard reaction, although it may be involved in caramelization.

EGGS

The coagulation of egg proteins during baking makes an important contribution to the structure of many quick breads. This is especially important because gluten structure is weak in these products. Popovers, in which eggs are a major ingredient, depend primarily on the coagulation of egg proteins for structure after steam has greatly expanded the volume. The lipoproteins of egg yolk are effective surface active agents and aid in distributing fat throughout the batter.

SALT AND LEAVENING

Salt is added to quick breads chiefly for flavor. However, it also affects the hydration of flour proteins. The amount of salt in a formula is decreased if a salted fat, such as butter or margarine, is used.

Baking powder is commonly used as a source of carbon dioxide for leavening. However, soda and an acid-containing ingredient such as buttermilk, fruit juice, or molasses may be employed. (Leavening agents are discussed in Chapter 28.)

30.2

METHODS OF MIXING

Three basic methods of mixing flour products have been used traditionally. Many modifications of these methods are used in various baked mixtures. The basic methods are 1. the muffin method, 2. the pastry or biscuit method, and 3. the conventional cake method.

The muffin method of mixing consists of blending milk, eggs, and melted fat together and adding the liquid mixture all at once to the sifted dry ingredients. This is the usual method for mixing muffins, as the name implies. Many quick breads are mixed by this method, especially those that are relatively low in fat. The amount of mixing after the ingredients are combined is limited in products that contain little fat and sugar in order to avoid toughening and tunnel formation. Shortened cakes made by this method tend to stale more quickly than those made by conventional or modified conventional methods.

In the pastry or biscuit method of mixing, the fat is cut into the flour and salt mixture until it is similar to a coarse meal. The liquid is then stirred into the flour–fat mixture. Baking powder biscuits, as well as plain pastry, are usually mixed by this method. Biscuits are generally kneaded slightly before being rolled out and cut.

The conventional cake method involves creaming a plastic fat with sugar, after which egg is added. The sifted dry ingredients are then added in portions, alternately with portions of the milk. Mixing is done after each addition. Shortened cakes were traditionally mixed by this method, particularly when fats that were not precreamed, such as lard and butter, were used. Air incorporated in the fat during the creaming stage formed most of the tiny gas nuclei that affected the finished cake structure. Muffins that contain relatively high levels of fat and sugar may be mixed by this method.

30.3

MUFFINS

Muffins are made from a drop batter that has a fairly thick consistency. The proportions of fat and sugar in the batter are relatively small (see Table 30.1). Consequently, conditions are favorable for the development of gluten with overmixing. Gluten development in muffins is undesirable because it results in peaks and tunnels and a toughened product. Figure 30.1 shows a properly mixed muffin and other muffins that have been subjected to increased periods of mixing. Tunnel development and peaking are evident in the overmixed muffins. Properly mixed muffins have an even texture although the grain is somewhat open and more coarse than that of shortened cakes. The crumb is tender. The surface is symmetrical and has a slightly rough appearance. The overmixed muffin has a smoother surface with a definite peak. The texture is compact between tunnels which are oriented upward toward the peak.

Production of tunnels in muffins is due to the over-development of gluten and loss of carbon dioxide during the period of overmixing. The development of gluten is apparent as the batter changes from a somewhat lumpy, noncohesive character to a more smooth, extensible, elastic mass. The development of gluten is not usually uniform throughout the batter, however. With loss of additional carbon dioxide, the rising of the batter in the oven is delayed and a crust begins to form. When the batter is heated and expansion of gases does occur, the gases push the dough in tunnels through the most extensible areas to the top of the muffin, which forms a peak. Tunnels that contain relatively high proportions of fat and sugar tolerate more mixing before tunnel formation occurs. Substitution of cornmeal for part of the flour in muffin batter also decreases the likelihood of tunnel formation with mixing. Cornmeal contains no gluten-forming proteins. Muffins made with whole wheat flour are less susceptible to tunnel formation since the particles of bran interfere with gluten development.

30.4

BISCUITS

The leavening agent in biscuits is often baking powder. However, buttermilk and soda are also used for the production of carbon dioxide in this product. Flakiness is a characteristic that is often desired in

Figure 30.1

Plain Muffins (*a*) dry ingredients just dampened (*b*) mixed 20 strokes (*c*) mixed 35 strokes.

(a)

(b)

(c)

biscuits. This characteristic is achieved most effectively by cutting a plastic fat into the dry ingredients until the mixture resembles a coarse meal. Milk is then added all at once and stirring is continued until a soft dough is formed. The dough is placed on a lightly floured hard surface and kneaded gently for 10–20 times to develop some gluten and orient all of the developed strands in the same direction. After kneading, the dough is rolled out to the desired thickness and cut. Letting the cut biscuits stand for 15–30 minutes at room temperature does not affect the quality of the biscuits, if they are covered so that the surface does not become excessively dry. In fact, cut biscuits may be refrigerated for several hours or frozen for a few weeks without detrimental effects if they are properly packaged. When baked in a hot oven, the fat melts and steam aids in separating the layers of dough that have been produced by the kneading and rolling process and flakiness results.

Mathews and Dawson (1963) studied the characteristics of baking powder biscuits made from several different fats. Hydrogenated fats were better shortening agents in biscuits than was lard. The smaller stable crystals in the hydrogenated fats covered a larger surface area than did the larger lard crystals. Flakier biscuits also were rated by panel members as more tender.

If the pH of the biscuit is slightly acid, the crumb will be white. If excess soda has been used in the preparation of the dough, a yellow color develops. The texture tends to be coarse and the flavor alkaline and slightly soapy. This is because of the production of the alkaline salt, sodium carbonate, as discussed in Section 29.2. The excess sodium present may form soaps with fatty acids that are derived from the fat in the dough. Briant and Hutchins (1946) found that biscuits prepared with SAS-phosphate baking powder often had cracks on the sides. The dough did not stretch sufficiently during baking.

The amount of fat in biscuits affects the flakiness and tenderness and also the optimum amount of manipulation to be used. With increased amounts of shortening, more mixing is desirable. The recombination of various fractions of fractionated flour to produce a product similar to hard wheat bread flour caused biscuits to be darker in crust color, larger in volume, and less tender than when fractions were combined to simulate soft wheat pastry flour (Zaehringer et al., 1956). Briant and Hutchins (1946) reported that biscuits made with fresh whole milk were more tender, more compressible, higher in volume, and had better flavor than biscuits made with diluted evaporated milk, reconstituted dry whole milk, or water. The effects of the type of milk were less pronounced when the dough was not kneaded but baked as drop biscuits by Kirkpatrick et al. (1961). However, there was a tendency for drop biscuits made with fresh whole or fresh skim milk to be more tender than those made with some processed milks. A larger quantity of some of the processed milks was required to hydrate the dry ingredients. The amount of milk added in making rolled biscuits is variable, depending upon the hydration capacity of the flour being used.

30.5

PASTRY

The term *pastry* may be used in a broad sense to include a variety of products made from doughs that are relatively high in fat. This includes sweet rolls and puff pastry. However, the term is more commonly used to mean plain pastry or pie crust.

CHARACTERISTICS OF PASTRY

Both flakiness and tenderness are desirable characteristics of pastry. A flaky pastry depends on a certain physical orientation of ingredients in the dough. Some degree of separation of fat and water is necessary to produce flakiness. Layers of dough are formed by hydration of flour that has particles of fat distributed throughout. Water is absorbed by the flour less readily when the flour is in direct contact with fat. Hydration of some of the flour allows gluten to be formed which contributes to the strength of the layers of dough.

During baking in a hot oven, steam separates the layers of dough. Expansion of air on heating probably also contributes to the separation of layers. The fat melts and spreads over the dough.

A mealy crust is nonflaky. In the preparation of a mealy crust, mixing is done in such a way that nearly all of the fat combines with the flour. Practically none remains in the form of discrete particles (Preonas *et al.*, 1967). The spreading of fat over flour particles decreases the formation of gluten strands as water is added to the fat–flour mixture. Soft wheat flours tend to give more mealy pastries than do hard wheat flours.

Tenderness is at a maximum when the fat coats the flour in such a way that hydration of the flour particles is prevented. When this occurs, gluten formation is inhibited.

The ability of a fat to tenderize is called *shortening power*. A number of early research studies were concerned with the shortening power of various fats in the preparation of pastry. Denton and Lowe (1924) found that generally the fats having the highest percentage of unsaturated glycerides gave the most tender pastries. Fisher (1933) reported that the shortening power in pastry of lard was greater than that of any other plastic fats tested. Hornstein *et al.* (1943) found that a hydrogenated vegetable oil gave the most tender pastry among those tested. Second in tenderness were a refined lard, butter oil, and butter. In third place were another hydrogenated vegetable oil sample, a hydrogenated lard, and another butter. The fat giving the least tender pastry was an oleomargarine. Advances in food technology are apparent in the types of fats marketed in recent years. Matthews and Dawson compared some of the processed fats on the retail market in 1963. They measured the tenderness of pastries made with increasing amounts of various fats, comprising from 25 to 51 percent of the weight of the flour. Optimum tenderness was reached at lower fat levels for oils than for solid fats. It would appear that unsaturated fats produce more tender pastries than do fats that are saturated to a greater degree. Oils generally produce more tender pastries than do plastic fats. However, relationships are not always clearcut when a wide variety of fats is compared. Other undefined factors associated with the fats also appear to affect tenderness.

MEASUREMENT OF TENDERNESS AND FLAKINESS

Tenderness of pastry samples may be measured by subjective and objective methods. Flakiness is usually evaluated only by subjective means. A judging panel evaluates pastry subjectively. In addition to tenderness and flakiness, flavor and color are usually assessed.

For many years, pastry tenderness has been evaluated objectively by use of the Bailey shortometer. This instrument is designed to measure the force required to break (breaking strength) small wafers of plain pastry, crackers, or cookies (Bailey, 1934). The measurement of tenderness by the shortometer is a more sensitive assessment of this characteristic in pastry than is organoleptic evaluation, according to a study carried out by Briant and Snow (1947). However, Matthews and Dawson (1963) reported a highly significant negative correlation between tenderness scores judged by panel members and breaking strength values determined by the shortometer. A large number of samples should be measured with the shortometer because variation from one sample to another is fairly large.

Four methods for the evaluation of pastry tenderness were compared by Stinson and Huck (1969). Scores from the subjective evaluation by a trained sensory panel were compared with scores from three objective evaluations. These included the Bailey shortometer, a L.E.E.-Kramer shear press, and a tenderpen. The *L.E.E.-Kramer shear press* is a shearing device that has been successfully used for the evaluation of texture in meat, poultry, fruits, vegetables, and other food products. The *tenderpen* apparatus was devised specifically to measure pastry tenderness. It consists of a pendulum that swings into a pastry sample and breaks it, as shown in Figure 30.2. If the sample is tender,

Figure 30.2

Tenderpen apparatus showing the pendulum in motion. (From Stinson, C. G. and M. B. Huck. 1969. A comparison of four methods for pastry tenderness evaluation. *Journal of Food Science* 34, 537. With permission.)

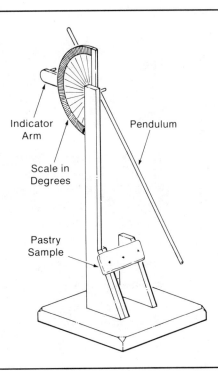

Indicator Arm

Pendulum

Scale in Degrees

Pastry Sample

the swing of the pendulum is inhibited to a lesser degree than if the sample is tough. Tenderness values are obtained by subtracting the number of degrees through which the pendulum swings from 100. The tougher samples, therefore, have higher readings.

Stinson and Huck reported that all of the methods of evaluation investigated could detect significant differences in pastry tenderness. Highly significant correlations were found between the subjective and objective methods of evaluation. The panel and the shear press rated all of the four types of examined pastries in the same order. The panel and the shortometer values disagreed on the tenderness of only one type of pastry out of four. The tenderpen and the panel ranked two of the four types similarly.

Differences in flakiness of pastry are shown in Figure 30.3. Scoring of these pastries was done by a panel using a scale of 1–7. The optimum value was five. Scores above and below this value reflect observable defects (Preonas *et al.,* 1967). Many thin layers are considered optimal for flakiness in pastry.

INGREDIENTS IN PASTRY

Fat   A variety of liquid and plastic fats is used in the preparation of pastry. As previously discussed, the more unsaturated oils tend to produce greater tenderness than do the more saturated plastic fats. Tenderness increases with increasing amounts of any fat. Matthews and Dawson (1963) reported that oil pastries were nearest their optimal

Figure 30.3

The pie crust samples were scored for flakiness on a scale of 1 to 7 with 5 being the most desirable. A score of 7 indicates a mealy pastry; 6, indistinct layers; 5, many thin layers; 4, thin layers; and 3, thick and thin layers. These samples scored 3, 4, 5, 6, and 7, respectively, from (a) to (e). (Reprinted with permission from Preonas, D. L., A. I. Nelson, and M. P. Steinberg. 1967. Continuous production of pie dough. *Bakers Digest* 41 [No. 6], 34.)

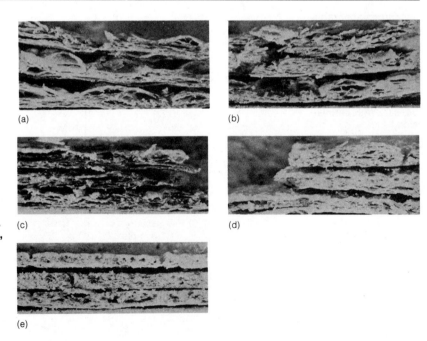

(a)

(b)

(c)

(d)

(e)

score for tenderness at a level of 45 percent of the weight of the flour and solid fats were optimal at 51 percent. Pastries made with oils at 51 percent of the weight of the flour and solid fats at 68 percent levels were considered to be too tender. Pastries that scored high in tenderness also scored high in flakiness. However, Miller and Trimbo (1970) reported that flakiness was not a requisite for tenderness. Pie crust can be flaky and tender, flaky and tough, mealy and tender, mealy and tough, or somewhere between these extremes.

In general, from $\frac{1}{4}$ to $\frac{1}{3}$ cup of fat is used for each cup of flour in making a pastry of acceptable tenderness. Butter or margarine contain approximately 80 percent fat. The same weight or measure of these fats is therefore expected to have less shortening power than similar amounts of shortening such as hydrogenated shortening and lard that are essentially 100 percent fat.

Flour The type of flour used in pastry affects tenderness and flakiness. Soft wheat flours of relatively low protein content give more tender pastries than do hard wheat flours (Denton *et al.*, 1933). Miller and Trimbo (1970) found that the tenderness of pie crust was a function of

Figure 30.4

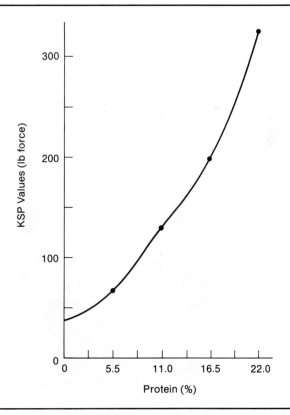

Effect of flour protein content on the force required to shear pie crust made from dough mixed with an electric mixer. (From Miller, B. S. and H. B. Trimbo. 1970. Factors affecting the quality of pie dough and pie crust. *Bakers Digest* 44 [No. 1], 46. With permission.)

the protein content of the flour. This relationship is shown in Figure 30.4. The toughening effect of flour protein on pie crust was also found to be accentuated by increasing the level of water in the pie dough.

Hydration of flour proteins and mixing result in gluten development. The formation of gluten into definite strands was very evident in pastry dough produced with excessive manipulation (Hirahara and Simpson, 1961). A photomicrograph of this pastry dough is seen in Figure 30.5. Large gluten strands did not form in the standard dough. The breaking strength of wafers baked from the over-manipulated dough was greater than was the breaking strength of those baked from the standard dough. A relationship is thus established between the development of gluten in the dough and the tenderness of the baked pastry.

Liquid Liquid in pastry dough hydrates the flour enough to produce cohesiveness. It also provides steam to leaven the pastry during baking and contributes to flakiness. When the water in pastry dough is increased, the breaking strength of wafers baked from this dough is increased (Swartz, 1943). Figure 30.5 shows a photomicrograph of pastry dough prepared with excess water by Hirahara and Simpson (1961). A larger amount of gluten is present in this dough than in a standard dough. The gluten does not appear to be in long strands, however, as it is in the dough prepared with excess manipulation. Nevertheless, the pastry baked from the dough with excess water was less tender than wafers baked from the standard dough.

Figure 30.5

Photomicrographs of raw pastry doughs: (a) Standard dough (b) Dough with excess manipulation (c) Dough with excess water. (Reprinted with permission from Hirahara, S. and J. I. Simpson. 1961. Microscopic appearance of gluten in pastry dough and its relation to the tenderness of baked pastry. *Journal of Home Economics* 53, 681.)

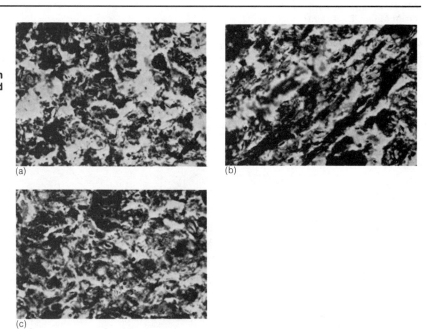

(a)

(b)

(c)

A wide variety of methods for mixing pastry dough may successfully be employed. These include the traditional method of cutting fat into the flour and salt mixture before adding water with a minimum of stirring. Methods also include combining the fat with boiling water and stirring this mixture into the flour. Rose *et al.* (1952) found that pastry made by the boiling water method was more tender than that prepared by cutting the solid fat into the flour. They also found that the fat was more evenly distributed throughout the dough when mixed by the boiling water method. Often pastry becomes mealy and less flaky as the fat is more finely dispersed throughout the dough.

Decreased breaking strength, indicating more tender pastry, was reported by Swartz (1943) when ingredients were at room temperature during mixing instead of at refrigerator temperature. Warm fat undoubtedly coats the flour more completely than does cold fat and shortening power is thereby increased. Swartz also found that increased mixing time after adding the water decreased tenderness when the ingredients were cold. However, when the fat and water were at room temperature, the mixing time had little effect. When a relatively high level of fat is present in the mixture, increased mixing of the dough up to an optimum amount actually increases tenderness because of finer distribution of the fat. Miller and Trimbo (1970) reported that pie crust lost flakiness and became mealy with increased mixing but tenderness was increased.

Pastry is generally baked at a relatively high oven temperature. Bernds (1937) found that baking temperatures of 185°–245°C (301°– 409°F) produced no significant differences in breaking strengths of the pastries. However, the pastries baked at the higher temperatures were judged to be more palatable. They were browner and had a more desirable flavor.

SUMMARY

The term quick breads distinguishes from yeast breads this group of relatively quickly prepared flour mixtures that is leavened primarily by chemical agents, steam, and/or air. It includes muffins, biscuits, and popovers.

Batters and doughs may be classified according to consistency. They include pour batters (1:1 ratio of liquid to flour), drop batters (1:2 ratio), soft doughs (1:3 ratio), and stiff doughs. Liquid in batters and doughs acts as a dispersing medium. It also hydrates the proteins and starch granules of flour. Flour provides the basic structure for quick breads. The starch in flour plays a particularly important role in structure after gelatinization. The texture of quick breads is generally more crumbly than that of yeast breads because gluten is not developed into cohesive, elastic strands.

Fat is a tenderizing agent. It spreads over the moistened flour particles in batters and doughs. The greater the spreading power of a fat, the greater its shortening power. Quick breads generally contain relatively small amounts of fat. Sugar is present in many quick breads in minimal amounts. It contributes sweetness and it tenderizes. The coagulation of egg proteins during baking makes an important contribution to the structure of many quick breads. This is especially important because gluten structure is weak in these products. Baking powder is a common leavening agent in quick breads. However, soda and an acid-containing ingredient may be employed.

Three basic methods of mixing flour products are the muffin method, the pastry or biscuit method, and the conventional cake method. Quick breads may be mixed by any of these methods.

Conditions are favorable for the development of gluten with over-mixing of muffins because the proportions of fat and sugar are low and the consistency of the batter is thick. Overmixing results in the production of tunnels and surface peaks. Gluten is developed, although not uniformly, and excessive carbon dioxide is lost during overmixing. When the batter is heated during baking, a crust begins to form before the product has expanded sufficiently. When it does expand, the heated gases push the dough in tunnels through the most extensible areas to the top of the muffin, which forms a peak.

Flakiness is a desirable characteristic in biscuits. It is achieved most effectively by cutting a plastic fat into the dry ingredients and then stirring in the liquid to form a soft dough. The dough is kneaded somewhat to develop gluten and orient the developed strands in the same direction. When baked in a hot oven, the fat melts and steam aids in separating the layers of dough. The amount of fat in biscuits affects flakiness and tenderness.

Both flakiness and tenderness are desirable characteristics of pastry. The production of flakiness depends on an imperfect blend of fat and water. Tenderness is at a maximum when the fat coats the flour in such a way that hydration of the flour particles is prevented. The shortening power of a fat appears to be related to its degree of unsaturation, with the more unsaturated fats producing more tender pastries.

The tenderness of pastry is measured subjectively by sensory panels. It is measured objectively by use of the shortometer, the L.E.E.-Kramer shear press, a tenderpen, and similar types of instruments. Subjective and objective methods have been shown to be correlated with each other.

Pastry ingredients include fat, flour, water, and salt. Tenderness increases with increasing amounts of fat. In general, from $\frac{1}{4}$ to $\frac{1}{3}$ cup of fat is used for each cup of flour in making a pastry of acceptable tenderness. The tenderness of pie crust is a function of the protein content of the flour. Tenderness decreases with increasing protein content. Over-manipulation of pastry dough develops gluten strands that increase the toughness of the baked pastry. Increasing the liquid in pastry dough also increases the gluten content and toughness.

Acceptable pastry may be prepared by a wide variety of mixing methods. When fat is more evenly and finely distributed throughout the dough, as in the boiling water method, tenderness increases. Flakiness, however, may be decreased. More tender pastry is produced when ingredients are at room temperature before they are mixed than when they are at refrigerator temperature. Warm fat is more readily dispersed with the flour. More palatable pastry is produced by baking at high than at lower oven temperatures.

STUDY QUESTIONS

Quick breads are leavened primarily by chemical agents, steam, and/or air.

1. What are quick breads? Give several examples.
2. Describe the major roles of liquid, flour, fat, sugar, and eggs in quick breads.
3. What are the major steps involved in the muffin method of mixing? In the pastry method? In the conventional cake method? Give examples of products that are commonly mixed by each method.
4. Explain how and why tunnel formation occurs in muffins.
5. Explain how flakiness is produced in biscuits.

Both flakiness and tenderness are desirable characteristics of pastry.

6. What factors influence the development of flakiness in pastry? Of tenderness? Explain.
7. Describe both subjective and objective methods for evaluating the tenderness of pastry.
8. How does the degree of saturation of fat affect tenderness in pastry? Give a possible explanation for this effect.
9. Describe the relationship between protein content of flour and tenderness in pastry.
10. What role does gluten play in production of pastry? Under what conditions of preparation is gluten development encouraged?
11. Describe changes occurring in pastry as it bakes. Explain why a hot oven temperature is usually recommended.

REFERENCES

1. American Home Economics Association. 1975. *Handbook of Food Preparation,* 7th edition. Washington, D.C.

2. Bailey, C. H. 1934. An automatic shortometer. *Cereal Chemistry* 11, 160.

3. Bernds, M. W. 1937. Factors affecting the shortening power of fat in pastry. M. S. Thesis. Iowa State University Library.

4. Briant, A. M. and M. R. Hutchins. 1946. Influence of ingredients on thiamine retention and quality in baking powder biscuits. *Cereal Chemistry* 23, 512.

5. Briant, A. M. and P. R. Snow. 1957. Freezer storage of pie shells. *American Dietetic Association Journal* 33, 796.

6. Denton, M. D., B. Gordon, and B. Sperry. 1933. Study of the tenderness in pastries made with flours of varying strength. *Cereal Chemistry* 10, 156.

7. Denton, M. C. and B. Lowe. 1924. The shortening power of fats. Unpublished paper. Bureau of Home Economics.

8. Fisher, J. D. 1933. Shortening value of plastic fats. *Industrial and Engineering Chemistry* 25, 1171.

9. Hirahara, S. and J. I. Simpson. 1961. Microscopic appearance of gluten in pastry dough and its relation to the tenderness of baked pastry. *Journal of Home Economics* 53, 681.

10. Hornstein, L. R., F. B. King, and F. Benedict. 1943. Comparative shortening value of some commercial fats. *Food Research* 8, 1.

11. Kirkpatrick, M. E., R. H. Matthews, and J. C. Collie. 1961. Use of different market forms of milk in biscuits. *Journal of Home Economics* 53, 201.

12. Matthews, R. H. and E. H. Dawson. 1963. Performance of fats and oils in pastry and biscuits. *Cereal Chemistry* 40, 291.

13. Miller, B. S. and H. B. Trimbo. 1970. Factors affecting the quality of pie dough and pie crust. *Bakers Digest* 44 (No. 1), 46.

14. Preonas, D. L., A. I. Nelson, and M. P. Steinberg. 1967. Continuous production of pie dough. *Bakers Digest* 41 (No. 6), 34.

15. Rose, I., M. E. Dressler, and K. A. Johnston. 1942. The effect of the method of fat and water incorporation on the average shortness and uniformity of tenderness of pastry. *Journal of Home Economics* 44, 707.

16. Stinson, C. G. and M. B. Huck. 1969. A comparison of four methods for pastry tenderness evaluation. *Journal of Food Science* 34, 537.

17. Swartz, V. 1943. Effect of certain variables in technique on the breaking strength of lard pastry wafers. *Cereal Chemistry* 20, 120.

18. Zaehringer, M. V., A. M. Briant, and C. J. Personius. 1956. Effects on baking powder biscuits of four flour components used in two proportions. *Cereal Chemistry* 33, 170.

CHAPTER 31

SHORTENED CAKES

Shortened cake batter represents an already complex multi-component system that undergoes additional complex changes during baking. The ingredients must be balanced in type and proportion for the preparation of a cake of high quality.

31.1

INGREDIENTS

A variety of ingredients may be used in the formulation of shortened cakes. These generally include flour, sugar, fat, liquid, eggs, leavening agent, and flavoring materials. Emulsifiers, particularly mono- and diglycerides, are often contained in shortenings that may be used in cake preparation at home. Mono- and diglycerides were the first commercial emulsifiers and their addition to shortening allowed bakers to use higher levels of sugar and water and lower amounts of fat in cake batters. These batters are called *high ratio* cake formulas. Emulsifier systems in shortenings gradually became more sophisticated until it is now possible for the commercial baker to use either fluid shortening or crystalline fat in cake manufacture.

FLOUR

A short patent flour of low protein content is commonly used in the production of shortened layer cakes. Cakes made with all-purpose flour are generally lower in volume, less tender, and less fine in texture than those made with cake flour. Substituting 2 tbsp of cornstarch for 2 tbsp of the all-purpose flour per 1 cup produces a cake with intermediate characteristics between those made with cake flour and those made with all-purpose flour.

Cake flours are treated with chlorine after milling. This has an improving effect in terms of the performance of the flour in cake baking. The chlorine treatment reduces the pH of cake flour to approximately 4.8. A cake flour that has not been treated with chlorine produces a layer cake with thick-walled cells, soggy crumb, and coarse appearance. The volume is small and the layer is flat-topped or fallen at the center. If chlorine is added in progressively increasing amounts, the volume of the cake increases, the crumb ceases to be soggy, and the structure improves. With excessive amounts of chlorine the volume of the cake decreases somewhat, the crumb becomes dry, and the texture too fine. There is thus an optimum level for chlorine application to a given volume of flour (Wilson and Donelson, 1963).

The granulation of flour affects cake quality. Shellenberger *et al.* (1950) compared three levels of particle size in cake flour. The flour of smallest particle size, which was also lowest in protein, produced cakes of highest quality.

The flour protein probably plays some role in the development of cake structure. However, flour protein is of much lesser importance in the structure of cakes than it is in yeast breads. Starch plays a more important role in cake structure. Intact starch granules are essential in achieving proper setting of cake structure during baking (Howard *et al.*, 1968). Miller and Trimbo (1965) found that the temperature of initial gelatinization of starch in cake flour and the associated high consistency of white cake batter after the initial swelling of the starch were important to cake quality. A deficiency of water in the batter and a high concentration of sucrose depressed the gelatinization of starch and resulted in a dip in the center of the cake. They observed a natural tendency of the starch in some flours to gelatinize at a lower temperature than did the starch in other flours. The flours with the earliest gelatinization behavior were best adapted to the preparation of white cake batters with low levels of liquid.

SUGAR

Sugar tenderizes and gives flavor to a shortened cake. High levels of sugar generally increase tenderness and moistness. Cakes were prepared using a high-, a medium-, and a low-sugar formula by Hunter *et al.* (1950). Three different methods of mixing, three fats, and three levels of baking powder were also evaluated. The levels of liquid, fat, and egg were increased as the sugar was increased by 25 and 40 percent of the low-sugar formula. With the higher proportions of sugar and fat, the cell structure of the cakes was finer and more uniform and the crumb increased in velvetiness and tenderness. Cakes of high quality were prepared from high- and medium-sugar formulas by all three methods of mixing that included the conventional, pastry-blend, and single-stage methods. Cakes of good quality were prepared with the low-sugar formula and the conventional method of mixing. Those low-sugar cakes prepared by the other two mixing methods were less desirable.

High levels of sugar inhibit starch gelatinization, as previously indicated. Therefore, increased liquid generally accompanies high sugar levels in shortened cakes to encourage adequate starch gelatinization. Sugar interferes with the development of gluten. Although gluten is not the major structural component of cake, the coagulation of gluten on baking apparently contributes to some degree to the final structure of the cake. Cakes containing relatively high levels of sugar require additional beating in order to avoid a coarse-textured product with a dip in the center. Possibly the additional mixing is necessary to adequately develop gluten.

Sweeteners other than sucrose may be used in baked products. However, direct substitution of products such as glucose, or dextrose, corn sirup, and honey is usually not possible. If the sweeteners are sirups containing water, adjustment must be made in the liquid ingredients of the formula. Browning is much more extensive when glucose and fructose are used in place of sucrose. The reducing sugars, glucose and fructose, readily participate in the Maillard reaction.

The use of high fructose corn sirup (HFCS) in white layer cake was evaluated by Volpe and Meres (1976). They found that a lower level of browning occurred in the cakes when the pH of the crumb was below 6. They substituted HFCS for 60 percent of the sucrose in the formula. Three leavening acids, differing in residual acidity, were compared. The HFCS cake made with sodium acid pyrophosphate baking powder had a pH of 7.0. The pH of the cake made with glucono-delta-lactone was 5.7. Glucono-delta-lactone is the lactone of gluconic acid, a derivative of glucose. The HFCS cake made with sodium aluminum phosphate-monocalcium phosphate monohydrate had a pH of 5.6. Figure 31.1 shows three HFCS cakes made with the various leavening agents in comparison to a cake containing sucrose only. The marked browning in the cake with a pH of 7.0 is apparent. Volpe and Meres concluded that highly acceptable cakes can be produced with HFCS; however, further adjustments in flavoring systems are needed to compensate for the excessive acidity of the cakes.

Crystalline sugar aids in the incorporation of air into fats as they are creamed. The sharp edges of the crystals have air adhering to their sides. The air is then beaten into the fat. Cake volume increases as the granulation of sugar becomes finer (Dunn and White, 1937).

FAT

The chief functions of fat in shortened cakes are to impart moistness, tenderness, and keeping quality. Fat also plays a critical role in incorporating air into the batter. The crystalline structure of a plastic fat affects its ability to perform satisfactorily in cakes. (The various forms of crystalline fats (polymorphism) are discussed in Section 18.2.) Asymmetrical triglyceride molecules that form small stable crystals in the beta prime (β') form are ideal for use in shortened cakes. An optimal percentage of solids in the shortening system is also an important factor in its performance as a component of cakes.

Several fats may be used for the preparation of shortened cake at home. Matthews and Dawson (1966) compared white cakes made with five fats produced for the retail market. These included two hydrogenated fats with mono- and diglycerides added; butter; and two kinds of margarine, an unsaturated corn oil type and a regular type made from a mixture of soybean and cottonseed oils. Each fat was used at

Figure 31.1

Effect of leavening acids on high fructose corn syrup (HFCS) layer cakes: (*A*) Sucrose-sodium acid pyrophosphate (SAPP); (*B*) HFCS-SAPP, (*C*) HFCS-glucono-delta-lactone; (*D*) HFCS-sodium aluminum phosphate-monocalcium phosphate monohydrate. (Reprinted with permission from Volpe, T. and C. Meres. 1976. Use of high fructose syrups in white layer cake. *Bakers Digest* 50 [Apr.], 38.)

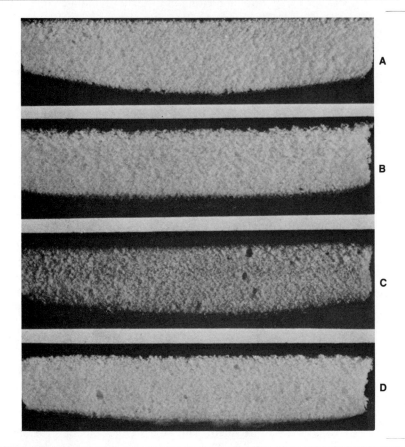

five levels, ranging from 12.5 to 100 percent of the weight of the flour. They reported that batters became lighter with increased levels of each fat. However, batters made with margarines were less light and less viscous than were batters made from the other fats, as indicated by a higher specific gravity with margarine. Hydrogenated fats produced batters of a low specific gravity and high viscosity. Cakes made with butter rated highest for tenderness and velvetiness. Those made with hydrogenated fat rated highest for evenness of grain.

Hunter *et al.* (1950) found that hydrogenated shortening creamed well and was readily dispersed in the batters. Its use resulted in high quality cakes over a wide range of ingredient temperatures and by both the conventional and pastry-blend methods of mixing. Good cakes were made with hydrogenated shortening using the single stage method of mixing when the ingredients were at about 22°C (72°F). Margarine creamed well but was not readily dispersed in the batters. Margarine cakes ranged from good to fair in quality and tended to be better when mixed by the pastry-blend than by the conventional method. Lard creamed poorly but was readily dispersed in a batter. Lard cakes generally ranged from fair to poor in quality. However, good lard cakes were produced by the pastry-blend method when ingredients were at 30°C (86°F). Fat appeared to be the ingredient most influential in determining the amount of air entrapped in the batter.

Emulsifiers Mono- and diglycerides are widely employed as emulsifiers in hydrogenated shortenings used in cake production. Carlin reported in 1944 that monoglycerides produce a finer dispersion of fat throughout shortened cake batter than occurs when no emulsifier is present. Hunt and Green (1955) prepared plain cake with butter, both with and without added mono- and diglycerides. Batters made with no added emulsifier were well aerated and relatively viscous, but had a curdled appearance. Addition of the emulsifying agent resulted in batters that were smooth and nonviscous and had a higher specific gravity (indicating less incorporated air) than did batters without emulsifier. The volume of the finished cake was slightly improved with the addition of emulsifier. Histological examination indicated that the fat and air cells were more finely distributed throughout the batter in the emulsified product. Figure 31.2 shows microphotographs of cake batters containing increasing levels of emulsifying agents. As the air cells become smaller and more numerous, the finished cake gains in volume and fine texture (Moncrieff, 1970).

Emulsifiers seem to perform many of the same functions as do shor-

Figure 31.2

Photomicrographs of cake batter showing the effect of increasing levels of emulsifying agents, from (a) to (c), on the relative size and number of air cells. (Reprinted with permission from Moncrieff, J. 1970. Shortenings and emulsifiers for cakes and icings. *Bakers Digest* 44 [Oct.], 60.)

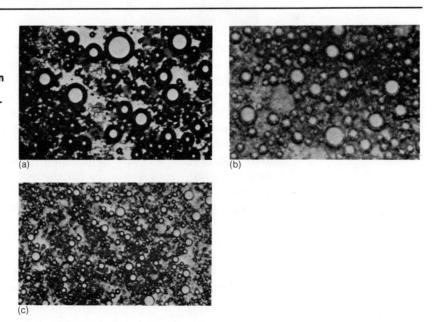

(a)

(b)

(c)

tenings in cakes and thereby extend the effectiveness of the shortening. They aid in aerating the batter, lubricate the movement of other ingredients, and retard staling of the baked cake. They apparently function as anti-staling agents by combining in some way with starch components (Moncrieff, 1970).

Several other types of emulsifying agents, in addition to mono- and diglycerides, have become available to the commercial baker in recent years. With use of the new surface active agents, marked improvement has been seen in emulsification and air incorporation in cake batters. These effects result in increased volume and finer grain of the finished cakes over cakes produced by the addition of mono- and diglycerides. Examples of such emulsifiers include lactoylated glycerides, propylene glycol monostearate, and 1-acetyl-3-monostearin. Liquid shortenings with propylene glycol monostearate and stearic acid added have been developed for commercial use in cake production (Wootton et al., 1967; Howard, 1972).

It has been suggested that the new shortening additives enhance the incorporation of air into cake batter systems because of their unique behavior at the fat–water interface. If the concentration of these substances at the interface exceeds the solubility limit, they crystallize in a stable crystalline form (alpha crystals). The interfacial film formed possesses waxlike properties and encapsulates the dispersed shortening droplets within a protective coating. A typical film formed by 1-acetyl-3-monostearin is shown in Figure 31.3. Wootton et al. (1967) have suggested that the encapsulation of fat encourages the incorporation of air into the batter by preventing fat migration into the aqueous phase of the batter and thus interfering with the aeration process.

LIQUID

Milk is the liquid usually employed in shortened cake formulas. The milk solids contribute to browning because of the lactose and protein present in them. Milk proteins probably aid in stabilizing the foam in cake batter and contribute to the formation of cake structure (Howard, 1972).

The role of liquid in the formation of layer cake structure was studied by Wilson and Donelson (1963). They reported that liquid concentration had a critical effect on the extent of starch gelatinization during baking, which in turn determined the type of crumb structure formed. Liquid is also necessary for the development of gluten. The amount of liquid in the formulation affects the consistency of the batter. Too little liquid has an effect similar to too much flour. The batter is stiff and difficult to mix adequately and the cake is dry.

EGGS

Whole eggs, egg whites, or egg yolks may be used in various shortened cake formulations. Dried egg products are also employed. Fresh eggs contribute moisture to the batter. Egg proteins coagulate on heating. They play an important role in stabilizing the foam structure, particu-

Figure 31.3

(*A*) Appearance of air dispersion in single-stage cake batter made with fluid shortening containing 12 percent 1-acetyl-3-monostearin. (*B*) Microscopic appearance of oil/water interfacial film of 1-acetyl-3-monostearin at 21°C (70°F). The distorted water drop was hanging from needle tip in cottonseed oil containing the emulsifier. Some water was withdrawn from the drop to collapse the film and emphasize the properties of the adsorbed interfacial film. (*C*) Effect of concentration of 1-acetyl-3-monostearin on the interfacial strength of an oil/water interface. The high values at 70° and 80°F indicate conditions at which films were formed. (Batters mixed at 90°F did not incorporate air during mixing.) (Reprinted with permission from Howard, N. B. 1972. The role of some essential ingredients in the formation of layer cake structures. *Bakers Digest* 46 [Oct.], 28.)

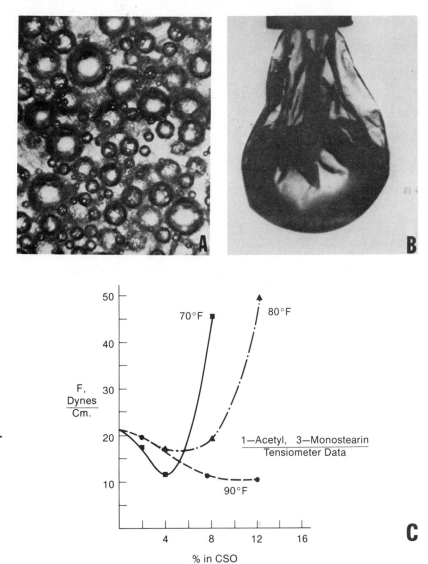

larly during the early stages of baking (Howard, 1972). The lipoproteins of egg yolk are also effective emulsifying agents.

Eggs act as toughening components of cake batters. As the level of whole, fresh eggs is increased without any other change in the formula, the cakes become more tough. The volume increases at first and then decreases. If compensation is made in the formulation for the added liquid from the eggs, the volume of the cake continues to rise (Pyke and

Johnson, 1940). Increased amounts of egg are generally balanced in recipe formulation by increased content of fat and sugar.

The size of eggs varies widely. Therefore, it is desirable to measure egg volume especially when a high proportion of them is used in a cake recipe. Eggs are weighed when they are used in cakes that are baked for purposes of research.

LEAVENING

The aeration of shortened cake batters is dependent on more than the addition of leavening agents such as baking powder. In aeration the role of emulsifiers in shortening has been mentioned previously. Soluble proteins in the batter contribute greatly to the stability of the foam structure in fluid cake batter while it is being heated. The setting of the final structure by the gelatinization of starch also affects the lightness of the finished cake.

Baking powder is commonly used in shortened cakes for the production of carbon dioxide. However, other sources of carbon dioxide may be employed, such as buttermilk and soda. An excess of soda produces a coarse, uneven texture. This may be partially due to overexpansion of the cake structure. Too much baking powder in a formula produces a similar effect.

The pH is a critical factor in cake formulation and quality control. The pH is usually controlled by adjustment of the chemical leavening components. It affects cake color, flavor, volume, and texture. Typical pH values for shortened cakes are given in Table 31.1.

A cake that is too acidic has a tart and biting flavor. On the other hand, a cake that is too alkaline has a bitter and soapy taste. However, within typical pH ranges, small differences in pH do not appear to markedly affect flavor. Generally, typical cake flavors are best and most pronounced if the cake is slightly acid or neutral. Chocolate and devil's food cakes are exceptions because they require an alkaline pH for characteristic flavor and color (Ash and Colmey, 1973). The pigments in chocolate change in color with a changing pH. A chocolate cake will vary from a cinnamon color at a pH of 5.5 to a brown color at pH 7.0. As the pH increases above 7.0, the crumb becomes a darker brown and then starts to take on a reddish cast at pH values near or above 8.0. The Maillard reaction increases with increasing alkalinity.

Table 31.1 Typical Cake pH Values

Type of Cake	pH Range
Chocolate	7.5–8.0
Devils food	8.0–9.0
White layer	7.0–7.5
Yellow layer	6.7–7.5

Source: From Ash and Colmey, 1973

Therefore, as the pH of the cake batter is increased, the rate or degree of crust browning increases. The texture of cakes is very fine at low pH values and the volume is decreased. As the pH is raised above the optimum range, the grain becomes more open and coarse with thick cell walls (Ash and Colmey, 1973).

FORMULA BALANCE

The rules for formula balance have changed with the development of new emulsifier systems and with the use of fluid cake shortening in commercial operations. The following rules have been suggested (Lawson, 1970):

1. The weight of the sugar should exceed the weight of the flour. Most cakes made by wholesale bakers have a sugar : flour ratio of about 115 : 100. This may range from 120 to 140 : 100 for high quality white and yellow layer cakes.
2. The weight of the shortening should generally not exceed the weight of the eggs.
3. The weight of the liquid (fluid milk or water and eggs) should equal or exceed the weight of the sugar. Higher levels of liquids may be used with fluid cake shortenings than with plastic fat products.

31.2

STRUCTURE

In cake batter, fat globules are dispersed throughout an aqueous medium. Other ingredients are suspended or dissolved in the aqueous phase. Sugars and salts are in true solution. Proteins are colloidally dispersed and starch granules are suspended in the watery base. Air is also dispersed in the batter to produce a foam. Carlin (1944) studied the structure of cake batters microscopically. He reported that tiny bubbles of air are enclosed in "lakes" of fat during mixing. Little, if any, liquid appears to be emulsified in the fat. During baking, the fat melts and releases its suspended air to the aqueous medium. Carlin further suggested that gas produced by baking powder goes into the air spaces already existing within the batter. Movement of air spaces occurs at all times during the baking process until the structure is set.

Other researchers have also reported that air is dispersed in the fat globules of cake batter. Mackey (1955) found the clustering of closely packed small air bubbles within fat particles in freshly prepared cake batters. The air bubble clusters were much less numerous in frozen batters. However, the air remained dispersed in the fat globules even after freezing.

A different arrangement of air bubbles was reported by Pohl *et al.* (1968) when cake batter was prepared for microscopic study through the technique of freeze-drying, followed by fixation and staining of the fat, infiltration with paraffin, and sectioning. Microscopic examination of cake batter prepared in this way revealed an emulsion of fat in an aerated aqueous phase. This structure is shown in Figure 31.4. The fat, which appears black in the photograph, is dispersed throughout the aqueous starch-protein system. The air bubbles are also dispersed in the aqueous medium rather than in the fat. However, Pohl *et al.* suggested that fat aided in aeration because gas pockets formed most readily at points of cleavage between fat globules and the watery portion of the dough mass. The dispersion of air in water in cake batters may make easier the visualization of steam and carbon dioxide diffusing into the already formed air bubbles, as has been suggested. Diffusion would apparently be more difficult if the air cells were entrapped in fat (Paul and Palmer, 1972). The precise distribution of air and fat in cake batter remains to be clarified, however.

Howard (1972) studied the role of essential layer cake ingredients in the formation of the porous, expanded structure of the finished cake. For this purpose, he divided the baking cycle into three stages: aeration during batter mixing, the early stage of baking while the batter emulsion is still fluid, and the thermal-setting stage when starch gelatinizes. He suggested that soluble protein is the key aerating ingredient, being responsible for the incorporation of air. This protein may come from the eggs and milk in the batter. The emulsifiers, particularly those having the ability to form alpha crystals at the fat–water interface, contribute to aeration indirectly. They surround the fat phase and prevent it from interfering with the foaming properties of the proteins.

Figure 31.4

Photomicrograph of cake batter made with a common household shortening. Fat is stained black, air bubbles are clear, aqueous phase is lacy in appearance, and starch grains may be clearly seen. (Reprinted with permission from Pohl, P. H., A. C. Mackey, and B. L. Cornelia. 1968. Freeze-drying cake batter for microscopic study. *Journal of Food Science* 33, 318.)

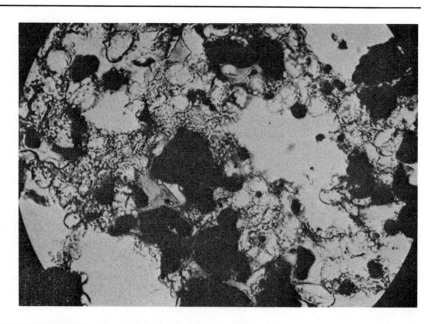

Howard suggested that most of the air is present within the fat phase, except when mixing is done by the single-stage method. In this case, the air is dispersed in the aqueous phase. During baking, the fat gradually melts and releases air bubbles into the aqueous phase. The batter is stabilized in the early baking period by the soluble proteins, polyvalent cations such as calcium, and surface active lipids such as stearic acid. The gelatinization of starch is primarily responsible for the setting of a solid, porous structure during the final stages of baking. Wheat starch absorbs water and gelatinizes at the baking temperatures usually achieved.

31.3

MIXING METHODS

The mixing method plays an important role in the production of quality cakes. Many methods have been used to mix cakes both by hand and by machine. In addition to the conventional cake and muffin methods described in Section 29.2, methods have included the conventional-meringue; the pastry-blend; and the single-stage, one-bowl, or quick-mix.

In the *conventional-meringue method,* approximately half of the sugar is beaten into egg whites to form a meringue. This is added to the batter at the end of mixing by the conventional method in which egg yolk rather than whole egg is added to the creamed fat and sugar mixture. The *pastry-blend method* involves first blending together the fat and flour. Sugar, baking powder, and half of the milk are then mixed with the fat–flour blend. This is followed by the egg and the remainder of the milk. The *quick-mix* method is the method most commonly used at home. In this method, all of the ingredients, including plastic fat at room temperature, are mixed together in a single step or in two steps. If two steps are used, part of the liquid and the eggs are added in the second phase of mixing.

The commercial baker generally uses a two-stage method of mixing in which part of the liquid ingredients are added in the second stage. The use of fluid cake shortenings facilitates the bulk handling of ingredients. Fluid shortening may be metered and pumped easily. *Continuous cake mixing systems* are also in operation. In this case ingredients are usually premixed into a slurry and continuously fed into a final mixer (Lawson, 1970).

Hunter *et al.* (1950) compared the conventional, pastry-blend, and one-bowl methods of mixing cakes made with hydrogenated shortening, margarine, or lard. The method of mixing affected the density of batters, depending upon the kind of fat and the temperature of the ingredients. The pastry-blend method appeared to be adapted to a wider range of ingredient conditions for the production of high quality cakes than was the conventional method.

31.4

BAKING

The size and shape of the baking pan affects cake quality. Charley (1952) found that cakes baked in shallow pans tended to be larger and more tender than those baked in deep pans when the amount of batter was proportional to the size of the pans. A humped crust with a crack tended to form on the tops of cakes baked in deep pans because crust formed while batter was still soft in the center of the pan.

The material of which a baking pan is made affects the rate of heat penetration and the speed of baking. Dark colored pans with a dull finish promote rapid baking because they absorb heat readily and transmit it to the batter. Charley (1950) reported that there was a greater tendency for the tops of cakes to hump and for browning to be uneven and excessive when the cakes were baked at 185°C (365°F) in dark or dull pans that when they were baked in pans with a bright finish. It was not possible to compensate for the effects of the baking pan material by adjusting the oven temperature (Charley, 1956).

Oven temperature affects heat penetration and the quality of the cake. Jooste and Mackey (1952) baked cakes at oven temperatures of 149°, 163°, 191°, and 218°C (300°, 325°, 375°, and 425°F). Cake quality improved with each temperature increase. Cakes baked at the higher temperatures had small air cells with thin cell walls. The crusts were thin and tender. Cakes had some tendency to peak when baked at 218°C.

31.5

CAKE MIXES

Since World War II, the use of cake mixes by the homemaker for the preparation of all types of cakes has gradually expanded. The first mixes on the market had a very short shelf life and were frequently unusable after a few weeks or months (Matz *et al.,* 1955). Many improvements in cake mixes have been implemented over the past few decades.

Several factors may affect the storage life of a mix. Dried eggs, particularly whole eggs, have limited keeping quality and decrease the stability of the mix. For this reason, and also because the consumer may prefer to add fresh eggs when the cake is prepared, dried eggs are omitted from most cake mixes marketed today. Shortening may become rancid on storage. Antioxidants are used to retard the onset of rancidity. Emulsifiers are added to improve the baking characteristics of the fat. Phosphate baking powders that dissolve slowly, including sodium aluminum phosphate and sodium acid pyrophosphate, aid in avoiding the premature action of the leavening agent during storage. A low moisture level in the flour is essential in preventing the loss of carbon dioxide from the baking powder in the mix. Matz *et al.* (1955) reported that cake mixes formulated with flour of 7.4 percent moisture content or less were generally resistant to loss of leavening gas during storage for periods up to 18 months. Modified starches, lecithin, and various vegetable gums are often added to cake mixes as stabilizers and improvers.

SUMMARY

Shortened cake batter is a complex multi-component system. Ingredients interact in a variety of ways. Flour, sugar, fat, liquid, eggs, leavening agent, and flavoring materials are usually included. A short patent cake flour of low protein content is commonly used. The flour is treated with chlorine for an improving effect. Although gluten makes a small contribution to cake structure, gelatinization of starch granules is of major importance.

Sugar tenderizes and gives flavor to a shortened cake. With higher proportions of sugar and fat, the cell structure of the cakes is fine and uniform and the crumb is velvety and tender. High levels of sugar inhibit starch gelatinization and gluten formation, however, and high sugar cakes require additional beating to avoid a coarse texture. A high fructose corn sirup has been successfully substituted for 80 percent of the sucrose in a layer cake. Crystalline sugar aids in the incorporation of air into fats during creaming. The chief functions of fat in shortened cakes are to impart moistness, tenderness, and keeping quality. Fat also plays a critical role in incorporating air into the batter. A variety of fats may be used in cake production. Hydrogenated fats produce cakes of fine, even grain. Cakes made with butter are tender and velvety. Mono- and diglycerides added to shortening as emulsifiers cause the fat to be more finely dispersed in cake batter. The batter is also better aerated and the finished cake has an increased volume and a fine texture. Emulsifiers extend the effectiveness of shortening. They aid in aerating the batter, lubricate the movement of other ingredients, and retard staling. Newer emulsifiers produce marked improvement in emulsification and air incorporation over mono- and diglycerides. They form strong films around fat globules and possibly prevent them from interfering with the foaming ability of soluble proteins in the batter.

Milk is the liquid usually employed in cakes. The milk solids contribute to browning. Milk proteins aid in stabilizing the foam in cake batter and contribute to cake structure. The concentration of liquid has a critical effect on the extent of starch gelatinization during baking, which in turn determines the type of crumb structure formed. Eggs play an important role in stabilizing the foam structure. Upon heating (baking) they coagulate and act as the toughening components of cakes.

The pH of a cake is usually controlled by adjusting the chemical leavening components. Baking powder is commonly used for the production of carbon dioxide but buttermilk and soda may be employed. The final pH affects cake color, flavor, volume, and texture. The pigments in chocolate change color with changing pH. They are dark brown or red at alkaline pH levels. The texture of cakes becomes coarse and open as the pH is raised to very alkaline values.

Some rules for formula balance have been suggested. The weight of the sugar should exceed the weight of the flour. The weight of the shortening should not exceed the weight of the eggs. The weight of the liquids should equal or exceed the weight of the sugar.

Fat globules are dispersed throughout an aqueous medium in cake batter. Other ingredients are suspended or dissolved in the aqueous phase. Several investigators have reported that air is dispersed in the globules or "lakes" of fat during mixing. Using a freeze-drying technique for the preparation of slides, however, air appeared to be dispersed in the aqueous phase. The precise distribution of air and fat in cake batter remains to be clarified. It has been suggested that soluble protein is the key aerating ingredient in cake batter. The emulsifier indirectly contributes to aeration by encapsulating the fat globules so that they do not interfere with the action of the proteins. The batter is stabilized in the early baking period by the soluble proteins, polyvalent cations, and surface active lipids. The gelatinization of starch sets the solid, porous structure during the final stages of baking.

Mixing methods for cakes include the conventional, muffin, conventional-meringue, pastry-blend, and one-bowl or quick-mix. The quick-mix method is most commonly used at home. It requires higher proportions of sugar and liquid than do other methods.

Several factors concerned with baking affect the quality of a shortened cake. These include size and shape of the baking pan, the material of which the pan is made, and the oven temperature. Oven temperatures of 191° and 218°C produce improved quality over temperatures of 149° and 163°C.

The use of commercial cake mixes has greatly expanded since World War II. The shelf life and quality of the mixes has gradually improved. Antioxidants retard the development of rancidity. Emulsifiers improve the baking characteristics of the fat. Slow dissolving phosphate baking powders are used. A low flour moisture level prevents loss of carbon dioxide from the premature action of baking powder. Various stabilizers and improvers are often added.

STUDY QUESTIONS

Each ingredient in shortened cakes plays a specific role(s) in the production of the finished cake.

1. Explain the major purpose(s) of flour, sugar, fat, liquid, eggs, and leavening agent in the production of shortened cakes.
2. Describe and explain the expected results in baked cakes from: too much

sugar, too little beating, too much fat, too much flour, too much liquid, too many eggs, too much baking powder, and too little baking powder.

3. Suggest several rules for balancing ingredients in a shortened cake formula.
4. A baked yellow layer cake is evenly browned but has a slightly concave center. The surface of the cake is not particularly bright or glistening in appearance. The texture of the cut cake is open and coarse appearing. The cake is crumbly. Some individuals who taste it find it has a slightly bitter aftertaste. Suggest what might have produced this type of cake and why. Recommend to the young cook who prepared it what might be done to assure a finer texture, symmetrical appearance, and acceptable flavor when the cake is made again.

Several factors operate and interact to determine the structure of cake batter and the finished cake.

5. Describe and explain the effects of an added emulsifier on a cake batter and on the finished cake. Compare the effects of mono-diglycerides to those of emulsifiers such as lactoylated glycerides and 1-acetyl-3-monostearin.
6. Describe the probable structure of a shortened cake batter and explain how this changes to produce typical characteristics of a good quality finished cake.
7. Describe several methods for mixing shortened cakes. How would you decide which method to use and why?

Commercial cake mixes are specially formulated and packaged to achieve good storage life and quality.

8. Describe and explain special precautions that are used in producing cake mixes for usual market channels.

REFERENCES

1. Ash, D. J. and J. C. Colmey. 1973. The role of pH in cake baking. *Bakers Digest* 47 (No. 1), 36.

2. Carlin, G. T. 1944. A microscopic study of the behavior of fats in cake batters. *Cereal Chemistry* 21, 189.

3. Charley, H. 1956. Characteristics of shortened cake baked in a fast- and in a slow-baking pan at different oven temperatures. *Food Research* 21, 302.

4. Charley, H. 1952. Effects of the size and shape of the baking pan on the quality of shortened cakes. *Journal of Home Economics* 44, 115.

5. Charley, H. 1950. Effect of baking pan material on heat penetration during baking and on quality of cakes made with fat. *Food Research* 15, 155.

6. Dunn, J. A. and J. R. White. 1937. Factor control in cake baking. *Cereal Chemistry* 14, 783.

7. Howard, N. B. 1972. The role of some essential ingredients in the formation of layer cake structures. *Bakers Digest* 46 (Oct.), 28.

8. Howard, N. B., D. H. Hughes, and R. G. K. Strobel. 1968. Function of the starch granule in the formation of layer cake structure. *Cereal Chemistry* 45, 329.

9. Hunt, F. E. and M. E. Green. 1955. Physical properties of cake as affected by method of butter manufacture and addition of an emulsifying agent. *Food Technology* 9, 241.

10. Hunter, M. B., A. M. Briant, and C. J. Personius. 1950. Cake quality and batter structure. Cornell University Agricultural Experiment Station Bulletin No. 860.

11. Jooste, M. E. and A. O. Mackey. 1952. Cake structure and palatability as affected by emulsifying agents and baking temperatures. *Food Research* 17, 185.

12. Lawson, H. W. 1970. Functions and applications of ingredients for cake. *Bakers Digest* 44 (Dec.), 36.

13. Mackey, A. O. 1955. Microscopic structure of frozen cake batters. *Food Technology* 9, 261.

14. Matthews, R. H. and E. H. Dawson. 1966. Performance of fats in white cake. *Cereal Chemistry* 43, 538.

15. Matz, S. C., C. S. McWilliams, R. A. Larsen, J. H. Mitchell, Jr., J. McMullen, and B. Layman. 1955. The effect of variations in moisture content on the storage deterioration rate of cake mixes. *Food Technology* 9, 276.

16. Miller, B. S. and H. B. Trimbo. 1965. Gelatinization of starch and white layer cake quality. *Food Technology* 19, 208.

17. Moncrieff, J. 1970. Shortenings and emulsifiers for cakes and icings. *Bakers Digest* 44 (Oct.), 60.

18. Paul, P. C. and H. H. Palmer. 1972. *Food Theory and Applications*. New York: Wiley.

19. Pohl, P. H., A. C. Mackey, and B. L. Cornelia. 1968. Freeze-drying cake batter for microscopic study. *Journal of Food Science* 33, 318.

20. Pyke, W. E. and G. Johnson. 1940. Relation of mixing methods and a balanced formula to quality and economy in high-sugar-ratio cakes. *Food Research* 5, 335.

21. Shellenberger, J. A., F. W. Wichser, and R. C. Lakamp. 1950. Cake properties in relation to flour particle size fractions. *Cereal Chemistry* 27, 106.

22. Volpe, T. and C. Meres. 1976. Use of high fructose syrups in white layer cake. *Bakers Digest* 50 (Apr.), 38.

23. Wilson, J. T. and D. H. Donelson. 1963. Studies on the dynamics of cake-baking. I. The role of water in formation of layer cake structure. *Cereal Chemistry* 40, 466.

24. Wootton, J. C., N. B. Howard, J. B. Martin, D. E. McOsker, and J. Holme. 1967. The role of emulsifiers in the incorporation of air into layer cake batter systems. *Cereal Chemistry* 44, 333.

CHAPTER 32

YEAST BREADS

Breadmaking is an ancient art. Its development, from the simple unleavened product made in early times to the complex mixture produced in the mechanized bakeries of modern society, has paralleled the development of man's civilization. Most of the bread consumed in the United States today is produced in commercial bakeries. Many changes have occurred in bakery technology, even in recent years. Continuous breadmaking processes carried out in large, consolidated operations require carefully specified ingredients of uniform quality.

Although much of the bread consumed today is commercially produced, breadmaking at home is still a popular art. The methods and equipment used at home are vastly different from those commonly employed commercially. However, the same basic principles controlling quality in the finished product are operating in both the industrial bakery and the home kitchen.

32.1

INGREDIENTS

A Standard of Identity for bread has been established by the U. S. Food and Drug Administration. It prescribes certain ingredients, specifically flour, water, yeast, and salt. Bread may be made with only these ingredients, but usually contains others as well. A number of ingredients are listed as optional. These include shortening, milk, sugars, and eggs. Other optional ingredients that may be added by the commercial baker include dough softeners or emulsifiers, malt, enzyme preparations, yeast food, oxidizing agents, and preservatives.

As bread is made in the home it commonly contains flour, yeast, milk, salt, sugar, and fat. Milk (or other liquid), salt, sugar, and fat are usually mixed together in fixed amounts in any one recipe or formulation. The amount of flour added to a specified quantity of the liquid mixture varies, depending upon its absorptive properties. High protein flour generally absorbs more liquid than does a flour of lower protein content. The amount of yeast may be varied in accordance with the desired fermentation time. Eggs are sometimes used as ingredients in yeast breads. They provide color and contribute to the structure of the loaf as their proteins are coagulated by heating.

YEAST

Yeast is a microscopic one-celled plant, belonging to the group of plants without stems or chlorophyll that are called *fungi*. Yeast differs from other fungi, such as molds and mushrooms, in that it usually multiplies by a process called *budding* (see Figures 32.1 and 32.2). Yeast ferments sugar to produce ethanol, carbon dioxide (CO_2), and various by-products. (Some characteristics of yeast are discussed in Section 5.2.)

The yeast that is used in breadmaking is *Saccharomyces cerevisiae*, commonly called *baker's yeast*. The basic functions of yeast in the making of bread are 1. to leaven the dough by the CO_2 that it produces, 2. to contribute to bread flavor as a consequence of the formation of alcohols, acids, esters, and other flavor precursors, and 3. to participate in dough development as a result of the total fermentation process (Cooper and Reed, 1968). Dough development during fermentation results from a number of effects on other components of the system. For example, CO_2 contributes to a decrease in pH that may affect gluten proteins. The expansion of the dough by the CO_2 affects the extensibility of the gluten structure. Various enzymes produced by the yeast catalyze oxidation–reduction reactions that involve other substances in the dough. Many complex interactions occur.

The production and marketing of live microorganisms, as is carried out by the yeast industry, requires considerable technology. Environmental conditions must be carefully controlled at all times. Strains of *S. cerevisiae* are selected for qualities that are important in baking, including good CO_2 production, development of desirable flavor, and adequate keeping qualities. Cultures may be gradually built up from single

Figure 32.1

Two stages in the commercial production of yeast, illustrating the budding phenomenon by which yeast cells propagate (1200× magnification). (Reprinted with permission from Buckheit, J. T. 1971. Yeast, its controlled handling in the bakery. *Bakers Digest* 45 [Feb.], 46.)

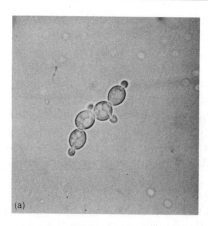 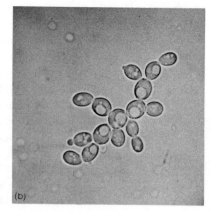

(a) (b)

Figure 32.2

A scanning electron photomicrograph of bakers yeast. (Reprinted with permission from Magoffin, C. D. and R. C. Hoseney. 1974. A review of fermentation. *Bakers Digest* 48 [Dec.], 22.)

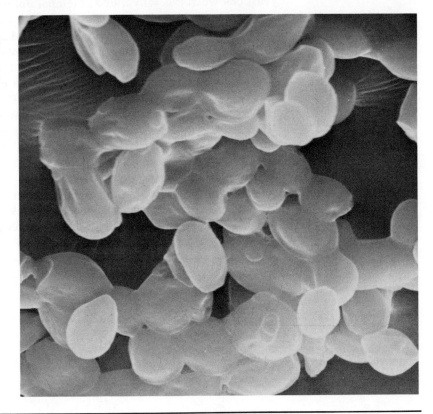

cell isolates. Compressed yeast, which is used predominantly by the baking industry, contains 69–71 percent moisture and 20–24 billion cells per wet gram. Although it is perishable, it loses little fermentation power during refrigeration for four to five weeks and can be stored in the frozen state for months (Matz, 1960). However, compressed yeast is particularly sensitive to temperatures above 30°C (86°F) and loses fermentation power when stored at these temperatures (Hautera and Lovgren, 1975). Heat activates proteolytic enzymes present in the yeast cell and, under extreme conditions, the cell may destroy itself in a process called *autolysis* (Buckheit, 1971).

Active dry yeast is prepared from certain strains of baker's yeast that possess special abilities to withstand the drying treatment. The dried product is ground and packaged in sealed containers. Prepared bread and roll mixes generally contain active dry yeast. It is the least stable component of these mixes (Stacey, 1964). Active dry yeast should be rehydrated in water at 37.8°–46°C (100°–115°F). At higher temperatures the yeast will be inactivated. At lower temperatures the normal cell constituents tend to be leached out of the cell. *Glutathione,* a *reducing tripeptide,* is one of the substances that is leached from the yeast cell when it is rehydrated at temperatures below 38°C. In excessive amounts, this substance causes bread dough to soften because of the reducing effect it has on flour proteins (Matz, 1960).

Yeast has an optimal pH range for fermentation of 4–6, but it can tolerate extremes of pH for short periods of time. Temperature has a large effect on the rate of fermentation. Glucose fermentation by yeast was reported to be twice as fast at 35°C (95°F) as at 25°C (77°F). However, as the temperature increases above 38°–42°C (100.4°–107.6°F), the rate of yeast inactivation may more than balance the increase in fermentation rate (Pomper, 1969). A temperature of about 30°–35°C (86°–95°F) is probably optimal for dough fermentation.

Osmotic pressure produced in the dough by solutes affects yeast activity. Figure 32.3 shows the inhibiting effect of sugar concentration on the rate of yeast fermentation. Increased levels of yeast are required in sweet doughs containing more than 10 percent sugar to achieve the

Figure 32.3

Effect of sugar concentration on the rate of yeast fermentation. (From Pomper, S. 1969. Biochemistry of yeast fermentation. *Bakers Digest* 43 [Apr.], 32. With permission.)

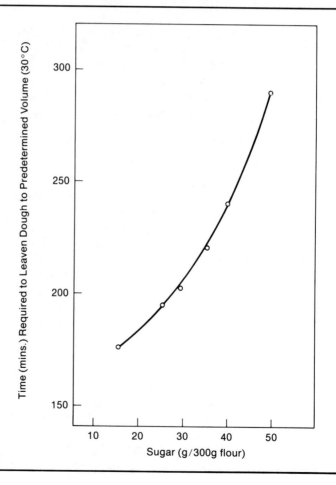

same rate of fermentation as occurs in doughs with lesser amounts of this substance. Salt also increases osmotic pressure and restricts the rate of yeast fermentation. High osmotic pressure probably has a dehydrating effect on the yeast cells (Pomper, 1969).

For optimum yeast activity, required nutritional factors must be present in the dough. The yeast requires sources of carbon, nitrogen, potassium, magnesium, sulfur, phosphorus, thiamin, pyridoxine, and nicotinic acid. While yeast food other than the usual dough ingredients is not commonly used when bread is made at home, it is usually added by commercial bakers. Calcium and ammonium salts are common ingredients of yeast food mixtures. Calcium also has a toughening effect on doughs.

The fermentation of sugar by yeast is generally an anaerobic process and it involves a large number of biochemical reactions. The overall reaction is:

$$C_6H_{12}O_6 \rightarrow 2C_2H_5OH + 2CO_2$$
$$\text{glucose} \quad\quad \text{ethanol} \quad\quad \text{carbon dioxide}$$

The yeast cell elaborates many enzymes that catalyze various steps in the overall reaction. In addition, some enzymes such as beta-amylase are present in flour and play a role in the fermentation process.

The sugar substrate for yeast fermentation in dough may come from several sources. First, flour contains small amounts of sugars (about 1.2 percent), including glucose, fructose, sucrose, and other oligosaccharides. Yeast produces an invertase enzyme that in many strains of yeast can hydrolyze not only sucrose but other oligosaccharides as well, yielding simple sugars (Biltcliffe, 1972). Second, beta-amylase activity in flour may produce some maltose from the hydrolysis of starch in damaged granules. Alpha-amylase produces some glucose. Alpha-amylase activity in flour is low but a source of this enzyme is often added in commercial breadmaking. Baker's yeast readily ferments maltose only after the more easily fermentable hexoses, glucose, and fructose, are exhausted from the medium (Pomper, 1969). Third, small quantities of sugar, usually sucrose, are added in making bread dough. Sucrose is hydrolyzed to glucose and fructose by yeast invertase. This provides a readily available substrate for the early production of CO_2 by the yeast cells. When sugar is present, the yeast fermentation of bread dough begins immediately upon mixing. Yeast growth, which involves the production of new yeast cells, does not generally occur in the first two hours of dough fermentation. Some yeast growth takes place in two to four hours, if that much time is allowed before baking, and then growth declines after four to six hours (Frazier, 1967).

A wide variety of compounds has been found in fermented yeast doughs. These include acetone, acetaldehyde, n-butyraldehyde, n-hexanal, pyruvaldehyde, benzaldehyde, acetic acid, lactic acid, pyruvic acid, and various higher alcohols. At least some of these substances probably participate in the development of typical bread flavor (Pomper, 1969).

FLOUR

Wheat flour is unique among the cereal flours in that, when mixed with liquid in correct proportions, the proteins will form an elastic dough structure that is capable of holding gas and which will set to a firm, spongy texture when baked. Production of fine grained bread with large volume in relation to its weight is therefore possible using wheat flour. The wheat proteins, glutenin and gliadin, form the elastic gluten during hydration and mixing. Bread flour is produced from hard wheats that contain relatively high levels of protein. This flour is used by the commercial baker because of the large amount of protein and the strength of the gluten formed. Although bread flour may be used in making bread at home, all-purpose flour is more commonly available and more likely to be used. A satisfactory loaf can be produced with all-purpose flour with the methods commonly employed in home preparation. (The milling of flour is discussed in Section 15.4.)

LIQUID

Water may be used in making bread. However, milk is the liquid more commonly utilized. Reasons for using milk in commercial breadmaking involve added nutrition, finer texture, improved crust and crumb color, flavor, and buffering value. The principal form used is nonfat dry milk (NDM). Various whey products are also used to some extent (Pomeranz, 1971). Due to increasing costs for NDM in recent years, milk replacers containing isolated milk and vegetable proteins have become popular (Cobb, 1976).

If milk is not sufficiently heated before its use in bread, the dough is more slack and sticky than a normal dough and yields loaves with reduced volume, open grain, and poor texture. The volume-depressing factor appears to be associated with the whey proteins of milk. The dough-softening substance seems to be eliminated after an interaction occurs during heating between the whey proteins, especially beta-lactoglobulin, and kappa-casein (Pomeranz, 1971). Special heat-treated milk is available for use by the commercial baker.

Water hydrates proteins and starch in the flour and is essential for gluten development. Flours may absorb liquid in amounts ranging between 50 and 65 percent of the flour weight. Greater amounts of liquid are absorbed by flours with higher protein content. Some of the water is bound rather firmly to the flour protein molecules during the mixing process. Unbound water contributes to dough motility.

SALT

Salt generally improves the taste of bread; however, it has other effects as well. Salt is added in amounts that usually do not exceed about 2 percent of the weight of the flour. It has a stabilizing influence on yeast fermentation, slowing its activity to some degree. Dough made without salt rises very rapidly. Figure 32.4 shows the effect of salt on yeast fermentation. This effect of salt probably results from its influence on the osmotic pressure of the mixture. Salt inhibits the action of proteases in dough. It also has a firming effect on gluten and changes the rheological properties of the dough. The water holding capacity of flour is decreased and the mixing requirement of a dough is increased (Hlynka, 1962). Because of these effects, the presence of salt in a dough mixed by a commercial continuous process may be undesirable. Fortmann *et al.* (1969) suggested the use of salt granules coated with a high melting point edible fat so that they do not dissolve until the later stages of mixing. Special breads without salt are prepared for individuals on low sodium diets.

SUGAR

Sugar provides a readily available substrate for yeast fermentation. The usual amount of sugar added in commercial breads has increased from about 2 percent of the weight of the flour in the 1920s to up to 8 percent in the 1970s. The additional sugar is added primarily to provide residual sweetness to the bread. Corn sweeteners are becoming widely used. Tang *et al.* (1972) reported that breads made with the same ingredients but by different processes varied greatly in the type of residual sugar, although the total content was between 2–3 percent of the moist crumb. Bread made by the straight-dough method had a relatively high maltose content while the glucose and fructose had been largely fermented. Sponge-dough bread contained the least maltose and larger amounts of fructose and glucose.

Figure 32.4

Effect of salt on gassing power of yeast in liquid ferment. (From Fortmann, K., H. Welcker, and F. Barrett. 1969. Effect of modified salt on dough development. *Bakers Digest* **43 [No. 5], 50. With permission.)**

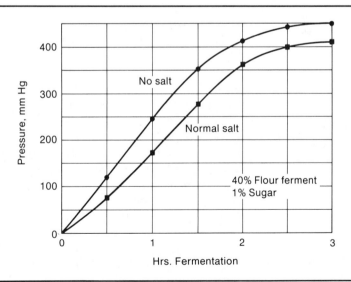

Sugar generally has a tenderizing effect by interfering with gluten development. However, when relatively small amounts of sugar are used in bread this effect is minimal. Tenderization is not the primary purpose of sugar in yeast bread.

FAT

Fat is used in bread because it increases loaf volume, gives a more uniform tender crumb, enhances keeping qualities, and improves slicing properties. The improvement in volume occurs mostly with 0.5–1.5 percent fat. Levels above 3 percent of the weight of the flour do not increase volume further and may actually decrease it to a slight degree. Plastic fats perform more satisfactorily in bread than do oils. An effective fat apparently must provide a sufficient level of solids during the proofing and baking stages (Pomeranz, 1971). Fat improvement in bread is thought to be a purely physical effect of high-melting point lipid finely dispersed through the dough matrix composed of gluten and small amounts of natural flour lipid material. The improvement in volume and texture is mostly seen shortly after the loaf enters the oven when crumb temperature is rising. During this period, the release of CO_2 from the loaf is delayed and the period of loaf expansion is extended when hard fat is present in the dough (Morrison, 1976). Large amounts of fat may physically interfere with the development of gluten strands during mixing.

Shortening mixtures that are fluid at room temperature yet contain about 27 percent saturated fatty acids have become available to the baker in recent years. They generally contain vegetable oil with micro-dispersed hard fats. Monoglycerides or other emulsifiers are added. They offer advantages to the baking industry because they can be automatically measured and pumped in mechanized baking systems (Pomeranz, 1971; Petricca, 1976).

A number of polar and nonpolar lipid materials are naturally present in flour. Although they occur in comparatively minor quantities, they play important roles in the development of gluten in doughs.

ADDITIVES

Several additives are commonly used in commercial bread production. Yeast foods have been previously mentioned. Calcium and ammonium salts present in yeast foods supply the nutrient needs of yeast cells and provide a slight buffering action. Calcium also has a firming effect on gluten. In addition to these salts, yeast foods often contain oxidizing agents, such as potassium or calcium bromates and iodates and azodicarbonamide. Each of the oxidizing agents affects dough a little differently and specific ones are chosen on the basis of the flour quality and production methods used. In general, oxidizing agents appear to oxidize sulfhydryl groups on gluten to disulfide groups (Johnston and Mauseth, 1972; Barrett, 1968). Sulfhydryl groups are potentially capable of undergoing cross-linking reactions as they form disulfide bridges between gluten protein chains, setting the structure of the protein network in the dough.

$$\text{\large$\langle$}\!\!-\text{SH} \quad \text{HS}\!-\!\!\text{\large$\rangle$} \xrightarrow{\text{oxidation}} \text{\large$\langle$}\!\!-\text{S}\!-\!\!-\text{S}\!-\!\!\text{\large$\rangle$}$$

sulfhydryls   disulfide

A wide variety of surface active agents classified as dough conditioners and softeners are available for use in bread and other baked products. Conditioners strengthen the gluten structure of dough and thus improve its gas retaining ability. Examples of these substances include polyoxyethylene monostearate and polysorbate 60. Softeners contribute to an increased shelf life for bread by retarding the firming of the crumb. Monoglycerides are examples of these types of agents. Some substances have both a conditioning and softening effect. Sodium stearoyl-2 lactylate and diacetyltartaric acid esters of monoglycerides are such substances. These additives have a shortening-sparing effect (Knightly, 1973; Tsen and Hoover, 1971; Hoseney *et al.*, 1976).

Enzymes may be added in the preparation of bread dough. Milled flour contains some beta-amylase but little alpha-amylase activity. Alpha-amylase is provided by the addition of malt made from sprouted grains or by use of fungal and bacterial amylase preparations. Good gassing power is achieved in dough when both beta- and alpha-amylases are present. Alpha-amylase acts on damaged starch granules and breaks them into dextrins. Beta-amylase converts the resulting dextrins into maltose. The action of these enzymes is described in Section 16.2. Alpha-amylase may continue to produce dextrins during the early stages of baking bread. Malt sources of alpha-amylase are not rapidly denatured until the temperature of the loaf reaches about 75°C (167°F). Wheat starch begins to gelatinize between 60°–75°C (between 140°–167°F) and thereby provides starch that is available for enzyme attack. Beta-amylase is destroyed at a lower temperature than is alpha-amylase and dextrins produced by alpha-amylase may accumulate in the bread. A small quantity of dextrins has a softening effect on the baked product. However, excessive alpha-amylase activity leads to stickiness and decreased volume (Cole, 1973; Finney *et al.*, 1972).

Proteases from fungal or vegetable sources are sometimes added to bread dough in carefully controlled amounts. Their major function is to partially degrade gluten proteins, thereby reducing the required input of mechanical energy during mixing. Protease treatment also provides improved dough handling properties and increased dough extensibility (Cole, 1973).

White bread produced commercially often contains the antimolding agents, sodium or calcium propionate. These substances also inhibit the growth of the spore-forming organism, *Bacillus subtilis* var. *mesen-*

tericus, which causes a condition known as *rope. Ropy bread* is characterized by the presence in the crumb of yellow-brown sticky spots and an objectionable odor that has been described as being similar to that of overripe melon. Hydrolytic enzymes produced by the bacterium are apparently responsible for the effects. Acid conditions in the dough discourage proliferation of this bacterium (Kent, 1975).

The importance of dietary fiber in nutrition has been emphasized and bread has been proposed as a vehicle for fiber enrichment. The commercial production of low-calorie, high-fiber breads has been described, the breads ranging in fiber content from 4.5 to 7.5 percent. The major source of fiber in these breads is cellulose, although wheat bran has also been used. The addition of wheat gluten in high-fiber breads is necessary to alleviate the increased strain on the natural gluten in terms of bread structure that results from the additional cellulose or bran material. Some of the major problems in the commercial production of high-fiber breads are weakness of the dough, blisters, and holes under the top crust. The use of a strong wheat flour and optimizing yeast and bread additives are aids in the production of a high-fiber bread of acceptable quality (Pomeranz, 1977).

32.2

MIXING THE DOUGH

Bread is made by mixing ingredients into a dough and allowing the dough to ferment at a temperature of 27°–30°C (80.6°–86°F) before baking. Either a straight-dough or sponge method may be satisfactorily employed in mixing the dough.

When bread is mixed at home by the straight dough method, milk is scalded to prevent later softening of the dough and then cooled to the proper temperature for yeast dispersion, which varies with the type of yeast used. The softened shortening, sugar, and salt are dispersed in the liquid. Flour is gradually added to the liquid mixture until a soft dough is formed. The dough is kneaded to adequately develop the gluten into an elastic mass that will retain gas during fermentation and proofing. The process of kneading is illustrated in Figure 32.5. (The gluten complex is discussed in Section 28.2 and its relationship to baking quality is described in Section 28.4.)

The sponge method of mixing dough involves combining all of the liquid with the yeast and part of the flour and allowing this batter (sponge) to ferment for some hours before completing the mixing of the dough. Part of the sugar may be added to the sponge, if desired, but the salt and fat are withheld until after the sponge has undergone fermentation. The remainder of the flour is then added and mixing completed as in the straight-dough method. The straight-dough method is most commonly used for making bread at home.

Adequate development of the gluten structure in dough during the

Figure 32.5

Kneading yeast dough. (Courtesy U. S. Department of Agriculture.)

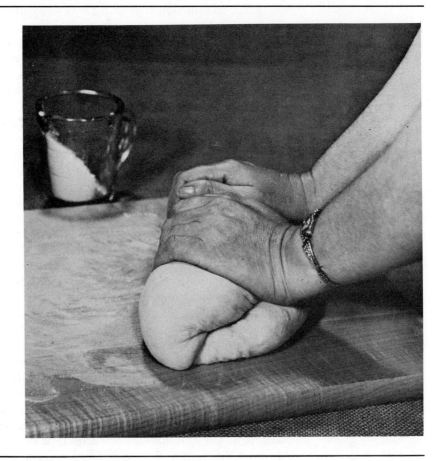

process of mixing is essential to the preparation of high quality bread. Little research has been reported on the preparation of whole wheat bread. Desirable characteristics in baked white bread are fine grain with thin cell walls, uniform texture, tender though elastic crumb, well shaped symmetrical appearance of the loaf, relatively large volume in proportion to weight, and golden brown crust color. To achieve these characteristics the dough should be smooth, elastic, and nonsticky. It should be extensible but not too soft. Numerous air cells are incorporated into the dough during mixing, surrounded by thin elastic gluten walls. These are expanded as carbon dioxide is produced during fermentation. Optimum mixing depends on the flour strength and formulation of the mixture. A bread dough may be overkneaded, in which case the gluten loses its elasticity and strength, the volume of the loaf is low, and the texture is coarse. Dough is not likely to be overkneaded when this operation is performed by hand. However, overmixing may occur when bread is made with an electric mixer. Bread mixers have dough hooks that mix the dough in such a way as to allow maximum development of the gluten strands.

Continuous breadmaking is a commercial process that substitutes intense mechanical energy to a large degree for traditional bulk fermentation. A critical speed and energy input are necessary to bring about satisfactory development of the gluten network in dough (Tipples and Kilborn, 1974). A liquid ferment of yeast, containing all of the yeast for the formula, about 15–20 percent of the water, and a small part of the sugar, is prepared separate from the dough. The purpose of the ferment is to precondition and stimulate the yeast for uniform and optimum gassing power and to develop flavor components (Olsen, 1974). The yeast ferment is blended with other ingredients into a homogeneous dough that is then pumped to the developer for intense mixing and is extruded directly into baking pans without a fermentation period. This procedure reduces processing time and floor space in the commercial bakery and saves labor costs (Pomeranz, 1971).

Dough development may also be accelerated by the use of reducing substances such as the amino acid cysteine. This treatment is followed by oxidation with bromate or other oxidizing agents. With these added chemical substances and their effects on the gluten proteins, mixing action and fermentation may be less intense (Tsen, 1970 and 1973).

Several instruments are used in the laboratory to give some indication of dough handling properties for various flour samples. For example, the *farinograph* is a recording dough mixer. It records on a graph the resistance that the dough offers to the mixing blades during a prolonged and relatively gentle mixing action at constant temperature. The shape of the curve gives information concerning the mixing behavior of the dough. The *mixograph* is a second type of recording dough mixer. An instrument called the *extensigraph* measures the extensibility of a piece of dough. A cylinder of dough is stretched to the breaking point and the force required for this operation is recorded on a graph (Shuey, 1963).

32.3

FERMENTATION AND PROOFING

After the dough has been developed by mixing and kneading, it is placed in a warm environment (usually 25°–30°C) for several hours as fermentation proceeds. Dough development occurs during fermentation as well as during mixing. The changes in dough structure during fermentation appear to be separate and different from those occurring during mixing. Fermentation apparently has a pronounced effect on the nature of the gluten complex. During this period a balance is produced between gluten's ability to form thin, extensible films and the properties of the dough that allow for maximum gas retention by these films. The final balance may result from a combination of proteolysis, accumulated fermentation by-products, and hydrogen ion concentration change affecting the colloidal behavior of gluten (Magoffin and Hoseney, 1974).

The decrease in pH that occurs during fermentation results chiefly from production of carbon dioxide and lactic acid and from assimilation of ammonia. The reduction of pH significantly affects the hydration and swelling of gluten, the reaction rate of enzymes, and various other chemical reactions. Production of some acid favors the action of amylases in dough. Gluten becomes less soluble, less sticky, and more extensible as the pH of dough decreases from about 6 to 5.5–5.0. Oxidation occurring in the dough may affect the sulfhydryl groups, as discussed in Section 32.1. The extent of this process during fermentation has not been clarified.

After the dough has risen until it is doubled or tripled in volume, it is punched down to bring about a subdivision of gas cells and a uniform distribution throughout the dough. A test for sufficient lightness in bread dough made at home is shown in Figure 32.6. If depressions in the dough do not immediately fill in because of dough elasticity, it is light enough to be molded into a loaf.

Figure 32.6

A test for dough lightness. (Courtesy U. S. Department of Agriculture.)

The structure of fermented bread dough was examined by Bechtel *et al.* (1978) with use of electron microscopy. After mixing, the gluten strands provided a matrix network in the dough, as shown in Figure 32.7. Small vacuoles could be seen in the gluten. Starch granules were surrounded by thin protein sheets and strands. Yeast cells were evenly distributed throughout the dough. Large lipid droplets that were formed from the added shortening were also scattered in the dough and did not seem to be consistently associated with either protein or starch. After fermentation and before punching down, the structure appeared to be similar except that gas vacuoles had started to form because of the action of the yeast. Figure 32.8 shows the dough after the first punching down. Fine protein strands, dispersed starch granules, and shortening globules can be seen. The number of vacuoles in the gluten had decreased from the unfermented dough. In these studies, Bechtel *et al.* found that poor quality flours gave protein strands that broke

Figure 32.7

An electron photomicrograph of optimally mixed complete dough shows yeast cell (Y), highly vacuolated protein strand (P) surrounding shortening (S) and starch granule (ST). (Figures 32.7, 32.8, and 32.9 courtesy of Donald B. Bechtel, North Central Region U. S. Grain Marketing Research Laboratory. Reprinted from Bechtel, D. B., Y. Pomeranz, and A. de Francisco. 1978. Breadmaking studied by light and transmission electron microscopy. *Cereal Chemistry* 55, 392.)

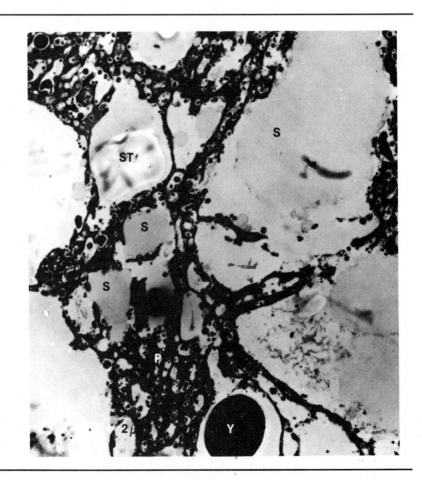

Figure 32.8

An electron photomi-crograph of complete dough after first punch. Note fine protein strands (*arrow*), starch granule (*ST*) and shor-tening (*S*). Also note that the number of vacuoles has decreased com-pared with optimally mixed dough (Figure 32.7).

easily. Overmixed doughs also contained broken protein strands and many large vacuoles were seen in the protein.

Proofing is the process of allowing the dough to rise in the pan after fermentation before baking. A temperature of 25°–30°C (77°–86°F) should be maintained during this process as the dough approximately doubles in volume. If proofing is continued until the dough is too light, the texture of the baked loaf is coarse and crumbly. If proofing is insufficient, the loaf shows wide and broken margin (shred) along one or both sides where expansion occurs after the crust has started to set.

32.4

BAKING

Dough is transformed into bread by the process of baking. During this short period of time, the pale, plastic dough rapidly expands and then sets to a self-supporting structure with a soft but resilient internal tex-ture and an attractive outer color and appearance. The physical and chemical changes taking place during baking are complex and depend on a number of interacting factors (Marston and Wannan, 1976).

Within the first few minutes of baking, the volume of the loaf in-creases markedly in what is called *oven spring*. Adequate volume in-crease is dependent upon the ability of the cell walls in the dough to stretch evenly while still retaining gas up to the point that they become rigid. Yeast activity is initially stimulated by heat and the release of carbon dioxide provides the main impetus for cell expansion. The yeast

Figure 32.9

Top center of loaf imme-
diately after baking.
Note gelatinized starch
(*F*) between thin protein
strands. Note lack of
vacuoles in protein (*P*).
Gas vacuoles (*G*).

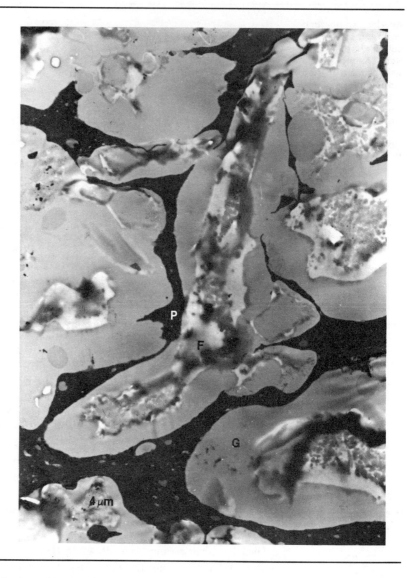

is inactivated at approximately 60°C (140°F). Water is vaporized at higher temperatures and provides steam for further expansion. Alcohol is also vaporized and all of the gasses themselves expand on heating (Marston and Wannan, 1976).

The dough becomes more fluid as the temperature rises to about 65°C (149°F). Hydrolysis of starch by amylases contributes to this change in consistency. Starch gelatinization and protein denaturation by heat then reduce dough fluidity and a semi-rigid structure is formed by the time the temperature reaches 90°C (194°F). Although some water migrates from gluten to starch during baking, the amount of water in the dough is insufficient for the complete gelatinization of starch (Willhoft, 1971). The granules lose birefringence but still retain their shapes. At approximately 95°C (203°F) the structure is well formed. It does not become stable until it has cooled, however. Crust formation gives strength to the hot loaf (Marston and Wannan, 1976).

The evaporation of water from the exposed surface of the bread dries the outer layers of cells and allows the surface temperature to rise well above the boiling point of water. The Maillard reaction proceeds at a significant rate above 160°C (320°F) at the usual pH of dough. This reaction involving aldehyde groups from sugars and amino groups from proteins is primarily responsible for the characteristic brown color of baked bread. Some caramelization of sugar may contribute to crust color when a relatively high proportion of sugar is used. These reactions also contribute to bread flavor.

An electron micrograph of bread immediately after baking is shown in Figure 32.9. Much of the starch is gelatinized. The granules have expanded into long, bulky fibrous strands interwoven with the protein. The gelatinized starch is linked to the protein strands by thin fibrils. The protein has smooth edges and does not contain vacuoles. The shortening is not consistently associated with any structures in baked loaf. Gas vacuoles are dispersed throughout the structure (Bechtel *et al.*, 1978).

32.5

BREAD FLAVOR AND STALING

Few odors produced during food preparation are more appreciated than is the aroma created during the baking of bread. This aroma is undoubtedly related to fermentation by the yeast cells. The use of gas chromatography has helped the researcher to detect and identify many of the volatile compounds in bread that contribute to its characteristic aroma. These include alcohols, acids, esters, and various carbonyl compounds. Total bread aroma is ascribed to a complex mixture of many substances that apparently include more than 60 different compounds (Johnson and Sanchez, 1973).

Organic acids produced during fermentation contribute to the taste of bread. Acid taste is particularly prominent in sour dough breads. Some bitter compounds are formed in the crust through the Maillard reaction. Most white bread made commercially in the United States has enough residual sugar to contribute to a sweet taste. Bakers add sugar because of assumed consumer preference.

Caul and Vaden (1972) applied the flavor profile method to a study of flavor events occurring as white bread aged for 96 hours. The bread was baked by professional bakers, sliced, wrapped, and stored at room temperature. The terms sweet, alcoholic, estery, yeasty, doughy, and wheaty were used to describe the crumb flavor of fresh bread. Sweet, caramel, browned flour, and wheaty depicted its top crust flavor.

Crumb aging was found to be continuous over the 96 hour period. It was reflected by a decrease in the amplitude of the flavor, a loss of sweet aromatics and sweet taste, an increasing sour impression, deterioration in yeast character, and a change from doughy to starchy. The top crust lost amplitude of flavor, sweet aromatics and taste, and developed a flat character.

The staling of bread is a very complex phenomenon. It is not simply a loss of moisture by evaporation. Changes in the starch and other components also take place. During staling there is (Knightly, 1977):

1. a change in taste and aroma.
2. increased hardness, opacity, and crumbliness of crumb.
3. increased starch crystallization.
4. decreased absorptive capacity of crumb.
5. decreased susceptibility of crumb to action of beta-amylase.
6. decreased soluble starch content.

Changes in the starch component of bread appear to be of major importance in the staling process. Aged crumb shows X-ray diffraction patterns that are characteristic of crystalline or retrograded starch. When heated under moist conditions, stale bread reverts to a fresher state and gives diffraction patterns that are less crystalline. Early workers in the field assumed that the amylose fraction of starch was the cause of staling because of its tendency to retrograde. However, later work has pointed to the amylopectin fraction as the most important participant in staling. Amylose is apparently already retrograded and made insoluble by the time the baked bread is cool. It thus seems unlikely that it is the cause of changes occurring with aging. The manner in which amylopectin participates in the staling process requires further clarification. It has been proposed that the branches of the amylopectin molecules within the swollen starch granules of freshly baked bread are dilated and the granules are soft and extensible. During staling, the branched molecules may undergo a sort of retrogradation, whereby the dilated branches gradually fold up and associate with one another. Apparently this produces a slow rigidification of the bread structure (Schoch, 1965). Many questions concerning bread staling remain unanswered. These include questions about the precise roles of the surfactant bread softeners in inhibiting the staling process (Knightly, 1977; Zobel, 1973).

SUMMARY

A Standard of Identity for bread prescribes flour, water, yeast, and salt as ingredients. Optional ingredients include shortening, milk, sugars, and eggs. The commercial baker may also add dough softeners or emulsifiers, malt, enzyme preparations, yeast foods, oxidizing agents, and preservatives.

The yeast that is used in breadmaking is *Saccharomyces cerevisiae*. Its basic functions are 1. to leaven the dough by the carbon dioxide that it produces, 2. to contribute to bread flavor as a consequence of the formation of a number of chemical substances, and 3. to participate in dough development as a result of the total fermentation process.

Strains of *S. cerevisiae* are selected for qualities that are important in baking. Cultures may be gradually built up from single cell isolates. Compressed and dry active yeasts are marketed. Compressed yeast requires refrigeration unless it is frozen. Active dry yeast should be rehydrated in water at 37.8°–46°C to avoid the leaching of cell contents into the liquid. Yeast has an optimal pH range for fermentation of 4–6, but can tolerate extremes of pH for short periods. A temperature of about 30°–35°C is optimal. High osmotic pressure inhibits yeast activity, therefore, salt and sugar, in more than small amounts, significantly decrease the rate of fermentation. Certain nutritional factors are required for optimum yeast activity. Yeast food is commonly added to bread doughs by commercial bakers.

The fermentation of sugar by yeast produces ethanol and carbon dioxide from glucose. The yeast cell elaborates many enzymes that catalyze various steps in this overall reaction. The sugar substrate comes from small amounts already present in flour, that produced by hydrolysis of starch, and sugar added as a dough ingredient.

Wheat flour provides the proteins from which gluten is developed. Bread flour contains more protein than all-purpose flour but satisfactory bread may be made at home using all-purpose flour.

Milk is the liquid most commonly utilized in breadmaking. It adds nutrients; gives a finer texture; improves crust and crumb color and flavor; and has some buffering effect. The principal form used is nonfat dry milk. Milk replacers containing protein isolates are now available. Milk must be adequately heated before its use in bread to eliminate a dough-softening and volume depressing factor that is associated with the protein fraction. Liquid in bread is necessary to hydrate proteins and starch and is essential for gluten development.

Salt improves the taste of bread. However, it also inhibits yeast fermentation and changes the rheological properties of the dough. It has a firming effect on gluten. Although sugar in comparatively large quantities inhibits yeast activity, a small amount provides a readily available substrate for immediate gas production by yeast.

Fat in amounts of up to 3 percent of the weight of the flour increases loaf volume; gives a more uniform, tender crumb; enhances keeping qualities; and improves slicing properties. An effective fat apparently must be hard enough to provide a certain level of solids during the proofing and baking stages. A number of polar and nonpolar lipids are naturally present in flour and play important roles in the development of gluten in doughs.

Either a straight-dough or sponge method may be satisfactorily employed in mixing bread. Adequate development of the gluten structure in dough during mixing is essential to the preparation of high quality bread. Additional dough development occurs during fermentation. A decrease in pH and the production of a variety of substances by the yeast cells probably contribute to changes in the gluten structure. Continuous breadmaking is a commercial process that substitutes intense mixing for bulk fermentation to some degree.

The structure of bread dough after mixing, as seen by electron microscopy, consists of a matrix network of gluten strands containing small vacuoles. Starch granules are surrounded by thin protein sheets and strands. Yeast cells and fat droplets are distributed throughout the dough. After fermentation, many gas vacuoles are formed in the mixture. The small vacuoles in the gluten decrease. After baking, much of the starch is gelatinized. The granules expand into long, fibrous strands interwoven with the protein. Gas vacuoles are dispersed throughout the structure.

Within the first few minutes of baking, yeast activity is stimulated and the loaf volume increases markedly in oven spring. Adequate volume is dependent upon the ability of the gluten mass to expand and produce thin cell walls that hold gas up to the point of setting the structure. Partial gelatinization of starch and protein denaturation by heat are instrumental in changing the fluid dough to a relatively rigid loaf of bread.

The characteristic flavor of freshly baked bread is related to volatile and nonvolatile substances produced during fermentation. This flavor begins to change within a matter of hours after baking as staling occurs. Staling is a complex phenomenon that appears to involve chiefly the amylopectin fraction of starch. It has been suggested that amylopectin undergoes a type of retrogradation during staling as its branches fold up and associate with one another.

STUDY QUESTIONS

The fermentation of sugar by yeast is a vitally important reaction in the production of yeast bread.

1. Name the strain of yeast that is commonly called baker's yeast.
2. Describe the storage stability and the recommended temperature of liquid for dispersing compressed yeast; for active dry yeast. Explain why in each case.
3. Write an overall reaction showing the beginning and ending components for the anaerobic fermentation of sugar by yeast. What agents catalyze the many steps involved in this overall reaction?
4. Describe three general sources of sugar in bread dough that are available for yeast fermentation.
5. What are the basic functions of yeast in breadmaking?

6. What are optimal conditions for yeast fermentation?

Each ingredient in yeast bread plays a specific role(s) in the production of the finished loaf.

7. What are the characteristics of good quality white bread?
8. Describe and explain the major role(s) of flour, of liquid, of yeast, of sugar, of salt, and of fat in the production of a light, fine-textured loaf of bread.
9. Why does the commercial baker often use each of the following additives in breadmaking: yeast food, oxidizing agents, surface active agents, enzymes, and preservatives?

Several different methods of mixing bread will each produce satisfactory results.

10. Compare the straight dough method, the sponge method, and the batter method for mixing yeast bread at home.
11. What are distinguishing features of continuous breadmaking?
12. Why is milk scalded before use in making yeast bread? Explain.
13. Explain the importance of adequately kneading bread dough.
14. How might oxidizing agents contribute to the structure of gluten in dough? Explain.

A number of important changes occur in bread dough during fermentation.

15. Outline some major enzymatic changes that occur in bread dough during the fermentation period.
16. Account for changes in pH during fermentation.
17. What effect does fermentation have on gluten?

Bread dough is a complex system of dispersed ingredients that changes as bread is baked and held after baking.

18. Draw and explain a diagram showing the internal structure of bread dough after mixing and after fermentation and of the baked loaf. Include the distribution of protein, starch, yeast, fat, and gas.
19. Describe and explain the major changes occurring as bread bakes, including those induced by alpha-amylase.
20. Why is it important to proof a loaf of bread to precisely the proper degree before baking? What are the consequences of not doing so?
21. Describe the major changes associated with staling of bread.
22. Suggest a theory involving amylopectin that has been proposed as an explanation of the staling phenomenon. Suggest evidence that might eliminate amylose from a staling theory.

REFERENCES

1. Barrett, F. F. 1968. Oxidation how and why. *Bakers Digest* 42 (Dec.), 56.

2. Bechtel, D. B., Y. Pomeranz, and A. de Francisco. 1978. Breadmaking studied by light and transmission electron microscopy. *Cereal Chemistry* 55, 392.

3. Biltcliffe, D. O. 1972. Active dried baker's yeast. II. Factors involved in the fermentation of flour. *Journal of Food Technology* 7, 63.

4. Buckheit, J. T. 1971. Yeast, its controlled handling in the bakery. *Bakers Digest* 45 (Feb.), 46.

5. Caul, J. F. and A. G. Vaden. 1972. Flavor of white bread as it ages. *Bakers Digest* 46 (Feb.), 39.

6. Cobb, S. G. 1976. Alternatives to nonfat dry milk. *Bakers Digest* 50 (June), 41.

7. Cole, M. S. 1973. An overview of modern dough conditioners. *Bakers Digest* 47 (Dec.), 21.

8. Cooper, E. J. and G. Reed. 1968. Yeast fermentation. *Bakers Digest* 42 (Dec.), 22.

9. Finney, K. F., M. D. Shogren, Y. Pomeranz, and L. C. Bolte. 1972. Cereal malts in breadmaking. *Bakers Digest* 46 (Feb.), 36.

10. Fortmann, K., H. Welcker, and F. Barrett. 1969. Effect of modified salt on dough development. *Bakers Digest* 43 (Oct.), 50.

11. Frazier, W. C. 1967. *Food Microbiology,* 2nd edition. New York: McGraw-Hill.

12. Hautera, P. and T. Lovgren. 1975. The fermentation activity of baker's yeast. *Bakers Digest* 49 (June), 36.

13. Hlynka, I. 1962. Influence of temperature, speed of mixing, and salt on some rheological properties of dough in the Farinograph. *Cereal Chemistry* 39, 286.

14. Hoseney, R. C., K. H. Hsu, and R. S. Ling. 1976. Use of diacetyltartaric acid esters of monoglycerides in breadmaking. *Bakers Digest* 50 (Apr.), 28.

15. Johnson, J. A. and C. R. S. Sanchez. 1973. The nature of bread flavor. *Bakers Digest* 47 (Oct.), 48.

16. Johnston, W. R. and R. E. Mauseth. 1972. The interrelations of oxidants and reductants in dough development. *Bakers Digest* 46 (Apr.), 20.

17. Kent, N. L. 1975. *Technology of Cereals,* 2nd edition. New York: Pergamon Press.

18. Knightly, W. H. 1977. The staling of bread. *Bakers Digest* 51 (Oct.), 52.

19. Knightly, W. H. 1973. The evolution of softeners and conditioners used in baked foods. *Bakers Digest* 47 (Oct.), 64.

20. Magoffin, C. D. and R. C. Hoseney. 1974. A review of fermentation. *Bakers Digest* 48 (Dec.), 22.

21. Marston, P. E. and T. L. Wannan. 1976. Bread baking. *Bakers Digest* 50 (Aug.), 24.

22. Matz, S. A. 1960. *Bakery Technology and Engineering.* Westport, Conn.: Avi Publishing Company.

23. Morrison, W. R. 1976. Lipids in flour, dough and bread. *Bakers Digest* 50 (Aug.), 29.

24. Olsen, C. M. 1974. No-time doughs. *Bakers Digest* 48 (Apr.), 24.

25. Petricca, T. 1976. Fluid bakery shortenings. *Bakers Digest* 50 (Oct.), 39.

26. Pomeranz, Y. 1977. Fiber in breadmaking. *Bakers Digest* 51 (Oct.), 94.

27. Pomeranz, Y. 1971. *Wheat Chemistry and Technology.* St. Paul, Minn.: American Association of Cereal Chemists.

28. Pomper, S. 1969. Biochemistry of yeast fermentation. *Bakers Digest* 43 (Apr.), 32.

29. Schoch, T. J. 1965. Starch in bakery products. *Bakers Digest* 38 (Apr.), 48.

30. Shuey, W. C. 1963. Physical testing and dough properties. *Bakers Digest* 36 (Aug.), 61.

31. Stacey, N. E. 1964. A comparison of active dried yeast produced in different areas of the world. *Cereal Chemistry* 41, 149.

32. Tang, R. T., R. J. Robinson, and W. C. Hurley. 1972. Quantitative changes in various sugar concentrations during breadmaking. *Bakers Digest* 46 (Aug.), 48.

33. Tipples, K. H. and R. H. Kilborn. 1974. Dough development for shorter breadmaking processes. *Bakers Digest* 48 (Oct.), 34.

34. Tsen, C. C. 1973. Chemical dough development. *Bakers Digest* 47 (Oct.), 44.

35. Tsen, C. C. 1970. Chemical dough development. *Bakers Digest* 44 (Aug.), 28.

36. Tsen, C. C. and W. J. Hoover. 1971. The shortening-sparing effect of sodium stearoyl-2 lactylate and calcium stearoyl-2 lactylate in bread baking. *Bakers Digest* 45 (June), 38.

37. Willhoft, E. M. A. 1971. Bread staling. I. Experimental study. *Journal of the Science of Food and Agriculture* 22, 176.

38. Zobel, H. F. 1973. A review of bread staling. *Bakers Digest* 47 (Oct.), 52.

INDEX

81 82 83 9 8 7 6 5 4 3